EXPLORING CORRECTIONS

EXPLORING CORRECTIONS
A BOOK OF READINGS

Edited By
TARA GRAY

New Mexico State University

Foreword By
ROBERT JOHNSON

ALLYN AND BACON

Boston • London • Toronto • Sydney • Tokyo • Singapore

Series Editor: Jennifer Jacobson
Editor-in Chief, Social Sciences: Karen Hanson
Series Editorial Assistant: Tom Jefferies
Marketing Manager: Judeth Hall
Editorial-Production Service: Omegatype Typography, Inc.
Composition and Prepress Buyer: Linda Cox
Manufacturing Buyer: Joanne Sweeney
Cover Administrator: Kristina Mose-Libon
Cover Designer: Joel Gendron
Electronic Composition: Omegatype Typography, Inc.

Library of Congress Cataloging-in-Publication Data
Exploring corrections : a book of readings/edited by Tara Gray; with a foreword by Robert Johnson.
       p.   cm.
    Includes bibliographical references and index.
    ISBN 0-205-32776-1 (alk. paper)
       1. Corrections–United States.   I. Gray, Tara.
HV9471 .E96 2001
364.6–dc21

                                                          2001031599

Printed in the United States of America
10   9   8   7   6   5   4   3   2   1   06   05   04   03   02   01

To
Dale W. Robison
for sharing a marriage,
our ring of fire.

CONTENTS

PART TWO
LIVING AND WORKING IN PRISONS
AND JAILS   31

PART THREE
PRISON ADMINISTRATION   141

The Glen Mills Reform School resembles an excellent
prep school; it assumes the students are normal and
requires them to conform to more than a hundred
group norms, which helps them excel and reduces
recidivism.

The readaptation model helps inmates live in the freeworld by making life on the inside much like life on
the outside in terms of work and family, which has
resulted in very low recidivism.

CONTROL MECHANISMS

Correctional officers *seem* to have total power over
inmates, but they don't, and their job design further
erodes their power. In the end, officers control inmates
through the privilege system, a system that needs
tightening.

Correctional officers have allowed prison sex as a way
to divide and conquer inmates, but this practice must
be stopped because prison sex involves coercion that
borders on rape and leads to other violence.

PART FIVE
DO ALTERNATIVES TO PRISON WORK? 267

FOREWORD

We've heard a lot about prison escapes lately. Some thirteen high-security prisoners broke out of prison within just a three-month period—seven from Texas and six from Alabama. In each case, the prisoners worked in groups. Some of the men were heavily armed; all were dangerous. Citizens in neighboring areas and states were understandably frightened, and at least one life was lost—that of a young police officer—at the hands of the so-called Texas Seven. Prison breakouts are a serious concern, and a group escape is nothing short of terrifying. But escapes occur rarely. In recent years, about one-half of one percent of our nation's prisoners escape, and most are "walk-aways" from minimum security prisons and community corrections facilities. All fugitives are returned, dead or alive, to face a long prison term. Still, escapes capture the public mind, feeding a popular call for repression that takes the now-familiar form of more punishment and less correction in our nation's growing penal archipelago.

The general public cares about prisons when a crisis—an escape or a riot—takes place. A few of us care about prisons on a full-time basis. One such person is Tara Gray, a thoughtful scholar who cares deeply about corrections. Her passion for fairness and her empathy for others comes through clearly in her superb anthology, *Exploring Corrections: A Book of Readings*. The book is an antidote to short-term thinking; and it has many virtues. It is well organized, engaging, timely, and comprehensive. It is also well named. The reader is treated to a wide-ranging and fair-minded exploration of corrections, learning who is confined and for what crimes, the nature of daily life and existence experienced by the various inhabitants of penal institutions (the inmates who live there as well as the staff who work there), how penal institutions are run, and how they might be changed to make them more humane and, in the long run, more effective. The laudable if undervalued goal of rehabilitation is examined in the prison context and in the context of alternative sanctions.

If you are the kind of person who believes that a close look at prisons is an invitation to look elsewhere for effective and humane sanctions for a sizeable segment of offenders, this is your book. Prisons have promise, to be sure, and Gray is open to that promise. (The book covers intriguing possibilities for innovative correctional management, from Tom Murton in Arkansas's Cummins Prison Farm, to Dennis Luther in the Federal Correctional Institution at McKean—two pioneers in the humanization of prisons.) But the limits of the prison as a sanction come across clearly, so clearly in fact that the reader is left wondering how we, as a society, locked ourselves into a correctional strategy that is so prison-heavy as to be oppressive for all of us—victim and offender, keeper and kept, and of course the trusty and trusting citizen who pays the bills in the form of a growing tax burden and a shrinking return in social and educational services.

Corrections raises big issues, and this is, appropriately, an ambitious book. Gray examines prisons, jails, and community sanctions, which in turn are viewed from a variety of perspectives, including those of inmates and clients, line and executive staff, the general public, and the researcher. The focus is on prisons, which is sensible in light of the "imprisonment binge" we have engaged upon for the last few decades. We now lead the world in the prison business, surely a dubious distinction. We build and operate institutions of confinement that are chock full of men and women, boys and girls, and people of color—especially poor people of color, and most especially young black men. Other penal institutions (such as jails or boot camps) and other penal sanctions (such as intensive probation) are examined as precursors to prison or alternatives to prison, or both, which indeed they are. The groundwork is laid for creative thinking about ways to rethink and reshape corrections. Students are challenged to do just this, as are concerned citizens, who have much to learn from this anthology.

Exploring Corrections is a delightful read. Each chapter is annotated in the Contents, which gives the reader the lay of the land—a map to guide his or her exploration of the corrections field. Readings include a mix of works that are summarized (succinctly and clearly) by Gray, and essays by others that are excerpted from journals and books. The sections of the book flow easily across the main contours of the field; each section is introduced with an objective and even-handed summary. Sensible short-answer and essay questions are asked. Lists of websites appear throughout the book.

Each of the readings was "test-driven" by Gray's students over the past several years, and it shows. The entries are engrossing and the format is inviting. To call this book user-friendly is an understatement. It is easy and fun to use, and remarkably informative. I plan to use it in my corrections courses. My students deserve the best, and I'm not one to stand in their way.

Robert Johnson
Department of Justice, Law, and Society
American University

PREFACE

I compiled this book because I wanted readings that were written in a lively and compelling style to provoke thought and spark discussion. To this end, I began this book eight years ago and worked closely with students in my classes to delete less effective readings and replace them with better, more current readings. After many heated discussions—and many substitutions—here is the book.

This book offers a frank exploration of corrections in the United States today. Readers explore corrections by touring the underside of prison life as well as the most hopeful forms of prison administration and its alternatives. Readers weigh and consider contrasting views on what is needed to improve corrections. These views range from the belief that prison administrators need more control, to the view that inmates need to participate meaningfully in prison administrations, to the idea that the system needs more and better alternatives to prison.

Part One asks the question, Who gets convicted and why? In fact, an increasing number of people do: The United States now incarcerates a higher proportion of our population than any other country. Several experts argue that this "incarceration binge" needs to be reversed for both men and women (see John Irwin, James Austin, and Meda Chesney-Lind). Although some prisoners are very serious criminals indeed, the typical prisoner is not a serious criminal and may have been discriminated against in terms of class or race (see Jeffrey Reiman; Samuel Walker, Cassia Spohn, and Miriam DeLone).

Part Two explores the experience of living and working in prisons and jails, including the challenges faced by both correctional officers and inmates. Three readings discuss working as correctional officers in prison and jail. Other topics include prison and jail life for men, women, and juveniles, as well as living with the threat of rape, living with AIDS, and life in "the hole" or on death row. Authors in Part Two include inmate Jack Abbott, as well as Clemens Bartollas, Robert Johnson, Lucien X. Lombardo, Gary Webb, and Linda Zupan.

Part Three presents several models of how best to administer prisons, ranging from controlling to participatory models, and including unit management (see Robert Levinson). John DiIulio, Jr., and Gresham Sykes argue for the need to give prison administrators and correctional officers more control. Other authors argue against the current level of control, opposing control units and other control mechanisms such as psychotropic drugs (see inmate Victor Hassine), prison sex (see James Gilligan), and prison gangs. Exceptional wardens who have had tremendous success with prison administration are also featured, including Tom Murton, the real "Brubaker" of Arkansas fame; Dennis Luther of FCI McKean; Sam Ferrainola of Glen Mills Reform School; and Jorge Duarte of La Mesa Prison in Tijuana, Mexico. These futuristic models show what is possible in prison and keep hope alive.

Part Four debates whether prisons really work—and whether rehabilitation works. Two authors disagree about whether prisons meet their goals: One contends that they do, with the possible exception of rehabilitation. The other argues that prisons do not meet their goals: They incapacitate only temporarily; they do not deter; and instead of rehabilitating inmates, they make them more dangerous. Next, James Q. Wilson and Elliott Currie square off regarding whether rehabilitation can be successful. Wilson argues that rehabilitation doesn't work: It is unreasonable to expect it to work, and we should probably put our efforts into controlling offenders, rather than reforming them. Elliott Currie disagrees vigorously. He argues that rehabilitation has never been tried seriously on a large scale, but it can work.

Part Five discusses the extent to which prison alternatives work, including boot camps, restorative justice, and probation. Alternatives to prison are designed to reduce prison overcrowding and save money; at the same time, they are intended to provide rehabilitation and sufficient incapacitation, deterrence, and retribution. The critics of alternatives charge that some of these programs may fail to meet these goals, and, instead of providing an alternative to prison, they may replace probation or "widen the net." Others argue forcefully that, as with prisons, it is too soon to give up on the alternatives; instead, we must remain serious about reducing crime by working to improve both prisons and their alternatives.

WHAT STUDENTS AND FACULTY SAY ABOUT THIS BOOK

I asked students who read this book for class whether it helped them learn, and if so, how. Students report that they learn from this book because it reads well and presents different perspectives:

Compared to other books I've read in college, this was the one I couldn't put down.

Martin Martos

This book was a great source of many heated discussions in our class. Every corrections student should read this text.

Elizabeth Parra

Dr. Gray is fair in her findings and presents issues from all perspectives, which allows students to draw their own conclusions.

Romo Villegas

I also asked experts for their views of the book. Faculty echoed the comments of students and added a few observations of their own:

Exploring Corrections *touches all the bases and lets all the players speak. Readings describe what prison life is like for adult and juvenile inmates and what prison work is like for guards and administrators. Their authors are not only scholars, but also prisoners, wardens, probation officers and attorneys. The key debates—whether prison works, whether rehabilitation works, whether prisoners should be more controlled or have more control—are here, as well as issues too rarely discussed—violence, sexual abuse, gangs, the prevalence of AIDS, the experience of death row. Finally, an extensive section of the book is devoted to alternatives to prisons—boot camps, probation, electronic monitoring, community service and others.* Exploring Corrections *is a lively, balanced and comprehensive anthology.*

Jeffrey Reiman
William Fraser McDowell Professor of Philosophy
American University, Washington, DC

Nature takes a grain of sand and builds a pearl around it. A human takes a handful of these pearls and strings them together into a beautiful necklace. In comparable fashion, Dr. Gray has constructed a lustrous volume. It examines the field of corrections from a variety of viewpoints, all of which are arranged so that those interested in this profession find themselves agreeing with some experts and challenging others. Students will find concepts on both sides of the book's five central themes which they can discuss far into the night.

Robert Levinson
Special Projects Manager
American Correctional Association

Tara Gray has done a remarkable job of assembling a wide variety of topics and viewpoints in her book, Exploring Corrections: A Book of Readings. *Some of the selections in this reader are classics, while others are recent publications. Some sweep broadly, while others examine the microcosm of prison life. All of the sections are written in a lively and engaging way. Many readers have been put together in sociology and corrections, but this one stands above the rest.*

Clemens Bartollas
Department of Sociology
University of Northern Iowa

FEATURES THAT MAKE THIS BOOK DISTINCTIVE

I want this book to help teachers teach and students learn. To this end, the book includes study questions after each reading to help focus the attention of students on main points as they read. Teachers may require students to complete these questions as a way of giving them a focus and a reason to read. Teachers may want to promote student accountability by regularly using these questions for quizzes.

Essay questions appear at the end of each part, and the instructor's manual includes multiple-choice test questions and table summaries for each reading. Each table summary includes the author's thesis at the top, followed by the key arguments in the left column, and supporting evidence in the right column. The table summaries are formatted one on each page so that they can be easily photocopied onto an overhead transparency and will be readable in a large classroom, thus making them useful for lecture outlines.

ACKNOWLEDGMENTS

I could not have compiled this book alone. The book truly stands on the shoulders of giants. I especially thank the following people:

Laura Madson, my colleague and friend, who reads much of my work. She is gracious enough to read for me on short notice, she seems to enjoy what she reads, and she gives world-class suggestions for change.

Karen Hanson and Jennifer Jacobson, of Allyn and Bacon, who patiently answered my daily queries with great aplomb and expertise. They were ably assisted by two editorial assistants, Sarah McGaughey and Tom Jefferies. Each of these professionals provided a seamless transition to the next, which made working with Allyn and Bacon a joy.

The editorial production team at Omegatype Typography, Inc., especially Shannon Foreman for her patience and attention to detail.

My students in corrections classes, who "test drove" each reading in the book and told me which readings would best help them learn.

My research assistant, Reina Acosta, who left no stone unturned and tirelessly pursued every possible research lead.

My colleagues in criminal justice at New Mexico State University, who make it an amazing place to live and work. Two of these colleagues—Jody Crowley and Sami Halbert—ably critiqued parts of the manuscript. Larry Mays suggested that I compile this book in the first place.

The following experts, who gave sometimes disturbing, but very profound, suggestions for change, and made me think harder than ever about corrections:

Leo Carroll, University of Rhode Island
Meda Chesney-Lind, University of Hawaii at Manoa
John Irwin, San Francisco State University
Robert Johnson, American University
Robert Levinson, American Correctional Association
Lucien X. Lombardo, Old Dominion University
Jeffrey Reiman, American University
Hans Toch, State University of New York, Albany

The reviewers of this edition:

Clemens Bartollas, University of Northern Iowa
Charles B. Fields, Eastern Kentucky University

As you read this book, please note systematically any suggestions you have, and contact me. I want to hear from you and your students, my readers.

Tara Gray
tgray@nmsu.edu
www.taragray.com

ABOUT THE CONTRIBUTORS

Tara Gray, the editor of *Exploring Corrections,* serves as an associate professor of criminal justice at New Mexico State University. Dr. Gray publishes in the field of corrections. In addition, she gives workshops across the country on improving teaching and scholarly productivity. Dr. Gray has received awards for her spirited teaching, as well as for community service. She chose these readings to reflect her passion for prisons—and her commitment to improving them and their alternatives.

Jack Abbott, Inmate-Author, *In the Belly of the Beast: Letters from Prison*

Linda R. Acorn, Former Associate Editor, *Corrections Today*

James Austin, Professor, The George Washington University

Clemens Bartollas, Professor of Sociology, University of Northern Iowa

Phyllis Jo Baunach, Former Attorney, U.S. Department of Justice

Daniel J. Bayse, Founder and Executive Director, Prison Family Foundation, Inc.

Lawrence A. Bennett, Former Director of the Crime Prevention and Police Research Division, National Institute of Justice

Meda Chesney-Lind, Professor of Women's Studies, University of Hawaii

Terry D. Childers, Senior United States Probation Officer, Northern District of Illinois

Elliott Currie, Professor of Legal Studies, University of California–Berkeley

Miriam DeLone, Associate Professor, University of Nebraska at Omaha

Thomas L. Densmore, Senior United States Probation Officer, Northern District of Texas

John J. DiIulio, Jr., Professor of Political Science, University of Pennsylvania

Fay Dowker, Member, Committee to End the Marion Lockdown

Billie S. Erwin, Former Senior Operations Analyst, Office of Research and Evaluation, Georgia Department of Corrections

James Gilligan, Former Director, Center of the Study of Violence, Harvard Medical School; Former Director, Bridgewater State Hospital for the Criminally Insane; Former Director of Mental Health, Massachusetts Prison System

Glenn Good, Member, Committee to End the Marion Lockdown

Angela R. Gover, University of Maryland

Victor Hassine, Inmate-Author, *Life Without Parole: Living in Prison Today*

Geoffrey Hunt, Institute for Scientific Analysis

John Irwin, Professor Emeritus of Sociology, San Francisco State University

Robert Johnson, Professor of Justice, Law and Society, American University

Richard Lawrence, Professor of Criminal Justice, St. Cloud State University

Robert Levinson, Special Projects Manager, American Correctional Association

Douglas Litowitz, Visiting Professor of Law, Florida Coastal University

Lucien X. Lombardo, Professor of Sociology and Criminal Justice, Old Dominion University

Doris Layton MacKenzie, Professor of Criminal Justice and Criminology, University of Maryland

Omar Madruga, Senior United States Probation Officer, Southern District of Florida

Julie C. Martin, Attorney, Columbus, Ohio

Jon'a Meyer, Assistant Professor of Sociology, Rutgers University

Andrew Metz, Staff Writer, *Newsday*

Tomas Morales, Institute for Scientific Analysis

David G. Morris, Sociologist, Menaul Penitentiary

Donald J. Newman, Late Dean of the School of Criminal Justice, State University of New York at Albany

Tom Peters, Author, *Liberation Management*

E. Jane Pierson, Senior United States Probation Officer, Eastern District of California

Orville B. Pung, Retired Deputy Commissioner, Minnesota Department of Corrections

Jeffrey Reiman, William Fraser McDowell Professor of Philosophy, American University

Stephanie Riegel, Institute for Scientific Analysis

John M. Shevlin, Supervising United States Probation Officer, Southern District of Florida

Charles Shireman, Professor of Social Work, Portland State University

Nina Siegal, Reporter, *The New York Times*

Cassia Spohn, Professor of Criminal Justice, University of Nebraska at Omaha

Gaylene J. F. Styve, University of Maryland

Gresham M. Sykes, Professor Emeritus of Sociology, University of Virginia

Mark S. Umbreit, Director of the Center for Restorative Justice and Peacemaking, Professor of Social Work, University of Minnesota

Dan Waldorf, Institute for Scientific Analysis

Samuel Walker, Professor of Criminal Justice, University of Nebraska at Omaha

Gary L. Webb, Professor of Criminal Justice, Ball State University

James Q. Wilson, James A. Collins Professor Emeritus in Management, University of California at Los Angeles

Linda L. Zupan, Professor, Northern Michigan University

WHO GETS CONVICTED AND WHY?

Part One of this book asks the question, "Who gets convicted and why?" The data show an increasing number of people do. The United States now incarcerates six times as many people as it did in 1973, which is more than any other country in the world. Although some offenders are serious criminals indeed, these authors argue that the typical prisoner is not a serious criminal and may have experienced discrimination in terms of race, gender, or class.

The first reading in Part One is an overview of a book by James Austin and John Irwin titled *It's About Time: America's Imprisonment Binge*. Irwin and Austin argue that our unprecedented imprisonment binge is based on three myths: the beliefs that most prisoners are serious criminals; that the public demands long sentences; and that imprisonment reduces crime. Irwin and Austin found that, by the public's own definition of crime seriousness, only 4 percent of those in prison were there for "very serious" crimes, but a full 52 percent were there for crimes that qualified as "petty." In addition, the authors learned that the so-called punitive public does not support imprisonment for nonviolent crimes, which constitute most of the crimes for which people are incarcerated. Finally, the authors found that states with higher incarceration rates do not have lower crime rates. As a result, Irwin and Austin suggest that states cut prison sentences by 90 days across the board. Illinois did this and saved $90 million per year, with only one percent of crime stemming from the early release.

The imprisonment binge also affects women. Although women make up only 6 percent of those imprisoned, their rate of imprisonment is increasing twice as fast as men's. Meda Chesney-Lind argues that many of these women could be better served by community corrections; the women's imprisonment binge did not stem from an increase in women's crime, and women have more difficult personal histories than men do. In the last ten years, women's arrests increased by about 30 percent, but the increase in imprisoned women was about 160 percent. Further, of the male and female prisoners surveyed about childhood abuse, 43 percent of women but only 12 percent of the men had been abused at least once. This pattern continues into adulthood, with 25 percent of women versus 3 percent of men having been abused as adults. Therefore, Chesney-Lind argues that many of these women can be safely housed in the community but they continue to be imprisoned in increasing numbers because of "vengeful equity," which emphasizes, in the name of justice, treating women offenders as though they were men, particularly when the outcome is punitive.

The next reading comes from Samuel Walker, Cassia Spohn, and Miriam DeLone's book, *The Color of Justice*. The authors argue that racial minorities, especially blacks, are disproportionately represented in the correctional system; that the disparity cannot be fully explained by differences in crime commission; and this disparity is worsening over time. More African Americans are under correctional supervision than are attending college. In contrast, four times as many whites attend college, and African American males are seven times more likely to go to prison than are white males. The authors conclude that some of this racial gap can be explained by the fact that racial minorities commit more street crimes than whites do; however, some of the gap can be explained only by racial discrimination. Although African Americans have always been sentenced to prison disproportionately, they are *increasingly* overrepresented; since 1926, their representation has nearly doubled.

The last reading in Part One is an overview of the book *The Rich Get Richer and the Poor Get Prison,* by Jeffrey Reiman. Reiman asserts that upper- and middle-class people receive preferential treatment from the justice system both when they commit street crimes and when they commit white-collar crime, often considered a "higher class" of crime. Indeed, many people feel that a kinder, gentler treatment of white-collar criminals is justified because, although they steal far more dollars than street criminals do, they do not kill or injure people. Reiman shows that white-collar criminals actually do kill and injure more people than street criminals do, but they are punished more leniently because of the way crime is defined and because excuses are made for "higher class" criminals.

AMERICA'S IMPRISONMENT BINGE
AN OVERVIEW OF THE BOOK BY
JOHN IRWIN AND JAMES AUSTIN

TARA GRAY

It's About Time: America's Imprisonment Binge is an ambitious book, which offers a powerful response to those who would have us continue a "lock 'em up" strategy, even though the United States now sports the biggest and fastest-rising prison population in the world (p. 1). . . . According to authors John Irwin and James Austin, America is engaged in an unprecedented imprisonment binge. . . . We now imprison more than a million people, with another half a million in jail, half a million on parole, and 3 million on probation (p. 3). We incarcerate more people than live in any of our thirteen smallest states (p. 1). . . . For white men in their twenties, we incarcerate one out of every 15; for Hispanics, one in 10; for blacks, one in three (p. 3).

THE COSTS OF CRIME AND PUNISHMENT

The cost of this imprisonment binge is staggering. The book includes some absurd stories about individual offenders. One man returned items he had stolen, which were worth $200, and turned himself in, only to receive a prison sentence that will cost Florida almost $65,000 (p. 44). On a broader scale, every year Americans spend $112 billion on criminal justice. . . . In contrast, the cost of crime, including the economic losses from theft or damage, medical expenses, loss of pay, and related costs, comes to $17.6 billion per year, or $500 per crime (the majority of victims suffer losses below $100) (p. 13). In other words, we spend six times as much to solve the problem of crime as crime itself costs. If the purpose of the justice system is to reduce the cost of crime, it would seem impossible to get our money's worth.

Incarceration imposes human as well as economic costs, and Irwin and Austin devote half the book to these costs. To understand the human costs, we must understand what happens to inmates in prison and after release. As more and more people have been sent to prison, there has been a shift towards more security and away from rehabilitation; this shift has served only to "widen the gap of hostility, hate and violence between guards and prisoners" (p. 97). Or, as Jack Abbott writes, a prisoner today "cannot imagine what forgiveness is, or mercy or tolerance, because he has no experience of such values" (p. 111).

WHY DO WE IMPRISON SO MANY PEOPLE?

If incarceration is so costly in both human and monetary terms, why are we incarcerating larger and larger numbers of people? Perhaps it is necessary to do so, in the eyes of the public, because the inmates have committed heinous crimes. To determine public perception of the seriousness of these crimes, Irwin and Austin analyzed the responses from another study in which 52,000 Americans were asked to assign a level of seriousness to a short description of 204 briefly described criminal acts (pp. 25–26). From these findings, Irwin and Austin developed the following classifications of seriousness:

SERIOUSNESS	POINTS	CHARACTERISTICS
Petty	1–4	No injury or threat of injury, no weapon, no theft over $1,000, and no use of heroin or sale of marijuana
Moderate	5–9	Minor injury or threat of injury, a weapon, theft over $1,000, or use of heroin or sale of marijuana
Serious	10–14	Serious injury, attempted murder, theft over $10,000, or sales of heroin or smuggling narcotics
Very Serious	15+	Rape, manslaughter or homicide, kidnapping, or a child victim.

Next, Irwin and Austin examined official records, and conducted lengthy interviews with 154 male prisoners, randomly selected from the intake populations of Washington, Nevada, and Illinois (p. 26).[1] Of the crimes that sent these men to prison, 52 percent qualify as petty. Twenty-nine percent of the remaining crimes were moderate, 13 percent serious, and five percent very serious (pp. 26–27). Irwin and Austin conclude that "rather than being vicious predators, most [prisoners] were disorganized, unskilled, undisciplined petty criminals who very seldom engaged in violence or made any significant amount of money from their criminal acts" (p. 41).

Clearly, our prisons are not full because the people in them are vicious predators. Instead, our imprisonment binge stems from incarcerating a large proportion of convicted felons for relatively long periods, and reincarcerating record numbers of parolees. Although the public may believe that relatively few convicted felons are incarcerated, almost two-thirds are. For prisoners, the average time served is 25 months, which does not include the 5–6 months the average defendant spends in jail before sentencing (p. 20). . . . Once an offender is released from prison, his or her parole can be violated by any of a long list of items including failing a drug test and failing to get and keep employment. . . . These technical violations accounted for more than two-thirds of all parole failures in 1996 (p. 144). Currently, about one-third of released prisoners were returned to prison for new crimes or parole violations within three years, which is just less than the number previously returned to prison in a lifetime (29–42 percent) (p. 144). The long and short of it is, the revolving door is revolving a lot faster than it used to.

Why are we incarcerating a high proportion of convicted felons for relatively long periods, and reincarcerating a record number of parolees? Traditionally, researchers blame the punitive public. In recent years, the Bureau of Justice Statistics and its researchers have argued that "the public wants long prison sentences for most crimes" (p. 47). Irwin and Austin point out that the Bureau arrived at this conclusion by presenting the public with very serious examples of crime that are not representative of the crimes inmates typically commit. In their robbery scenario, for example, $1,000 was taken, the offender brandished a gun, and the victim was hospitalized. In the Irwin and Austin classification scheme, this crime would be classified as serious, and would represent the crimes committed by only 5 percent of the people sentenced to prison (p. 47). Irwin and Austin cite a number of studies finding that when more realistic scenarios are presented, the majority of citizens would not recommend imprisonment (p. 47). In fact, the public may be less punitive than the Bureau of Justice Statistics would have us believe.

Insofar as the public is punitive, researchers may be partly responsible. According to Irwin and Austin,

The public reacts to crime with fear and intensity because they have been led to believe by the media and public officials that thousands of vicious, intractable street criminals menace innocent citizens . . . For years, criminologists debunked the 'evil person' theory of crime and instead attributed the crime problem to social and economic conditions. But recently, many researchers, perhaps swayed by the general conservative shift or lured by government incentives in the form of grants, jobs, and recognition, have resurrected

*old theories of "crime" and the "criminal type" (now
most often labeled the "career criminal") (pp. 17–18).*

The interest in career criminals began in 1970 with the
idea that a few criminals commit most of the crime,
and with the hope that we could identify them before
they embarked on a lifetime of crime. By 1986, Gottfredson and Hirschi noted that "the criminal career
notion so dominates discussion of criminal justice policy and so controls expenditure of federal research
funds that it may now be said that criminal justice research in this country is indeed centrally planned"
(p. 19).

    This plan, directed by the Department of Justice,
would have us believe that career criminals are a huge
problem and that the imprisonment binge is the solution. In 1991, the Justice Department concluded, "Statisticians and criminal justice researchers have
consistently found that falling crime rates are associated with rising imprisonment rates" (p. 225). Later
that year, former Attorney General William Barr reit-
erated this position, arguing that the country has a
" 'clear choice' between building more prisons and
tolerating higher violent crime rates" (p. 225).

    According to Irwin and Austin, prison does not
reduce the crime rate. It is not enough to blame the
public for America's imprisonment binge—not when
the federal government, and the many researchers who
work for it, publish information like this. . . . Irwin and
Austin test the hypothesis that incarceration reduces
crime in a number of ways. For example, they compare the crime and incarceration rates among the 50

states and find that "greater increases in imprisonment
did not produce decreases in crime" (p. 228). Further,
despite steady increases in incarceration rates, crime
has been relatively stable in the beginning of each
decade since the 1960s . . . Clearly, raising the incarceration rate has not systematically lowered the crime
rate (p. 227).

WHAT IS THE SOLUTION?

If the imprisonment binge does not reduce crime
significantly, then what should be done? Irwin and
Austin argue that

> *The single most direct solution that would have an im-
> mediate, dramatic impact on prison crowding and
> would not affect public safety is to shorten prison
> terms. This can be done swiftly and fairly through a
> number of existing mechanisms, such as greater use
> of existing good-time credit statutes, accelerating pa-
> role eligibility, developing re-entry programs for in-
> mates, and altering existing parole revocation policies
> (p. 246).*

Some states have shortened prison sentences. Between
1980 and 1983, Illinois reduced most sentences by 90
days; the prisoners who were released early were responsible for less than a 1 percent increase in crime.
The experiment was considered so successful that Illinois shortened sentences another 90 days, and now
saves $90 million a year. Other states should follow
suit instead of fanning the flames of America's imprisonment binge.

ENDNOTES

1. Irwin and Austin point out that this research method con-
trasts sharply with that of many social scientists who form

    most of their ideas in "armchairs" . . . using evidence
    that is unreliable and skimpy—police arrest records,
    prison files, and convicts' penciled-in answers to

questionnaires. . . . Very few of these criminologists
have spent any significant time observing or talking
to our subjects, the prisoners, something absolutely
necessary to develop an accurate understanding of
offenders' motives and criminal practices (p. 19).

REFERENCES

Irwin, John and James Austin. 1997. 2nd edition. *It's About
    Time: America's Imprisonment Binge.* Belmont, CA:
    Wadsworth.

STUDY QUESTIONS FOR READING 1

1. Irwin and Austin explain the extent of our incarceration binge in terms of the total numbers incarcerated, the number of people in our smallest states, and the different ethnic groups. Explain each.

2. The book includes some absurd stories about individual offenders, one of whom turned himself in and returned the T.V. and microwave he had stolen, only to receive a prison sentence that will cost Florida how much? How does the cost of crime compare to the cost of criminal justice?

3. What are some of the human costs of imprisonment?

4. Irwin and Austin argue that we may imprison so many people, despite the high costs, because the public imagines that the typical inmate has committed heinous crimes. To what extent is this true? To answer this question, use the classification of crime seriousness the authors developed from public opinion. Explain what constitutes a "very serious" crime and what constitutes a "petty" crime.

5. Irwin and Austin conclude that we incarcerate a high proportion of convicted felons for long periods of time. What percentage of convicted felons are incarcerated? How long is the average time served?

6. It has been said that "the revolving door is revolving a lot faster than it used to." To understand this statement, tell what fraction of inmates *return* to prison for either a new crime or a technical violation. In 1985, how long did it take for approximately the same fraction of inmates to be returned to prison? In your answer, give examples of "technical violations."

7. In Irwin and Austin's view, is the Bureau of Justice Statistics right when it asserts that the public wants "long prison sentences for most crimes"?

8. Why do Irwin and Austin believe that researchers may be partly responsible for the extent to which the public is punitive?

9. What does the Department of Justice believe about imprisonment as a solution to the crime problem?

10. According to Irwin and Austin, does incarceration reduce crime? What evidence do they give? In your answer, explain how they compare incarceration rates across states and how they compare the steady rise of incarceration rates to the changes in crime rates.

11. According to Irwin and Austin, if the imprisonment binge does not reduce crime significantly what should be done? When sentences were shortened in Illinois, what happened?

THE FORGOTTEN OFFENDER
WOMEN IN PRISON: FROM PARTIAL JUSTICE TO VENGEFUL EQUITY

MEDA CHESNEY-LIND

Throughout most of our nation's history, women in prison have been correctional afterthoughts. Ignored because of their small numbers, female inmates tended to complain, not riot, making it even easier for institutions to overlook their unique needs. Perhaps as a consequence, the United States never developed a correctional system for women to replace the reformatory system that fell into disuse shortly before World War II. In fact, by the mid-70s, only about half of the states and territories had separate prisons for women, and many jurisdictions housed women inmates in male facilities or in women's facilities in other states.

Something dramatic happened to this picture in the 1980s: During that decade, the number of women in U.S. prisons jumped dramatically. In 1980, there were just over 12,000 women in U.S. state and federal prisons. By 1997, that number had increased to almost 80,000. In about a decade and a half, the number of women incarcerated in the nation's prisons had increased sixfold.

This astonishing increase should not be seen simply as a reflection of the increase in male incarceration during the same period. Women's "share" of total imprisonment has more than doubled in the past three decades, from 3 percent in 1970 to 6.4 percent in 1997.

The rate of growth in female imprisonment also has outpaced that of men; since 1985 the annual rate of growth in the number of female inmates has averaged 11.1 percent, higher than the 7.6 percent average increase in male inmates. In 1996 alone, the number of females grew at a rate nearly double that of males (9.5 percent, compared to 4.8 percent for males).

Similar patterns have been seen in adult jails: Women constituted 7 percent of the population in the mid-80s, but today they account for 11 percent of the population. Likewise, the rate of increase in female incarceration in local jails since 1985 has been 9.9 percent for women, compared to 6.4 percent for men.

Finally, the rate of women's imprisonment is at a historic high, increasing from a low of six sentenced female inmates per 100,000 U.S. women in 1925 to 54 per 100,000 in 1997. In 1997, California led the nation with 11,076 women in prison, followed by Texas with 10,549, New York with 3,584 and Florida with 3,404.

The correctional establishment, long used to forgetting about women, was taken almost completely by surprise when this change started. Initially, women inmates were housed virtually anywhere (remodeled hospitals, abandoned training schools and converted motels) as jurisdictions struggled to cope with the soaring increase in women's imprisonment. Increasingly, though, states have begun to open new units and facilities to house female inmates. Data collected by Nicole Rafter, author of *Partial Justice: Women, Prisons and Social Control,* document this clearly. Between 1930 and 1950, the United States opened approximately two to three facilities for women each decade, but during the 1980s alone, more than 34 were opened. By 1990, the nation had 71 female-only facilities; in 1995, the number of female facilities had jumped to 104—an increase of 46.5 percent.

What has caused this shift in the way that we respond to women's crime? What unique challenges have these women inmates produced? And what could we do better or differently, as we struggle to create a woman-oriented response to the current state of affairs?

WOMEN'S CRIMINAL ACTIVITY

Is the dramatic increase in women's imprisonment a response to a women's crime problem spiraling out of control? Empirical indicators give little evidence of this. For example, the total number of arrests of adult women, which might be seen as a measure of women's criminal activity, increased by 31.4 percent between 1987 and 1996, while the number of women in prison increased by 159 percent.

And despite media images of hyper-violent female offenders, the proportion of women doing time in state prisons for violent offenses has been declining steadily from about half (48.9 percent) in 1979 to just over a quarter (27.6 percent) in 1997. In states like California, which runs the two largest women's prisons in the nation, the decline is even sharper. In 1992, 16 percent of the women admitted to the California prison system were incarcerated for violent crimes, compared to 37.2 percent in 1982. What explains the increase? A recent study by the Bureau of Justice Statistics (BJS) indicates that growth in the number of violent offenders has been the major factor for male prison population growth, but for the female prison population, "drug offenders were the largest source of growth." One explanation, then, is that the "war on drugs" has become a largely unannounced war on women. In 1979, one in 10 women in prison was doing time for drugs. Today, drug offenders account for more than a third of the female prison population (37.4 percent). Finally, while the intent of "get tough" policies was to rid society of drug dealers and so-called drug kingpins, more than a third (35.9 percent) of the women serving time for drug offenses in state prisons are there on charges of possession.[1]

POLICIES IMPACTING WOMEN'S IMPRISONMENT

Many observers suspect that the increase in women's imprisonment is due to an array of policy changes within the criminal justice system, rather than a change in the seriousness of women's crime.

Certainly, as data on the characteristics of women in prison indicate, the passage of increased penalties for drug offenses has been a major factor. Also important has been the implementation of a variety of sentencing reform initiatives which, while devoted to reducing class and race disparities in male sentencing, pay little attention to gender.[2]

The scant evidence we have suggests that sentencing reform has played a major role in the soaring increase of women in federal prisons. In 1988, before full implementation of sentencing guidelines, women comprised 6.5 percent of those in federal institutions; by 1992, that figure had jumped to 8 percent. The number of women in federal prisons climbed by 97.4 percent in the space of three years.

Data on the offense characteristics of women in federal institutions further confirm the role played by policy shifts in response to drug convictions. In 1989, 44.5 percent of the women incarcerated in federal institutions were being held for drug offenses. Two years later, this figure was up to 68 percent.[3] Twenty years ago, nearly two-thirds of the women convicted of federal felonies were granted probation, but in 1991, only 28 percent were given straight probation. The mean time to be served by female drug offenders increased from 27 months in July 1984 to 67 months in June 1990.

As a result of these pressures, the federal prison system holds 8,306 women, and the number of women incarcerated in federal facilities continues to increase at an even faster pace than that found in state prisons. Additionally, women comprise an even larger proportion of those incarcerated in federal prisons (7.4 percent, compared to 6.3 percent in state prisons).

Other less obvious policy changes also have played a role in increasing women's imprisonment. For example, look at new technologies for determining drug use (e.g., urinalysis). Many women are being returned to prison for technical parole violations because they fail to pass random drug tests. Of the 6,000 women incarcerated in California in 1993, approximately one-third (32 percent) were imprisoned on parole violations. In Hawaii, 55 percent of new admissions to the women's prison during a two-month period in 1991 had been returned to prison for parole violations (largely drug violations). Finally, in Oregon, during a one-year period from October 1992 to September 1993, only 16 percent of females admitted to institutions were incarcerated for new convictions; the rest were probation and parole violators.

The impact of gender-blind sentencing, coupled with what might be seen as increased policing of women's behavior while on probation or parole, have played major, though largely hidden, roles in the growth of women's imprisonment.

VENGEFUL EQUITY?

What has happened in the last few decades signals a major change in the way the country is responding to women's offending. Without much fanfare and certainly with little public discussion or debate, the male model of incarceration has been increasingly accessed in response to the soaring number of women inmates.

Some might argue that this pattern is simply the product of a lack of reflection or imagination on the part of those charged with administering the nation's prison systems. They are, after all, used to running prisons built around the male model of inmate. However, an additional theme also is emerging in modern correctional response to women inmates: vengeful equity. This is the dark side of the equity or parity model of justice—one which emphasizes treating women offenders as though they were men, particularly when the outcome is punitive, in the name of equal justice.

Perhaps the starkest expression of this impulse has been the creation of chain gangs for women. While these have surfaced in several states, the most publicized example comes from Arizona. There, a sheriff pronounced himself an "equal opportunity incarcerator" and encouraged women "now locked up with three or four others in dank, cramped disciplinary cells" to "volunteer" for a 15-woman chain gang. Defending his controversial move, he commented, "If women can fight for their country, and bless them for that, if they can walk a beat, if they can protect the people and arrest violators of the law, then they should have no problem with picking up trash in 120 degrees." Other examples of vengeful equity can be

found in the creation of women's boot camps, and in the argument that women should be subjected to capital punishment at the same rate as men.

FEMALE OFFENDER CHARACTERISTICS

But who are these women inmates, and does it make sense to treat women in prison as though they were men? BJS recently conducted a national survey of imprisoned women in the United States and found that women in prison have far higher rates of physical and sexual abuse than their male counterparts. Forty-three percent of the women surveyed "reported they had been abused at least once" before their current admission to prison; the comparable figure for men was 12.2 percent.

For about a third of all women in prison (31.7 percent), the abuse started when they were young girls, but continued as they became adults. A key gender difference emerges here. A number of imprisoned young men (10.7 percent) also report abuse as boys, but the abuse generally does not continue into adulthood. One in four women reported that the abuse started during adulthood, compared to just 3 percent of male offenders. Fully 33.5 percent of the women surveyed reported physical abuse, and a slightly higher number (33.9 percent) had been sexually abused either as girls or young women, compared to relatively small percentages of men (10 percent of boys and 5.3 percent of adult men in prison).

A look at the offenses for which women are incarcerated quickly puts to rest the notion of hyperviolent, nontraditional women offenders. Nearly half of all women in prison are serving sentences for nonviolent offenses and have been convicted in the past of only nonviolent offenses. By 1996, about two-thirds of women in the nation's prisons were serving time either for drug offenses or property offenses.

Even when women commit violent offenses, gender plays an important role. Research indicates, for example, that of women convicted of murder or manslaughter, many had killed husbands or boyfriends who had repeatedly and violently abused them. In New York, of the women committed to the state's prisons for homicide in 1986, 49 percent had been the victims of abuse at some point in their lives and

59 percent of the women who killed someone close to them were being abused at the time of the offense. For half of the women committed for homicide, it was their first and only offense.

As with previous studies of women in prison, the BJS survey found that two-thirds of the women had at least one child under 18, yet more than half had never received visits from their children. Most of the women who did receive visits from their children saw them once a month or less frequently. More women were able to phone or send mail to their children, but one in five never sent mail to or received mail from their children, and one in four never talked on the phone with them. This was despite the fact that many of these women, prior to their incarceration, were taking care of their children (unlike their male counterparts).

Just under three-quarters of the women had children who had lived with them before going to prison, compared to slightly more than half (52.9 percent) of incarcerated men. In most cases, the imprisoned women's mothers (the children's grandmothers) take care of their children, while male inmates are more likely to be able to count on the children's mothers (89.7 percent). These patterns are particularly pronounced among African-American and Hispanic women.

Most importantly, the BJS study, like those done before, clearly documents the number of women of color behind bars. The numbers indicate that nearly half of the women in the nation's prisons are African American (46 percent) and Hispanic (14.2 percent). These data begin to hint at another important theme: The surge in women's imprisonment, particularly in the area of drug offenses, has disproportionately hit women of color in the United States. Specifically, while the number of women in state prisons for drug sales has increased by 433 percent between 1986 and 1991, this increase is far steeper for African-American women (828 percent) and Hispanic women (328 percent) than for Caucasian women (241 percent).

Women in prison, then, have different personal histories than their male counterparts and less serious offense backgrounds. In particular, women's long histories of victimization, coupled with the relative nonviolence of their crimes, suggests that extensive reliance on imprisonment could easily be rethought without compromising public safety.

WHAT COULD WE DO DIFFERENTLY?

Inattention to gender difference, willful or otherwise, has meant that many modern women's prisons have encountered serious, and unanticipated, difficulties in managing this population. Jails and prisons are generally unprepared for the large number of pregnant women in their custody (some estimates put this at one in 10). The sexual harassment of women inmates also is an increasingly well-documented problem that is receiving both national and international attention. Finally, procedures that have been routine in corrections for decades (strip searches) are now being understood as problematic in women's prisons (particularly when dealing with victims of past sexual traumas). To put it simply, gender matters in corrections, and a woman in prison is not, and never will be, identical to her male counterpart.

Given the backgrounds of women in prison, many would argue that they could be better served in the community due to the decreased seriousness of their crimes and the treatable antecedents to their criminality. Since the expansion of the female prison population has been fueled primarily by increased rates of incarceration for drug offenses, not by commitments for crimes of violence, women in prison seem to be obvious candidates for alternative, in-community sentencing. To make this shift requires both planning and focus—something that has been absent in U.S. corrections with reference to women in prison.

We could, though, look north to Canada, where a high-level Task Force on Federally Sentenced Women was convened by the prime minister to deal with the long-standing problems within that nation's federal facility, as well as to lay out a national plan for women's corrections in Canada. California also has convened the Commission on Female Inmate and Parolee Issues to examine the unique needs of women offenders in that state.

It is clear that the United States should consider a national initiative similar to the Canadian task force; the numbers alone argue for a more coherent and planned national strategy regarding women in jail and prison.

The United States now imprisons more people than at any time in its history, and it has the world's second highest incarceration rate (behind the newly created nation of Russia). Women's share of the nation's prison population, measured in either absolute or relative terms, has never been higher. All of this has occurred without serious planning, consideration or debate.

As a nation, we face a choice. We can continue to spend tax dollars on the costly incarceration of women guilty of petty drug and property crimes, or we can seek other solutions to the problems of drug-dependent women. Given the characteristics of the women in prison, it is clear that the decarceration of large numbers of women in prison would not jeopardize public safety. Further, the money saved could be reinvested in programs designed to meet women's needs, which would enrich not only their lives but the lives of many other women who are at risk for criminal involvement.

Clearly, any in-community or alternative sentencing programs should be crafted with women's needs at the center. For example, many traditional forms of in-community sentences involve home detention—clearly unworkable for women with abusive boyfriends or husbands, but also problematic for women who are drug-dependent and/or unemployed. Restitution also is not a viable choice for some women offenders for many of the same reasons.

Women's programs must, first and foremost, give participants strategies to deal with their profound substance abuse problems. They must also be gender-sensitive in additional ways: they must understand that most women take drugs as a form of self-medication (rather than for adventure or challenge), and they must be sensitive to women's unique circumstances (by providing such services as child care and transportation). Community programs must also deal with women's immediate needs for safe housing and stable employment.

By moving dollars from women's imprisonment to women's services in the community, we not only will help women—we also will help their children. In the process, we are helping to break the cycle of poverty, desperation, crime and imprisonment that burdens so many of these women and their families.

ENDNOTES

1. In 1979, 26 percent of women doing time in state prison for drug offenses were incarcerated solely for possession.

2. Myrna Raeder notes, for example, that judges are constrained by federal guidelines from considering family responsibilities, particularly pregnancy and motherhood, which in the past may have kept women out of prison. Yet the impact of these "neutral" guidelines is to eliminate from consideration the unique situation of mothers, especially single mothers, unless their situation can be established to be "extraordinary." Nearly 90 percent of male inmates report that their wives or girlfriends are taking care of their children; by contrast, only 22 percent of mothers in prison could count on the fathers of their children to care for them during imprisonment. This means that many women in prison, the majority of whom are mothers, face the potential, if not actual, loss of their children. This is not a penalty that men in prison experience.

3. The comparable male figure was 58 percent in 1993, up from 39.6 percent in 1989.

REFERENCES

Adams, Rukaiyah, David Onek and Alissa Riker. 1998. *Double jeopardy: An assessment of the felony drug provision of the Welfare Reform Act.* San Francisco: Justice Policy Institute.

Adelberg, Ellen and Claudia Currie. 1993. *In conflict with the law: Women and the Canadian criminal justice system.* Vancouver: Press Gang Publishers.

Bloom, Barbara and David Steinhart. 1993. *Why punish the children?* San Francisco: National Council on Crime and Delinquency.

Bloom, Barbara, Meda Chesney-Lind and Barbara Owen. 1994. *Women in prison in California: Hidden victims of the war on drugs.* San Francisco: Center on Juvenile and Criminal Justice.

Bureau of Justice Statistics. 1988. *Profile of state prison inmates, 1986.* Washington, D.C.: U.S. Department of Justice.

Bureau of Justice Statistics. 1989. *Prisoners in 1988.* Washington, D.C.: U.S. Department of Justice.

Bureau of Justice Statistics. 1993. *Prisoners in 1992.* Washington, D.C.: U.S. Department of Justice.

Bureau of Justice Statistics. 1994. *Women in Prison.* Washington, D.C.: U.S. Department of Justice.

Bureau of Justice Statistics, 1998a. *Prisoners in 1997.* Washington, D.C.: U.S. Department of Justice.

Bureau of Justice Statistics, 1998b. *Prison and jail inmates at mid-year 1997.* Washington, D.C.: U.S. Department of Justice.

Calahan, Margaret, 1986. *Historical corrections: Statistics in the United States, 1850–1984.* Washington, D.C.: Bureau of Justice Statistics.

Chesney-Lind, Meda. 1997. *The female offender: Girls, women and crime.* Thousand Oaks, Calif.: Sage Publications.

Federal Bureau of Investigation. 1997. *Crime in the United States: 1996 Uniform Crime Reports.* Washington, D.C.: U.S. Department of Justice.

Huling, Tracy. 1991. *Breaking the silence.* Correctional Association of New York, March 4, mimeo.

Immarigeon, Russ and Meda Chesney-Lind. 1992. *Women's prisons: Overcrowded and overused.* San Francisco: National Council on Crime and Delinquency.

Kim, E. 1996. Sheriff says he'll have chain gangs for women. *Tuscaloosa News* (August 16, p. Al).

Mauer, Marc. 1994. *Americans behind bars: The international use of incarceration, 1992–1993.* Washington, D.C.: The Sentencing Project (September).

Mauer, Marc and Tracy Huling. 1995. *Young black Americans and the criminal justice system: Five years later.* Washington, D.C.: The Sentencing Project.

O'Brien, Patricia. 1998. *Women in prison: Making it in the free world.* University of Illinois at Chicago: School of Social Work.

Raeder, Myrna. 1993. Gender and sentencing: Single moms, battered women and other sex-based anomalies in the gender-free world of the federal sentencing guidelines. *Pepperdine Law Review 20*(3):905–990.

Rafter, Nicole Hahn. 1990. *Partial justice: Women, prisons and social control.* New Brunswick, N.J.: Transaction Books.

Singer, Linda R. 1973. Women and the correctional process. *American Criminal Law Review,* 11:295–308.

Snell, Tracy L. and Danielle C. Morton. 1994. *Women in prison.* Washington, D.C.: Bureau of Justice Statistics, Special Report.

STUDY QUESTIONS FOR READING 2

1. How much faster is the incarceration binge taking place for women? Women now make up what percent of the prison population?

2. Did the increase in women's incarceration stem from an increase in women's criminal activity or women's violence? How do you know?

3. In 1980 and today, what percentage of women serving prison time were serving it for drug offenses? Of those serving time for drug offenses in state prisons, what percentage are serving time for possession rather than sales?

4. What is vengeful equity?

5. What are some examples of vengeful equity?

6. What numbers does Chesney-Lind use to show that women prisoners have been abused more than male prisoners, and that some of this abuse occurs in adulthood?

7. How does Chesney-Lind argue that women are less serious offenders than men?

8. What fraction of imprisoned mothers had children living with them prior to incarceration? What fraction of imprisoned fathers had children living with them prior to incarceration? For children with mothers in prison, most are cared for by their maternal grandmothers. For children with fathers in prison, what percentage are cared for by their mothers? Why does this make community programs for women especially important?

9. To summarize, why does Chesney-Lind believe community corrections would be better for many incarcerated women without jeopardizing community safety?

CORRECTIONS
A PICTURE IN BLACK AND WHITE

SAMUEL WALKER
CASSIA SPOHN
MIRIAM DeLONE

PRISON VERSUS COLLEGE:
MINORITIES IN SOCIETY

In 1996, more African Americans were under some form of correctional supervision (jail, prison, probation, and parole)[1] than were enrolled in college:[2] 2,099,500 versus 1,505,600. Among whites, the situation is just the opposite: more than ten million in college[3] and just over three million under correctional supervision.[4] These data dramatize the most compelling fact about the U.S. correctional system: African Americans are overrepresented at all levels. To put it another way, roughly 10 percent of those seeking degrees are African American, whereas half of those under correctional supervision are African American.

GOALS OF THE CHAPTER

This chapter describes various disparities in the ethnic and racial makeup of the U.S. correctional system. It examines which groups are overrepresented in situations of incarceration and supervision in the community. The extent of minority overrepresentation also is explored in relation to federal versus state populations, regional differences, historical fluctuations, gender distinctions, and juvenile populations.

This descriptive information is supplemented by a discussion of current research on discrimination in the correctional setting. Finally, the inmate social system, which reflects key aspects of prison life, is discussed. This section focuses on the influence of minority group status on prison subcultures and religion.

THE INCARCERATED: PRISON AND
JAIL POPULATIONS

Describing incarcerated populations in the United States is a complicated task. The answer to the question, Who is locked up? depends on what penal institution and which inmates we are discussing. There are a number of important distinctions between prisons and jails, federal and state institutions, and male and female inmates. In addition, important changes occur over time.

Prisons are distinct from jails because they serve different functions in the criminal justice system.[5] Federal and state prisons must be examined separately because of the differences in federal and state crime.[6] These differences result in different levels of minority overrepresentation. Male and female inmate populations also have different racial and ethnic compositions.

Minority Overrepresentation

The primary observation to be made about the prison population in the United States is that African Americans are strikingly overrepresented compared to their presence in the general population. They are less than 15 percent of the U.S. population but nearly 55 percent of all incarcerated offenders. Conversely, whites are underrepresented compared to their presence in the population: over 80 percent of the population but just under half of the prison population.

Not all racial and ethnic minorities show the same pattern of overrepresentation in prison populations. Hispanics comprise about 10 percent of the U.S. population, but are roughly 16 percent of the prison population. In recent years, Hispanics have represented the fastest growing minority group being imprisoned: In 1985 they were 10.5 percent of the prison populations, and in 1996 they were 17.7 percent. These increases reflect a rate twice as high as the increase for African American and white inmates.[7] With little information about the number of Asian and Native American prisoners, it appears their representation is not substantially greater than their representation in the general population.

The preceding numbers reflect the combined figures of state and federal prison populations. Although state prison populations account for the majority (nearly 90 percent) of incarcerated offenders, a look at the racial and ethnic percentages in state and federal populations separately is warranted. Just as state and federal laws differ, so will their prison populations, as they present different offenses and unique sentencing practices. An important implication for federal prisoners is that they can expect to serve more of their original sentence than state inmates do (by up to 50 percent).[8]

In data from 1996, the magnitude of racial and ethnic differences in state versus federal prison populations is noticeable.[9] African Americans are more seriously overrepresented in the state prison populations than in federal prison populations (nearly 55 percent versus less than 40 percent). In contrast, when these data are disaggregated, Hispanics and Native American populations are more seriously overrepresented in federal prison populations. That is, the percentage of federal inmates who are identified as Hispanic and Native Americans is slightly higher than their representation in the general population. Thus, the representation of both Hispanics and Native Americans appears closer to their distribution in the general population when it comes to state prisons.

These differences in disparity among racial and ethnic groups are explained in large part by different patterns of offending. Whites are relatively more likely to commit and be convicted of federal offenses. African Americans, conversely, are relatively more likely to be arrested and convicted for index crimes, which are generally state offenses. Hispanics are consistently overrepresented among convicted drug offenders at the federal level and immigration law offenders.[10] Finally, Native Americans are substantially impacted by the Major Crimes Act that brings many offenders into federal courts.[11]

Differences in the magnitude of racial disparity among the various racial and ethnic groups in prison offer more support that the impact of race and ethnicity is not a constant. That is, the impact of overrepresentation in incarceration settings varies in magnitude and quality. One of the differences manifests itself in the release figures of state and federal prisons. There are important implications for those groups that spend more time in federal prison than in state prisons, given that federal prisoners can expect to serve 50 percent more of their original sentence than state inmates.[12] This differential has the most detrimental impact on Hispanics, who are a substantially larger part of the federal population than the state population.

Racial and Ethnic Female Prisoners

Women make up less than 10 percent of federal and state prison populations.[13] Prison populations have increased drastically in the last several years, and the increase for female inmates is almost twice that for male inmates (9.1 percent versus 4.7 percent in 1996).[14] Among female prisoners, there are similar patterns of overrepresentation in terms of the racial and ethnic makeup compared to the overall (predominately male) prison population discussed earlier. Just over half of the female prison population is African American, with just under half identified as white females.

Comparing available demographic information from state and federal prison populations, African American females represent a higher percentage of state than federal inmates (just over one third of female federal prisoners are reported as African American).[15] However, Hispanic females account for almost one fourth of the female federal prison popu-

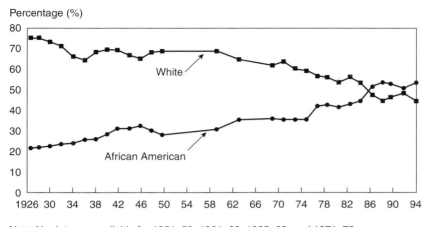

Percentage (%)

Note: No data are available for 1951–59, 1961–63, 1965–69, and 1971–73.

FIGURE 3.1   Admissions to State and Federal Prison, by Race, 1926–1996
Original, plus: BJS, *Correctional Populations in the United States, 1996* (Washington, D.C.: U.S. Department of Justice, 1999).

lation, leaving the percentage of state offenders similar to the representation of Hispanic females in the general population. Once again, this aspect of differential disparity in federal and state demographic descriptions of inmates has implications for the time racial and ethnic minorities actually serve in prison. As noted, the federal inmates serve, on average, 50 percent more of their sentence than state offenders.[16] Thus, Hispanic females are not merely overrepresented in federal prison populations, but are also subject to the longer federal sentences.

Historical Trends

The overrepresentation of African Americans in state and federal prisons is not a new phenomenon. Figure 3.1 provides a graphic illustration of the changing demographic composition of the prison population from 1926 to 1996. Reviewing this figure we can document a disproportionate number of African Americans in the prison population since 1926 (the beginning of national-level data collection on prison populations). The racial disparity has increased in recent years, however. In 1926, African Americans represented 9 percent of the population and 21 percent of the prison

population.[17] Over time, the proportion of the population of African Americans increased steadily, reaching 30 percent in the 1940s, 35 percent in 1960, 44 percent in 1980, and leveling off to around 50 percent in the 1990s. The 1926 figure represented an African American prisoner population ratio of 2.5 to 1; the current ratio is 4 to 1.

Impact of the War on Drugs

Dramatic increases in the overrepresentation of African Americans in the prison population have occurred in a context of generally increasing prison population totals and rising incarceration rates since the early 1970s. Although the incarceration binge surely has multiple sources, it may reflect an impact of the war on drugs. Tonry,[18] for example, argued that the war on drugs has had a particularly detrimental effect on African American males. Evidence of this impact, he argued, can be seen by focusing on the key years affected by the war on drugs: 1980 to 1992. During this period, the number of white males incarcerated in state and federal prison increased by 143 percent; for African American males the number increased by 186 percent.[19]

Correctional Personnel: Similarities and Differences on the Basis of Race

Currently, federal and state prisons have fairly equitable minority representation among correctional officers and supervisors, compared to the general population.[20] The important reasons for achieving such goals are numerous. Ensuring fair employment practices in government hiring is one goal, and others champion the importance of minority decision makers as having a beneficial (and perhaps less discriminatory) impact on the treatment of minority populations.

Author's[21] review of the research in the area of attitudes and beliefs of correctional officers toward inmates and punishment ideologies suggests that respondents' views do appear to differ in many ways on the basis of race. In particular, he noted that African American officers appear to have more positive attitudes toward inmates than white officers. However, others have found that black officers expressed a preference for greater distance between officers and inmates than did white officers. Additionally, neither white nor

African American correction officers reflect an ability to correctly identify the self-reported needs of prison inmates.

In relation to ideological issues, African American officers were more often supportive of rehabilitation than their white counterparts. African American officers also appear to be more ambivalent about the current punitive nature of the criminal justice system, indicating that the court system is often too harsh.

In short, current research does not offer a definitive answer to the question of whether minority correctional officers make different decisions. Assuming that differential decision making by correction officers could be both a positive and negative exercise of discretion, at what point are differential decisions beneficial to inmates versus unprofessional or unjust? What research could be done to resolve the issue of the presence or absence of differential decision making by correctional officers on the basis of race?

Statisticians for the federal Bureau of Justice Statistics argue that the sources of growth for prison populations differ for white and African American inmates. Specifically, drug offenses and violent offenses account for the largest source of growth among state prison inmates. During the ten-year period from 1985 to 1995, "the increasing number of drug offenders accounted for 42 percent of the total growth of black inmates and 26 percent of the growth among white inmates."[22] Similarly, the number of black inmates serving time for violent offenses rose by 37 percent, whereas growth among white inmates was at a higher 47 percent.[23]

The differential impact of the war on drugs may be due more to the enforcement strategies of law enforcement than higher patterns of minority drug use. Critics argue that whereas the police are *reactive* in responding to robbery, burglary, and other index offenses, they are *proactive* in dealing with drug offenses. There is evidence to suggest that they target minority communities—where drug dealing is more

visible and where it is thus easier to make arrests—and tend to give less attention to drug activities in other neighborhoods.

Incarceration Rates

Another way to describe the makeup of U.S. prisons is to examine incarceration rates. The information offered by incarceration rates expands the picture of the prison inmate offered in population totals and percentages (given earlier). Incarceration rates offer the most vivid picture of the overrepresentation of African Americans in prison populations. Rates allow for the standardization of population figures that can be calculated over a particular target population. For example, the general incarceration rate in 1995 was 615 per 100,000 population. This number can be further explored by calculating rates that reflect the number of one race group in the prison population relative to the number of that population in the overall U.S. population.

Over a ten-year period, African Americans and Hispanics are substantially more likely than whites to be incarcerated in state and federal prisons. Although rates for all groups are increasing, the rate for African American males remained the highest, which was six to seven times higher than that for white males. Hispanic rates were also higher than the rates for whites, but lower than the rates for African Americans. Note that rates of incarceration for females are substantially lower than male rates, but they are increasing over time, with African American female rates of incarceration nearly seven times higher than those for white females.[24]

JAILS AND MINORITIES

The Role of Jail

Jail populations are significantly different than prison populations. Because jails serve a different function in the criminal justice system, they are subject to different dynamics in terms of admissions and releases. The Annual Survey of Jails[25] reveals that approximately half of the daily population of jail inmates is convicted offenders and half are awaiting trial. Those awaiting trial are in jail because they cannot raise bail or they are denied bail altogether. The other inmates are convicted offenders who have been sentenced to serve time in jail. Although the vast majority of these inmates have been convicted of misdemeanors, some convicted felons are given a "split sentence" involving jail followed by probation.

Because of the jail's role as a pretrial detention center, there is a high rate of turnover among the jail population. Thus, *daily* population of jails is lower than prisons, but the *annual* total of people incarcerated in jails is higher.

Minority Overrepresentation

African Americans and Hispanics are overrepresented in jails (41.2 and 15.5 percent, respectively), whereas whites are underrepresented (41.3 percent) in jail populations compared to the general population. The picture depicted by these numbers is similar to the reflection of race and ethnicity in prison populations.

(These data represent a static one-day count, as opposed to an annual total of all people who pass through the jail system.) Although these data combine race and ethnicity into one category, as opposed to distinction of ethnicity as separate from race, limited comparisons to prison figures can be made. Keep in mind that some portion of the Hispanic population in a separate category system would fall in to the white race category, whereas others would fall in the African American or "other" categories.

Because of the jail's function as a pretrial detention center, jail population is heavily influenced by bail decisions. If more people are released on nonfinancial considerations, the number of people in jail will be lower. This raises the questions of racial discrimination in bail setting. There is evidence that judges impose higher bail—or are more likely to deny bail altogether—if the defendant is a racial minority.

PAROLE: EARLY RELEASE FROM PRISON

Parole is a form of early release from prison under supervision in the community. Not surprisingly, therefore, parole populations are similar in racial and ethnic distribution to federal and state prison populations. In 1997, 54 percent of the inmates released on parole were white, 45 percent were African American, and less than 1 percent were of other races.[26] Similarly, about 21 percent of the parole entrants were designated as Hispanic.

The benevolent side of this observation is that African Americans and Hispanics are making the transition to parole (arguably a positive move) in proportions similar to prison population figures. However, parole revocation figures require a closer look.

Success and Failure on Parole

A parolee "succeeds" on parole if he or she completes the terms of supervision without violations. A parolee can "fail" in one of two ways: by either being arrested for another crime or by violating one of the conditions of parole release (using drugs, possessing a weapon, violating curfew, etc.). In either case, parole authorities can revoke parole and send the person back to prison.

Box 3.1

International Comparisons

In the international arena, the United States has one of the highest incarceration rates in the world. According to the Sentencing Project,[27] in 1993 we had 519 people incarcerated in jails and prisons for every 100,000 people in the general population, second only to Russia (558 persons per 100,000 population). The next closest country was South Africa with the substantially lower rate of 368 per 100,000 people. European countries have much lower rates: England/Wales at 93, Germany at 80, and Sweden at 69.

The Sentencing Project also calculated that the incarceration rate for African American males in the United States is more than four times the rate for South Africa in the last years of apartheid. That is, in 1993, the incarceration rate for African American males was 3,822 per 100,000 compared to the rate of 815 per 100,000 for South African black males.

The data ... also illustrate that African American males have been incarcerated at higher rates than white males. Specifically since 1985, the incarceration rates for African American males have increased at a more rapid pace than incarceration rates for white males.

The racial disparity in the nation's prison populations is revealed even more dramatically by data from the Sentencing Project that estimate that on any given day 42 percent of the young African American men in Washington, D.C. were under some form of correctional supervision. In contrast, the U.S. Department of Justice estimates that less than 3 percent of the adult U.S. population is under correctional supervision.

Parole revocation, therefore, is nearly equivalent to the judge's power to sentence an offender in the first place, because it can mean that the offender will return to prison. The decision to revoke parole is discretionary; parole authorities may choose to overlook a violation and not send the person back to prison. This opens the door for possible discrimination.

The revocation data reveal more disparity at this stage of decision making than at the entrance to parole.[28] Overall, 37 percent of all parolees at the state level successfully completed parole in 1990. The success rate varied somewhat by racial and ethnic groups: 39 percent of whites, 34 percent of African Americans, 35 percent of other races, and 31 percent of Hispanics. The percentage of parolees returning to prison complements these proportions, with Hispanics having the highest return rates and whites the lowest.

Recent data on federal parole revocations[29] reveal that approximately 69 percent of federal parole discharges were from successful completion of parole conditions. Once again, these rates vary by minority group status. Whites and other races had the highest

Box 3.2

Supervision in the Community: An Uneven Playing Field?

Both parole and probation involve supervision in the community under a set of specific provisions for client behavior. One of the most common provisions is the requirement of employment. Not being able to attain or retain employment may lead to a violation of supervision conditions and unsuccessful discharge of an individual from probation or parole. Essentially, a person could be sent to prison for being unemployed. It is possible that the employment provision creates uneven hardships for minorities. In 1993, unemployment rates were 6 percent for whites, 12.5 percent for African Americans, and 10.5 percent for Hispanics.[30] That is, ethnic- and race-specific unemployment rates vary substantially, showing the disadvantaged status of minorities in the labor market. Does this aspect of the general economy adversely affect minorities on probation and parole? If yes, what should be done?

successful completion rate of 76 percent, followed by Hispanics at 68 percent, and African Americans with the lowest at 53 percent. Similarly, African Americans had the highest return to prison rates (36 percent), with all other groups exhibiting a return rate of less than 20 percent.

PROBATION: A CASE OF SENTENCING DISCRIMINATION?

Probation is an alternative to incarceration, a sentence to supervision in the community. The majority of all the people under correctional supervision are on probation, totaling over three million people.

African Americans are overrepresented (35 percent) in the probation population relative to their presence in the general population.[31] Correspondingly, whites are underrepresented at 64 percent of all probationers.[32] The ethnic breakdown of those under sentence of probation reveals Hispanics are again overrepresented compared to non-Hispanics (16 percent versus 84 percent).[33]

It is immediately apparent that the racial disparity for probation is not as great as it is for the prison population, however. Given that probation is a less severe sentence than prison, this difference may indicate that the advantage of receiving the less severe sentence of probation is reserved for whites. In a study of sentencing in California, Petersilia found that 71 percent of whites convicted of a felony were granted probation, compared with 67 percent of African Americans and 65 percent of Hispanics.[34] Similarly, Spohn and colleagues found that in "borderline cases" in which judges could impose either a long probation sentence or a short prison sentence, whites were more likely to get probation and African Americans were more likely to get prison.

PERSPECTIVES ON THE RACIAL DISTRIBUTION OF CORRECTIONAL POPULATIONS

Several theoretical arguments are advanced to explain the overwhelming overrepresentation of African Americans in the correctional system. The most fundamental question is whether prison populations reflect discrimination in the criminal justice system or other factors. One view is that the overrepresentation reflects widespread discrimination; the alternative view is that the overrepresentation results from a disproportionate involvement in criminal activity on the part of minorities. Mann[35] argued that there is systematic discrimination based on color, whereas Wilbanks[36] contended that the idea of systematic discrimination is a "myth."

The work of Alfred Blumstein offers a benchmark to explore the results of such research. Focusing on 1979 prison population data, Blumstein sought to isolate the impact of discrimination from other possible factors. The key element of his research is the following formula:[37]

> X = *ratio of expected black-to-white incarceration rates based only on arrest disproportionality/ ratio of black-to-white incarceration rates actually observed.*

Essentially, this formula compares the expected black–white disparity (X) in state prison populations based on recorded black–white disparity in arrest rates (numerator) over the observed black–white disparity in incarceration rates (denominator). Thus, accepting the argument that arrest rates are not a reflection of discrimination, Blumstein's formula calculates the portion of the prison population left unexplained by the disproportionate representation of African Americans at the arrest stage. In short, this figure is the amount of actual racial disproportionality in incarceration rates that is open to an explanation or charge of discrimination.

Overall, Blumstein found that 20 percent of the racial disparity in incarceration rates is left unexplained by the overrepresentation of African Americans at the arrest stage. Crime-specific rates indicate that results vary by crime type:[38]

All offenses	20.0 percent
Homicide	2.8 percent
Aggravated assault	5.2 percent
Robbery	15.6 percent
Rape	26.3 percent
Burglary	33.1 percent
Larceny/auto theft	45.6 percent
Drugs	48.9 percent

Arguably, the main implication of this list is that the level of unexplained disproportionality is "directly related to the discretion permitted or used in handling each of the offenses, which tends to be related to offense seriousness—the less serious the offenses (and the greater discretion), the greater the amount of the disproportionality in prison that must be accounted for on grounds other than differences in arrest."[39]

This observation is particularly salient in the context of drug offenses. . . . [Some] arguments . . . contend that drug arrest decisions are subject to more proactive enforcement than most offenses. Combine this observation with the fact that during the recent surge of incarceration rates (1980–1996), drug offenses have had the greatest impact on new commitments to prison. In short, the offense category indicated to suffer from the broad use of discrimination and the most opportunity for discrimination is the fastest growing portion of new commitments to prison. Thus, Blumstein's findings, although generally not an indictment of the criminal justice system, suggest an ominous warning for the presence of discrimination during the era of the war on drugs.

Langan[40] reexamined Blumstein's argument, contending that he relied on an inappropriate data set. Langan argued that prison admissions offered a more appropriate comparison to arrest differentials than prison populations. Langan also incorporated victim identification data as a substitute for arrest data to circumvent the biases associated with arrest. In addition to altering Blumstein's formula, he looked at three years of data (1973, 1979, 1982) across five offense types (robbery, aggravated assault, simple assault, burglary, and larceny). Even after making these modifications, Langan confirmed Blumstein's findings: About 20 percent of the racial overrepresentation in prison admissions was left unexplained.

In an updated analysis with 1990 prison population data, Blumstein found that the amount of unexplained variation in racially disproportionate prison populations on the basis of arrest data increased from 20 to 24 percent. In addition, the differentials dis-

---

FOCUS ON AN ISSUE

Civil Rights of Convicted Felons

Individuals convicted of felonies in the United States may experience a range of sentences from incarceration to probation. Such sentences in effect limit the civil rights of the convicted. No longer do we live in a society that views the convicted felon from the legal status of civil death, literally a slave of the state, but some civil rights restrictions endure after the convicted serves a judicially imposed sentence. *Collateral consequences* is a term used to refer to the statutory restrictions imposed by a legislative body on a convicted felon's rights. Such restrictions vary by state, but they include restrictions on employment, carrying firearms, holding public office, and voting.

Forty-six states have some restriction on the rights of convicted felons to vote. In most states the right to vote can be restored (automatically or by petition) after completion of the sentence (or within a fixed number of years). However, in fourteen states the legal prohibition on voting is permanent. Given the current increases in incarceration rates across the country, the additional penalty of disenfranchisement for convicted felons becomes an increasing concern. In short, the permanence of this measure may have unanticipated consequences.

Given the overrepresentation of African American males in our prisons, "significant proportions of the black population in some states have been locked out of the voting booth."[41] For example, in the state of Florida, which denies voting rights permanently to convicted felons, nearly one third of the African American male population is not eligible to vote. Arguably, laws such as these, which have the effect of barring a substantial portion of the minority population from voting, fail to promote a racially diverse society. Should convicted offenders be allowed to earn back their right to vote as recognition of their efforts at rehabilitation? Should we change laws that have a racial impact, even if the intent is not racially motivated?

cussed earlier on the basis of discretion and serious-ness increased for drug crimes and less serious crimes, decreasing only for homicide and robbery.[42] This seems to confirm the argument that the war on drugs has increased the racial disparities in prison popula-tions. . . .

Women in Prison

Studies addressing the "prisonization" of women are less numerous than those for men, but they are in-creasing in number. Within this growing body of re-search, the issue of race is not routinely addressed, either. When race is assessed the comparisons are gen-erally limited to African Americans and whites. The evidence is mixed on the issue of whether race affects the adjustment of women to prison life.

MacKenzie[43] explained the behaviors (conflicts and misconduct reports) of women in prison on the basis of age and attitudes (anxiety, fear of victimiza-tion). She commented that the four prisons she ex-amined are similar in racial composition, but she failed to comment on whether she explored differ-ences by race in relation to attitudes and aggressive behavior. Such research ignores the possibility that race may influence one's perception of prison life, tendencies toward aggression, age of inmate, or length of time in prison.

MacKenzie and others[44] did, in later works, ad-dress race in the demographic description of the in-carcerated women. In a study of one women's prison in Louisiana, for example, they found that nonwhite women were severely overrepresented among all pris-oners and even more likely to be serving long sen-tences. Their findings indicate unique adjustment problems for long-term inmates, but they failed to in-corporate race into their explanatory observations about institutional misconduct. This omission seems contrary to the observation that nonwhite women are more likely to have longer sentences.

Race has specifically been recognized as a factor in research addressing the issue of sexual deprivation among incarcerated women. Leger[45] identified racial dimensions to several key explanatory factors in the participation of female prisoners in lesbianism. First, the demographic information reveals that most lesbian relationships are intraracial and that no distinctions emerged by race in participation in the gay or straight groups. Second, once dividing the group by the char-acteristics of previous confinements (yes or no) and age at first gay experience, the pattern of even repre-sentation of whites and African Americans changed. African American females were overrepresented in the group indicating previous confinement, and the in-formation about age at first arrest indicates that African American females are more likely to have en-gaged in their first lesbian act prior to their first arrest.

Juveniles Under Correctional Supervision

Juvenile court statistics reveal that the racial makeup of juveniles at key stages of the system varies by de-cision type. Generally, nonwhite youth (the majority of whom are African American) are overrepresented at every stage of decision making. They are also at greater risk of receiving harsher sanctions than white youth. At the stage of deciding whether to detain a ju-venile before the hearing, nonwhite youth are detained in secure custody prior to their hearing at rates that ex-ceed those for white youth, regardless of delinquency offense. Specifically, 26 percent of nonwhite youth were detained, whereas 17 percent of whites were in custody in 1993.[46]

A look at national juvenile populations under cor-rectional supervision for those placed on probation and for those placed in secure and nonsecure facilities after adjudication reveal familiar disparities as well. Whites are more likely to receive the benevolent sanc-tion of probation,[47] and nonwhites are at greater risk of receiving the harsher sanction of confinement.[48]

Juvenile offenders are confined in both private and public facilities. More than half of the juveniles in public facilities are minorities, with the largest cat-egory of these juveniles identified as African Ameri-cans. Hispanics are overrepresented also, but other races are not. More African Americans and Hispanics are detained in public juvenile correctional facilities, whereas the private populations are predominately white. African Americans are still overrepresented in private facilities, compared to their distribution in the general population. Both Hispanics and juveniles or other races are evenly represented in private facilities compared to their distribution in the general population. One probable explanation for the discrepancies in the nature of admissions decisions to public versus private facilities involves the costs that the parents may have to assume when children are confined to the latter. Private facilities may not be an option for parents of African American and Hispanic youth, given overrepresentation of these groups under the poverty level.

CONCLUSION

The picture of the American correctional system is most vivid in black and white. Such basic questions as who is in prison and how individuals survive in prison cannot be divorced from the issues of race. The most salient observation about minorities and corrections is the strong overrepresentation of African Americans in prison populations. In addition, this overrepresentation is gradually increasing in new court commitments and population figures. Explanations for this increasing overrepresentation are complex.

The most obvious possibility is that African American criminality is increasing. This explanation has been soundly challenged by Tonry's work, which compares the stability of African American arrest rates since the mid-1970s to the explosive African American incarceration rates of the same period.[49] He argued that a better explanation may be the racial impact of the war on drugs.

Blumstein's analysis offers another clue to the continuing increase in the African American portion of the prison population that links discretion and the war on drugs. His work suggests that the racial disparities in incarceration rates for drug offenses are not well-explained by racial disparities in drug arrest rates. Thus, the war on drugs and its impact on imprisonment may be fostering the "malign neglect" Tonry charged.

ENDNOTES

1. Estimates calculated from Christopher J. Mumola and Allen J. Beck, *Prisoners, 1996* (Washington, D.C.: U.S. Department of Justice, 1997) and *Correctional Populations in the US, 1995* (Washington, D.C.: U.S. Department of Justice, 1997).

2. *Chronicle of Higher Education,* August 28,1998.

3. Ibid.

4. Estimates calculated from Mumola and Beck, *Prisoners, 1996* and *Correctional Populations in the US, 1995.*

5. Harry E. Allen and Clifford E. Simonson, *Corrections in America: An Introduction,* 7th ed. (Englewood Cliffs, NJ: Prentice-Hall, 1995).

6. Ibid.

7. Mumola and Beck, *Prisoners, 1996.*

8. Bureau of Justice Statistics, *Comparing State and Federal Inmates, 1991* (Washington, D.C.: U.S. Government Printing Office, 1993).

9. Bureau of Justice Statistics, *Correctional Populations in the United States, 1996* (Washington, D.C.: U.S. Department of Justice, 1999).

10. Bureau of Justice Statistics, *Comparing State and Federal Inmates, 1991.*

11. For a review of these issues, see Marjorie S. Zatz, Carol Chiago Lujan, and Zoann K. Snyder-Joy, "American Indians and Criminal Justice: Some Conceptual and Methodological Considerations," in *Race and Criminal Justice,* ed. Michael Lynch and E. Britt Paterson (New York: Harrow & Heston, 1995).

12. Bureau of Justice Statistics, *Comparing State and Federal Inmates, 1991.*

13. Bureau of Justice Statistics, *Correctional Populations, 1996.*

14. Bureau of Justice Statistics, *Prisoners, 1996.*

15. Bureau of Justice Statistics, *Correctional Populations, 1996.*

16. Bureau of Justice Statistics, *Comparing State and Federal Inmates, 1991.*

17. Margaret Werner Calahan, *Historical Corrections Statistics in the United States, 1850–1984* (Washington, D.C.: U.S. Government Printing Office, 1986), pp. 65–66.

18. Michael Tonry, *Malign Neglect* (New York: Oxford University Press, 1995).

19. Ibid.

20. *1993 Directory of Juvenile and Adult Correctional Departments, Institutions, Agencies and Paroling Authorities* (Laurel, MD: American Correctional Association, 1993).

21. John A. Author, "Correctional Ideology of Black Correctional Officers," *Federal Probation,* 58 (1994): 57–65.

22. Tonry, *Malign Neglect,* p. 21.

23. Ibid.

24. Ibid.

25. Darrell K. Gilliard, *Prison and Jail Inmates at Midyear 1998* (Washington, D.C.: U.S. Department of Justice, 1999).

26. *Probation and Parole, 1997* (Washington, D.C.: U.S. Department of Justice, 1998).

27. Marc Mauer, *Americans Behind Bars: A Comparison of International Rates of Incarceration.* Washington, D.C.: The Sentencing Project, 1991).

28. Louis W. Jankowski, *Correctional Populations in the U.S., 1990* (Washington, D.C.: U.S. Department of Justice, 1992).

29. Ibid.

30. Ibid.

31. Ibid.

32. Ibid.

33. Ibid.

34. Joan Petersilia, *Racial Disparities in the Criminal Justice System* (Santa Monica, CA: Rand, 1983), p. 28.

35. Coramae Richey Mann, *Unequal Justice: A Question of Color* (Bloomington: Indiana University Press, 1993).

36. William Wilbanks, *The Myth of the Racist Criminal Justice System* (Monterey, CA: Brooks/Cole, 1987).

37. Alfred Blumstein, "On the Disproportionality of United States' Prison Populations," *Journal of Criminal Law and Criminology* 73 (1982): 1259–1281.

38. Ibid., p. 1274.

39. Ibid.

40. Patrick Langan, "Racism on Trial: New Evidence to Explain the Racial Composition of Prisons in the United States," *Journal of Criminal Law and Criminology* 76 (1985): 666–683.

41. *Omaha World Herald* (March 3, 1999), p. 22.

42. Alfred Blumstein, "Racial Disproportionality in U.S. Prisons Revisited," *University of Colorado Law Review* 64 (1993): 743–760.

43. Doris L. MacKenzie, "Age and Adjustment to Prison: Interactions With Attitudes and Anxiety," *Criminal Justice and Behavior* 14 (1987): 427–447.

44. Doris L. MacKenzie, James Robinson, and Carol Campbell, "Long-Term Incarceration of Female Offenders: Prison Adjustment and Coping," *Criminal Justice and Behavior* 16 (1989): 223–238.

45. Robert G. Leger, "Lesbianism Among Women Prisoners: Participants and Nonparticipants," *Criminal Justice and Behavior* 14 (1987): 448–467.

46. National Center for Juvenile Justice, *Juvenile Court Statistics, 1993* (Washington, D.C.: National Center for Juvenile Justice, 1996).

47. Ibid.

48. U.S. Department of Justice, *National Juvenile Custody Trends, 1979–1989* (Washington, D.C.: U.S. Government Printing Office, 1992).

49. Tonry, *Malign Neglect.*

STUDY QUESTIONS FOR READING 3

1. It is often said that more African Americans are in prison than college. More accurately, more African Americans are under correctional supervision (prison, jail, probation, or parole) than in college. How many times more whites are in college than under correctional supervision?

2. What percentage of the U.S. population and the prison population are African American?

3. What percentage of the U.S. population and the prison population are Hispanic?

4. The percentage of African Americans as a proportion of the population has risen slowly from 9 percent in 1926 to 15 percent currently. Is the rate of incarceration increasing at a faster or slower rate?

5. In 1995, the incarceration rates in England, Germany, and Sweden were all under 100 people per 100,000. In contrast, America had the highest incarceration rate in the world. Its closest competitors were Russia and South Africa. What were these three incarceration rates?

6. What is the U.S. incarceration rate for African American men? This is how many times the rate of incarceration for black men in South Africa during the last years of apartheid?

7. The incarceration rate for African American men is how many times as high as that for white men? Is this ratio higher, lower, or about the same for African American women as compared to white women?

8. Why might some authorities argue that we are "criminalizing unemployment"? Why does this issue have a racial dimension?

9. According to Blumstein, what percent of the disparity between African Americans and whites sent to prison can be explained by the disparity in arrests? This percentage assumes that the arrest disparity does not represent discrimination. However, it may represent discrimination, especially in regard to crimes that account for the fastest growing proportion of the prison population. What type of crime is this, and why may there be more discrimination in these arrests?

THE RICH GET RICHER AND THE POOR GET PRISON
AN OVERVIEW OF THE BOOK BY JEFFREY REIMAN

TARA GRAY

In his thought-provoking book *The Rich Get Richer and the Poor Get Prison,* Jeffrey Reiman shows that the criminal justice system favors upper-class criminals over poor criminals, whether they commit street crime or white-collar crime. First, poor people are more likely than rich people to be arrested, charged, convicted, and sentenced to prison for street crimes (Reiman, 2001:110). For example, one study found that boys from the lowest socioeconomic class committed street crimes at a rate 1.5 times higher than boys in the highest socioeconomic class; however, boys from the lowest class were arrested five times as often as those in the highest class (Gold as cited in Reiman:115). Similarly, the ratio of sentences given for possession of powder cocaine to crack cocaine is 1 to 100. This difference is significant because powder cocaine is popular in suburbs, but crack is popular in poor, inner-city neighborhoods. Federal laws require a five-year mandatory sentence for either 500 grams of powder cocaine, or only 5 grams of crack cocaine. This means that a first-time drug offense for possession of crack with no aggravating factors yields a sentence harsher than that for kidnapping, and only slightly less harsh than that for attempted murder. (McDonald and Carlson, as cited in Reiman:130).

Second, the wealthy disproportionately commit white-collar crimes, which are not always defined as crimes and are punished less severely than street crimes. White-collar crimes are sometimes called occupational crimes because they are committed "in the course of a legal business or profession" (Cole, 1995:47). Reiman tells us that white-collar crime is serious, but its treatment is lenient. He addresses the myths that surround white-collar crime, especially the myth that such offenses are not serious because they do not typically result in injury or death. Reiman argues that the way we define crime has meant that white-collar crime is not even defined as illegal behavior. And when we do acknowledge the deeds of white-collar offenders as crime, we still make excuses for their actions, and punish them leniently. In contrast, we demonize street criminals and punish them harshly. Why? Reiman explains that people in power benefit when they scrutinize the "criminal" actions of the poor, while ignoring the actions of the rich. In summary, Reiman asserts that white-collar crime is more serious than street crime but is punished leniently because of the way crime is defined, and excuses are made for "higher-class" criminals—excuses that serve the interests of people in power.

WHITE-COLLAR CRIME—SERIOUS, BUT PUNISHED LENIENTLY

There are many ways to steal, including crimes such as fraud and embezzlement, and they all cost Americans a great deal of money, but white-collar crimes are not as easy to understand as street-level theft. For example, fraud is stealing through deceit or misrepresentation. Embezzlement occurs when someone steals or "misappropriates" money or property entrusted to his or her care, usually because the person is in a position of power or responsibility. Many people assume that the losses from this kind of theft are absorbed by big corporations, but they are not. Corporations pass their losses onto consumers by charging higher prices. In fact, white-collar criminals "take money out of the very same pocket muggers do: yours!" (Reiman:124).

Most people know that white-collar criminals steal far more in dollars than street criminals do, but white-collar criminals are punished less often and less severely. In 1997, the cost of embezzlement alone was more than four-fifths the total value of all stolen property and money listed in the FBI Index of street-level crimes. That is, one type of white-collar crime cost almost as much as the most serious street level property crimes combined. Although the costs were comparable, the number of arrests made for street crimes in 1997 was 90 times greater than arrests for white-collar crime; there was one arrest for every $8,000 stolen but one for every $726,000 "misappropriated" (Reiman: 124). The biggest case of fraud ever recorded was the savings and loan scandal, involving about 400 billion dollars. Considering the amount stolen, the punishments were very small. The average savings and loan officer stole $500,000 in contrast to the average property offender who steals only $1,250; however, the average prison sentences were similar: 36 months for the savings and loan officers, and 38 months for motor vehicle theft. Reiman quotes one official who concluded, "The best way to rob a bank is to own one" (Reiman 136–137).

Many people assume that white-collar crime is relatively harmless, but it is actually deadly. Reiman cites several studies that estimate the number of deaths due to unnecessary surgery, which was not performed to save the life of the patient. In one study, the number of deaths resulting from surgeries recommended and performed by doctors who are paid for individual operations they do was compared to the number of deaths resulting from surgeries recommended and performed by salaried doctors who receive no extra income from surgery. According to this research, about 16,000 people die every year from unnecessary surgery (Wolfe, as cited in Reiman:85–86). Far fewer

people die from what the FBI calls a "cutting or stabbing instrument." Reiman concludes that:

> *obviously the FBI does not include the scalpel as a cutting or stabbing instrument . . . No matter how you slice it, the scalpel may be more dangerous than the switchblade (86).*

Moreover, work may also be dangerous to your health. In 1997, the number of work-related deaths was 31,000; in contrast the number of workers murdered was about 9,000 (75). The typical murderer serves eight years in prison, but the typical fine to a company for a work-related death is only $480 (84).

Pollution is the single biggest killer of Americans: One in four of us will die of cancer, with 70 to 90 percent of these deaths caused by pollution, which is theoretically preventable. Of course, reducing pollution would require a massive effort and an incredible amount of money. Nonetheless, Reiman suggests that we would make this kind of effort if another nation were systematically killing this many people: "How much of an effort . . . would the nation make to stop a foreign invader who was killing a thousand people a day and bent on capturing one-quarter of the present population?" (88). In 1992, the United States allocated only $1.9 billion to the National Cancer Institute, but spent at least $45 billion to fight the Persian Gulf War.

> *The simple truth is that the government that strove so mightily to protect the borders of a small, undemocratic nation 7,000 miles away is doing next to nothing to protect us against the chemical war in our midst (Reiman:88–89).*

There is a moral to this story: When the harm caused is one-on-one, we take notice and punish the crime severely; however, when the harm is caused less directly, we turn a blind eye.

HOW WHITE-COLLAR CRIME IS EXCUSED

We excuse white-collar criminals in several ways: we define crime in a way that excludes white-collar crime, we focus on criminal intent, we emphasize that one-on-one crime is more terrifying, we consider corporate crime a means to a legitimate end, and we assume that workers freely choose the dangers of the workplace. Reiman acknowledges that each of these views has some merit; however, in each case, he asks whether the idea has enough merit to justify vast differences between the treatment of street criminals and white-collar criminals.

First, we define crime so that white-collar crime does not fit our definition:

> *The fact is that the label "crime" is not used in America to name all or the worst of the actions that cause misery and suffering to Americans. It is primarily reserved for the dangerous actions of the poor (Reiman:58).*

Reiman cites the example of a 1993 mining accident in which ten workers died. The company plead guilty to a "pattern of safety misconduct," including falsifying reports of methane levels, requiring miners to work beneath unsupported roofs, and systematically hiding these violations from safety inspectors. The company was fined $3.75 million (59). The acting foreman of the mine was the only person charged with a crime, but because he cooperated with the investigation, prosecutors recommended that he receive the minimum sentence—probation to six months incarceration (59). In contrast, in another 1993 incident, a man boarded a commuter train in Long Island, New York, and shot passengers, killing five and wounding eighteen. This man was clearly a murderer. But were those responsible for the death of miners also murderers?

> *Why do ten dead miners amount to "an accident," a "tragedy," and five dead commuters a "mass murder"? "Murder" suggests a murderer, whereas "accident" and "tragedy" suggest the work of impersonal forces (Reiman:59).*

Note that "even the language becomes more delicate as we deal with a better class of crook" (Reiman:124). In the end, we need to reexamine "*what* will be called crime and *who* will be treated as a criminal" (Reiman:60).

We also excuse corporate crime by saying that the degree of intent is less for the executive who kills than for the street murderer. Indeed, the intent of street murderers is clearer because they harm purposefully, but executives often do not. Still, executive killers may be punished criminally because we have criminal laws against both reckless and negligent acts. And although

the street criminal purposefully harms a particular person, the executive criminal knowingly risks the lives of a large number of workers. The street criminal may act in the heat of passion, whereas the executive may act with cool reckoning:

> *Two lovers or neighbors or relatives find themselves in a heated argument. One (often it is a matter of chance which one) picks up a weapon and strikes a fatal blow. Such a person is clearly a murderer and rightly subject to punishment by the criminal justice system. Is this person more evil than the executive who, knowing the risks, calmly chooses not to pay for safety equipment (Reiman:74)?*

Although executive killers may have weaker intent, their crimes are still serious because they risk more people's lives, and they kill with premeditation, not in the heat of passion.

We also excuse white-collar crime by emphasizing that direct personal injury is more terrifying than indirect personal injury—and it is. But both types of crime have very serious consequences:

> *After all, although it is worse to be injured with terror than without, it is still the injury that constitutes the worst part of violent crime. Given the choice, seriously injured victims of crime would surely rather have been terrorized and not injured than injured and not terrorized (Reiman:76).*

Therefore, we should not treat a workplace "tragedy" as a minor crime or a regulatory matter. Instead, despite different levels of terror, we should acknowledge that both street murder and corporate murder are dangerous acts with grave consequences.

Another excuse we make for white-collar crime is that street crimes are committed for self-interest, but corporate crimes are a means to an important end (i.e., productivity and profit). However, in neither case does the end justify the means. Besides, in one important sense, the corporate criminal actually does act in self-interest because he or she is likely to be rewarded for keeping costs down, even though his or her actions could lead to increased workplace injury and death.

The final excuse made for white-collar crime is that workers freely choose to work, and thus they consent to the dangers of the job in advance. However, workers can consent to dangers only if they know about them, and the dangers are often concealed. Although it is true that "no one is forced at gunpoint to accept a particular job" (Reiman:76), virtually everyone must take some job. In an economy where there are more workers than jobs, some workers end up with dangerous jobs, and these workers may or may not know the risks of the jobs they take. In the end, this excuse like each of the others, has some merit, but not enough merit to account for the vast difference in the treatment of white-collar criminals compared to that of street criminals.

EXCUSES SERVE PEOPLE IN POWER

The excuses we make for white-collar criminals serve the self-interests of people in power because they suggest two other self-serving ideas: that there is a real threat to law-abiding middle America, and it comes from the poor, not the rich; and that the poor are criminally inclined and therefore are moral degenerates who deserve poverty. If it were true that the real threat always comes from the poor, then the public would be wise to ignore the way it is injured and robbed by the rich, and focus instead on law-and-order tactics aimed at the poor. These tactics take the heat off the rich and mask white-collar crime.

If it were true that the poor are always criminally inclined and moral degenerates, then the public should not demand a more equal economic system, which again would help the rich by leaving them rich and leaving the poor, poor. Indeed, those in power benefit when others do not demand a more equal economic system:

> The have-nots and the have-littles could have more if they decided to take it from the have-plenties. . . . [Therefore], the have-nots and the have-littles must believe it would not be right or reasonable to take away what the have-plenties have. In other words, they must believe that for all its problems the present social, political, and economic order, with its disparities of wealth and power and privileges, is about the best that human beings can [reasonably do] (Reiman:178).

However, it is a myth that our system is "about the best that human beings can [reasonably do]." The distribution of wealth in this country is very unequal, and

is becoming more skewed over time. At no time in our history has the majority of our population owned more than about ten percent of the nation's wealth. The top one-fifth of households, by contrast, owns 84 percent of our wealth (Reiman:179). Reiman concludes that

> Because we are nowhere near offering all Americans a good education and an equal opportunity to get ahead, we have no right to think that the distribution of income reflects what people have truly earned. . . . Few people who are well off can honestly claim they deserve all they have. Those who think they do should ask themselves where they would be today if they had been born to migrant laborers in California or to a poor black family in the Harlem ghetto (179–180).

The have-plenties need everyone else to believe the system is fair as it is. If we accept this, we will not demand changes that will adversely affect the have-plenties.

CONCLUSION

If our justice system is to be truly just, we must work hard to educate the public about the seriousness of white-collar crime. To do so, we must redefine crime to include all dangerous actions rather than only the dangerous actions of the poor, and we must redefine the image of the typical criminal to include the upper-class criminal. We must stop making excuses for white-collar crimes. This is difficult because excuses make the lives of the have-plenties easier in two ways: The excuses keep the "heat" on street criminals rather than on those in power, and they demonize poor people so that there is little popular support for reducing poverty.

Those in power do not intentionally downplay the seriousness of white-collar crime. Historically, one-on-one crimes have been the main way that people have harmed each other, especially in pre-industrial societies. Therefore, confusion about the seriousness of white-collar crime comes not from a conspiracy on the part of the rich, but from historical inertia. The current system generates no effective demand for change (Reiman:161). As a result, those in power continue to focus on individual wrongdoers, which means the attention of the public is diverted away from issues of equality. To focus on individual guilt is to ask

whether the individual has fulfilled his or her obligations to society—but not whether the society has fulfilled its obligations to the individual. Reiman states,
"Justice is a two-way street—but criminal justice [has
become] a one-way street" (157).

*The author thanks Jeffrey Reiman for his helpful com-
ments on this overview.*

REFERENCES

Cole, George. 1995. *The American System of Criminal Justice.* Belmont, CA: Wadsworth.

Gold, Martin. 1966. Undetected Delinquent Behavior. *Journal of Research in Crime and Delinquency* 3(1): 27–46.

McDonald, Douglas, and Ken Carlson. 1993. *Sentencing in
the Federal Courts: Does Race Matter?* Washington,
D.C.: Bureau of Justice Statistics.

Reiman, Jeffrey. 2001. *The Rich Get Richer and the Poor
Get Prison: Ideology, Class and Criminal Justice.*
Boston: Allyn and Bacon.

Wolfe, Dr. Sidney. 1975. *The Washington Post* (16 July):
A3.

STUDY QUESTIONS FOR READING 4

1. In the first central idea of the book, Reiman argues that even when poor people
   commit the same crimes that richer people commit, the poor are more likely to be
   arrested, charged, convicted, and sentenced to prison. What evidence does he
   give to support his point?

2. What is the second central idea of the book, and how is it summarized?

3. Do corporations "absorb" the costs of white-collar crimes? Why or why not?

4. In 1997, the cost of embezzlement alone cost almost as much as the total value of
   all stolen property and money in the FBI Index of property crimes *combined.*
   How much was this? Although the cost of embezzlement and street crimes are
   comparable, the number of arrests made for street crimes was not. That is, one arrest was made for how many dollars stolen? One arrest was made for how many
   dollars embezzled?

5. How much does the average savings and loan officer steal? How much does the
   average property thief steal? How did the average prison sentence for a savings
   and loan officer compare to that of a motor vehicle thief?

6. In 1993, how did the number of work-related deaths compare to the number of
   workers murdered? How many years does the typical murderer serve? What is the
   corporate fine for the typical work-related death?

7. What is the single biggest killer of Americans? What proportion of Americans
   will die of this? Why does Reiman compare this type of killing to the way people are killed in a war? What does this comparison show us about how we treat
   harm that is inflicted directly versus indirectly?

8. According to Reiman, we excuse white-collar crime in five ways. What are they,
   and what problems are there with each?

9. The excuses we make for white-collar crime are self-serving for people in power
   in two ways. What are they, and why is Reiman skeptical of each?

10. In Reiman's view, what is ultimately wrong with focusing on individual guilt?

ESSAY QUESTION FOR PART ONE

In your answers, be sure to use one sentence at the end of your first paragraph to offer a clear thesis statement—that is, a statement of your point of view and your arguments for it. Then, in each paragraph of your answer, give evidence to support one of your arguments. Cite specific authors and give specific, concrete support for your point of view by offering statistics, case studies, examples, quotations, expert opinions, and so on.

1. Who goes to prison in terms of the

   - seriousness of crime committed?
   - gender, ethnicity, and class of offender?
   - class of crime (white-collar versus street crime)?

WEBSITES

The following websites provide valuable information about corrections as well as excellent listings of other websites and printed sources:

> **www.prisonwall.org**
> Maintained by attorney Arnold Erickson, who has won many awards for this web
>   page.

> **www.ojp.usdoj.gov/nij/corrdocs.htm**
> National Institute of Justice

> **www.nicic.org**
> National Institute of Corrections

> **www.ojp.usdoj.gov/bjs/welcome.html**
> Bureau of Justice Statistics

> **www.damascusway.com/links.htm**
> Damascus Way Reentry Center

PART TWO

LIVING AND WORKING IN PRISONS AND JAILS

The Supreme Court ruled in *Rhodes v. Chapman* that prisons are not supposed to be comfortable because people are sent there for punishment. "The Constitution does not mandate comfortable prisons. . . . [Prisons,] which house persons convicted of serious crimes, cannot be free of discomfort." Nonetheless, the question remains, How uncomfortable are prisons, and how uncomfortable should they be? Part Two presents various views of life and work in prisons and jails for men, women, and juveniles. This part also explores living in prison with the threat of rape, with AIDS, and in "the hole" (solitary confinement), or on death row.

The first reading in Part Two comes from Linda Zupan's book *Jail Reform and the New Generation Philosophy.* Zupan describes jails as loud, filthy, scary places that are overcrowded. She points out that jail conditions are worse than prison conditions, which is ironic because half of all jail inmates have not yet been convicted and should still be presumed innocent. Jail conditions are worse than prison conditions because jails are under local, rather than state or federal, control, which lowers the standards for administrators and workers alike. Jail workers are among the most poorly trained, least educated, and worst paid in the justice system. Jail administrators are usually sheriffs who are not required to have any training in corrections and devote less than 10 percent of their time to administering jails. Zupan points out that every major study in the last sixty years has recommended replacing the sheriff as the chief jail administrator and abolishing local control. Six states have taken their jail systems over, but unfortunately, political considerations have prevented this elsewhere.

The next reading explains life for jailers in Nassau County Jail and how they feel about their jobs, including the pay, the public's perception of correctional officers, their life expectancy, and the best tools for getting the job done. In 1999, pay for new jailers was almost $30,000 per year. These jailers resent that the public feels officers are brutes, and they point out that only a few officers abuse inmates. These officers do not want to be called guards "because guards work at Macy's and don't stop dead in their tracks when they hear, 'Yo, C.O.!' as they leave the mall and see five former inmates behind them." The life expectancy for correctional officers is only fifty-nine years, due to high rates of hypertension, ulcers, and heart attacks, not to mention burnout, alcohol abuse, divorce, and suicide. In 1998, seven correctional officers in the United States died in the line of duty, and 14,000 were seriously assaulted. In this jail, jailers are unarmed, but their supervisors carry pepper spray. The greatest tools, they say, are composure and communication.

The next reading describes the process of being socialized as a correctional officer in prison. New officers learn to fit in when they realize that an officer's power comes from the interpretation of rules, and when they adopt the "officer's view" of inmates, social service personnel, administrators, and the public. Officers view security as their number-one priority, and discipline as a means to an end. Officers are ambivalent about rules, and guards acknowledge that they derive their power through their *interpretation* of rules, rather than from the rules themselves. One guard states, "Every guard interprets the rules a little different. I even interpret the rules differently on different days." Inmates are seen as untrustworthy, and officers are said to be "con-wise" if they are aware of the frequency with which they will be lied to, deceived, and manipulated. Officers become con-wise by getting "burned" or "conned" by inmates. In contrast, officers view social service personnel as extremely gullible regarding inmates; the officers believe that social service workers coddle inmates and act as inmate advocates by overemphasizing treatment programs at the expense of security. Officers perceive administrators as outsiders with political connections and arbitrary power, and they see the public as too kind in its views towards inmates, and too harsh on officers: "They feel sorry for murderers, rapists, and robbers; they resent us." By adopting these attitudes and views, the author says new officers can fit into the officer world.

The next reading is an overview of the book *Guards Imprisoned,* by Lucien X. Lombardo. According to Lombardo, because guards lack employment alternatives, they feel imprisoned. Like inmates, guards develop coping mechanisms for whatever chain binds them most: Some avoid inmates, others seek active jobs to avoid boredom, and others seek jobs with relatively more autonomy to avoid administrators. Indeed, sixty percent of the officers interviewed reported that the pay and job security are the "best" things about the job "for the work we do" or "for the education" level they have reached. Twenty-five percent of the officers said there was nothing they would describe as most satisfying about their jobs, however, and another twenty-five percent of the officers selected for interviews never showed up. One officer defended his decision not to be interviewed this way: "I don't have any regard for the job. I never did, and I don't want to talk about it." Boredom is another problem. One-third of the officers said their jobs were boring—so boring that they didn't discuss their jobs—even with their families. Some officers coped with boredom by devising elaborate, time-consuming ways to keep records, and most officers chose a job within the prison because of the activity it provided. Most officers worried about the danger posed by inmates, and some found inmates rude and uncooperative. Officers coped with these problems either by improving their ability to manage inmates, or by seeking posts where they could avoid them. Officers also felt ignored and disrespected by administrators, and some officers responded to this by seeking jobs where they could work without much supervision.

The next several readings examine prisons primarily from the perspectives of inmates. First, Clemens Bartollas argues that incarcerated juveniles must prove themselves to other inmates and must please staff, often through manipulation and conning. New inmates must appear strong enough to protect themselves from predatory peers who "accidentally" bump them, "palm" them (grab their buttocks), "sucker punch" them (strike them in the face or stomach without warning), or even rape them. But new inmates must not appear too strong, or they will be seen as a threat to the inmate leaders who will then "test" them even more. First-time offenders often emit fear and anxiety, which causes them to be victimized. In contrast, juveniles with street experience know how to carry themselves and how to respond to a direct confrontation or challenge. These inmates know that if confronted, they must retaliate immediately. All inmates have a contentious relationship with staff because they quickly discover that staff make all the important decisions about privileges, promotions, visits, and sometimes even release. Therefore, inmates have to impress staff. As one inmate put it, "You've got to kiss a lot of ass to get out of here." Any staff member in a prison will have to deal with hostile and manipulative inmates—hostile because they are confined against their will, and manipulative because they are powerless to ask for what they want directly. These traits create a never-ending cycle of problems between inmates and staff.

The following reading is an overview by Robert Johnson of the book *In the Belly of the Beast,* by Jack Abbott. Johnson describes how Abbott argues that inmates feel violated and victimized in prison; this leads some inmates to conclude that violence is necessary and justified, and therefore they become more violent. Abbott describes in detail the wrongs he suffered in prison, including lengthy periods of solitary confinement, mind-altering drugs, and overt violence. However, Johnson points out that Abbott takes no responsibility for anything that happened to him, seeing only the fault of the guards. Abbott writes,

> *He who is state-raised—reared by the state from an early age after he is taken from what the state calls a "broken home"—learns over and over and all the days of his life that people in society can do anything to him and not be punished by the law. Do anything to him with the full force of the state behind them.*

Abbott comes to see himself and other inmates as victims who are therefore justified in further victimizing and doing violence to others:

> *[Inmates] must avenge even the slightest insult that might cast doubt on their manliness, brook any authority that would curtail their sense of self. To do less, as they see it, is to be demeaned as a man.*

Abbott's book, a powerful account of one man's journey through the prison system, demonstrates how prisons can contribute to a cycle of violence.

The next reading is an excerpt from Jack Abbott's book *In the Belly of the Beast.* Abbott argues that living in "the hole," prison slang for solitary confinement, is really a living death because imagination must replace actual experience. Abbott reports being thrown in the hole brutally by a team of guards, and then finding that

> *Time descends in your cell like the lid of a coffin in which you lie and watch as it slowly closes over you. When you neither move nor think in your cell, you are awash in pure nothingness.*

Abbott says this living death means you will eventually stop doing push-ups or walking in your cell—you will even stop masturbating. Abbott comes to realize that the routine and monotony will bury him alive if he is not careful, and he will lose his mind. He responds by reading anything and everything, and by beginning to remember and imagine. He says imagination replaces experience in the hole, and he concludes that "when a man is taken farther and farther away from experience, he is being taken to his death."

The next reading comes from Robert Johnson's book, *Death Work: A Study of the Modern Execution Process.* Johnson argues that the goal of death row is "human storage"; this affects inmate life as well as the way guards think and feel about inmates. Death row inmates say they are treated as if they were already dead. Because the goal of death row is human storage, guards treat prisoners as bodies to be kept alive to be killed. Inmates are seen as objects, not actors in their own right. As a result, guards say, "I'm going to shower the row now." The training of guards emphasizes combat duty and makes no attempt to help guards approach the extremely difficult task of human relations. Extreme suspiciousness results because guards feel these men are known to be violent and have little to lose. Even the kinder guards avoid contact with the inmates because they need to protect themselves from the pain of "losing" these men to execution. Outsiders begin to think of death row inmates as dead too. When visits do occur, they sometimes resemble wakes. Johnson describes visits that involve no contact—the inmate sits alone in an enclosed chamber, neatly dressed and carefully groomed, as if on display for his loved ones.

Aside from death row, AIDS is another increasingly common cause of death in prison. Two percent of all inmates (23,000) are HIV positive, and half a percent have full blown AIDS. AIDS is six times more common among inmates than in the larger community. Nina Siegal argues that good health care for these inmates means the community standard of care; when this is not available, terminally ill prisoners should obtain early medical release. In reality, inmates with AIDS, especially women inmates, seem to receive very poor care. Linda Cortez spent three years in prison and contracted an AIDS-related herpes illness that spread from her leg to her eyes and caused blindness. No one in the prison acknowledged that she couldn't see or helped her navigate the prison. No one told her, for example, when her breakfast tray was there. When she left prison, Cortez weighed 92 pounds and was unable to walk. Once she was given AIDS medication, taught how to use her legs again, and placed on an appropriate diet, she learned how to manage her disease herself, regained weight, and became self-sufficient. In contrast to Cortez's neglect in prison, the community standard of care includes access to all eighteen of the anti-HIV drugs currently approved by the FDA, medication for opportunistic infections, and alternative therapies, where appropriate. Thirty-one state systems and the Bureau of Prisons (BOP) do have compassionate-release or medical-parole programs, but the application process is long and complicated.

In the next reading, Phyllis Jo Baunach tells us that prisons for women tend to look nicer than prisons for men, with a campus environment, well-trimmed hedges and neat flower gardens, and with no gun towers, armed guards, or razor wire. Despite the nice appearance of women's prisons, however, women in prison suffer especially from separation from their children, and they are offered far fewer programs than men are. Incarcerated mothers experience severe depression, shock, and loss of self-esteem. The placement of their children with other caregivers is painful, especially when they are placed with strangers, and on a permanent basis, which is standard for children born to incarcerated mothers. This separation is also a special concern to society because most of these mothers were raising their children before they were incarcerated, and they may still be the best parents available upon their release. Some prisons have experimented with extended visitation for women and children, including overnight visitation, which may help both the mother and child adjust to separation and to life after the mother is released. A second key problem for women is that prisons provide far fewer technical and vocational training programs to women than to men. For women, training programs are very traditional, as if geared toward married women who will be providing only supplemental income. Training includes feminine hygiene, makeup, home decorating, sewing, gardening, cooking, nursing, and other domestic services, with the biggest focus on cosmetology, clerical work, and food service. In one state, women could participate in training for either keypunch operator or food service work, whereas men could participate in any of a dozen programs, including training for welding, auto body repair, drafting, computer programming, or work as a medical lab or X-ray technician. If women are to be less dependent on "finding a man" and less likely to commit crimes upon release, they need to be taught more marketable skills so that they can care for themselves and their children.

Sex between women inmates and prison staff seems epidemic, but the courts are beginning to intervene and require anonymous hotlines for inmates, and an all-female staff may be a necessary next step. This last reading in Part Two describes how staff lure inmates into sex by offering cigarettes, phone calls, preferred job assignments, and even drugs. Sometimes these staff members use actual or threatened physical force. In 1992 in Georgia, 17 staff were indicted for misconduct over a period of 14 years. One lieutenant was indicted for having sex with at least seven prisoners. None were convicted, but several lost their jobs. In 1993 in Washington, D.C., the prison staff involved in sex with inmates included chaplains, administrators, deputy wardens, contractors and food service workers, and women as well as men. More recently, in a federal prison in California, three female inmates were sold as sex slaves to male inmates by guards who allowed the males to enter the women's cells. In 1998, the Federal Bureau of Prisons settled out of court. Human Rights Watch and others recommend anonymous hotlines for all women inmates. In addition, Amnesty International recommends that women prisoners be attended only by women officers, which is in accordance with United Nations Standard Minimum Rules for the Treatment of Prisoners. Amnesty International argues that it may be fair to men to restrict their employment this way since there are many more men's prisons than women's.

THE PERSISTENT PROBLEMS PLAGUING MODERN JAILS

LINDA L. ZUPAN

The Law Enforcement Assistance Administration defines the jail as "any facility operated by a local government for the detention or correction of adults suspected or convicted of a crime and which has authority to detain longer than forty-eight hours" (quoted in Flynn, 1973:55). As the "hybrid" of American correctional institutions, the jail's role is two-fold: to act as a "way-station" for those awaiting action by other components of the criminal justice system, and to act as a penal institution for those who have been convicted and sentenced to less than one year's incarceration. This dual role gives the jail jurisdiction over a broad range of people. Inmates of a jail may include people awaiting trial, arraignment or sentencing; those serving sentences of less than one year; and persons who are awaiting transfer to other jurisdictions or correctional institutions. On any given day, 49% of the people in jail are serving sentences while 51% are pretrial detainees who have yet to be convicted of a crime but are detained because they cannot raise the funds necessary for bail or because they are declared a risk by the courts (U.S. Department of Justice, 1990:4).[1]

Although the jail is the oldest of American penal institutions, it is the least studied of all correctional institutions.[2] Only since 1970 have statistics on jail populations been systematically collected at the national level. In 1970, the National Criminal Justice Information and Statistics Service completed the first comprehensive census of county and city jails. Subsequent censuses were conducted by the Bureau of Justice Statistics in 1973, 1978, 1983, and 1988, and are planned for subsequent five-year periods.

From these censuses we know that approximately 9.7 million people are incarcerated annually in the nation's 3,316 jails. About 343,000 people are in jail on any given day—roughly equivalent to the entire 1984 population of Toledo, Ohio (U.S. Department of Justice, 1990). We also know that ethnic minorities, the poor, and the undereducated make up a major proportion of the jail's population. According to the 1978 Census of Jails conducted by the Department of Justice, the typical inmate is a young, minority male with an annual income slightly above the "poverty line" as defined by the U.S. government. Fifty-six percent of jail inmates are black or Hispanic (U.S. Department of Justice, 1990). While 1 out of every 10 persons in the general population is black, four out of every 10 male inmates and 5 out of 10 female inmates are black. Forty-five percent of jail inmates have annual incomes below the "poverty line," while one out of four have no source of income and are dependent on welfare, social security or unemployment benefits (U.S. Department of Justice, 1980a:2–7). A majority of jail inmates are high school dropouts. Only 40% of the jail population have completed high school. In contrast, 75% of the general population of comparable age have high school diplomas (U.S. Department of Justice, 1980a:4).

Although sociodemographic data of this nature is necessary to determine who is in American jails, it says little about the nature of jail incarceration or the conditions within these facilities. The information that does exist comes from journalistic exposés, personal narratives of those who have been incarcerated, court documents in cases involving jails, and a handful of scholarly studies. All four sources concur in depicting conditions in most jails as bleak indeed.

In an attempt to understand the nature of the jail situation, the Advisory Commission on Intergovernmental Relations (1984:5) concluded that the " 'jail problem' is not simply a problem—if it were, its solution would probably not be so hard to attain. Rather, the 'jail problem' is a complex collection of problems, including jurisdictional authority and responsibility, constitutional rights, sociological and medical opinions, basic public safety, and perhaps most difficult, the allotment of increasingly scarce resources for the benefit of an exceedingly unpopular constituency." The most commonly cited and serious problems affecting modern American jails are misuse and overuse of detention; decrepit and substandard physical plants; overcrowding; administrative arrangements; staffing and personnel deficiencies; and substandard inmate care and treatment.

MISUSE AND OVERUSE OF DETENTION

Soon after their development jails evolved into catch-all institutions into which were thrown the ill, the addicted, the young, and other social misfits. Today, jails continue to serve as dumping grounds for society's more troubled members. Alcoholics, the mentally ill, juveniles, and women are among the individuals routinely detained in jails. In many instances, these individuals are incarcerated for offenses that are not fundamentally criminal; their primary offense is that they offend public tastes rather than threatening the safety or well-being of the community. Rather than detaining these individuals because they are a danger to the community or because they might flee prosecution, the jail functions primarily as a mechanism of social sanitation, concealing from public view those members of society who offend and repulse.

The jail, however, is ill-equipped to deal with the special and varied problems of alcoholics, the mentally ill, juveniles, and women. Geared primarily to the goals of custody and security, jails have neither the staff nor the resources to provide for the physical, medical, psychological or social needs of these individuals. The warehouse mentality of the jail makes physical and psychological deterioration inevitable as well as leading to a vulnerability to suicide, medical trauma and victimization by staff and other inmates.

Alcoholics

Street alcoholics, particularly skid row drunks, are vulnerable to arrest by virtue of their being drunk in public. Consequently, they make up a substantial proportion of the jail population. In 1970, the Law Enforcement Assistance Administration estimated that of the 67,000 inmates incarcerated on any given day in the nation's 4,037 local jail facilities, 30,000 were alcoholics (Law Enforcement Assistance Administration, 1971). It is believed that 20% to 40% of the jail population nationwide is incarcerated for public intoxication. The large number of alcoholics in jails is the consequence of a large number of arrests for public drunkenness. One out of every ten arrests in the United States is for public intoxication. According to the Federal Bureau of Investigation's Uniform Crime Reports, an estimated 933,900 arrests were made for drunkenness in 1986. This figure does not include the increasing number of arrests annually made for driving while intoxicated or disorderly conduct, for which public inebriates are often jailed in states which have decriminalized public intoxication. Frequently, the same individuals are arrested and booked into jail over and over again.[3]

The impact of these arrests on the jail is immense, particularly in terms of cost and wasted jail space. It is estimated that 400 million dollars is expended each year in trying and jailing public inebriates (American Correctional Association, 1985). Given the critical problem of jail overcrowding, jailing public inebriates has been criticized as a waste of precious jail space that could be used to detain more serious offenders (American Correctional Association, 1985).

Alcoholic inmates also pose special problems for the jail, particularly with regard to their medical needs. Even a short stay in jail may produce *delirium tremens,* which can be fatal if medical attention is not available. And, not surprisingly, alcoholic inmates suffer from a wide range of other medical problems. In a study of 3,000 public inebriates in New York, researchers found that 50% had wounds, cuts or burns; 25% suffered from seizure disorders; 20% had bone fractures; 20% experienced hallucinations; 20% had severe brain damage; 20% had severe gastrointestinal bleeding; and, 15% had cardiopulmonary problems (American Correctional Association, 1985). Yet the level of medical facilities available to these, as well as other, jail inmates is surprisingly poor. A 1972 American Medical Association (1973:ii) survey found that "65.5% of the responding jails had only first aid facilities, while 16.7% had no internal medical facilities. In only 38% of responding jails were physicians available on a regularly scheduled basis, and in only 50.6% . . . were physicians available on an on-call basis. In 31.1% no physicians were available." A more recent study conducted by the National Institute of Justice (U.S. Department of Justice, 1980b:209) reported that 77% of American jails had no medical facilities, 70% did not give inmates medical examinations upon entry into the jail, and only 15% gave medical examinations to those inmates who were "obviously" ill at the time of their incarceration. By 1980, only 67 jails in the country were accredited by the American Medical Association for meeting the minimum standards of health care. The National Sheriffs' Association jail study in 1981 found that only 16.6% of the responding jails had an in-house infirmary and that slightly more than 40% conducted initial medical screening of inmates or took inmates' medical histories.

Alcoholics are also vulnerable to suicide during their jail incarceration. Suicides are more common among inmates in jail for public intoxication and under the influence of alcohol at the time of their incarceration (Hayes, 1983).

Many criminal justice reformers have argued that public drunkenness is a type of offense that is not fundamentally a crime and therefore, should not be under the purview of the criminal justice system (Miller, 1978). Rather than threaten the safety and well-being of the public, street alcoholics offend public tastes. It is recommended that alcoholics be treated for their disease rather than incarcerated. On the heels of this recommendation, many states have acted to decriminalize public drunkenness and to establish public health centers for the detoxification and treatment of alcoholics. However, despite these efforts, public inebriates continue to be arrested and jailed for such offenses as disorderly conduct, disturbing the peace or littering.[4]

Juveniles

On June 30, 1988, 1,676 juveniles were incarcerated in the nation's jails (U.S. Department of Justice, 1990). Even though many states forbid the practice of incarcerating juveniles in adult detention facilities, over 100,000 juveniles annually pass through adult jails (U.S. Department of Justice, 1988). A study conducted in Minnesota (Schwartz, Harris and Levy, 1988) found that 4,000 juveniles were admitted to the state's jails and police lockups in 1986, a 5% increase in the number admitted the previous year. More surprising was the fact that many were very young. Two hundred and fifty of the youths were 13 years old or younger. The same study found that the majority of the juveniles had committed no crime or only petty offenses.

The incarceration of juveniles in adult jails has been criticized for a number of reasons. First, the comingling of adults and juveniles places young people in greater risk of being physically, sexually and mentally abused by adult offenders and defendants (Advisory Commission on Intergovernmental Relations, 1984:12). Juvenile girls, in particular, are vulnerable to sexual assault by jail guards (Chesney-Lind, 1988; Soler, 1988; Children's Defense Fund, 1976).[5] Juveniles are also more susceptible to suicide. For every 100,000 juveniles incarcerated in adult jails, 12 commit suicide. Flaherty (cited in the Advisory Commission on Intergovernmental Relations, 1984:12) noted that "the rate of suicide among children held in adult jails and lockups [is] significantly higher than among children in juvenile detention centers and children in the general population of the United States." Reports indicate that the suicide rate among juveniles in adult jails is 7.7 times higher than among juveniles in juvenile detention centers and 4.6 times higher than among juveniles in the general population (U.S. Department of Justice, 1983b).

The higher rates of suicide can be attributed to a number of factors. First, in jails which have made efforts to conform to the 1974 Juvenile Justice and Delinquency Prevention Act's mandate that juveniles and adults be completely separated during confinement, juveniles are often placed in isolated parts of the jails where they receive little staff support or supervision (Steinhart, 1988). Second, jail staff are typically not trained to recognize signs of severe depression in juveniles. Finally, juvenile girls with a history of sexual and physical abuse may be more vulnerable to depression and suicide while incarcerated (Chesney-Lind, 1988).

The nature of the alleged offenses for which juveniles are incarcerated is also an issue of concern. According to the Children's Defense Fund (1976:3–4), "17.9% of jailed children . . . had committed 'status offenses,' i.e., actions which would not be crimes if done by adults, such as running away or truancy." The same study found that 4.3% of incarcerated juveniles had committed no crimes but were taken to jail by the police for their own protection and because there were no alternatives available other than jail. Only in 11.7% of the cases were youths incarcerated for having committed serious criminal offenses. In the Minnesota study (Schwartz, Harris and Levi, 1988), most of the juveniles were being held for minor or petty crimes. Twenty-eight percent were confined for public order offenses (e.g., vandalism, possessing or receiving stolen property, driving while intoxicated); 17% for status offenses (e.g., running away, truancy, incorrigibility, loitering, curfew violations); and 10% for probation violation or contempt of court.

In 1975, Congress passed the Juvenile Justice and Delinquency Prevention Act which placed restrictions on the confinement of juveniles in adult facilities in states participating in the federal juvenile justice program. Initially, the Act allowed the incarceration of juveniles if they were housed in a part of the jail where they were out of sight and sound of adult prisoners. In 1980, the Act was amended to totally eliminate the practice of jailing juveniles in adult facilities. A deadline for removing juveniles was set for 1985, but was later extended to January, 1988. However, by 1987, 22 states participating in the program had failed to comply with this mandate (*Criminal Justice Newsletter,* 1987).

A number of reasons have been offered as to why the practice of jailing juveniles in adult facilities continues. In interviews with key juvenile justice and jail figures in Minnesota, Schwartz, Harris and Levi (1988) found that the lack of available alternatives for the detention of juveniles was the most important obstacle. Also cited were: the perception among key criminal justice figures that it was not a real problem; the belief that jailing juveniles was necessary for public safety; and the belief that jail serves a deterrent effect among juveniles. Steinhart (1988), in an analysis of a California law abolishing the jailing of juveniles, found that political leaders in smaller counties opposed the ban because they had so few juvenile offenders that the construction and operation of a juvenile detention facility would be cost prohibitive. They also were reluctant to transport juveniles to detention facilities in other counties because of the manpower and transportation costs.

Mentally Ill

The mentally ill are also overrepresented in the jail population. It is estimated that the lifetime prevalence of psychiatric disorders in the general population is 33%, yet among the jail population anywhere from 35% to 60% of inmates suffer from some form of mental illness (U.S. General Accounting Office, 1980:1).[6] The National Institute of Corrections estimated that 60% of all inmates suffer from mental disorders (cited in U.S. General Accounting Office, 1980:1). In a study conducted at the Philadelphia County Prison (Jail) system, psychopathology was diagnosed in 75% of the 493 newly admitted inmates systematically selected by the researchers (Guy, et al., 1985). In a study of 445 inmates referred for mental health evaluations in the Denver County Jail, 22.9% (102) were diagnosed as suffering from functional psychosis, 14.4% had previously been hospitalized for less than one month for mental problems and 27.9% had experienced long term or multiple hospitalizations (Swank and Winer, 1976). So numerous are the mentally ill in the nation's jails that an American Medical Association representative reported that "the jail is turning into a second-rate mental hospital" (cited in Wilson, 1980:14).

Some researchers have suggested that the jail is replacing the mental hospital as a "dumping ground" for the mentally ill. A number of reasons have been offered for this shift, including a general movement toward deinstitutionalization,[7] stricter commitment laws, less stringent discharge criteria, and reductions or curtailment of public funding for residential and outpatient treatment programs. According to one report:

> One of the most serious problems in the L.A. County Jail is a backlog of mental health cases waiting for transfer to state mental health facilities. In California, as in most other states, the closing of state mental hospitals, together with a general tightening of the civil commitment laws, has meant that increasing numbers of mentally ill people are on the streets. According to the [American Medical Associations' Joseph] Rowen, that has meant that growing numbers of former mental patients, as well as people whose bizarre behavior might have landed them in a hospital bed a few years ago, are now being arrested and are ending up in jail (Wilson, 1980:14).

Poor planning on the part of the federal government and local communities, further exacerbated the problem:

> Federal mental-health planners envisioned the flowering of a network of support services to care for deinstitutionalized patients at the community level through the stimulus of Federal seed money. But 1,300 of the 2,000 community mental-health centers projected for 1980 have failed to materialize and many that did have failed to service this chronically ill population. Deinstitutionalization, and ostensibly humane treatment programs, has denigrated into a tragic crisis. . . . Planners, without real consultation, assumed strong communities would accept the chronically ill. When few welcomed large numbers of these troubled people, patients were steered to transitional neighborhoods that would not put up a fuss, but the strong community support factor essential for successful aftercare was absent. The result was city streets became wards of mental hospitals, and it was out of the snakepits and into the gutter for victims of deinstitutionalization policy (cited in Advisory Commission on Intergovernmental Relations, 1984:14).

Most jails have neither the personnel nor the facilities to humanely deal with the mentally ill. The American Medical Associations' (1973) survey of medical care in jails found that only 14.2% of the 1,159 responding jails had facilities for the mentally ill while only 15.2% of the jails made a psychologist available to prisoners. In the absence of appropriate

personnel and facilities, some jail officials and staff have resorted to inhumane techniques to restrain mentally ill inmates. In an Allegheny County (Pennsylvania) jail, for example, mentally ill inmates "clothed in hospital gowns or left naked, were bound to canvas cots with a hole cut in the middle. A tub was placed underneath the hole to collect the body wastes. Prisoners also were required to sleep in canvas cots, many of which were discolored by vomit, feces, and urine" (U.S. General Accounting Office, 1980:9).

Women

Women comprise only a small percent of the total inmate population; however, census data reveal that their number is increasing at a faster rate than males. On June 30, 1983, less than 7% of the total jail population were female (U.S. Department of Justice, 1988). Five years later, on June 30, 1988, women comprised almost 9% of the total jail population. In real figures the number of women incarcerated in jail climbed from 15,652 to 30,299 in the five-year period—an increase of approximately 94% (U.S. Department of Justice, 1988). In contrast, the number of males increased by 51% during the same period.

The typical female inmate is a poor, undereducated, young, minority (American Correctional Association, 1985). Sixty-six percent of female jail inmates were unemployed prior to their incarceration and 47% have one or more children dependent upon them (American Correctional Association, 1985). Some scholars suggest that many women in jail do not pose a threat to the community but are incarcerated because their limited financial resources make raising the necessary bail difficult, if not impossible. An examination of the offenses for which women are incarcerated demonstrates that many were arrested for victimless crimes. A 1981 study of women booked into the San Francisco jail reveals that 40% were arrested for prostitution, 30.3% for property crimes (theft, shoplifting, forgery, fraud), 12.1% for drug offenses, and 6.1% for violent offenses (cited in American Correctional Association, 1985).

Jailed women seldom have access to programs and services provided to male inmates. Furthermore, because so few women are incarcerated in jails, special programs designed specifically for their unique needs are not offered:

> *Many women in jails are mothers with sole responsibility for the support of their children. Separated from their children, they live in fear of losing custody of their offspring to the state. Many jails do not permit children to visit their mothers in jail or severely restrict those visits. There is a lack of gynecological care for jailed women and seldom any special health care for pregnant women; use of contraceptive pills is often interrupted because they are not available in jail (American Correctional Association, 1985:24).*

Another deficiency in the treatment of female inmates concerns jail staffing. In a number of the nation's jails, female corrections officers are not employed by the jail or too few are employed to ensure around-the-clock supervision of female inmates (Kerle, 1985). A 1982 study found that in almost 23% of the 2,664 responding jails, women corrections officers are not always on duty when female inmates are housed in the facility (National Sheriffs' Association, 1982). While the lack of female employees is understandable in small jail facilities where resources and personnel are often limited, it also exists in a number of large facilities. In over 13% of the largest jails in the country (63 beds or more), women officers are not always on duty when female inmates are detained (National Sheriffs' Association, 1982). In many of these facilities male corrections officers are deployed to supervise female inmates.

The absence of female staff, even if only for limited periods of the day or night, leaves women inmates particularly vulnerable to exploitation and abuse by male staff. Take, for example, the controversial case of Joan Little. Little, a 20-year-old black woman, was the only woman inmate in the Beaufort County (North Carolina) Jail. She had been in the jail for 81 days on a charge of breaking and entering, and was awaiting transfer to a state prison for women (Reston, 1975). During her stay in the jail, she was supervised entirely by males; the jail did not employ female guards for women prisoners (*Newsweek*, 1975:86). According to Little, in the early morning hours of August 27, 1974, 62-year-old Clarence Alligood, a white jail guard, entered her cell and sexually attacked her. Little claimed

that in self-defense she killed Alligood with an icepick he had brought into the cell. In her trial for murder, the prosecution claimed that Little had willingly engaged in sexual intercourse with Alligood on previous occasions in return for special privileges and sandwiches, but that on the morning of August 27th, Little "had taken the ice pick from Alligood's desk while making a telephone call, cooperated in a sexual act and then murdered him" (*Time*, 1975:19). The trial became a *cause celebre* for feminists and civil rights activists, and in the end, the jury found Little not guilty of murder.

PHYSICAL AND SANITARY CONDITIONS OF JAILS

Although the "typical" American jail has been described as a "relatively small institution with less than twenty-five cells, built between 1880 and 1920, located in a small town, frequently the county seat of a rural county (Mattick, 1974:785–786) the description is somewhat misleading. Although 44% of the nation's jails are small (less than 25 cells), they hold only 4% of the nation's inmates. In contrast, only 4% of the nation's jails hold over 45% of all jail prisoners. Typically, these large facilities are located in major metropolitan and urban areas (Advisory Commission on Intergovernmental Relations, 1984:6). Decrepit and decaying physical facilities are common to both the small and large jails. While these conditions exist in small, rural facilities because of fiscal and administrative neglect, they exist in large, urban facilities because of overuse and overcrowding (Flynn, 1973:64).

A common complaint leveled at the modern jail concerns deficiencies in its architectural design. In his scathing commentary on prison and jail architecture, Norman Johnston (1973:54) concluded that:

> *[T]he history of prison architecture stands as a discouraging testament of our sometimes intentional, sometimes accidental degradation of our fellow man. Prison structures have continued to be built in a way which manages by one means or another to brutalize their occupants and to deprive them of their privacy, dignity, and self-esteem, while at the same time strengthening their criminality. The 19th century contemporary prison seems to allow mechanical con-*

trivances to dominate the prisoner. Architects in the future must share some responsibility for the unintended indignities made possible by their works.

Deficiencies in jail architecture can be traced, in part, to the assumptions that have traditionally directed institutional designs. William G. Nagel (1973:18–19), in the definitive study of modern jail architecture, argued that facility administrators, consultants and architects develop jail and prison designs with four assumptions in mind:

1. Jailers are not wise enough to recognize which inmates might try to escape. They, therefore, must apply maximum custody provisions to all.
2. Jails must be designed to compensate for the inadequacies and transience of personnel.
3. Jails receive the most destructive elements of society, who have, during confinement, much idle time for the venting of their destructive impulses. The masonry, hardware, and furnishings, therefore, must be virtually destruction-proof.
4. Jails must be built as cheaply as possible. Since the concrete and hardware needed to provide the desired level of physical security are expensive, costs must be kept down by housing detainees in wards and by keeping the amount of activity space provided to a minimum.

The impact of these assumptions on the architecture and interior design of jails is immense. Jails are massive, concrete and metal constructions resembling fortresses on the outside and cages on the inside. The implicit belief that prisoners must be restrained and constrained is overemphasized in the architecture and furnishings. The bars, the strategically placed video cameras and the deliberately located eavesdropping equipment are all geared to the effective and efficient supervision, control, and surveillance of inmates.

In the typical jail facility, inmates are housed in two-, four-, six-, and eight-person cells or in multiple-occupancy dormitories. Although both the American Correctional Association and the National Jail Association recommended single-occupancy cells, few jails are designed to provide them (American Correctional Association, 1981:30). Even in some facilities featuring single cells, overcrowding has forced double- or even triple-bunking. Ironically, inmate living space is even less in double-bunked single cells than in multiple-occupancy cells.

Single-occupancy cells are recommended over multiple-occupancy cells (particularly dormitories) for a number of reasons. First, they provide greater security against escapes. Second, they allow greater flexibility in the classification and segregation of different categories of inmates. Third, they provide better security for jail personnel. Fourth, they prevent homosexual activities among inmates. Fifth, they assist in reducing aberrant inmate behavior such as assaults, extortion, etc. Sixth, they fulfill inmate privacy needs (Nagel, 1973:24). A majority of jail experts and administrators acknowledge that the most critical problem associated with the lack of single cells is the violence that occurs between inmates in multiple-occupancy cells and dormitories.

The most economical housing arrangement, in terms of building costs and space utilization, is the use of dormitories. Over 51% of confinement space in local facilities is composed of dormitory units that house between 11 and 50 prisoners (U.S. Department of Justice, 1980b:80). In many jails, dormitories provide inmates with less than the 60 square feet of floor space recommended by the American Correctional Association and the Commission on Accreditation for Corrections (American Correctional Association, 1981:30). Revealingly referred to as "jungles" by correctional personnel and inmates, dormitories are the most detrimental of housing arrangements in terms of their impact on staff and inmates. According to Nagel (1973:24), dormitories provide greater opportunities for sexual exploitation, moral contamination and physical exploitation among inmates; they deprive inmates of privacy, prevent appropriate classification or separation of prisoners, and pose serious threats to the safety of staff.

As discussed previously, most jails, regardless of their age, were built in a traditional, linear/intermittent surveillance architectural style. The inability of the custodial staff to adequately supervise inmates and their activities is a consequence of this architectural design. In more modern facilities, sophisticated electronic equipment has been installed to improve institutional surveillance of inmates. However, over-reliance on these technological mechanisms significantly reduces contact between inmates and staff and promotes the impression that "inmates are literally held in the system—they are mere items" (Nagel, 1973:29). For inmates, the effect of mechanical bugging devices and short-circuit television systems is often dehumanizing. One inmate, for example, complained that the jail "is the only place in the world where a man can urinate, defecate and masturbate knowing full well that some bastard is watching him on the boob tube" (quoted in Nagel, 1973:64, 67).

In the typical jail cell at least one wall consists of bars; the other three are cement or cinderblock. The bars give the cell its cage-like appearance and effectively reduce inmate privacy. Where cells are equipped with toilets, no effort is made to shield inmates from the view of others. Anyone walking by the cell can look in on inmates as they use the toilets. Toilets are left unscreened for purported security and surveillance reasons.

Rugs, curtains, soft furniture or other materials that absorb sound are absent from most cells. Jail furniture is typically made of heavy, durable metal to prevent inmate vandalism. In most cases, pieces of furniture are bolted to the floor so inmates cannot use them as weapons to throw at other inmates or staff members. Because of the lack of effective sound absorbing components, noise levels are often exceedingly high. Without appropriate absorption materials, sounds from the locking and unlocking of the metal doors, from televisions and radios, and from the inmates themselves are magnified. One inmate commented that "all night the jail sounds like a nuthouse. All the junkies are screaming their guts out going through cold turkey" (quoted in Reid, 1976:369). After spending a night in a Boston jail, a federal judge complained that "the noise seemed to increase after midnight and approached a virtual bedlam which lasted until dawn" (*Inmates of the Suffolk County Jail v. Eisenstadt,* 1973:680–681).

In many modern facilities, cells are equipped with stainless steel toilets and sinks. Often, the toilet can only be flushed from outside the cell by corrections officers and toilet tissue is provided only upon request.

In some older facilities, cells are not equipped with either toilets or sinks. Still in existence in some jails is the "honey bucket" system wherein a bucket serves as a toilet. The plumbing is so antiquated in other facilities that toilets may not flush or may occasionally back up. In these cases, persistent and unpleasant smells permeate the cells.

Adequate lighting is also a problem in many facilities. Since many jails are designed without windows, natural light may be totally absent. The assumption is that windows threaten the security of the facility. There is, however, little evidence to support this belief. Artificial light may also be inadequate for inmate activities. In many facilities, the lack of light gives a dark, dreary and depressing appearance to the living area.[8]

In a survey sponsored by the National Sheriffs' Association (1982), 11% or 262 of the 2,373 responding jails were built in the 1800s; 26% or 612 of the responding facilities were built sometime between 1900 and 1920. Older jails have myriad problems involving, in particular, inadequacies in the physical plant. Many of these facilities have antiquated ventilation and heating/cooling systems. While the jail is hot in the summer, it is inevitably cold in the winter. Nonfunctioning ventilation systems have been credited with the spread of aerobic viruses that cause illnesses among inmates and staff. A typical problem in aging facilities is plumbing that leaks water onto the floor. In a number of these facilities, overcrowding forces inmates to sleep on floors, and, consequently, in puddles of water.

Common to many jail facilities is a lack of cleanliness—both of the facility and of inmates. As succinctly stated by Mattick (1974:802), "if cleanliness is next to godliness, most jails lie securely in the province of hell." Jail inmates suffer high rates of venereal disease, tuberculosis and infectious hepatitis (Mattick, 1974:802). Yet the lack of cleanliness and sanitation makes it inevitable that these diseases are passed from inmate to inmate, or even from inmate to staff. In some facilities elementary personal hygiene materials such as soap, towels, toothbrushes, clean clothes and bedding are in short supply or, in some cases, absent. Even shower facilities may be inadequate. Often the ratio of showerheads to inmates is so high that it is necessary for inmates to compete for the opportunity to shower. In addition, communal showers provided in many facilities make showering a dangerous task. Often unsupervised, the shower area is a common site for sexual assaults.

The age and decrepit condition of the facility also contribute to its uncleanliness. In older facilities, any remedial measure taken cannot overcome the physical deterioration that contributes to an unclean and unsanitary environment.

> *Extensive cleaning is not possible in some old jails because the ironwork is rusted, the cement floors are broken, and the walls would disintegrate. Such jails are havens for rodents, body lice, and other vermin that can successfully survive sporadic attempts at extermination. Where jails can be cleaned, this is usually done by the inmates themselves (Mattick, 1974:802).*

A final problem concerning the physical plant of modern jail facilities is the lack of space for inmate programs such as counseling, educational and vocational classes, recreation, and visitation. In a survey of 2,452 facilities, the National Sheriffs' Association (1982) reported that only 35.1% have space for medical services; 29.2% have space for counseling or educational programming; 28.6% have space for outdoor recreation; 27.9% have space for contact visits; 25.6% of the responding facilities have specifically designated space for library services; 25.4% have space for indoor recreation; 17.8% have space for dining; and 7.1% have space for vocational programming.

Even more surprising is that only 45% of the facilities have dayroom space.[9] As a result of the lack of space, inmate programming is minimal at best, and, in many cases, nonexistent.

In the last two decades there has been a movement for greater state involvement in jail administration, largely as a consequence of burgeoning inmate litigation challenging the constitutionality of jail conditions, particularly those concerning the physical plant of the facility. The focus of this involvement has been primarily on the establishment and enforcement of minimum standards for the operation, construction and renovation of local jail facilities. In 1966, 40% of

states had adopted comprehensive standards. Twelve years later, 45 states had implemented jail standards, the majority of which were mandatory.

In most cases, the standards adopted by states are those delineated by federal courts in actions brought by inmates and by professional correctional associations such as the American Correctional Association and the National Sheriffs' Association (Advisory Commission on Intergovernmental Relations, 1984:97–98). The most comprehensive set of standards was promulgated by the American Correctional Association. These standards focused on such issues as minimum floor space provided to inmates, lighting, noise levels, air circulation, temperatures, toilet and shower facilities, recreation, visitation and inmate program space, and other aspects of the physical environment of the jail.[10]

While it was hoped that these new standards, particularly those that were mandatory, would improve jail conditions, the evidence suggests that their impact has been modest at best. Establishment and enforcement of minimum standards is a highly political exercise. Products of political bargaining and consensus-building, the standards adopted by states are often vague and unenforceable. Some argue that accreditation by the state is based more upon "who you know" than upon actual compliance with the standards. One jail administrator commented that "the only difference in this state between an accredited jail and one that isn't, is the plaque on the wall of the Sheriff whose jail is accredited" (cited in Advisory Commission on Intergovernmental Relations, 1984:103). In many states, jail inspection amounts to a "bad joke" (Allinson, 1982:22).

Although no one has yet made a comprehensive evaluation of the impact of state standards on jail conditions, indirect evidence suggests that full compliance has yet to be attained. According to a joint study conducted by the Advisory Commission on Intergovernmental Relations and the National Association of Counties, 16 states with mandatory minimum standards had jails under court order to revise conditions (cited in Advisory Commission on Intergovernmental Relations, 1984:103). This evidence suggests that even where states have adopted standards, local jails have failed to live up to them.

OVERCROWDING

Survey after survey has revealed that overcrowding is the most critical problem facing urban jail administrators today. In a survey of 35 jail administrators and social services providers, Gibbs (1983) found that overcrowding was listed as the most serious of 24 jail problems. In a study conducted by the National Sheriffs' Association, 795 out of 2,452 jails listed overcrowding as the greatest problem affecting their facility.

Prior to 1980, jail populations remained relatively stable. The average annual population of the nation's jails in the 1970s hovered at around 158,000. In the 1980s, there has been a dramatic upswing in the jail population. The Bureau of Justice Statistics (U.S. Department of Justice, 1983a) reported that by 1982 the national annual jail population jumped to approximately 212,000, an increase of about 26% between 1978 and 1982. Between 1983 and 1988, jail populations grew from a daily rate of 223,551 to 343,569 inmates—an increase of 54% (U.S. Department of Justice, 1990).

The 100 largest facilities in the United States have been the hardest hit by the overcrowding problem. In these facilities inmate populations consistently exceed designed capacity (U.S. Department of Justice, 1983a:2). In some cases the problem is so pronounced that many inmates are forced to sleep on the floors or in dayrooms when cell capacity is surpassed. Although smaller facilities seldom exceed their capacities, they nevertheless feel the effects of too many inmates. In the National Sheriffs' Association (1982) jail survey, small facilities rated overcrowding as the most serious problem affecting their facility even though they were the least likely to be operating at capacity. On closer examination, the authors of the report concluded that:

many participants cited overcrowding as an issue which at times didn't square with the figures cited as their daily inmate population. What some of these people probably mean is there aren't enough staff on shift to handle the workload properly. Even if a jail does have a bed space for every prisoner, jail officers think of it as overcrowded if, due to staff shortages, the inmate counts, bed checks, and cell searches are over- *looked and inmate programs such as outdoor recreation are postponed (National Sheriffs' Association, 1982:231).*

The jail overcrowding problem involves a number of factors, including: a judicial movement toward stricter penalties for crimes, such as mandatory sentences for driving while intoxicated; state restructuring of sentencing, particularly from indeterminate to determinate sentencing, that has resulted in the diversion of many offenders from prisons to jails; general increases in crime rates; and, finally, overcrowding in state prisons.[11] The U.S. Department of Justice (1983a:3) concluded that "during 1981, the number of states under court orders to reduce overcrowding rose from 28 to 31, while the number involved in litigation about overall prison conditions increased from 32 to 37." This litigation has had a tremendous impact on local jails.

When [prison administrators] are forced to reduce the inmate population, many simply refuse to accept sentenced prisoners. Consequently, jails must retain inmates until the prison will accept them. In 1981, 8,576 state prisoners were being held in local jails (U.S. Department of Justice, 1983a:3). In New Jersey during the same year, 945 (11%) of the state's 8,692 prisoners were housed in 21 county jails that were themselves overcrowded (Carney, 1982:24). In Mississippi, the prison system was so overcrowded that 1,300 inmates were backed up in local jails awaiting transfer to prison.[12] Some jail administrators and sheriffs have become so frustrated with the overflow of state prisoners that they have taken extraordinary steps to alleviate the problem, including suing the state to force them to accept their own prisoners. In one case, the sheriff in Pulaski County, Arkansas, chained 19 state prisoners housed in his jail to posts and fences outside of two prisons. He had been forced to house the prisoners until the state could meet a court order to alleviate overcrowding in the prisons. By 1988, the problem intensified. On June 30, 1988, 28,481 state prisoners were being held in local jails because there was no bed space available in state prisons (U.S. Department of Justice, 1990).

While many jails grapple with the problem of "spill-over" from overcrowded state prisons, the courts have made it clear that overcrowding in jails will not be tolerated. In the 1979 case of *Bell v. Wolfish,* the U.S. Supreme Court concluded that "a detainee may not be punished prior to an adjudication of guilt."[13] Because, on the average, around 60% of all persons in jail are pretrial detainees—who under our system of law are presumed to be innocent—the courts have stipulated that any condition of detainment which in effect punishes pretrial detainees violates their constitutional rights. In the case of *Gross v. Tazewell County Jail* (1982), the U.S. District Court summarized its rationale for prohibiting overcrowding in jails:

> It is abundantly clear that extreme overcrowding in a local jail is of greater practical effect and constitutional consequence than in a larger institution or a common road camp. Perhaps more importantly, the local jail houses a high percentage of pretrial detainees. . . . As a matter of common sense and fundamental fairness, the criminal justice system must insure that pretrial detainees are not housed in more deprived circumstances than those accorded to convicted persons. . . . Overcrowding in a local jail cannot be qualitatively equated with overcrowding in a state penal institution.

Overcrowding is the most common basis on which inmates challenge the constitutionality of jail conditions. Of the 285 facilities under court order in 1982, overcrowding was the primary cause for court action in 73%, or 209, of the cases (National Sheriffs' Association, 1982:45). Of the nation's 612 largest jails, 23%, or 139, were under court order in 1986 to reduce inmate populations (U.S. Department of Justice, 1987).

While overcrowding has a number of consequences for jail administrators, it also has tremendous impact on the inmates housed in overcrowded facilities.[14] First, overcrowding places excessive strain on the resources of the jail, particularly with regard to programs, goods and services provided to inmates. The availability of telephones, televisions, recreation and visitation time, counseling and educational programs, and medical and mental health treatment is significantly reduced as a result of overcrowding, and in some cases, may be denied to all inmates. The amount of personal space provided to each inmate is also reduced, thereby removing any opportunity for privacy. Even basic hygiene facilities such as a shower or a change of clothing and bedding may not be readily accessible in a facility that is overcrowded.

While reductions in services, programs and goods produce feelings of frustration and perhaps anger among inmates, some scholars suggest that overcrowding stimulates aberrant inmate and staff behavior.[15] Although only a limited amount of research has been conducted on the impact of crowding in correctional institutions, existing research suggests that overcrowding has psychological and physical consequences for inmates. Clear and Cole (1986:225) summarized the effect of overcrowding on inmates as follows:

> Cells intended to hold one or two persons are holding three, four, even five. It is not uncommon for prisoners to sleep in hallways, with or without mattresses. Direct and immediate consequences of overcrowding are violence, rape, and a variety of health disorders. There is some evidence that prolonged exposure to seriously crowded conditions reduces the expected life span of inmates. Certainly tempers flare in close quarters and the vulnerable inmate becomes a more likely victim. What makes these facts even more depressing to contemplate is that many of the persons subjected to these conditions have not yet been tried and must be presumed to be innocent.

ADMINISTRATIVE ARRANGEMENTS

From the time of their inception jails were administered by county sheriffs. Through default, sheriffs have remained the titular heads of most local facilities. Only in six states are local jails administered by state officials rather than by county sheriffs. These states include Alaska, Connecticut, Delaware, Hawaii, Rhode Island, and Vermont. In a small number of local jurisdictions, jails are administered by county-level departments of correction. In Kentucky, all counties (except those containing a city over 100,000) separately elect county jailers who have custody and control over the jail.

Burns (1975) suggested that the jail has remained under the jurisdiction of county sheriffs because of self-interest, particularly in regard to the monies that could be made through extortion of prisoners. In earlier days, the jails' fee systems provided sheriffs with a fairly substantial income. Under the fee system, sheriffs received a set amount of money per day for the care of prisoners. In addition to the widespread abuses previously discussed, the fee system encouraged wholesale arrests of nondangerous social outcasts in order to increase the jail population and the fees paid to the sheriff (Miller, 1978:23). The fee system provided the incentive for sheriffs to detain prisoners for as long as possible.[16] The prisoner fees paid to the sheriff made the position highly desirable and much sought after. In some localities, the local sheriff earned more money than the President of the United States (Burns, 1975:157)!

Today, jail administration by county sheriffs is commonly cited as the major cause of jail problems and a formidable obstacle to reform efforts. The majority of the criticisms directed at jail administration by county sheriffs focuses on the sheriffs' preoccupation with their law enforcement role and neglect of the correctional role. For the most part, sheriffs tend to have little interest in or knowledge about jail administration. Twenty years ago the President's Commission on Law Enforcement and Administration of Justice (1967) observed that "the basic police mission of apprehending offenders usually leaves little time, commitment, or expertise for the development of rehabilitative programs, although notable exceptions demonstrate that jails can indeed be settings for correctional treatment." Years later, Flynn (1973:59) commented that sheriffs "view the jail as an adjunct to their law enforcement activities and as a place for the temporary detention and warehousing of inmates."

The background, education, training and interests of most sheriffs are in law enforcement. Few have the expertise, training or incentive to spend inordinate amounts of time on jail concerns. In a study of local jails in Illinois conducted by the University of Chicago's Center for Studies in Criminal Justice, it was found that "the sheriffs and their deputies, or the Police authorities, who are responsible for the jails, spend 10 percent or less of their time doing any jail work" (cited in Mattick; and Aikman 1969:112). Nor is it politically expedient for sheriffs to devote time and energy to the jail. More often than not, sheriffs are elected on the basis of their crime control and law enforcement abilities, not their skills as jail administra-

tors. It is certainly more glamorous and attractive to be a crimefighter than a jail keeper. For elected sheriffs, there is truth in Huey Long's adage: "There ain't no votes in prisons."

Although every comprehensive jail study conducted within the last 60 years has recommended either replacing the sheriff as the chief jail administrator with an appointed, correctional specialist or abolishing local jail control (Fishman, 1923; Robinson, 1944; Richmond, 1965; Flynn, 1973; Mattick, 1974), jails remain firmly dominated by local political officials. These reforms would reduce the number of locally elected positions, reduce patronage opportunities, and damage the interests of local bailsbondsmen and tradesmen who regularly deal with the jail. These lost opportunities ensure that local opposition is fierce and prolonged.

PERSONNEL

In a 1982 survey of jails sponsored by the National Sheriffs' Association (NSA) respondents were asked to identify five of the most serious problems in their facility. Of the 2,452 responding facilities, 1,209 ranked "personnel" among their top five problems (1982:225). Ken Kerle, a jail consultant and coauthor of the NSA report, stated that: "personnel is still the number one problem of jails. . . . Start paying decent salaries and developing decent training and you can start to attract bright young people to jobs in jails. If you don't do this, you'll continue to see the issue of personnel as the number one problem of jails for the next 100 years" (cited in Advisory Commission of Intergovernmental Relations, 1984:7).

Clear and Cole (1986:221) summarized the jail personnel conundrum as follows: "Local corrections workers are among the most poorly trained, least educated, and worst paid employees in the criminal justice system." The personnel problems cited by authorities in the field include inappropriate selection and training programs, substandard salaries, understaffing, and low job prestige (Advisory Commission on Intergovernmental Relations, 1984; Mattick, 1974; National Sheriffs Association, 1982; Miller, 1978; Flynn, 1973).

The impact of these personnel problems on the jail and its operation is tremendous. Clear and Cole (1986:221) observed that turnover in jails is extraordinarily high and that many jails report complete staff turnover once every two or three years. Mattick (1974:804) concluded that "if a jail's staff is inadequate in its initial qualifications for the job, in screening, in training, in numbers, and in motivation and morale, even the most modern, well-designed, and fully equipped penal plant will be defeated in its every function and purpose."

The personnel problem most often discussed by correctional scholars is that of understaffing. Approximately 99,000 people are employed in the nation's jails; of this number, 74% perform custodial duties (U.S. Department of Justice, 1990). A Law Enforcement Assistance Administration study (1971) concluded that there were 1.6 full-time staff members per jail per shift.[17] On average, each staff member is in charge of 40 inmates. Many small and rural counties do not employ custodial personnel, but rely instead on local police or sheriff s employees to make periodic checks of the jail to ensure that inmates have not escaped, killed themselves, or killed one another.

Understaffing, and in some cases a complete lack of staff, has been criticized for a number of reasons—primary among them the threat it poses to inmate safety and security. Many jail officials deal with inadequate staffing levels by locking inmates in their cells to prevent escape and ease the handling of prisoners. Without appropriate staff supervision, however, little can be done to protect inmates locked in multiple-occupancy cells from one another. Inmates themselves express concern over the lack of adequate supervision. According to one inmate in the San Francisco jail, "I was here three days and didn't sleep a wink because I was scared. You know what was scariest of all? Never seeing a guard" (quoted in *Newsweek,* 1980:77).

A second personnel dilemma concerns the lack of adequate systems for the recruitment, selection, training, and compensation of correctional staff. The National Sheriffs' Association's comprehensive study of jails provided a number of insights into the deficiencies of most personnel systems.

On Recruitment: "Too often, there are no standards for recruitment and warm bodies are taken off the street, put into uniform, given a set of keys, and told to go to work. At times, one finds line officers in the golden age category—a job men and women take to supplement a social security or retirement check. Most people in the over 60 bracket are not physically capable of handling the younger inmates who act out in a physically violent manner" (1982:231).

On Screening Job Applicants: "Most [jails] are deficient in the areas of physical, written, and psychological testing. . . . Many jails which we have examined have no educational requirement at all for the jail officer position although a few states require a high school diploma or a GED (general equivalency diploma) certificate" (1982:119).[18]

On Training: " . . . jail training is still an extremely low priority in local facilities. Jail training today is where police training was 20 years ago. Until sheriffs and county governing personnel understand the necessity of a well-trained jail staff, problems will continue to plague jails.[19] Training seems to be the most expendable item in budgets and frequently budget cuts are given as the excuse for not conducting training . . . Most state and local governments have defaulted on their responsibility to give training to jail officers on any consistent basis" (1982:125–127).

On Salaries: "Jail officer careers will never achieve the status they deserve so long as counties continue to pay jail officers less money than the officers assigned to police duties.[20] Part of the problem facing counties today is not only the lack of sufficiently trained staff, but the lack of qualified staff in terms of education. Education relates to salaries. No person wants to make a career where the reward is lousy wages. You can't attract the people who have the potential to be the best officers by paying them wages in the poverty range" (1982:151).

With an apparent lack of quality control in most jails' personnel systems, it is more than likely that people unfit for correctional work are hired and retained. An example of unfit officers was found in the 1969 investigation of the Nassau County (New Jersey) Jail. To investigate the validity of rumors concerning brutality and corruption among corrections officers, undercover private investigators were sent into the jail to pose as inmates. The investigators found that, in general, the facility was well run; however, they also uncovered a number of problems concerning staff attitudes and performance.

> Investigative reports dealing with the attitude and performance of the guards revealed that, while most did their jobs with insight, understanding, and courtesy, some performed indifferently and behaved arrogantly. As the investigation proceeded, it became more and more obvious that the entirely unprofessional attitude and behavior of this latter group had a serious detrimental effect on the best interests and concerns of the institution. These guards seemed less intent on doing their jobs than on demonstrating their superiority and dominance over the inmates. Although at times this behavior appeared consciously directed at specific individuals purely for purposes of harassment, it was just as prevalent as a simple reflexive response to any inmate's request or expression of human sentiment (Cahn, 1973:8).

Among the behaviors exhibited by the unprofessional officers were threats issued against inmates, insults, profanity, name-calling (e.g., "chump," "punk," "honky"), ignoring or responding with sarcasm to legitimate requests and complaints, belittling and degrading comments, minor physical abuse, and general harassment.[21] The most serious form of abuse found by the undercover agents was the granting of special privileges to organized crime figures. In addition to treating these prisoners with dignity and respect, the officers delivered illicit liquor and narcotics to them. In one case, a female prisoner was supplied to a mobster for his sexual pleasure.

Inmates reacted to the degrading treatment with anger, frustration, resentment and aggression. When officers continued to ignore complaints that coffee or Kool-Aid was not being delivered with meals, inmates staged a hunger strike to get their attention. It is apparent that if inmates are pushed too far by uncaring and rude corrections officers, a hunger strike can easily erupt into a more serious demonstration.

A more serious case of officer misconduct occurred in the Okaloosa County (Florida) Jail. While checking the detoxification unit at about 10:00 one evening, a female corrections officer found a male inmate with one end of a shoestring tied around his neck and the other end tied to the bunk directly above him. After removing the shoestring and determining that the inmate still had a pulse, the officer left the man in his cell. The officer did not notify her supervisor or call for medical assistance. The next morning, the inmate was found dead. The autopsy showed that the inmate had died about two hours after he was found hanging by the officer. An investigation into the suicide revealed that the inmate had threatened to kill himself when booked into the jail and that the officer had failed to notify her supervisor of the threat or to initiate 15-minute observations required for suicidal inmates. The officer was suspended without pay for five days and received a written reprimand (*Daily Home Sun,* 1989:23).

Available research on correctional employees tends to suggest that, in general, corrections officers are largely a disaffected group.[22] Symptoms of their plight include high levels of stress (Stinchcomb, 1986), cynicism (Farmer, 1977), alienation (Toch and Klofas, 1982; Poole and Regoli, 1981), and occupational tedium (Shamir and Drory, 1982); low levels of job satisfaction (Hays and Tompkins, 1986); and high turnover rates (May, 1980; Jurik and Winn, 1986; *Corrections Compendium,* 1987; Benton, Rosen and Peters, 1982).

Scholars have offered a variety of reasons to explain why corrections officers are such a troubled group. Some authorities suggest that the nature and design of the work performed by corrections officers is an important factor in the problems they experience (Brief, Munro and Aldag, 1976; Toch and Grant, 1982). Herzberg, Mausner and Snyderman (1959) argued that people find satisfaction in their work when it is interesting and challenging, when it provides genuine responsibility, and when it presents opportunities for achievement, personal growth and individual advancement. The design of the job performed by corrections officers has been criticized by several scholars as incapable of providing these sources of satisfaction.

The work performed by corrections officers in jails is best described as fragmented, routinized and menial—in a word, impoverished. An examination of officer activities, tasks and assignments illustrates this point. The following tasks have been emphasized for a New York corrections officer: "Checks inmate passes and records inmates' movements in and out of areas"; "Watches for unusual incidents and reports any to his supervisor either verbally or in writing"; "Makes periodic rounds of assigned areas checking for faulty bars, gates, etc. and checks areas for daily fire report"; "Supervises bathing", "Announces sick call" (Toch and Grant, 1982:85–86). These obligations appear to be bureaucratic chores that require little or no judgment, initiative or skill on the part of officers. Consequently, the nature and design of the job can frustrate fulfillment of officers' personal needs for recognition, challenge, responsibility, and achievement, and produce officers who are dissatisfied, apathetic, unmotivated, alienated from their jobs and uncommitted to the goals of the jail.

Another source of dissatisfaction for jail guards is the lack of well-defined and clearly articulated organizational goals. In part, this lack of goals is due to an ambiguity about the role of the jail within the criminal justice system and within society as a whole. By default, security and custodial convenience have emerged as the underlying forces that direct the operations of the jail.[23]

The persistence of incoherent and ambiguous goals has important consequences for custodial personnel. First, it prevents officers from clearly identifying the obligations of the job and the organization's expectations of their performance. Deprived of these guidelines, officers must second guess the organization or rely on co-workers (or even inmates) to provide clarity. In either case, the risk is high that the officer will perform tasks in direct opposition to what the facility's administration desires. Second, officers lack the ability to assess whether their performance has a positive effect on attainment of the organization's goals. In essence, the performance of officers under these circumstances is without direction or purpose.

A third source of dissatisfaction is the classical hierarchical authority structure of the jail organization. As with most police agencies, the jail hierarchy is organized along paramilitary lines, with graded levels of authority that are assigned specific military ranks. Corresponding to Weber's organization model, authority, power and control increase as one ascends the hierarchy. Jail guards, who occupy the lowest level of the hierarchy, are vested with little authority and control. Likewise, jail policies formulated by those at the upper levels of the hierarchy direct and control the behavior of those at the lower levels.

In the hierarchical organization of the jail, firsthand factual reports about what is occurring in the facility are communicated upward by corrections officers, and policies, directives, and orders are communicated downward by the administration. Schrag (1961) argued that this arrangement alienates corrections officers in three ways. First, although corrections officers are closest to the situations involving inmates and know the most about them, they have little input in the decision-making process. Their role is to follow orders, not to evaluate them. Second, because the administration is so far removed from situations involving inmates, they must rely on officer reports that may be distorted in the communication process. Consequently, their decisions may be inappropriate to the situation. The decisions, however, are communicated in the form of commands and officers have no recourse but to follow orders. Finally, because communication between the administration and subordinates is limited, officers are not privy to reasons and rationales for the various rules and regulations that direct their every action. Without an understanding of the reasons for the rules, officers are more inclined to unofficially reinterpret them or to simply ignore them.

Another source of guard dissatisfaction is the overabundance of formal institutional rules and regulations for the control of inmate and staff behavior. There are few activities or situations involving inmates which are not covered by an institutional rule or regulation. Corrections officers, whose primary responsibility is to control inmates, are also governed by an exhaustive list of rules that prescribe expected behavior in all situations.

Cressey (1968) observed that the organization's concern for obedience to rules and regulations places corrections officers in a precarious position. Although his observations were specifically intended for prison organizations, they are applicable to the equally rule-bound jail organization. As managers of inmates, corrections officers need flexibility and discretion to deal with the myriad situations they encounter. However, the organization's preoccupation with rules does not provide this necessary flexibility and discretion. Cressey (1968:494) summarized the situation as follows:

> *Prisons differ significantly if not uniquely, from other organizations, because their personnel hierarchies are organized down to the lower level of the administration of the daily activities of men. The guard, who is the lowest level worker in a prison, is also a manager. He is managed in a system of regulations and controls from above, but he also manages, by a corresponding system of regulations, the inmates who are in his charge. Essentially because he is a worker, he cannot be given full discretion to produce a desired end product such as inmate docility or inmate rehabilitation, and essentially because he is a manager his activities cannot be bureaucratized in a set of routine procedures.*

A consequence of the overabundance of jail rules is the conflict that results when obedience to rules is not compatible with other organizational expectations. This incompatibility is often found in the potentially conflicting expectations of rule enforcement and order maintenance. While officers are expected to enforce all facility rules, they are also expected to maintain order among inmates. The two expectations can conflict when excessive rule enforcement leads to inmate unrest. Another source of conflict among organizational expectations of rule enforcement was offered by Schrag (1961). He argued that it would require the repeated use of force and the issuance of a number of official rule-infraction reports for officers to enforce all facility rules. Such a flurry of activity would cause administrators to question the competency of the officer and his or her ability to control inmates.

Another source of dissatisfaction is the lack of adequate organizational resources available to officers for performing the required tasks of the job. One of the most important resources in short supply are the means necessary to control inmate behavior. Although officers are legitimately empowered to use coercion (e.g., force, threats and physical punishments) to control inmates, administrators actively discourage its use. Coercion is costly in terms of manpower and resources; its use breaks down any chance of peaceful control, and public opinion will eventually condemn its excessive use (Schrag, 1961). Consequently, officers are caught in a quandary. Because inmates do not view officers as possessing legitimate control, coercion is the only means of control that they possess (Sykes, 1958). However, if coercion is used too often, officers risk disciplinary action by the jail administration.

Some scholars have argued that the involuntary and hostile nature of the clientele with whom corrections officers routinely interact is a source of irritation for the officers (Lipsky, 1980). Client-centered organizations such as jails require officers to work intensively and intimately with other people. Over an extended period of time such contact can be particularly wearing and stress-inducing (Shamir and Drory, 1982). The situation is made worse by the fact that officers receive very little esteem from their work with inmates. The job performed by officers places them in intimate contact with inmates who tend to be neither respectful, appreciative, nor supportive of their work.

INMATE CARE AND TREATMENT

A final component of the jail problem concerns the care and treatment provided to inmates. As noted previously, the decrepit state of the jail's physical plant, overcrowding and inadequate personnel place undue stress on prisoners. Inmate stress is further aggravated by the difficulties many prisoners experience while adapting to the jail environment and by the treatment they receive in the facility.

Jail incarceration is a totally disrupting event for those who must endure it. The shock that accompanies initial entry into the jail and the rapid transition from freedom to captivity are particularly difficult (Gibbs, 1982; Toch, 1975). Flynn (1973:68) described jail entry as a watershed where a "person first loses contact with family, employer, friends, personal belongings and clothes, and with every other symbol of his individuality and humanity." Those who have been arrested but not convicted must wrestle with a number of questions concerning how long they will be in jail, the chance of securing bail, the abilities of their attorney, and the extent of their legal predicaments. However, their inability to freely contact and consult with others leaves many of these questions unanswered. In *The Felon,* Irwin (1970:39–40) described prisoners' reactions to processing by the criminal justice system and the jail experience:

These experiences—arrest, trial, and conviction— threaten the structure of his life in two separate ways. First, the disjointed experience of being suddenly extracted from a relatively orderly and familiar routine and cast into a completely unfamiliar and seemingly chaotic one where the ordering of events is completely out of his control has a shattering impact upon his personality structure. One's identity, one's personality system, one's coherent thinking about himself depend upon a relatively familiar, continuous, and predictable stream of events. In a Kafkaesque world of the booking room, the jail cell, the interrogation room, and the visiting room, the boundaries of the self collapse.

While this collapse is occurring, the prisoner's network of social relations is being torn apart. The insulation between social worlds, an insulation necessary for the orderly maintenance of his social life, is punctured. Many persons learn about facets of his life that were previously unknown to them. Their "business is in the streets." Furthermore, a multitude of minor exigencies that must be met to maintain social relationships go unattended. Bills are not paid, friends are not befriended, families are not fed, consoled, advised, disciplined; businesses go unattended; obligations and duties cannot be fulfilled—in other words, roles cannot be performed. Unattended, the structure of the prisoner's social relations collapse.

The rapid transition from street to jail is so highly disruptive, debilitating and traumatic that it can result in serious psychological disturbances in prisoners and even lead to self-injury and suicide (Gibbs, 1982). In 1988, 287 jail inmates killed themselves (U.S. Department of Justice, 1990). According to a national study on jail suicides, "for the approximately 200,000 inmates in county jails and police lockups on any given day . . . , at least one person will kill himself"

(Hayes, 1983:480). The suicide rate in jails is 16 times greater than in a city with a population comparable in size. The typical jail suicide is a 22-year-old, single, white male who has been arrested for an alcohol-related offense. The suicide usually occurs within 24 hours of arrest (Hayes, 1983:467–470). Research findings indicate that suicide is more prevalent in jails than it is in prisons (Danto, 1973), and that self-injury is greater among pretrial jail prisoners than in those serving sentences (Esparza, 1973; Heilig, 1973). Bowker (1982:312) argued that inmates react to the psychological stress associated with jail incarceration by becoming either resentful and uncooperative or depressed and suicidal.

The stress caused by the rapid transition from street to jail and uncertainty over legal matters is further aggravated by the treatment prisoners receive during the booking process. In addition to the loss of freedom and contact with friends and family, inmates are forced to undergo a series of degradations that include strip searches and delousing conducted by facility personnel. Barbara Deming (1972:152), arrested in Albany, Georgia, for participating in an integrated cross-country peace march, provides an example of the indignities prisoners experience when booked into jail:

A policewoman takes us into a small room in the building where we are arraigned. She searches our handbags for sharp objects; we take off most of our clothing for her, unfasten the rest as she peers at us. The guard outside the temporary detention cell examines our bags for a second time, removes a few more possessions. At the House of Detention, a third guard empties the bags, keeps every remaining article. We have packed a few things with which to keep ourselves decent: comb, toothbrush, deodorant, a change of underclothes. She takes them all—even, in my case, some pieces of Kleenex. And if I have to blow my nose? "Find something else to blow it on," she tells me cheerfully. She explains then: I might be smuggling in dope this way. I am led into a large shower room and told to strip. Another guard shakes out each piece of clothing. Hands on her hips, she watches me closely as I take my shower, and I struggle hard now for self-possession. Her stance reminds me a little of that of an animal trainer. Now she asks me to hold my arms wide for a moment, turn my back and squat. I ask the reason. She, too, is searching for dope—or for concealed weapons. One of my companions has been led in by another woman and has stripped and is sitting on the toilet there. Her face is anguished. She explains her predicament to the guard: she is menstruating, but her extra sanitary napkins have been taken from her. "Just don't think about it," the woman tells her. I don't know how to help her; catch her eye and look away. I am given a very short hospital gown and led now into a small medical-examination room. Another of my companions is just leaving the room and smiles at me wanly. I climb up on the table. I assume that the examination performed is to check for venereal disease. The woman in the white smock grins at me and then at her assistant, who grins back. No, this too is a search for concealed dope or dangerous weapons.

Once in jail, prisoners are exposed to a number of irritants to which they must adapt, the most common of which is prolonged inactivity. In a survey of jail administrators and social service providers (Gibbs, 1983), insufficient activities for prisoners was ranked as the third most serious problem encountered in jails. Overcrowding and inmates with psychological problems were the only other problems ranking higher than inmate idleness. Almost half of the respondents indicated that boredom was the most serious problem facing jail prisoners.

For inmates, boredom and idleness are constant sources of irritation and stress. Some spend inordinate amounts of time worrying about their situation and about what is occurring outside the jail. In the words of one inmate:

You're in the cell most of the day. You're locked in. And you have nothing to do but think. You get tired of playing cards. That's all they got here is cards. You get tired of that after a while. You get sick of that. And you got to think. And what do you think about? You think about home, girl friends, things that you'd be doing, like if it was Friday night or Thursday night, what you'd be doing. And, like, when I lay down, I think of things like that. I try not to, but I can't help it. And I see things that I would be doing. I know what I'd be doing, and I can see this. . . . I just couldn't take it (cited in Toch, 1975:148).

In the investigation of the Nassau County Jail, undercover agents sent into the facility recounted their experiences as inmates. For one female operative, the enforced boredom was almost unbearable.

My immediate feeling that [first] morning was of excitement and in less than fifteen minutes, my cell was straight and I was dressed . . . and then it struck me that I had nowhere to go, nothing to do or see . . . that my freedom of choice for the rest of the day consisted solely in whether I ate or didn't eat the food that would be slid under my door, and whether I passed the time by sleeping, or reading one book or the other. My eagerness to be involved in the jail, just like any other desire, was utterly irrelevant. I think I could have become frightened at this first emotional realization of incarceration, but I was helped out, as at many later bad moments, by my knowledge of why I was here . . . that my responses were to be noted, not feared; emotions were grist to my mill, so I shrugged and noted it, and lay down on my bed with Kiss Me Again, Stranger, *until breakfast arrived (Cahn, 1973:4).*

An accounting of inmate services offered in the nation's jails indicates that only the largest jails offer educational, counseling and recreational programs to inmates; smaller jails have neither the facilities nor the money to provide inmate programs. The National Sheriffs' Association (1982:193, 199) survey found that of 2,452 facilities only 49.6% offered personal counseling; 38.1% offered substance abuse counseling; 29.1% offered the GED (general equivalency diploma); 21.7% offered group counseling; and 14.4% offered adult basic education.

The same study found that a majority of jails (55.5%) allowed inmates only one or two visits from friends and relatives per week.[24] On average, inmates were provided 14.5 hours of outdoor recreation per week and 6.3 hours of indoor recreation per week.[25] Analysis by the size of the facility indicated that, in general, the larger the jail facilities, the wider the variety of programs for inmates. The smallest facilities had the fewest inmate programs. In summary, jails offer few activities for inmates except for "ubiquitous television viewing, card playing, perhaps ping-pong" (Flynn, 1973:63).

A commonly cited obstacle to offering educational and counseling programs to inmates in jails is the diversity of the inmate population. Types of jail inmates run the gamut from sentenced to unsentenced; women to men; young to old; employed to unemployed; educated to uneducated. The problems that these people face also vary and include alcohol and narcotic addiction, personality disorders, psychiatric disorders, learning disabilities, mental illness, physical illness and disabilities, lack of education and job training.

Another reason given for the lack of adequate programs is the belief that they threaten the security of the facility. It is assumed that when inmates are provided with opportunities to leave the living area and to associate with other inmates during the counseling or educational sessions, facility security is reduced. Some, however, including the American Correctional Association, argue that programming and activities enhance facility security.

> *Perhaps, in the final analysis, the soundest and safest security measure of all* is the existence of a positive program of inmate activities. *Such a program includes all the things such as work, recreation, and education. . . . Such multifaceted programs are sometimes referred to as "calculated risks" against security. Actually, these positive programs have become important security factors in well-managed institutions of all types and have become primary security features in many institutions. . . . Prisoners who are receiving decent food and humane treatment and who are busily engaged in self-improvement, seldom resort to disturbances or escape attempts. No matter how modern the buildings, how secure the facilities, how efficient the operating procedures may be, or how well the personnel may be trained, it should be emphasized that security cannot be assured if it is predicated entirely on procedures which are operated wholly against the will of the prisoners. If the prisoners are committed to inactivity, moral degradation, humiliation and mental stultification, then the desire within them to escape or throw off the shackles of these unnatural restraints will become so strong that security facilities and procedures will be breached sooner or later* (American Correctional Association, 1966:367).

In addition to idleness and inactivity, prisoners are exposed to a number of other stress-inducing irritants in the jail environment. Jails have been aptly characterized as "revolving doors" because of the high number of people that pass through them and the rel-

atively short duration of most incarcerations. The average inmate stay in a jail is 11 days (U.S. Department of Justice, 1983a). Such a high rate of turnover makes it difficult for inmates to establish and maintain relationships with other inmates and, consequently, produces an environment perceived by inmates as both unstable and unpredictable.

The poor quality of the food provided by the facility is another source of irritation. In many cases, jail food tends to be unpalatable, contaminated and insufficient (Flynn, 1973). More often than not, by the time the food is served to inmates it is lukewarm. In cases where trustees are serving inmate meals, favoritism often prevails; the amount of food inmates receive depends on their relationship with a trustee or on what they can give the trustee in return.[26]

Another problem that inmates must deal with is unsafe conditions within the jail. Four factors contribute to inmate feelings of personal danger and insecurity: overcrowding, inadequate inmate classification, jail architecture and the lack of staff supervision. Overcrowding reduces the amount of space and privacy provided to inmates and forces them into close physical proximity with each other. Because of overcrowding, cells designed to hold one prisoner are used to house two or more. According to one court (*Inmates of the Suffolk County Jail v. Eisenstadt*, 1973:676, 679), "it is impossible for two men to occupy one of these cells without regular, inadvertent physical contact, inevitably exacerbating tensions and creating interpersonal friction." In addition, multiple occupancy cells provide ample opportunities for abusive inmates to prey upon more vulnerable jail residents.

In many facilities, classification for purposes of segregating inmate types is rudimentary at best, and nonexistent at worst. In most jails, classification and segregation are exclusively based on obvious inmate categories such as male/female and adult/juvenile (Mattick, 1974). No attempt is made to segregate experienced inmates from the inexperienced, predatory inmates from the vulnerable, or even sick inmates from healthy ones.[27] Mattick (1974:812) commented that "jailers often *intentionally* fail to separate prisoner types for lack of staff to supervise them; drunks and suicide risks are placed with others 'for their protection,' and juveniles may be mixed with adults so the latter can 'straighten them out'." Hence, without adequate classification and segregation, inmates are confined in close quarters with others who may be predatory, physically ill or mentally unbalanced.

The architecture of the facility and the lack of supervision interact to increase inmate safety concerns. In many traditional facilities, there are "blind spots" that make it difficult, if not impossible, for staff to observe inmate behavior and activities. Blind spots are those physical locations where staff surveillance is blocked by design features such as grillwork, walls, or dead-end corridors (Atlas, 1986). Many argue that the existence of blind spots provides predatory inmates with opportunities to assault (even murder) other inmates without being detected by staff. Even without the presence of "blind spots," the lack of adequate supervision provides opportunities for assaultive behavior. Inadequate supervision, whether a consequence of an architectural design that makes it difficult for staff to continually observe inmates, or whether a result of understaffing, often invites assaults between inmates as well as other types of aberrant inmate behavior.

A final irritant is the treatment inmates receive from staff. As demonstrated in earlier sections of this chapter, inmates do not always receive fair and consistent treatment from corrections officers. In a substantial number of cases, inmates are harassed, brutalized, and degraded by their keepers. The brutal nature of those hired as jail guards is commonly cited as a reason for this treatment.

A frequently stated homily is that guards differ little from the people they guard. Research on correctional staff backgrounds suggests strongly that this is particularly true in regard to the level of education and the socioeconomic characteristics of both groups (Mattick, 1974:804). Others, however, have found that this similarity extends to psychological attributes as well. After administering a series of psychological tests to corrections officer candidates and prison inmates, psychologist Allan Berman found that each group was almost identical in regard to their "violence potential," with inmates scoring as slightly less violence-prone than the officers. According to Berman (cited in Mitford, 1973:9), the findings "imply that the

officer group actually has the potential for even more unexplained lashing out than does the inmate group." He concluded that " . . . the officer candidates are as likely as the inmates to engage in assaultive behavior. This would carry along the correlative implication that the reasons why one group is behind bars and the other group is guarding them may be due to incidental factors . . . "

Others argue that authoritarian behavior on the part of guards is actually a product of the social institution of the jail rather than a reflection of the individual characteristics or pathologies of the guards. The crux of this viewpoint is that situational as opposed to dispositional factors contribute to staff brutality and aggression. Although often criticized for its methodological deficiencies, the simulated prison experiment conducted by Haney, Banks and Zimbardo (1973) supports this argument. In that research, 22 "physically and mentally stable" male college students were randomly assigned to the role of guard or inmate and situated in a simulated prison. According to the authors, extreme reactions by both groups were almost immediately apparent.

> While guards and prisoners were essentially free to engage in any form of interaction (positive or negative, supportive or affrontive, etc.), the characteristic nature of their encounters tended to be negative, hostile, affrontive, and dehumanizing. Prisoners immediately adopted a generally passive style of responding, while guards assumed a very active initiative role in all interactions. Throughout the experiment, commands were the most frequent form of verbal behavior and, generally, verbal exchanges were strikingly impersonal, with few references to individual identity. Although it was clear to all subjects that the experimenters would not permit physical violence to take place, varieties of less direct aggressive behavior was observed frequently (especially on the part of guards). In fact, varieties of verbal affronts became the most frequent form of interpersonal contact between guards and prisoners (1973:164).

CONCLUSIONS

The history of the jail provides an important lesson about the insidious nature of the problems affecting modern detention facilities. More than 350 years of intensive industrial and technological growth and development have passed, yet the modern jail still retains elements of the inhumane conditions and custodial practices that prevailed in the first jails. Early English gaols were "dumping grounds" into which were thrown children, the physically infirmed, the mentally ill, and other social outcasts deemed offensive to public taste and sensibilities. The modern American jail continues to function as a catch-all institution for the more troubled and troublesome members of society. Inadequate physical facilities, unsanitary living conditions, overcrowding, the lack of segregation, uncaring personnel, idleness and boredom were common in feudal, English gaols as they are in modern American jails.

For many who pass through the portals of the contemporary American jail the experience is one of inhumane brutality. In *The New Red Barn*, Nagel (1973:188) captured in a photograph the sentiment of prisoners and staff alike. Scrawled on the wall of a cell were these words:

> *To the builders of this nitemare though you may never get to read these words. I pity you; for the cruelity of your minds have designed this hell; if men's buildings are a reflection of what they are, this one portraits the ugliness of all humanity. If only you had some compassion.*

ENDNOTES

1. For years, in keeping with the judicial axiom that an individual was presumed innocent until proved guilty, bail was routinely granted to any criminal offender. In cases where it was probable that the defendant would not appear in court, bail was set exceedingly high to ensure that it could not be met. However, the 1984 Bail Reform Act included provisions for "preventative detention," that allowed courts to deny bail to some federal suspects. The law was directed at organized crime suspects and drug dealers who, in most cases, could afford to meet high bail. In May, 1987, the U.S. Supreme Court upheld the preventative detention aspect of the Act, paving the way for states to pass similar laws (*Time*, 1987:69).

2. The number of inmates annually incarcerated in jails is approximately 30 times the number of prisoners handled by state and federal prisons (Irwin, 1985:XI). The jail is also the first, and often only, experience people have with incarceration. Yet the jail has been virtually ignored by correctional scholars. In a review of the *Criminal Justice Periodical Index,* Mays and Thompson (1988) find that in a four-year period, fewer than ten articles about jails appeared in scholarly journals. It is not clear why there is such a lack of scholarly interest in jails, as compared to prisons. One reason may be because the transitory nature of inmates makes it difficult to undertake long-term studies of inmate cultures. Another reason may be because jails are such troubled institutions that few want to undertake the task of unraveling their problems. A final reason may be because of difficulty in gaining access to these locally run facilities. Whatever the reasons, Irwin (1985:xi) argues that studies on jails, rather than prisons, are more urgently needed: "First, many more people pass through the jail. . . . Second, when persons are arrested, the most critical decisions about their future freedom are made while they are either in jail or attached to it by a bail bond. These decisions, like the decision to arrest, are often highly discretionary and raise disturbing questions about the whole criminal justice system. Third, the experiences prisoners endure while passing through the jail often drastically influence their lives. Finally, the jail, not the prison, imposes the cruelest form of punishment in the United States."

3. At a medium-sized jail in Texas, I was shown the booking record of a middle-aged male who had been arrested and booked into the jail 72 times for public intoxication. On a few occasions, the man was arrested just hours after his release from the jail.

4. Drug addiction among jail inmates is also a critical issue in jail administration. The 1978 *Profile of Jail Inmates* reported that 40% of jail inmates were drug addicts or daily users, 8% used drugs less than daily but at least weekly, and 20% took drugs less than weekly (U.S. Department of Justice, 1980). More recent studies of the extent of drug use among jail inmates are unavailable; however, data compiled from other sources suggest that the proportion of inmates who use drugs is high. The results from the National Institute of Justice Drug Use Forecasting, for example, indicates that between 56% and 84% of males arrestees in 16 large cities test positive for drugs and between 58% and 88% of female arrestees test positive (U.S. Department of Justice, 1989). The study also reports that "recent drug use in arrestees is more than 10 times higher than is reported in surveys of persons in households or senior high schools" (U.S. Department of Justice, 1989:2). While many alcoholics are arrested simply because they are intoxicated, most drug users are arrested because they *commit a criminal offense while on drugs.* As with alcoholics, drug-addicted inmates pose special problems for the jail in terms of their medical needs and their susceptibility to suicide. Although narcotic withdrawal is less likely to be fatal than alcohol withdrawal, drug addicts are more likely to successfully commit suicide than are nonaddicts (U.S. Congress, 1970).

5. A number of cases involving the victimization of juveniles in adult facilities have received national media coverage, as well as stimulating litigation against the jails. In Ohio, a 15-year-old girl, ordered by the judge to 5 days in jail to "teach her a lesson," was raped by a jail guard. In Wisconsin, a 13-year-old boy, held in jail for 11 days, was repeatedly beaten by other juveniles while the guard ignored the assault. In Idaho, a 15-year-old boy, jailed for failing to pay $73 in traffic fines, was tortured and beaten to death by other inmates. For a discussion of these cases, see Soler (1988).

6. Gibbs (1987) questions the validity of studies that have accessed the prevalence of psychopathology among jail inmates. Typically, these studies are conducted on newly admitted inmates who are still experiencing the stress of adapting to the jail environment and incarceration. Gibbs argued, with some empirical support, that the symptoms of psychopathology prevalent in the inmate population may actually be "situational," and produced by the harsh environment and conditions of the jail. His own research indicated that inmates with no history of mental illness displayed symptoms of psychopathology in the early stages of their incarceration.

7. In the first half of the twentieth century, the number of patients confined to mental hospitals steadily increased. Yet, beginning in the 1950s, patient numbers have steadily decreased. From 1955 to 1975, the number of mental patients decreased to 25% of maximum hospital capacity (Pollack, 1977).

8. While conducting research in Washington state jails in the spring of 1983, I visited one small jail in the western part of the state. The jail consisted of a ship's brig set into a large, double-story room. While the conditions of this jail were deplorable for a number of reasons, they were made worse by a serious lack of light. The only source of natural light was a small window located at the uppermost part of the room; this light was supplemented by one small, bare light bulb

hanging from the ceiling. Neither the window nor the light bulb provided sufficient light to enable inmates to read.

9. Dayrooms are typically adjacent to the living cell area, and, like the cells, are separated from the remainder of the facility by bars. Usually, inmates have unlimited access to the dayroom during the day but are locked in their cells at night. Many dayrooms are equipped with television and recreational equipment (e.g., card and board games). In most facilities, dayrooms are furnished with metal or hard plastic furniture that make it less than comfortable for inmates.

10. The standards established by the American Correctional Association cover a broad range of issues including fiscal management, personnel training and staff development, inmate records, safety and emergency procedures, food service, security and control, inmate rights, inmate rules and discipline, classification, and so forth (American Correctional Association, 1981).

11. Since passage of the 1984 Bail Reform Act, federal detention facilities have witnessed a 36% increase in pretrial detainees. Preventative detention, permitted by the Act, has increased the demand for space in federal lockups (Clear and Cole, 1986:213–214). The U.S. Supreme Court recently upheld the preventative detention clause in the Act. If other states follow the precedent established by the U.S. Congress and pass similar laws, local jails may experience further increases in population, adding to the already burdensome problem of overcrowding.

12. In many cases, jail conditions are so poor compared to those in prisons that inmates "have actually protested in an effort to get *into* prison" (cited in *Newsweek,* 1980:76).

13. The case of *Bell v. Wolfish* represents a dramatic shift from over a decade of court intervention into the administration of correctional institutions. In this case, the Supreme Court decided that double-bunking in the Federal Metropolitan Correctional Center (MCC), a podular/direct supervision facility, did not violate the Due Process Clause of the Fifth Amendment that prohibits the punishment of pretrial detainees. The Court cited several facts specific to the situation at the MCC in its decision. First, inmates in the facility spent relatively few hours in the confines of their cells. Prisoners usually were confined only for sleeping. The Court believed that 75 feet per cell was adequate space for two prisoners to sleep. Second, the inmates in the facility were exposed to the conditions of the facility for relatively short periods. Eighty-five percent of the pretrial detainees were released within 60 days. Finally, the court noted that the MCC was unlike most traditional jail facilities. Legal scholars are uncertain of what the Court meant by this. According to Call (1983:25–26), "It is unclear whether by this implied reference to MCC as a nontraditional jail the Court meant to suggest that the modern design of MCC and its cells with doors rather than solid walls also militated in favor of its decision." Following the *Wolfish* decision, lower courts continued to find overcrowded jail conditions unconstitutional. These courts either ignored *Wolfish* or made brief mention of it without analysis of its applicability to the case at hand. In an assessment of the impact of *Wolfish*, Call (1983) concluded that the decision had little effect on subsequent lower court actions. These courts continued to find overcrowding unconstitutional.

14. In some cases, overcrowding has resulted in the "emergency" suspension of state standards for local jail operations. In Oklahoma, the legislature eliminated 94 of the 172 state standards. The rationale was that the standards were "frivolous" or "too excessive" (Allinson, 1982:22).

15. Research on the effects of overcrowding is discussed in greater detail in Chapter 5.

16. For a discussion of how the fee system promotes incarceration and overcrowding in jails, see *Behind Bars: Kentucky Looks at its County Jails* (1981), an investigation of Kentucky jails prepared by the Kentucky Department of Justice.

17. This figure does not take into account vacation, sick leave or other absences by the correctional staff. If these were included, the ratio would be much smaller.

18. In many jails, staff selection is based on patronage. When the sheriff leaves office, so do the jailers who were appointed by him/her. In some areas, sheriffs are prohibited from holding office for two consecutive terms. Hence, complete staff turnover occurs every four years (Flynn, 1973; Mattick, 1974).

19. In discussing the inadequacies of corrections officer training, Miller (1978:28) characterizes most jail training as " 'good luck' on-the-job training."

20. The survey results revealed that, on average, the starting salary for corrections officers is 14% less than for sheriff's patrol officers.

21. Cahn (1973:9) recounts examples of harassment where "inmates on their way to the visiting room would have to wait for ten minutes for a door to be opened while the officer with the key stood a few feet away chatting with a colleague." In the meantime, the inmates lost ten minutes of visitation time that could have been spent with their families or friends.

22. The plight of corrections officers in local detention facilities has been virtually ignored by correctional scholars. Consequently, much of the following section relies on re-search conducted among corrections officers in prisons. Although some scholars argue that the two types of institutions are vastly different, in several respects they are highly similar—particularly in regard to the nature of their clientele, the work performed by officers, and their organizational and work environments. While caution must be exercised in generalizing the results of personnel-related research findings from the prison to the jail setting, they at least provide some hint of the problems that may be plaguing corrections officers in jails.

23. Flynn (1973:66) defined custodial convenience as the facility's preoccupation with ensuring that inmates do not escape: "As much as possible, jails are geared to the fullest possible supervision, control, and surveillance of inmates. Physical structures, program choices—if any—and operational policies optimize security and administration convenience and restrict the inmate's movement to the point of removing all of his control over his environment."

24. Almost 15% of the surveyed jails had unlimited visitation while 17.2% allowed from three to five visits per week.

25. Although it could be argued that 20.8 hours per week is an adequate amount of recreation time, it must be remembered that with the exception of sleeping, eating, reading and watching television, there are few activities to fill the remaining 315.2 hours of the week.

26. Trustees are prisoners who have been given work responsibilities in the jail. Some argue that without trustees many jails would be unable to function due to understaffing. Trustees may be responsible for cleaning, preparing meals, washing laundry, etc. In order to accomplish these tasks, trustees are given the run of the facility. Trustees are usually inmates serving a longer jail sentence who have been deemed reliable and responsible by the jail staff. In one facility I worked at, a trustee who was serving a one-year sentence on involuntary manslaughter regularly advised staff on jail and sheriffs' operations. Because the jail had no full-time jailers, sheriff's officer dispatchers were responsible for the well-being of inmates. High personnel turnover meant that the sheriff's office and the jail were being run by inexperienced and untrained staff. Because the trustee had been in the facility much longer than the staff, he was often able to advise them on how to perform the job. He was even able to show the dispatchers how to handle emergency police calls.

27. Small jail facilities are often deterred from classification because, even if they had a well conceived system, the lack of space makes segregation according to inmate characteristics almost impossible.

REFERENCES

Advisory Commission on Intergovernmental Relations (1984). *Jails: Intergovernmental Dimensions of a Local Problem, A Commission Report.* Washington. DC: U.S. Government Printing Office.

Allinson, R. (1982). "Crisis in the Jails: Overcrowding Is Now a National Epidemic." *Corrections Magazine.* April:18–40.

American Correctional Association (1985). *Jails in America: An Overview of Issues.* College Park, Maryland: American Correctional Association.

American Correctional Association (1981). *Standards for Adult Local Detention Facilities.* College Park, Maryland: American Correctional Association.

American Correctional Association (1966). *Manual of Correctional Standards.* Washington, DC: American Correctional Association.

American Medical Association (1973). *Medical Care in U.S. Jails: Report of the 1972 AMA Medical Survey of the U.S. Jail System.* Chicago: American Medical Association.

Atlas, R. (1986). "Crime Site Selection for Assaults in Four Florida Prisons." A paper presented at the annual meeting of the Academy of Criminal Justice Sciences, in Orlando, Florida, March, 1986.

Benton, F. W., E. D. Rosen and J. L. Peters (1982). "National Survey of Correctional Institution Employee Attrition." New York: National Center for Public Productivity.

Bowker, L. H. (1982). *Corrections: The Science and the Art.* New York: Macmillan Publishing Co., Inc.

Brief, A. P., J. Munro and R. J. Aldag (1976). "Correctional Employees' Reaction to Job Characteristics: A Data Based Argument for Job Enrichment." *Journal of Criminal Justice.* 4:223–230.

Burns, H. (1975). *Corrections: Organization and Administration.* St. Paul, Minnesota: West Publishing Co.

Cahn, W. (1973). "Report on the Nassau County Jail." *Crime and Delinquency.* 19:1–14.

Call, J. E. (1983). "Recent Case Law on Overcrowded Conditions of Confinement." *Federal Probation.* 47:23–32.

Carney, R. (1982). "New Jersey—Overcrowding Is Blamed on the State." *Corrections Magazine.* April:24–27.

Chesney-Lind, M. (1988). "Girls in Jail." *Crime and Delinquency.* 34:150–168.

Children's Defense Fund (1976). *Children in Adult Jails.* Washington, DC: Children's Defense Fund.

Clear, T. D. and G. F. Cole (1986). *American Corrections.* Monterey, California: Brooks/Cole Publishing Company.

Corrections Compendium (1987). "Survey: COs In Demand in Many States."

Cressey, D. R. (1968). "Contradictory Directives in Complex Organizations: The Case of the Prison." In L. E. Hazelrigg (ed.) *Prison Within Society.* Springfield, Illinois: Charles C Thomas.

Criminal Justice Newsletter (1987). "OJJDP to Award Some Funds to States for Jail Removal Efforts." 18:17.

Daily Home Sun (Talladega, Alabama). "Two Jailers Disciplined for Inmate Death." February 19, 1989:23.

Danto, D. (1973). "Suicide at the Wayne County Jail: 1967–70." In L. Danto (ed.) *Jail House Blues.* Orchard Lake, Michigan: Epic.

Deming, B. (1972). "Prisoners Don't Exist." in D. M. Petersen and M. Truzzi (eds.) *Criminal Life: Views from the Inside.* Englewood Cliffs, New Jersey: Prentice-Hall, Inc.

Esparza, R. (1973). "Attempted and Committed Suicides in County Jails." In L. Danto (ed.) *Jail House Blues.* Orchard Lake, Michigan: Epic.

Farmer, R. E. (1977). "Cynicism: A Factor in Corrections Work." *Journal of Criminal Justice.* 5:237–246.

Fishman, J. F. (1923). *Crucibles of Crime: The Shocking Story of the American Jail.* Montclair, New Jersey: Patterson Smith.

Flynn, E. E. (1973). "Jails and Criminal Justice." In L. E. Ohlin (ed.) *Prisoners in America.* Englewood Cliffs, New Jersey: Prentice-Hall, Inc.

Gibbs, J. (1987). "Symptoms of Psychopathology Among Jail Prisoners." *Criminal Justice and Behavior.* 14:288–310.

Gibbs, J. (1982). "The First Cut is the Deepest: Psychological Breakdown and Survival in the Detention Setting." In R. Johnson and H. Toch (eds.) *The Pains of Imprisonment.* Beverly Hills: Sage Publications, Inc.

Gibbs, J. (1983). "Problems and Priorities: Perceptions of Jail Custodians and Social Service Providers." *Journal of Criminal Justice.* 11:327–338.

Gross v. Tazewell County Jail. 31 Cr. L. 2061 (W.D. V. 1982).

Guy, E., J. J. Platt, I. Zwerling, and S. Bullock (1985). "Mental Health Status of Prisoners in an Urban Jail." *Criminal Justice and Behavior.* 12:29–53.

Haney, C., W. C. Banks and P. G. Zimbardo (1973). "Interpersonal Dynamics in a Simulated Prison." *International Journal of Criminology and Penology.* 1:69–97.

Hayes, L. M. (1983). "And Darkness Closes In . . . A National Study of Jail Suicides." *Criminal Justice and Behavior.* 10:461–484.

Heilig, S. (1973). "Suicides in Jails." In L. Danto (ed.) *Jail House Blues*. Orchard Lake, Michigan: Epic.

Herzberg. F., B. Mausner and B. B. Snyderman (1959). *The Motivation to Work*. New York: John Wiley & Sons, Inc.

Inmates of the Suffolk County Jail v. Eisenstadt, 360 F. Supp. 676, 679 (1973).

Irwin, J. (1985). *The Jail: Managing the Underclass in American Society*. Berkeley, California: University of California Press.

Irwin, J. (1970). *The Felon*. Englewood Cliffs, New Jersey: Prentice-Hall, Inc.

Johnston, N. (1973). *The Human Cage: A Brief History of Prison Architecture*. New York: The American Foundation, Inc.

Jurik, N. C. and R. Winn (1986). "Describing Correctional Security Dropouts and Rejects: An Individual or Organizational Profile?" Presented at the annual meeting of the Academy of Criminal Justice Sciences in Orlando, Florida, March, 1986.

Kerle, K. E. (1985). "The American Woman County Jail Officer." In I. L. Moyer (ed.) *The Changing Role of Women in the Criminal Justice System*. Prospect Heights, Illinois: Waveland Press, Inc.

Law Enforcement Assistance Administration (1971). *National Jail Census—1970*. Washington, DC: U.S. Government Printing Office.

Lipsky, M. (1980). *Street Level Bureaucracy*. New York: Russell Sage.

Mattick, H. W. and A. B. Aikman (1969). "The Cloacal Region of American Corrections." *The Annals of the American Academy of Political and Social Science*. 381:109–118.

Mattick, H. W. (1974). "The Contemporary Jails of the United States: An Unknown and Neglected Area of Justice." In D. Glaser (ed.) *Handbook of Criminology*. Chicago: Rand McNally.

May, E. (1980). "Prison Guards in America—The Inside Story." In B. M. Crouch (ed.) *The Keepers: Prison Guards and Contemporary Corrections*. Springfield, Illinois: Charles C Thomas Publishers.

Mays, G. L. and J. A. Thompson (1988). "Mayberry Revisited: The Characteristics and Operations of America's Small Jails." *Justice Quarterly*. 5:421–440.

Miller, E. E. (1978). *Jail Management: Problems, Programs and Perspectives*. Lexington, Massachusetts: Lexington Books.

Mitford, J. (1973). *Kind and Usual Punishment: The Prison Business*. New York: Alfred A. Knopf.

Nagel, W. G. (1973). *The New Red Barn: A Critical Look at the Modern American Prison*. New York: Walker and Company.

National Sheriffs' Association (1982). *The State of Our Nation's Jails, 1982*. Washington, DC: National Sheriffs' Association.

Newsweek (1975). "Joan Little's Defense." (February 24):86.

Newsweek (1980). "The Scandalous U.S. Jails." (August 18):74–77.

Pollack, S. (1977). *Resident Patient Rate in State Mental Hospitals Reduced to One-Fourth the 1955 Rate*. Memorandum No. 6. Rockville, Maryland: National Institute of Mental Health.

Poole, E. D. and R. M. Regoli (1981). "Alienation in Prison." *Criminology*. 12:251–270.

President's Commission on Law Enforcement and Administration of Justice (1967). *Task Force Report: Corrections*. Washington, DC: U.S. Government Printing Office.

Reid, S. T. (1976). *Crime and Criminology*. Hinsdale, Illinois: Dryden Press.

Richmond, M. S. (1965). "The Jail Blight." *Crime and Delinquency*. 11:132–141.

Robinson, L. N. (1944). *Jails*. Philadelphia: John C. Winston.

Schrag, C. (1961). "Some Foundations For a Theory of Correction." In D. R. Cressey (ed.) *The Prison: Studies in Institutional Organization and Change*. New York: Holt, Rinehart and Winston, Inc.

Schwartz, I. M., L. Harris and L. Levi (1988). "The Jailing of Juveniles in Minnesota: A Case Study." *Crime and Delinquency*. 34:138–149.

Shamir, B. and A. Drory (1982). "Occupational Tedium Among Prison Officers." *Criminal Justice and Behavior*. 19:79–99.

Soler, M. (1988). "Litigation on Behalf of Children in Adult Jails." *Crime and Delinquency*. 34:190–208.

Steinhart, D. (1988). "California Legislature Ends the Jailing of Children: The Story of a Policy Reversal." *Crime and Delinquency*. 34:169–189.

Stinchcomb, J. B. (1986). "Correctional Officer Stress: Looking at the Causes; You *May* Be the Cure." Presented at the annual meeting of the Academy of Criminal Justice Sciences, Orlando, Florida, March, 1986.

Swank, G. E. and D. Winer (1976). "Occurrence of Psychiatric Disorder in a County Jail Population." *American Journal of Psychiatry*. 133:1331–1333.

Sykes, G. M. (1958). *The Society of Captives.* Princeton, New Jersey: Princeton University Press.

Time (1975). "A Case of Rape or Seduction?" (July 28):19.

Time (1987). "First the Sentence, Then the Trial." (June 8):69.

Toch, H. (1975). *Men in Crisis: Human Breakdown in Prison.* Chicago: Aldine Publishing Company.

Toch, H. and J. D. Grant (1982). *Reforming Human Services.* Beverly Hills: Sage Publications.

Toch, H. and J. Klofas (1982). "Alienation and Desire for Job Enrichment Among Correction Officers." *Federal Probation.* 46:35–44.

U.S. Congress. House Select Committee on Crime (1970). *Crime in America: Heroin Importation, Distribution, Packaging, and Paraphernalia.* 91st Congress, 2nd Session. 214–222. Testimony of G. McGrath.

U.S. Department of Justice, Bureau of Justice Statistics (1980). *Profile of Jail Inmates: Sociodemographic Findings From the 1978 Survey of Inmates of Local Jails.* Washington, DC: U.S. Government Printing Office.

U.S. Department of Justice, Bureau of Justice Statistics (1983a). *Jail Inmates, 1982.* Washington, DC: U.S. Government Printing Office.

U.S. Department of Justice, Bureau of Justice Statistics (1983b). *Juvenile Suicides in Adult Jails: Findings from a National Survey of Juveniles in Secure Detention Facilities.* Washington, DC: U.S. Government Printing Office.

U.S. Department of Justice, Bureau of Justice Statistics (1987). *Jail Inmates, 1986.* Washington, DC: U.S. Government Printing Office.

U.S. Department of Justice, Bureau of Justice Statistics (1988). *Census of Local Jails, 1983.* Washington, DC: U.S. Government Printing Office.

U.S. Department of Justice, Bureau of Justice Statistics (1990). *Census of Local Jails, 1988.* Washington, DC: U.S. Government Printing Office.

U.S. Department of Justice, National Institute of Justice, Office of Justice Programs (1989). *Drug Use Forecasting, April to June, 1989.* Washington, DC: Government Printing Office.

U.S. Department of Justice, National Institute of Justice, Office of Research Programs (1980a). *American Prisons and Jails, Vol. I: Summary and Police Implications of a National Survey.* Washington, DC: U.S. Government Printing Office.

U.S. Department of Justice, National Institute of Justice, Office of Research Programs (1980b). *American Prisons and Jails, Vol. III: Conditions and Costs of Confinement.* Washington, DC: U.S. Government Printing Office.

U.S. General Accounting Office (1980). *Jail Inmates' Mental Health Care Neglected; State and Federal Attention Needed.* Washington, DC: U.S. Government Printing Office.

Wilson, R. (1980). "Who Will Care for the 'Mad and Bad'." *Corrections Magazine.* (February):4.

STUDY QUESTIONS FOR READING 5

1. The jail serves two roles: What are they, and what fraction of inmates does each role account for?

2. Public intoxication accounts for what percent of all arrests and what percent of all jail inmates? Prosecution and jailing these offenders costs how much per year?

3. Many criminal justice reformers want public intoxication decriminalized. Explain their argument.

4. Many experts call jails "dumping grounds for the mentally ill." According to the National Institute of Corrections, about what percentage of jail inmates are mentally ill? What percentage of jails make psychologists available to inmates or have mental health facilities?

5. Of the juveniles in jail, what percentage had committed serious offenses? Status offenses? No offenses, but they needed protection?

6. Women make up what percent of all jail inmates? How fast is this number growing compared to men?

7. Tell the story of Joan Little. What has it come to represent?

8. Almost half of the nation's jails are small (25 cells or less), but they hold what percent of all jail inmates?

9. Your kid brother has constant scrapes with the law. You warn him that he will land himself in jail some day, but he tells you he knows all about jail. According to your brother, jail is characterized by a life where you don't have to go to school; instead, you play hoops and cards and shoot the breeze with your friends all day. Unlike the joint your folks are running, he's heard that the rooms are really nice, and you usually get one to yourself with a T.V. He's tired of the constant supervision of home, he tells you, and ready for some peace and quiet. Besides, he's tired of waiting in line for the bathroom and having to clean house every Saturday. He says prison might be pretty scary, but he is actually looking forward to some time in jail.

   You are concerned that your brother has an idealized idea of jail life, and you want to "scare him straight" with some of the facts in this article, and especially from the section on "Physical and Sanitary Conditions of Jails." What facts could you use to refute each of his ideas?

10. How does jail life compare to prison life? What's the irony here?

11. Who usually administers jails? What percent of their time is spent on jail issues? What training in corrections is required?

12. According to jail administrators, what is the major cause of jail problems?

13. In contrast, what do researchers find to be the biggest obstacle to reform? As a result, what has every comprehensive study of jails recommended for the last 60 years? What have some states done about it? Why doesn't this happen in other states?

14. Discuss jail staff in terms of understaffing, recruitment, training, and salaries.

15. What did undercover investigators learn about the way guards did their jobs?

16. Correctional employees tend to have a lot of work-related problems. What are they?

17. The work of corrections officers in jails has been described as "fragmented, routinized and menial—in a word, impoverished." Give examples of routine duties for an officer.

18. How does communication occur in a hierarchical organization? What are the problems with this approach?

19. Explain how classification works in jails.

20. Do guards really differ from the people they guard? Explain in terms of education and socioeconomic characteristics.

21. Do guards and inmates come to the jail with the same personality traits, or do they develop them there? What position did the Haney, Banks and Zimbardo study take on this issue and why?

22. The Haney, Banks, and Zimbardo study was dramatized in the film *Quite Rage: The Stanford Prison Study.* The film shows that the guard role fosters sadism and the inmate role fosters shame. Why do you think the guard role fosters sadism?

LIFE ON THE INSIDE: THE JAILERS

ANDREW METZ

This is the job: One unarmed correction officer and 60 inmates, the jailer and the jailed, warily taking each other's measure, sparring for control. Right now, the officer is Cpl. William Roulis, and though it's only 6:30 in the morning, he's already on edge. Purple crescents hammock his eyes as he moves about a locked, windowed room in a second-floor cellblock at the Nassau County jail.

The inmates, men in orange jail jumpsuits, in on mostly drug and alcohol offenses, sluggishly walk through breakfast lines, picking up plastic trays of scrambled eggs, boxes of Fruit Loops, half-pints of milk, slices of white bread.

"Although we are charged with watching them, they watch us," Roulis says, studying through the glass one of the men who is using an empty peanut-butter jar as an oversized coffee cup. "They know what cologne you wear, the click of your heels."

Of all the things Roulis has learned over 10 years at the jail in East Meadow, the most important may be this: "You don't know what is going to happen, or when it is going to happen."

When two inmates will abruptly start brawling in front of the shower stalls, and he will have to order over the loud speaker, "lock in; everybody lock in *now*." Or when an inmate will barricade himself in his cell, and three officers will have to drag him out by the arms and legs. Or when an inmate will taunt him from behind the bars, "I'm going to ____ me a Greek boy."

So, the 44-year-old officer is cynical, always expecting to be had. And this constant tension, this nerve-wracking wait-and-see imprisons him, too.

"You do 25 years, but a day at a time, a week at a time," he says, parting his lips in a faint smile. "When

you come through the gates, you're in a different world."

There are about 1.8 million people in jails and prisons around the country, roughly 3,600 in Nassau and Suffolk awaiting trial or serving sentences of up to a year. But even as the public cheers the get-tough policing that fills correctional institutions, correction officers believe they are seen as brutes, only a shade better than the people behind bars.

This stigma is a sort of occupational hazard that is usually sloughed off. But for officers at the Nassau County Correctional Center, the past three months have brought the stereotype painfully close to home.

After an inmate was allegedly beaten to death by officers inside the jail in January, federal authorities stepped in to investigate the homicide and whether there is a pattern of brutality. And the whole situation has revealed a bevy of complaints and lawsuits brought by inmates with wide-ranging claims of mistreatment.

Inside lunch rooms and control rooms, in the trailers that function as the training academy and in dozens of posts throughout the facility, morale is dark. Officers say they have been wounded by recent headlines and newscasts.

They tell of being looked at askance by neighbors. Of wives being insulted in supermarkets. Of children confused by what they hear.

Few deny that abuses have occurred. But they insist any misbehavior is limited to rogues, to officers unable to rise above the depravity of jail culture.

"We spend our day with the kind of people you don't want next door," says Officer Bob Shanlin, 41, who in his years at the jail has twice saved inmates who were trying to hang themselves with bedsheets.

"We're like offensive linemen. You only hear our name when something goes wrong. . . . The vast majority of people here are not beating people. I wouldn't work with people that were."

One thousand and ten correction officers and commanders work at the jail, one of the largest county lockups in the country. In three shifts of around 120 officers each, they supervise and provide for about 1,800 inmates.

While keeping some of the jail off limits, including the building where the inmate allegedly was beaten in January, correction officials permitted closely monitored visits inside the jail in recent weeks. Days of observation and interviews—14 hours on one day a week—show just how complicated life on the inside can be. Locked in, officer and inmate move in a suspicious waltz, staking out positions, enduring the monotony, the indignities, the dependence.

One minute an officer is handing out toilet paper, the next he is explaining court papers. An officer is joking with two inmates playing checkers, and in an instant, he is ordering everyone to their cells.

This is the job: Put on a blue-and-gray uniform, pin a silver sheriff's badge to your shirt pocket and lace up black work shoes. Drive to a sprawling complex of concrete and metal, through 18-foot-high fences topped with thick coils of razor wire.

In a two-story building called the 832, bars open and seal shut behind you, and as you walk to the Muster Room to get your assignment, the odor of floor cleaner, the industrial kitchen and too many bodies carries you forward.

Soon you are locked inside a cellblock. You are outnumbered. Your only weapons are the wits you walked in with and the alarm on your waist. And when you set that off, officers come running, and more often than not it means inmates are swinging fists or throwing feces or food. For sure, they're yelling and swearing and refusing to lock down. Your life could be in danger.

You're enraged, and if you're honest, you're scared.

"Anytime a body alarm goes off, your adrenaline starts pumping because you are running into a situation and you don't know what it is going to be like and it could be a war," says Shanlin, who can't recall being assaulted in his career, but has had a jar of urine thrown at him and has been insulted and threatened countless times. "You're an idiot if you . . . are not scared."

But all-out violence is rare, and you know it as you settle down behind a desk at the center of the cellblock. You supervise the "feedings," keeping track of each meal tray because almost anything can be made into a weapon.

Usually, the closest you come to using force is an unequivocal command or a firm grip on an elbow. No one wants to be locked down. No one wants weightlifting canceled.

At least every half-hour, you get up and pace the dimensions of the dorm, peering into each cell and inserting a key in a slot to record your passage. You sock away the paychecks that don't ever seem fat enough, rack up the overtime when you can and push your union to get a 20-year retirement clause in your contract. Police have one, after all.

You bristle when you're called a guard because guards work at Macy's and banks and don't stop dead in their tracks when they hear, "Yo, C.O.!" as they leave a mall and see five former inmates behind them. At the end of a day, you decompress however you can, if you can, and tell yourself you're an integral part of the criminal justice system.

"The public doesn't want to know about them," Officer Robert Koplar, 35, who has worked at the jail for 14 years, says of the inmates. "After they are caught, they forget about the other part. Where are you supposed to store them? Not the Marriott.

" . . . Someone has to watch them 24–7. Someone has to do it."

Few people actually plan on a career in corrections.

"I don't think you'll talk to anyone that says, 'Since I was 12 years old I wanted to be a correction officer,' " says Lt. Richard Plantamura, who is in charge of the jail's training academy.

Of the dozens of new officers who each year routinely join the Nassau County Sheriff's Department, Division of Correction, most say they were looking for a position as a police officer.

They had taken a slew of civil service exams, perhaps not scoring high enough to land a police job at first. Then the jail made an offer.

Some eventually move to the Suffolk or Nassau police departments, where salaries are significantly higher. The first year of employment at the jail, base pay is about $28,000. A rookie Suffolk police officer makes about $45,000. And after two years, so does a new officer in Nassau.

Still, jail officials say attrition is low, and for men and women shopping for a civil service job, a job that doesn't require any college and eventually promises salaries more than $50,000, thousands in overtime, security and benefits, corrections is a coveted career.

"I love what I do," says Officer Ronald Lanier, a former Army enlisted man, who was driving a Drake's delivery route in Brooklyn when he was offered a post at the jail eight years ago.

Standing tall, his black oxfords reflecting like mirrors, Lanier is monitoring visiting hours. As inmates hug mothers and girlfriends and wives, the 35-year-old says he sees his work as a calling.

"A lot of these guys I went to school with," he says, nodding his chin to the inmates. "I am here to do a job, but I care."

One of roughly 150 black officers, Lanier says he is a mentor for African-American inmates, who make up about half the jail population.

Lanier says he has been in only one physical tussle in his eight years and that was while breaking up a fight. Holding ground in a cellblock rarely comes down to force, he says. He lets the inmates know they're in his "house" now, and "this is how it's done."

"I don't go straight to C," he says. "I start at A and nine times out of 10 we end up at A."

And that, in the simplest sense, is the philosophy officers say they carry with them day to day: Force is supposed to be the last resort, and when it's doled out, it is meant to be measured.

As a rule, officers are unarmed. Supervisors have a can of pepper spray. The greatest tools, officers say, are composure and communication.

"The way you present yourself to people, how you communicate with people is going to get you through 90 percent of the time," says Sgt. Daniel Doo-

ley, who teaches recruits. "Your communication skills will get you through. It's the easiest way to go."

In a cavernous jail gymnasium, Officer Kenny Sellers says he puts this to the test everyday. During a midmorning recreation period, 77 inmates are pumping iron and dribbling basketballs and jogging. Sellers mingles with them all, smiles a lot. In small groups, he tries to quell brewing discontent this day, because both basketball hoops are being repaired.

The inmates are disappointed, but "they don't want to fight because they know if they do, they will lose out," says Sellers, 41, who at 6-foot-2, 240 pounds is as rippled as they come.

During 12 years as an officer, he says, he has forged a respectful discourse with inmates, giving them space—and sometimes advice on how to bulk up.

"They respect me," he says. "They know me."

This is the job: A 40-year-old officer makes a patrol along a guardwalk one Christmas. He sees the lights and snow outside and thinks of his family. He passes cell after cell and is pinched by a sorrow that takes years for him to understand.

"I thought, just on the other side of the bars are people thinking the same things I am," Lt. Richard Levering recalls.

Now, more than two decades later, Levering describes what hit him as the "incarceration feeling." . . . "We are all locked in here," says Levering, 66.

And that's a universal feeling for correction officers. Mel Grieshaber, of Michigan, who is the immediate past president of the International Association of Correctional Officers, likens corrections to combat.

"You are there coaching Little League one moment, then you get up the next day, brush your teeth and go to this . . . 100-percent hostile environment," says Grieshaber. "A lot of jobs are stressful, however this is the type of job where everything can be calm for periods of time, but you are always dealing with this little voice way deep down that says something could happen. So there is a certain edge all the time."

Up-to-date figures on the effects of corrections work are scarce and are more anecdotal than scientific. However, most correction experts agree that officers have excessively high rates of suicide, burn-out, divorce and alcohol abuse. Studies have shown they have heart attacks, hypertension and ulcers more than almost any other employment group. And a 1980s report by the American Federation of State and County Municipal Employees put their life expectancy at 59.

Nationally, officials estimate that seven died in the line of duty last year and more than 14,000 were seriously assaulted. At the Nassau jail, there were 38 assaults against officers last year, and two so far in 1999. Inmates assaulted one another 39 times last year, and already 35 times this year.

"It's a hard life to grow up in," Levering says. "I have often thought that no one should come on this job before 28 or 30."

He has had to tell inmates that relatives were killed, separate a baby from a mother, cut down a prisoner trying to hang himself.

Mostly, officers hope for a humdrum day. "A good day for me is when none of my officers get hurt," says Cpl. Bob Zizza, 37, who in 12 years has been assaulted five times.

In 1971, two professors in California embarked on a study of the psychology of imprisonment. In what became known as the Stanford Prison Experiment, they cast a group of college students in the roles of correction officers and inmates for six days. The results, the authors, Craig Haney and Philip Zimbardo declared, were shocking, and forced them to halt the experiment.

In under a week, they witnessed mock inmates and officers suffer trauma and stress. They watched many of the "officers," particularly those on the night shifts, harass and degrade and mistreat inmates. Others stood by and failed to report the abuses.

"You are talking about an environment that is constantly pushing against people," says Haney, a professor of psychology at the University of California at Santa Cruz. "This is really antithetical to what people are, and so prisoners are not at their best and not surprisingly correction officers aren't either."

And while the national corps of correction officers is more diverse, better educated and instructed than at any other time, according to experts, abuses persist.

Bob Gangi, head of the Correctional Association of New York, a nonprofit watchdog group, says that while the job breeds brutality, "correction officers have legitimate beefs that we as a society throw them down into the pits and ask them to do the dirty work and often don't really care about what goes on."

And so, correction officials and critics agree, in this field that constantly challenges moral bearings, rules and regulations are crucial compasses.

"You have to have structure for both the inmates and the officers," says Lt. Jerry Magnus, a supervisor who has worked in the Nassau jail for 27 years. He says the officers' rulebook is voluminous and "tells you how to do everything here except go to the bathroom."

Since the jailhouse death in January of Thomas Pizzuto and the federal probe, he says inmates are "thriving on the media," concocting accusations, even inflicting injuries on themselves and threatening to blame officers.

These are trying times, he says. "People have to put themselves in our place."

This is the job: Twelve hours after he first walked into his cellblock, Cpl. Roulis is in the same small bubble, monitoring the men in his charge.

It is 6:30 p.m. and the last feeding has finished. Inmates are talking on phones, talking to one another. Two TVs broadcast hazy images. A wiry, gray-haired inmate is sitting at a table, staring blankly at the floor.

"Look at that guy over there," says Roulis, a father of three. "He's done. He's left it all here."

A few minutes later, a mountainous man with thick hair bursting from his shirttop and a beard waits to be let inside the dorm. He is glowering and doesn't even turn his eyes as Roulis pushes a button to open the gate.

Roulis shakes his head. He says he "shudders to think if . . . [his children] ever got trapped in this world and couldn't get out."

In four hours, his double shift will be done. Then he'll drive home around 10:30 P.M. At 4 A.M., he'll pull himself out of bed again.

"Tomorrow's my last," before the weekend, he says, "and when I walk out of here, I'm running out of here. When I hit that parking lot, it's like I left the burden of the world behind me."

STUDY QUESTIONS FOR READING 6

1. How do correctional officers think they are seen by the public?

2. What do the officers at the Nassau County Correctional Center say about the recent charges of abuse?

3. How is it explained that correctional officers don't like to be called guards?

4. How high is the base pay at the jail? What about at the nearby Suffolk police department?

5. Are officers armed? Are supervisors? What do officers say their greatest tools are?

6. What is the life expectancy of correctional officers? What are some reasons it might be so short?

WORKING AS A PRISON GUARD

GARY L. WEBB
DAVID G. MORRIS

Occupational groups, according to Howard S. Becker (1963:80) have common understandings and thus a culture. Members of such groups develop perspectives of themselves and their activities. Similarly Robert Redfield (1941:132) has stated, "Wherever some group of people have a bit of common life with a modicum of isolation from other people, a common corner in society, common problems and perhaps a couple of common enemies, there culture grows."

This paper is intended to provide a glimpse at the culture and perspectives of prison guards.[1] The absence of attention to this occupational group is reflected by the lack of reported findings in the professional literature. However, a better understanding of the guard's culture and perspectives is imperative if the prison environment is to be comprehended.

Almost without exception prison guards are pictured as villainous. Movies, television, and literature have consistently depicted the guard disparagingly. Celebrated former offenders (turned to by a curious public for a glimpse of what it's really like inside a prison) usually castigate guards as representatives of a repressive, demeaning system. And prison administrators, fearful of ridicule and public misunderstanding, have contributed to this negative image of guards by shielding their institutions from scrutiny.

It might be argued that Americans, taught from an early age to value freedom above virtually all else, are reluctant to openly accept those individuals who are seen to earn their livings by depriving others of their freedom. However, other occupational groups in the administration of justice process, which are more directly involved in the stripping of basic freedom to those individuals incarcerated in penitentiaries, are not nearly as stigmatized as prison guards. To illustrate the low status afforded prison guards we need only think about the answers offered by children when asked what they want to be when they "grow up." Children not infrequently report their desires to be a policeman. . . . But to date the authors of this paper have not been informed of a single case where a child has reported his desire to become a prison guard.

Nevertheless, the prison guard is not totally disvalued. While his assumed behavior may be distressing to many, others generally remember that the people he guards are murderers, rapists, child molesters, robbers, thieves, and the like. As with Whittemore's cops (1969:11), prison guards may be seen as "complex and sometimes confused individuals grappling firsthand with the sickness of society while the rest of us theorize about prevention and cure."

More than anyone else, the guard represents the prison to its captives. The guard is always there, while the prisoner works, plays, eats, sleeps, etc. "In his supervision over a period of years the guard's relationship may become more constant than the relationship which may have existed between the prisoner and his parents" (Sacks, 1948:85). The development of close relationships between guards and inmates is recognized by prison administrators. In fact, rules and regulations are written by prison administrators explicitly forbidding "socializing" between guards and inmates. One such Administrative Regulation in force at Menaul Penitentiary[2] reads as follows:

> *No employee of the Adult Division of the Department of Corrections is permitted to socialize with residents (inmates) who are currently in custody in any of the state correctional institutions or facilities, parolees,*

mandatory or conditional releases, or any of their relatives or close associates, except under special circumstances which are known to and approved by the employee's Chief Administrative Officer.

Any employee who violates this regulation may be subject to suspension and/or discharge from employment with the Department of Corrections.[3]

The authors of this paper represent ten years experience at Menaul Penitentiary. The first author, Gary L. Webb, was employed as a Correctional Sociologist [for two years]. The second author, David G. Morris, was employed as a Correctional Counselor [for eight years]. The first author actually worked as a guard for two weeks, while undergoing what was termed guard training. However, both authors have had extensive interaction with prison guards, thus gaining access to the culture of this occupational group. For a cumulative total of ten years, the authors have worked with prison guards and watched them at work. We have talked with them and with their families. We have shared their companionship in leisure activities. Therefore, our frame of reference is, to some extent, that of "insiders," who through affiliation with guards, have gleaned an understanding of their viewpoints.

The prison that serves as a setting for this research may be described as fairly typical in respect to the administrative practices, programming, discipline, and work opportunities found in most "correctional" institutions. Menaul is a maximum security state prison, built before the turn of the century and surrounded by thirty-foot walls and gun towers. Menaul has been characterized in the professional literature as "just another place where men do time" (Clemmer, 1940:XV).

During the reporting period (1970–1978), this prison has been administered by five different wardens, appointed by four different departmental directors, appointed by three different governors. In spite of these administrative changes there is a certain continuity in evidence.

There have been policy changes affecting both staff and inmates, too numerous to mention. Two organized disturbances in which hostages were taken have occurred, as well as many lesser incidents.

The inmate population has fluctuated between 1,300 and 2,600 adult males, and at this time numbers around 2,600. The staff consists of 654 employees, of whom 391[4] or fifty-nine percent are guards (Menaul, 1978).

METHOD OF STUDY

The experiences and observations accomplished through both writers' employment are, in essence, the methodology. Some of the material for this study was gathered by participant observation, i.e., actually working with guards in related tasks, e.g., feeding inmates during lockups, joint committee assignments, and performing guard duties during guard training. We did not conduct formal interviews, in that formal interviews were not necessary in view of our daily conversations with guards and their willingness to discuss virtually any topic we mentioned in informal conversations. Throughout this paper we have reconstructed conversations that have occurred over the years, as well as our notes and memories will allow. Consequently, the quotes attributed to guards have been reported as faithfully as possible but may contain some slight, unintentional rephrasing.

The major focal points of this paper will be: (1) the process by which one is acculturated into the world of the prison guard; (2) the guards' conceptions of themselves and the other individuals who people their world, i.e., the administrators, the various social service personnel, and of course, the inmates; (3) resultant conflicts inherent with these other people; and (4) the guards' feelings of isolation from the larger society and how they cope with it.

I. ON BECOMING A GUARD

At this point in time, anyone seeking employment as a guard at Menaul Penitentiary must file a written application at the institution. Periodically, a number of applicants are called to take a civil service examination, which consists of an oral interview by a panel of three prison officials. The applicant is graded on such items as his attitude, interest in the job, ability to follow instructions, adaptability, and appearance (Menaul, 1978). The applicant's grades are forwarded to the Department of Personnel, where his placement on an eligibility list is determined. Federal hiring guidelines are followed, and veterans are given preference.

Guards hired prior to 1968 took written examinations to determine their eligibility. Civil service practices were not in effect prior to the fifties, and old-timers still talk about the "suitcase parades," i.e., massive turnovers of personnel that followed general elections.

Merely being hired does not make one a guard in the truest sense of the word. The new guard must first become "con-wise." That is, he must come to have an understanding of the inmate culture, certain expectations of inmates, and a method of interacting with inmates that is common to guards. Failures in this regard may result in denial of acceptance into the camaraderie of the guards' world, invariable inter-personal conflicts, and perhaps acquisition of the label "pro-inmate."

It takes time to become con-wise. New employees are expected to be sympathetic[5] in their attitudes toward inmates, but they should begin showing signs of "hardening" within a few months. If after six months to one year of employment, a guard is not regarded as con-wise, he is generally seen as pro-inmate. This term clearly implies the nature of the guard-inmate relationship. However, being pro-inmate does not necessarily mean the guard is on the inmates's side, as much as it implies that his view of inmates is different when compared with the views of the other guards.

The pro-inmate label when applied to a guard is much more derogatory than when said of non-guards, who are often thought of as extremely gullible where inmates are concerned. However, employees other than guards can become con-wise. When this happens, the non-guard employee is afforded greater acceptance by the guards. He is kept on the perimeter of the guards' world only by his position, although he may come to be thought of as "alright." This label is not freely given, it must be earned by repeated demonstrations of being like guards in ideation. Counselors, teachers, psychologists, sociologists, chaplains, etc., are expected to be more sympathetic and remain that way longer; their education is considered a liability in dealing with inmates.

It is generally agreed that the best experience for a new guard is what the guards call "getting burned" or "being conned." This refers to being deceived or manipulated by an inmate. It is a virtual initiation rite into their culture. Those experiences in which a guard is "burned" or "conned" are those experiences which lead to the attitude described as "con-wise."

The guard who is subjected to this experience on numerous occasions and does not become increasingly skeptical is observed with caution. Experienced guards may begin to think there is "something wrong with him," and he is apt to become regarded as pro-inmate.

It is not unusual to hear an experienced guard make reference to rigid skepticism, in a joking manner, when counseling a new guard. For example, such statements as "if an inmate tells you what time it is, look at your watch," are not uncommon. Similarly, the first author's third day in the prison (second day in guard training, dressed as a guard, and working in a cell house), he was approached by an inmate in a very cordial manner. The conversation was very one-sided, lasted ten to fifteen minutes, and consisted primarily of flattery directed toward the assumed new guard. The inmate explained in great detail that it was easy to spot an intelligent, compassionate new guard. Shortly after the inmate left, a young but experienced guard, who had obviously observed the conversation from a distance, commented to the intelligent, compassionate, guard-like first author, "he's just throwing some bait out, like bass fishing, waiting for you to bite, so he can reel you in."

Informal counseling by experienced guards is an attempt to reduce the new guards' gullibility, but a new guard is expected to be gullible. It is expected that a new guard will be "conned." In fact, vulnerability to deception or manipulation by an inmate does not end with experience.

One is expected to be far less vulnerable to manipulation or deception if he is considered "con-wise," but all guards are vulnerable. The term "con-wise" simply means the individual is aware of the frequency with which he is apt to be lied to, deceived, and/or manipulated. The term "con-wise" does not imply immunity. In fact the authors doubt that a single guard, interacting regularly with inmates (i.e., not working in a guard tower or a comparable position of insulation), would have the audacity to state to his fellow officers that he had not been "conned" to some extent in the past 12 months, regardless of his experience.

In those instances when the new guard is not viewed as more sympathetic and gullible than experienced guards, he may be viewed as peculiar, strange, or even paranoid. Hard skepticism is expected of a guard after he has dealt with hundreds of inmates. However, hard skepticism is viewed as genuinely odd when prison experience is lacking.

Becoming a guard necessitates becoming conwise. Remaining a guard in the guards' world also requires rigid loyalty. Loyalty as reflected in a former guard's statement, "The majority of guards work together to help one another. Ninety percent of them. I enjoyed working with most of them."

A guard assigned to the segregation unit described the scene as a lone guard, encountering trouble on one of the galleries, called for help. "Everybody jumped to his feet, chairs flying every which-a-way. You should have seen it when eight of us went busting up those stairs."

The we-feeling of the guards' world and its importance is exemplified by the following comments of a former guard:

> It was fun to go to work in the morning. I enjoyed the fellowship with the other guards. I used to like most having breakfast with the guys. We'd all get in the dining room about six-thirty and eat breakfast and swap stories over coffee for half an hour before making roll call up in the guard hall.

II. GUARDS' CONCEPTIONS: THEMSELVES

It is not unusual to hear a first-time visitor to Menaul Penitentiary comment, "Why, it's like a little city in here." Within this miniature community, as one guard stated, "the guards are the police force." The identification with police roles is such that many of the guards are active members of police organizations. The image of guards as policemen is also conveyed by the inmates in whose specialized language guards are referred to as "the police," "the man," and "pigs," just as are policemen in major cities throughout the United States. In fact, the term "police" is used quite regularly by inmates at Menaul when referring to guards.

The management of guards, as with police officers, is regulated in a military manner. Guards wear uniforms, follow orders, relieve one another at assigned "posts," practice on firing ranges, place people "on report," may be promoted to sergeant, lieutenant, captain, or major and in earlier times even saluted guards and officials of "superior rank."

Key concepts in this para-militaristic culture are the terms "security" and "discipline." Maintaining security is the guards' function, as seen by the guards. They view the prison as a place that serves to protect their communities by confining lawless and oftentimes dangerous men, and they see themselves as "the back-bone" of the institution—the ones who see that the day-to-day operations of the prison are carried out.

Security is viewed as the end result of their roles, the means to that end is expressed as "discipline." Guards frequently comment on "the need for discipline."

"We all need rules and regulations."

"If these men had had discipline, they wouldn't be here today."

"Strict discipline is good for them."

Despite the above quotes, rigidity is disvalued, guards are quick to point out "you can't go strictly by the book," "rules are made to be broken." They argue that one must take a common-sense approach in "enforcing discipline."

"None of the rules are enforced all the time, I guess," a lieutenant with considerable experience confided. "They have to be ignored at times. Rules aren't absolutes."

In an institution such as Menaul, there is an absence of informal communication between those who establish procedures and those who carry them out.

Thus, administrative regulations are subject to interpretation. And, it is in this area of interpretation that the guard draws his power. He decides whether a disciplinary report is required or if an incident can be handled "by other available means." The administrative regulations, as pointed out by one of our respondents, contain an abundance of ambiguous phraseology, e.g., "minimum force" and "normal conditions."

For the past few years, there has been considerable pressure for changes in the management of correctional institutions, and to the guards what appears as an atmosphere of constant change provides even greater room for circumvention of policy. It is not uncommon to hear guards complain about the labyrinth of prison rules. Written rules are not viewed as the ultimate authority to check when the correct or official procedure is not known. In such cases, fellow guards or those of superior rank are consulted.

The guards believe that through their work experience and daily interaction with inmates they have a better understanding of inmates than do "dumb-ass experts in cozy offices who wouldn't know an inmate if one fell through the ceiling." As is reflected by the quoted comment, guards tend to be adamant about their self-perceived superior understanding of inmates.

Which rules are strictly enforced and which aren't? "Each guard interprets the rules a little different. I even interpret the rules differently on different days," one guard commented. The following comment from a guard provides some insight:

I've met some inmates who will actually help you. If you're on a job where you don't know what the hell you're doing, they'll tell you what has to be done, even who to watch out for. They know what kind of officer you are. They'll try to keep you straight. If they have a good job, they don't want a lot of heat, so they aren't going to let you get things messed up. Oh sure they do some conniving. What the heck. I would too.

This guard is expressing a belief shared by many guards that bartering or trading among inmates is not a serious breach of discipline.

In this regard, the first author (while in guard training, dressed as a guard) was assigned to escort approximately forty inmates to the commissary.[6] Since currency is not allowed, all transactions at the commissary are conducted by ledger.[7] Therefore, it is impossible for a guard to purchase a soft drink at the commissary.

Noticing the absence of money, but experiencing some thirst, the first author asked an experienced guard about the procedure necessary to acquire a soft drink. The guard simply walked to the commissary counter and spoke with an "inmate commissary employee"; seconds later the inmate handed the guard two Cokes. The guard returned and as we stood drinking our Cokes, he explained that it was impossible to pay for them but that he would do the inmate a favor someday like fixing a ticket.[8] That is to say he would "fix" the ticket in the same sense that a police officer would fix a traffic ticket.

Many guards feel that gambling is not a serious breach of discipline. Some even feel that an inmate who is guilty of being intoxicated has not committed a serious breach of discipline. In fact, during the first author's guard experience, an experienced guard commented that a certain inmate was "alright" because he caught an inmate fellating this inmate's penis and the inmate referred to as "alright" (the recipient of the act) later thanked him for not reporting the incident. Generally considered as the more serious inmate offenses are physically assaulting or threatening a guard, impudence or disrespect toward a guard, or refusing to work or to comply with an order.

Regulations governing inmate behavior are not the only regulations subject to circumvention by the guards. Some guards fail to follow rules governing their own conduct. Most guards tell that they would not traffic with inmates and deplore the fact that others do. But, it seems highly probable that because of their loyalty to one another they would be most reluctant to inform on a "fellow guard."

A stereotypical image of the prison guard is seen by them as unrealistic and serves to intensify their perspectives and conceptions of themselves as protectors of an unappreciative society. The stereotyped image of a prison guard as brutal and sadistic particularly irritates them. Guards are quick to point out that they did not take their positions because of a desire to fulfill such a role.[9] Rather most guards tell that they took their jobs because it was the best available in the area, the highest paying job available, or because it was steady work, not subject to the layoffs they had experienced elsewhere.

"I did it (accepted a guard position) with the full intent of finding something else as soon as possible," one guard, who started in 1963, stated. Another guard accepted his position ten months ago with apparently a similar attitude. He says he plans to obtain employment at a coal mine in the near future.

Most guards indicated what they liked most about their jobs was being able to remain in the rural area where the prison is located or the companionship of their fellow guards. They dislike the lack of advancement opportunities, the perceived role played by "politics," the constant pressure for change, the physical conditions of the institution, and above all else, recent administrations which have been viewed as lacking experience or insight, prone to coddle inmates, and "out to get us" ("us" referring to guards).

There is discontent over being assigned on manhunts when an inmate escapes, but this has been relieved somewhat by the recently implemented policy of paying overtime to participants. Surprisingly, the seemingly monotonous tasks of supervising line movements, the perpetual locking and unlocking of doors, and the constant watching of inmates elicits very little complaining. However, most guards do express a decided preference for working on the ground as opposed to working in a gun tower. Interestingly, guards assigned to tower duty generally have less status among the guards.

II. GUARDS' CONCEPTIONS: SOCIAL SERVICES PERSONNEL

The world of the custodial officer is of course not limited to guards and inmates. Many employees fill non-custodial roles, including: psychiatrists, doctors, sociologists, psychologists, counselors, chaplains, teachers, vocational instructors, nurses, dieticians, secretaries, and clerks.

At Menaul, all employees are divided into two groups; one is said to work in either security or treatment. The guards are thought of as the security staff, and play the more dominant role in the institution. Nonuniformed personnel are generally thought of by older guards as counselors, no matter what their position might be.

The treatment and security categories are treated as somehow divorced one from the other. A strong belief exists throughout the institution that these categories are incompatible, even detrimental, each to the efforts of the other. They are separate but unequal. The second author remembers one of the wardens telling a group of counselors to stay away from the guards. "You have your job to do, and they have theirs," he said.

In April of 1973, inmates seized control of the commissary and took a guard hostage. A local newspaper ran a related story on May 3, 1973 (Sec. 1, p. 1), citing " . . . a high degree of unrest among the inmates at Menaul for several months, according to security officers." This story continued: "The atmosphere in the prison stems from coddling the prisoner, inmate counselors who have become in fact inmate advocates in almost every disciplinary action by the security force, and an overemphasis on social and educational programs within the prison."

How representative of the guard force was the phrase, "according to security officers"? We can never know for certain. Most of the guards with whom we discussed non-guards, expressed the belief that counseling and educational services are needed and that those persons assigned these roles are for the most part "alright," which is the ultimate respect afforded a "treatment employee." But of course, due to our status as "treatment employees" their remarks are necessarily subject to propriety, as well as to honesty. Indeed, many guards speak disdainfully of "counselors" and graciously exclude the authors of this paper. Most guards, while indicating that rehabilitative programs are necessary, indicate that they believe they are ineffective because they are "overloaded." Some guards seem to possess considerable insight into the goals, functions, and problems of social service personnel, while others seem to have little, if any idea of why such employees are even in the prison.

"I think the programs here are crap. Very few enable the inmate to get a job on the street. The programs right now serve as recreational periods to get the men out of their cells and keep them busy. If the programs are not stiff and worthwhile, they're a waste of time," one guard commented.

Because of the two-staff approach, most guards and most non-guards aren't too familiar with one another. Also, as conveyed by the two-staff concept, most guards see their jobs as unrelated to the rehabilitative process. However, most also see their jobs as more utilitarian than those of the non-guards.

Guards frequently express the belief that they are by the nature of their roles tougher than "counselors" (who are viewed as permissive) and therefore better able to relate to inmates. Several guards noted that in the past guards were required to do many of the things presently handled by counselors, and they indicate a measure of resentment because of this.

In conclusion, gaining acceptance by the guards is the responsibility of the non-guard employee, for he is the newcomer to the microcosmic world within the prison walls. He becomes "alright" with the guards first by getting to know them. No matter how much he might be like the guards philosophically, they will regard him as an outsider if they do not know him. Then, of course, he must reflect an attitude of sympathetic support for them, value discipline, and naturally, become "con-wise."

II. GUARDS' CONCEPTIONS: ADMINISTRATORS

"The administrators are drunk with power. Their idea is to have us do whatever they say. We have no input; we can't relate to them. They radiate the idea that they're a controlling force. I don't like the feeling of so much power over my head." These comments made recently by an experienced guard express the sense of fear conveyed by many others.

Though subject to superiors in a hierarchy, a prison warden does in fact have at his command discretionary use of dictatorial powers in administering his institution that are similar to the authority of the captain of a sea-going vessel. It is this aura of absolute authority that creates an atmosphere of fear, as exemplified by the guard who stated, "They seem to be out to get everyone. After thirty-four years, I find myself worrying about holding onto my job."

Wardens are generally viewed as outsiders. At Menaul they are not subject to civil service requirements, as are their counterparts in federal prisons; and wardens have traditionally been appointed on the basis of political patronage.

The view of the warden as an outsider is especially true in the case of recent wardens. Recent wardens have had little prior experience in prison work. Key administrative posts have been assigned to the

warden's associates, further alienating the staff, who not only see these administrators as outsiders but as "Johnny Come Latelies." Guards and non-guards alike feel "stalemated" in terms of advancement and it is generally felt that promotion is dependent on one's political contacts.

Most guards say that they believe administrators should work their way up and be subject to civil service requirements that emphasize experience. They favor "a prison man," as they put it. The last warden at Menaul considered to be a "prison man" was replaced in 1973. He began as a guard approximately thirty years before, was stabbed and nearly died trying to quell a riot, and worked his way up the promotional ladder. He was eventually named assistant warden and then acting warden upon the resignation of his predecessor. He served as warden for approximately six months.

The guards greatly admired this man. "He was the best. The guards would do anything for him. The inmates respected him, too."[10] There is general agreement that it will take someone like him to "put the place back together again."

Of course, the warden is not the whole administration, and the guards understand this. "It's run by remote control. Somebody in the capital says to do this, and it's relayed to us."

The "somebodies" in the state capital are viewed as unknowledgeable about prisons in general and about Menaul in particular. The guards witness "a trial and error approach" and become frustrated. But mostly, the guards see the administration as politically motivated. As one guard commented, "They all use statistics to make themselves look good." Guards see the purchase of expensive office machinery as political graft and question the rationale for such purchases in view of existing shortages of foodstuffs and toilet paper. Rumors of "tapped" telephones and suppressed information are rampant.

In short, guards see prison administrators at all levels as outsiders with political connections and arbitrary power determined to "look good." They lack the guards' knowledge of the institution and its population. They are viewed as a necessary evil; something that in good times may support them and in bad times will blame them when things go wrong. "When some dumb-ass expert dreams up a new theory, we're the ones who have to try it out. And, if it backfires, it's a guard that gets hurt. Then these bastards in their plush offices in the state capital or up in front of the double gate (reference to the warden) sit back and defend their stupid theories and place the blame for their failures on us overreacting guards." And, in the guards' final analysis of the administrators, "They all come and go."

II. GUARDS' CONCEPTIONS: INMATES

There is, of course, no such thing as an average inmate, nor is there such a thing as an average conception of inmates. Each guard brings to his encounters within the walls a world view that is uniquely his own, but due to the commonality of their relationships with one another and with the other people present in the institution, their views tend to become rather uniform in many areas.

This uniformity of perception becomes most splintered in the area of what inmates are like. While there may be a consensus that inmates are evil, there is no consensus on how or why they are evil, or to what extent they are evil. A guard asked to tell what inmates are like is going to predicate his answer to a great degree on his personal knowledge of inmates, what he has heard others say about inmates, his ability or inability to get along with people in general, and, of course, on his most recent dealings with inmates.

Guards' views of inmates may be seen as resting between two hypothetical poles; at one extreme would be the concept that inmates are just like the guards. On the other extreme would be the concept that inmates are the exact opposite of guards.

"I'd say eighty percent are no different personality-wise than the people you meet on the street. Moral-wise, they're different."

"Inmates aren't like anybody else. That's bunk. They're different. No doubt about it. Their feelings of right and wrong are different than most people's."

The comments above reflect the disparity between two guards' views, and yet an area of consensus.

Some guards indicate that they dislike inmates and manifest a critical attitude:

"Most (inmates) don't take too much pride in their personal appearance."

"These guys are like kids, always butting into someone else's business."

"They think they're better than everybody else."

Some guards indicate that they like inmates and manifest a tolerant attitude:

"There's some decent ones down there. The majority just want to do their time and get the hell out."

"Out of 2,000 people, you're bound to find some you like. I like the way some of them are very outgoing and uninhibited."

"Just because they're inmates doesn't keep me from liking them as people. Some people on the outside I like; some I don't. It's the same with inmates."

How do you make friends with inmates, if you are their keeper? "How do you make friends with people you meet anywhere?", one guard answered. He pointed out that in time, you come to see the inmates as people, rather than as "oddities." "Remember how when you first started you automatically wondered, whenever you had any dealings with an inmate, what's he in for? And, then eventually you just don't wonder about it anymore."

It seems probable that the opposite effect also occurs with the passage of time, i.e., a dehumanization process going from a view of inmates as people to a view of them as work, cases, or numbers. This process may be viewed as a natural out-growth of becoming "con-wise." A young experienced guard commented, "I guess I was like everybody else. My heart bled for them when I first started at the prison. Gradually, you feel less sorry for them and more like they're responsible for their being here."

The relationship between guards and inmates is peculiarly intimate. When interacting with inmates, guards are bound to have favorites, no matter how diligently they might try not to. This is not a condemnation, but a fact common to all interpersonal relationships. Coaches have favorite athletes, teachers have favorite students, parents even have favorite children. And, in prison, this type of relationship is labeled as a father-son situation. "He's his kid"[11] is said about an obvious favorite inmate of any given guard. Similarly it might be said that the guard is the kid's "dad," or "daddy."[12] The term "kid," "dad," "daddy," and the like, used in this fashion imply no disrespect, unless applied to a pro-inmate guard.

One important factor involved in the guard's view of inmates, which shall be discussed at greater length in the next section, is their fear of them. When asked what he disliked most about inmates, one guard answered, "The fact that they can smile at you and stab you in the back." This statement is very representative of a guard's fear in that it may be viewed as a metaphor (as is the most common usage of the phrase by guards) or it may be used literally. In a literal sense, many guards are afraid of inmates and are very concerned with their safety. In a figurative sense, many guards fear "being stabbed in the back," i.e., duped or in some way made to look poorly before other guards or the administration.

In describing what inmates are like, some guards allude to what may be termed peer pressure among inmates.

"I don't like the general idea that they have to be sneaky about everything. Most of them take pride in the fact that they were able to obtain some trinkets by illegal means. And, it's catching. If they didn't do it when they first came here, eventually they get around to it."

"I've never found one that was really honest, because he is playing a game. And, he's going to play this game as long as he's inside the institution because they all do." The majority of the guards at Menaul appear to reflect what might be termed a fundamentally pragmatic conception of inmates. Inmates are regarded as individuals who may or may not be likeable but who are almost without exception untrustworthy.

"Understanding that some thieving, conniving son-of-a-bitch behaves the way he does because he's black and his mother was a whore and he never knew his father and he had to steal to eat—understanding that—is important, but it don't alter the fact the son-of-a-bitch is still a son-of-a-bitch."

III. CONFLICT: ADMINISTRATORS

In any situation where a number of individuals are drawn together a certain amount of conflict is inevitable, and the guards' culture contributes to magnification of their personal conflicts into we-they

situations. In the guard's day-to-day interactions with the administrators—whose orders he carries out, the other employees—with whom he works, and the inmates—whom he watches and supervises, conflict and its resolution seems at times to be his principal preoccupation. However, he is comforted by the knowledge that his side will be taken by his fellow guards.

As with all management-employee relations, the conflict between guards and administrators reflects upon the managerial abilities of the men in charge, their ability to communicate their objectives, their ability to promote harmony, and their ability to garner staff support.

Very little conflict existed between the guards and the first two administrations covered by this research. One of the administrations was headed by a former state police captain, who was viewed almost immediately as physically and mentally tough, worthy of respect, and con-wise. The other was an up-through-the-ranks guard. The last three wardens[13] have been viewed differently, not just from the other two administrations covered in this research, but from any and all administrations, according to the guards. One veteran guard's response is somewhat typical, "I've never seen anything like this bunch."

The three most recent wardens have been viewed by the guards as pro-inmate and antagonistic toward their (the guards') values. Consequently, the existing conflict between the guards and their supervisors is of such proportion as to equal, if not surpass, even their incessant conflict with the inmate population.

The guards' chief complaints are as follows: (1) they feel that they are jeopardized by administrative decisions, (2) they voice the chronic complaint of lack of communication, and (3) they resent what they interpret as arrogance and ambition of not only outsiders, but out-of-staters.

The most significant area of conflict is in the area of administrative decisions affecting the running of the institution. Many such decisions upset the guards, who see threats in these decisions to the status quo, their jobs, and their personal safety. Probably the most criticized decision concerned the placement of guards to duty posts. In May of 1974, the Superintendent[14] decided not to assign guards to the guntowers in the East Cell House, and during that month, rebellious inmates seized control of the cell house and took four guards hostage.[15] Armed guards in the guntowers could have prevented the over-powering of four lone sentries by hundreds of prisoners, the guards argue. The guards also point out the increased number of fights and physical assaults by inmates on other inmates, the high number of escapes, the fact that some guards have been injured or taken hostage, and the contracting of an outside agency to collect trash inside the institution because (inmate labor can't or won't do so) as verification of their belief that the administration "has lost control" of the inmates.

The complaint, "we're always the last to know" has been heard with tiresome regularity in recent years. Guards frequently complain that they are never consulted by the administrators. As one guard commented, "their attitude is don't call us, we'll call you."

Stories pertaining to the arrogance, vindictiveness, and incompetence of recent administrators abound. However, the guards' methods of resolving conflict between themselves and the administration is quite limited, because of the latter's authority to discipline and discharge employees. Still, such authority is not without limits.

Many guards are openly critical of the administration. And, needless to say, they need to look no further than their captives for ways and means of undermining the administrator's authority. Many do nothing that they are not told to do, or they do exactly what they are told to do. "The best way to change a rule is to follow it exactly," one guard explained.

For many years, the guards have had a labor union, and it has functioned primarily in the area of negotiating pay scales and obtaining fringe benefits. Those guards who belonged to it in the past admitted its weaknesses. However, during recent years, the union's membership has increased dramatically as the union has initiated numerous grievance procedures against administrators for alleged abuses.

Both authors have attended union meetings at which discussions centered on gaining leverage in dealing with the administration through winning public support. Measures such as letters to editors, petitions to the Governor and legislators, pressuring civic and business leaders in the community, and even

strikes were examined. But, most guards, mindful of the "suitcase parades" and schooled in the belief that what goes on inside the prison should stay inside the prison, do very little to resolve their personal conflicts. They manifest attitudes of apathy and hope that the next general election will restore things to their former state. They condone acquiescence in the face of this type of conflict and frequently echo the often-repeated statement, "Like it or not, they're running it."

III. CONFLICT: SOCIAL SERVICE PERSONNEL

The increased conflict with administrators in recent years has had the effect of reducing conflict between prison guards and other prison employees. Guards express opinions that for the most part reflect acceptance of social services personnel as non-threatening and possibly even needed. This has not always been the case, and even now may be superficial.

In the past, the conflict between the so-called treatment and security staffs has generally taken a form similar to sibling rivalry with each side vying for administrative support. Thus, to some extent the guards and non-guards are more unified than in the past due to the presence of administrators perceived by both groups as outsiders.

The newest treatment personnel are the "correctional counselors." During the early years of the reporting period, they were viewed as threatening, not only by the guards but by other treatment personnel as well. The role of uninitiated newcomers is still ascribed to them. They aren't subjected to the open contempt with which counselors were first met in 1970 and 1971, but privately they are still viewed by many guards as "pretty pathetic."

In the past, guards resolved most conflicts with counselors by ignoring them. Call tickets for inmates, made out by counselors, were often ignored or responded to at times other than specified. Stories of counselor's ineptness in dealing with inmates abounded. Disturbances were linked to group therapy programs conducted by counselors.

Following the take-over of the East Cell House in 1974, the guards' union met and forwarded demands to the Director of Corrections through legislators sympathetic to their cause, and one of their demands was that no new counselors be hired until an alleged shortage of guards was alleviated.

III. CONFLICT: INMATES

Ultimately the conflict central to prison life is that which exists between the keepers and the kept. This conflict has been the theme of much of what has been written about prisons, both fact and fiction. And, this theme has been employed so dramatically and imaginatively as to elicit at least passing interest from almost everyone. Its impact is such as to challenge the researcher in this area to separate myth from reality.

According to the myth, prisoners and guards are avowed enemies engaged in a constant combat, where, depending upon one's point of view, either dedicated or desperate men strive and plan to seize the moment to regain their lost freedom by the overthrow of their captors or by executing a cunning escape.

The major focus of the guards' conflict with inmates, if the myth were true, would be fear, and certainly much of the conflict they experience is born of their fear of their charges. In an institution where custody is stressed, where there are high walls and guntowers, where many employees can vividly recall the deaths of guards at inmates' hands in 1965, fear is a natural thing, perhaps a necessary thing.

It is also only natural that this fear be handled differently by different people, and some guards are obviously far more concerned with their physical safety than are others. "He can't work around inmates," is said by one guard about another, whose fear of inmates is known to be problematic. Such guards are generally assigned duties not involving direct supervision of inmates.

The major focus of the guards' conflict with inmates is not fear, however, but frustration—the frustration which results from daily hassles with inmates, who argue that they were not sent to prison to follow rules or to work, but to be rehabilitated. And the guards' frustration is intensified as more and more limitations are placed on their authority to "discipline" inmates.

The traditional resolution to guard-inmate conflict has been the writing of a disciplinary ticket, which previously brought the inmate to the attention

of the yard office captain (a senior guard of considerable experience) who controlled job placements and meted out disciplinary measures. The yard office captain knew the guards and frequently knew more about their conflicts than was communicated on the disciplinary ticket. He resolved conflict/problems through whatever punitive measures he felt appropriate, including segregation, denial of privileges, and compulsory assignment transfers.

Now a disciplinary ticket brings the inmate to the attention of one of two committees composed of rotating members. The perceived seriousness of the disciplinary ticket is used to determine which committee will hear the ticket. The committee which hears[16] the less serious tickets is referred to as the "Program Team."[17] This committee is composed of one counselor, one guard, and a third member such as a food service employee or maintenance man (the third member must be an employee other than a counselor or guard). If the inmate pleads guilty or is found guilty by the committee, he most frequently receives a reprimand, i.e., the chairman tells him it was wrong and asks or tells him not to do it again. Of course, many of the tickets are just dismissed, and the third most frequent punishment is to not allow the inmate to watch a show or visit the recreation room for a few days. Commissary privileges cannot be "taken" nor can his recreation in the prison yard, unless the infraction occurred in the yard. In addition, all decisions by the Program Team are subject to inmate grievance proceedings, which involve still more committees, hearings, and decisions. Thus the "Program Team's" disciplinary function is viewed in large part as a "joke" or a sham.

If an inmate receives a disciplinary ticket for a violation of the rules which is perceived to be a major ticket, that is a serious rule violation, he must then appear before the "Adjustment Committee."[18] A serious rule violation is generally viewed as something more serious than pretty theft or telling a guard to engage in sexual congress with himself. In fact, swearing is ignored in large part, regardless of prison rules to the contrary.[19] Major rule violations are such things as assaulting a guard, assaulting another inmate, possessing illegal drugs, alcohol, or marijuana, or possessing a knife or club. The Adjustment Committee is composed of three members, a guard, a counselor, and a department head or assistant warden on a rotating bases. Thus, one day the head of the school program will chair the Adjustment Committee, the next day an assistant warden, the following day the head counselor, then the supervisor of the Reception and Classification Unit, etc. The disciplinary measures available to the committee include reduction in grade (withholding a portion of the inmate's privileges), assignment to segregation,[20] and forfeiture of good time (generally three months or less for offenses punishable by a year or more in prison if committed in the free community.) Thus, the most severe punishment at Menaul is in large part nominal. As one inmate commented as he was complaining about the lax security and nominal punishment at Menaul, "If the laws didn't deter us on the street, then for damn sure that Mickey Mouse segregation won't deter anybody."[21] In fact it is both authors' opinion that the discipline and punishment offered by the armed forces is far more demanding and severe than what is or has been available in recent years at Menaul Penitentiary. Thus, as might be expected, there is a general consensus among the guards that conflicts with inmates must frequently go unresolved because of a lack of administrative support in the area of disciplinary measures and decision making.

Racial conflict is also present at Menaul as it is in the broader society. Many guards have known few blacks other than those they've met at Menaul serving time. Separated by cultural differences and the enforced gulf between guard and inmate, both find solace in their prejudices. Many guard-inmate conflicts are so rooted, and conflict seems inevitable whenever interaction occurs between a white guard and a black-racist inmate; a black guard and a white-racist inmate; a white racist guard and a black inmate; or a black racist guard and a white inmate.

IV. FEELINGS OF ISOLATION

Guards feel isolated from the broader society, and they draw support from one another, in part, to compensate for a lack of prestige from outsiders, whom they call "civilians." The use of this term is most indicative of the martial perceptions guards have of themselves.

This image carries with it certain perplexities. For example, guards resent a public view of prisons as primitive and punitive institutions and of themselves as brutal, dehumanized enforcers of rigid rules. However, they do relish the images of toughness and coolness under pressure that may be ascribed to them by many of those who see prisons in this light.

The guards' isolation from the larger society can be seen in the following comments about the guards interactions with outsiders:

"I don't talk about it (the prison), unless someone else brings it up."

"Even in (the name of the small town closest to Menaul Penitentiary) you have the stereotype (of guards) from late movies on TV."

"They feel sorry for murders, rapists, and robbers, they resent us," one lieutenant generalized of the people he has conducted through Menaul on countless tours.

"Whenever people find out you're a guard, they ask a lot of dumb questions."

"There are state laws that prohibit corporal punishment that say that inmates have to be fed, housed, clothed, provided free medical care, exercise, recreation, and access to legal services. Then they (inmates) get to go to college free, and get paid while they're in here. Hell, when I take college courses, I have to pay for them like everybody else."

"It makes me sick to hear people moaning about poor, unfortunate inmates. What about the goddamn victims? When's the last time you heard somebody bitching about the poor unfortunate victims who are murdered, beaten, crippled, raped, and just basically shit on? Jesus Christ, victims even have to pay their own hospital bills. The way things are today you can be beaten, butt-fucked, and burned at the stake, and God help you if you live, you'll go broke trying to pay for what some crazy bastard did to you. But, the crazy bastard that did it will go to college and come out a counselor."

"A prison guard is viewed as someone who can't do anything else," a former guard commented. "I don't believe that myself, but most people do."

A young guard with less than a year's experience says he does not like being a guard, and he may reflect something of the outsider's attitude noted above. He says, "The ones that stay are either lazy when they came here or they get that way. They're friendly and decent enough. They're just the kind of people who sit on a bank fishing with a cane pole."

As evidenced by the above quotes, guards are concerned that their occupational status is disvalued. However, of at least equal significance appears to be their evaluation of the public's perception of inmates as poor unfortunates suffering at the hands of guards. When, in fact, guards view their roles as a police action—protecting people in society from those who have committed serious crimes.

CONCLUSION

There seems to be a general consensus in this society that a prison exists for the combined purposes of isolating convicted criminals from the community, favorably affecting changes in them, and exacting some societal vengeance and thereby reaffirming the rightness of the existing normative order. In this regard the correctional bureaucracy is confronted with the problem of turning these purposes into unified policies, but the prison employee, especially the guard, must convert policy into practice. Guards believe that they should have more influence in shaping policy. They argue that they have a considerably better understanding of confined men than do the "liberals" who

"dream up theories" without the benefit of "first-hand knowledge." "They don't know anything about inmates but they think their theories will work," was the way one veteran guard put it. While a newer guard said, "We have no input. We can't relate to them." A more bitter guard expresses his opinion this way: "When some dumb-ass expert dreams up a new theory, we're the ones who have to try it out."

Perhaps, an important element related to the guards' feelings of isolation can best be explained by pointing out that the "they" referred to by the guards quoted above are essentially unidentifiable. The guards know that some of the "theys" are key administrators in the Department of Corrections, but others are only identified as "so-called experts" who somehow are able to shape things over which the guards have no control. So-called "invisible," unidentified experts who somehow shape policy and thus the guards' world.

The guards at Menaul reflect feelings of frustration and impotence. Their world continues to change and those who have shaped and will shape their world have paid little attention to them. Those concerned with prison reform have traditionally ignored prison guards. Their opinions and perceptions have not been sought. They resent their historical and present exclusion in policy making and theory development. They fear it will continue.

ENDNOTES

1. Although the terms "prison guard" or "guard" are used throughout this paper, perhaps it should be mentioned that prison guards are generally referred to as "correctional officers." The term "guard" is in large part passé.
2. Menaul Penitentiary is the . . . actual name of the prison. . . . It is the same prison Donald Clemmer wrote about in his classic work, *The Prison Community,* 1940. . . .
3. Administrative Regulation #213 at Menaul Penitentiary. Most recently rewritten on July 7, 1975.
4. This number includes 29 guards listed as "trainees."
5. The word sympathetic in this paper is used in the sense that it also implies gullibility or credulity.
6. The term commissary at Menaul Penitentiary refers to the store, i.e., a retail establishment where goods such as food stuffs (ice cream, soda, potato chips, etc.) and toilet articles (hair dressing, deodorant, combs, etc.) are purchased by inmates.

7. A record of all money transactions is kept including credits and debits. Inmates are not allowed to make a purchase unless they have enough money on the ledger to pay for the items they select. The amount of their purchase is deducted from their balance.
8. The term "ticket" at Menaul refers to disciplinary reports written on inmates by guards for violating prison rules. The term has probably evolved in part because the disciplinary report forms are small (approximately twice the size of a pack of cigarettes) and resemble "traffic tickets."
9. In fact, anyone familiar with the restrictions placed upon guards at Menaul would hardly suspect them of brutality or sadism. Guards are not allowed to carry saps, sticks, or even penknives. A weapon of any kind is not allowed. The only armed guards are in the gun towers. Guards at Menaul are not even allowed to carry mace. Guards are armed only with a pen or pencil to record the number of an inmate who

misbehaves. In essence, a guard is helpless in large part if attacked by an inmate. He has only his bare hands and the help of fellow unarmed guards as a defense, with exception of assaults occurring near gun towers. Needless to say guards are assaulted with some regularity.

10. Interestingly, the inmates also respected this man a great deal as evidenced by literally hundreds of unsolicited comments offered by the approximately 2,000 inmates the authors of this paper have interviewed during the past five years.

11. In this sense, the word "kid" has no sexual overtones. However, when it is said that one inmate is another's "kid" the word "kid" does have explicit sexual overtones. Such usage generally refers to a young inmate who is cared for and protected by an older inmate. In exchange, the young inmate "services" the older inmate, i.e., he allows himself to be sodomized and/or fellates the older inmate's penis on a regular basis.

12. In this sense, the word "dad" or in more common usage, the word "daddy" has no sexual overtones. However, when the term "daddy" is applied to an inmate it refers to the fact that he has a "kid" (a young inmate who services him sexually).

13. From 1973 to 1978, Menaul Penitentiary has been governed by three different wardens.

14. In May of 1974 the young man who was holding the position of Warden referred to himself as "Superintendent." Interestingly, he stopped using the title of Superintendent in the summer of 1975 and referred to himself and signed all correspondence as "Warden" until his resignation in August of 1976. His resignation was obviously prompted by political considerations. His benefactor, the Director of Corrections (himself a recent out-of-state political appointment) appointed this young man (also from the same state that the director hailed from) superintendent (warden) in 1973. However, in 1976, when the incumbent Governor, attempting a second term of office, lost in the democratic primary, administrators in the department of corrections began to flee the state. Their flight was hastened undoubtedly by the fact that the winner of the democratic primary in 1973 had listed their names and salaries in a political newspaper ad prior to the democratic primary. The ad, published by a newspaper in the southern part of the state which appeared on March 10, 1976, (paid for by two different county democratic committees) reads as follows:

> *Following are just some of the more outlandish examples of out-of-state residents to whom (the incumbent Governor's last name) gave jobs in our state government during his administration.*

Following the above quote, twenty-nine top-ranking state officials were listed by name, job (title), state they emigrated from, and salary. Included on the list was the Director of Corrections, the Warden at Menaul, the Assistant Warden at Menaul, the Wardens at the other three maximum security prisons in the state, two individuals—both with the title "Chief of Program Services, Department of Corrections," Coordinator between Children and Family Services and Department of Corrections, Supervisor of the Training Academy for the State Law Enforcement Agency, and an individual with the title of Executive Director of the State Law Enforcement Commission at a salary of $38,000 per year.

The Director of Corrections resigned in 1976, after his patron (the Governor) lost in the primary. He left and was appointed Director of Corrections in an adjacent state. Shortly thereafter, in August of 1976, the Warden at Menaul was hired by his benefactor, (the Director of Corrections) as warden of a penitentiary in the newly infiltrated adjacent state. Thus, the political overtones in the field of corrections are all too palpable.

15. Interestingly, guards had manned the guntowers in the East Cell House for five decades. (East Cell House contains 500 two-man cells. Thus, when full, 1,000 inmates are housed there.) This may be viewed as a classic example of a young, inexperienced, out-of-state, politically-appointed Warden endangering the lives of experienced guards.

This same Warden, who made the decision to remove the guards in the East Cell House guntowers, was lauded by the mass media when appointed in 1973, as reflective of a progressive administration concerned with college training. As might be expected, the guards didn't share the mass media's enthusiasm. The Warden, the mass media praised and pointed to as the youngest in the nation in charge of a maximum security prison, was quickly labeled as the "dumbest in America" by the guards. One senior guard captain, who has worked at Menaul since the 1930's—spanning five decades—probably summed up the guards' feelings best when he commented, "I don't believe these people . . . it's like a bunch of little kids playing prison."

16. The chairman of the committee interviews the inmate, asks what his explanation is, and whether or not he (the inmate) pleads guilty or not guilty. Then the committee decides guilt or innocence and the punishment to be imposed, if any, based on the evidence. Majority rules, that is, if two out of the three agree on a disposition, it is decided.

17. The second author, David G. Morris, has chaired this committee on numerous occasions.

18. The first author, Gary L. Webb, has chaired this committee on numerous occasions.

19. While in guard training, the first author observed, as an inmate in the vocational school explained to a uniformed guard that he (the guard) was a big-cunted mother fucker. Needless to say, the inmate's tone was loud and insulting. The guard didn't even write the inmate a disciplinary ticket. Similarly, weeks later, two inmates were observed telling a third inmate that they were going to get his pussy. The inmate recipient of the comments, obviously disturbed, left immediately. Two guards standing closer than the author ignored the incident.

20. Segregation, contrary to traditional folklore, does not entail sensory deprivation, loss of all privileges and no yard. To the contrary, approximately two-thirds of all inmates housed in the cell house referred to as segregation are voluntary, that is, they have requested segregation placement for protection, to avoid the extortionary demands of inmate gangs, which are prevalent at Menaul Penitentiary. While in segregation, inmates watch televisions supplied by the state, have commissary privileges (although they may be reduced), and they have yard privileges, i.e., a special recreational yard for all of those in segregation both disciplinary and voluntary has been created in recent years. Thus, the most severe punishment at Menaul is also viewed as somewhat of a "joke" or a sham.

In fact, in September and October of 1975, the Adjustment Committee was actually removing voluntary commitments to segregations and forcing them to re-enter the general population so there would be room for disciplinary cases in the segregation unit. The first author actually witnessed a department head recommending to an inmate (who had been raped and who was being forced to pay protection to live in his cell—the inmate claimed $50.00 a week) that he (the inmate) should commit a serious rule violation so he would be placed in segregation if he encountered difficulties when attempting to sign himself into segregation, which was probable.

The second author worked in the segregation building (unit) from April 1977 to February 1978 as a "segregation counselor." His entire caseload consisted of those inmates in segregation. The segregation unit is presently populated by approximately 450 inmates. Approximately 300 or two-thirds are voluntary commitments, i.e., they have requested segregation placement. Thus, only approximately 150 or roughly one-third of the inmates in segregation have been placed there because of serious rule violations.

21. This comment is not, as may be suspected, unusual. It is very common to hear inmates complain about the lax security, and nominal punishment. Obviously, inmates suffer most when security is relaxed, because the weaker inmates are forced to pay protection, surrender their belongings and submit to sexual perversions. On the other hand, gang leaders, gang members, and others who prey on the weaker inmates, enjoy the reduced discipline and frequently file grievances, and complain to attorneys and the mass media that discipline and punishment is too strict in prison.

REFERENCES

Becker, Howard S. 1963. *Outsiders: Studies in the Sociology of Deviance.* New York: MacMillan.

Clemmer, Donald. 1940. *The Prison Community.* New York: Holt, Rinehart and Winston.

Menaul Penitentiary. Information supplied by Personnel Department. 1975–April 10, 1978.

Redfield, Robert. 1941. *The Folk Culture of Yucatan.* Chicago: University of Chicago Press.

Sacks, Jerome Gerald. 1948. *Troublemaking in Prison.* Washington, D.C.: The Catholic University Press.

Whittemore, L. H. 1969. *Cop: A Closeup of Violence and Tragedy.* Greenwich, Conn.: Fawcett World Library.

STUDY QUESTIONS FOR READING 7

1. How do established officers expect new officers to feel toward inmates? How do they expect this to change over time? Explain the terms "con-wise" and "pro-inmate."

2. What is the guard's view of rules and their proper enforcement? How do guards get their power? In one guard's view, what is "the best way to change a rule"?

3. How did the new guard (Webb) get a soft drink?

4. What infractions are seen as serious by these guards? Not serious?

5. What is the attitude toward treatment staff (social services), administrators, and the public? Explain.

GUARDS IMPRISONED
AN OVERVIEW OF THE BOOK BY LUCIEN X. LOMBARDO

TARA GRAY

Guards Imprisoned: Correctional Officers at Work is a book by Lucien X. Lombardo about the work of correctional officers, as they perceive it. In the foreword to the book, Hans Toch asks, "What makes Lombardo's book different?" and he answers, "He talked to the guards" (cited in Lombardo, 1989:vii). Indeed, before writing the book, Lombardo spent 160 hours inteviewing correctional officers, including fifty officers in 1976 as well as seventeen of those same officers again in 1986, plus five new ones (Lombardo, 1989:v). The officers interviewed all worked at Auburn Correctional Institution in New York, where Lombardo was a prison teacher for six years. Toch points out that because Lombardo is an insider–outsider, he speaks the language and does not make the mistake of replacing old stereotypes about prison with new ones (Lombardo, 1989:xiii).

As prisons go, Auburn is a better place to live and work than most. Auburn provided the "training ground for Thomas Mott Osborne, the well-known prison reformer of the early 1900s" (Lombardo, 1989:8). Through much of its history Auburn has been known for its quality programming. For decades, officers at Auburn took pride in the fact that inmates who wanted an education would be sent there. Increasingly, however, the toughest inmates are sent there. As a result, Auburn is developing a reputation as the institution that handles the most difficult inmates with the lowest number of problems (17). One sign that Auburn is a fairly good place to work is its low turnover of correctional officers: At a time when the comparable turnover rate was 51 percent according to a national study, the turnover at Auburn was only 7.5 percent (137–138).

Nonetheless, as Lombardo's book unfolds, it becomes clear that these officers feel stuck—they do not feel free to leave their job because they lack employment alternatives. Correctional officers feel imprisoned. Like inmates, they develop coping mechanisms for whatever chain binds them most: Some seek active jobs to avoid boredom, others avoid inmates, and yet others avoid administrators by seeking jobs with relatively more autonomy.

LACK OF EMPLOYMENT ALTERNATIVES

People become correctional officers because they want stable jobs with steady pay and good benefits. Indeed, 60 percent of the officers interviewed reported that the pay and job security are the "best" things about the job "for the work we do" or "for the education [level we have attained]" (Lombardo 177–178). It wasn't the nature of the work that attracted them; it was avoiding less attractive work. One officer explains:

> *"I had two uncles and a cousin who worked [at Auburn Prison]. They came home clean, no dirt. They said you didn't really have to work." (29)*

Another officer joined the prison when he was on strike at the plant he worked at previously. He reports that:

> *"I never had a worry since then about layoffs. It takes a load off your mind. I'm secure now. I can go out and do the things I've always wanted to do." (28)*

Although administrators like to tell officers they can "leave" if they don't like it, many officers feel imprisoned financially as much as inmates are imprisoned by the law (138). The officers are not only physically confined, but they feel they cannot leave for better jobs. When asked, 25 percent of the officers said there was "nothing" they would describe as most satisfying about their jobs (177). And 25 percent of the officers originally selected for interviews (13 of 52) never showed up. One said, " 'I don't have any regard for the job. I never did and I don't want to talk about it' " (11).

Many officers actually perceived their careers as a sentence, or, in inmate slang, a "bit." One officer characterized his career as "my 25-to-life bit" (58).

BOREDOM

Inmates report that boredom is a key problem of prison, and it is also a problem for officers. When asked about it, one-third of the officers said boredom is a problem, and some spoke passionately about it (163):

> "Can you stand boredom, idleness? If you can't, don't take the job. I've gone backwards since I started. The job's made me lazy. . . . I found myself having trouble spelling simple words. We just sit and watch." (163)

> "Boredom is one of the greatest killers on the job. It stifles mental growth, it really does. It's not healthy for officers or inmates. It's one of the worst hazards of prison. It leads to laziness and every other bad thing. . . . If my job was all I had to do, I wouldn't know what day it was." (163)

One reflection of officer boredom is officers' reluctance to talk about their work, even with their families. When these male officers were interviewed in their homes, their wives often sat in a nearby room and listened. Afterwards, one wife remarked:

> "He's been an officer for 20 years and this [interview] is the first time I've ever heard him talk about his work." (31)

One officer explained his reluctance to talk about the job, even with his wife:

> "What am I going to say? 'Gee, honey, I looked in three guys' assholes for contraband today?; or 'boy, I

wrote a guy up for taking an extra pork chop.' Hardly exciting stuff." (31)

To cope with boredom, a few officers created unnecessary work and many sought the more active jobs. Some officers create unnecessary work in the form of "elaborately color-coded record-keeping systems," which demand their constant attention. Such record keeping is not required, nor is it likely to bring recognition, but it helps these officers "manage their boredom" (164). When choosing job assignments, the single-most desired characteristic in a job was activity. These officers wanted to experience "fast" eight-hour days (57). To make days go faster, one officer even agreed to work in the kitchen, where inmates are assigned to work as punishment when they have had trouble working anywhere else. This officer says:

> "It's one of the worst jobs and I've got to be crazy to work [in the kitchen], but I thought it would make the job go faster." (58, 96).

To this officer and others like him, anything that made the job go faster, even if it meant more and harder work, was preferable because these guards seemed to fear boredom more than anything else.

PROBLEMS WITH INMATES

When asked to identify the worst or most difficult thing about their jobs, some officers pointed to various problems with working with inmates, especially the potential for violence, and to a lesser degree, the bad attitudes of inmates. Danger and mental tension were seen as the "worst thing" about the job by one-third of officers, and were seen as the "most difficult" aspect of the job by one-fifth. One officer pointed out that violence is not common, but the worry is always there:

> "You can go in there every day for 20 years and never break up a fight, never get assaulted. But the thought's there that it can always happen." (140)

Officers who were hired more recently, when inmate problems were becoming more common, were more likely to apply negative stereotypes to inmates. This stereotyping was unlikely when Lombardo first began his interviews (76, 167). When asked to name the worst thing about the job, one of these recently hired officers discussed his fear of riots:

> *"Knowing collectively that they're animals and that they'll do hideous things to you and to themselves if they get the chance." (167)*

Another officer complained about the stereotyping of guards by inmates:

> *"They don't understand what your job is, but they want you to understand their problems in doing their time. They want officers to take them as individuals, but they take officers as a group." (142)*

Other officers focused on the rudeness of inmates and the difficulties of getting them to cooperate. These officers said the "most difficult" thing was:

> *"Just getting these characters to shower and keep their cells clean. Being able to take a little guff, sarcasm and insults from inmates." (143)*

Guards responded to the difficulties of working with inmates either by learning to handle inmates better, or by seeking jobs with less inmate contact. Some guards responded to the fear—and the other problems of working with inmates—by seeking jobs away from inmates, in the tower or in the administration building. Other officers still wanted to work with inmates, perhaps for the activity it represented, and they coped by learning to effectively exert their authority. These guards report that it took five or ten years to develop an authority that could be established with a new group of inmates in a short period of time. To develop this authority, they recommended that new officers let inmates know who is boss initially, pointing out that officers can always ease up later (94).

TREATMENT BY ADMINISTRATORS

If inmates are seen as a problem by some guards, the administration is seen as a much bigger problem. After interviewing all these guards, Lombardo concludes that:

> *From the guard's perspective, inmates are a relatively minor problem. . . . It is the prison administration that commits a multitude of sins. . . . For the guard, his work is simple, if only the administration would let him do it. (164)*

Officers complain that administrators ignore their ideas and treat them with disregard. Two officers explain how their ideas are commonly ignored:

> *"You can't do anything new, you can't innovate, even if your ideas are better, even if it's common sense. It's frustrating." (147)*

> *"They should compile information from the people actually working the jobs . . . I'm not saying we're always right, but we should at least have a say." (148–149)*

Two other officers explain how administrators treat officers with disregard:

> *"We are professionals, not children. We're men, not complete idiots. Sometimes we're treated like children or mental defectives." (158)*

> *"I don't think they have any regard for the officers. They use you like a number . . . If you complain, they say 'There's the door.' " (158)*

Another officer even laments one way in which officers are not treated as well as inmates:

> *"Why can't our grievances be responded to within fixed time limits like those of inmates[?]; they [the administration] would probably have a lot less problems." (78)*

Some guards coped with the problem of dealing with administrators by seeking jobs where they worked without much supervision, such as on the "tower," and therefore they had more autonomy.

CHANGES OVER TIME

Because Lombardo interviewed correctional officers in both 1976 and 1986, he showed that their situation changed a lot in ten years. When Lombardo interviewed guards in 1976, most came from manufacturing jobs; by 1986, most guards had come from service jobs. On entering the prison, the guards hired in 1986 received formal on-the-job training, with jobs defined by formal policies and procedures rather than informal rules. However, upon becoming correctional officers, these recruits were to experience a greater degree of "negative reality shock" for several reasons (48). Correctional officers in 1976 worried about individual inmate violence; by 1986, they worried about gang violence. The language of corrections had also changed, with punitive philosophies becoming dominant. As a result of all these changes, the social distance between officers and inmates increased.

CONCLUSION

Clearly, if prisons are to be better places to live and work, prison administrators must make further changes, starting with treating officers, and their ideas, with more respect. In the foreword to Lombardo's book, Hans Toch notes that assembly line workers are increasingly charged with planning and rethinking their work, but officers, whose jobs are infinitely more complicated, are treated in stone age management terms (Lombardo, 1989:ix). Indeed, officers have good ideas about the daily operations of prisons, and administrators should establish mechanisms for listening to them. To this end, Lombardo suggests training sessions designed to encourage officers to share information with each other and with the administration. These sessions could provide valuable insights for administrators about the realities of policy implementation, and they might help reduce officers' sense of isolation from each other and from the administration. The interchanges might also give officers a greater stake in prison policies and a greater desire to carry them out (207). It is time to change the way administrators treat officers—this can improve the lot of all those caught up in the prison system, including inmates, officers, and even administrators.

The author thanks Lucien X. Lombardo for his helpful comments on this overview.

REFERENCE

Lombardo, Lucien X. 1989. *Guards Imprisoned: Correctional Officers at Work.* Cincinnati: Anderson.

STUDY QUESTIONS FOR READING 8

1. In the foreword to this book, Toch mentions two ways in which the book is different. What are they, and why?
2. What makes Auburn a better prison to work in than most? How is this shown by lower turnover of officers?
3. Why then do Auburn officers feel imprisoned?
4. Why do people become correctional officers?
5. What other evidence does the author give that suggests officers feel imprisoned by their jobs?
6. What evidence does the author give that suggests officers feel bored?
7. How do officers deal with boredom?
8. Some officers say "working with inmates" is the worst part of the job. Of these officers, what do they complain about most? What else do they complain about?
9. In what two key ways did officers cope with the difficulties of working with inmates?
10. Some officers say "working with administrators" is the worst part of the job, even worse than "working with inmates." What problems does "working with administrators" present?
11. How do some officers cope with the problem of dealing with administrators?
12. What should administrators change about their dealings with officers and why?

LIVING IN A JUVENILE PRISON

CLEMENS BARTOLLAS

Institutionalization is a painful process for most offenders, though it is clearly more painful for some than for others. Persons from different racial or ethnic groups, women, and the mentally ill, often show distinctive patterns of adjustment and breakdown in confinement. Adolescent offenders, too, have special problems and concerns. For most adolescents, imprisonment is an extremely stressful experience, whether they are confined in adult jails or prisons (Cottle, 1977; Toch, 1975; Johnson, 1978), youthful offender prisons (Johnson, 1978), or training schools (Bartollas et al., 1976). In this chapter I examine the psychological survival problems of boys and girls confined in training schools.

As juvenile inmates see it, institutionalization means that they are told when to arise and when to go to bed, are required to eat institutional food, are frequently escorted to institutional activities, are often supervised by uncaring or even brutal staff, are sometimes required to attend religious services, are subjected to various means to remake or rehabilitate them, are made to jump through a number of staff-imposed hoops to be released from their confinement, and are separated from family and friends. All youths experience the stresses of the loss of liberty, the coerciveness of a punishment-oriented environment, and the deprivations of caring relationships they would have in their home communities. Moreover, they find they must learn to make it in a "strong shall survive" setting. From the day they first enter the training school to the day they leave, they will be tested and confronted by predatory peers. If they have learned how to take care of themselves on the streets, it of course becomes easier to cope with juvenile institutionalization. But if they have not, their period of confinement is likely to be difficult and even traumatic. Some in-

stitutional victims make it; some do not and choose to run away, to withdraw into their own world, or even to "hang it up" (commit suicide). In view of what juveniles experience in training schools, it is not surprising that juvenile correctional institutions have more enemies than friends.

To examine more carefully the stresses of institutionalization, this chapter considers the following aspects of confinement: initial traumas, making it with peers, supervision of staff, pains of imprisonment, and coping with confinement. After this review, I will recommend four changes that are needed to make this nation's training schools more humane and less harmful to offenders.

INITIAL TRAUMAS

Youthful offenders hear rumors about state and private juvenile institutions, and sometimes they know youths who have served time in one or more of these facilities. Ranches, farms, and forestry camps usually are considered "easy time," but end-of-the-line facilities frequently provoke considerable anxiety among youths sentenced to them for the first time. The Bartollas et al. (1976, pp. 52–53) study of a maximum security training school for boys in Ohio reported fearful rumors residents had heard about this institution before their arrival:

> *I heard that all the staff were black, and that all the guys were big and tough and they messed over you. I also heard there was a lot of homosexuality up here. And that the institution wasn't together. It was more like a racial problem.*
>
> *I was scared, because when I was at [another institution], everyone was telling me [present institution] was supposed to be a bad place. Everybody was*

getting pushed around, jumped on all the time, fighting all the time, and all of this. Always being locked up, and they said [present institution] was underground.

I heard that when you first came that they took your handcuffs off, then hit you in the head, shaved your head, and beat you up before they put you in your cell in the ground.

That all the students would jump on you and try to get to you, and that all the staff members ever did was beat you up during the time you were here. And that you had to stay here three years.

Initial Interaction with Peers

New admissions are handled in one of three ways: They are placed in an orientation cottage with other new residents, assigned to a cottage that has residents with similar personality characteristics or world views, or assigned to whatever cottage has space for them. All residents then go through a period of testing from other residents; those who are able to stay in an orientation cottage for a few weeks probably run less of a gauntlet than those residents who are immediately sent to whatever cottage has room for them.

Cottage residents are typically experts in sizing up a newcomer. One strong white youth tells how the diagnosis is arrived at:

By the way you talk and the way you act, when they talk to you they find out what you've done and they kind of put it all together in their own little way to determine whether you're bad or not. Whether you can fit in with them or not. If you just seem like some silly little kid off the streets, you're the scapegoat—like a few people in this cottage. If you don't know how to handle yourself, then somebody is always picking on you [Bartollas et al., 1976, p. 54].

New residents are forced to walk a fine line. They must appear strong enough that predatory peers will not exploit them; yet if they put up too big a "front," they know that inmate leaders will look upon them as a threat to their social positions and, therefore, will physically and emotionally test them even more.

But regardless of how good newcomers' skills at impression management are, they will be tested. Predatory peers may demand their institutional food, weekend canteen, food brought from home, or cigarettes. In a juvenile state correctional system in the South, a favorite predatory practice is to line up at the "chow line" ahead of new residents and take all the desired foods before the new inmates arrive at the front of the line. The victimization process sometimes takes more verbally or physically aggressive forms: A youth may be verbally accosted, may be "accidentally," bumped by another, may be "palmed" (grabbed on the buttocks), or may be "sucker punched" (struck in the face or stomach without warning).

Unfortunately, some neophytes are sexually assaulted during this initial period. A black youth in a southern training school was greeted with a "blanket party" during his first few days; a blanket was thrown over his head and he was gang raped. In another southern training school, a girl was grabbed in the shower and three other girls sexually penetrated her with a metal object. A lower-class white in a midwestern training school was sodomized by three black residents and was so shattered by this experience that he suffered a psychological breakdown. Another youth in a midwestern state training school was forced to commit oral sodomy on sixteen youths his second night in the institution.

MAKING IT WITH PEERS

. . .

Race, street sophistication, degree of exploitation experienced within training schools, crimes committed in the community, and personality characteristics are the most important variables affecting the social role adopted by the new resident.

In most juvenile correctional institutions, whites adopt the more passive roles while blacks and other minority groups assume the more aggressive roles. (This is often the case in adult institutions as well.) This means that blacks make up the leadership of the cottage and whites serve as the victims or scapegoats. Street sophistication and previous institutional experience are also important in determining where a youth fits in the cottage pecking order. The streetwise youth knows how to carry himself or herself; this youth knows how to respond to a direct confrontation or challenge. But the first-time offender, instead of knowing the techniques of impression management needed to impress peers, frequently emits fear and anxiety about his or her present placement. Furthermore, the more a youth permits himself or herself to be victimized, the lower this youth will be placed in the social hierarchy of the cottage. For example, the sexual scapegoat is sometimes regarded as a social outcast and is avoided by nonpredatory peers in the cottage. Offense is also of consequence in determining a youth's social standing. The youth who has committed a murder in the community is regarded quite differently than the runaway. One youth put this quite well when he said, "He hasn't done shit! What's he doing here?"

Finally, personality characteristics affect where a youth will fit on the social hierarchy: A resident who exhibits aggressiveness and makes "dominance gestures" will take over highly esteemed roles, but those inmates who are passive and make "submissive gestures" will take over the more unacceptable roles (Mazur, 1973).

This inmate social system causes considerable stress, especially for the less advantaged inmates. Those who have the credentials and desire to adopt more highly esteemed roles know that they must claw their way to the top. If they are confronted verbally or physically, they must retaliate immediately and must be certain that they do not exhibit weakness in any way. To impress peers it may be necessary for them to confront staff, with the consequence of prolonging their institutionalization. Once they have earned highly esteemed roles, they cannot relax because there are always others who desire their social position.

Those who lack the credentials to impress peers are faced with being forced into lowly social positions. Although they are aware that they must avoid victimization, they may not be able to protect themselves against predatory peers. Staff generally offer little help, and may even inform potential victims, "If you are a man, you'll protect yourself." In older male institutions there may be a respected inmate who is willing to protect others against predatory peers, but the price of protection is steep—the protégé must become his "boy" or "sweet boy." A sexual victim finds himself on the last rung of the social hierarchy, nearly engulfed in a social role from which escape is very difficult.

The degradation of victim status presents nearly overwhelming stress to a youth. In a revealing incident, a resident was making fun of a scapegoat one day when the scapegoat, to the surprise of everyone, attacked the supposedly more aggressive youth. In the fight that ensued, the scapegoat clearly got the better of the other youth. Staff locked both youths in their rooms until a disciplinary meeting could be held. The youth who had a higher position in the cottage until the fight tried to commit suicide by setting his room on fire; he clearly preferred to die rather than take the place of the scapegoat. This youth did become the cottage scapegoat and later confessed to a staff member that he was committing oral sodomy on half the youths in the cottage.

The Inmate Code

As is the case with adult prisoners, the inmate social system sometimes develops conduct norms, or an inmate code, that all residents are expected to follow. Bartollas et al. (1976, pp. 63–64) discovered that the general inmate code of the maximum security youth institution consisted of the following tenets: "Exploit whomever you can," "Don't kiss ass," "Don't rat on your peers," "Don't give up your ass," "Be cool," "Don't get involved in another inmate's affairs," "Don't steal 'squares,' " and "Don't buy the mindfucking." In their study of a coeducational correctional system, Sieverdes and Bartollas (1982a) found the existence of the following reference norms: (1) an unwillingness to inform on peers; (2) an expectation that nobody else within the institution is likely to snitch on the respondent or on a third party; (3) a lack of feeling of trust and confidence in staff; (4) a willingness to manipulate and play games against staff members; (5) a perception that staff view the respondent as a troublemaker; and (6) a feeling of antagonism toward staff.

Both McEwen's (1978) study of training schools in Massachusetts before they were closed and Sieverdes and Bartollas's (1982a) study of coeducational training schools in a southeastern state revealed that the widely accepted informal norm was the one against informing, variously called "snatching," "ratting," "finking," or "dime dropping." Sieverdes and Bartollas also found that a number of sexual, racial, and institutional variables affected the response of residents to the code. Black youths usually upheld the informal norms more than did the white and American Indian youths. Black females were somewhat more supportive of the code than black males, while American Indian males generally adopted the code more than white males, white females, and American Indian females. Residents in the maximum security training school also supported the code slightly more than those in the minimum and medium security facilities. Finally, long-termers and the elites supported the code more than short-termers and lower-status types.

Residents are most troubled by the norms of the code that forbid informing on peers and that advocate resisting the supervision of staff. Should a peer "snitch" on another who stole his radio or cigarettes, or should he settle the matter himself? Should a sexually victimized youth "rat" on his exploiter or should he follow the tenet of the code and remain quiet? In terms of "taking on" staff, residents would literally be cutting their own throats because the "keepers" control institutional privileges and usually determine the length of confinement. The ideal solution is to make it appear to peers that the resident is resistant to the control and norms of staff but at the same time convince staff that he or she has changed and is ready to return to the community.

Supervision by Staff

McEwen (1978, pp. 64–66) found in his study of 23 institutional and community-based programs in Massachusetts that organizational arrangements and expectations of staff either increased or reduced the resistance of residents to staff. The most important variables negatively correlated with the resistance of residents to staff were informal exchanges with staff, no isolation cells, no locks on the doors of living units, no limitations on smoking, permission to wear one's own clothing, youthful staff, and ex-offender staff.

In observing juvenile institutions in five states, the same staff patterns consistently appear in living units: one staff member is exemplary with youth, one receives a very negative response and is sometimes involved in brutality if the correctional system permits physical force, and the rest are on the short end of the

ineffectiveness continuum. Exemplary staff members are typically nonprofessionals who are genuinely interested in their charges, have remarkable insight into their needs, are able to reinforce them when it is needed, and are able to discipline them effectively when appropriate.

However, this positive and caring person is usually matched by another staff member who has considerable problems working with adolescents. This person is often overloaded with personal problems and has a tendency to vent repressed anger on residents. The present author has seen these ineffective staff become involved in such incidents as splitting a resident's head open with a pool stick, bashing youths in the head with a flashlight, and giving the room key of a passive inmate to sexual exploiters. These staff members commonly create considerable turmoil among residents; one inmate expressed the sort of angry feelings that are generated when he said, "Man, when I get out of here, I'm going to get that MF."

The remainder of the staff usually came into the institution intending to guide wayward youth back to more constructive lives. However, when they are met with manipulation and hostility rather than appreciation from their charges, they eventually lose interest in their jobs and develop the attitudes of "Don't do more than you get paid for" and "Beat the punishment-oriented system as much as you can."

The supervision patterns of staff pose several problems for the "kept." First, residents quickly discover that staff make all the important decisions relevant to them during their institutional stay. They usually decide when residents will be promoted to the next status or level, when and what privileges will be given, whether or not residents will be permitted home visits, off-campus visits, or work release in the community, and perhaps even when they will be released. Thus it becomes imperative that residents make a "good presentation of self" (Goffman, 1959) to the cottage staff. Most youths handle this challenge by manipulating or "conning" staff (Bartollas et al., 1976; Bartollas & Sieverdes, 1982).

Second, residents are commonly resistant to authority and are therefore apt to resent staff control. Status offenders, especially, are known for their refusal to comply with authority and rules; their typical response to orders is "I ain't going to do it." Sieverdes and Bartollas's (1982b) study of a training school for boys in a southeastern state suggested that the longer a resident remained at the facility, the less likely it was that he would have effective and open communication with staff: 16.7 percent of the early-phase, 37.7 percent of the middle-phase, and 46.3 percent of the late-phase inmates reported that communication with staff was difficult. Sieverdes and Bartollas's (1982a) study of the coeducational training schools in another southeastern state revealed that inmates in the maximum security institution were more hostile to staff than those in minimum and medium security institutions.

Third, inconsistencies among staff members create suspicion and disrespect among residents. Although the institutional rules specify procedures of cottage life, staff members commonly vary in what rules they enforce. For example, one youth supervisor will permit residents to roam the cottage, whereas the other on duty keeps them in one place. The enforcement of rules sometimes varies from one cottage shift to the next, and there is usually also some variation among cottages (McEwen, 1978, p. 71). For example:

> Mr. Simmons does not see the prohibition against smoking, which is an institutional rule, as making much sense. The school rule is that the boys are not allowed to carry their own cigarettes and are only supposed to smoke at specified times during the day, when the masters hand out cigarettes to the boys. The rule at Elms [Mr. Simmons's cottage] is that kids can keep their own cigarettes but that they cannot smoke in specified areas and that they cannot carry cigarettes around the grounds; Mr. Simmons told me that the school superintendent knows of his transgression of the school rule but that he apparently condones it.

On one hand, staff inconsistencies promote gaming and manipulative behavior as residents end up playing one staff member against another. But on the other hand, the lack of consistency in their environment engenders anxiety and insecurity among inmates.

Fourth, because the institutional release process usually depends on the whims and sometimes capricious judgments of cottage staff, this process creates considerable anxiety among residents. Inmates know that they can be turned down for release because of lack of rapport with staff members, for failure to do

their work detail or to keep a neat room, for poor personal hygiene, for an altercation with peers, or for inadequate performance in school. Residents are aware that various staff members may feel differently about their being released and that the vote, therefore, depends on who is present at the meeting. One indignant inmate who spoke about the lack of fairness in the release process summarized consensus when he noted, "You've got to kiss a staff member's ass to get out of here. . . ."

PAINS OF IMPRISONMENT

Recent reforms have removed some of the psychic discomforts of juvenile institutionalization. Required short haircuts have disappeared in most settings. No longer are most residents required to wear drab institutional clothing. Residents also have more privacy in personal correspondence than they had in the past; most staff no longer open outgoing mail and only check incoming mail for contraband. With the establishment of coeducational institutions in some states, residents also enjoy the benefits of a more normal social environment than they had in the past. The typical institutional stay is much shorter than it used to be; indeed, a commitment to a training school may now mean a shorter period of confinement than a disposition to a group home. Training schools also are smaller than they were in the past; the large fortress-like training school holding 600 or more residents has largely passed from the scene.

But some psychic humiliations still remain. Residents are still typically run through showers like cattle and given a limited time to dry. When they first come to the institution and when they return from each trip off campus, residents still receive a strip search. The food varies in quantity and quality from institution to institution, but it is generally starchy and bland. Although being locked in one's room at night with an emergency pail is humiliating enough, it can be a terrifying ordeal if residents become ill and are unable to convince staff that they need medical attention. Youths have nearly died at night because of their inability to convince staff that they had a genuine medical problem. Inmates who become sexual victims must deal with this devastating blow to their self-esteem, and must worry that the news of their "degradation status" may be spread around their home communities. One youth, in this regard, said:

> I'm afraid of going home. I'm afraid that it's all around the neighborhood what I've done here. If my mother and brothers and sisters find out about it, I couldn't handle it.

The emotional deprivations of institutional life are among the sharpest pains of imprisonment. In the junglelike setting of many training schools, inmates know that they must constantly guard against "bogarting" peers who bully and push them around. They are aware that the best way to handle institutional life is to keep their distance from others. Some youths are fortunate to have an occasional visit from their parents; other youths have no contact with those at home. It becomes painful to display photographs of a girlfriend or sister when other residents can make derogatory sexual comments about them. Boyfriends or girlfriends are sometimes not even permitted to visit because they are underage. The sexual deprivations of confinement are a painful factor of institutional life because most incarcerated youths have had more or less regular sexual relations since their early teens or so.

The memory of good times in the community is also considered a pain of confinement. Many youthful offenders, especially those who have dropped out of school, stay up a good part of the night and sleep until the late afternoon. They enjoy loafing with friends, listening to music, playing pool, and committing their capers. They often are free to come and go as they please because of the laxity of home supervision. Juvenile offenders, most of whom abused drugs in the community, particularly miss "getting high" because few residents are as resourceful as adult prisoners in getting drugs smuggled into the facility or in making alcohol.

"Prison time" becomes extremely hard to handle the final few weeks before release. It is painful for a youth to be locked up for any length of time, much less for many months or several years. Time goes by very slowly, aggravated by the typically monotonous daily existence of training school life. But when a youth receives his or her release date, time becomes

even harder to handle. Allen (1969, p. 300) describes the experience:

> When a boy is within a few weeks or a few months of release, either on parole or on mandatory release, he becomes a "short timer.". . . He counts the days remaining and tells the others, which is called "signifying" and for which he is chided in a good-natured way by the other boys. This often initiates a period of considerable turmoil, during which many seek out a staff member—sometimes the psychiatrist. There is depression at leaving one's friends, the institution, the staff, the ordered and well-looked-after existence, and the place one has made for oneself. There is anxiety at returning to the community, family, wife, or nothing at all, depending on the case. Initially, there is jubilation and a false sense of euphoria; however, insomnia, hyperactivity, and nightmares indicate that this is a dysphoria rather than a euphoria. A general withdrawal and depression may develop, and irritability, fighting, and generally impulsive behavior may occur.

COPING WITH CONFINEMENT

The Bartollas et al. (1976) study of a maximum-security training school for boys in the Midwest found that most residents exhibited the following emotions about their confinement: righteous indignation, rage, fear and anxiety, shame and humiliation, and despair and hopelessness. The ways in which inmates attempted to cope with their confinement depended largely upon which of these emotions was the strongest.

The most popular mode of adaptation was making the most of institutional life. Residents attempted to satisfy their creature comforts with this adaptation: They tried to get more food, to find ways to avoid unpleasant talks, and to be given all possible institutional privileges. Inmate leaders were the most effective in getting their needs met.

The least popular way to cope with institutional life was to adopt prosocial attitudes and to use the training school experience to prepare for the future; only a few youths over a period of four years were receptive to this mode. A third mode of adaptation was to "play it cool." The inmate was simply "doing time" and gave allegiance to neither staff nor peers. He learned to keep his emotions under control and to do whatever was necessary to shorten the institutional stay.

Rebellion was a fourth way of coping with the training school; in this mode, inmates confronted staff in every possible way. They were filled with rage toward their confinement and instigated others to rebel against staff, to stage a protest, and even to set institutional fires. Withdrawal, another extreme type of adaptation, was usually accompanied by feelings of anxiety, humiliation, and hopelessness. Whites were more prone to this mode of coping than blacks, and victims were the most likely of all to withdraw. Runaway behavior was the favorite means of withdrawal, but other means included drugs, mental breakdown, and suicide (Bartollas et al., 1976, pp. 172–178).

POSSIBLE INTERVENTIONS

It is not difficult to understand why training schools have few friends. There is too much truth in the accusations that they are inhumane and unsafe for residents, that they are schools for crime, and that they are prohibitively expensive. Improvements in juvenile correctional institutions must include steps to assure that they are safe for all offenders, provide positive experiences for residents, enlarge the personal and group decision-making responsibilities of residents, and normalize the atmosphere as much as possible.

The safety of training schools is a first priority. Society is responsible for providing safe settings in which inmates will not be victimized or intimidated by either peers or staff. Some institutions are safer than others, some racial groups are safer than others, and some staff are better than others in protecting residents. But in conducting empirical studies in three states and in interviewing institutional residents in two other states, this author has not found a single training school that adequately protects residents.

How can training schools be made safe? Staff appear to be the most important variable. Some staff are very skillful in protecting residents but, unfortunately, many do not care. The amount of indefensible space also becomes an important variable because predatory peers can use indefensible space to victimize peers. Finally, the more staff can help to turn around the

"strong shall survive" nature of the peer culture, the safer the institution will be.

Second, training schools must provide positive experiences for residents. A good relationship with a concerned staff member can help generate a lot of positive feelings in a youth. To learn social survival skills, to develop vocational and educational skills, and to gain positive feelings from doing something well are other constructive experiences that confined offenders usually need. Some residents have felt good about their involvement in a sailing program or a wilderness experience, in a treatment modality such as transactional analysis (TA), or in a vocational shop experience such as automotive design, printing, or welding.

Providing more opportunities for decision making and making offenders responsible for their behavior is a third reform that is needed in most training schools. The danger, of course, is that increasing the amount of responsibility given to residents might result in their creating more of a lawless society within the walls. However, the effective staff person can usually determine when a youth is ready to accept greater responsibility. The development of a logical consequences model, in which residents are taught the consequences of behavior, may be a step in the establishment of a more responsible peer culture.

Finally, correctional administrators should make every effort to simulate a normal atmosphere within the institution. Coeducational institutions are a good beginning because they constitute a more normal setting than a single-sex institution. Frequent contacts with the community, with residents going to the community and with the community (family, friends, and volunteers) coming to the residents, are also necessary in order to make training schools more humane.

SUMMARY

The average training school is clearly better today than it was a decade ago. However, there is still evidence that these long-term juvenile institutions do damage to many residents. The stresses of confinement begin when a youth hears that he or she has been committed to a training school; they do not end until the youth establishes some semblance of a satisfying community adjustment upon release. Some youths have the credentials to handle the stresses of confinement; other residents find confinement an extremely painful experience. The goals of policymakers must be to make juvenile institutions as humane as possible and to create as little pain as possible for those confined within them. A society that supposedly cares about youth must do a better job of confining those who need secure detention.

REFERENCES

Allen, T. E. Psychiatric observations on an adolescent inmate social system and culture. *Psychiatry,* 1969, 32, 292–302.

Bartollas, C., Miller, S. J., & Dinitz, S. *Juvenile victimization: The institutional paradox.* New York: Halsted, 1976.

Bartollas, C., & Sieverdes, C. M. *Institutional games played by confined juveniles.* Unpublished manuscript, 1982.

Breed, A. Inmate subcultures. *California Youth Authority,* 1963, 16, 6–7.

Cottle, T. J. *Children in jail.* Boston: Beacon, 1977.

Goffman, E. *The presentation of self in everyday life.* Garden City, NY: Doubleday, 1959.

Johnson, R. Youth in crisis: Dimensions of self-destructive conduct among adolescent prisoners. *Adolescence,* 1978, 13, 461–482.

McEwen, C. A. *Designing correctional organizations for youths: Dilemmas of subcultural development.* Cambridge, MA: Ballinger, 1978.

Mazur, A. A cross-species comparison of status in small established groups. *American Sociological Review,* 1973, 38, 513–530.

Sieverdes, C. M., & Bartollas, C. *Adherence to an inmate code in minimum, medium, and maximum security juvenile institutions.* Unpublished manuscript, 1982. (a)

Sieverdes, C. M., & Bartollas, C. *Coping and adjustment patterns among institutionalized juvenile offenders.* Unpublished manuscript, 1982. (b)

Toch, H. *Men in crisis: Human breakdowns in prison.* Chicago: Aldine, 1975.

STUDY QUESTIONS FOR READING 9

1. What does institutionalization mean to juvenile inmates?

2. What is the fine line that new residents are forced to walk? What kind of tests may they face?

3. Explain how race, being streetwise, and personality affect the social role of incarcerated youth.

4. In the inmate culture, how do youth climb to the more highly esteemed roles?

5. Tell the story of the scapegoat who traded places with another resident.

6. What is the ideal solution for inmates in regard to resisting staff at the same time they impress staff?

7. Explain each of the three types of staff that the author observed over and over again in juvenile institutions in five states.

8. Residents in a maximum security training facility for boys coped in five ways. What were they? Which was the most popular? Which was the least popular?

9. According to the author, how should training schools be changed?

LIFE *IN THE BELLY OF THE BEAST*

ROBERT JOHNSON

Sociological portraits of the state-raised convict depict him as a man at home in the prison, inured to its abuses and coldly dispensing violence to achieve his selfish ends. He typically moves in predatory cliques, but whether alone or in gangs he is adept at exploiting the weak and defenseless. He finds sexual gratification in the violation of other men; paradoxically, these encounters prove his manliness. He succeeds as a convict because the prison is the only world he knows.

> *He was raised in a world where "punks" and "queens" have replaced women, "bonaroos" [specially pressed prison outfits] are the only fashionable clothing, and cigarettes are money. This is a world where disputes are settled with a pipe or a knife, and the individual must form tight cliques for protection. His senses are attuned to iron doors banging, locks turning, shakedowns, and long lines of [uniformed] convicts. He knows how to survive, in fact prosper, in the world, how to get a cell change and a good work assignment, how to score for nutmeg, cough syrup, or other narcotics. More important, he knows hundreds of youths like himself who grew up in the youth prisons and are now in the adult prisons. (Irwin, 1970:74)*

State-raised convicts adapt to prison life and even dominate the public culture of the prison, but they are by no means immune to the pains and deprivations of confinement. In fact, many of these men are deeply scarred by a life of imprisonment, and these wounds are apparent in the lives they lead in the prison world.

The most striking thing about state-raised convicts is their facade of adult maturity, their veneer of cool, hard manliness. Yet this demeanor and their sometimes casual use of violence are not badges of strength, but tragic testimony to the violence prison has done to them. They were reared in a world where they were susceptible to flagrant abuse. More than other prisoners, they know in their guts what it means to be locked up—to be "helpless and vulnerable" and hence at the "matrix of disaster" while in the arms of the law. In the words of Jack Abbott (1981:12), in many ways to prototype of the state-raised convict,

> *He who is state-raised—reared by the state from an early age after he is taken from what the state calls a "broken home"—learns over and over and all the days of his life that people in society can do anything to him and not be punished by the law. Do anything to him with the full force of the state behind them.*

Abbott speaks with some authority in this matter for, sad to say, Abbott's credentials as a state-raised youth are unimpeachable.[1] His life is a study in neglect and abuse, in the free world and in the prison (see Nusser, 1982). His parents separated when he was quite young, breaking up what was a turbulent and no doubt abusive home. He was passed from one foster home to another over a period of years, during which time he was physically beaten and sexually abused. He dropped out of school after the sixth grade. Within a year, "he was committed to the Utah State Industrial School for Boys for 'failing to adjust.' He was twelve years old. He stayed there until his release at age eighteen" (Nusser, 1982:560). His adjustment never improved. If anything, his lengthy stay in training school—most juveniles serve short terms—indicates that his adjustment worsened over time.

Abbott's marginal adjustment to life continued into adulthood. On release he developed a drinking problem. He issued fraudulent checks, for which he was sent to prison. In prison, as a young adult, he appears to have fully cultivated his propensity to violence.

While serving his court-imposed sentence, Abbott stabbed another inmate to death for informing on him. He was convicted and sent back to prison with an additional twenty years, but not before throwing a water pitcher at the judge and trying to choke one of the jurors. (Nusser, 1982:560)

At one point Abbott escaped from prison briefly, robbed a bank, and was confined once again with an additional nineteen years to serve. At this point his fate was sealed. He was truly a state-raised man, a product of institutions. "Uncaring and impersonal, each of these institutions compounded and passed on responsibility for the problem" (Nusser, 1982:560).

A substantial part of "the problem" in Abbott, and in other state-raised convicts, is chronic defensiveness. Abbott assumes a tough and menacing pose because he is angry and frightened, and because he sees no other way to keep a hostile and rejecting world at bay. And because this world is almost a caricature of the abusive worlds that spawn the chronic felons who later come to share adult prisons with him, the state-raised convict typically becomes the most impulsive of prison's hasty hedonists, the most cunning and lethal of its jungle cats.

The state-raised convict's predatory pose has a distinctively adolescent character. And for good reason. Prison life equates the normal dependency of childhood with vulnerability and makes adult independence impossible. Life on these terms is likely to leave the prisoner emotionally stunted, a perpetual, impulsive adolescent. "You hear a lot about 'arrested adolescence' nowadays," observes Abbott (1981:13), "and I believe this concept touches the nub of the instability of prisoners like myself." The state-raised prisoner, Abbott continues, does not have a chance to mature normally. "As a boy in reform school, he is punished for being a little boy. In prison, he is punished for trying to be a man" (Abbott, 1981:14). At best, "he is treated as an adolescent in prison" (Abbott, 1981:15).

Abbott's point has been made before, notably by Sing Sing's Warden Lawes, who quotes an English penal authority who observed the "the trouble with the American Reformatory idea"—an idea that shaped many of the prisons that shaped Abbott—"was that it made youths out of adults and adults out of youths, subjecting both to all the odious and cruel oppressions that prevailed in prisons for men steeped in crime and viciousness" (Lawes, 1932:36). More recently, Zamble, Porporino, and Kalotay's research supports Abbott's analysis of the chronic prisoner's adolescent character. "Imprisonment," they found,

deprives people of the usual experience necessary for the development of coping, and in this way it freezes development at the point when a person enters the institution. Thus, we can see why the behavior of habitual offenders resembles that of adolescents in many ways, e.g., in the dependence on peer groups, emphasis on physical dominance, and [a] generally impulsive behavioral style. It also follows that imprisonment at an early age will have more effect on subsequent behavior than at a later time, since that is when the greater development is normally occurring. Finally, we can also predict that those who have spent the most time in prison will be those who cope most poorly when they are on the outside. (Zamble, Porporino & Kalotay, 1984:137).

The result for the state-raised convict, in Abbott's (1981:15) words, is that "he lacks experience and, hence, maturity. His judgment is untempered, rash; his emotions are impulsive, raw, unmellowed" (see also Myers & Ley, 1978; Higgins & Thies, 1981).

The "raw" emotions of the state-raised convict are not those of the typical adolescent, however. Unlike adolescents in the free world, prison's adolescents have never been taken seriously or cared for as individuals. These prisoners, then, are not only consigned to a lifetime of adolescence, a painful experience in itself, but are also burdened with chronic self-doubt, the often crippling corollary of rejection that reads, "I must be unlovable if I am unloved; I must be bad to be treated badly." Moreover, it is likely that this self-doubt will escalate over time and become personally disabling. A lifetime in prison means emotional and sometimes physical abuse. These experiences produce a legacy of impotent rage (because one is helpless to defend oneself) and ultimately self-hatred (a product of one's sense of shame and contamination). The result, in Abbott's view, is a kind of "prison paranoia" that reduces one's life to a daily struggle to maintain sanity and self-control.

> *When I walk past a glass window in the corridor and happen to see my reflection, I get angry on impulse. I feel shame and hatred at such times. When I'm forced by circumstances to be in a crowd of prisoners, it's all I can do to refrain from attack. I feel such hostility, such hatred, I can't help this anger. All these years I have felt it. Paranoid. I can control it. I never seek a confrontation. I have to intentionally gauge my voice in a conversation to cover up the anger I feel, the chaos and pain just beneath the surface of what we commonly recognize as reality. Paranoia is an illness I contracted in institutions. It is not the reason for my sentences to reform school and prison. It is the effect, not the cause. (1981:5)*

To my knowledge, Abbott has never been diagnosed as a paranoid psychotic, though this diagnosis is unusually common among prison populations.[2] Yet Abbott is, like all paranoids, profoundly self-centered; his fragile sense of self is always hanging in the balance. His personality is marred by suspicion of others, doubt in himself, and an ugly festering rage and hate that touch virtually everything and everyone in his world. There is no rest for Abbott, no chance to let his defenses down. His image in the mirror is simply a poignant reflection of the continuing struggle he must wage against the pain of the prison world and the hurt he carries within himself.

Prisons thus raise men who are as much at war with themselves as with the world around them. On both fronts they are threatened: internally, with the knowledge of their inadequacy; externally, with the knowledge of their vulnerability. Failure in social encounters, even the slightest hint of defeat, at once exposes their weaknesses to themselves and others. To guard against this, they must avenge even the slightest insult that might cast doubt on their manliness, brook any authority that would curtail their sense of self. To do less, as they see it, is to be demeaned as a man (see Abbott, 1981:78–79).

The difficulty is that encounters in which such a fragile notion of dignity might be shattered are quite common in prison. Prisoners vie for status and routinely make invidious comparisons among themselves; guards issue and enforce countless orders every day. Under this continuing assault upon their self-esteem—for state-raised convicts, such encounters feel like personal attacks—state-raised convicts readily come to see themselves as innocent victims of an arbitrary world who have no choice but to strike out in their own defense. Their behavior is, for the most part, wildly disproportionate to the objective pressures at hand. Sadly, their justifications for their conduct are transparently false and self-serving to everyone but themselves.

Perhaps the root of the problem with state-raised convicts, and why so many of them appear as pathetic but dangerous adolescents, is that they simply cannot see the world from the other person's point of view. At best, others emerge as pale reflections of their own inner worlds, as persons distorted by the the same forces that shaped and ultimately distorted the prisoners themselves. Thus Abbott sees others as contemptible, just as he holds himself in contempt, and as sources of danger, just as he knows the danger within himself. The state-raised youth's dealings with others routinely involve manipulation and deception; that is, he believes, what others deserve and what is required to succeed in life. Yet these stratagems typically fail, at least in one's dealings with other savvy state-raised convicts, and hence one must fall back on violence as the final measure of worth.

Prisoners like Abbott are all the more dangerous, moreover, because the lesson they learn from their redundant interpersonal failures is that violence is in fact their *only* means of becoming men of consequence who are taken seriously. Life is reduced to an either/or proposition: either you or me. As a result, these men have a personal stake in violence, and they protect it jealously. Thus Abbott (1981:15 & 149–50) speaks almost reverently of

> *the high esteem we naturally have for violence, force. It is what makes us effective, men whose judgment impinges on others, on the world: Dangerous killers who act alone and without emotion, who act with calculation and principles, to avenge themselves, establish and defend their principles with acts of murder that usually evade prosecution by law; this is the state-raised convicts' conception of manhood, in the highest sense. . . . Here in prison the most respected and hon-*

*ored men among us are those who have killed other
men. . . . It is not merely fear, but respect.*

One such prisoner bragged to a television reporter
about the raw, brutal violence he had used to kill a
guard, who had been chosen at random, merely to impress other convicts. He concluded by saying, on cam-
era, "This has just begun for me. I'm only thirty-one
years old. I got a lot of bodies to collect yet" (Early,
1992:305).

Abbott sees his violence as a dignified, one might
almost say solemn, obligation of manhood. This self-
serving view is no doubt shared by other convicts and
helps them to glorify their explosive tantrums. (If this
sounds harsh, remember that Abbott himself traced
the "nub" of his character to "arrested adolescence.")
This violence does in fact command respect from
other prisoners, but on the grounds that its authors are
the most unrestrained, emotionally immature, and
hence dangerous men in the institution. There is even
an awareness among the prisoners that this behavior
reflects a kind of mental instability not far from Abbott's conception of prison paranoia. In the words of
Schroeder (1976:23), an ex-inmate,

> *if you clearly didn't care, if you could convince in-
> mates and guards that you had absolutely nothing to
> lose and that your countermeasures to even the most
> trivial provocation would be totally unrestrained and
> pursued to the utmost of your abilities—then you were
> given respect and a wide berth, and people looked to
> you for leadership and advice. "He's crazy," they'd
> say admiringly, even longingly, when the name came
> up. "He's just totally, completely insane."*

Hence it is that the prisoners who are least equipped
for life in the civil world set the tone of adjustment on
the prison yard.

The threat of violence, even lethal violence, is a
salient norm in the convict world. It begins at the
point of entry into the prison, when the young convict must protect himself from the predations of others. But the use of violence to establish one's manly
image never stops here, even if one humiliates one's
opponents (see Abbott, 1981:93–94). Violence continues because there is no mechanism within the
convict culture that allows prisoners to make peace
with one another, to break with the violence of the

past and embark on a nonviolent future. Convicts,
ever on the defensive, felt they must draw lines in
the prison yard, as it were, demarcating that point beyond which others cannot cross for fear of retaliatory
violence; to do less is to live without principle or
honor in the prison community (see Early, 1992:186).
The difficulty is that for many convicts, the very
presence of such lines is an open invitation to test the
prisoner's mettle, to see if he will in fact defend himself. The drawing and crossing of lines of permissible
behavior occur endlessly in the prison community,
leaving in their wake a history of insult and retaliation that seems endless. . . .

The convict world is populated by men who
doubt their worth as human beings, and who feel they
must constantly find occasions to "prove" themselves.
In this world, there is no such thing as an accident, and
hence "there are no innocent bystanders." Here, Lip-
man continues, "paranoia is nothing more than increased awareness" (Bruchac, 1984:193). While an
apology may often suffice to resolve a conflict among
regular inmates (see Cooley, 1992:36), being a convict is, apparently, never having to say you are sorry,
and certainly never accepting an apology at face value
because it is almost certainly a ploy, a trick. For convicts, every insult is premeditated, a planned assault
demanding a vengeful response that provides tangible
evidence of one's worth. The only proofs of worth that
matter in this context are those that entail the subjugation of other men.

The convict world is a world of continuing—and
generally escalating—conflict. Aggrieved parties cannot afford to back down, for then they are seen as
weak and hence vulnerable to more abuse. Violence
in the convict world establishes one's competence as a
man who can survive in a human jungle. The ultimate
paradox of this world is that only lethal violence can
truly assure one's peace of mind:

> *To a prisoner it is an insult to grapple hand-to-hand
> with anyone. If someone ever strikes him with his hand
> (another prisoner), he has to kill him with a knife. If he
> doesn't he will be fistfighting with him everyday. He
> might be killed. . . . All violence in prison is geared for
> murder, nothing else. You can't have someone with ill
> feelings for you walking around. He could drop a knife
> in you any day. . . . . [Y]ou are not killing in physical*

self-defense. You're killing someone in order to live respectably in prison. Moral self-defense. (Abbott, 1981:88–89)

As simple and straightforward as this code of violence may be, the notion that when in doubt, one should hurt or kill one's neighbor produces a bleak and solitary prison "community" in which "most prisoners fear almost every other prisoner around them" (Abbott, 1981:85). In fact, in the convict world,

> Everyone *is afraid. It is not an emotional, psychological fear. It is a practical matter. If you do not threaten someone at the very least someone will threaten you. When you walk across the yard or down the tier to your cell, you stand out like a sore thumb if you do not appear either callously unconcerned or cold and ready to kill. Many times you have to "prey" on someone, or you will be "preyed" on yourself. After so many years,* you are not bluffing. *No one is. (Abbott, 1981:144).*

In the convict world, day-to-day relations among prisoners are at best distant and tense, with simple co-existence a major achievement. One is vividly reminded of Sartre's notion of hell as a circumscribed world with "no exit," and hence no escape from people you hold in contempt.

> *You don't comfort one another; you humor one another. You extend that confusion about this reality of one another by lying to one another. You can't stand the sight of each other and yet you are doomed to stand and face one another every moment of every day for years without end. You must bathe together, defecate and urinate together, eat and sleep together, talk together, work together. (Abbott, 1981:102)*

To be sure, other prisoners may feel less bitter than Abbott, but the quality of their interpersonal relations with fellow prisoners is often much the same.

Relations between convicts and staff are, if anything, even worse. (There is no exit here either.) Convicts' perceptions of guards are suffused with resentment. Officers are hacks who comprise a monolithic caste of oppressors; the convicts are their hapless victims. The standard notion that is "us" against "them" doesn't fully capture the animosity the state-raised convict feels toward his keepers. "Us" against "that" comes closer to the mark.

> *Among themselves, the guards are human. Among themselves, the prisoners are human. Yet between these two the relationship is not human. It is animal. Only in reflection—subjective reflection—do they acknowledge sharing a common consciousness. What is that common consciousness? It is the consciousness that we belong to a* common species *of life. But this is not the consciousness of society. It is not humanistic; it is animalistic.*
>
> *What I am saying is that the prisoner is closer to humanity than the guard: because he is* deprived *by the guard. That is why I say that evil exists—not in the prisoner, but in the guard. Intentions play none but an illusory role. In fact, the guard is evil. His* society *is demonic. I don't care if he likes the same food I do or the same music—or whatever: this is the illusory role intentions play. Animals can enjoy the same music or food we do. (Abbott, 1981:70–71)*

It is almost as if the state-raised convict is impelled into destructive encounters with his keepers. When they treat him in a standard but impersonal way, this is an affront. When they vary their treatment of prisoners, they are revealed as arbitrary tyrants (see Abbott, 1981:65–66). One senses that guards, by the very exercise of authority, imperil the state-raised convict's tenuous sense of autonomy. The prisoner's only course of action, then, is to rebel and deny the possibility of legitimate prison authority—to "beat the man" by breaking every rule you can, all the while nurturing an unremitting hatred for them and everything they stand for (see Earley, 1992:282–83). This stance has both tragic and comic elements, and both are grasped by Abbott.

> *It's impossible. I'm the kind of fool who, facing Caesar and his starving lions, need only retract a statement to walk away scot-free but instead cannot suppress saying "fuck you" to Caesar—knowing full well the consequences. What is more, I refuse to be* martyred: *I don't accept the consequences, and whine all the way to my death. A death, it seems, that I chose.*
>
> *If I could* please *Caesar, I would, I gladly would. It's a fucked-up world, but it's all I got. (Abbott, 1981:18)*

The punishment system within the prison that is invoked to handle these degenerating encounters is, as the state-raised convict sees it, by definition a sham, a mockery of any notion of justice (see Abbott,

1981:139–40). The prisoner knows himself to be helpless before a powerful and malevolent opponent whose goal is to crush one's manhood. Still he rebels and gets the worst punishments prisons have to offer. This includes, in at least some instances, flagrant acts of brutality.

Abbott, for instance, records a litany of punishments comprised of lengthy solitary confinement, mind-altering drugs, and overt physical violence (1981:44–45). These punishments have almost certainly been embellished with time, but the more important point is that in no instance can Abbott see his own role in precipitating these abuses, even though he freely admits to insulting and even attacking "the pigs" at will. Nor can he put himself in the shoes of his punishers or even acknowledge the pain and rage that move them to primitive violence. Always he is utterly innocent; always they are unremittingly brutal. He suffers—and he does suffer—but somehow they only mete out pain. If he errs at all, as Abbott sees things, it is in being too stubbornly faithful to the convict code of manliness even as he nurses his wounds.

There is a saying: The first cut is the deepest. *Do not believe that. The first cut is nothing. You can spit in my face once or twice and it is nothing. You can take something away that belongs to me and I can learn to live without it.*

But you cannot spit in my face every day for ten thousand days; you cannot take all that belongs to me, one thing at a time, until you have gotten down to reaching for my eyes, my voice, my hands, my heart. You can't do this and say it is nothing.

I have been made oversensitive—my very flesh *has been made to suffer sensations and longings I never had before. I have been chopped to pieces by a life of deprivation of sensations; by beatings so frequent I am now a piece of meat and bone; by lies and by drugs that attack my nervous system. I have had my mind turned into steel by the endless smelter of* time *in confinement.*

I have been twisted by justice the way other men can be twisted by love. (Abbott, 1981:44–45)

The hurt generated by these encounters seems endless, and still there is no effort on Abbott's part to learn from them, to approach problems differently in the future.

ENDNOTES

1. Many of the more telling and tragic observations made by Abbott about the life of the state-raised youth are confirmed and amplified in the work of Dwight Edgar Abbot (1991).

2. The prison is "rigidly hierarchical and routinized, cold and impersonal" (Johnson, 1976:111). As such, it "parallels the classic paranoid image of conspiratorial control" (Johnson, 1976:111). Psychiatric research reveals that prison attracts a disproportionate number of people with paranoid dispositions and then reinforces their suspicious worldview. Prison also independently creates this disposition. Diagnosis and treatment of prison paranoia are therefore difficult, because the adaptive and maladaptive aspects of paranoid views may be hard to separate (see Thurrell, Halleck & Johnson, 1965; and Hamburger, 1967).

REFERENCES

Abbot, D. E. *I Cried, You Didn't Listen: A Survivor's Exposé of the California Youth Authority.* Portland, OR: Feral House, 1991.

Abbott, J. H. *In the Belly of the Beast.* New York: Vintage, 1981.

Bruchac, J. (ed.). *The Light From Another Country: Poetry From American Prisons.* New York: Greenfield Review Press, 1984.

Cooley, M. "Prison victimization and the informal rules of social control." *Forum on Corrections Research* 4(3) 1992:31–36.

Earley, P. *The Hot House: Life Inside Leavenworth.* New York: Bantam Books, 1992.

Hamburger, E. "The penitentiary and paranoia." *Correctional Psychiatry and Journal of Social Therapy* 13(4) 1967:225–30.

Irwin, J. *The Felon.* Englewood Cliffs, NJ: Prentice-Hall, 1970.

Johnson, R. *Culture and Crisis in Confinement.* Lexington: Lexington Books, 1976.

Lawes, L. E. *Twenty Thousand Years in Sing Sing.* New York: Ray Long and Richard R. Smith, 1932.

Myers, L., and G. W. Levy. "Description and prediction of the intractable inmate." *Journal of Research in Crime and Delinquency* 15(2) 1978:214–28.

Nusser, N. "The epitome of failure: Jack Abbott." *Crime and Delinquency* 28(4) 1982:557–66. (Note that various inmate writers are featured in this article.)

Schroeder, A. *Shaking It Rough.* Garden City, NY: Doubleday, 1976:23.

Thurrell, R. J., S. L. Halleck, and A. F. Johnson. "Psychosis in prison." *The Journal of Criminology and Police Science* 56(3) 1965:271–76.

Zamble, E., F. Porporino and J. Kalotay. *An Analysis of Coping Behavior in Prison Inmates.* Ministry of the Solicitor General of Canada: Programs Branch User Report, 1984.

STUDY QUESTIONS FOR READING 10

1. How was Jack Abbott parented? When did he drop out of school? When was he first incarcerated and for how many years?

2. Once released from reform school, Abbott developed a drinking problem and committed a crime. What was the first crime? What was the second crime? How did he behave in the courtroom?

3. Johnson argues that prison life makes it difficult to grow up emotionally: It freezes development. What does Abbott say about this?

4. In addition to remaining immature, state-raised youth are full of self-hatred. Why? And to what extent?

5. Inmates feel that, to guard against seeming weak, they must avenge even the slightest insult that might cast doubt on their manliness. To do less is to demean themselves as a man. What is the problem they immediately encounter? How do they come to see themselves?

6. For state-raised youths, violence is the *only* means of being taken seriously as a man. What are some of the results of this in terms of who is respected, the use of apologies, and the escalation of violence?

7. Abbott felt that because he had been victimized he had a right to violate others. He could not comprehend that he had no such right. Explain in terms of his behavior upon release.

8. What is the real tragedy of Jack Abbott, and how can the cycle of violence be broken?

THE HOLE: SOLITARY CONFINEMENT

JACK ABBOTT

There is only *one man* in a cell in the hole for it to really be "the hole." There are rows of cells on a tier, but in the hole—the genuine hole—no two prisoners are ever out of their cells at the same time.

There are always voices in the hole. It's a strange thing. I have seen *wars* take place in the hole. I have seen sexual love take place in the hole. I have seen, as a matter of fact, the most impossible things *happen* under these conditions. Let us say a kind of movement that is not really movement exists there. To illustrate: to walk ten miles in an enclosed space of ten feet is not really movement. There are not ten miles of space, only time. You do not go ten miles. To write about the hole, in other words, I would have to explore such common places.

. . . I have been dragged to the hole fighting back many times. I was once carried to the hole in Leavenworth by the security force (goon squad). My hands were cuffed behind me. A pig about six feet two inches who weighed about two hundred and fifty pounds was the boss. He was about forty-five, but he was hard as a rock. The pigs had me face down on the concrete floor, punching and kicking me. It was exactly like a pack of dogs on me. The big one, the boss, ordered me to stand up. He motioned to the others to stand back—and I swear to God, you won't believe this, he knocked my clothes off me with a few swipes of his hands.

The cloth tore my skin like knife cuts. I hit the floor, he hit my shoes (high tops) and knocked them off (broke the laces). All through this thing I tried to keep my head by acting passive and smiling. I thought they were so afraid of me it made them animals, which was true, but I couldn't calm them. That was the time they threw me face down in a dungeon cell.

They stood on me while one unhandcuffed me. The pig who knocked my clothes off was the last to leave the cell. I heard them back out of the cell and I rolled over onto my side. I was hurting everywhere. Well, this pig, who had seemed the least emotional of them all, had his cock out and his face was wrinkled up in a grin and he kind of bounced up and down by bending his knees. He was pretending to jerk off. Then he zipped his fly and left the cell kind of chuckling.

. . . You sit in solitary confinement stewing in nothingness, not merely your own nothingness but the nothingness of society, others, the world. The lethargy of months that add up to years in a cell, alone, entwines itself about every "physical" activity of the living body and strangles it slowly to death, the horrible decay of truly living death. You no longer do push-ups or other physical exercises in your small cell; you no longer pace the four steps back and forth across your cell. You no longer masturbate; you can call forth no vision of eroticism in any form, and your genitals, like the limbs of your body, function only to keep your body alive.

Time descends in your cell like the lid of a coffin in which you lie and watch it as it slowly closes over you. When you neither move nor think in your cell, you are awash in pure nothingness.

Solitary confinement in prison can alter the ontological makeup of a stone.

. . . My years in solitary confinement altered me more than I care to admit, even to myself. But I will try to relate the experience, because you're understanding, and what you do not understand is only what you cannot because *you* have not experienced the hole for years. You *listen* and that is all that counts.

It is hard for me to begin. Beginnings are like that for me now.

But something happens down there in the hole, something like an event, but this event can only occur over a span of years. It cannot take place in time and space the way we ordinarily know them.

Not many prisoners have experienced this event. It *never* fails: most prisoners I know who have been in prison off and on all their lives will tell you they have served *five years* in the hole. Everyone is lying, and I do not know why they must say they served *five years* in the hole. Why *five years?* I cannot understand why that particular duration occurs to all of them. They do not say "I served *four years* or *three years*"—nor even six or seven years. It is *always* five years. I *do* know perhaps a half dozen who *have* indeed served five years or six years, but they are so few and so far between.

At any rate, let me return to the point. Let us say you are in a cell ten feet long and seven feet wide. That means seventy feet of *floor* space. But your bunk is just over three feet wide and six and a half feet long. Your iron toilet and sink combination covers a floor space of at least three feet by two feet. All tallied, you have approximately forty-seven square feet of space on the floor. It works out to a pathway seven feet long and about three feet wide—the excess is taken up by odd spaces between your commode and wall, between the foot of the bunk and the wall.

If I were an animal housed in a zoo in quarters of these dimensions, the Humane Society would have the zookeeper arrested for cruelty. It is illegal to house an animal in such confines.

But I am not an animal, so I do not insist on such rights.

My body communicates with the cell. We exchange temperatures and air currents, smells and leavings on the floor and walls. I try to keep it clean, to wash away my evidence, for the first year or two, then let it go at that.

I have experienced everything possible to experience in a cell in a short time—a day or so if I'm active, a week or two if I'm sluggish.

I must fight, from that point on, the routine, the monotony that will bury me alive if I am not careful. I must do that, and do it without losing my mind. So I read, read anything and everything. So I mutter to myself sometimes; sometimes recite poetry.

I have my memories. I have the good ones, the bad ones, the ones that are neither of these. So I have *myself.*

I have my seven-by-three-feet pathway, and I pace, at various speeds, depending on my mood. I think. I remember. I think. I remember.

Memory is arrested in the hole. I think about each remembered thing, study it in detail, over and over. I unite it with others, under headings for how I feel about it. Finally it changes and begins to tear itself free from facts and joins my imagination. Someone said *being is memory.*

It travels the terrain of time in a pure way, unfettered by what is, reckless of what was, what will become of it. Memory is not enriched by any further experience. It is *deprived* memory, memory deprived of every movement but the isolated body traveling thousands of miles in the confines of my prison cell.

My body plays with my mind; my mind plays with my body; the further I go into that terrain of time, into my memories, the more they enter my imagination. The imagination—bringing this memory into that, and that into this, every possible permutation and combination—replaces further experience, which would, if not enhance it, at least leave it intact.

I remember well, with such clarity, I am blinded by the memory. It is as if I had forgotten—but it is that I remember so well, too well:

Why am I here? Because I needed the money? Or was it the palmprint on the counter? What was it—a theft? Or was it that girl by the pond in the flowery dress who smiled at me . . . ?

Where was I?

Every memory has an element of pain or disappointment. It scolds a little and in its own way. These elements are normally overshadowed by a familiarity we can live with—we happily forget the rest. The rest: there is no rest—but a quality we can live with in comfort, a degree of quietude.

In the hole after a while the painful elements begin to throw out shoots and sprout like brittle weeds in the garden of memory—until finally, after so long, they choke to death everything else in the garden.

You are left with a wild wasteland of scrubby weeds and flinty stone and dusty soil. They call it *psyche-pain.*

It is the same with ideals. Everyone has a few: a touch of idealism, a little of passion. As life in the hole, in the pure terrain of time, continues, your passions are aroused less and less with the help of memories and more and more by your ideals. Love, Hate, Equality, Justice, Freedom, War, Peace, Beauty, Truth—they all eventually become Idols, pure and empty abstract gods that demand your fealty, your undying obedience. Little Hitlers come from every precious feeling, every innocent notion you ever entertained, every thought about yourself, your people, the world—all become so many idols, oblivious to each other, that stridently dictate to you in the prison hole.

You cannot fill them up with your days, your years, for they are empty too. But you try—God, how you try.

The wasteland that is your memory now comes under the absolute dictatorship of idols too terrible to envision.

They are the hard, driving winds that torture the tumbleweeds across the prairie desert of memory—the crazy, hard winds that whip up smaller chaotic columns of dust that twist a few feet in the air like little tornadoes. They are the scorching suns that wither the scrubby vegetation and torture the air that shimmers in waves of suffocating heat that rises from the dead, hard stone. They are the cold, merciless nights of the desert that offer surcease only to the fanged serpents: the *punishment* unfolds.

Don't go near yourself.

Then the mirages in the wasteland. You are far from insanity; you are only living through an experience, an event. The mirages are real reflections of how far you have journeyed into that pure terrain of time. They *are* real. They bring the now out-of-place things back into the desert that was once the felicitous garden of your memory. *There a cherished woman passes into existence and you approach, draw close to her, and you touch her and she caresses you and then she vanishes in a shimmer to reveal the man masturbating that you have become and are caressing so tenderly. A beautiful flower is seen at a small distance*

and opens its radiant wings in a promise of spring among the dusty weeds. More suddenly than it appeared, it disappears to reveal a dark splotch on the wall in the fetid, musky cell. A brook bubbles over the dusty pebbles of the wasteland, promising to quench, to quench—and as you turn, it disappears in a flush of the toilet.

Anything you can experience in the hole, you do to yourself, and after an indecent interval, each occasional experience recalls the old, nice quality of a memory which lies fallow beneath the wasteland. A word in a sentence; a tone in a voice or sound; a fleeting essence in a taste or odor; a momentary texture in a tactile sensation, or a combination of motion and form and color caught by the tail of your visual field. These can revive a good thing. Real things: these are the mirages in the desert.

The real world is out of place in the hole, but the hole is nonetheless really there. It is time that no longer moves forward in human experience. You can walk, placing one foot before the other, across eternity in time. All the space you need is six or seven feet. The hole furnishes only that provision: you are living a demonstration of the theory of the infinite within the finite; the dream within the reality.

But the hole is not the stuff of dreams, of fantasies: it is all quite real. In fact, it's so real it haunts you.

Experience occurs seldom and only in extremes: vividly intense or drably monotonous. Surreal paintings have tried to capture—with some success, I might add—the relationships that are very real in life in the prison hole. It is *not* a dream. *To you* it is not a dream. Your words and thoughts can only reflect this condition of your sensations, your feelings; they do not know their plight. Few thoughts in the hole are conscious of their true grounds.

You become silent, contemplative, because you have become inverted. Your sense perception, having taken in everything, including yourself, within the finite confines of the hole, passes through the monotony and now rises up from the *other side,* the infinite, to haunt you with reality. Those outside the hole, at that moment, would call it a dream—but you inside the hole are in reality, not a dream:

What am I? Do I exist? Does the world exist? Will I awaken to find this is all a dream? Is there a God? Am I the devil? What is it like to be dead? What does toilet water taste like? What is it like to put a finger up my butt? What would happen should I shit on the floor? Or piss down my legs? Am I homosexual? What is it like to sleep on this filthy concrete floor?

The mind deprived of experience because of social sensory deprivation in the hole conceives its intellectual faculty to be capable of putting to use a fictional apparatus in the brain. It will believe that somehow it can learn to control this apparatus and use it to move material things, to destroy or change or create physically real things. Shorn of a gracious God, the mind surrenders to nothing, to Nothingness:

If I concentrated, could I melt or bend the bars of my cell? (Yes. Ommmm.) Should I first try to concentrate to move that scrap of dust on the floor? (Yes. Ommmm.) Did it move? (I saw it move just a hair.)

The intelligence recedes, no more a tool of learning—because knowledge is based on experience—but a tool of the outside world it is deprived of knowing. It tries to contact other minds by telepathy; it becomes the Ancestor. *Words* and *Numbers* come to bold mystic significance: they were invented by some arcane magic older than man. The line between the word and the thing vanishes; the intervals of numbers in infinity collapse with infinity.

The mind now crouches in fear and superstition before the idols of the hole, terrified:

I do not want to talk any more. There is nothing you can say of interest. I cannot remember ever being happy. No one has ever been kind to me. Everyone betrays me. No one can possibly understand—they are too ignorant. You have not suffered what I have endured. You call me names (homosexual). You do not understand. You mock me (screwball). This world is nothing. An illusion. Death is the release.

But a kind of genius can come of this deprivation of sensation, of experience. It has been mistaken as naïve intelligence, when in fact it is *empty* intelligence, pure intelligence. *The composition of the mind is altered.* Its previous cultivation is disintegrated and it has greater access to the *brain, the body:* it is Supersanity.

Learning is turned inside out. You have to start from the top and work your way down. You must study mathematical theory before simple arithmetic; theoretical physics before applied physics; anatomy, you might say, before you can walk.

You have to study philosophy in depth before you can understand the simplest categorical differences assumed in language or in any simple commonplace moral or ethical maxim.

Indeed, it is almost a rule that the more simple and commonplace something is, the more difficult to understand it.

You have come the full circle; experienced that single event that happens down there in the prison hole. How long does it take? Years. I would say five years or more.

. . . They finally put a name on what I have suffered in solitary: *sensory deprivation.* The first few times I served a couple of years like that, I saw only three or four drab colors. I felt only concrete and steel. When I was let out, I could not orient myself. The dull prison-blue shirts struck me, dazzled me with a beauty they never had. All colors dazzled me. A piece of wood fascinated me by its feel, its texture. The movements of things, the many prisoners walking about, and their multitude of voices—all going in different directions—bewildered me. I was slow and slack-jawed and confused—but beneath the surface I raged.

I can guess how wasted I have become now by the fact that I am no longer disoriented by solitary confinement. It has finally wormed its way into my heart: I cannot measure my deprivation any longer.

Let us say I can no longer measure my *feelings*. I can draw the proportions mentally, however.

. . . I explained to you the other day that the cell regulates the moods of the body. The mind does not regulate its own condition. Mental depression, for example, is a state of the mind caused by the body. In a cell in the hole it only *seems* that there is a separation of mind and body—in fact, the body's condition (of deprivations of sensations; experiences, functions, and so on) controls the moods of the mind more than in any other situation I can think of.

William James described this relationship when he said we become sad because we shed tears: we do not shed tears because we are sad. That is our original condition as living beings.

A long time ago in the hole, when I first entered prison, I was on the floor lying on my stomach writing a letter, with my elbows propping me up. So I was bent directly over the page I was writing on.

My mood was "normal"—I mean the normal mood of a prisoner in the hole. I remember I noticed, as I was writing, little spots of water appearing on the paper. I touched them with a finger and wondered at the phenomenon—when suddenly I realized tears were falling from my eyes, and immediately I began to weep uncontrollably. It was the first and only time I have wept since I was a child. I do not know *why* now, nor did I know the cause of it then. I must have been weeping over everything, all of it.

. . . A man is taken away from his experience of society, taken away from the experience of a living planet of living things, when he is sent to prison.

A man is taken away from other prisoners, from his experience of other people, when he is locked away in solitary confinement in the hole.

Every step of the way removes him from experience and narrows it down to only the experience of himself.

There is a *thing* called death and we have all seen it. It brings to an end a life, an individual living thing. When life ends, the living thing ceases to experience.

The *concept* of death is simple: it is when a living thing no longer entertains experience.

So when a man is taken farther and farther away from experience, he is being taken to his death.

STUDY QUESTIONS FOR READING 11

1. How does time "kill" you in the hole? What does this "living death" mean you will eventually stop doing?

2. Abbott says if he were an animal in a zoo the Humane Society would have his keeper arrested. Why?

3. What does Abbott do to keep the routine and monotony from burying him alive?

4. According to Abbott, what replaces experience in the hole? How does he relate this to death?

LIVING AND WORKING ON DEATH ROW

ROBERT JOHNSON

At its best, life on death row amounts to long hours of "dead time," as the inmates are wont to put it, spent in either single or congregate cells. That such an existence is a psychological nightmare hardly requires elaboration. With only rare exceptions, condemned prisoners are demoralized by their bleak confinement and defeated by the awesome prospect of death by execution. Worn down in small and almost imperceptible ways, gradually but inexorably they become less than fully human. At the end, the prisoners are helpless captives of the modern execution drill.

The dehumanization condemned prisoners experience is in no way reduced by recent reforms of some death rows. In no instance in even the most extensively reformed death row are condemned prisoners prepared in any way for the ordeal they must face. And as executions occur with increasing frequency, a trend that has gathered momentum since the advent of the death row reforms discussed in the preceding chapter, there is every reason to believe that conditions of confinement on death rows will become more rather than less restrictive.

Preliminary evidence from an American Correctional Association (ACA) survey of death row conditions, conducted in 1987, suggests that this is indeed the case. There is, according to the ACA survey, a definite trend toward increased security on death rows, as well as toward maximum separation of individual prisoners.[1] A return to a standard regime of solitary confinement is a real possibility.

Moreover, none of the recent death row reforms affects the deathwatch, the period that culminates death row confinement and ends in the execution of the prisoner. This period continues to be one of virtually unmitigated solitary confinement under condi-

tions of total security. As we shall see, the stress of life under sentence of death reaches its zenith during the deathwatch.

LIVING ON DEATH ROW: THE PSYCHOLOGY OF HUMAN WAREHOUSING

The bleak quality of life on all death rows, reformed and unreformed, reflects their common goal: human storage. This goal dictates that condemned prisoners be treated essentially as bodies kept alive to be killed. This concern for preserving the body without regard to the quality of life reaches an extreme in suicide prevention efforts that amount to treating the person like a piece of meat.

Philip Brasfield, for example, reported that a suicidal prisoner on death row in Texas, where Brasfield himself was also confined while under sentence of death, was

> placed in a straightjacket that was left open at the back to secure him to a bare mattress on the bunk. In addition, handcuffs were placed on his wrists. A crash helmet much like a motorcyclist would wear, was placed on his head and there he lay for weeks, helpless, alone, and drugged. The care and feeding he received was from the inmate porters. At times, he'd call for assistance for over an hour before a guard would open the door and untie him so he could urinate.[2]

Similar procedures apply to inmates whose mental health problems present trouble. On the reformed death row I studied, an inmate testified to these procedures:

> Should any individual with psychiatric problems present a problem [to staff], his cell will be stripped of all belongings (including clothing and hygiene items),

and he is subject to be chained to the cell's bare steel bunk. This has happened to me, personally, and I have seen the same happen to other men.

Yet another example of preserving the body but ignoring the person was related to me by Alvin Bronstein of the American Civil Liberties Union's (ACLU's) National Prison Project. One of his condemned clients required triple-bypass heart surgery but refused treatment. Officials allegedly urged the prisoner to undergo surgery so he could be alive for his execution, at one point asking Bronstein to argue their case with his reluctant client. Bronstein declined. The prisoner subsequently died of a heart attack.[3]

Daily procedures on death row embody the storage premise quite explicitly. "Neat and efficient," in the words of Jackson and Christian, these procedures are tellingly described in terms that objectify the prisoners. For instance, Jackson and Christian tell us that

death row inmates get showers one at a time. The noun takes a verb form: "I'm going to shower the row now," the guard says. "I'm opening one-row cell 13 to shower Jones." One is "being showered" rather than "taking a shower." The option is the guards', always. The same thing happens with recreation; it becomes a verb: "I'm going to recreate group three now," the guard says, meaning he will let one-quarter of the men on the row out of their cells and into the small dayroom.[4]

The immediate result of such efficient storage arrangements is a radical reduction in the prisoner's privacy. Indeed, prisoners typically claim that on death row one has no privacy at all! In the words of Caryl Chessman, who spent twelve years on San Quentin's death row before his execution in 1962,

You have no privacy. Day and night, you're watched closely. Having claimed it, the state is jealous of your life. Every possible safeguard is taken to prevent you from cheating the executioner—by digging, cutting, or assaulting your way to stolen freedom; by self-destruction; by fleeing to the world of the insane. You've come to the wrong place if curious eyes and the probing beams of flashlights make you uneasy.[5]

A present-day death row prisoner seconded Chessman's observations, reminding us that nothing essential has changed on the row:

They read your mail. Take a visit, they're standing over your shoulder. They know everything you're saying. You shower and they're watching you. At night they're shining flashlights in your cell. You never have a free moment.[6]

Regular prisoners are permitted to develop an informal society and, to some extent at least, police themselves.[7] But the margin for failures of control on death row is exceedingly narrow. The prisoners are watched closely, though not continuously, and without apology.[8]

Held powerless on death row, condemned prisoners also come to feel powerless—that is, alone and vulnerable. Many—as many as seven out of every ten[9]—deteriorate in measurable ways. All are to some degree weakened and demoralized. Those condemned prisoners who reach the deathwatch . . . are subjected to constant surveillance and complete loss of privacy. Made susceptible by their death row confinement, they collapse under the substantial pressure of the deathwatch. In the final analysis, they are reduced to dehumanized objects that are mere pawns in the modern execution process.

Powerlessness

Close confinement combined with almost constant surveillance renders death row inmates powerless to alter or influence their daily existence in any meaningful way. Their lives are monotonous and lonely, and they are predictably bored, tense, and depressed. Chronic irritability and periodic lapses in personal control can leave prisoners feeling alienated from themselves. The prisoner comes to see himself as essentially a stranger in a strange land.[10] Powerlessness and its emotional sequelae, established in the *Harries* case as key factors in the cruelty of Tennessee's death row, affect prisoners of all death rows. The reason is straightforward: All death rows are, at bottom, sterile, eventless, oppressive environments that demoralize their inhabitants as a direct function of the setting's emphasis on custodial repression.

The experience of powerlessness is magnified on solitary-confinement death rows, in which warehousing for death takes its most blatant, unvarnished form.

The barren dimensions of the condemned prisoners' lives on such death rows are evident in the empty diversions they employ to occupy their time. In the prisoners' words,

- I have got so bored at times, I used to hook cockroaches together, sort of like they was a team of mules, to drag a matchbox around on the floor to pass time. I mean that may sound weird to you or somebody else, and it might be. Matter of fact I just flushed a little frog down the shit jack the other day that I had back there [in my cell]. It came up through the shit jack. I kept him back there a couple of weeks and I kicked roaches and things to feed him. Just any little old thing. . . . To more or less keep your mind off the damned chair and the things that you're seeing around you. Anything to occupy your mind.

- I got a big dictionary. I look in there and I read—just look at words, I can't even pronounce the words I be looking at, you know, but I read the meaning to them. I like doing stuff like that. It's hard to stay at that thing, you get sleepy—without moving—you can't stay up but an hour at a time, you have to lay back down. I can't seem to settle down in my cell. Like, I spend 23½ hours in there and I can't ever come to peace with myself. It irritates me all the time.[11]

Long hours in the cell are a source of psychological pressure and emotional turmoil. All prisoners experience some pressure; for some, the experience is almost disabling. For example,

I sit in that cell, you know, and it seems like I'm just ready to scream or go crazy or something. And you know, the pressure, it builds up, and it feels like everything is—you're sitting there and things start, you know, not hearing things, things start to coming in your mind. You start to remember certain events that happened, bad things. It just gets to a person. I sit up at night, you know. You just sit there, and it seems like you're going to go crazy. You've got three walls around you and bars in front of you, and you start looking around, you know, and it seems like things are closing in on you. Like last night, when I sit in there and everything's real quiet, things, just a buzzing noise gets to going in my ears. And I sit there, and I con-

sciously think, "Am I going to go crazy?" And the buzzing gets louder; and you sit there and you want to scream and tell somebody to stop it. And most of the time you get up—if I start making some noise in my cell, it will slack off. And it sounds stupid, I know, but it happens. . . . [S]ometimes I wonder if I don't get it stopped, I'm going crazy or something. . . . And you know, maybe tonight when I lay down it's not going to break when I get up and try to make some noise.[12]

Against the suffocating vacuum of the cells, a chance to place a simple order at the commissary can be an exhilarating, liberating experience—a small freedom so sweet it accentuates the bitter constraints that envelop one's life on death row.

They have one day which is a store day. That one day actually is to these people on death row like Christmas and all they actually get is cigarettes and candy or cookies, and that's actually become to be a thing like Christmas. I've surveyed it from watching the guys and everybody gets excited and they are actually more happy on Tuesday when they get that little package. But you see this is actually what we have been reduced to as far as being men, trying to be a man, finally enjoying a little thing like a cookie. To me it's actually absurd, this actually affects me to that point and there is no way out of it, there is no way to rebel against it.[13]

Prisoners on reformed death rows generally have more autonomy than those on solitary-confinement death rows. (I say generally because reformed death rows go through periodic lockdowns, during which the prisoners are kept in solitary confinement as punishment. On the reformed death row I studied, one such lockdown lasted a full five months.) These prisoners normally have the company of their dayroom companions to fall back on, and this can, no doubt, be a source of comfort, giving them a sense of a more normal and at least minimally autonomous daily life. Contact with other prisoners, however, can be a double-edged sword. One's fellows can be a source of pressure, harassment, and sometimes violent victimization, all of which add to feelings of helplessness. As a case in point, on our reformed death row, one man was brutally attacked by a fellow prisoner in the dayroom. The victim was paralyzed for life.

Even congenial conversations in dayrooms (for those on reformed death rows) or with men in neighboring cells (for those in solitary confinement) offer only limited opportunities for autonomous action or emotional support. Eventually, one says and does all that one can say and do in the compressed world that is death row. One's social life, as it were, becomes numbingly redundant and oppressive in its own right. It is worth recalling that Sartre's notion of hell was being confined for eternity with people one despises. For at least some prisoners, especially on reformed death rows, the fact that they have "no exit" from the other condemned prisoners may make their confinement a kind of hell.

The enduring difficulty is that on death row—any death row—everything remains the same. "It's continuously having the same walls, the same bars, the same papers, the same books," said one condemned prisoner. "Nothing changes. Only the outside, the light. We have day and we have night, we have day and then we have night." People become fixtures, as unchanging as the schedule. A paradoxical dependence is bred; routines come to hold in check the very resentments they produce. "If something changes, it's like a shock to you," observed one inmate. "You'll hear them yelling and screaming and everything else."[14] With the inexorable return of routine, the inmates retreat once more into the familiar, however impoverished it may be.

Loneliness

Though familiar, the routine on death row offers little real comfort—to the prisoners, that is. For the staff, routine can become an end in itself, a means of distancing themselves from the prisoners. Too often, the staff become insensitive to the human tragedies unfolding among the condemned; they seem unwilling or unable to offer meaningful support. "Caring," observed one group of researchers studying death row officers, "is simply not part of the job."[15] "Nobody is going to help you," confirmed an inmate. "Nobody is going to give you a kind word. Nobody is going to ask you, 'How's it going, how's your day? Is everything coming out okay?' You're totally ignored." Nor do other prison officials fill the emotional void. Like the occasional citizen's groups that tour death rows, "they just look in the cave and they go away."[16] Though

these are almost surely overstatements on the part of the inmates—some officers and officials say they care, and try to show it—they indicate widely and firmly held perceptions of the social reality on death row. Almost to a man, condemned prisoners feel abandoned by the prison staff, denied simple human compassion, treated "as if already dead."[17]

Feeling abandoned by the prison staff often goes hand in hand with feeling abandoned by the world. The custodial regime not only insulates guards from prisoners, it also isolates prisoners from the moral and social community of the outside world. Inmates suffer "a symbolic isolation that comes from living with the fact that 12 members of your community have determined that you are a worthless person who should no longer be permitted to exist." Prisoners may feel "so isolated that it is nearly impossible to share a religion with those on the outside." As time passes and they gradually exhaust their appeals, prisoners may feel further removed from the world of the living. One reason is that fewer people are apt to write or visit in support of a lost (or losing) cause.[18] Another is that failed appeals mark progressive stages in the killing and dying process, "pull[ing] layers of legal legitimacy over a corpse that hasn't quit moving and complaining yet."[19]

Their isolation on death row contributes to the weakening and often the dissolution of the prisoners' relationships with their loved ones. In one condemned man's words, "While most people rely on their families for their major source of support, it is not at all uncommon for this resource to be unavailable to death row prisoners."[20] One reflection of this sad fact is an empty visiting room. "On the death row visiting day," Jackson and Christian tell us, "the room is usually empty. It is rare for even two death row inmates to get a visit at the same time."[21]

Visits are a precious but rare—and precarious—commodity in the eyes of the condemned. Visits are not matters of right but rather privileges that can be—and, in fact, regularly are—suspended at the discretion of prison officials.[22] Officials discourage visits through a variety of restrictive rules and regulations. For example, visits can take place only on certain days and for limited periods of time. This creates logistical problems for the prisoners' loved ones. And though no physical contact is allowed during typical visits, the staff nevertheless carefully monitor all visits. What is worse, after all visits, inmates are shackled and subjected to thorough body searches, even when the visits involved no physical contact. For some prisoners, the pain and humiliation engendered by such treatment outweigh the pleasure of the visit. One prisoner could barely suppress his rage when describing his experience with visits.

Your people come to this place. You go down and you sit down for an hour or whatever you stayed and you get your mind away from this place. And just as soon as you come in after having enjoyed yourself for a little bit, just as soon as you get up from out there and walk in here, they strip you, look up your asshole and in your mouth and strip search you and handcuff you behind your back and drag you back up that hall. Well, you see, they just broke your whole fucking visit. You would have been better off, in a way, if you'd just stayed in your cell and if you could have slept through that hour. . . . I mean that's the kind of attitude that leaves you with after they fuck with you. Knowing your people drove and went through all this trouble to come see you, to give you an hour or something. Then they have taken the fucking time to figure out a way to fuck it up for you.[23]

Condemned prisoners tend to see the death row regime as a calculated and gratuitous assault on their humanity. For them, the physical setting is punitively spartan; rules and regulations are means to inflict pain.[24] The intrusive procedures associated with visits do much to fuel the prisoners' angry perception that their keepers mean them harm.

Aside from humiliating searches, the rules regulating visits with condemned prisoners make these encounters strained and potentially divisive. Visiting arrangements for Florida's condemned, under which visitors are continuously observed, have been found to impede the flow of information and emotional support between families and condemned prisoners, "thereby sustaining rather than alleviating feelings of isolation and uncertainty."[25] The visiting routine on Alabama's death row frustrates any attempt at congenial conversation. The visiting situation in Alabama, as I stated after observing visits there firsthand, is more akin to a wake than to a supportive family gathering.

The priorities on [Alabama's] death row seem almost unforgivable in regard to visits. The routine surrounding visits might be compared with the preparations for a funeral. Noncontact visits, in particular, seem peculiarly reminiscent of the viewing at a wake. The inmate sits alone in an enclosed chamber, neatly dressed and carefully groomed, almost as if on display for his loved ones. The need to shout across the barrier separating the inmate and his visitors precludes intimate conversation and results in awkward interludes of silence. Visitors speak as much among themselves as with their prisoner; they appear nervous and out of place. The prisoners, too, seem ill at ease.[26]

It is hard to be natural when yelling to loved ones or when officers are looking over your shoulder, perhaps eavesdropping as well. In turn, truncated conversations and awkward interludes of silence can leave people feeling confused and lonely: What did she *really* mean by this pause or that phrase? The prisoner, on returning to his cell, is left to wonder. And worry.

The empty existence on death row may, in any case, render prisoners mute during visits. They and their loved ones live in utterly different worlds, with little or no common ground to draw on to sustain communication (though more accommodating visiting conditions would certainly improve matters). Unrewarding visits reflect and reinforce the prisoners' basic sense of alienation. The custodial milieu of death row thus tends to corrode relationships. As a result, most condemned prisoners describe themselves as abandoned by the free world and left to their own devices to endure their confinement.[27]

Vulnerability

Held powerless under conditions of indifference and neglect, prisoners tend to resent their guards, who are the nearest at hand to blame for their helpless and lonely state. Prisoners also come to feel vulnerable to harm by their keepers. Alone and defenseless when in their cells, living at all times in harsh and deprived conditions, convenient objects of contempt, condemned prisoners feel vulnerable to abuse from their keepers. Condemned prisoners are usually held in the most secluded quarters of the prison—a condition that, absent effective supervision of the guard force, invites, indeed almost authorizes, abuse. Their stark vulnerability may be apparent from the moment prisoners set foot on death row. One prisoner put the matter like this:

> The biggest fear is when you walk onto this place. I've seen one man walk out there and he stood right there and he broke down and cried. I've seen more come in here and live three days and start praying. I've seen them come in here and cuss the day they was born because of fear. I've seen grown men come in here and get down and pray like kids. And cry.[28]

Condemned prisoners see death row as a law unto itself, one based on the premise "Might makes right." As one prisoner observed, "They can do anything they want to you. Who's going to stop them?" Power, many say, emanates from the butt end of the baton or billy club that is often standard equipment for death row officers. This weapon, sometimes tellingly called an axe handle by the prisoners, can function as both a symbol of violence and an instrument of social control. As one prisoner observed,

> You have to more or less watch what you say to these guys because if they want to get you back, they could easily do that. You're on your way out to the yard, the guy could say as soon as you get out of the center—around that little bend—where the rest of the guys couldn't see you, they could easily claim "well, he turned around and hit me," "he turned around and I thought he was attacking me," or "he pushed me." And one whack with one of those axe handles up against your head, if you're not going to be dead, you're going to be insane for the rest of your life. And then you're not going to be able to help no one. . . . I am really afraid of that. I'm trying to hold on to my own common sense, you know, because I feel that is one of the main factors that I do have that is still mine. My knowledge that I can think and my ability to learn and do my own research on my own case. I feel that if I got hit with one of those sticks, I wouldn't have that much sense. So, I live in constant fear of that actually all the time."[29]

Abuse, including violence, may also be implicitly authorized in the training of death row officers. Colin Turnbull's research revealed that death row officers' training emphasized "combat duty" and made "no attempt to help the guard approach the extremely

difficult task of maintaining appropriate human relations [with condemned prisoners]."[30] The profound suspiciousness of the officers on the reformed death row I studied, a suspiciousness demanded by their superior officer, promoted a combat mentality among many of these officers. Informal socialization on the job, moreover, is apt to alert the guards of any death row to the potential dangers of their work, reinforcing the apparent value of a cold and even pugnacious stance with the inmates. One prisoner put this matter plainly:

> They got us one sorry motherfucker right here and that's the only way I know how to put it. One of the most sorriest motherfuckers right here that could be working in a penitentiary. Now he comes to work and sits his ass down right up there, and sits there and tries to figure out a way to fuck somebody back there on death row. And he's the one that shows the others how to do us. . . . It's just like father teach son—that's their routine. When a guard comes here, instead of giving him [formal] training and everything and teach him how he should cope with these things in prison and stuff, they bring him right up here, put him under one of the worst sons-of-bitches there is here. Then father teach son. Then it's just a very short period of time until they have built up this attitude and they look at you the same way he does. . . . Now I been in down here since way back. So a whole lot about the outside, I don't know nothing about it. But about these sons-of-bitches, I do. And that's why I say, when a guy come into here and he say, "Well, there goes a good guard." Shit. It won't be three days before he's just as sorry as the next motherfucker.[31]

Many condemned prisoners believe that their keepers, with or without provocation, would resort to violence.[32] Indeed, some prisoners' fear of violence from their keepers merges with their fear of execution. One prisoner, visibly afraid, had this to say:

> When you're on death row and you're laying down in your cell and you hear a door cracking, you'll think of where it comes from. When you hear it crack. And when you hear the keys and everything, when something like this happens, the keys come through here: I'm up. I'm up because you don't know when it's going to take place. The courts give you an execution date, that's true. But you don't know what's going to take place between then and your execution date. You

don't know when you're going to be moved around to the silent cell over here. That's right down the hall, what they call a waiting cell. You don't know when you're going to be moved down there. And this keeps you jumpy, and it keeps you nervous, and it keeps you scared.[33]

Such fear, which borders at times on raw panic, may be more prevalent among condemned prisoners than one would imagine. It bespeaks the profound vulnerability these prisoners feel, and the deep distrust they have for their keepers.

A Living Death

The cumulative impact of death row, as noted by the court in the *Harries* case, is an "overall sense of defeat."[34] Hopelessness is the condemned prisoner's cellmate. In one prisoner's words,

You can hear its empty sound in the clanging of the steel doors, in the rattle of chains, in the body searches, in the lack of privacy, in the night sounds of death row, and you can see it in the eyes of the guards who never look really at you, but are always watching to see that you do not commit suicide.[35]

The *normal* reaction in such an environment, observed the noted psychiatrist Seymour Halleck, who testified as an expert in the *Harries* case, features "depression and lethargy."[36] (Harries himself showed signs of psychological deterioration that a number of experts attributed to the conditions of his confinement on death row, an attribution supported by a body of empirical research and accepted by the court.)[37] Prisoners of other death rows bear out this observation, describing death row as a "living death" and themselves as the "living dead.[38] As one prisoner poignantly observed, "You need love and it just ain't there. It leaves you empty inside, dead inside. Really, you just stop caring."

Death row prisoners, to restate Halleck's point, give up on life as we normally know it. They exist rather than live. That existence, however, can be deceptive to outside observers, even to correctional officers and officials on the scene. For on a social level, death row prisoners, and, to a lesser extent, their keepers, create a make-believe world premised on

denying the reality of the death penalty. Prisoners talk tough and act cool, posturing even within the cells that cage them, desperate to deceive themselves and those around them. Humor, in particular, is used to bolster a facade of manliness, as well as to direct attention from inner doubts and turmoil. But denial is a psychological gambit that always comes home to roost. As one prisoner of a solitary-confinement death row put it,

The row ain't serious; it's a lot of funny things happening on the row. Everybody seeing who can be the funniest, you know. So, I contribute in that there, too. I figure if I contribute in that, that will keep me going halfway. But I figure now when things really get hard and everybody stops joking, that's when you are going to see about ten people just bug out from the jump. All of us are going to bug out sooner or later.[39]

Things "get hard," to complete the prisoner's point, when someone is executed—as happens these days with increasing regularity. These executions would seem to be both the logical and the psychological culmination of death row confinement.

WORKING ON DEATH ROW

Tension and Fear

The condemned prisoner's life on death row is grim. The lot of those who guard death row is singularly unrewarding as well. Work on death row is, in fact, a stressful and often frightening assignment that lends itself to indifferent and even abusive treatment of the condemned prisoners. Death row guards are enjoined solely to preserve the corpus of the condemned—to feed them in their cells or in common areas, to conduct them to out-of-cell activities, to watch them at all times. In large measure, the officers are reduced to intrusive waiters and unwanted escorts. Moreover, the death row guard's role is in some respects an impersonal and hence symbolically dehumanized one: The officer's character as a distinctive person, though not stripped from him, is rendered largely irrelevant to how he carries out his work as a death row officer. Unsurprisingly, like the prisoners, the guards are bored and tense much of the time. Some even report being depressed by their circumscribed, thankless jobs.

Relations between guards and inmates have been described as either overtly hostile, with harassment and counterharassment a common form of exchange,[40] or impersonal, with little or no contact.[41] Still, the condemned and the keepers usually accommodate one another to some degree, and a few death row officers are even able to transcend the limitations of their role and develop normal, if superficial, relationships with death row prisoners. Nonetheless, death row officers are, at best, professional custodians, they may be tactful and even courteous, but not "chummy."[42] "They don't make friends," said one prisoner of such guards, "they just do their job and go home."[43] Tension is high, affecting officers and inmates alike.

Neither is fear of violence restricted to inmates. Officers, too, feel vulnerable as they go about the work of guarding condemned prisoners. Officers regularly cite the dangers posed by the prisoners as justification for the custodial restrictions on death row. Guards are quick to point out that condemned prisoners are men of proven violence with little to lose in trying to escape. It is widely believed that because the prisoners face execution and often live in the most depriving environment the prison has to offer, they feel free to attack or even kill guards. What more can we do to them? worried officers ask. The guards thus come to fear the potential violence of their captives just as the prisoners fear the potential violence of their keepers. Too often, shared fears give way to mutual hate.[44] The peace on death row can seem precarious indeed.

Fears harbored by officers may be especially pronounced on reformed death rows, because the inmates are out of their cells in small groups and hence are a more potent threat. The security-related concerns of many of the officers on our reformed death row appeared to be rooted, at least in part, in fear.

For some of these officers, my interviews revealed, fear lurks in the background. Said one officer, "You know in the back of your mind who you're dealing with, what they are, but still you don't bring it to the surface." Other officers spoke of conscious fears. The prisoners, they believe, are violent men bent on escape. These officers work under constant pressure. As one said, "They will hurt you to get away. You've got to watch them all the time. You know if these guys get a chance, you're gone. They'll kill you. They've all killed before." In the words of another officer, "There was always that thought in my mind, 'If they ever get out of here, I'm as good as dead.' I feel they don't have anything to lose. If we get in their way, they just get rid of us quick." Security procedures are in place to restrain the prisoners and protect the officers, but they fail to reassure. Assessed against a backdrop of fear, regulations appear flawed. "If they want to escape, they can," said one officer with an air of futility. "Somebody's going to slip up somewhere along the line."

The officers' fears are not indiscriminate. There are periods of high risk and hence high anxiety, though different officers expressed different concerns. For one, it was "taking inmates to recreation" that required extreme caution. For another, "Counts are scary. I worry there'll be one hiding 'round the corner and I'll have to go and find him." According to a third, "Open areas bother me. I'm uncomfortable working in the open area [in the hall] near the control station." One officer, though calm on the surface, found almost *any* occasion a source of fear because he was intimidated by the prisoners' crimes. He readily admitted that some prisoners were less fierce than one would expect, given their crimes, but he took no comfort in this. "You can't judge a book by its cover. You've never seen him mad."

A troubling and pervasive sign of fear is that officers see themselves as potential hostages. "The inmates constantly threaten to take hostages," said one officer. Some of it is joking, he acknowledged, but the risk of one day becoming a hostage "is very real." That fearful eventuality preoccupies a number of officers, who envision scenarios that would result in their being taken hostage. A common fear is that a harried, and thus distracted, control officer will open the wrong door at the wrong time, unleashing a group of inmates on a defenseless hall officer. The officers respond to such intimidating contingencies with a grim fatalism, taking the attitude that they should do what they can to control their own lives and let other matters sort themselves out.

Anybody can get attacked or taken hostage at any time. But I just have a job to do, and I just go ahead and do it and hope that nothing will happen. I just try to do my job, be alert and observant, and nothing should go wrong. If it does, I'd just have to deal with it.

As another officer put it, "You know who you're with, *what* you're dealing with, but you have to deal with it as it comes. You do what you have to do in the line of your duties, your job. You focus on what you're doing."

Fear can directly affect the way officers do their jobs. A common but dangerous temptation, born of fear, is to appease prisoners to gain their cooperation. (Inmates do not note or mention officers' use of this approach, perhaps because they see such officers as friendly to their immediate interests.) One officer stated the premise underlying appeasement quite baldly: "Anybody facing death, they gotta be dangerous. If he calls and he needs something, you got to try to get it for him." Such officers are said by their colleagues to bend or even ignore the rules "to keep it calm in there and to make their day go by." Other officers are said to get "too personally involved." They "play" with inmates rather than controlling them, and are "slap happy" and "sloppy" in following procedures. These officers, according to their colleagues, say to inmates, " 'You're my buddy.' Slap 'em on the back and say, 'You're my partner. I know you're not going to hurt me because we're stick buddies.' This is no place to play. If you get that far gone, I think, you better get out." Obsequious guards make their fellow officers nervous. The problem for the staff, and for the weaker inmates they must protect, is that appeasement corrodes the officers' authority and undermines control, lowering the general level of security. "We're supposed to be a team," complained one officer, "and what happens to them happens to me." If a colleague trembles visibly, he is useless as an officer. What is worse, his presence emboldens the more predatory prisoners, which in the long run spells trouble for officers and inmates alike.

Some officers go to the other extreme and become overbearing and abusive. This response, as we have seen, is salient in the minds of the prisoners. As Radelet et al. observed, "Relations with the correctional officers are fragile, with one hostile guard eas-

ily able to overshadow relationships with those who are more humane."[45] A major reason for this fragility is fear. Ever on the defensive, abusive officers are quick to take personal offense and quick to intimidate and harass prisoners in retaliation. Under conditions of solitary confinement, officers of this type may have the upper hand because prisoners are locked in their cells. They may even set the example for other officers to follow.[46] On less restrictive death rows, however, abusive officers are more apt to be seen by their colleagues as a liability.

Contrary to appearances (and inmate perceptions), these abusive officers are not gratuitously hostile. Rather, condemned prisoners are a trial for them, taxing their limited self-control. Though the prisoners are, in the view of most officers I interviewed, reasonably well behaved on a day-to-day basis, the officers pointed out that the prisoners are not easy to be around. They characterized the inmates as impatient, touchy, demanding, and given to wide mood swings that sometimes end in tirades. Such, said the officers, is the pressure of life on death row. To get into a "cursing match" with the prisoners is tempting, noted one officer, but he resists because to do so "would put me at their level." Unfortunately, this officer felt that some of his colleagues regularly lower themselves to the level of the prisoners, becoming defensive about their authority and abusive with prisoners. Wherever these officers go, this man maintained, they stir up trouble.

We have some hard cases. I could have everything calm, but this one guy wouldn't be there but two seconds and he'd rile 'em up so. When he left, you could hear the inmates down the hall, he'd rile 'em up so. . . . Just some small remark or something he'd know would get 'em riled.

Since trouble is seen as contagious, given the pressure of life on death row, abusive officers are as much of a problem as their lax colleagues. In the one instance, abuse may provoke an incident. In the other, timidity may invite trouble. Either way, other officers—and the prisoners—suffer.

The fears of the prisoners and guards, though quite real, are not necessarily realistic. It is by no means clear that death row guards would be eager to harm their captives if the opportunity arose. Certainly the officers cannot simply enter prisoners' cells and carry them off to the execution chamber on a whim. (Fearful prisoners can acknowledge this last point intellectually, by the way, but not emotionally. They still feel starkly vulnerable.) Nor is it clear that condemned prisoners, most of whom face years of legal appeals and therefore have reason to hope for reprieve, are desperate enough to callously harm or kill a guard to escape the executioner or to exact revenge.

But the fear persists on this and other death rows, with harmful consequences. A prisoner of a solitary-confinement death row described the consequences as follows:

> There seems to be too much security. There seems to be an abnormal amount of fear in the guards simply because we have a death sentence and that makes it hard for us to have the same courtesies that we should—that other inmates have. For example, the guards are so afraid of us where they won't get close to us or they won't come up and talk to us when we need something done seriously. It could be a medical problem or something. And because of this fear in the guards, we don't get the assistance we need like other inmates do. . . . You can easily tell it's fear in the officers and other employees of the institution. Just because we have this death sentence, people are so afraid of us that they don't want to get close to us and because of this very thing we just don't get what I would say [is] the compassion that we need or the assistance that we need. Sometimes it's hard to find the right word, but I know that it is something that we don't get that every man, regardless of his condition, should have.[47]

The main casualty of fear, then, is simple human compassion, the absence of which contributes to the distinctively cold interpersonal climate on death row.

Human Services

Yet fear need not contaminate all encounters on death row. Implicit in the above-quoted prisoner's insightful observations about the corrosive effect of fear is the hope that individual officers and inmates can, through more open interaction, come to know one another and use that knowledge to suspend, or at least place in perspective, the stereotypes that divide them.

That hope sometimes bears fruit. On the reformed death row I studied, three officers, admittedly a minority, suppressed their fears and went about their jobs as responsible correctional officers. Two of these officers were women. Like good officers of either gender in any correctional setting, they saw themselves as figures of authority whose job was to help the inmates cope with the pains of imprisonment.[48] In their view, condemned prisoners, like all other prisoners, are entitled to a range of basic human services, and these officers provided those services as a matter of course.

One officer ticked off by rote some examples of human services provided on death row: "You must provide phone calls, supplies, commissary, legal and personal calls [call the switchboard for them], toilet paper, soap, towels. The list goes on. . . ." Paradoxically, security is on that list of services, even on death row. For these officers, security means more than merely preventing escape. It also means protecting the inmates and the officers. In one guard's words,

> This is a security job: to keep them protected while they're here and to keep them from getting out. Anytime they go anyplace within the building or outside it, they have to have waist chains, leg irons, and all this stuff. So you have to act as a buffer between them and the inmates who are "free." So it's a form of protective custody. You have to protect them from the other inmates because they can't protect themselves.

Condemned prisoners need protection from each other as well. Stress builds up on death row, and men under pressure sometimes act out. Violent men sometimes act out violently, so fights are one periodic symptom of stress on death row with which the officers must deal. Such fights are usually broken up on command. When they are not, the regular death row officers do not enter the dayroom, where they might be taken hostage, but instead call in a twelve-man tactical team, which restrains the prisoners. In this way, both the inmates and the officers are protected.

Sometimes officers go a step beyond efficient provision of services. In the words of one such officer, they "develop a friendly-type relationship" with the prisoners. Having come to empathize with the prisoners in their difficult situation, they are moved to respond to the prisoners' legitimate concerns. "It may be a simple thing to you and me, but if it's something that's pressing them, then they want it done today. They don't have a lot of business. The least thing that comes up is important."

These more responsive officers occasionally find themselves in a helping role. Interactions may start with a request for a basic commodity, such as toilet paper, and end in an informal counseling session.

The man may start a conversation which eventually brings out a problem they're struggling with. For example, problems with girlfriends. They ask me because I'm a female. Or [problems with] kids or cooking, things they know I know about.

At other times, such officers may simply offer a friendly word to lift a prisoner's spirits. "Sometimes you just smile to cheer them up sometimes. Sometimes they're looking sad, you say, 'What's wrong? It's not that bad. Cheer up.' " The fact that prisoners may not tell them what's wrong or visibly cheer up is a disappointment—none of the officers claimed success as informal counselors—but it does not discourage the officers from trying to be of help. Their job, they say, is a thankless one. These officers behave as they do to satisfy their own personal and professional standards, not to win praise or recognition from the prisoners.

Such officers are explicitly aware of the limits of a human-service role on death row. Quite consciously, they try to be friendly without becoming friends, to be responsive without kowtowing. They don't appease; they simply care enough to serve and protect. In their view, the ideal officer "doesn't get too close but gets close enough to deal with them and accept them for who they are." If a guard gets too friendly, prisoners "can ask you for favors, and you can get caught up in things." The objective is to be a concerned professional that is, "to deal with them on a one-to-one basis but not get emotionally involved with them." These officers see themselves as correctional professionals who must go about their work in a civil and responsive but fundamentally businesslike way.

Us and Them: The Divisive Role of Executions

Executions cast a long shadow over death row and impose a stark limit on the degree of emotional involvement that is possible between officers and inmates. As one prisoner on a solitary-confinement death row observed, "We know within ourselves that no matter how courteous a guard tries to be to us, we know what he will do in the end. And so that right there makes us guard against them."[49] Contrary to the view of this and, indeed, most condemned prisoners, death row officers normally are not involved in executions; the execution team is assembled from officers who have had little or no contact with the prisoner prior to the deathwatch. Still, complicity is obvious in that the death row officers expressly hold the prisoners for the purpose of execution. Some of the guards of our reformed death row recognized this complicity; others did not. In any case, the prisoners hold each and every officer accountable. "You can feel the tension in the air after an execution," observed one officer. "I think they are angry at anybody with a [correctional] uniform."

Anger is not the only emotion to follow in the wake of executions. Prisoners may also feel a sense of loss. Some condemned prisoners, on this and other death rows, develop among themselves a primitive notion of community.[50] The execution of one of their fellows is therefore a loss. Their sense of loss accentuates feelings of powerlessness and vulnerability; it reaffirms in no uncertain terms the lonely fate that awaits the condemned prisoners. The complicated mix of sentiments evoked by the execution of their fellows can seem overwhelming and inexplicable; only rage at the death row officers, the culprits once removed from the execution team, offers relief. In the words of one prisoner,

I wanted to understand why Mike was being taken from me, but it was impossible. Each day I have to interact with the same guards who came to the unit and took him from me. These guards were the same guards who were telling me, "Joe, Mike is a good man. They shouldn't kill him." Each time I heard a guard say that, I could feel the anger within me. What they were saying made no sense to me. I wanted to scream, "NO!" I wanted to tear down the prison walls and make them stop. I hated them. . . . Before that day four other friends had been executed: whom I ate with, talked with, played with, argued with—men whom I came to know as friends and shared a life bond with. Men whom no matter what their crimes, I could not see as anything but human beings . . . men whose tears I saw, whose flesh I touched, whose pain I still feel. I still know the hopelessness, I am still with the guards who took them away to be executed, and I am still trying to understand.[51]

Some of the death row officers, too, develop a sense of community with at least some of the prisoners. The executions of these prisoners are a loss for the staff as well. Parting with prisoners one has come to know and like can be at once touching and depressing. An officer on our reformed death row, supervising a prisoner's last visit with his family, reacted in a revealing way.

The reality of that last family visit really made me feel bad. His daughter didn't even know him. It was depressing to be there. . . . It's supposed to be part of the job, like being a doctor or something. You lose a patient and that's just it, but it's not that easy. You never forget this type of thing, but you can put it behind you.

For this officer, one "loses" a prisoner to execution. Like any genuine loss, it doesn't come easily.

To be sure, officers on this and other death rows more typically remain aloof from condemned prisoners or even treat them abusively. They do not see executions as emotionally wrenching events, nor do they take pleasure in them. They behave as they do, in part, to avoid the emotional hurt that involvement with prisoners would bring. "You can't be buddy-buddy," said one officer, "you've got to keep it business." This business is a matter of life and death, killing and dying. Death row officers, however, are not simply waiting to kill the prisoners, whatever the prisoners may feel. In many ways, the officers, too, are pawns in the death penalty drama. The officers know that condemned prisoners either have their sentences changed by appeal or commutation, in which case they never see them again, or the prisoners are executed. In either case, but particularly when prisoners are executed, most officers feel it is better not to have known them well.

More concretely, one officer told me that he kept his emotional distance from the condemned because he might be the one to escort them to the death house. The death house, which in the state under study is located in another prison, is where the executions occur. There another group of correctional officers takes over, conducting the deathwatch and carrying out the execution. . . .

ENDNOTES

1. C. A. Nesbitt and R. L. Howard, *Management of Death Row Inmates: An Examination of the Issues* (Laurel, Md.: American Correctional Association, 1988). See especially Chap. 3, p. 8, and Chap. 5, p. 4. The ACA disseminates this monograph only to prison officials and their consultants. A shorter version is available to the public. See *Managing Death-Sentenced Inmates: A Survey of Practices* (Laurel, Md.: American Correctional Association, 1989).

2. P. Brasfield with J. M. Elliot, *Deathman Pass Me By* (San Bernardino: Borgo Press, 1983), 91–92.

3. A. Bronstein, personal communication.

4. B. Jackson and D. Christian, *Death Row* (Boston: Beacon Press, 1980), 14.

5. C. Chessman, "Trial by Ordeal," in *Death Row: An Affirmation of Life,* ed. S. Levine (New York: Balantine, 1972), 4.

6. Jackson and Christian (n. 4), 94.

7. See G. Sykes, *The Society of Captives* (New York: Atheneum, 1966); J. Irwin, *Prisons in Turmoil* (Boston: Little, Brown, 1980); and R. Johnson, *Hard Time: Understanding and Reforming the Prison* (Pacific Grove, Calif.: Brooks/Cole, 1987).

8. B. Schwartz, "Deprivation of Privacy as a 'Functional Prerequisite': The Case of the Prison," *Journal of Criminal Law and Criminology* 63 (1972):235–236.

9. I and Professor Stanley Brodsky of the University of Alabama independently found 70 percent of Alabama's condemned prisoners to be showing signs of deterioration. My finding, based on content analysis of interviews, was that "7 of every 10 prisoners diagnosed themselves as suffering physical, mental or emotional deterioration in what was typically portrayed as the interpersonal vacuum constituting the human environment of death row." See R. Johnson, "Life under Sentence of Death," in *The Pains of Imprisonment,* ed. R. Johnson and H. Toch (Prospect Heights, Ill.: Waveland Press, 1988), 132. Brodsky found a 70 percent deterioration rate for this same population using objective personality tests. Brodsky's results are reported in depositions pertaining to Jacobs v. Britton, No. 78–309H et al. (S.D. Ala., 1979).

Other studies have described the problem of deterioration as common among condemned prisoners but have not provided statistics on the prevalence of symptoms. See R. Johnson, *Condemned to Die: Life under Sentence of Death* (Prospect Heights., Ill.: Waveland Press, 1989). . . . Jackson and Christian (n. 4), 174–189 (examining Texas's death row); L. West, "Psychiatric Reflections on the Death Penalty," *American Journal of Orthopsychiatry* 45 (1975):689–700 (covering death row prisoners generally); H. Bluestone and C. L. McGahee, "Reaction to Extreme Stress: Impending Death by Execution," *American Journal of Psychiatry* 119 (1962):393–396 (covering death row prisoners at Sing Sing); and J. Gallemore and J. Panton, "Inmate Responses to Lengthy Death Row Confinement," *American Journal of Psychiatry* 129 (1972):167–172 (covering death row prisoners in North Carolina). In 1968, Congress heard testimony on the problem of deterioration among the condemned. See U.S. Congress, Senate Committee on the Judiciary, *To Abolish the Death Penalty: Hearings before the Subcommittee on Criminal Laws and Procedures,* 90th Cong., 2nd sess., March 20 and 21 and July 2, 1968, S. 1760.

10. C. M. Lambrix, "The Isolation of Death Row," in *Facing the Death Penalty: Essays on a Cruel and Unusual Punishment,* ed. M. L. Radelet (Philadelphia: Temple University Press, 1989), 199.

11. Johnson, *Condemned* (n. 9), 48, 48.

12. Ibid., 49.

13. Ibid., 51.

14. Jackson and Christian (n. 4), 232, 226.

15. M. L. Radelet, M. Vandiver, and F. Berardo, "Families, Prisons, and Men with Death Sentences: The Human Impact of Structured Uncertainty," *Journal of Family Issues* 4(4):596 (December 1983). For many regular prison guards, caring, expressed as a concern for delivering human services and thereby ameliorating the stresses of confinement, is a central feature of their work. See H. Toch, "Is a Correctional Officer, by Any Other Name, a 'Screw'?" *Criminal Justice Review* 3 (1978):19–35; R. Johnson and J. Price, "The Complete Correctional Officer: Human Service and the Human Environment of Prison," *Criminal Justice and Behavior* 8(3):343–373 (1981); L. Lombardo, *Guards Imprisoned: Correctional Officers at Work* (New York: Elsevier, 1981); and R. Johnson, *Hard Time* (n. 7), Chap. 8.

16. Jackson and Christian (n. 4), 90, 19.

17. Brasfield (n. 2), 80.

18. Lambrix (n. 10), 198, 200, 200.

19. Jackson and Christian (n. 4) 31. See also Lambrix (n. 10).

20. Lambrix (n. 10). 199.

21. Jackson and Christian (n. 4), 15. See also Johnson, *Condemned* (n. 9); Radelet et al. (n. 15); and B. Eshelman, *Death Row Chaplain* (New York: Signet Books, 1972).

22. M. Vandiver, "Coping with Death: Families of the Terminally Ill, Homicide Victims, and Condemned Prisoners," in *Facing the Death Penalty: Essays on a Cruel and Unusual Punishment,* ed. M. L. Radelet (Philadelphia: Temple University Press, 1989), 133.

23. Johnson, *Condemned* (n. 9), 54.

24. Ibid., 50.

25. Radelet et al. (n. 15), 605.

26. Johnson, *Condemned* (n. 9), 115.

27. Ibid., Chap. 1; Radelet et al. (n. 15); Jackson and Christian (n. 4), 100–109.

28. Jackson and Christian (n. 4), 78.

29. Johnson, *Condemned* (n. 9), 70–71, 71.

30. C. Turnbull, "Death by Decree: An Anthropological Approach to Capital Punishment," *Natural History* 87 (1978):54.

31. Johnson, *Condemned* (n. 9), 65.

32. Ibid., Chap. 4.

33. Ibid., 74.

34. Groseclose v. Dutton, 609 F. Supp. 1432 (D.C. Tenn. 1985), 1436.

35. J. M. Giarratano, "The Pains of Life," in *Facing the Death Penalty: Essays on a Cruel and Unusual Punishment,* ed. M. L. Radelet (Philadelphia: Temple University Press, 1989), 195.

36. *Groseclose* (n. 34), 1436.

37. See n. 9.

38. Johnson, *Condemned* (n. 9); Jackson and Christian (n. 4).

39. Johnson (n. 9), 112, 96.

40. Ibid., Chap. 3.

41. Radelet et al. (n. 15); Jackson and Christian (n. 4).

42. Toch (n. 15).

43. Personal communication from a death row inmate, as part of an unpublished survey of death row living conditions conducted by John Conrad and myself (1984).

44. Johnson, *Condemned* (n. 9), 69.

45. Radelet et al. (n. 15).

46. Johnson, *Condemned* (n. 9), 69.

47. Ibid., 60.

48. Lombardo (n. 15); Johnson, *Hard Time* (n. 17).

49. Johnson, *Condemned* (n. 9), 64.

50. Ibid., Chap. 7.

51. Giarratano (n. 35), 194–195.

STUDY QUESTIONS FOR READING 12_____

1. What is the goal on all death rows? What does this mean for how death row prisoners are treated? How is this attitude reflected in the language guards use?

2. How do the reformed death rows differ from the traditional solitary-confinement death rows?

3. Death row inmates say they are treated as if they are already dead. How does this affect their religion and visits from family?

4. What do visits on death row in Alabama resemble?

5. What was emphasized in the training of officers for death row? What was not emphasized?

6. Why are guards so suspicious on death row?

7. How do the more human relations–oriented guards act on death row? Why are even these guards so cautious?

LETHAL LOTTERY

NINA SIEGAL

Standing in the hospice of the California Medical Facility at Vacaville, with its brightly waxed floors and whitewashed walls and the sharp smell of pine cleaner in the air, you can forget you're in a maximum-security prison. It is quiet here, the only sounds the low murmur of a television set and the hushed voices of two inmates: a pastoral care worker and a patient.

Down the hallway and beyond the glass doors, it's another world entirely.

A cacophony of sounds bounces off the walls of the prison's long, bleak central corridor, called the "main line." Pallid inmates, dressed in light blue shirts and jeans, walk jagged paths down the hall; klatches of correctional officers, clad in pressed brown and teal, are poised nearby. Inflexible but not particularly orderly, with constant talking and yelling, it seems like some form of underground military, preparing for war.

Although the hospice and prison are both antiseptic, institutional environments, it is odd to find two such seemingly opposed institutions joined together—the focused, attentive culture of quality medical care, and the austere, forbidding and impersonal world of corrections. But it is an increasingly common juxtaposition.

Since the mid-'80s, new "tough on crime" laws have caused the nation's prison population to swell to more than 1.7 million. In the past decade, the number of incarcerated men and women has more than doubled, due in large part to mandatory drug-sentencing guidelines at both the federal and state levels. Since the percentage of inmate substance users continues to surge, more prisoners are at risk for a panoply of health problems related to drugs and the hard life of

the streets. Topping the list is HIV, now one of the most common diseases among the incarcerated. Some sick inmates end up in decent hospices like Vacaville's, but the majority receive substandard care all around.

In August 1997, the Bureau of Justice Statistics (BJS) of the U.S. Department of Justice put out a special report on HIV in Prisons and Jails, using data culled in 1995. According to the survey, 24,226 state and federal prison inmates—2.3 percent of the total incarcerated population—had HIV. The vast majority—23,404—were in state facilities (state prisons house the vast majority of inmates), while 822 were in federal institutions. The same report indicated that 0.5 percent of the total U.S. prison population had AIDS, more than six times the rate of the general population, 0.08 percent.

In the past few years, prisons nationwide have been confronted with the problem of treating the growing numbers of HIV positive inmates, and most have been slow to respond to their new, complex and ever-changing needs. In some prisons, campaigns by AIDS activists and class-action lawsuits alleging gross violations of inmates' civil and constitutional rights have instigated change.

Faced with court-ordered consent decrees requiring them to improve their medical care, some prison systems, such as the Connecticut Department of Corrections, have made impressive unprovements. Others, such as the Alabama Department of Corrections, remain health-care backwaters, where treatment and care are dangerously inadequate. As a result, the type of health care for those with HIV in state prisons ranges from relatively good to cruelly poor. Since inmates are often moved from one institution to another and denied access to basic information and services, such uneven care poses a significant health hazard, not just to prisoners but to the public at large as well.

THE RIGHT STUFF

What is "good" care in the prison setting? Simply put, it is the same standard of care that people with HIV on the outside deserve: access to all 11 anti-HIV drugs currently approved by the FDA, medicine for opportunistic infections and alternative therapies where appropriate.

But there are additional burdens on physicians and other health care workers who treat HIV in prisons: They must be able to help inmates comply with the complicated dosing schedules of combination regimens and to ensure that inmates get consistent treatment even if under lockdown, at parole hearings or in court, or transferred to another institution. Finding a knowledgeable doctor in a prison setting is no simple feat. Anne S. De Groot, MD, an assistant professor of medicine at Brown University Medical School who has worked in prisons for 10 years, says that there are a handful of prison doctors nationwide [who are] compassionate and interested in their patients, but otherwise the doctors inside are far from the best in their fields. "There are a lot of doctors who didn't succeed in community-based or academic-based facilities," she says. "They didn't have the people skills. So they ended up in prison, and the patients can't do anything about it."

When adequate care is not available, caregivers should help prisoners gain access to outside hospitals and infectious-diseases specialists and, when appropriate, help terminally ill prisoners get early medical release—known as "compassionate release"—so they won't die inside.

Even though protease inhibitors have recently become widely available in many prisons, it is difficult to determine how many inmates are on combination therapy. A 1997 report by Abt Associates Inc., a public-health research firm in Cambridge, Massachusetts, found that 90 percent of all state prison systems claimed to provide protease-based combos to their inmates, 100 percent claimed they conducted CD4 monitoring, and 80 percent claimed they administered viral load tests. But Theodore M. Hammett, the author of the study, admits that the statistics may be misleading. "Those numbers look good, but there's quite a bit of information showing that there are a number of problems with access," he says. "The picture is not as rosy as it seems."

Frederick Altice, MD, an assistant professor of medicine at Yale University, director of the college's HIV in Prisons Program and a national expert on HIV care in prison, says the Abt numbers are more than dubious. "If a prison has just one patient on a protease inhibitor, they can say on those surveys, 'Yes, we provide it,' " Altice says. "States don't want to say they are not providing the community standard of care. They can't afford to, because it's mud on their face. The real question would be, 'What percentage of inmates with HIV have access to protease inhibitors?' "

Altice conducted his own study in the Connecticut prison system and determined that 80 percent of all inmates with HIV were on protease inhibitors. But he guesses that the total would be much lower nationwide—about 40 percent—although he knows of no official studies.

De Groot agrees that Hammett's numbers are too optimistic. "Institutions will tell you that they have combination therapies when saquinavir is the only protease inhibitor they have," she says. "If you come in on Crixivan, too bad—you get saquinavir. If you get sick from saquinavir, tough luck. Triple therapy really means having access to all 11 possible drugs, and having a qualified physician helping you to make decisions about which are the best ones for you."

Patients on combination therapies often have debilitating side effects, ranging from nausea and dizziness to kidney stones or neuropathy. But there is an equally grave danger when those on combo-therapy fail to adhere to dosing requirements: Their virus can become resistant to entire classes of drugs, aborting future treatment options. Drug resistance is not just bad for the one patient—it can be disastrous for the whole community because these super-resistant strains may be spread.

Fewer than 20 state prison systems—including California, Florida, Illinois, Massachusetts, New Jersey, New York and Texas—and the federal Bureau of Prisons (BOP) have written policies stating that they will provide the federally endorsed standard of care, according to Michael Haggerty, the executive director of the Correctional HIV Consortium in California.

Even in relatively enlightened systems, however, prison docs often have trouble ensuring that prisoners get their medications on time (and with meals if necessary), are supplied with timely refills and have access to the necessary supplements, prophylactic medications or painkillers. Judy Greenspan, chair of the HIV in Prison Committee of California Prison Focus, says she knows of no prison that adapts meal times to a prisoner's drug-compliance needs. Only a few facilities nationwide go out of their way to provide HIV positive inmates with medically specialized diets, although some offer larger portions. And only on a case-by-case basis do prisons give inmates medication to take on their own a few hours after a meal or offer snacks for HIV drugs that must be taken with food.

Thirty-one state systems and the BOP have compassionate-release or medical-parole programs, but the process is usually long and complicated. In California, for example, a prison doctor may initiate early release if an inmate is judged to be within six months of death. The application has to be approved by the prison counselor, the warden and the director of the Department of Corrections. A judge makes the ultimate decision, in some cases only after convening a hearing.

A HEALTH CARE CRAPSHOOT

To generalize about HIV care in prison is hard because it is not standardized across the nation. Each state system has its own set of policies and procedures for treating inmates, and the federal prison system, too, operates under its own guidelines. Even within each state, the quality of treatment programs varies widely from facility to facility.

Most advocates agree that Alabama's prison system represents the bottom rung of AIDS care. Its 200-plus HIV positive inmates are segregated from the general population and denied access to programs. The state contracts out its medical care to a St. Louis company called Correctional Medical Systems, but according to one longtime volunteer who doesn't want to be identified, inmates have a hard time even getting

CD4 counts. "You are in the system for 30 days and if you test positive, you're segregated, " she says. "Then you just stay there and vegetate."

Jackie Walker, AIDS information coordinator for the ACLU's National Prison Project, agrees that Alabama's care is the nation's worst. "Being in Alabama, or being in a small county jail anywhere, are the worst places if you're a prisoner with HIV," she says. "Alabama punishes prisoners for being HIV positive. You don't have access to the work that inmates in the regular population get, you can't get educational or vocational programs, you can't get substance-abuse programs, you can't get work release."

In 1988, the ACLU filed a class-action suit, Onishea v. Hopper, on behalf of the HIV positive inmates in Alabama's state system, challenging their segregation and exclusion from prison programs and activities. U.S. District Judge Robert E. Varner ruled against the prisoners twice, saying that the danger of transmission was too great to allow inmates with HIV into the general prison population. The case is in its second appeals process.

By comparison, care in New York state, with the highest proportion (10.7 percent) of HIV positive inmates—about 7,500 of more than 70,000 prisoners—is near the gold standard, at least on paper. It is one of the few states that has all 11 FDA-approved HIV drugs in all 69 state prisons as well as a statewide standard of care, established by the New York State AIDS Institute. Available programs include confidential testing, education, support services, one-on-one and group counseling, and transitional and pre-release counseling. Of course, even with all this, there are still many complaints about care, and the system has a long way to go before all inmates are treated adequately.

THE CASE OF CALIFORNIA

Mid-range in terms of quality AIDS care lies California, the state with the fourth-largest HIV positive prison population. (Only New York, Florida and Texas have more.) According to recent estimates, there are 1,300 known HIV cases in California's prison system, about 0.8 percent of the state's inmates. California is one of only three states (the others are Alabama and

Mississippi) that segregate their HIV positive inmates by housing them in separate units in each prison.

By and large, the care for California inmates depends on who is in charge. For instance, Joe Bick, MD, chief medical officer at Vacaville since 1993, is credited with making its HIV care perhaps the best in the nation. Bick is assisted by a court mandate: In the late '80s, the prison was ordered by a California judge to improve its medical care.

Care for the 500 HIV positive men at Vacaville is a top institutional priority, says Bick. All FDA-approved drugs are available. The clinic physicians keep charts of all meds about to expire so that patients do not have to request refills, and they clock the time it takes between an inmate's request for a visit and when he is seen. Bick says the wait is rarely more than a week.

And there is an effort to minimize the amount of time that care is interrupted by the special circumstances of prison life. During lockdowns, or if an inmate is transferred to administrative segregation—under lock and key 23 hours a day—clinic staff make cell calls so inmates get treatments on time. Bick even makes it a priority to prescribe reasonable doses of pain medications, famously difficult to get in prisons because of the security risk of distribution.

Even some of the most vocal critics of HIV treatment in correctional settings concede that the medical facility is doing a good job. "I believe that Vacaville is a model for what can be done within a prison setting," says advocate Greenspan. "I would wager that it is one of the best medical facilities for prisoners in the country."

But Vacaville's achievements do not translate into good care throughout the state. Just look south, to Corcoran State Prison, for a dramatically different picture of health care. Quentin Hicks, a 33-year-old inmate serving a five-year sentence for fraud, says that he has refused to start a triple-combination regimen because the average wait for refills at Corcoran is three weeks, and he knows that irregular dosing can lead to drug resistance. "If I'm going to take protease inhibitors, I want it to work," says Hicks. "I don't want to mess up my chances of it working in the future."

According to a peer educator, who wanted to be identified only as C.K., most inmates at Corcoran are offered just one protease inhibitor—Crixivan—even if they are on a different regimen when they arrive at the prison. Some report getting double-combination therapy (which is universally acknowledged as substandard). Although viral load tests should be done once every three months, prisoners at Corcoran report getting them only every six months. "My greatest concern about Corcoran is that once I got very sick, I would not receive proper care, and I would die miserably," wrote C.K. in a medical questionnaire.

WOMEN DO WORSE

The level of care is even worse in California's women's prisons. There are an estimated 1,000 HIV positive inmates in the state's four female facilities, or about 4 percent of all women prisoners. In general, women in prison are more likely to be HIV positive than male inmates; according to the BJS, nationwide 4 percent of all women prisoners are positive, compared with 2.3 percent of all men. But prisoner advocates agree that women have a harder time getting treatment than men do, and rarely have access to combination therapy. While there are four men's facilities in the state with licensed medical care facilities, there is only one licensed medical facility for women—the Skilled Nursing Facility at the Central California Women's Facility (CCWF) in Chowchilla, notorious for its inadequate care.

Linda Cortez, incarcerated at CCWF in 1995 where she was diagnosed with AIDS, knows that all too well. Arrested in January 1994 in Riverside County for possession of an unregistered firearm and violating her parole, Cortez spent almost three years in CCWF before compassionate release sent her home in December 1996. While at CCWF, she came down with AIDS-related herpes zoster on her leg, which looked like a series of dark-red, blistering cigarette burns, but she says the doctor didn't admit her to the infirmary. The herpes spread to her eyes, and she went blind.

Brown Medical School's De Groot says that herpes zoster is a common complication of HIV that, if properly treated, should never lead to permanent disability. "If it was herpes that blinded her, that is unacceptable," says De Groot. "It could happen in Africa where there is inadequate medical care overall, but it should never have happened in the United States."

But Cortez's bad luck didn't end there. After she was returned to her old cell, she says that no one acknowledged that she couldn't see or taught her how to get around or made sure that she got breakfast—when she was brought a breakfast tray, no one told her it was there. When she finally left prison in December 1996, Cortez weighed 92 pounds, was unable to walk and was convinced that she was about to die. "My care at Chowchilla?" said Cortez recently. "I'll put it like this: If you were dying of thirst and I stuck you in the desert with no water, how would you feel? You would die from dehydration." She paused. "To put it even more bluntly: They didn't give a fuck."

After leaving prison, Cortez was treated at the University of Southern California Medical Center in Los Angeles, where she was given AIDS meds, taught how to use her legs again and placed on an appropriate diet. Since then, she has learned how to manage her HIV herself, regained weight and begun working with the Braille Center to become self-sufficient.

In May 1995, hundreds of inmates at CCWF and the California Institute for Women (CIW) in Frontera filed a class-action lawsuit in the U.S. District Court for Eastern California against the California Department of Corrections, alleging that their rights were violated because they were provided inadequate health care, including inmates with chronic and terminal conditions such as HIV. Cynthia Chandler, director of the Women's Positive Legal Action Network, based in Oakland, California, describes the care at CCWF as "dangerously, negligently lacking. It was like watching torture in progress."

The disparity in care between Vacaville and Corcoran or CCWF brings into sharp focus the essential problem in California: It is so uneven that when an inmate is moved, it's a crapshoot as to what kind of medication, education or services they get. Chandler says that typically, when an inmate is moved from one prison to another, he or she is taken off all meds, retested for HIV and placed on an entirely new drug regimen. Medical files are routinely lost and may not show up for years.

Stories of negligence and abuse are repeated again and again across the nation. In some cases, inmates with HIV may be sent to the nearest outside hospital, whether or not it has an infectious-disease specialist. But many inmates in state and federal prisons simply go untreated and end up in prison infirmaries or hospitals where they are left to die.

Increasingly, the final, short reprieve provided by compassionate release is unavailable, as many facilities send inmates to in-prison hospices. The Vacaville hospice, with its sparkling floors and countertops, hires inmates as pastoral care workers to comfort the dying, and the care is sensitive and timely. But now there is talk of building hospices in prisons such as CCWF, where inmates serve longer sentences. Many advocates call this trend dangerous because prisons cannot be relied upon to provide even basic services. "I worry about setting up a hospice in a prison unit with no medical care," Greenspan says. "In a prison with no medical care, a hospice unit becomes a death camp."

STUDY QUESTIONS FOR READING 13

1. In 1997, how many thousands of inmates were HIV positive? What percentage had full-blown AIDS? How does this compare to the rest of the population?

2. According to Siegal, what is good care in the prison setting? How does actual prison care compare to this standard?

3. What should happen when the community standard of care is not available for an inmate? Is this what usually happens?

4. Compare the standards of care in Alabama to New York. What is the rate of HIV infection in New York prisons?

5. How does the care differ between women and men? Between the prison and the community? Illustrate your points by telling the story of Linda Cortez.

6. What are the pros and cons of hospice care behind prison walls? In the worst case, what does Greenspan compare prison hospices to? Why?

CRITICAL PROBLEMS OF
WOMEN IN PRISON

PHYLLIS JO BAUNACH

Until recently, the problems confronting incarcerated women offenders have been largely ignored. The massive ten volume report issued in 1967 by the President's Commission on Law Enforcement and the Administration of Justice made no mention of women offenders (Murton and Baunach, 1973:543). The Department of Labor Manpower Administration devoted only about one half of a page of its 113 page report dealing with research efforts in correction to incarcerated women because those offenders "did not play a major role in the offender projects" (McArthur, 1974:8).

The primary reason that women offenders of all ages have been neglected is that there are so few of them in American jails and prisons. Surveys in 1970 indicated that only one in seven persons arrested (FBI, 1970:12) and only one in ten persons incarcerated (National Prisoner Statistics, 1972:6) was a woman over 18 years old. Some authors suggested in the mid-1970s that these statistics remained accurate (Simon, 1975:108).

More recent figures indicate that the percentage of women incarcerated in the United States increased from 4.4 percent to 5.7 percent (Bureau of Justice Statistics, 1990). Immarigeon and Chesney-Lind (1991:5–6) argue that:

> *Women have been hit hard by our nation's punitive policies. In recent years, female populations in jails and prisons have increased disproportionately to the increase of women's involvement in serious crime. The U.S. Bureau of Justice Statistics (BJS) reports that the average daily population of women confined in local jails rose by 82 percent between 1984 and 1988. The number of men in jail increased by 44 percent during this period. . . . In 1979, there were 12,005 women in our nation's prisons. By 1988, that number had grown to 32,691, an increase of 172 percent.*

Thus, despite the fact that there are fewer women than men incarcerated in American jails and prisons, the number of women incarcerated is rising dramatically. Therefore, the needs of incarcerated women must be understood in order to deal more effectively with this increasing population. With these points in mind, this chapter will describe conditions of confinement, programmatic inadequacies, and potential means of alleviating problems encountered by women offenders.

THE CONDITIONS OF
WOMEN'S CONFINEMENT

Unlike prisons for men, many women's prisons resemble college campuses, rather than fortress penitentiaries.[1] Often, there are no gun towers, no armed guards and no stone walls or fences with concertina wire strung on top. Neatly pruned hedges, well-kept flower gardens, attractive brick buildings and wide paved walkways greet the visitor's eye at women's prisons in many states. Often these institutions are located in rural, pastoral settings which may suggest tranquility and well-being to the casual observer.

However, placid external appearances are not indicative of the psychological environment of incarceration from an inmate's perspective. The freedom of movement and choice of daily activities we take for granted may be nonexistent in a prison setting. Regulations formulated by those in authority guide the inmate's life. Close personal contacts may be forbidden to minimize the potential development of homosexual relationships. However, these restrictions may limit the formation of more acceptable interpersonal relationships as well. Security requirements dictate searching letters, packages and incoming inmates for contraband. After a brief "incarceration" in the Women's Detention Center in Washington, D.C., journalist Jessica Mitford perceived prison life as "planned, unrelieved inactivity and boredom . . . no overt brutality but plenty of random, largely unintentional cruelty" (Mitford, 1973:27).

The lack of autonomy, the loss of identity, and powerlessness create an exaggerated dependency upon those in authority for incarcerated women. Burkhart's descriptions suggest that reactions to this environment may entail despondency, frustrations, heightened tensions, anxiety and apathy. As one inmate said:

> You start losing your identity when you get locked up. You stop seeking things, you stop doing things for yourself, you stop looking for things. You feel nothing's gonna be all right again . . . (Burkhart, 1973:120).

Two major problems confronting incarcerated women are the loss of love and family and the lack of meaningful training programs.

THE LOSS OF LOVE AND FAMILY

Perhaps one of the most serious problems faced by incarcerated women is separation from their loved ones. Anecdotal and limited statistical evidence suggest that one of the greatest concerns of confined women is their children (Glick and Neto, 1977:116). In their study of the women at the California Institution of Women (CIW) at Frontera, Ward and Kassebaum found that 43 percent of the women incarcerated for less than six months, 42 percent of the women incarcerated for six months to a year, and 38 percent of the women incarcerated for more than a year responded that the most difficult aspect of adjustment to prison was the absence of home and family (Ward and Kassebaum, 1965:120). At the time they conducted their study, the authors noted that problems of the separation of women from their children were especially felt among the women at CIW, as 59 percent of them had minor children and 68 percent were mothers (Ward and Kassebaum, 1965:15). More recently, the National Study of Women's Correctional

Programs reported that of approximately 6,300 incarcerated women studied in fourteen states, 56.3 percent had one or more dependent children living with them prior to incarceration (Glick and Neto, 1977:116).

Inmate mothers are especially concerned about the custody and care of their children during their confinement. Children most often stay with their maternal grandmothers. Other caretakers include the child's father or other relatives. However, incarcerated mothers express the most satisfaction when their children are placed with their maternal grandmothers and when they have participated in the decision as to where the child will live. Involvement in the decision-making process to place children gives inmate-mothers some peace of mind that their children will live in safe surroundings. Moreover, in placing children with maternal grandmothers, inmate-mothers feel sure that they will encounter minimal difficulties in taking the child back after release (Baunach, 1984).

Children may, however, be placed in foster homes or put up for adoption if suitable alternatives are unavailable. This might occur if the woman's mother is not a viable placement; if the child's father cannot be located or is in prison himself; or if there are no other relatives to care for the child. In the long run, this separation may severely damage the family relationship (Female Offender Resource Center, 1976:12; LEAA Task Force on Women 1975:5). Moreover, sometimes the careful arrangements made by women prior to incarceration for the care of their children may be reversed by authorities who "know what is best" for the child's welfare. For instance, a black inmate in Washington state had procured placement for her eight children with white members of her congregation. Despite the inmate's efforts, and the help of her Christian friends, a young social worker decided that the children should be placed with black families. The inmate objected that her children would be happier with white friends than with black strangers, and responded, "They're not like kittens where you give half the litter away" (O'Brien, 1974:3).

Incarcerated mothers are burdened not only with the stigma associated with imprisonment but also with the knowledge that their own behavior has caused the separation from children. The psychological consequences experienced by these women often are very severe (Lundberg, et al., 1975:36). For instance, mothering seems to be an "axis of self-esteem" (Lundberg, et al., 1975:36) for incarcerated women. The separation generates feelings of emptiness, helplessness, anger and bitterness, guilt and fear of loss or rejection by the children. DuBose (1975:8) similarly found that with prolonged separation, mothers feared that children might establish bonds of affection more closely with caretakers than their mothers. Moreover, mothers feared that teenage children who stayed with elderly grandparents would be arrested because supervision was inadequate.

Baunach (1984) studied the effects of the separation from their children on 138 inmate mothers incarcerated in prisons in Washington state and Kentucky. Her findings revealed that regardless of race or age, women expressed guilt and shame that they committed crimes which separated them from their children. Moreover, for any women drug users, incarceration was the first extended time period they were not using drugs and had an opportunity to consider the effects of their behavior upon their children. Many wondered how they would remain "clean" once released and reunited with their children. Other women were bitter and angry at "the system" because they had pled guilty or because they felt that they had been convicted unfairly. These women thus felt that the separation from their children was unjust.

Most of the women with older children indicated that their children knew that their mothers were locked up for "being bad." Some mothers wanted this situation to serve as an example to their children of what would happen if they, too, broke the law. In addition, many mothers told their children where they were, because these mothers preferred to have a "straight relationship" with their children. On the other hand, women with very young children often did not tell their children that they were in prison because they felt the children were too young to understand or would suffer negative reprisals from playmates (Baunach, 1984).

The emotional pains of separation may be especially acute for women who are pregnant when incarcerated. These women bear their children in the prison maternity ward or at a nearby hospital and within a short time are compelled to give them up, possibly to foster parents or adoption agencies. One effect of this separation may be severe depression, shock or loss of self-esteem.[2]

In addition, although varying among institutions, visitation policies and procedures determine the extent to which a woman can maintain contact with her children. Sometimes, this contact is minimal. For example, the Washington, D.C. Citizen's Council issued a report in 1972 which noted, among other things, that women at the Washington, D.C. Detention Center had only two one-hour visits each week. Moreover, there had been no provisions made for the mothers, who comprised some 86 percent of the inmate population, to visit their children (Murton and Baunach, 1973:548).

It must be noted that whether or not an inmate-mother should retain or relinquish her parental rights to her child(ren) during or following incarceration involves both moral and legal decisions which in some ways may overlap. From a legal perspective, Palmer (1972) argued that incarceration, per se, does not provide adequate evidence that a parent is unfit. Rather, he suggested that the courts should consider additional factors, such as the woman's relationship to the offspring prior to incarceration and the causal relationship between the criminal act and the mother's ability to perform her parental role. With these points in mind, judges would be better able to determine the mother's parental fitness and to decide whether or not the child(ren) should be placed in her custody after her release.

A further argument raised along these lines was that legislative guidelines limit the extent to which the courts may modify their procedures for deciding parental fitness. Guidelines currently consider the best interests of the child(ren), but simultaneously treat the issue of parental fitness inequitably. Established standards such as nonsupport, child abuse, neglect, desertion, drunkenness, adultery, mental illness and incarceration have been regarded as manifestations of the abandonment of parental responsibilities and their justification for the termination of parental rights. The author pointed out that these interpretations are erroneous and that a reassessment of the standards is required (Palmer, 1972).

The court's consideration of a mother's criminal act and subsequent incarceration as a voluntary relinquishment of her parental rights was decided in re: Jameson (1967). In this case, the court held that the mother knew prior to committing the act that she would be incarcerated for it if convicted. Palmer challenged this justification as illogical, since the women's intention may have been to obtain money or food with no intention of getting caught. Furthermore, he noted, if she wished to abandon her child, the woman probably could have devised alternative means which would not have been detrimental or discomforting to herself.

The author suggested that imprisonment in and of itself does not constitute abandonment. Rather, additional factors, such as parental neglect and withholding affection, should be used to substantiate claims of abandonment. Given this background, Palmer recommended legislative reform, such as allowing an inmate to live with her children (under two years old) in prison, in conditions conducive to positive interaction; devising "mother release" programs to enable inmate-mothers to stay with their children in the community; and reforming visitation practices to allow for more relaxed visits in less security-oriented surroundings.

With respect to legislation, a few states have legislation allowing children under two years old to live with their mothers in prison; however, this practice is not currently used regularly. In addition, there has been a growing concern for the legal rights and rehabilitative needs of inmate-mothers and their children. This concern was reflected in a California lawsuit regarding an inmate-mother's right to have her children live with her in prison. The suit, however, was denied in court. Arguments raised included the effects that the prison environment and procedures could have on the child and the potential effects of the child's presence on the prison and other inmates (La Point, 1977:13–14; Shepard and Zemans, 1950).

Baunach (1984) explored some of the inmates' attitudes toward allowing children to stay in the prison for short periods of time (i.e., all day or overnight). Regardless of whether or not they have children of their own, women in prison tend to respond favorably to the presence of children. Many women indicated that they try to "clean up their language and behavior" when children are present, and enjoy watching or playing with children. However, to date, there has been no research on the effects on the children of being in a prison with mothers for short or long periods of time.

LACK OF MEANINGFUL TRAINING PROGRAMS

Since the social roles of women in our culture traditionally have been oriented toward homemaker and mother, incarcerated women usually have been trained to assume these roles upon release. Thus, training programs for women offenders include feminine hygiene, makeup application, cosmetology, home decorating, sewing, gardening, cooking, nursing and other domestic services. In addition, some institutions offer training programs which include business courses, such as typing, bookkeeping or key punch.

The National Study of Women's Correctional Programs found that the most frequently offered training programs in the jails and prisons studied included clerical skills, cosmetology, and food services. In addition, six prisons provided training in keypunch; two prisons offered graphic arts and one prison offered training in banking through the Chase Manhattan Bank. However, in the latter program only four of 365 incarcerated women were involved in the program (Glick and Neto, 1977:73).

Although the Manual of Correctional Standards suggests that incarcerated women should be taught a marketable skill, as Burkhart points out, the manual "gets back to reality when it states: 'Perhaps the largest number of inmates are placed in work assignments necessary for maintaining the institution' " (Burkhart, 1973:296). Just as are incarcerated men, women inmates are required to drive garbage trucks, operate lawn mowers, cook, clean, wash clothes, and haul heavy sacks of supplies to keep the institution running. In addition, women offenders often provide a cheap labor force in prison industries which make goods for their own institutions or for other agencies.

Although work of this nature sometimes has been considered as "on-the-job training" programs, the likelihood that women will be employed in similar positions upon release is minimal. In fact, the machinery employed in prison industries is often outdated and not used commercially outside the prison (Burkhart, 1973:294). Therefore, women cannot transfer acquired skills to jobs even if they are able to secure employment upon release. One inmate described the limitations of programs at the Women's Detention Center in Washington, D.C. as follows:

> *Vocational training programs? There's eight old broken-down typewriters somewhere in the building. I don't know if anybody ever uses them, though. Or you can go down to group theory. But who wants it? A bunch of us [and] . . . our deprived lives? (Mitford, 1973:19).*

Although there may be deficiencies in the programs provided for male inmates in this country, male inmates are afforded better opportunities to learn meaningful, marketable skills during incarceration than their female counterparts. A recent General Accounting Office study (1980) points out that in comparison with men, women inmates have "unequal access" to available training facilities. One reason cited for this discrepancy is that male inmates may have the opportunity to transfer between institutions within the state or within the federal prison system and may thus take advantage of a variety of programs. Confined women, on the other hand, have little opportunity to transfer to other facilities that might offer training programs because there are none (General Accounting Office, 1980:12). For instance, in one state, GAO researchers observed that there were eighty-five correctional facilities in sixty-seven counties. Women were housed in only one primary institution and four halfway houses (General Accounting Office, 1980:15).

Further, the study reported a wide disparity in the number and types of training programs provided for male and female inmates. In one state visited in the study, the researchers noted that women housed in a single facility could learn keypunch and food services; men housed in one of the two prisons in the state could participate in thirteen vocational and on-the-job training programs. These programs included welding, auto body repair, drafting, computer programming, medical lab assistance and X-ray technician. Similarly, the other prison for men in the state had eleven such programs (General Accounting Office, 1980:18).

Within the federal prisons, men have had better access than women to industries which provide both a training and work environment and an hourly wage.

Of eighty-four industrial operations, male offenders may take part in eighty-two. However, women offenders may participate in only thirteen; eleven of these programs for women are located in co-correctional facilities and thus are available to male offenders as well (General Accounting Office, 1980:19).

In recent years, the GAO report noted that the federal prison system has, however, made some attempt to improve the training opportunities for women inmates. The Federal Women's Reformatory at Alderson now has programs for women inmates in apprenticeship trade areas credited by the U.S. Department of Labor. What the report did not mention, but what is needed to assess the effectiveness of this effort, is careful research on the extent to which women graduates of this program are better equipped to and actually do pursue training and work opportunities following release.

WHERE DO WE GO FROM HERE?

The conditions and problems of women's confinement outlined previously suggested a need to explore alternatives to the traditional modes of dealing with women offenders. Recognizing the deficiencies of the current system, the National Advisory Commission on Criminal Justice Standards and Goals urged all states to "reexamine" and "readjust" their "policies, procedures, and programs" to make them "more relevant to the problems and needs of women." Among other things, the Commission has argued for a comprehensive evaluation of women offenders' needs in each state, and the development of adequate diversion and alternative programs in community centers (National Advisory Commission on Criminal Justice Standards and Goals, 1973:378).

If a woman has a job and some source of emotional support, it may be more beneficial to her and less costly to the state or county to keep her at home and require restitution or community service. The Des Moines Project, cited a few years ago by the National Institute of Justice as an Exemplary Project, affords one such possibility. For women requiring more secure placement, live-in residential halfway houses may provide an appropriate alternative. When it was operative, Project ELAN in Minneapolis, Minnesota enabled both women and their children to live together in a community setting. For live-in programs, requiring women to pay at least part of their costs for room and board would assist in defraying the program costs. This is especially important since, given the number of women served, many community programs may be as expensive as prisons (Glick and Neto, 1977:181).

However, whether women are incarcerated in detention centers, prisons, or community facilities, the environment and relationships with others are important in determining the attitudes of the offender when she is released. Adherence to the old medical model which suggests that offenders are "sick and must be cured" prior to release means that things must be done to or for the offender rather than with her.

An alternative approach to this traditional medical model is participatory management. In this approach, inmates are given an opportunity to develop responsible decision-making skills (Murton, 1973). The underlying assumption is that despite the type of offense, sex, or age of the offender, a person who has committed a crime has demonstrated her lack of behaving responsibly toward herself or others. Therefore, one of the most valuable activities is to engage in making decisions about her own life while she is incarcerated. If incarcerated women are taught only to conform to institutional rules for several months or years, it should be no surprise that they cannot adequately handle difficulties that arise after they are released.

In this approach, the superintendent strives to provide an environment conducive to the growth and development of offenders, one in which inmates may learn respect for themselves and others. Yet the superintendent does not coddle the inmates or relinquish her authority over the institution to them. Rather, she involves staff and inmates jointly with her in making decisions that affect the institution. Areas of decision-making might, for instance, include jointly developing rules that govern curfews, noise level or even inmate discipline.

One way in which this involvement may be brought about is by the creation of staff-inmate councils where staff and inmates elect peers to discuss matters of importance to them both. Inclusion of staff in the councils is important to assist in reducing the "We-They" syndrome characteristic of prison life. Work-

ing together for common goals would enable each group to see the other in a different light.

Everyone should be able to vote or run for office. Enabling women and staff to elect council members also entails their responsibility for the people elected. Therefore, if they are dissatisfied with the council's work, they may elect new people at the next election or they may run for office themselves. Realizing that their decisions will affect their own well-being in the institution, women (and staff) may feel a vested interest in the process (Baunach, 1981).

Whether or not this type of participatory management could be introduced into a prison or community facility, of course, depends upon the interest and willingness of the superintendent or director to do so. However, the literature indicated that at least four prisons in different parts of the world and at different time periods successfully developed participatory management for male offenders (Murton and Baunach, 1973; Baunach, 1981). If men are capable of developing and engaging in participatory management, then women can do equally as well. In addition, careful documentation of the council's evolution and evaluation of its effectiveness must be done to indicate the process others might use in developing similar approaches and the ways it might be improved.

Another way in which women with children might be given a chance to develop responsible decision-making skills is to involve them in dealing with their children on a routine basis prior to release. Mothers who plan to reunite with children upon release (as most do), need the opportunity to interact with them during incarceration. Mothers need to learn their own strengths and weaknesses as a parent by accepting this important responsibility. Moreover, they need to determine if they really want to be mothers and if they are able to handle problems of discipline, demands, and routine care for children. Parental responsibility entails far more than simply showing off a child to others or sitting together during regular visiting hours.

Some states (i.e., Minnesota, Nebraska, Tennessee, Kentucky, Washington, New York, California) allow children to stay overnight with mothers in prison. However, in developing this type of program, care should be taken to ensure that the welfare of both mother and child are considered. For some women, having the responsibility of children may make it more difficult to deal with their own problems. Thus, even the decision allowing inmate mothers to be involved with their own children during incarceration should be made jointly with the inmate-mothers. Many women feel that unless they want to be with their children, they will be viewed as "bad mothers" by those around them. In fact, many of these women may feel insecure as mothers and fear they could not handle the responsibilities adequately. Thus, parenting programs such as those at the Kentucky Correctional Institution for Women, Minnesota Correctional Institution for Women or Purdy Treatment Center (Washington) may be helpful. Some of these programs attempt to combine textbook information with actual interactions with children.

Finally, a need exists to identify and examine more systematically particular issues pertaining to women offenders. For instance, research on the long range effects of the separation on children or the possible impacts of involvement with the mother in a prison setting need to be determined before live-in programs in prison are created extensively.

Careful research should address the problems encountered by women of all ages from the time of arrest and processing through the courts, through the time served in detention centers or prisons or on probation or parole. Studies, such as that by Kruttschnitt (1982) which suggests that sentencing may be affected by both sex and economic dependency status of the defendant, need to be expanded and refined. In-depth analyses of specific problem areas such as sentencing will provide valuable information which may be useful to administrators and practitioners in planning and developing appropriate programs designed to meet the needs of women offenders as effectively and efficiently as possible.

ENDNOTES

The views in this chapter are those of the author and do not reflect the policies or opinions of the Bureau of Justice Statistics or the U.S. Department of Justice.

1. The published National Study of Women's Correctional Programs identified four designs among the sixteen women's prisons studied: four prisons had a complex of buildings each with one or more functions, surrounding a central administration building; two had a single building which housed all the functions of the prison; six had a campus design which included a group of buildings each with a separate function and grassy areas within which inmates might move; one had a cottage design which consisted of several small buildings that look like multiple-family dwellings; and three had designs which were variations of these four basic designs (Glick and Neto, 1977:20–25).

2. Tom Murton, former Warden of the Arkansas prison system, reported the incident of a woman inmate who gave birth to a child while incarcerated. Murton reported that immediately following the baby's birth, the welfare department planned to put the baby up for adoption. The impact on the inmate was "semi-shock and depression." Murton, however, retrieved the child and for a short time, at least, the child lived with foster parents who worked at the prison and lived directly adjacent to the prison grounds on the "free line." Thus, the inmate-mother responded positively to the brief chance she had to maintain contact with the newborn child before she voluntarily surrendered the baby to the welfare department (Murton and Hyams, 1969:170–181).

REFERENCES

Baunach, Phyllis Jo. 1984. *Mothers in Prison.* New Brunswick: Transaction.

Baunach, Phyllis Jo. 1981. "Participating Management: Restructuring the Prison Environment." Pp. 196–218 in D. Fogel and J. Hudson (eds.), *Justice as Fairness.* Cincinnati, OH: Anderson Publishing Company.

Bureau of Justice Statistics Bulletin. 1990. "Prisoners in 1989." Washington, D.C.: Department of Justice.

Burkhart, Katheryn. 1973. *Women in Prison.* New York: Doubleday and Company, Inc.

DuBose, D. 1975. "Problems of Children Whose Mothers are Imprisoned." New York: Institute of Women's Wrongs.

Federal Bureau of Investigation. 1970. *Crime in the United States: 1970.* Washington, D.C.: U.S. Department of Justice.

Female Offender Resource Center. 1976. *Female Offenders: Problems and Programs.* Washington, D.C.: American Bar Association.

General Accounting Office. 1980. *Women in Prison: Inequitable Treatment Requires Action.* Washington, D.C.: U.S. General Accounting Office.

Glick, Ruth and Virginia Neto. 1977. *National Study of Women's Correctional Programs.* Washington, D.C.: National Institute of Law Enforcement and Criminal Justice.

Immarigeon, Russ and Meda Chesney-Lind. 1991. *Women's Prisons: Overcrowded and Overused.* Washington, D.C.: National Council on Crime and Delinquency.

Kruttschnitt, Candace. 1982. "Women, Crime, and Dependency: An Application of the Theory of Law." *Criminology* 19(4)495–513.

La Point, Velma. 1977. "Child Development During Maternal Separation: via Incarceration." Washington, D.C.: NIMH (unpublished).

LEAA Task Force on Women. 1975. The Report of the LEAA Task Force on Women. Washington, D.C.: Law Enforcement Assistant Administration.

Lundberg, O., A. Scheckley and T. Voelkar. 1975. "An Exploration of the Feelings and Attitudes of Women Separated From Their Children due to Incarceration." Masters thesis. Portland: Portland State University.

McArthur, Virginia. 1974. *From Convict to Citizen: Programs for the Women Offender.* Washington, D.C.: U.S. Department of Labor.

Mitford, Jessica. 1973. *Kind and Usual Punishment.* New York: Alfred A. Knopf.

Murton, Thomas O. 1975. *Shared Decision-making as a Treatment Technique in Prison Management.* Minneapolis: Murton Foundation for Criminal Justice.

Murton, Thomas O. and Joe Hyams. 1969. *Accomplices to the Crime: The Arkansas Prison Scandal.* New York: Grove Press, Inc.

Murton, Thomas O. and Phyllis Jo Baunach. 1973. "Shared Decision-making in Prison Management: A Survey of Demonstrations Involving the Inmate in Participatory Management." Pp. 543–573 in M. G. Herman and M. G. Haft (eds.), *Prisoner's Rights Sourcebook.* New York: Clark Boardman Company.

Murton, Thomas O. and Phyllis Jo Baunach. 1973. "Women in Prison." *The Freeworld Times* 2 (June–July).

National Advisory Commission on Criminal Justice Standards and Goals. 1973. *Corrections.* Washington, D.C.: U.S. Department of Justice.

National Prison Statistics. 1972. *Prisoners in State and Federal Institutions for Adult Felons.* Washington, D.C.: U.S. Department of Justice.

O'Brien, Lois. 1974. "Women in Prison." *The Freeworld Times* 3 (March).

Palmer, D. 1972. "The Prisoner-mother and her Child." *Capital University Law Review* 1:127–44.

Shepard, Dean and Eugene Zemans. 1950. *Prison Babies.* Chicago: John Howard Association.

Simon, Rita. 1975. *Women and Crime.* Lexington, MA: D.C. Heath and Company.

Ward, David and Gene Kassebaum. 1965. *Women's Prison.* Chicago: Aldine Publishing Company, Inc.

STUDY QUESTIONS FOR READING 14_____

1. Describe the appearance of women's prisons.

2. Many authors have argued that women's prisons are marked by a more exaggerated dependency upon those in authority, but Baunach focuses on two other problems. What are they?

3. One of the biggest concerns of women inmates is their separation from their children. Why might this be an important concern to society? How have some prisons helped incarcerated women and their children adjust better to separation and to life after the mother's release?

4. What kind of programs were found to be offered most often to women inmates? In the one state described in detail here, what and how many training programs were offered for men and for women? What are the problems with these differences?

5. What are some of the alternatives to incarceration for women?

6. Why might participatory management help incarcerated women? How might women participate in management?

READING 15

STOPPING ABUSE IN PRISON

NINA SIEGAL

Widespread abuses of women behind bars barely received notice until seven or eight years ago. Across the country, there were incidents of prison or jail staff sexually molesting inmates with impunity. Slowly but surely, the nation's correctional facilities are responding to this abuse.

"Ten years ago, I think we knew it was going on, but we hadn't named it," says Brenda Smith, a Practitioner-in-Residence at Washington College of Law at American University. "Until you raise it as a problem, and until people start coming forward and talking about it, it is not perceived as a problem."

The changes are the result of several landmark legal cases, a shift in government policy, and the attention of human-rights groups. Still, problems remain. Guards continue to rape women inmates. But now there's a process to bring them to justice.

The stories were too consistent to be ignored. Numerous female inmates in three Washington, D.C., prison and jail facilities said they had been awakened at two or three in the morning for a "medical visit" or a "legal visit" only to be led into the kitchen, the clinic, the visiting hall, or a closet to have sex. Many inmates were becoming pregnant in a system that allowed no conjugal visits.

"There were a lot of places where people could have sex," says Smith. "A lot of it was in exchange for cigarettes." Prison employees offered other deals: " 'I will give you phone calls, I will make sure you get a better job assignment, I'll give you drugs if you have sex with me.' The sex involved not just correctional officers. It involved chaplains, administration, deputy wardens, contractors, and food-service workers. It involved not just male staff but female staff as well," Smith says.

In 1993, the National Women's Law Center and a District of Columbia law firm filed a class-action suit, *Women Prisoners vs. District of Columbia Department of Corrections*, in U.S. District Court. The suit alleged a pattern of discrimination against women in the jail, the Correctional Treatment Facility, and the Lorton Minimum Security Annex, a D.C. facility in Lorton, Virginia. A large portion of the case focused on issues of sexual misconduct, based on evidence that the law firm had collected during an investigation. The following year, a judge found that there was a pattern and practice of misconduct so severe that it violated the Eighth Amendment protection against cruel and unusual punishment. The decision was appealed and is still in court.

As extreme as the D.C. situation was, it was not unique.

Lawyers in Georgia had been preparing a class-action suit on behalf of men and women in the state's prisons for almost ten years when they began to come across striking charges of sexual misconduct in the Georgia Women's Correctional Facility in Milledgeville and the nearby camp, Colony Farm. The alleged activities included rape, criminal sexual contact, leering, and abusive catcalling of inmates. One lieutenant had sex with at least seven prisoners from 1987 to 1991, directing women to meet him in various locations in the prisons for sex.

In 1992, the lawyers for the suit, *Cason V. Seckinger,* amended their complaint to add allegations of sexual abuse that had taken place over a period of fourteen years. Seventeen staff members were indicted. None were convicted, though several were dismissed from their jobs as a result of the lawsuit. The suit resulted in a number of federal court orders requiring the department to rectify many of its practices.

It also influenced the department to close Milledge-ville and move all the female inmates to a different facility.

These two suits—and the criminal prosecutions that ensued—were the first major legal attempts to address a problem that had been plaguing the criminal justice system for decades.

One of the biggest cases for the rights of women prisoners was settled last year. The case (*Lucas vs. White*) involved three inmates of a federal facility in Pleasanton, California, called FCI Dublin, who were sold as sex slaves to male inmates in an adjoining facility. Inmates paid guards to allow them into the cells of female inmates who were being held in the men's detention center, which is across the street from Dublin.

The plaintiffs settled their civil suit against the Federal Bureau of Prisons for $500,000 and forced the agency to make dramatic changes in the way it handles allegations of misconduct. According to the settlement, the Bureau of Prisons was to set up a confidential hotline, or some other reporting mechanism, so that inmates and staff can inform the authorities of problems inside. It was also supposed to provide medical and psychological treatment for inmates who have been victimized and establish new training programs for staff and inmates.

Geri Lynn Green, one of the two attorneys for the *Lucas* case, has been monitoring the changes at the prison since the case settled. After the lawsuit and the subsequent training, she says, "it appears there was a tremendous impact."

Brett Dignam, clinical professor of law at Yale University, agrees that the *Lucas* case made a big difference: "More prison staff members are resigning over issues of sexual misconduct."

Human rights advocates, too, have taken up the cause. In 1996, the Women's Rights Project at Human Rights Watch issued "All Too Familiar: Sexual Abuse of Women in U.S. Prisons."

The 347-page report detailed problems in California, Washington, D.C., Michigan, Georgia, and New York. "We have found that male correctional employees have vaginally, anally, and orally raped female prisoners and sexually assaulted and abused them,"

says the report. "We found that in the course of committing such gross misconduct, male officers have not only used actual or threatened physical force, but have also used their near total authority to provide or deny goods and privileges to female prisoners to compel them to have sex or, in other cases, to reward them for having done so."

Last June, the United Nations sent a special rapporteur, Radhika Coomaraswamy, to the United States to investigate sexual misconduct in the nation's women's facilities. She argued that stronger monitoring was needed to control widespread abuses.

"We concluded that there has been widespread sexual misconduct in U.S. prisons, but there is a diversity—some are dealing with it better than others," Reuters reported her saying in December. "Georgia has sexual misconduct but has set up a very strong scheme to deal with it. In California and Michigan, nothing has been done and the issue is very prevalent." In April, Coomaraswamy will give a final report to the U.N. Commission on Human Rights.

This March, Amnesty International released its own report, " 'Not Part of My Sentence': Violations of the Human Rights of Women in Custody," which includes a section on sexual abuse. "Many women inmates are subjected to sexual abuse by prison officials, including: sexually offensive language, observation by male officers while showering and dressing, groping during daily pat-down searches, and rape." In addition to the problems detailed in the Human Rights Watch report, Amnesty investigators found problems in Illinois, Massachusetts, New Hampshire, Texas, West Virginia, and Wyoming.

Lawyers and human rights groups have won some important reforms. In 1990, only seventeen states had a law on the books defining sexual misconduct in prisons as either a misdemeanor or a felony offense. Today, there are only twelve states left that do not criminalize sexual relations between staff and inmates—Alabama, Kentucky, Massachusetts, Minnesota, Missouri, Montana, Nebraska, Oregon, Utah, Vermont, West Virginia, and Wisconsin—according to Amnesty International, which is campaigning to get all these states to pass their own laws.

The U.S. Justice Department is also taking a more active role. It has filed two suits charging that the correctional systems in Michigan and Arizona were responsible for violations of prisoners' constitutional rights. The suits cite numerous allegations of abuse, including rape, lack of privacy, prurient viewing, and invasive pat searches. Both cases are still pending.

Meanwhile, state prison systems are training personnel. Andie Moss was a project director with the Georgia Department of Corrections in 1992 when the department was asked to help interview inmates for the class-action lawsuit. She ended up culling information from women who said they had been subjected to misconduct over a fourteen-year period. Today, Moss works with the National Institute of Corrections, part of the Bureau of Prisons. Her primary responsibility is to develop training programs to educate both staff and inmates about sexual misconduct, the new laws, and their rights.

Since her program, "Addressing Staff Sexual Misconduct," was initiated in early 1997, Moss and her team have provided training for more than thirty state correctional systems, and she expects to complete training for all fifty states by the end of 1999.

The training involves four basic elements: clarifying the departments' sexual misconduct policy, informing inmates and staff of the law in their state, telling inmates and staff how to report abuse that they witness, and giving examples of how people have intervened in the past.

"We know it's still an issue. We know corrections departments still need to work diligently on this," says Moss. "It's a constant effort because it is a cultural change. But if you could follow the change in the law, the change in policy and practice, there's been an amazing effort in the last three years."

Despite all the positive steps, however, women are still being abused in America's prisons and jails. Investigators from a number of California-based law firms who recently visited the Valley State Prison for Women in Chowchilla, California, heard stories of at least a dozen assaults by specific guards. They also found "a climate of sexual terror that women are subjected to on a daily basis," says Ellen Barry, founding director of Legal Services for Prisoners with Children, based in San Francisco.

"The instances of both physical and sexual abuse are much higher than any other institution where I've interviewed women," she says. "The guards are really brutalizing women in a way that we really haven't seen before."

Valley State Prison inmate Denise Dalton told investigators that a doctor at the facility groped her and conducts inappropriate pelvic exams. "If I need Tylenol, all I need to do is ask him for a pelvic and he will give me whatever I want," she said.

But most of the abusive conduct was of the type that, Barry says, made for "a climate of sexual terror" in the prison. Coreen Sanchez, another inmate, said that in December, she entered the dayroom at the facility and asked a correctional officer if the sergeant had come in, and he responded by saying, "Yeah, he came in your mouth." She also reported seeing correctional officers flaunt their erections in front of inmates.

Advocates for prisoners say there still needs to be a dramatic cultural shift within the system before women are safe from the people who guard them behind bars.

"I think we have to keep in perspective the limitations of litigation and advocacy work for truly making a change in this arena," says Barry.

One problem that advocates cite is the recalcitrance of the unions that represent prison guards. "The people we really have to win over are not legislators, but the unions," says Christine Doyle, research coordinator for Amnesty International U.S.A. "Guards look at this as a workplace violation, as something fun to do on the job. They don't look at these women as human beings. The message that these are human beings they are exploiting isn't getting through."

For them to get that message, says Doyle, corrections officers will have to hear it from within the unions, and not from any set of codes, procedures, or laws. "We have states that have legislation, and some of them are just as bad, if not worse, than states without legislation," Doyle says. "So, obviously, that doesn't work. If it comes from within, and the unions themselves say, 'We can do this internally,' workers will respond better."

Human rights groups, for now, are focusing on legislative solutions. In 1996, Human Rights Watch recommended that Congress require all states, as a precondition of receiving federal funding for prisons, criminalize all sexual conduct between staff and inmates. It also urged the Department of Justice to establish secure toll-free telephone hotlines for reporting complaints.

Amnesty International's new report takes an additional step, arguing that the role of male staff be restricted in accordance with the United Nations' Standard Minimum Rules for the Treatment of Prisoners, which state that "women prisoners shall be attended and supervised only by women officers."

Debra LaBelle, a civil rights attorney who filed a class-action suit on behalf of abused women inmates in Michigan, says she would like to see men taken out of women's institutions altogether.

"I resisted going there for a long time, but I don't know another solution," she says. "When we started out, they didn't do any training, much supervision, investigation. In the last three years, they've changed countless policies and yet it is still happening. Get them out of there. It's not like they're losing employment opportunities. There are, unfortunately, many more facilities that men can work in."

Sheila Dauer, director of the Women's Human Rights Program for Amnesty International, says the group's report aims to persuade the final thirteen states without laws against sexual misconduct to initiate legislation, starting with eight state campaigns this year. She says the campaign will also lend support to a federal bill that would do the same thing.

Amnesty's report, she says, is designed to "wake up the American public to the horrible abuses that women inmates are suffering in prison and stop the suffering."

STUDY QUESTIONS FOR READING 15

1. How do correctional staff entice women inmates into having sex? How do they force women into sex? In the D.C. sex scandal, what staff were involved?

2. What happened regarding sex and women inmates in the Bureau of Prisons in California? How was the case resolved?

3. In Georgia, how many staff were indicted? What was one lieutenant indicted for? Were these staff convicted? Were they fired?

4. Amnesty International recommends two changes in women's prisons. What are they? What are the precedents for these changes? Are these changes fair to men who seek employment as correctional officers?

ESSAY QUESTIONS FOR PART TWO_____

In your answers, be sure to use one sentence at the end of your first paragraph to offer a clear thesis statement—that is, a statement of your point of view and your arguments for it. Then, in each paragraph of your answer, give evidence to support one of your arguments. Cite specific authors and give specific, concrete support for your point of view by offering statistics, case studies, examples, quotations, expert opinions and so on.

1. Compare and contrast prisons and jails in terms of the effect that local control has on various conditions for inmates, including the quality of staff and administrators.

2. Discuss the job of a guard from the point of view of inmates as well as guards.

3. Compare and contrast the experience of living in prison for men, women, and juveniles.

4. Discuss the possibility that the ways inmates are violated and victimized may actually make them more violent and criminal.

WEBSITES_____

www.jpp.org
Back issues of the *Journal of Prisoners on Prisons*

sun.soci.niu.edu/~critcrim/prisons/prisons.html
The Critical Criminology Division of the American Society of Criminology

PRISON ADMINISTRATION

Some prison workers and administrators think of inmates as degenerates, but others disagree pointedly. These two opposing views can be summarized by two groups of prison administrators, one group that says, "We can't do anything with these inmates," and the other group that says, "We can and we must do something." The first view is sometimes expressed when assaults, rapes, and brutality in prisons are exposed, and an administrator replies by pointing out the criminal nature of the prisoners. Such administrators conclude that the best way to manage a prison is to control inmates tightly; this view represents the core value of the control model of prison administration. In contrast, the inmate-participation model contends that, because more than 90 percent of all inmates will be released one day, life on the inside should be less tightly controlled so that inmates are prepared for life on the outside. This view represents the core value of the participatory model of prison administration.

The first reading in Part Three compares the control model and the inmate-participation model of prison administration. These two models were made famous in the 1960s by George Beto in Texas and Tom Murton in Arkansas (the real "Brubaker"), respectively. Both models are important today, but for different reasons. The control model has greatly influenced current prison administration, especially as shown by the development of control units. The inmate-participation model, however, although unusual, promises a more hopeful future. Unlike the control model, the inmate-participation model assumes inmates should be viewed not as convicted criminals, but as incarcerated citizens. This model asserts that inmates should learn to follow rules not by being "made" to follow them, but by having a stake in rules that they help create. Further, inmates should learn how to live not in a totalitarian society, but in a representative democracy. According to the control model, inmates should be treated as convicted criminals because of their criminal past. In the participation model, however, almost all inmates will be released some day, so prison administrators should view inmates as incarcerated citizens and focus on the inmates' future. In the control model, rules "were followed closely and enforced rigorously. . . . Inmates were required to walk between lines painted on the floors. . . . Talking too loud was a punishable offense" (DiIulio, 1987: 105). By contrast, the participation model recognizes that such rules can be enforced in prison, but not on the outside; therefore inmates should help create the rules so that they have a stake in following them. According to the control model, prisons should be "benevolent, paternalistic despotisms" (DiIulio, 1987: 179). Advocates of the inmate-participation model, on the other hand, feel that although a totalitarian prison might prepare inmates for life in Nazi Germany, a representative democracy should be used to prepare inmates for freedom in the United States: "It is liberty alone that fits men for liberty" (Osborne cited in Murton, 1976: 202). This reading tells a success story about inmates who were allowed to help govern an Arkansas prison for five months:

During that time, in a prison characterized by violence, terror, and many escapes, there were no fights or assaults and only one escape (Murton, 1976: 219).

The second reading comes from John DiIulio, Jr.'s, book *Governing Prisons: A Comparative Study of Correctional Management.* DiIulio compares the responsibility model of prison management, which allows inmates choices so that they learn responsibility, to the control model, which focuses on controlling inmate behavior tightly. DiIulio argues that the responsibility model is less successful than the control model because of differing views on four issues: rule enforcement, the idea that individuals should serve their own time, classification of inmates, and the paramilitary aspects of prison life. Under the responsibility model, "the rule book reminded officers (in bold letters) that 'there is no requirement that every rule violation' be treated formally, noting that in 'many cases verbal counseling or summary action should be the first response.' " In the control model, on the other hand, "rules and regulations were followed closely and enforced rigorously" (DiIulio, 1987: 108), punishment was swift and certain. The responsibility model "normalizes" life by fostering community, but the control model divides the inmate community by formally encouraging each inmate to "do your own time." As for classification of inmates, the responsibility model places inmates in the most appropriate but least restrictive setting because secure institutions are considered "expensive to build and operate, and counterproductive, except where really needed" (DiIulio, 1987: 119). In the control model, however, every prison is a maximum-security facility. Finally, the responsibility model minimizes the paramilitary aspects of prison life, whereas the control model maximizes them. DiIulio argues that the paramilitary model is favored by officers. He cites a Michigan correctional officer who complained about the lack of uniforms: "We look like some bartenders' union. We got rid of the symbols of authority. But we lost more than the symbols . . . " (DiIulio, 1987: 124). Another officer said, "We want uniforms, the stripes." DiIulio concludes that when it comes to high-security prisons, "Those that govern most, govern best."

The next reading is an overview of Robert Levinson's book, *Unit Management in Prisons and Jails.* Levinson argues that the benefits of unit management can be maximized when the key requirements are met. These requirements include a stable population in each unit, an adequate staff–inmate ratio, decentralized decision making, internal classification of inmates, and a team approach to management. The fundamental assumption of unit management is that cooperation among inmates is most likely to occur in small groups with lengthy interactions; therefore, stable populations and an adequate staff–inmate ratio are essential. Further, unit management requires decentralized decision making, which in turn allows decisions to be made more quickly by people who better know the inmates. Internal classification of inmates lowers violent incidents, improves the social climate, and allows staff to be matched to inmates. A team approach to management helps unite correctional officers and unit staff members and it helps ensure that inmate voices are heard. When these requirements are met, unit management can maximize control, as well as improve the quality of relationships and decision making. However, in one survey of correctional managers, only one state out of twenty-eight reported following each of the key requirements.

PARTICIPATORY MODELS

The next three readings describe three different models for allowing inmates more participation in prison: the two-way communication model, the use of group norms, and the readaptation model. The two-way communication model was developed by Warden Dennis Luther who spent his career in the federal system and who eventually served as warden for the McKean Federal Correctional Institution in Bradford, Pennsylvania. The two-way communication model demonstrates that if prison administrators show respect for and listen to officers, officers will do the same for inmates, and prisons will be much better places to live and work. To this end, Warden Luther and his administration set the tone for two-way communication with inmates by treating correctional officers with respect. As Luther puts it, correctional officers "have good ideas, not only about how to do their job, but how to do *your* job better." At meetings, staff members are asked to bring one concrete suggestion for improvement. Officers and administrators alike are told to treat inmates with respect by never lying and by always keeping promises. Two-way communication with inmates is encouraged through town-hall meetings and "customer surveys." Luther used this management philosophy at McKean for three years and boasted no escapes, murders, suicides, sexual assaults, or serious assaults on inmates or staff. The American Correctional Association rated this facility only one of two prisons ever to be rated outstanding for *both* inmates and staff.

The Glen Mills Reform School applies similar participatory principles to male juvenile delinquents, as described in the next reading, an overview of the book *Without Locks and Bars: Reforming the Reform Schools*. Glen Mills resembles a top-flight prep school; it assumes the students are normal and requires them to conform to more than a hundred group norms, which helps them excel and reduces recidivism. The norms include the expectations that at Glen Mills, the students will establish eye contact and greet visitors, show pride in their own and others' achievements, and treat all others with respect. Violators of these norms are confronted in a small group setting and asked to own up and apologize for their behaviors. The school tries in every way possible to "go first class" and implement a "why not the best" philosophy that promotes student pride in themselves and their institution. This means top-quality furnishings, clothing, and food, as well as educational and athletic facilities. The school pays for all home visits, and most students go on one long trip, usually to Florida. Still, this private institution costs less than half the cost of public reform schools in Pennsylvania. The school assumes that its students are as "normal" as other youth; that is, they suffer from no more serious psychological problems and they have the same potential for growth. Students excel in this environment. For example, Glen Mills athletic teams have achieved excellent records, and several boys have received athletic scholarships to universities. At any given time, there are always at least twenty students on campus who won scholarships to return to Glen Mills to complete academic programs or compete in athletics. Students at Glen Mills recidivate only somewhat less than students at other institutions, which may be because no school can inoculate youth against the extreme difficulties they will face upon release. Clearly, a better aftercare program is needed, even though the school provides a good model for future reform schools.

The readaptation model was developed by Warden Jorge Duarte at La Mesa Prison in Tijuana, Mexico. The readaptation model helps inmates live in the outside world by making life on the inside much like life on the outside in terms of work and family. This model has resulted in very low recidivism. Indeed, the 2,500 inmates that live in this Mexican prison retain many of the rights and responsibilities of free people. For example, inmates established and ran about 70 small businesses, mostly stores. And inmates reduced the overcrowding problem by building apartments for themselves, which they could either own and live in or rent or sell to others. Finally, inmates are allowed to have their families live with them behind prison walls, which resulted in 500 "permanent visitors." Through these measures, Duarte feels inmates get the practice necessary to live successfully on the outside and will leave the prison "without anger, without hate, and ready to live in society." Indeed, La Mesa boasts that only 20 percent of inmates return.

CONTROL MECHANISMS

The previous several readings explored the promise of participatory models, but these models are unusual. The next few readings describe the far more typical use of control mechanisms.

First is a reading from Gresham Sykes' book *The Society of Captives*. Many people assume that in a prison, officers should give the orders and inmates should follow them exactly, but this doesn't always happen. Officers may seem to have total power over inmates, but they actually don't, and the job design of officers further erodes their power, according to Sykes. In the end, officers actually control inmates through the privilege system, a system of rewards and punishments, and this system needs tightening. Officers seem to have total power over inmates who say, "They have the guns and we don't." However, Sykes points out that officers lack the mark of total power, the "unchallenged right to be capricious." Further, the job design of officers erodes their power. For example, officers become friends with inmates because they are in close, intimate association with inmates all day. Officers also need the support of inmates to do their jobs well. "A noisy, dirty cellblock reflects on the officer's ability to 'handle' prisoners." Officers rely on help from inmates to do their jobs, which results in sharing power with inmates. Officers ultimately control inmates through the privilege system, a system of rewards and punishments. Unfortunately, the rewards are given at the time of admission (including good time, recreation, mail and visiting privileges). Instead of awarding privileges on admission and revoking them for misbehavior, Sykes says privileges should be awarded one by one, thus giving inmates hope for progress. This incentive would help inmates have a stake in the system, and it would reduce threats and rudeness.

The second reading is from prison psychiatrist James Gilligan's book *Violence: Reflections on a National Epidemic*. Gilligan acknowledges that correctional officers and administrators feel outnumbered and "out of control" in the cell blocks. Officers resort to using prison sex as a control mechanism, that is, as a means to "divide and conquer" inmates. This practice should be stopped because prison sex involves coercion that borders on rape, which leads to additional violence. According to Gilligan, officers accommodate the rapists ("you scratch my back and I'll scratch yours") by allowing them whatever gratification they get from raping weaker inmates. In return, the rapists cooperate with the officers by submitting to the prison system as a whole—that is, they refrain from assaulting officers, protesting conditions, and organizing riots. Prisoners are also less likely to unite against officers because they have been divided into two groups, the rapists and the raped. Indeed, prison sex amounts to little more than prison rape because sexual choices in prison are so constrained that words such as "free" or "voluntary" don't apply. The vast majority of sexual relationships in prison occur in a context of coercion, either through force or violence, or its credible threat. The relatively stable "marriages" between dominant and submissive partners constitute a form of chronic, ongoing, and repeated rape. Officers should stop using prison sex as a way of controlling inmates because men will fight—often to the death—to avoid being raped. Fighting rape proves that they are "real" men and not homosexuals (as these words are defined in the macho, homophobic subculture).

The following reading is an excerpt from inmate Victor Hassine's book *Life Without Parole.* Hassine argues that prison authorities freely dispense mind- and mood-altering psychotropic drugs. Hassine interviews "Chaser," a medication addict who reports that psychotropic medications (tranquilizers, amphetamines, and barbiturates) are easier to obtain in prison than phone privileges or access to the chapel. To get these drugs, an inmate need only say that he wants "to kill himself." The effects of these drugs are chilling: the shakes, very slow disjointed movement, and noticeable scars on the wrists from razor cuts (when these drugs increase an inmate's depression). Chaser concludes that prison administrators and guards seem to think that "a medicated inmate is a controlled inmate," controlled by the use of "chemical shackles."

Are prison authorities truly victims of prison gangs that are "out of control"? Or do prison authorities use prison gangs as another control mechanism to divide and conquer inmates? Of course, the official view is that prison gangs should be eradicated. However, there is often a considerable discrepancy between the official stance and what actually takes place in prisons. Some prison authorities hold a more pragmatic view of prison gangs, saying that gangs have had "little negative impact on the regular running of prison operations." The authors of the next reading interview a sample of ex-inmates, who point out several reasons for the growth of prison gangs, including prison overcrowding, and what they see as the immaturity of new inmates and the trouble they cause. These inmates also reveal that officers sometimes accept and even encourage prison gangs because officers profit by selling drugs, weapons, and food to prison gangs; and because gangs create a "threat to security," which means overtime for officers. Some officers give false information to different gangs, so that each gang prepares for conflict with the other, which results in overtime for the officers. Sometimes officers encourage prison gangs because if inmates are spending their time fighting each other, they have no time to fight the officers. The inmates interviewed also reported an increase in the use of snitches. For example, officers reward snitches for giving confidential information about other inmates. The officers can then permanently transfer the inmate snitched on to maxi-max special housing units for stricter confinement—unless that inmate, in turn, snitches on someone else.

"Control units" are perhaps the ultimate way of controlling inmates by separating them from each other. These maxi-max facilities keep inmates in solitary confinement for twenty-two or twenty-three hours a day. Fay Dowker and Glenn Good argue in the next reading that control units should be abolished because they fail to meet their stated goals: housing "the worst of the worst," and reducing violence and the need for heightened security at other prisons. They point out that housing an inmate in a control unit is considered an "administrative" rather than a "disciplinary" measure, which means that no due process is required by law, and inmates can be sent to control units indefinitely, with no reason given. As a result of this system, many political prisoners are held at the federal penitentiary in Marion, Illinois, and many were sentenced there directly from court, before they could possibly misbehave in prison. In 1984, Marion was the only level 6 federal prison, but a congressional committee found that, according to the BOP's own classification procedures, 80 percent of the prisoners were not rated as level 6 prisoners. After this revelation, instead of reducing the number of inmates at Marion, the procedures were changed. Every inmate at

Marion was reclassified appropriately for Marion, regardless of his crime. Dowker and Good contend therefore that control units do not reduce violence in other prisons because they do not house "the worst of the worst." Rather, they express concern that control units will *increase* violence on the outside because they produce mental deterioration and feelings of rage. Further, Marion has served as a model for other state prison systems: Thirty-eight states now have control units, and more are being built. When lawsuits are brought against these state prisons, the prisons use their similarity to Marion as a defense. Instead of improving conditions at other prisons, Marion's example has "dragged them downwards toward greater brutality."

REFERENCES

DiIulio, John J., Jr. 1987. *Governing Prisons: A Comparative Study of Correctional Management.* New York: The Free Press.
Murton, Thomas O. 1976. *The Dilemma of Prison Reform.* New York: Holt, Rinehart and Winston.

WHY INMATE PARTICIPATION IS BETTER WHEN MANAGING PRISONS

TARA GRAY
JON'A MEYER

Since 1973, America's prison population has increased sixfold (Irwin & Austin, 2001). Someone new to the criminal justice system might assume that such a dramatic increase would have nipped America's crime problem in the bud. But this 600 percent increase in America's prison population has not been matched by a decrease in crime. Instead, "the prevailing notion [about prisons] is that . . . they function as 'breeding grounds for crime' " (Toch & Adams, 1989, 210).

Many experts agree that prison administrators must take steps to stem the tide of crime, but there is little agreement about what these steps should be. As we search for solutions for the future of prisons, this [reading] looks back at two prison models of the 1960s. Why the 1960s? What do such *old* models have to offer for the future? The control model is studied here because much of current prison practice involves trying to solve problems by increasing control over inmates through the expanded use of lockdowns, special housing units, and maxi-max prisons. The more participatory models, on the other hand, are far less common today and have been practiced by only a few wardens, including Warden Luther, who recently retired from McKean Federal Correctional Institution (Peters, 1992). The inmate participation model will be studied here because it stands in stark contrast to the control model. It argues that more control offers nothing but more of the same, that it will never solve our prison problems, and that it is responsible for some of the problems we now face.

The control model was developed by the late George Beto, Director of Corrections in Texas from 1962 to 1972. Although Beto held a doctorate in educational administration, he did not publish his views on prison administration. They were best articulated by John J. DiIulio, the political scientist and Princeton scholar who wrote the compelling book, *Governing Prisons*. DiIulio argues that the brightest moments of prison history occurred under Beto's control model, in which inmates were tightly controlled and rule violations resulted in certain and swift punishments.

The inmate participation model was championed by the late Tom Murton, who served as warden at several other institutions before becoming warden of two Arkansas prison farms between 1967 and 1968. He co-authored a book about his experience in Arkansas, *Accomplices to the Crime,* which was made into the 1980 movie, *Brubaker.* Murton went on to earn a doctorate in criminology and to write a book about prison administration, *The Dilemma of Prison Reform.* He values order, as DiIulio does, but places less of a premium on it. When two correctional officers were murdered at Marion in October of 1983, DiIulio applauded the way officials responded by locking down the institution. He points out that "more than 98 percent of Marion's nearly 400 inmates have a history of violent behavior, including homicide and assault" (DiIulio, 1989, 83). In contrast, Murton was appalled at the assumption that the violent nature of the inmates was the source of the unrest. Instead, he urged officials to correct the problems that made Marion far more violent than other prisons.

Murton's (1976, xi) inmate participation model begins with the premise that 95 percent of the inmates will return to society, so the main purpose of prison is to help inmates learn to live in a *free* society. Therefore, the inmate participation model strives to make the prison society less totalitarian and more like life in a representative democracy. To accomplish this goal, inmates elect their own representatives to an inmate council, which operates as a legislative body.

A BRIEF HISTORY OF PRISONS IN TEXAS FROM 1962 TO 1986

Much has been written about the history of the Texas Department of Corrections (TDC), a system which has been widely heralded:

> *Academic and practicing penologists came from all over to see the spotlessly clean prisons inhabited by prisoners dressed in spotlessly clean white uniforms and dining well in spotless mess halls. The educational system was and still is handsomely funded. During the Beto days and for several years thereafter there was virtually no prisoner idleness. The system was almost self-supporting. (Conrad, 1988, 66)*

One reason that the Texas system was self-supporting was that it was a farm system, with many inmates working in the fields. In addition, "everything from food to inmate clothing was produced, as Beto phrased it, 'by the inmates for the inmates' " (DiIulio, 1987, 200). Beto lobbied for a bill that enabled the system to sell its industrial goods to other state agencies, which were required to buy its goods as long as "the quality was satisfactory and the price was right" (DiIulio, 1987, 200). The Texas system was also characterized by about half as many guards as other prisons (Conrad, 1988, 66). To bolster the power of the guards, the system used inmate guards who were called Building Tenders or BTs. With the help of the BTs, the Texas system was sometimes heralded as "the prison system that works" (Crouch & Marquart, 1990, 99).

When Beto retired in 1972, he was replaced by his hand-picked successor, W. J. Estelle, who would serve as Director until 1983 (DiIulio, 1987, 111). During this time, however, the prison population increased dramatically. DiIulio argues that the change in leadership and the increase in prison population marked the beginning of many problems:

> *Though in most respects a brilliant prison man, Estelle was no Beto. Under Beto, the BT system was like an overly sharp knife wielded by a master chef in a calm kitchen. This knife was handed to Estelle who, by comparison, was a good short-order cook behind a busy counter. (DiIulio, 1987, 208).*

Abuses by guards and BTs kept surfacing, and these abuses became nationally known during the court case, *Ruiz v. Estelle*. In the trial, much testimony was given about inmates who were beaten with fists and clubs, kicked, and maced. One medical doctor testified that he had seen "hundreds" of cases where "it happened to be obvious that another human being . . . had inflicted the injuries." As a result of this testimony, Judge Justice found that "brutality against inmates [was] nothing short of routine" (Ruiz v. Estelle, 1980, 1299).

DiIulio acknowledges that, by the mid-1970s, the BTs became nothing more than con-bosses. They were allowed to carry weapons and were given unauthorized privileges for 'keeping things quiet,' which sometimes involved beating other prisoners who wouldn't work or who defied prison staff. In exchange, the BTs were allowed to choose their own cellmates and break some prison rules, especially those prohibiting possession and sale of illicit items, such as drugs and alcohol. In a few institutions, the administration became a "virtual hostage" to the BTs, who conducted counts and cell searches and performed other necessary tasks (DiIulio, 1987, 209).

According to DiIulio (1987, 39), however, the BTs got out of control only after Beto relinquished control of the TDC:

> *So long as the building tenders were selected with extreme care and monitored closely, they served their purpose and rarely abused their special status. But as soon as the tight administrative controls on the building tenders were relaxed—that is, as soon as the system became one of genuine inmate self-government—terrible abuses of inmates by other inmates followed. (DiIulio, 1987, 39)*

Crouch and Marquart (1990, 100) agree that the BTs were better behaved during the Beto years when officer-inmate ratios were lower: "BTs appear to have been somewhat better controlled, relatively less free to abuse prisoners." However, they disagree that the BTs were not violent under Beto, stating that "there were always abuses of authority by these inmate elites" (1990, 99).

Other critics of Beto agree that the brutality of the system was well-established long before Beto left in September of 1972:

> During the course of the hearing in Dreyer v. Jalet *in 1972, prisoners testified that building tenders routinely were given access to pipes, bats and clubs to administer discipline. Dr. Beto, in his testimony in that case, defended the appointment of inmates with histories of predatory and vicious behavior to serve as building tenders. Other credible allegations regarding the role of building tenders during this period included a complaint filed in 1970 in* Jimenez v. Beto *to the effect that ten building tenders, armed with axe handles, wood clubs, iron pipes and blackjacks, assaulted a group of prisoners in the company of an assistant warden and several officers. (Nathan, 1988)*

This testimony helped establish the willingness of TDC officials and BTs to use "whatever means necessary." By May 1973, the abuses of the BTs were well enough established to justify a court injunction forbidding them. Some experts concluded that the TDC under Beto presented "a clean and well-ordered facade to the casual observer," but underneath was a system that subjected inmates to a "brutal, repressive and dangerous reality" (Feeley & Rubin, 1992, 134). In this view, the building-tender system was the foundation for a "terror-based system of control" (Feeley & Rubin, 1992, 135).

A BRIEF HISTORY OF PRISONS IN ARKANSAS FROM 1967 TO 1968

Murton wrote extensively about the abuses he encountered in Arkansas when he arrived in 1967 as warden of Tucker State Prison Farm and later of Cummins State Prison Farm (Murton & Hyams, 1969; Murton, 1976):

> *The first thing that struck me was the atmosphere of total despair. The inmates did not smile, laugh or talk. (Murton, 1972, 170)*
>
> *Inmates in these institutions were literally worked from dawn to dark, six or seven days a week, in all*

> *kinds of weather, at menial, hard, slave-labor chores. They were housed in 100-man barracks and subjected to theft of property, abuse, assaults, and gang rape. . . . No underwear, boots, jackets or gloves were ever issued; food consisted of watery rice or weevils and beans; meat in the form of hog-head stew was received only annually; milk was never provided. At the time of the police investigation in 1966, the inmates were observed to be at least 40 pounds underweight. (Murton, 1976, 146–147)*

The starvation was especially noteworthy, given that Tucker and Cummins were prison *farms* that flourished by the use of free inmate labor and always turned a profit. Clearly, someone was reaping the benefit of the harvests, but it wasn't the inmates.

Rackets abounded in Arkansas, and these rackets forced inmates to pay bribes in order to receive goods and services to which they were already entitled. For example, inmates who ran the kitchen charged other inmates for food. Inmates who could not pay the bribes did not get enough to eat. In the hospital, a prison doctor paid each inmate $5 for blood plasma, which he sold to a laboratory for $15, making an estimated $140,000 a year (Murton & Hyams, 1969, 109). Rackets were one of the abuses Murton eliminated first.

Murton was also faced with extreme shortages of freeworld (paid) staff, with only six paid staff for 300 inmates at Tucker and only 18 for 1,200 inmates at Cummins. To make up for the shortage of freeworld guards, armed inmate guards called "trusties" were used. Both guards and trusties resorted to violence, including:

> *. . . lashing an inmate ten times a day with the "hide," a five-foot leather strap capable of maiming. This official method of discipline was augmented by such illegal but customary techniques as inserting needles under the fingernails, crushing knuckles and testicles with pliers, hitting the inmate with a club, blackjack, or "anything you can lay your hands on," kicking inmates in the groin, mouth, or testicles—and, of course, use of the infamous "Tucker Telephone." (Murton, 1976, 147)*

The Tucker Telephone was a torture device adapted from a rural telephone that was used to punish or extract information from inmates. Wires were attached from the telephone terminals to the inmate's penis, and the shock caused terrible pain (Murton, 1976, 94). Murton immediately abolished corporal punishment and brutality. He wanted to "demonstrate to the people of Arkansas that a prison could be run without torture and violence—a foreign concept at the time" (Murton, 1976, 148).

Murton was also concerned because there were more than 200 "escapees" who had never been heard from again, a far greater number than would be expected (Murton & Hyams, 1969, 183). The prison physician, Dr. Barron, had discovered a remarkably high death rate: in a four day period in 1959, six inmates were shown to have died of "heart disease." Other death certificates failed to list a cause of death at all, and many had no signature from the former prison physician. Dr. Barron talked with an inmate, Reuben Johnson, who told him he had seen the warden shoot one inmate through the heart. He said another man had his head chopped off by a warden, and the trusties had bludgeoned a third man to death with rifle butts. Johnson said he had helped bury all of them; he swore he could pinpoint the location of the graves. On January 29, 1968, Murton found the bodies in the exact location Reuben Johnson had described (Murton & Hyams, 1969, 182–3). As Johnson had predicted, one of the bodies was decapitated and another had its head crushed to the size of a grapefruit (Murton & Hyams, 1969,185).

During the next few weeks, the state conducted investigations. Some inmates alleged that they had witnessed the murders of inmates or had participated in their burials. Citizens and historians testified that the graves were from an old black church located across the river, and the state sided with them (Parker, 1986, 152). Murton maintained that the inmates were murdered. He argued that a system of terror like the one in Arkansas had to include the threat of death. "For this threat to be meaningful, it must, from time to time, be carried out" (Murton, 1976, 147). Besides, "it is not customary to decapitate indigents because they cannot afford the usual burial fee" (Murton, 1976, 149):

It would seem that one way to refute contentions that inmates have been murdered is to do the obvious: dig

up the remaining 200 bodies and demonstrate that they were not murdered. (Murton, 1976, 158)

In contrast, the Arkansas officials did *not* investigate further. Instead, Murton was threatened with serving 21 years as a prisoner in the Arkansas system for "grave robbing." He escaped prosecution, but on March 7, 1968, he was fired.

ADMINISTRATIVE PRINCIPLES: INMATE PARTICIPATION VERSUS THE CONTROL MODEL

The inmate participation model differs from the control model on many issues, including: the proper enforcement of prison rules; the extent to which inmates are thought to be responsible for their crimes; whether inmates should be viewed as convicted criminals or incarcerated citizens; and the success of two experiments with inmate participation.

In Texas, "rules were followed closely and enforced rigorously. . . . Talking too loud was a punishable offense" (DiIulio, 1987, 105). All prison administrators want inmates to behave responsibly, but in Texas they talk about "making" inmates behave that way (DiIulio, 1987, 147). By making inmates behave, they will learn to abide by prison rules and later by laws on the outside. The control model focused on the individual guilt of the convict:

Virtually none of the Texas keepers [correctional workers] looked beyond the individual offender in explaining criminality. They were well aware of the social, psychological, and economic explanations of criminality, but they rejected them in favor of explanations that laid greater stress on the criminal's personal culpability [guilt]. (DiIulio, 1987, 177)

The control model held that inmates should be viewed as convicted criminals rather than incarcerated citizens (DiIulio, 1987, 176). In Beto's words, "I never shake hands with an inmate. You must keep some social distance between the inmate and the free, law-abiding citizen. They neither are nor ought to be viewed as equals" (quoted in DiIulio, 1987, 177).

Murton also acknowledged the guilt of the individual inmate. In the movie *Brubaker,* Robert Redford makes a statement that was typical of Murton, when he declares to a large group of inmates that "most of you people deserve to be here." On the other hand, the movie addresses Murton's concerns about the "three strikes" which impose life sentences on offenders with three felony convictions. *Brubaker* features an inmate who was doing life for allegedly breaking a toilet seat while sharing a jail cell with five others. Anyone could have broken the toilet seat, and this inmate says he didn't. Nonetheless, it was his third felony conviction which meant life in prison. In Murton's writings, he points to other injustices, including death sentences for blacks. In Murton's view, "From the records, I felt sure that at least half of them were victims of the white power structure in Arkansas, and not guilty as charged" (Murton & Hyams, 1969, 77–78). Clearly, Murton held the view that, although most inmates were guilty, some were more guilty than others, and few were guilty enough for the punishment meted out in these prisons.

In contrast, the control model sees inmates as deserving of their punishment, as convicted criminals and therefore, as "persons who had a demonstrated inability to be self-governing" (DiIulio, 1987, 178). As Estelle put it, "A prison which dabbles in the 'democratic process' or participative management . . . is borrowing trouble" (quoted in DiIulio, 1987, 178). One guard, a veteran of two such experiments, agreed:

> *Boil it down, and the thing was to be nice to the inmates, to let them have a real hand in running the show. Some so-called experts discovered that these men had never had enough responsibility for themselves and that was why they had killed people, beat up teachers, raped, and so forth. . . . We used to say "do your own time." Now we say "do time in your own way"—you organize the place, you run it. Just don't try to escape or get too crazy on us. Common sense said the whole damn thing from A to Z was ridiculous, but sometimes folks have to get burnt before they stop playing with matches. And sometimes the more educated or high-and-mighty they are, the less they learn. (quoted in DiIulio, 1987, 37)*

In this view, prisons must be tightly governed by administrators, and run as "benevolent, paternalistic despotisms" [well-intended dictatorships] (DiIulio, 1987, 179).

Murton (1976, 165–166) disagreed, arguing that such an authoritarian model might prepare inmates for life in Nazi Germany, but not for freedom in the United States:

> *From the prison experience, the inmate learns that democracy is a fiction; that the treaters . . . profess to believe in the rights of man while tolerating and promoting the indignity of totalitarianism. (Murton, 1976, 72)*

Inmates cannot learn to dance by having their legs tied together. The only way to prepare them for life in a democracy is to expose them to democracy while they are incarcerated. Most inmates have not actively participated in our representative democracy: they have been told to follow rules (plenty of them), but they have never really had a stake in the system or helped to make it work. The only way to sell inmates on a democracy at this late date is to let them learn the way it is supposed to work and allow them to participate in governing their own prison. "It is liberty alone that fits men for liberty" (Gladstone, as quoted in Osborne, 1915, 451).

But can inmates actually govern themselves? DiIulio thinks not. In order to demonstrate the ineffectiveness of inmate self-government, DiIulio discusses Walla Walla Penitentiary which he calls "one of the most forthright experiments in inmate self-government" (DiIulio, 1987, 37):

> *The formal prison administration abdicated in favor of inmate leaders. Among those who came to rule the prison were the "Bikers," a prison gang which, when not terrorizing other inmates or the staff, extended its members the privilege of racing their motorcycles on the prison yard. The experiment ended when the internal situation became so thoroughly chaotic that public pressure mounted to regain control of the institution. (DiIulio, 1987, 37)*

DiIulio concludes his discussion by noting that hardline administrators are right when they argue "the more freedom inmates have, the more unsafe prisons will be" (Hoffman & McCoy, 1981, 193).

Murton also studied Walla Walla, noting that the Resident Government Council was the "most publicized inmate council in this country" (Murton, 1975, 115). Murton (1975, 107–116) discussed at length the continuous turmoil of the council and the seemingly constant erosion of its decision-making power. To Murton, the extent to which a model is truly participatory depends on the extent to which inmates share in decisionmaking (Murton, 1975, 29). Murton did find evidence of one successful experiment with inmate decisionmaking at Walla Walla. In the "Take a Lifer to Dinner" program, inmates serving life sentences (usually murderers) were allowed to leave the prison for eight hours for a visit in the community. Previously, inmates were chosen for the furlough program by prison staff. Under that system, of the 292 inmates sent on furlough in March 1972, 28 were late returning, 26 escaped and 17 violated the law. When one inmate committed an armed robbery and another killed a state trooper, furloughs were almost abolished. In response, 98 percent of the inmates signed a petition urging the administration to appoint five inmates to a screening committee. Once the inmate screening committee was established, no professional staff would be involved in the screening: only other lifers made decisions. With the lifers in charge, several hundred leaves resulted in only one violation. Why? Murton quotes an inmate, who writes: "We know the people. We're with them 24 hours a day. An inmate might look good on paper but we know the goof-ups" (Murton, 1976, 172).

Murton points out that what is common knowledge among inmates is often kept secret from staff, which makes an inmate council a perpetual source of information (Murton, 1976, 218). He advocates obtaining this information in an above-board way, rather than through the use of the traditional snitch system. Early in his term, Murton set out to break the power of the trusties, which resulted in a rash of escapes from a prison farm that had no walls and almost no perimeter security. In response to the escapes Murton established an inmate council, with members elected by other inmates. Because the inmate leaders were chosen by the inmates, they had credibility and were accountable to the inmate body (Murton, 1976, 217). Unlike the depiction of the inmate council in the movie, *Brubaker,* none of the men elected for the council were operators, and none had ever had any power in the prison before.

The inmate council included a classification committee that suggested many changes in security, including the removal of some of the inmate guards from critical posts (Murton, 1976, 218). One inmate came to the committee to request a job and custody change that seemed reasonable to Murton. However, the request was rejected unanimously by the inmate members of the committee. The committee explained that the inmate's mother had recently visited him and informed him that his wife had moved in with a male neighbor. The inmate wanted to be reassigned to a position from which he could easily escape. The results of decisions by the inmate classification committee were incredible for an institution that was previously characterized by violence, terror, and a steady stream of escapes: for the five months the inmate council was fully operational, there was only one escape and no fights or assaults (Murton, 1976, 219).

In just a few months at Tucker, Murton was able to adequately feed and clothe the inmates, hire competent staff, upgrade the agricultural programs, establish educational and vocational training programs, provide religious counseling and services, and eliminate corruption. He destroyed the illegitimate inmate power system and moved the trusties back into the barracks (Murton, 1976, 215 and 219). Murton also integrated the black inmates who were on death row into the activities of the all-white Tucker population. Two death row inmates participated in the new prison band that sometimes performed off the prison grounds. No condemned prisoner ever attempted to escape even when outside the prison (Murton, 1976, 219). Dances were held at the prison, which were attended by Tucker inmates, their wives or girlfriends, and the freeworld staff. The first interracial dances in Arkansas probably occurred at the Tucker prison farm (Murton, 1976, 215).

By Christmas of 1967, women were also integrated into the prison. Women worked in the prison, ate in the dining room, and taught classes without a guard present. These changes were not undertaken recklessly, but as part of a plan to help inmates participate more responsibly in society by practicing in a relatively free prison society. During Murton's tenure, no woman was ever assaulted, attacked, or even insulted inside the prison:

As long as I was superintendent, freeworld staff, women and children were free to mingle with the "convicts" without fear. But the most significant change was in the attitude of the inmates. Fear had disappeared, a new community had been created, and despair had been replaced by hope. (Murton, 1976, 219)

These changes seemed monumental to some experts who visited. Joseph Lohman, the Dean of Criminology at Berkeley, came and "expressed amazement at the peaceful revolution taking place within the prison . . . and reported that a 'renaissance in corrections' was taking place in Arkansas" (Murton & Hyams, 1969, 117). Other visitors were not as impressed: George Beto visited about the same time and remarked that the prison was 'not clean' (Steinmetz, 1967, 8).

After Murton's departure, the prison reverted to its old ways. Later that year, Robert Sarver became commissioner of corrections. In March of 1969, he testified before the U.S. Senate Committee on the judiciary (1971, 5253): "When I read of an exposé of homosexualities, bribings, escapes, political corruption in prisons, I think most knowledgeable correction administrators think: 'So what else is new?' " Despite Sarver's cavalier attitude about the problems in his prisons and elsewhere, Arkansas became the first prison system to be declared unconstitutional. Judge Henley found the system to be "not only shocking to 'standards of decency,' but immoral and criminal as well" (*Holt v. Sarver,* 1971, 310). Beto returned to inspect the prison that same year and testified before Judge Henley that, since the time Murton was fired, the prison system had been *improved* (quoted in Murton, 1976, 155–156).

CONCLUSION

For the last twenty years, the United States has tried to "build" our way out of the crime problem by constructing more prisons and by increasing rates and terms of incarceration to the point of rampant prison overcrowding. As we incarcerate more people under more security, the examples of Beto and DiIulio remain important, because so much of what they recommended has come to pass. Unfortunately, some scholars maintain that as more emphasis has been placed on control, it has served to "widen the gap of hostility, hate and violence between guards and prisoners" (Irwin & Austin, 2001, 71). A prisoner today "cannot imagine what forgiveness is, or mercy or tolerance, because he has no *experience* of such values" (Abbott, 1981, 13). It is possible that our prisons are doing as much to exacerbate the crime problem as to solve it.

Having failed to "build" our way out of the crime problem, we must also try to "manage" our way out. Even so, some experts might feel that Murton's success in Arkansas has little relevance. After all, his experiments are not in line with contemporary thinking. However, if we are dissatisfied with prisons today, we should ask ourselves whether prison reform is best served by ignoring the lessons of Murton in Arkansas. The control model encourages prison administrators to adopt the attitude that, except for controlling inmates more tightly, "you can't do anything with these people." It was not always so. We can and we must.

REFERENCES

Abbott, Jack H. 1981. *In the Belly of the Beast.* New York: Random House.

Conrad, John P. 1988. Research and Development in Corrections. *Federal Probation, 52* (March), 64–68.

Crouch, Ben M., and James W. Marquart. 1990. *Ruiz:* Intervention and Emergent Order in Texas Prisons, in *Courts, Corrections and the Constitution,* edited by John J. DiIulio, Jr. New York: Oxford University Press, pp. 94–114.

DiIulio, John J. 1987. *Governing Prisons: A Comparative Study of Correctional Management.* New York: The Free Press.

DiIulio, John J. 1989. Governing Prisons: Managing Constitutionally. *Society,* 81–83.

Dreyer v. Jalet, 349 F. Supp 452 (S.D. Texas, 1972).

Feeley, Malcolm M., and Edward Rubin. 1992. Prison Litigation and Bureaucratic Development. *Law and Social Inquiry,* 17(1): 125–145.

Hoffman, Ethan, and John McCoy. 1981. *Concrete Mama: Prison Profiles from Walla Walla.* London: University of Missouri Press.

Holt v. Sarver, 442 F.2d 304 (8th Cir., 1971).

Irwin, John. 1988. Donald Cressey and the Sociology of the Prison. *Crime and Delinquency. 34*(3), 328–337.

Irwin, John, and James Austin. 2001. *It's About Time: America's Imprisonment Binge.* Belmont, CA: Wadsworth Publishing Company.

Jimenez v. Beto, 468 F.2d 616 (5th Cir., 1972).

Mauer, Marc. 1994. *Americans Behind Bars: The International Use of Incarceration, 1992–1993.* Washington, DC: The Sentencing Project.

Murton, Tom, and Joe Hyams. 1969. *Accomplices to the Crime: The Arkansas Prison Scandal.* New York: Grove Press.

Murton, Tom. 1972. Too Good for Arkansas, in *Prisons, Protest and Politics,* edited by Burton M. Atkins and Henry R. Glick. Englewood Cliffs, New Jersey: Prentice Hall.

Murton, Tom. 1975. *Shared Decision-Making as a Treatment Technique in Prison Management.* Minneapolis: The Murton Foundation for Criminal Justice.

Murton, Thomas O. 1976. *The Dilemma of Prison Reform.* New York: Holt, Rinehart and Winston.

Nathan, Vincent. 1988. Reflections on Two Decades of Court Ordered Prison Reform. (A speech presented at the Southwestern Criminal Justice Association Meeting, Corpus Christi, Texas.)

Osborne, Thomas M. 1915. The New Methods at Sing Sing Prison. *The American Review of Reviews, 52*(4), 449–456.

Parker, Mary. 1986. *Judicial Intervention in Correctional Institutions: The Arkansas Odyssey.* PhD Dissertation: Sam Houston State University.

Peters, Tom. 1992. The Missing X-Factor: Trust. *Liberation Management.* New York: Knopf, 249–256.

Ruiz v. Estelle, 503 F.Supp 1265 (S.D. Texas, 1980).

Steinmetz, T. 1967, April 30. Texas prison chief tells study panel Arkansas prisons are 'not clean.' *Pine Bluff Commercial,* p. 8.

Toch, Hans and Kenneth Adams. 1989. *Coping: Maladaptation in Prisons.* New Brunswick: Transaction Publishers.

United States Senate Committee on the Judiciary. 1971. Conditions in Juvenile and Young Offender Institutions, in *Hearings Before the Subcommittee to Investigate Juvenile Delinquency,* part 20. Washington, DC: U.S. Government Printing Office.

STUDY QUESTIONS FOR READING 16

1. What makes the control model so important today? the inmate participation model?

2. What happened in the Federal Bureau of Prisons maxi-max prison in Marion, Illinois between 1980 and 1983? How did Murton and DiIulio react?

3. What were some of the advantages of the Texas Department of Corrections under Commissioner George Beto?

4. Were the Building Tenders (BTs) abusive under Beto? In your answer, include the views of DiIulio as well as Crouch and Marquart.

5. Dr. Beto was asked in court about his review of the appointment of BTs who had histories of predatory and vicious behavior. He was also asked whether he was "interested in prisoners bringing to the attention of the courts conditions which they do not consider fair or equitable or humane." In each case, what was his response for the court record?

6. To DiIulio, the BTs were the weakness, or the "rotten crutch" of the otherwise excellent control model. To his critics, the control model was a "terror-based" system of control, for which the BTs served as what?

7. In Arkansas, how did Warden Tom Murton begin to suspect that inmates were buried on prison grounds?

8. According to Beto, inmates are 100 percent responsible for their crimes, and therefore should be viewed as what? According to Murton, 95 percent of inmates will return to the free world someday, and therefore should be viewed as what?

9. According to Beto, what was the rationale for "making inmates behave"? How might Murton defend his view that wardens should have inmates help make the rules so the inmates will have a stake in them?

10. According to Beto, who should select inmate leaders and how should they be monitored? What would Murton say in response?

11. What governmental model did Murton adopt? Beto? What did Murton have to say about the contrast?

12. According to Murton, what alone fits men for liberty? According to DiIulio, where higher-custody prisons are concerned, those govern best who govern how?

13. How successful was the "Take a Lifer to Dinner" program at Walla Walla? The classification committee at Tucker prison farm?

14. How did Beto and Lohman (dean of Criminology at Berkeley) differ in their evaluation of the prison during Murton's tenure? How did Beto and Judge Henley differ three years after Murton left?

WHY MORE CONTROL IS BETTER WHEN *GOVERNING PRISONS*

JOHN J. DiIULIO, JR.

Whether a prison (or a prison system) is safe, humane, and treatment-oriented, on the one hand, or violent, harsh, and unproductive, on the other, may depend mainly on the character of its prison governance. Managerially, the Texas, Michigan, and California prison systems have differed dramatically. In this decade, the Texas prison system has undergone an administrative revolution. There have been, and continue to be, intrasystem differences in prison management, especially in California. These three sets of managerial differences—intersystem, historical, and intrasystem—parallel and, it will be argued, account for the differences in the quality of prison life. . . .

Unfortunately, this explanation for differences in the quality of prison life is far more messy and complex than most of its rivals—expenditure levels, overcrowding, staffing ratios, and so on. It may, however, have the virtue of being true. Let us begin to explore this thesis by way of a brief tour of the Texas, Michigan, and California prison systems.

A TOUR THROUGH TDC, CDC, AND MDC: THREE MODELS OF CORRECTIONAL MANAGEMENT

If you were blindfolded and taken into the building which is headquarters for the Texas Department of Corrections, within seconds of uncovering your eyes, you would probably know that you were someplace having to do with prisons. To your left you would see a showcase of weapons (crudely fashioned knives, handmade guns); makeshift escape ladders; and the "bat," a wooden-handled, rawhide belt, 3¼ feet long and 2½ inches wide, once used to administer whip-

pings of twenty lashes to those guilty of rule infractions. If you read the index cards beneath each object in the case and studied the photos on the walls, including pictures of present and past governors, prison board members, directors, and inmates, you would learn more than a little about the history of this prison bureaucracy. Even as a casual observer you would not miss the clean-shaven men in the crisp white uniforms, names written in black over their shirt pockets, busily washing windows, polishing floors, and nodding a greeting to each person who walked by them. Nor would you miss the other men (and women) in the crisp grey uniforms, some of them with silver bars on their shoulders or sergeant's stripes on their sleeves. But if, after these and similar observations, you were still in doubt about where you were, all doubts would end the moment you walked through the building and stepped out on the other side. There you would see a massive red brick structure with high walls, gun towers at each corner, and green-and-white uniforms in every direction.

If, on the other hand, you were blindfolded and taken into the building which is headquarters for the Michigan Department of Corrections, you would probably guess that you were someplace that housed government or business offices. Reading the office directory, you would know that you were in a government building. Exit the elevator a few floors up and, if you bothered to read the fine print on some of the notices hanging on the bulletin boards, you would believe that you were in the central offices of the Michigan prison system. You would, however, be only half right. To find the personnel or training offices of the department you would have to leave the building and drive (unblindfolded) several miles to another nondescript building. Once you stepped outside and looked across the street, you would see high brick walls, but they would belong to the Michigan Civic Center.

If, alas, you were blindfolded and taken to the building that is headquarters for the California Department of Corrections, you would not have the foggiest idea of where you were, unless and until you were past the enclosed reception area on the inside. If the blindfold were removed before you entered the building, and if (as I did) you missed the state flag flying in front and the unobtrusive nameplate, you would be sure that you were standing before a store in a shopping mall. All around, you would see stores and shoppers. (In fact, the building that now houses CDC was once a J.C. Penney store.) Once inside, however, you would see a few pictures of buildings that look like prisons and various announcements asking for votes in some upcoming ballot to decide which union will represent the line correctional staff.

Let us now move from headquarters into the field. If you enter a Texas or California prison, you are unlikely to have any problem sorting out who is who and who is in charge. Inside the Texas prison you will see inmates in white, officers in grey, and senior officers wearing various signs of rank. When the men in white speak to the men and women in grey, they usually do so in a calm voice, addressing the officers as "sir" or boss." Inside the California prison, you may have a bit more trouble sorting things out, but only slightly. The officers are the ones in the paramilitary green-and-tan uniforms. Some inmates are wearing state-issued blue pants and shirts, but most are in an assortment of "street duds"—jeans, T-shirts (often with lewd sayings on them), and (on cooler days) an occasional leather vest or jacket. When the inmates speak to the officers, it is not uncommon for them to do so in a very forward manner, often beginning with "Hey man!"

If you enter a Michigan prison, it is a fair bet that, unless you have been there before, you will have some initial difficulty telling who are the officers and who are the inmates. Even after you have spent much time inside the prison, you will be unable to tell senior officers from junior officers (unless, of course, you

come to know and associate names, ranks, and faces). The officers wear no visible signs of rank—no stripes, no bars, no insignias. Instead, they sport black pants and green or white "airline pilot" shirts. Some wear green blazers and black baseball caps. The inmates are in every imaginable garb. Few wear their state-issued "blues and shoes." Many are in "cool threads"—silky shirts, expensive (but untied) sneakers, one to three hats (usually baseball caps) on their heads, and gold chains. Stick around for a few minutes and you will almost surely hear inmates address officers with some vulgar epithet. Walk about alone or with a member of the nonuniformed staff (even the warden), and you are likely to hear much more of the same. If the staff person is female, much of the vulgarity will be sexual and threatening.

If you wished to avoid contacts with the inmates, you would be best able to do so in Texas and least able to do so in Michigan. In Texas inmates move about in a more or less orderly fashion with a correctional officer somewhere close at hand. There is little roaming about the cellblocks. It is rare for an inmate to initiate a conversation with a visitor and rarer still for a visitor to be shouted at, insulted, or threatened by inmates. In Michigan, it is virtually impossible to avoid interaction, friendly or unfriendly, with inmates. It is not uncommon for an inmate to demand an explanation of who you are and what you are doing. Indeed, it is common for inmates to bombard you (sometimes in groups of ten or fifteen) with their opinions about the institution, the administration, and other matters. The following is a sample of what you are likely to hear:

> *You got these f——ing idiots here (pointing to officers). You got an asshole for a warden.*

> *Hey b——h, hey sweet b——h I want you. I'll beat/rip your ass motherf——er (shouted from various cells).*

> *Tell them. You know who. Tell them of the injustice you witnessed here today.*

In Michigan, such behavior by inmates is considered typical, unexceptional, and requiring little or no response. In Texas, such behavior (the few times it occurs) will bring an immediate reprimand and in some cases disciplinary action. In California, how much of this type of inmate behavior you witness will depend largely on what prison you are visiting. San Quentin, for instance, is about as noisy and threatening as any prison could be. As you move from that prison to Folsom, Soledad, and CMC such behavior by inmates will become less likely. At CMC you will witness virtually none of this type of inmate behavior.

In California and Michigan prisons, inmates are more likely to register complaints with officers or other staff members in an aggressive way. Workers in both systems are as likely as not to respond to such complaints in a sympathetic manner and to do so in the inmates' argot. For instance, in Michigan an inmate screams in the face of a higher-level official: "I'm fed the f—— up with this s——t. I'll do my time! What can you do, put my ass in the hole? Big s——t! F—— the warden too." The official responds with repeated attempts to reason with the inmate, calling him by his nickname, making clear that he appreciates the problem, and repeating over and over the need to grasp the "real options." The inmate responds by shouting, "I'm a man, I'm sick and tired," turning his back on the official, and returning to his cell. Similarly, a California inmate accosts a staff person as follows: "Hey lady, who are you? [*to me*] Who are you? Why the hell am I here? I'm supposed to be at another unit. Why don't I have any socks? Do you have any power?" The official responds: "I can't help you man, you'll just have to hang on. . . . Send me a kite." (A "kite" is a written request or statement from an inmate to a prison official.) In another California prison, an inmate, subjected to a frisk on his way out of the dining hall, curses and criticizes the officer who is frisking him as a "low status man trying to act bad." The officer completes the frisk and then says, "Well, what's your claim to fame?"

In Texas, inmates rarely accost officials in this manner. When they do, a disciplinary report normally follows. Rather than automatically sympathizing with the complaint, Texas prison workers are more likely to weigh its legitimacy and remind the inmate of the limits both of the institution's resources and of the inmate's rights. For instance, it is recreation period and from the window of the office of the major—the highest-ranking uniformed worker in the prison—you see inmates playing basketball in the yard. One of them leaves the game and approaches the major's door. Without bothering to knock—there is a sign hanging on the door which says (in English and in Spanish) "Knock and wait for permission to enter"—the inmate enters the office and complains loudly: "Yeah, I'm here because I'm tired of being jacked around. I'm tired of the bulls——t that's going on here. I been real sick since I come here, but I can't get to a lower bunk. Some other man got one . . . a transit." (A "transit" is an inmate housed at the prison en route to another unit.) The major asks, "Why do you need a lower bunk?" The inmate replies, "I just told you! . . . Look, I'm a man too. Why does one guy get it and not another? I'm needing a lower bunk." At that point the major orders the inmate out of his office. The inmate complies but slams the door on the way out. As instructed, he waits on the major's doorstep until, some thirty minutes later, he is told to reenter. The major then addresses him as follows:

> *You slammed the door. Don't ever do that again. This is the penitentiary. There are rules to be followed. The man who is disrespectful isn't going to do well in here. . . . I checked on your request. You've been complaining about a hurt hand. You can't climb into an upper bunk, but you* can *play a mean game of basketball. The other man really did need that lower bunk. He has a bona fide medical problem. That is all. (Inmate says "Thank you, sir" and retires from the major's office, gently closing the door.)*

If you looked into the cells of prisoners in each state, you would find those of the Texas inmates to be most spartan and those of the Michigan inmates to be bursting with all manner of personal property—television sets, radios, games, books, clothes, sewing machines, and so on. In Michigan, you would see huge green canvas baskets being wheeled about by correctional officers. The baskets are used to transport inmate property in the event that the inmate is transferred to a new cell or out of the unit.

In Texas and California, prison officials may tease you, the naïve visitor, about the facilities available to the inmates: 'Want to see the swimming pool?" Having fallen for the joke in those two states, you will be prepared for it when your tour ends in Michigan. But do not be too quick to laugh. In at least one Michigan higher-custody prison, there was a heated, enclosed inmate swimming pool.

These and scores of like differences would impress you as your tour of prisons in each state came to an end. If you were then motivated to make some general sense out of what you observed, you would discover that the differences were indicative of three different models of correctional management: the Texas control model, the Michigan responsibility model, and what, for lack of an existing appellation, will be termed the California consensual model.

Elements of the Texas Control Model

Until recently, the Texas prison system ran according to what in corrections circles came to be known as the control model of correctional management. The chief architect of the control model was Dr. George Beto, director of the Texas Department of Corrections from 1962 to 1972. The control model was based on a correctional philosophy emphasizing inmate obedience, work, and education, roughly in that order.

One of the most telling facts about the control model is that, during its reign in Texas, a period stretching roughly from 1963 to 1983, every prison in the system was designated as a maximum-security institution and, for the most part, run accordingly. There were, to be sure, some differences in administrative practices from prison to prison, but in general the administrative routine inside Texas prisons was the same everywhere. In each prison, correctional officers were organized along strict paramilitary lines running from the warden and his assistants, to the major, all the way down to the most junior correctional officer. Official rules and regulations were followed closely and enforced rigorously. In the prison corridors, inmates were required to walk between lines painted on the floors rather than moving at random down the center. Talking too loud was a punishable offense. In short, daily life inside the prisons was a busy, but carefully orchestrated, routine of numbering, counting, checking, locking, and monitoring inmate movement to and from work activities and treatment programs.

As late as 1984, this system was still in existence at some Texas prisons. For instance, at the Huntsville "Walls" unit, the system's oldest and probably best-known institution, traces of the control model remained highly visible. Figure 17.1 is a schedule of the prison's daily activities. Things happened precisely when (and how) they were supposed to at this prison. Inmate movement was regulated tightly. The chain of command was followed rigorously. Officers had a sense of mission, an ésprit de corps, and an amazing knowledge of the system's history. Treatment and work opportunities were offered on a regular basis and were well administered. Tension between treatment and custody personnel was virtually nonexistent. In short, life inside the Walls was in general safe, humane, productive, calm, stable, and predictable. Such was life at most Texas prisons in the years when the control model was in effect.

In essence, the control model involved a mixture of correctional carrots and sticks. For inmates who violated the rules, punishment in the form of solitary confinement or extra work assignments was swift and certain. For inmates who "did their own time" and kept out of trouble, the rewards were equally swift and certain. Indeed, given that Texas used solitary confinement and related punishments less frequently than other systems, the rewards were vitally important in securing inmate compliance with official rules and regulations. Texas offered inmates some of the most liberal "good time" provisions in American corrections. Under its 1982 good time policies, for instance, a Texas prison inmate could earn as much as two days off of his term for every productive, problem-free day he served (see Table 17.1). Inmates who scored below a fifth-grade competency level on prison-administered tests were required to attend school at least one day each week. Each inmate spent his first six months in the prison working on the prison farms. Better jobs—in the industrial plants, kitchens, or elsewhere—awaited those who performed well. There was a "point-incentive system" whereby inmates could earn points for working, going to school, and other such positive endeavors. In general, the more points an inmate earned, the closer he moved to a trustyship. But any good time or associated privileges earned by an inmate could be taken from him for disciplinary reasons.[1]

By most accounts, this simple combination of—as one veteran Texas officer described it—"prods and prizes" enabled the Texas prison authorities to control the Texas prison inmates. One comparative measure

SO-4 Rev. 10-75

TEXAS DEPARTMENT OF CORRECTIONS
Inter-Office Communications

From _ _CPtn_ _ _ _ _ _ _ _ _ _ _ _ _ _   Date _ _JUNE_18,_1984_ _ _ _ _ _ _ _ _ _ _ _ _ _ _ _

To _ _ _ _Mr._Dilulio_ _ _ _ _ _ _ _ _ _   Subject _HUNTSVILLE_UNIT_TIME_SCHEDULE_ _

05:45 AM SHIFT CHANGE - FINISH FEEDING BREAKFAST

06:00 AM PROCESS PAROLES & DISCHARGES (SHOWERS)

06:15 AM START PILL LINE

07:00 AM WORK TURN OUT (IE LOWER YARD,MECH,DEPT,TEXTILE)
         START SICK CALL CHAIN BEGINS COMING IN.

08:00 AM TRANSIT SICK CALL-TRANSIT WRIT ROOM

08:45 AM SHUT DOWN PREPARE TO COUNT

09:00 AM COUNT TIME

10:00 AM OR AS SOON AS COUNT CLEARS START FEEDING LUNCH SHAKING
         DOWN IN COMING CHAIN

11:00 AM FEED ADMIN, SEG.-LOWER YARD TURNS IN FOR LUNCH

11:30 AM YARD OPENS

11:45 AM START 2nd PILL LINE

12:00 PM LOWER YARD TURNS BACK OUT

12:30 PM CLOSE DOWN CHOW HALL

13:30 PM CLOSE YARD-TRANSIT COMMISSARY

13:45 PM SHIFT CHANGE-2nd SHIFT BEGINS

14:45 PM BEGIN FEEDING SUPPER

16:00 PM LOWER YARD TURNS IN FROM WORK-GO's TO CHOW

17:00 PM END OF CHOW-ALL CHAIN SHOULD BE IN

17:30 PM BEGIN 3rd PILL LINE

18:00 PM SHUT DOWN PREPARE TO COUNT

18:30 PM START COUNT

19:00 PM OR WHEN COUNT CLEARS BEGIN DAYROOM RECREATION

20:00 PM LAST PILL LINE

21:30 PM ADMIN SEG GO TO WRIT ROOM

21:45 PM SHIFT CHANGE-3rd SHIFT BEGINS

FIGURE 17.1

```
SO-4 Rev. 10-75
                    TEXAS DEPARTMENT OF CORRECTIONS
                         Inter-Office Communications

From _ Cptn._____   Date _ JUNE 18, 1984_____

To ____ Mr. Dilulio_____   Subject HUNTSVILLE_UNIT_TIME_SCHEDULE___


    22:30 PM RACK UP

    23:30 PM 3rd SHIFT TEXTILE TURN OUT

    00:00 AM COUNT TIME

    02:00 AM COUNT TIME

    02:30 AM CHAIN TIME-BEGIN SHAKING DOWN & FEEDING OUT GOING CHAIN

    04:00 AM OUT GOING CHAIN TAKEN TO EAST GATE

    04:45 AM BEGIN FEEDING BREAKFAST, 1st CHAIN BUSES ARRIVE

    05:45 AM SHIFT CHANGE 1st SHIFT BEGINS
```

FIGURE 17.1   (cont.)

of just how well the control model worked is the degree to which antisocial or violent inmate associations appeared in Texas versus other systems. Until 1983–1984, a time during which the control model was rapidly disappearing from Texas prisons, the system experienced no significant gang problems, certainly nothing on the order of those that plagued California and many other states. Indeed, in the 1970s researchers and practitioners who sought an answer to the problem of gang-based prison violence looked to the large, racially diverse, but relatively gang-free Texas system. To my knowledge, however, none of them took away the most obvious lesson: Texas had little gang activity because prison gangs in Texas were few in number and weak; they were so weak because the administration saw to it that inmates were not allowed to associate freely in ways that might lead to the formation of stable, powerful prisoner groupings.

In general, under the control model, inmate movement was monitored too closely, rules were en-

TABLE 17.1   Good Time in Texas Prison System (1982)

TIME EARNING CLASS	SENTENCE SERVING BEGINNING 1-1-82	TIME SERVED	GOOD TIME CREDITED	TOTAL TIME CREDITED	DISCHARGE DATE
I	60 Mos	36 Mos	24 Mos	60 Mos	1-1-85
II	60 Mos	45 Mos	15 Mos	60 Mos	10-1-85
III	60 Mos	60 Mos	0 Mos	60 Mos	1-1-87
Trusty	60 Mos	30 Mos	30 Mos	60 Mos	7-1-84

forced too tightly, inmates were kept too busy, the punishments for misbehavior were too swift and certain, and the rewards to be earned in sentence reduction and other privileges were too great for inmates to commit many infractions.

Under the control model, a cardinal rule, well-understood and generally followed by all concerned, was that each inmate was to serve his sentence on his own. Criminalistic associations among inmates—to plot an escape, plan some violence, deal in contraband, or engage in some other form of misconduct—were checked. The principle that every inmate must "do his own time" was advanced and realized in a variety of ways. At the system's Diagnostic Center, the induction point for incoming inmates, the necessity of following the rules and avoiding troublesome contacts with other inmates was spelled out in handbooks and lectures. When an inmate reached the unit to which he was assigned, he would receive more documents and lectures to reinforce this message. In the units, the lectures were often conducted by the major on duty when the new inmates arrived. In a typical scene, a group of six to ten newly arrived inmates would be marched single file into the major's office, usually located at some central point inside the prison. In one of the instances I recorded, the major began by handing each inmate a copy of the prison's rulebook and then spoke to the group as follows:

> *You are in the custody of the Texas Department of Corrections. Stand where I can see you! [pause] That book I just gave you is the most important thing you'll ever receive here. It lists all the rules and regulations. You're responsible for knowing them. If you can't read, we'll have someone read it to you as many times as you need. . . . Now, if you need education—and we all do—we've got it right here. You can learn a skill in here, you can earn good time. . . . The best way to do time is to do your own time. Do your own time! Nobody else can do it for you. If you listen to some inmates inside, you'll have trouble for sure. You get in trouble, and you'll be right here with me for a longer time; I guarantee it. Now, you have family and friends waiting on you—don't let them down. Don't let yourself down. Do your own time, and you'll be fine. The rules are for your own protection and health. . . . There is a reason for each and every rule. They are to help you, to keep you whole.*

The control model did more than rely on such exhortation as a means of preventing individual or group misconduct, especially the sort that might threaten the safety of others or make escapes more likely. All rules, even the most minor ones, were enforced. Casual groupings of inmates in the cellblocks, on the yards, out in the fields, or at work in the plants were simply not permitted. Almost reflexively, officers would shout "Break it up!" or "Move out!" at the incipient stages of such gatherings. In sum, the control model involved administrative measures tight enough to check individual misdeeds as well as the maldevelopment of inmate society, but not so tight as to preclude the degree of inmate movement and interaction necessary for work and treatment opportunities.

Evolution of the Control Model

Dr. Beto's predecessor as director of the Texas prison system was O. B. Ellis. Ellis had served as director from 1947 till his death in 1961 at a Board of Corrections meeting. Ellis had come to Texas from correctional work in Tennessee. Beto, on the other hand, came to the helm of Texas corrections from a more unconventional background. An ordained Lutheran minister with a Doctorate in Education, he came to Texas from Illinois, where he had served on the Illinois Board of Parole and been active in other areas of criminal justice. In addition, he had been president of Concordia College in Texas and Concordia Theological Seminary in Illinois. While at the former, he had served on the Texas Board of Corrections. In corrections circles Beto earned the nickname "Walking George" because of his practice of making frequent and usually unannounced visits to the prisons.

It is important to note that one of the chief influences on Beto's thinking about prisons was Joseph Ragen, the famous warden of Illinois's Stateville penitentiary. Ragen's approach to correctional management was remarkably security-oriented. So far as the internal management of the prisons was concerned, Beto borrowed more than a few pages from Ragen's book, seeing to it that his subordinates at every level practiced an incredibly security-conscious yet treatment-oriented approach to running the prisons. In this effort, Beto was advantaged by having the kind of charismatic personality that led his subordinates to feel that he knew or could trace their every move; in fact, he normally could.

With Richard A. McGee, who directed the California prison system from 1944 into the 1960s, Beto was ahead of his time in being sensitive to the place of correctional agencies in the overall criminal justice system. Even more than McGee, however, Beto reached beyond the walls to master other parts of the criminal justice system and, more importantly, to bend the system's political environment to its best interests. Beto cultivated governors, legislators, prison board members, journalists, and other important constituencies beyond the walls. Largely because of his efforts, state laws were passed that, among other things, made it possible for the system to produce and sell a significant quantity of prisonmade goods. This enabled the system to develop a thriving industrial complex which could employ vast numbers of the prison population. Together with the system's enormous agribusiness complex, also developed largely under Beto's tutelage, it was possible for the system to keep per capita costs relatively low, far below the per capita costs of other major state systems. In Texas, a state where tax dollars for most public goods and services have traditionally been allocated in stingy and irregular amounts, this proved vital, for it helped to keep the system popular politically and enabled it to do more than merely warehouse inmates.

Beto's successor was W. J. Estelle. Estelle came to Texas after having been a ranking correctional worker in California and a warden in Montana. Estelle, whose family history in correctional administration stretches back to the late nineteenth century and includes the first warden of California's San Quentin prison, served as director of the Texas prison system from 1972 to 1983. He shared virtually all of Beto's correctional philosophy and saw it as his mission to further institutionalize the control model of management that, just about everybody agreed, had made Texas prisons safe, clean, treatment-oriented, and financially self-supporting.

As the Texas inmate newspaper noted in a 1984 article reviewing Estelle's administration "his 11½ years as director of TDC were highly successful in leading the Texas prison system through what were perhaps the most precarious years of its 140-year existence."[2] Estelle expanded the system's industrial and agricultural complexes, personnel training, and treatment programs.

Defects of the Control Model

There were at least two latent defects, one internal, the other external, in the model of prison administration bequeathed by Beto to Estelle. Internally, the control model involved what was known as the building-tender (BT) system.

BTs were inmates selected by the administration to assist correctional officers in running the cellblocks. The building-tender system grew out of Beto's theory, not untouched by readings of prison sociology, that inmates are bound to have leaders. Rather than allow the most aggressive and violent inmates to rule, Beto believed that prison officials could select exemplary inmates, give them special official status beyond a mere trustyship, and use them to preempt the influence of more hardcore, criminalistic, and violent inmates. "Either you pick their leaders," he explained, "or they do." Beto elaborated the idea as follows:

> *In any contemporary prison, there is bound to be some level of inmate organization, some manner of inmate society. . . . The question is this: who selects the leaders? Are the inmates to select them? Or is the administration to choose them or at least influence the choice? If the former, the extent of control over organized and semi-organized inmate life is lessened; if the latter, the measure of control is strengthened.*

The building-tender system was intended as a way of reducing the influence of aggressive, exploitative inmate leaders. It was, in effect, an attempt to make formal and legitimate what Gresham Sykes had characterized as the corrupt alliance between the inmates and the administration. It was designed as a way of avoiding a situation in which prison inmates rather than prison authorities determine the character of life behind bars. Under Beto, BTs were rewarded officially rather than informally with better job assignments and the like. But they were positively forbidden to use their positions for illicit gains and were, at least until the mid-1970s, largely prevented from doing so. Any BT who tried to exploit his position in this way would be in trouble with the authorities. Being a BT did not give an inmate the right to ignore the rules. In short, under Beto, the BT system worked as an alternative to the widely practiced con-boss system wherein favored inmates were given illicit privileges and allowed to abuse other inmates (and even the staff) in return for helping the administration to keep order.

But to keep the BT system from sliding into a con-boss system required enormous administrative energy spent selecting and monitoring the BTs. By all accounts, Beto saw to it that building tenders were chosen carefully and kept on a very short leash. As Beto himself recalled:

We would not select someone likely to abuse his position. All building-tender appointments had to be cleared by me or by the director of classification. No inmate could be appointed simply on a warden's say so. One day, for instance, during one of my tours I observed an inmate acting as a building tender. I knew this man's history. He was a very bad character, the type that would rape a snake through a brick wall. I said, "What in the world are you doing in this position?" He said that the warden or some other authority at the institution had given him the job. I saw to it that he was removed as a building tender—on the spot.

Estelle, like Beto, was a talented and energetic executive. During his tenure, however, the system more than doubled both in population and in number of units. Estelle was not given to the kind of super-close, hands-on supervision that marked Beto's directorship. Even if he were, however, it would have been virtually impossible for him to cover over two dozen institutions the way that Beto had covered twelve. Also, Estelle did not have the advantage of Beto's charismatic personality or reputation for omniscience concerning what was happening in the field. These factors combined to weaken the centralized control that was at the heart of the control model. Towards the end of Estelle's era, therefore, the BT system broke down and became a classical con-boss system. Under Estelle's successors, it evolved into a situation in which the leaders of various prison gangs, organized largely along racial and ethnic lines, ran major parts of the Texas prison system.

A second latent defect in the control model was essentially external and political. The Texas control model depended for its existence on an extraordinary degree of political support from powerful state leaders. For decades the Texas Board of Corrections, the body with immediate authority over the prison system, cast only unanimous votes in support of the administration's policies and was an effective public voice for the department's budgetary and other needs. Until the 1980s the board was composed almost entirely of the state's leading businessmen. Chief among them was H. H. "Pete" Coffield. Coffield, a member of the board since 1948, was its chairman from 1955 to 1974. He was a multimillionaire who had made money in a variety of endeavors. In his day, Coffield was considered to be, next to LBJ, the most powerful man in Texas.

Known affectionately as "Mr. Chairman," Coffield could be ruthless in pressing his will on state politicians and had much influence with the state's press. The Texas Department of Corrections was, in effect, the chief benefactor of his enormous power within the state. Beto used Coffield's influence sparingly but, nevertheless, had this political resource at his disposal to win key legislative or other battles. Coffield's dedication to the system was incredible. For example, on the department's behalf, he would sponsor (and pay for) lavish cocktail parties for the state's most influential citizens—legislators, corporate executives, and so on. He would come to the prisons and speak at inmate high school graduation ceremonies, a service valuable both for what he had to say and for the positive image it left with the public. In short, for twenty-eight years this important figure stood behind the Texas prison system in its efforts to become one of the nation's best. The system acknowledged his contributions when, in 1974, it dedicated a department-prepared history of the agency to him.[3]

Coffield, however, was not the only political pillar of the Texas control model. Equally important were key state legislators such as Bill Heatly, long-reigning chairman of the House Appropriations Committee. Known in Texas as the "Duke of Paducah" (Paducah being the Texas county from which he came), Heatly was for some twenty-eight years all-powerful in his control over the state's purse. Districts whose representatives opposed Heatly on even insignificant measures would get less funds for their roads, schools, and other state services. A "yellow dog" Texas Democrat (meaning a party loyalist who would "vote for a yellow dog over a Republican"), in 1972, Heatly was able to deliver his district for the wildly unpopular George McGovern. Heatly was a recovered alcoholic who was helped by Alcoholics Anonymous (AA). In gratitude, Heatly ran a loosely grouped AA chapter for people in state government. With one eye on the political significance of the act, Beto saw to it that the AA chapters in the prisons became an integral part of the formal treatment program. In later years Heatly repaid this gesture by giving Beto's agency what it needed (but not a penny more) budgetarily.[4]

Beto's ties to Heatly and other important state legislators were direct and intimate. Beto used various strategies to win and keep their support, but in general, he was simply relentless in his attempts to educate state political leaders about the system's needs. He encouraged them to visit and study the prisons. His powers of persuasion proved more than equal to the task of cultivating such support. Successive governors became highly interested in and supportive of his attempt to run the nation's best correctional agency.

In 1974, just two years into Estelle's tenure, the aging Pete Coffield retired from his chairmanship on the Board of Corrections. In 1978, William P. Clements, Jr. became the state's governor. Clements was the first Republican governor elected in Texas in 105 years. He made a number of appointments, including some to the Board of Corrections, that were intended to shake things up. Key supporters of the system began to retire or saw their influence wane. At the same time, the system was undergoing major litigation in federal court in the form of a class-action suit challenging the constitutionality of conditions inside the state's prisons. The presiding judge was William Wayne Justice. Judge Justice was known in Texas for his generally liberal views on such matters as busing. In 1980 "Willie Wayne," as he was called, handed down a decision ordering changes in virtually every part of the Texas prison system.

Judge Justice's opinion came at a time when the system's political support was already declining, albeit slowly. Estelle was known as a stubborn administrator, one dedicated to certain correctional principles (those of the control model). He was fiercely loyal to his subordinates and thoroughly opposed, on philosophical grounds, to the judiciary's attempt to order changes in prison operations and oversee their implementation. He thus made a vigorous defense of the system and its accomplishments against the court and its appointed monitors. By this time, the Board of Corrections was no longer solid in its support for the system. Unprecedented split votes were cast, and the Board, now composed of less powerful men and women of differing backgrounds, made its battles public. There soon followed an outpouring of news stories and editorials questioning, criticizing, or condemning the agency.[5] Clement's successor in the governor's office, Democrat Mark White, was no unbending supporter of the agency. In short, by 1984, the Texas prison system had gone from the sunniest political weather to a storm of thunderous dissent and protest.

Also during the latter part of Estelle's tenure, the state's oil revenues began to decline. The troubled prison system became a favorite target of those who wanted to spend less on the public sector. Estelle was unable to get the legislature to approve his package of budget requests. Recognizing that he had become a political liability to the agency, Estelle resigned in late 1983.

In a letter to me, former Texas Governor John Connally (1963–1969) summed up the transformation in the system's political environment leading up to Estelle's resignation:

> . . . the success of the Texas Department of Corrections was made possible by [a] supporting political environment which consisted of its Board of Corrections . . . [the] State Legislature, and . . . a favorable press. . . . We had the cooperation of men like Pete Coffield and Bill Heatly . . . and many many other people including the strong support of the Speaker of the House, Ben Barnes, who later became Lieutenant Governor.[6]

Connally implied that the loss of this support was responsible for the system's difficulties. Former Texas governor Preston Smith (1969–1973) made the same argument, though more directly. In a letter to me, Governor Smith wrote:

. . . it is rather ironical, but true, that politics has played a definite role in the overall operations of the Texas prison system. It's too bad, but true, that our system has not had the proper attention and support it had some years back.[7]

Smith went on to say that "we simply do not have the caliber of people on the board nor the executive, legislative, public support that was once available."

It is important to highlight the administrative consequences of this change in the organization's political environment.[8] The most important consequence was to undermine the system's organizational stability at all levels. From Beto's predecessor through Estelle, the Texas prison system had three directors in thirty-six years, a remarkable fact, given that the average tenure of state prison directors is roughly three years. Estelle was followed by D. V. "Red" McKaskle, who served several months as acting director. In mid-1984 Raymond P. Procunier, who had directed the California prison system from 1967 to 1975, was appointed director. Procunier's tenure lasted under two years; he was succeeded by his second-in-command O. L. McCotter, formerly an Army colonel in charge of the disciplinary barracks at Fort Leavenworth, Kansas. Since 1983, therefore, the system has gone through three directors, as many in the last few years as it had in the previous thirty.

Rates of turnover at lower levels increased as well. Veteran correctional officers, disgruntled by the administrative changes brought on by the Justice Justice's order and the new directorships, began to leave the system or seek early retirement. New recruits quit at rates as high as 90 percent per year. Meanwhile, policy and procedure manuals changed, multiplied, and thickened but the administrative routine grew less comprehensible and less predictable. Prison personnel became less certain about what rules were in effect, how to enforce them, and the extent of their authority in governing inmates. The sense of mission and esprit de corps of the lower ranks suffered. Officers who only months earlier had proudly boasted of their role in "the nation's best prison system" came to view their work as—in the words of one veteran officer—"just a job" in which the goal was to "get paid but not get injured, sued, or killed."

Though brief, Procunier's tenure as director of the Texas prison system was important and may be viewed as the final chapter in the demise of the Texas control model and the first in a sort of natural experiment in prison management. As noted, before coming to Texas, Procunier had been head of the California prison system. He had also served as director of the Virginia and Utah systems and was a consultant to the New Mexico prison system shortly before its major 1980 riot. Procunier was praised as a tough, energetic, and colorful administrator, a man of salty language who related to inmates and staff like an old-fashioned machine politician nailing down votes.

Procunier presided over California prisons during the years when four competing prison gangs became a major disruptive force in the system, a situation changed over the last decade only by the rise of new, still more violent gangs in that system. When he came to Texas, Procunier imported some of his old California subordinates with the idea that together they would implement changes in the way that Texas prisons were managed. Procunier took measures to dismantle the remaining elements of the control model and to erect something closer to the California consensual model of prison administration.

After an initial honeymoon period with state political leaders, prison reform groups, and the press, Procunier came under serious fire for unprecedented and rising levels of violence in the system. Then, as had occurred under his administration in California, Texas began to develop its first unabated prison gang problem. As the violence and the gang problem grew worse, Procunier's political support crumbled. As one local journalist stated, Procunier had been appointed to "come in, kick ass and clean house."[9] In the early months of his tenure, Procunier won a surprising measure of goodwill inside the organization from "old guard" wardens, the uniformed force, and other personnel. Soon, however, this internal support dwindled. For the first time ever Texas correctional officers began to unionize themselves. The sum of these and related developments proved too much, and Procunier, while having committed himself to two years at the helm of Texas prisons, retired from corrections in 1985.

The rising violence and the overall decline in the quality of prison life that characterized Texas prisons between 1983 and 1986 is attributable to these and associated changes in prison management. Now, however, let us turn to a model of correctional administration as different from the Texas control model as can be imagined: the Michigan responsibility model.

Elements of the Michigan Responsibility Model

The best way to introduce the Michigan responsibility model is to compare it to the Texas control model. Whereas the control model placed a premium on administrative measures that maximized control over inmates, the responsibility model placed a premium on measures that maximized inmates' responsibility for their own actions. Whereas the control model mandated that every prison be designated and run as a maximum-security facility, the responsibility model established a number of security levels and, through an inmate classification system leagues more sophisticated and elaborate than anything that has yet been developed in Texas and most other systems, attempted to fit inmates into the most appropriate but least-restrictive prison setting. Whereas the control model involved policies and procedures intended to maximize the paramilitary content of prison life, the responsibility model involved measures that minimized the symbols and substance of formal administrative authority over inmates.

The chief architect of the responsibility model was Perry M. Johnson, director of the Michigan Department of Corrections from August 1972 through June 1984. In 1955, Johnson began his career in corrections as a counselor at the State Prison of Southern Michigan. In 1959, he became supervisor of a minimum-security facility. Four years later he returned to Jackson prison as an administrative assistant to the warden. Between 1964 and 1969, he served as assistant deputy in charge of custody, first at Marquette Branch prison and later at Jackson. After about a year as deputy director of the department's Bureau of Correctional Facilities, he became warden of Jackson, a post he held until his appointment as director. After resigning as director, Johnson became deputy director of the department's Bureau of Field Services (BFS). As of this writing, Johnson is still deputy director of BFS.

Under the responsibility model, prisons are to be run in ways that impose minimum constraints on inmates. The 1979 *Employee Handbook* advised:

An important principle of Corrections is that no more custody and security should be imposed than are really necessary. People should be classified properly as to their security needs. This is true not only for reasons of humanity but also for economy. Secure institutions are expensive to build and operate, and are counterproductive except where really needed.[10]

Tight security is "counterproductive" because inmates ought to be given a chance to behave in acceptable ways. Rather than having their every move monitored inmates ought to be given the greatest measure of freedom consistent with basic security requirements and then be held strictly accountable for their actions.

Unlike Texas, but like California, the administration of prisons in Michigan is headed by a director who is also responsible for probation, parole, and other postsentencing ("field services") operations. According to the premises of the responsibility model, convicted offenders should, if at all possible, be given sentences that do not necessitate imprisonment. Only dangerous offenders should be sent to prison and only the most dangerous of those imprisoned should live under maximum-security conditions. Even those offenders who do end up in maximum-security prisons should not have to lead thoroughly regimented lives. They, too, should be given a significant degree of freedom—what in corrections is sometimes called "air"—and then be held to account for their actions. One upper-level administrator, familiar with the Texas system, explained:

We go by the idea that prison should be as unrestrictive as possible. Don't misunderstand. Order comes first. You have to keep control. Security is number one through one thousand. But we don't have to smother people to keep things under control. We try to show the inmates respect and expect it in return. We are more willing than Texas to give them air and then hold them accountable. . . . We attempt to operate safely in the least restrictive environment possible. . . . If Texas opts for the most restrictive, we opt for the least restrictive.

Predictably, the administrative routine of Michigan prisons has been quite different from that of Texas prisons. In Texas, for instance, there was an all-encompassing emphasis on the rules and their official enforcement. In Michigan, on the other hand, the rulebook reminded officers (in bold letters) that "there is no requirement that every rule violation" be treated formally, noting that in "many cases verbal counseling or summary action should be the first response to the apparent misconduct."[11] Rather than the tight routine of numbering, counting, checking, and locking that characterized Texas prisons, daily life inside Michigan prisons was a more loosely supervised, somewhat anarchic round of inmate movement punctuated by frequent counts of the population.

The responsibility model is highly consistent with attempts to give inmates a greater voice in prison affairs as well as opportunities for individual growth. For instance, a policy directive issued in 1981 stated that "prisoner organizations are to be encouraged as a means of prisoner self-expression and self-development."[12] Under the terms of this policy, it was not required that a member of the correctional staff be present to supervise inmate gatherings. Instead, the directive authorized "community volunteers" to supervise the meetings, requiring only that a staff member be available "for drop-in supervision."

As mentioned earlier, under the responsibility model, a premium is placed on assigning inmates to the lowest security setting consistent with basic custodial goals. This has necessitated the development of a complex classification system.[13] Regardless of security classification, Michigan inmates have been entitled to extensive visiting and other privileges such as frequent telephone calls. Until recently, Texas inmates were extended few such privileges.

Under the responsibility model, minimal emphasis is placed on exhorting or forcing inmates to "do their own time." Neither at the Reception and Guidance Center nor upon arrival at their assigned institu-

tions are inmates encouraged to isolate themselves, physically or psychologically, from other inmates. Such isolation would not be consistent with the attempt to "normalize" (a word commonly used by Michigan personnel in explaining their approach), so far as possible, life behind bars. If the Texas control model is an attempt to atomize the prisoner community, the Michigan responsibility model is an attempt to foster one. Many Michigan officials criticized the Texas approach as an attempt to "crush individuality" among the inmates.

Another element of the responsibility model is to invest in so-called Resident Unit Managers (RUMs) immediate authority for what goes on in the prison's living areas. RUMs are not correctional officers. They are, however, in charge of the officers in their units, adjudicate most minor disputes among prisoners, counsel inmates, and attempt to keep their areas clean. Michigan is by no means alone in its use of a unit management system. For instance, for most of the last decade virtually all federal prisons have used unit management. Michigan is unique, however, in that relatively few of its RUMs have risen through the custodial ranks or spent the bulk of their careers in uniform. In the federal system, and in several of the other states that have employed unit management, it is more common for unit supervisors to be ex-correctional officers.

Michigan prison authorities have worked closely with the American Correctional Association (ACA) and sought accreditation wherever possible. In some units staff members have spent virtually all of their time preparing for accreditation inspections. Michigan has also been in the forefront of attempts to hire and promote women and minorities, having perhaps the most aggressive affirmative action policy of any correctional department in the country. At some institutions these efforts have triggered conflicts between inmates and staff and between officers and their administrative superiors.

ENDNOTES

1. For a more detailed description of good time and the point-incentive program see *Texas Administrative Code, Annotated, Part 2,* sections 61.15 and 61.51 (State of Texas and McGraw-Hill, Inc., 1982).

2. J. T. Sullivan, "Estelle's Era," *The Echo: The Texas Prison Newspaper,* August/September 1984, p. 6.
3. *Texas Department of Corrections: 30 Years of Progress* (Huntsville, TX: Texas Department of Corrections, 1974), p. 4.

4. Among observers of the Texas political scene, Heatly's support for TDC and his ties to Beto were well known. See, for instance, Molly Ivins, "The Late Duke of Paducah Touched Every Texan's Life," *Dallas Times Herald,* February 28, 1984.

5. A representative list of these reports and other news stories related to Texas prisons is presented at the end of the notes for this chapter.

6. Hon. Governor John B. Connally of Texas, letter to the author, August 28, 1984. Interestingly, W. J. Estelle himself made a similar observation a decade earlier: "What remains unchanged is the formula necessary to realize our goals. As in the past, we must have the continuing support of the Texas citizenry; the intelligent support of the legislative and executive branches of government; a strong Board of Corrections, populated by leading business and professional persons. . . ." (*Texas Department of Corrections: 30 Years of Progress,* p. 72.)

7. Hon. Governor Preston Smith of Texas, letter to the author, August 28, 1984.

8. It is worth mentioning here that organization analysts, students of public administration and management among them, have only recently "discovered" that there are important connections between an organization's internal life and its political, economic, or other external circumstances. The reader who desires an explicit theoretical framework within which to place my account of each agency (particularly Texas) will find congenial candidates in the following: Gary L. Wamsley and Mayer N. Zald, *The Political Economy of Public Organizations* (Bloomington, IN, and London: Indiana University Press, 1976); Richard H. Hall, *Organizations: Structure and Process* (Englewood Cliffs,

NJ: Prentice-Hall, 1972), especially Part 4. I make no explicit or consistent use of any particular organization theory or mode of analysis because to do so would bog us down in esoteric conceptual and methodological issues, and because, to my knowledge, there is no such theory, which, if used in this way, would help rather than hinder clear understanding and exposition. The single theory which comes closest is known as "contingency theory." For an overview of this theory, see the following: Fred Luthans, *Introduction to Management: A Contingency Approach* (New York: McGraw-Hill, 1976); Roy R. Roberg, *Police Management and Organizational Behavior: A Contingency Approach* (St. Paul, MN: West, 1978); Claudia Bird Schoonhoven, "Problems with Contingency Theory: Testing Assumptions Hidden Within the Language of Contingency 'Theory'," *Administrative Science Quarterly* 26 (1981): 349–372.

9. Patrick Crimmins, reporter for the *Huntsville Morning News,* letter to the author, July 4, 1984.

10. Michigan Department of Corrections, "Purpose and History of the Michigan Department of Corrections," *Employee Handbook* (1979), p. 2.

11. Michigan Department of Corrections, "Introduction," *Pocket Guide For Prisoner Rule Violations* (1981).

12. Michigan Department of Corrections, *Policy Directive: Supervision of Prisoner Groups* (PD-BCF-30.10), December 1, 1981.

13. For an example of the kind of elaborate procedural guidelines on inmate processing necessitated by this classification system, see Michigan Department of Corrections, *Procedure: Intake Processing and Psychological Screening of R&CG* (Reception and Guidance Center) *Commitments* (OP-R&CG-40.07), July 15, 1983.

STUDY QUESTIONS FOR READING 17

1. Compare and contrast the control and responsibility models based on the criteria below. Take care to be very specific in your answers, quoting experts and giving concrete examples.
   a. Chief architects (and dates they served)
   b. Main goals
   c. Approach to inmate classification
   d. Emphasis on security
   e. Rule enforcement
   f. Building inmate community versus "Do your own time"

2. DiIulio considered the building tenders (BTs) the internal defect of the control model. Explain Beto's statement, "Either you pick their leaders or they do." According to DiIulio, how were the BTs picked under Beto?

UNIT MANAGEMENT IN PRISONS AND JAILS
AN OVERVIEW OF THE BOOK BY ROBERT LEVINSON

TARA GRAY

In his book *Unit Management in Prisons and Jails*, Robert Levinson points out that unit management became popular in the 1970s when the Federal Bureau of Prisons began implementing it. Now this concept has revolutionized prison management and is used throughout the federal system, in most of the fifty states, in several other countries, and in "direct supervision" jails (Levinson, 1999: 2). "Unit management is . . . the way we run institutions. It is a way of life for the Bureau of Prisons and for most states" (Dennis Johnson, quoted in Levinson: vi).

Unit management is based on the idea that cooperation is most likely in small groups that have lengthy interactions (12). A unit is a small, self-contained inmate living and office area, which is managed semi-autonomously within the larger institution (10). Unit management meets many goals; most importantly, it increases control and improves both communication and decision making. Unit management increases control because people in small groups are easier to control; it improves communication because it increases the frequency and intensity of relationships between inmates and staff; and it improves decisions because decisions about inmates are made more quickly by the people who really know them (2–3).

Unit management can best meet its goals when the guidelines for the model are carefully followed. However, like any management model that is widely used, sometimes it is implemented well, and sometimes poorly. In one survey of managers, only one state out of twenty-eight reported following all "ten commandments of unit management" (9, 15). When unit management seems to fail, it is wise to ask how well the guidelines were followed. There are numerous guidelines for successful unit management that are of special interest to students: direct supervision architecture, stable populations in each unit, an adequate staff–inmate ratio, decentralized decision making, effective internal classification, and a team approach to management.

Unit management works best with direct supervision units. That is, living units are built with cells in a square surrounding an open common area and staff offices that are on the unit. This architecture encourages staff–inmate communication and allows for direct supervision of inmates, which makes unit management easier. Buildings are "form givers" (Mote, quoted in Levinson: 1). That is, buildings create expectations, and prisoners respond to those expectations. However, architecture should never be used as an excuse to delay the implementation of unit management. "Architecture can help or hinder unit management, but it does not make or break it" (54).

Unit management is based on the idea, as mentioned earlier, that cooperation is most likely to occur in small groups that interact with each other over a long period of time (12). Therefore, stable unit populations and proper inmate–staff ratios should never be compromised. Under unit management, inmate, staff, and correctional officer populations are stable. Unit staff and inmates are assigned to units permanently. Therefore, staff cannot "ship" problem inmates to other units in the prison; instead, staff in each unit must deal with their own problem inmates. And inmates cannot manipulate staff to be placed in a "better" unit (9). Correctional officers are stationed in one unit for a minimum of nine months, which means inmates are not exposed to constantly changing interpretations of the rules (12).

Traditional correctional institutions make decisions through a centralized and hierarchical management structure, whereas unit management strives to decentralize decision making. In a centralized system, information flows both up and down the chain of command, but decisions are made at the top. In a decentralized system, whenever possible, decisions are made at the unit level. The combination of centralized and decentralized decision making ensures a level of uniformity between units, as well as individuality within any given unit. When decisions are made at the unit level, they are made with better information, and by people who know the inmates better.

Of course, decentralized decision making means that not all units will be managed in the same way, which is both a strength in terms of flexibility, and a weakness in terms of inconsistency. For example, sometimes the inmates in Unit A complain because they are not allowed to do something that the inmates in Unit B can do. And when staff were surveyed about problems with unit management, they listed "inconsistency among units" as the second biggest problem (43). To reduce this problem, Levinson encourages unit managers to meet weekly both to share ideas and to visit other units and observe how they operate (72, 98). Having different management methods in different units is also a strength because different inmates require differently managed units.

Therefore, internal classification is important—inmates who have been assigned to a given institution are assigned to a specific unit based on their personal characteristics. In general, internal classification is designed to separate predators from their victims and thereby reduce inmate violence and exploitation. Operationally, inmates in each institution are separated into three broad categories: The "Heavies" are predators; the "Lights" are victims; and the "Moderates" are inmates "who stand up to the former and who do not abuse the latter" (82). Levinson cautions that both

"good guys" and "bad guys" exist in each category of prisoners. Among the Heavies, less conflict occurs than one might expect because these inmates "respect" each other, and a "standoff," rather than a fight, occurs (86). Table 18.1 describes these three groups.

Ideally, inmates in one category are housed together, and staff can be matched with the type of inmate with whom they work best. Heavies and Lights cannot be mixed, but Moderates can be housed with either Heavies or Lights because they behave as neither predators nor prey. Moderates require fewer correctional officers to supervise them because they are independent and do not create problems. Correctional officers who like working with inmates by using a top-down, by-the-book approach work best with the Heavies, who are aggressive and hostile toward authority. In contrast, correctional officers who like to sit down and talk with inmates about their problems work best with the Lights, who are scared and rely heavily on staff support (88).

Unit management is controversial because some correctional professionals believe it leads to "labeling"; that is, these categories may become self-fulfilling prophecies. In other words, they cause inmates who are classified as Heavies to become difficult to control, and so on. As a result, in only fifteen states have the Department of Corrections and the Bureau of Prisons combined unit management with formal internal classification systems. Levinson, however, adamantly disagrees that internal classification labels cause inmate behavior, and he argues that it reduces violence and improves a prison's social climate (92–94). He points out that after internal classification was initiated, New Hampshire, Missouri, and one federal institution all reported radical drops in violence (93–94). In addition, inmates rate their institution's social climate higher than it was before unit management was used, and this is true for both tougher and for more vulnerable inmates (Hans Toch, cited in Levinson:93).

Unit management requires a team approach to staffing each unit. All staff members work in shifts and everyone in the unit reports to the unit manager. In the traditional model, treatment and custody staffs (called correctional unit staffs in the unit model) are separated by radically different work hours and by

TABLE 18.1   Internal Classification and the Characteristics of Inmates

INMATE CATEGORIES	POSITIVE DESCRIPTORS	OTHER DESCRIPTORS
Heavy	active in sports assertive energetic leaders outgoing quick decision makers shrewd stand up for opinions thrill seekers	aggressive confrontational manipulative hostile victimizers violent
Moderate	independent family oriented reliable studious	little criminal history minimal staff contact tend to remain uninvolved
Light	introspective interact regularly with staff reflective sensitive to others	inattentive moody passive prefer nonphysical activities rely heavily on staff self-absorbed short-fused tense withdrawn

Source: From Levinson, Robert B. 1999. *Unit Management in Prisons and Jails.* Lanham, MD: American Correctional Association.

reporting to different department heads. In the unit model, the two staffs are integrated, and the unit manager has supervisory responsibility over all staff members. Unit staff provide twelve-hour staff coverage, Monday through Friday, and eight-hour coverage on Saturday and Sunday (9). Every counselor, case manager, and unit manager works evening hours at least once a week. The staffing schedule is designed to integrate "custody" and "treatment" into one team. Although this new structure means correctional and unit staffs have to work together to reach their treatment and custody goals, the conflicts between two staffs have not ended. In fact, when staff were asked to identify the biggest problem with unit management, they answered "turf" battles between correctional and unit staff (41–42). Still, a well-managed unit takes impor-

tant steps to end this age-old problem by integrating these two approaches into one effective team.

Unit staff seek input from inmates, both in the form of an inmate advisory council and in regular town-hall meetings. Although inmate input will be considered, final decisions are made by staff, not by inmates (18). Admittedly, many experienced correctional workers have a negative attitude about inmate councils. They remember instances in which the toughest prisoners took over the council and used the time to attack the administration or intimidate other inmates. Levinson likens this view to that of "the unskilled carpenter who blames his tools" (72–73). He argues that effective unit managers must actively listen to inmates and that every unit should have its own inmate advisory council. Eligibility criteria should be clear, elections should be frequent, and terms should be short. In this way, one inmate (or group of inmates) cannot dominate the council. The council should meet weekly with the unit staff to share concerns and ideas that they have heard voiced in the unit. In addition, a town-hall meeting should also be held weekly, with all inmates and staff attending. This allows staff to inform inmates about new procedures, and inmates can share their ideas and concerns directly with staff (73).

Levinson gives many examples of studies that have shown that unit management works in a wide variety of institutions, when the guidelines for effective unit management are followed (101–118). One study showed that the effectiveness of unit management can be extended to jails and to youthful offenders. In a New York City jail for youth and adults, an equal number of inmates were placed under unit management and under traditional management. For both adults and youth, unit management was associated with a reduction in violence (117). As a top-level manager put it,

> *"Nobody thought it would work. The institution's architecture was against it working; so was the idea of trying it on adolescents. Now even the bad inmates want it. They see it is being fairer. Among the staff there is less 'ducking and hiding' which was the traditional way of handling problems. . . . The good guys won." (117–118)*

Ultimately, unit management means that both staff and inmates have more positive attitudes about working and living behind bars. Clearly unit management can work. Throughout his book, Levinson stresses the guidelines for unit management that, when followed carefully, yield important benefits for both inmates and staff.

The author thanks Robert Levinson for his helpful comments on this overview.

REFERENCE

Levinson, Robert B. 1999. *Unit Management in Prisons and Jails.* Lanham, MD: American Correctional Association.

STUDY QUESTIONS FOR READING 18

1. How common is unit management?

2. What idea is unit management based on?

3. What is a unit?

4. What are the most important goals of unit management? Why does it achieve each of these goals?

5. How widely were the "ten commandments of unit management" followed?

6. In his book, Levinson discusses numerous guidelines for unit management that are of special interest to students. What are they?

7. How should living units be designed for unit management? Should the implementation of unit management be delayed because an existing facility is built differently?

8. Why must unit populations be limited and appropriate staff–inmate ratios be maintained?

9. Why are stable inmate and staff populations important?

10. How do centralized and decentralized decision-making structures differ?

11. What does Levinson regard as the advantage of a mix between centralized and decentralized decision making?

12. Levinson discusses one more strength of decentralized decision making as well as a weakness. Describe each. What does he suggest should be done to rectify this weakness?

13. What is internal classification? In what three categories are inmates usually classified? What is distinctive about each category?

14. How is internal classification used to assign inmates and staff to housing units?

15. Why do some administrators oppose internal classification? How does Levinson support his argument that internal classification is effective?

16. How does unit management try to make one team out of the treatment and custody teams? How successful has this effort been?

17. In unit management, the management team also includes input from inmates. How is this input sought? Do inmates make decisions for the unit?

THE MISSING "X-FACTOR": TRUST

TOM PETERS

When Warden Dennis Luther calls inmates "constituents," that's a maverick position.
—Craig Apker, Associate Warden, Federal Correctional Institution, McKean

If you back a person into a corner and kick him and kick him and kick him, he will kick back. You've already backed the person into the corner by putting him in prison.
—Wayne Smith, Associate Warden, Federal Correctional Institution, McKean

Trust? "Good stuff," you say. "Now let's get down to the basics: How many levels of management? Exactly what should work team responsibilities be?"

That's the way it usually goes. Trust? Of course it's important. But what else can you say? A lot, I suggest. I'll at least say a little. We've already seen trust on the railroad, trust at a sausage maker. Now we'll get serious—how about trust at a federal pen?

Warden Dennis Luther opened Federal Correctional Institution McKean, in Bradford, Pennsylvania, in February 1989. In mid-1992, a staff of 334 oversaw 1,261 inmates—the medium-security facility was already at well over 100 percent of capacity.

Luther is a career prisons man who told us, when we interviewed him in 1991, that he went into the profession "out of altruism" instead of joining the ministry, his second choice. In the mid-'80s, Luther turned around the Federal Bureau of Prisons' Danbury operation, probably the most troubled institution in the system before his advent. He has a track record as a maverick and risk-taker.

"I don't think prison has to be a constant negative experience for staff and inmates," Luther said. The prisoner's punishment is being sent to prison, he

added. Punishing prisoners once they're inside is not the point. Luther insisted the prison can run smoothly if he can instill just that one notion.

AN UNORTHODOX CULTURE

"We could beat prisoners and build up hostility between the keeper and the kept," associate warden Wayne Smith told us, "but here we allow inmates to somewhat manage themselves." Establishing this new ethos hasn't been easy. Conservative staff members fought Luther under the generally unassailable banner of "compromising security." For example, when he decided to allow popcorn at special events like movies, some guards objected. Inmates would stuff the popcorn in the locks, they claimed. The popcorn was distributed. The locks stayed popcorn-free. (Not all staff can come to grips with the McKean approach. Luther eased out two associate wardens whose resistance persisted.)

Popcorn-free locks is the least of it, of course. Despite normal exterior security (electronically monitored chain-link fences, with coils of razor-sharp wire between them), you'll find no steel bars inside.

Wooden doors to the prisoners' rooms are kept unlocked and, unlike most prisons, McKean houses inmates without regard to race.

Inmate Roger Fields, who was released in mid-1992, was my original contact. He reported with bemusement that "if the staff isn't responsive to Luther's ideas, he deals with them." Another inmate, Steve Monsanto, confirmed Fields's comment, relating a story that could only come from McKean: Shakedowns take place in every federal prison. In other facilities, the guards usually tear the con's cell apart. At McKean, though, after a shakedown guards must replace everything exactly as they found it. Monsanto remembered returning to his cell once, to find it torn apart by a new officer. He told a lieutenant, who told Monsanto to leave the cell alone. "The new officer will put it back," he said.

More tribute to what Luther calls "an unorthodox culture" came from Mike Eger, warehouse foreman and, when we talked to him, head of the American Federal Government Employees Local. Eger has been at McKean from the start, signing up a record number of charter members in the union local. Washington officials were concerned. No matter, it turned out. "I've never had a grievance or a ULP [unfair labor practice] since we opened in October 1989," Eger told us. "The warden here is different. He tries things, simple things that make our life better." Eger contrasted his McKean experience with a previous posting at Lewisburg, where inmates were constantly fighting and harassing the staff. "Inmates here have a choice," he said, "and that choice is a high degree of self-management." Yet, Eger quickly added, it's no picnic: "They're not getting any more than any other inmate in the system." As to Luther's magic elixir, Eger was clear: "The best thing about the warden is that he never lies."

Respect for the Front Line

The success in getting front-line staffers to treat inmates with respect is a direct reflection of the respect top prison management shows for those staffers. (Yes, the same old story: If you want the customer to be treated well, treat the person who deals with the customer well. Ho hum. Ever wonder why it's still such

an exception? I do, every day.) Inmates are Luther's constituents. So are employees. Senior federal prison managers, Luther said, repeatedly overlook the role the front line can play. "Line-level people have good ideas, not only about how to do their job," he added, "but about how to do *your* job better."

Luther nurtures involvement by creating task groups for anything and everything. Task groups to explore using inmates in the nearby national forest. Task groups for expanding inmate programs, for teaching classes, for planning and putting on a community picnic. Such efforts are especially helpful in engaging those who normally aren't involved, he said.

"There's no correlation between creativity, intelligence, and [federal pay] grade level," Luther told us. "That's sweet music to most [McKean staff] people—but no one's ever told them that before." Luther expects staff contributions as a matter of course. At the biweekly meetings of department heads, for example, each attendee is expected to contribute at least one concrete suggestion for improvement.

The Line Staff Advisory Board, a rotating group of front-line workers, talks through suggestions, complaints, and rumors with Luther. Change comes all the time. Inmate food service workers, for example, used to be locked down (locked in their cells) when they weren't working. Now food service managers send them back to their dorm or to recreation when the job's done. Obvious? Not if you've spent a career being trained in *dis*trust.

FROM THE HORSE'S MOUTH

Maybe some of the ideas Luther espouses would be mouthed by other prison wardens. But one group is not likely to mince words—the prisoners themselves. My colleagues Deborah Hudson and Paul Cohen were allowed unfettered, no-administrators-present access to Luther's "constituents." Here's the sort of thing they heard: "I've been locked up fifteen years. I haven't seen people get along together regardless of race, creed, or color except here." "The warden channeled the staff so they treat the inmates like human beings." "I was awestruck. Two months after getting here I was still in a daze by the—I have to use the word—freedom." "There are very few incidents here. Why? Because inmates can use their skills and talents to benefit themselves and the institution. Where else could the inmates have a club with an office, their own phone, and the ability to talk to the administration whenever they want?" "This is as good as it gets inside. It's the best place in the system. You see an associate warden every day, and the warden every two or three days."

Abdul Adam was unofficial head of the prison's Sunni Muslims at the time of our visit: "I say to my people, if it gets any better, we're going to send for the wife and kids. Did I die and go to prison heaven?" Adam spent 10 years in Leavenworth, two in Terre Haute—where, reported one of McKean's associate wardens who "did time with him" (prison staff lingo), he was a first-class troublemaker. When new Muslim inmates got off the bus, they usually sought out Adam, and often asked him for a knife. "So we sit down and talk," he said, "and I tell them how it's run around here. They can't believe it."

Inmate Involvement

Regular "town hall" meetings with inmates are one part of a determined two-way communication process. Even more important, any proposed changes to regulations or procedures are brought to inmates first. The prisoners typically point out numerous subtleties which will help the program work better, or would torpedo it if not addressed, Luther said. In fact, inmate suggestions are now a routine part of McKean's day-to-day, culture: for example, recommendations about items to be offered in the commissary. (Sound small? Only if you're oblivious to prison psychology. Another "small" touch: The staff cafeteria serves exactly the same food as the inmate cafeteria.) The staff also conducts quarterly "customer"—that's right, inmate!—surveys.

The Inmate Benefit Fund

Attitude is all-important, but "structure" helps, too. Especially the McKean "clubs"—e.g., the Vegetarian Club, the Muslim Brotherhood, the Spanish Club. In addition to providing specific, useful outlets for in-

mates, the clubs also serve as "intake organizations" for arriving inmates—they're central, in fact, to transmitting McKean's unique culture.

The Inmate Benefit Fund, an umbrella organization representing all inmates, raises money, then spends it on charities, cultural affairs, leisure activities, and special programs. Inmates select representatives to the fund's board of directors, which also includes one senior prison staff member. The fund is audited annually by an outside CPA. "The strength of the Inmate Benefit Fund is that we can contribute to the running of the internal affairs of the prison," the prisoner who heads the Vegetarian Club told us.

The Inmate Benefit Fund is always moving, nudging. When Deborah Hudson visited, the fund was negotiating to become McKean's laundry vendor. Hudson also learned that the Music Appreciation Club was about to hold a fund-raiser—to expand its membership of 75 and to raise money to start a sheet-music library. (A club membership card permits you to check out musical equipment from the recreation center.) The Italian-American Club, 50 strong, had just held a fund-raiser, selling Italian meats and cheeses. Hudson was also invited to come back the evening of her visit to attend the West Indian Club's special ethnic dinner, followed by a video. (Subsequently, Hudson got a note from Luther, proudly reporting that the Inmate Benefit Fund's 1991 Christmas drive had netted $2,000 for needy local children. Overall, the IBF has raised more than $20,000 for local charities.)

"Thank You"

Father Henry Andrae, the Catholic prison chaplain, summed it up when he told us he'd gotten more thank-yous from McKean inmates in the last two years than during 12 years of teaching Catholic students. "The philosophy is 'whatever we can do to make this work better, let's give it a try,' " he added. "What's not accepted is, 'No, no, no, we can't have it, it doesn't work, go to your corner and shut up.' The philosophy is the same for staff and inmates."

Father Henry recalled a food strike right after the prison opened. It didn't turn into a major crisis, because the new leaders met, discussed the problem, and responded by communicating openly, honestly, and in a timely fashion with the inmates. Warden Luther said the strike "was a wonderful training experience. I'd open every prison with something like this! The issue is communication and responsiveness, and in a new facility, the staff was overwhelmed. The solution was walking and talking, getting out into the yard, comparing notes."

OK, OK, but does it work? In mid-1992, after more than three years of operation, the prison has had: no escapes, no murders, no serious assaults on inmates or staff, no sexual assaults, no suicides. McKean earned a 99.3 accreditation rating from the American Correctional Association, the highest in the Bureau of Prisons. "I've audited a hundred fifty prisons," the ACA's Richard Steinert told FCI McKean's staff, "and this is only the second one rated outstanding in quality of life for inmates and staff."

MCKEAN'S CREDO: "BELIEFS ABOUT THE TREATMENT OF INMATES"*

1. Inmates are sent to prison *as* punishment and not *for* punishment.

2. Correctional workers have a *responsibility* to ensure that inmates are returned to the community no more angry or hostile than when they were committed.

3. Inmates are *entitled* to a safe and humane environment while in prison.

4. You must believe in man's *capacity* to change his behavior.

5. Normalize the environment to the extent possible by providing programs, amenities and services. The denial of such must be related to maintaining order and security rather than punishment.

6. Most inmates will respond favorably to a clean and aesthetically pleasing physical environment and will not vandalize or destroy it.

7. We do not treat all inmates alike any more than we treat all people in the "free world" alike. We must

be sensitive to personality differences, cultural backgrounds, lifestyles and educational levels, and treat inmates as individuals.

8. Bringing racial bias into the institution that results in discriminatory actions can be every bit as dangerous to fellow staff members as the introduction of contraband.

9. Whenever possible, *provide explanations* for changes in policies and procedures that the inmate perceives as detracting from the quality of his life.

10. *Be responsive* to inmate requests for action or information. Respond in a timely manner and respond the first time an inmate makes a request.

11. *Be dependable* when dealing with inmates. If you say you are going to do something, do it.

12. It is important for staff to *model* the kind of behavior they expect to see duplicated by inmates.

13. The indiscriminate use of foul language by staff can only detract from the professional image staff must try to maintain.

14. There is *inherent value* in self-improvement programs such as education, whether or not these programs are related to recidivism.

15. Inmates need *legitimate opportunities* to enhance their self-esteem.

16. Inmates are to be treated *respectfully and with basic dignity*. Staff can treat inmates respectfully without compromising the essential element of professional distance.

17. Be courteous, polite and professional in all dealings with inmates, *regardless* of their behavior.

18. Staff *cannot,* because of their own insecurities, lack of self-esteem or concerns about their masculinity, condescend or degrade inmates.

19. Some inmates are very intelligent or knowledgeable. Don't be threatened but, rather, capitalize on their skills.

20. Never, *never lie* to an inmate.

21. Inmates will cooperate with staff to a much greater degree if motivated by *respect rather than fear.*

22. Don't impose rules, regulations or regimentation that cannot be *reasonably tied* to the need to maintain order and security.

23. Stress the value of rewarding good adjustment with privileges and amenities.

*Written by Dennis Luther, and widely distributed at FCI McKean.

24. Punish behavior that threatens order and security—swiftly and harshly.

25. Send clear messages regarding the kind of behavior that cannot be tolerated in an institution.

26. Inmate discipline must be consistent and fair.

27. Use only the amount of force, verbal or physical, needed to maintain order, security, and staff and inmate safety.

28. Do or say nothing to an inmate that you would not want to have videotaped for the warden's review!

STUDY QUESTIONS FOR READING 19_____

Editor's note: This model of prison administration is especially important because it has such a wide variety of supporters, including the American Correctional Association and John DiIulio, who favors the more controlling models of prison administration, as discussed earlier. DiIulio said "McKean is probably the best-managed prison in the country" (quoted by Robert Worth in "A Model Prison," *The Atlantic Monthly,* November 1995).

Warden Luther believes his two-way communication model would work in "any prison, even those most plagued with violence, overcrowding, and gangs." He had inmates transfer to McKean who were violent in other prisons, he says, and when they reached McKean, they tended to calm down. Still, he recognizes the challenges for the future of his model of prison administration.

> *Dennis Luther achieved his successes against the will of Bureau of Prisons senior management. The bureau declined to comment, but Luther claims that officials there saw him as 'a maverick, as someone who violates bureau policy flagrantly.' Some of the more successful programs at McKean—the Inmate Benefit Fund, for instance (which raised $50,000 a year, much of it for local charities)—have been cut by the bureau. . . . Inmates' access to computers and other amenities has been reduced in the past year, and now, with Luther retired, the trend may continue (as quoted by Robert Worth in "A Model Prison,"* The Atlantic Monthly, *November 1995).*

1. Warden Dennis Luther opened FCI McKean in Bradford, Pennsylvania in 1989. He says he can smoothly run a prison if he can instill just one notion in his staff. What is it?

2. This prison handles shakedowns differently than other prisons. How are they handled in other prisons? What incident in this prison shows that they are handled differently here? In your view, what did the lieutenant risk when he handled the incident this way?

3. What does the guard, Mike Eger, have to say about Luther's relationship with the guards? What does he say is the best thing about Luther?

4. According to Peters, what is the best way for Luther, or any warden, to make sure inmates are treated better? According to Luther, there's no correlation between creativity, intelligence, and what?

5. What are department heads expected to bring to staff meetings? How are other staff involved in decision making? Inmates?

6. How do inmates describe their time at McKean?

7. In this two-way communication model of prison administration, potential procedures and regulations are presented to inmates before they are instituted. Why? How are items for the inmate commissary chosen? How does the food served in the inmate and staff cafeterias differ?

8. After three years of operation, how much violence was there at McKean? What level of accreditation did McKean receive? How did ACA's Richard Steinert, who has evaluated 150 prisons, rate McKean?

9. According to McKean's Credo
   - Are inmates sent to prison *for* punishment or *as* punishment?
   - Bringing racial bias into an institution can be every bit as dangerous as bringing in what?
   - Staff should model the type of behavior they expect to see duplicated by whom?
   - What should staff never, never do to an inmate?
   - Inmates will cooperate better if motivated by what?
   - As staff interact with inmates, they should do or say nothing they would not want the warden to view how?

GROUP NORMS IN A REFORM SCHOOL
WITHOUT LOCKS AND BARS
AN OVERVIEW OF THE BOOK BY
GRANT R. GRISSOM AND
WILLIAM L. DUBNOV

CHARLES SHIREMAN

With this fascinating publication, Grissom and Dubnov interject an encouraging note of hope into the recent decade's quite gloomy discourse on the role, effectiveness, and future prospects of the American juvenile correctional institution. Rather widely shared current views of such institutions have been that the experiences they provide their charges too frequently drift toward depersonalization and even brutality or toward the rhetoric of treatment without its reality. Criminalization rather than rehabilitation is thought to be the likely consequence. These dangers are considered particularly pressing in the large institution; those, say, with populations approaching 100. Indeed, "deinstitutionalization" of delinquent youth has often seemed to achieve the status of an end in itself, quite apart from any analysis of what might become of the youth so deinstitutionalized.

A few studies providing a more optimistic picture have long been available. . . . Pennsylvania's Glen Mills School . . . can reasonably claim to be America's oldest juvenile correctional instititution. It is a direct descendant of the historic Quaker reform program, begun in 1787, at Philadelphia's Walnut Street Jail. By 1826, it was chartered as the House of Refuge for juveniles and relocated in 1892 to Glen Mills, Pennsylvania. No longer under Quaker auspices, the institution remains a nonstate venture administered by a private board that receives delinquent youth committed by a number of juvenile court jurisdictions, most—but not all—in Pennsylvania.

Although Glen Mills enjoyed a favorable reputation in its early history, the present story begins in 1975 with a rebuilding after several decades of depressing decline. At its nadir, the institution had declined to a population of only 30 boys living in the basements of three cottages condemned as unsafe by the Pennsylvania Department of Labor and Industry. Under new leadership, recovery was dramatic. By 1986, the school's population topped 600.

It had become a financially sound operation with a physical plant that, to quote the school's executive director, aspired to be one to which "Rockefeller would want to send his son." The driving force in this startling recovery was the school's executive director, Cosimo Ferrainola. When appointed, Ferrainola was an assistant professor of social work with experience in corrections, business management, and the study of organizational change. As is true of many successful organizations, Glen Mills today would seem to be the product of the skill, energy, and devoted leadership of one charismatic leader. Such organizations tend to become almost extensions of the personalities of their leaders. . . .

The Glen Mills program rests on the creation of a positive normative culture shared by staff and students. The central assumption expressed in every way possible is that the school's students are "normal": they "are no less deserving of dignity and respect and suffer from no more serious psychological problems than do their non-institutionalized peers, and have enormous potential for growth" (p. 2). Thus they are "students," not patients there to receive treatment for personality disorders. They are not "bad" youth requiring punishment as a means of "reform."

The all-important first task, then, is the establishment of a positive, campuswide normative culture, one first identified by leadership but then made familiar to, and adopted and expanded by, all staff and students. The norms of that culture are based on values of individual responsibility, self-respect, support and respect for others, and achievement in interpersonal relationships and in academic, vocational, and athletic training. These norms are expressly "middle class" in nature, in the belief that students are better equipped to succeed in life if they are accustomed to living and working in a middle-class world. The norms number upward of 100, some seemingly minor and others highly expressive of decent group living. As examples of their range, "at Glen Mills we: lace sneakers all the way up; establish eye contact and greet visitors; show pride in our own and others' achievements; and treat all others with respect" (p. 28).

The tale told here is of the apparently successful struggle to secure both staff and student allegiance to these norms. That tale will be of major interest to all juvenile justice practitioners. A major tool to this end is "guided group interaction" (also commonly referred to as "positive peer culture"), with its frequent small-group meetings in which students are required to be confronted by their peers with their negative behaviors and to own up, seek to understand, and apologize for them. They must also learn to confront others with their behaviors, and to do so in a manner that rejects negative behavior but retains deep, concerned respect for the person. Other tools include the identification of peer leaders and their enlistment in a "Bulls Club" charged with the provision of positive and creative leadership and, again, with confrontation of norm-violative behaviors. Members are trained to do this positively with respect for those involved.

A further important Glen Mills path to citizenship is wholehearted belief that the school should, in every way, "go first class." This means the provision of top-quality residence, furnishings, surroundings, clothing, food, and educational and athletic facilities. Most students take at least one extended trip during their stay, usually to Florida. The school pays transportation costs for all home visits. In these and other aspects, life at the school is said to resemble that at a topflight prep school. The thrust is to implement a "why not the best" philosophy and to promote student pride in their institution and thus in themselves.

. . . Glen Mills School [makes] extensive efforts to assess the effectiveness of its program. Data collection is done at several points during the student's residence and at departure. A random sample of each admissions cohort is tracked following departure. Extensive efforts are made to locate and interview the students who constitute this sample. Those in the sample who are not located are replaced by another random selection. Careful consideration is given the issues of the representativeness of the sample and other problems of validity and reliability. The court records of another random sample of 463 boys have recently been studied.

From this research, a number of conclusions emerge. Certainly, the short-term results are impressive. On the campus, students' behavior becomes more positive each year. The incidence of assaults by students on students or staff has markedly declined as the program has taken form. Destruction of property, AWOLs, truancy, and drug use have all become much rarer. Student acceptance of and pride in their Glen Mills experience is high. There are always a minimum of 20 once-discharged students on campus who have sought scholarships to return and complete academic programs or to compete in athletics. Glen Mills athletic teams have achieved enviable records, and a number of boys have received athletic scholarships to universities. Sixty-nine percent of former students disagreed with a statement that "they would have been better off if they had not been sent to Glen Mills." Only seven percent agreed. Ninety-two percent of the interviewees said that they had "never" been afraid of other students at the schools—a strong indication that the intimidation of students by their peers, which so plagues many correctional institutions, has been eliminated.

It does seem clear that Glen Mills has succeeded in establishing a humane environment expressive of decency in human relationships. Students have been provided with many of the fundamentals necessary to a fresh start in life. These are enormously heartening accomplishments. Also striking is the fact that this has been done at comparatively low cost. The per diem rate of the residential program in 1988 was $70. At Pennsylvania's other public facilities it averaged $150 in 1987. In spite of general inflation, the current Glen Mills costs of care have been reduced from $121 in 1975. It was not increased during the 13 years of Ferrainola's tenure prior to the writing of this book. Imaginative application of modern business methods to the correctional institution and the savings of scale have been achieved and have paid off.

The assessment of long-term effectiveness is difficult here as everywhere. The measurement of later careers of graduates of any institution is a most uncertain venture. Recidivism is the indicator commonly used, but it is a dubious measure at best. . . . By this dubious measure, Glen Mills's achievements seem generally positive. It appears that a true national rate of reincarceration for a new offense is at least 50 percent. For Glen Mills's students in nine successive annual cohorts the reincarceration rate has remained in the 40–50 percent range. Characteristics of the Glen Mills student population provide no basis for expectation that they, rather than the school's program, should account for any success that Glen Mills may have achieved in lowering recidivism rates below those of other institutions.

Measures of adjustment to the free community other than recidivism rates are difficult to come by. At the time of their interviews, some 51 percent of former students seemed to be coping with the life tasks of the young person, in that they were either in school or in some form of employment. Thirty-nine percent were unemployed and 13 percent were incarcerated. The percentage unemployed or incarcerated is disappointing, but these boys come from, and presumably returned to, frustrating social environments. The portion that would have "made it" in the absence of the Glen Mills experience cannot be determined.

The remaining, somewhat frustrating, question is why such impressive short-term success does not translate into more impressive indications of long-term life achievement in the free community. It is at this point that the reader must come to grips with one of the most ubiquitous aspects of yesterday's and to-day's American juvenile correctional scene: failure to provide adequate programs of assistance in reintegration into the free community. The juvenile justice system has long seemed to operate on the assumption that the correctional institution should somehow provide a sort of long-term immunization against the vicissitudes of the frustrating and defeating social environments from which many students come. These elements defeated them prior to their institutionalization and, without further intervention, may be expected to defeat them again. The student may leave the institution with enhanced feelings of self-worth, having experienced a life in many ways exemplifying that of a more advantaged world. He may be imbued with expectations of success. But his encounter with a familial and socioeconomic environment marked by lack of opportunity, failure, and despair may result in a sense of loss and resentment even more marked than before his glimpse of a possible better life. The Glen Mills "Why not the best?" motto may seem a bitter joke. The problem of effective assistance in reintegration into the community thus becomes one of the most pressing items on the agenda of the juvenile justice system—or, for that matter, of the adult criminal justice system as well.

Other, much more minor, caveats must be kept in mind when considering the utility of the Glen Mills program as an example for other correctional systems. Glen Mills is a private organization, not enmeshed in the personnel and other rigidities of a huge state bureaucracy. It can control its intake and dismiss students threatening the viability of the campus culture (though this is rarely done). It has been able to implement an aggressive recruiting campaign that reaches out to numerous jurisdictions, establishes relationships with referral sources (judges, probation departments, and social service workers), and educates them as to the type of student most appropriate for Glen Mills. Admission criteria emphasize the selection of the delinquent socialized into the delinquent subculture, possibly a gang member, but not presenting a severe physical handicap, a history of fire-setting or suicidal tendencies, severe emotional problems, or overt homosexuality. Otherwise, offense history is considered irrelevant to the admissions decisions.

It is difficult to assess the degree to which these factors contribute to Glen Mills's success. To me, they do not seem determinative. The type of boy sought by the school is the type filling most juvenile correctional institutions to the point of overflow. Once accepted, very few students, typically 2–4 percent, are returned to court for "failure to adjust." Such a "safety valve" probably exists, or could be developed, in most jurisdictions that administer or have access to multiple institutional resources. Certainly, the role of community-based programs and of other resources for the care of the severely emotionally disturbed delinquent remains to be further explored. But it seems probable that the Glen Mills experience may provide to many or most jurisdictions examples of what might become important aspects of a future enlightened juvenile correctional program. The book should be carefully read by juvenile justice system professionals, by those involved in juvenile justice policy development, and by citizens concerned about the relationship between our society and the frightening number of youngsters who have been so badly hurt in their early years and who, as a result, have become so hurtful of the security of the streets and neighborhoods of the world in which they must live.

STUDY QUESTIONS FOR READING 20

1. Is the Glen Mills School public or private? How many youth are committed there, and where are they from?

2. Who is credited with the school's current success, and what did he aspire to do?

3. What does it mean to assume the youth are students rather than patients or delinquents ("bad" youth)?

4. What are the norms at Glen Mills? These norms are enforced by confrontations. How are students trained to confront other students? What is the student who is confronted expected to do?

5. Glen Mills promotes student pride in themselves and their institution by trying in every way possible to "go first-class." How does the school achieve this goal?

6. What measures are used to show that this model works on campus and that students are excelling (i.e., less negative behavior and more positive behavior).

7. How do the costs at Glen Mills compare to the costs at public institutions in Pennsylvania? Why?

8. For juveniles, what is the national rate of re-incarceration for a new offense? What is the Glen Mills rate? What were the rates of employment, unemployment, and incarceration for boys studied after leaving the school?

9. Why are these rates disappointing in some ways, and what should be done about it?

10. What advantages does Glen Mills have as a private institution? How often does Glen Mills employ its "safety valve"?

11. What kinds of delinquents are accepted at Glen Mills? Do you think Robert Levinson (author of *Unit Management of Prisons and Jails*) would classify these boys as heavies, moderates, or lights? Why?

12. Once, Ferrainola issues a challenge to the state of Pennsylvania to send Glen Mills some of their *worst* boys—and they did. How do you think the boys adjusted? Why?

READADAPTATION: WORK AND FAMILY IN A MEXICAN PRISON VILLAGE

JON'A MEYER

The La Mesa Penitentiary in Tijuana, Mexico, is not your typical prison. It's not even your typical Mexican prison. This is not to say that it doesn't share many characteristics with other prisons. Its population of 2,500 inmates is housed for a variety of offenses, ranging from theft to murder: the average sentence length is five years. There's an administrative segregation unit that houses those who are unable to conform to prison rules. The 220 officers and 50 administrators, doctors, and psychologists on staff hope that the inmates don't return, but an estimated 20 percent do.

But that is where the similarities end. What make La Mesa truly different from its neighboring facilities is its prison management philosophy. In a nation where prisons are often characterized as brutal, the warden at La Mesa Penitentiary tries to allow the inmates to retain some of their humanity.

BRIEF HISTORY OF THE FACILITY

La Mesa Penitentiary was built in 1956 on the remote outskirts of Tijuana as a municipal jail for 500 inmates. Of course, little by little, the town grew until the building was located well within the city boundaries. Now it sits just off the main freeway, nestled among housing tracts and industry.

As time progressed, the flourishing economy near the border attracted more and more people to Tijuana. As the city grew, so did the prison population. The growth continued without respite, until it was intolerable. By the 1970s, 1,200 inmates were housed in space designed for 500.

Due to the overcrowding, the inmates asked for permission to build apartments for themselves. The administration granted the inmates' request so that the poorly funded prison did not have to build housing for the prisoners, whose numbers were increasing by leaps and bounds. The apartments, known as carracas, became a unique form of prison real estate. They remain the property of individual inmates and can be sold or rented to others. Many inmates buy a carraca when they enter the prison and sell it when they are released. In a sense, the inmates bought or rented their cells from other inmates.

The next step was to ask for work. The inmates had no means of supporting themselves and felt that they needed a legitimate way to earn money. Because many were from out of town, they could expect little or no support from their families. Once again, the administration agreed, and the inmates were allowed to establish small businesses, mostly stores. Parks and places of worship were also added to the miniature community. Little by little, La Mesa looked like a small town.

The last step was to bring family to La Mesa. Possibly the most unique aspect of this institution is that approximately 500 "permanent visitors" live on the prison grounds with their inmate spouses, lovers, and parents. This policy began when the inmates complained that they did not have enough money to pay for rentals for family or to support dependents. Some jealous men felt their wives might leave them for new companions on the outside. As a group, the inmates asked if their families could move in with them, and the prison agreed to this innovative idea.

These changes took place under the correctional philosophy that was popular in the 1970s. This approach, readaptation, focused on preparing inmates for life in the free world. It also firmly embraced the role played by family relations in helping inmates make it in general society. The dominant philosophy has now changed, however, to one that focuses on punishment. Readaptation, like our own rehabilitation, has lost its luster in the eyes of the public and is rapidly fading into history.

1995—A CURRENT VIEW

I was recently given the opportunity to spend a day at La Mesa and speak at length with its warden/director, Jorge Duarte Castillo. Señor Duarte is a soft-spoken man with an unspoken softness. He has served as warden since July 1992, after two stints as assistant warden that began in 1981. He also teaches law at the local university, where he tries to convey his correctional philosophy to his students: prison isn't for punishment, it's to help the inmates reintegrate into society. One way to achieve this task is to allow society to exist within the prison walls. Not a pseudocommunity, but as true a society as can be allowed.

During my visit, I noted the layout of the facility. The most striking difference to the casual visitor is the institution's appearance, an intriguing mix of town and prison. Several government buildings surrounded an impressive town square, complete with a miniature lighted nativity set built by the inmates after Duarte gave the project his blessing. A man and a woman sat on a park bench on the perimeter sharing Biblical scriptures. Another man held a woman's hand while watching the crowd that was gathering for a musical performance later that evening. Craftsmen were out in full force hawking their wares to a plethora of buyers. Children scampered about playing basketball or tag. An occasional chicken could be seen roaming the perimeter of the carracas complexes. It was impossible to distinguish the visitors from the inmates, who wore no uniforms.

The "town" was busy. The majority of the nearly 70 inmate-owned and operated businesses were open for commerce. Most of the enterprises were restaurants that serve to supplement inmates' prison diets and provide food to visitors and family members, who are on their own with respect to meals. Mexican, American, Chinese, and Italian food were advertised; some of the officers commented that the food was quite good. Other establishments sold grocery items and necessities such as soap.

I observed no arguments or disagreements. Many people were milling about, laughing and smiling. I found it very easy to forget that I was in a prison. If it hadn't been for my armed escort (Duarte doesn't take any chances and is always escorted while on the premises), I would have thought I was at any other town square in Mexico. No officers were visible except those patrolling on the walks above the facility and those who accompanied us on my tour. Duarte said they entered the grounds only when they were needed.

The inmates are allowed free rein of the town square from 8:00 AM until 10:00 PM. They have to return to their cells twice a day for counts. Those inmates who commit crimes against others in the prison or violate prison rules are kept in administrative segregation. These inmates are not allowed out during the day. If prisoners don't participate in a count, they get one day in segregation, while striking someone will fetch about two weeks. About 30 prisoners were in segregation the day I was there, some of whom chose to be there for their own protection.

PRISON PROGRAMS

Jorge Duarte knows that the inmates in his facility will someday be back in society. For this reason, he tries to ensure that adequate programming is available to help them reenter the free world. Besides, he notes, it's easier to help rather than punish inmates.

Medical needs are filled by eight doctors and a dentist. Routine medical care is dispensed on the prison grounds. For surgery and other complicated procedures, however, the inmates are transported to better prepared facilities. The medical and dental offices are housed in the administration building.

Duarte feels that education is a key element in preparing inmates for society. About 300 inmates participate in the prison's school programs, though he feels that at least 600 are in need of schooling. The prison is expanding its programs to meet the great need. At present, it offers kindergarten through high school sessions.

For others, there are a variety of vocational programs. Auto mechanics, electronics, and drawing workshops are offered on a regular basis. Inmates are also taught construction skills. Indeed, several of the buildings were built by inmates under the direction of professional carpenters and construction personnel. Duarte feels these are skills that will help the prisoners secure jobs after they are released.

With respect to alcohol abuse and addiction, there is an Alcoholics Anonymous chapter present on the premises. Others find help with such concerns through the religious personnel who are a regular fixture at the prison. Duarte recognizes the need for drug rehabilitation programs, but has been unsuccessful in implementing them due to budgetary constraints. He also hopes to set into motion parenting classes as he has noted that some of the inmates do not know how to best care for their children.

Duarte beams with pride when he mentions the fine arts programming available to the inmates. There are a variety of artistic programs for prisoners' personal development and enjoyment. One such program, the prison theater group, writes and performs its own plays. When the troupe asked to take the shows out into the community, Duarte was pleased to permit it. The inmates also have their own radio show, where they can sing or read poetry.

Because Duarte recognizes that sports are a useful way to teach inmates constructive use of their time and teamwork, several teams have been formed. The prison basketball team, for example, plays against teams in the community in addition to other prison teams. One professional boxer was allowed to leave the prison regularly to participate in his boxing career. His outfit, based on the stereotypical prisoner's stripes form the nineteenth century, was distasteful to Duarte because it harkened back to the days when prisons were dark and unenlightened. On the night of the inmate's release, the inmate won the match, and Duarte presented him with his walking papers in the ring. The audience gave him a standing ovation and the boxer cried.

WOMEN IN LA MESA

A substantial number of those in La Mesa are female. First, about 120 of the inmates are women, most of them drug mules. Duarte feels that he needs a separate facility for women, who for now are housed a few feet from the male inmates. During my tour, I visited one of the women's "cells." It was a conglomeration of three small bedrooms with low ceilings and three large, clean bathrooms. The dimly lit rooms were painted with several layers of pink paint that set off the white ceilings. Overall, the cell was cozy, and attempts had been made to make it visually appealing. Three-story bunkbeds were packed into the rooms like sardines. Many personal care items (e.g., shampoos and brushes) were neatly arranged on the inmates' desks. The women were very friendly and thanked me for coming to visit their cell. Four of them managed to jam themselves into one tiny room with myself, my mother, Duarte, the assistant warden, and our armed escorts. Due to space constraints, the inmates were forced to retreat to the lower bunks to make room, where they peered out at us with child-like wonder.

The other females at La Mesa are "permanent visitors." These women often leave during the day to work and return at night. On weekdays, they also deliver their children to the Tijuana city schools. This heavy traffic into and out of the facility creates quite a security risk for La Mesa (although there have been only three escapes during his tenure as warden). Duarte feels it is worth the benefits of having the women and children on the premises, however. In addition to maintaining the family, Duarte also feels the presence of loved ones reduces the occurrence of violence. The inmates feel that if they cause trouble, their families may be taken away. They are also less likely to participate in violence with children nearby.

One other female at La Mesa deserves special mention. Sister Antonia is a nun who has been at La Mesa for 19 years. Duarte feels she is good "for the inmates and for us . . . she helps us a lot." Sister Antonia lives in the prison and also operates a transition house for women. She is best known for the unconditional love and support she provides to the inmates, regardless of their crimes. She spoke fondly of one inmate who had brutally murdered a young girl by stabbing her 40 times, but who, nonetheless, deserved to be loved by someone.

JORGE DUARTE AND HIS PHILOSOPHY

There are no words that can truly describe Jorge Duarte. When I first met him, I immediately felt that he cared about his prison and the inmates that lived there. All through my tour, inmates approached and hugged him. Others shook his hand and called him friend.

Duarte feels his role in the criminal justice system is to work with the inmates and help them help themselves. He strives for the point where they can get into society "without anger, without hate, ready to live in society."

When asked about the recent move toward punishment, he is adamant that it is not the right path. "I don't believe in that," he says, "I prefer to go with the 1970s [approach] . . . I don't like the new." He feels that the new punishment-oriented group is getting ideas from other countries, including the United States. These ideas are being implemented wholesale without consideration for the differences between Mexico and other nations.

Duarte argues that the most important obstacle for him to overcome is the overcrowding at the prison. In 1990, a new building that houses 1,108 single inmates (7 per cell) was erected. This "free" housing was a very needed supplement for the privately owned and rented carracas. Still, there are about 150 homeless inmates who sleep in a large fenced area. On my tour, I saw the area, replete with dirty bedrolls and blankets. I noted that one inmate had a full "posturepedic" bed, probably a liability when it rains, as there is no roof for the homeless. During the day, the inmates are out in the square with their fellow prisoners. Duarte hopes that a planned facility will alleviate the crowding, although ground has yet to be broken.

Duarte is also quick to acknowledge that his prisoners do not represent the lowest of society. Only some killers are caught, and there are more drugs in the community than inside La Mesa. Taken together, he argues, there is "more trouble outside than inside."

Because of this, and his basic view of humanity, Duarte feels that inmates should have input into their prison. When the theater group wanted to move their performances into the community, he applauded their initiative. When the inmates want to change the physical appearance of the prison, he cheers them on. He guarantees that every prisoner has continued access to the press and to human rights organizations. Duarte is in a constant fight with those who want to change how his prison is run. When critics complain about the number of rights he extends to the inmates, he retorts, "Remember, they are people, not things." This is not to say that he surrenders all his decision-making authority to the inmates. He is careful to maintain control over his facility, while allowing the inmates some power. He acknowledges that some inmates cannot be reformed, but that does not stop him from trying. With respects to the model he employs at La Mesa, he simply comments, "It's human."

POSTSCRIPT

As I am finishing this article, I learn that Jorge Duarte was assassinated during the past week. An investigation is underway at this writing and there are many speculations as a city waits in shock for the answer to the question why. The world lost a good man and La Mesa lost its most powerful supporter.

During my visit to La Mesa, Duarte felt assured that one of his students at the university would carry on his work at La Mesa when he left. He didn't envision many changes and felt that the prison would be able to withstand the mounting criticism. We can only wait and see.

STUDY QUESTIONS FOR READING 21

1. Where is La Mesa Penitentiary? How many inmates reside there? How many officers work there? How many inmates was the facility designed for?

2. What are carracas? Why were they built in the 1970s? Who owns them?

3. Why did the inmates ask for legitimate work? What happened?

4. Why did the inmates ask to bring their families to La Mesa? What happened?

5. What is the correctional philosophy known as readaptation? What U.S. correctional philosophy does it resemble?

6. How does Warden Jorge Duarte explain his correctional philosophy?

7. What kind of activities and behaviors did the author see as she strolled around La Mesa?

8. Describe the programming that is available to La Mesa inmates and how this programming sometimes extends into the community.

9. Many family members leave La Mesa for work and/or take children to school, which creates quite a security hazard for the prison. How many escapes have there been in the four years Duarte has been warden? Why does he continue to allow "permanent visitors"?

10. How long has Sister Antonia lived at the prison? What is she best known for?

11. How did inmates relate to Warden Duarte as he toured the prison?

12. How does Warden Duarte feel about the punishment model of prisons, and why does he think it is becoming the popular model for Mexican prisons?

13. According to Warden Duarte, what is the biggest problem La Mesa faces? How many homeless inmates does La Mesa have?

14. According to Warden Duarte, there is "more trouble outside than inside." What evidence does he give?

15. What happened to Warden Duarte as this article went to press? In your opinion, what will happen to La Mesa?

THE NEED FOR MORE CONTROL IN THE *SOCIETY OF CAPTIVES*

GRESHAM M. SYKES

"For the needs of mass administration today," said Max Weber, "bureaucratic administration is completely indispensable. The choice is between bureaucracy and dilettantism in the field of administration."[1] To the officials of the New Jersey State Prison the choice is clear, as it is clear to the custodians of all maximum security prisons in the United States today. They are organized into a bureaucratic administrative staff—characterized by limited and specific rules, well-defined areas of competence and responsibility, impersonal standards of performance and promotion, and so on—which is similar in many respects to that of any modern, large-scale enterprise; and it is this staff which must see to the effective execution of the prison's routine procedures.

Of the approximately 300 employees of the New Jersey State Prison, more than two-thirds are directly concerned with the supervision and control of the inmate population. These form the so-called custodian force which is broken into three eight-hour shifts, each shift being arranged in a typical pyramid of authority. The day shift, however—on duty from 6:20 A.M. to 2:20 P.M.—is by far the largest. As in many organizations, the rhythm of life in the prison quickens with daybreak and trails off in the afternoon, and the period of greatest activity requires the largest number of administrative personnel.

In the bottom ranks are the Wing guards, the Tower guards, the guards assigned to the shops, and those with a miscellany of duties such as the guardianship of the receiving gate or the garage. Immediately above these men are a number of sergeants and lieutenants and these in turn are responsible to the Warden and his assistants.

The most striking fact about this [prison] bureaucracy of custodians is its unparalleled position of power—in formal terms, at least—vis-à-vis the body of men which it rules and from which it is supposed to extract compliance. The officials, after all, possess a monopoly on the legitimate means of coercion (or, as one prisoner has phrased it succinctly, "They have the guns and we don't"); and the officials can call on the armed might of the police and the National Guard in case of an overwhelming emergency. The 24-hour surveillance of the custodians represents the ultimate watchfulness and, presumably, noncompliance on the part of the inmates need not go long unchecked. The rulers of this society of captives nominally hold in their hands the sole right of granting rewards and inflicting punishments and it would seem that no prisoner could afford to ignore their demands for conformity. Centers of opposition in the inmate population—in the form of men recognized as leaders by fellow prisoners—can be neutralized through the use of solitary confinement or exile to other State institutions.[2] The custodians have the right not only to issue and administer the orders and regulations which are to guide the life of the prisoner, but also the right to detain, try, and punish any individual accused of disobedience—a merging of legislative, executive, and judicial functions which has long been regarded as the earmark of complete domination. The officials of the prison, in short, appear to be the possessors of almost infinite power within their realm; and, at least on the surface, the bureaucratic staff should experience no great difficulty in converting their rules and regulations—their blueprint for behavior—into a reality.

It is true, of course, that the power position of the custodial bureaucracy is not truly infinite. The objectives which the officials pursue are not completely of their own choosing and the means which they can use to achieve their objectives are far from limitless. The custodians are not total despots, able to exercise power at whim, and thus they lack the essential mark of infinite power, the unchallenged right of being capricious in their rule. It is this last which distinguishes terror from government, infinite power from almost infinite power, and the distinction is an important one. Neither by right nor by intention are the officials of the New Jersey State Prison free from a system of norms and laws which curb their actions. But within these limitations the bureaucracy of the prison is organized around a grant of power which is without an equal in American society; and if the rulers of any social system could secure compliance with their rules and regulations—however sullen or unwilling—it might be expected that the officials of the maximum security prison would be able to do so.

When we examine the New Jersey State Prison, however, we find that this expectation is not borne out in actuality. Indeed, the glaring conclusion is that despite the guns and the surveillance, the searches and the precautions of the custodians, the actual behavior of the inmate population differs markedly from that which is called for by official commands and decrees. Violence, fraud, theft, aberrant sexual behavior—all are common-place occurrences in the daily round of institutional existence in spite of the fact that the maximum security prison is conceived of by society as the ultimate weapon for the control of the criminal and his deviant actions. Far from being omnipotent rulers who have crushed all signs of rebellion against their regime, the custodians are engaged in a continuous struggle to maintain order—and it is a struggle in which the custodians frequently fail. Offenses committed by one inmate against another occur often, as do offenses committed by inmates against the officials and their rules. And the number of undetected offenses is, by universal agreement of both officials and inmates, far larger than the number of offenses which are discovered.

Some hint of the custodial bureaucracy's skirmishes with the population of prisoners is provided by the records of the disciplinary court which has the task of adjudicating charges brought by guards against their captives for offenses taking place within the walls. The following is a typical listing for a one-week period:

Charge	Disposition
1. Insolence and swearing while being interrogated	1. Continue in segregation
2. Threatening an inmate	2. Drop from job
3. Attempting to smuggle roll of tape into institution	3. 1 day in segregation with restricted diet
4. Possession of contraband	4. 30 days loss of privileges
5. Possession of pair of dice	5. 2 days in segregation with restricted diet
6. Insolence	6. Reprimand
7. Out of place	7. Drop from job. Refer to classification committee for reclassification
8. Possession of home-made knife, metal, and emery paper	8. 5 days in segregation with restricted diet
9. Suspicion of gambling or receiving bets	9. Drop from job and change Wing assignment
10. Out of place	10. 15 days loss of privileges
11. Possession of contraband	11. Reprimand
12. Creating disturbance in Wing	12. Continue in segregation
13. Swearing at an officer	13. Reprimand
14. Out of place	14. 15 days loss of privileges
15. Out of place	15. 15 days loss of privileges

Even more revealing, however, than this brief and somewhat enigmatic record are the so-called charge slips in which the guard is supposed to write out the derelictions of the prisoner in some detail. In the New

Jersey State Prison, Charge Slips form an administrative residue of past conflicts between captors and captives and the following accounts are a fair sample:

This inmate threatened an officer's life. When I informed this inmate he was to stay in to see the Chief Deputy on his charge he told me if he did not go to the yard I would get a shiv in my back.
                               Signed: Officer A_____

Inmate X cursing an officer. In mess hall inmate refused to put excess bread back on tray. Then he threw the tray on the floor. In the Center, inmate cursed both Officer Y and myself.   Signed: Officer B_____

This inmate has been condemning everyone about him for going to work. The Center gave orders for him to go to work this A.M. which he refused to do. While searching his cell I found drawings of picks and locks.
                               Signed: Officer C_____

Fighting. As this inmate came to 1 Wing entrance to go to yard this A.M. he struck inmate G in the face.
                               Signed: Officer D_____

Having fermented beverage in his cell. Found while inmate was in yard.   Signed: Officer E_____

Attempting to instigate wing disturbance. When I asked him why he discarded [sic] my order to quiet down he said he was going to talk any time he wanted to and _____ me and do whatever I wanted in regards to it.   Signed: Officer F_____

Possession of home-made shiv sharpened to razor edge on his person and possession of 2 more shivs in cell. When inmate was sent to 4 Wing officer H found 3-inch steel blade in pocket. I ordered Officer M to search his cell and he found 2 more shivs in process of being sharpened.   Signed: Officer G_____

Insolence. Inmate objected to my looking at papers he was carrying in pockets while going to the yard. He snatched them violently from my hand and gave me some very abusive talk. This man told me to_____ myself, and raised his hands as if to strike me. I grabbed him by the shirt and took him to the Center.
                               Signed: Officer H_____

Assault with knife on inmate K. During Idle Men's mess at approximately 11:10 A.M. this man assaulted Inmate K with a homemade knife. Inmate K was receiving his rations at the counter when Inmate B rushed up to him and plunged a knife in his chest, arm, and back. I grappled with him and with the assistance of Officers S and V, we disarmed the inmate and took him to the Center. Inmate K was immediately taken to the hospital.   Signed: Officer I_____

Sodomy. Found inmate W in cell with no clothing on and inmate Z on top of him with no clothing. Inmate W told me he was going to lie like a ____ ___ __ _____ to get out of it.   Signed: Officer J_____

Attempted escape on night of 4/15/53. This inmate along with inmates L and T succeeded in getting on roof of 6 Wing and having home-made bombs in their possession.   Signed: Officer K_____

Fighting and possession of home-made shiv. Struck first blow to Inmate P. He struck blow with a roll of black rubber rolled up in his fist. He then produced a knife made out of wire tied to a tooth brush.
                               Signed: Officer L_____

Refusing medication prescribed by Doctor W. Said "What do you think I am, a damn fool, taking that _____ for a headache, give it to the doctor."
                               Signed: Officer M_____

Inmate loitering on tier. There is a clique of several men who lock on top tier, who ignore rule of returning directly to their cells and attempt to hang out on the tier in a group.   Signed: Officer N_____

It is hardly surprising that when the guards at the New Jersey State Prison were asked what topics should be of first importance in a proposed in-service training program, 98 percent picked "what to do in event of trouble." The critical issue for the moment, however, is that the dominant position of the custodial staff is more fiction than reality, if we think of domination as something more than the outward forms and symbols of power. If power is viewed as the probability that orders and regulations will be obeyed by a given group of individuals, as Max Weber has suggested,[3] the New Jersey State Prison is perhaps more notable for the doubtfulness of obedience than its certainty. The weekly records of the disciplinary court and Charge Slips provide an admittedly poor index of offenses or acts of noncompliance committed within the walls, for these form only a small, visible segment of an iceberg whose greatest bulk lies beneath the surface of official recognition. The public is periodically made aware of the officials' battle to enforce their regime within the prison, commonly in the form of allegations in the newspapers concerning homosexuality, illegal use of drugs, assaults, and so on. But the ebb and flow of public attention given to these matters does not match the constancy of these problems for the prison officials who are all too well aware that "Incidents"—the very thing they try to minimize—are not isolated or rare events but are instead a commonplace. The number of "incidents" in the New Jersey State Prison is probably no greater than that to be found in most maximum security institutions in the United States and may, indeed, be smaller, although it is difficult to make comparisons. In any event, it seems clear that the custodians are bound to their captives in a relationship of conflict rather than compelled acquiescence, despite the custodians' theoretical supremacy, and we now need to see why this should be so.

II

In our examination of the forces which undermine the power position of the New Jersey State Prison's custodial bureaucracy, the most important fact is, perhaps, that the power of the custodians is not based on authority.

Now power based on authority is actually a complex social relationship in which an individual or a group of individuals is recognized as possessing a right to issue commands or regulations and those who receive these commands or regulations feel compelled to obey by a sense of duty. In its pure form, then, or as an ideal type, power based on authority has two essential elements: a rightful or legitimate effort to exercise control on the one hand and an inner, moral compulsion to obey, by those who are to be controlled, on the other. In reality, of course, the recognition of the legitimacy of efforts to exercise control may be qualified or partial and the sense of duty, as a motive for compliance, may be mixed with motives of fear or self-interest. But it is possible for theoretical purposes to think of power based on authority in its pure form and to use this as a baseline in describing the empirical case.[4]

It is the second element of authority—the sense of duty as a motive for compliance—which supplies the secret strength of most social organizations. Orders and rules can be issued with the expectation that they will be obeyed without the necessity of demonstrating in each case that compliance will advance the subordinate's interests. Obedience or conformity springs from an internalized morality which transcends the personal feelings of the individual; the fact that an order or a rule is an order or a rule becomes the basis for modifying one's behavior, rather than a rational calculation of the advantages which might be gained.

In the prison, however, it is precisely this sense of duty which is lacking in the general inmate population. The regime of the custodians is expressed as a mass of commands and regulations passing down a hierarchy of power. In general, these efforts at control are regarded as legitimate by individuals in the hierarchy, and individuals tend to respond because they feel they "should," down to the level of the guard in the cellblock, the industrial shop, or the recreation yard.[5] But now these commands and regulations must jump a gap which separates the captors from the captives. And it is at this point that a sense of duty tends to disappear and with it goes that easily-won obedience which many organizations take for granted in the naïveté of their unrecognized strength. In the prison power must be based on something other than internalized morality and the custodians find themselves confronting men who must be forced, bribed, or cajoled into compliance. This is not to say that inmates feel that the efforts of prison officials to exercise control are wrongful or illegitimate; in general, prisoners do not feel that the prison officials have usurped positions of power which are not rightfully theirs, nor do prisoners feel that the orders and regulations which descend upon them from above represent an illegal extension of their rulers' grant of government. Rather, the noteworthy fact about the social system of the New Jersey State Prison is that the bond between recognition of the legitimacy of control and the sense of duty has been torn apart. In these terms the social system of the prison is very similar to a *Gebietsverband*, a territorial group living under a regime imposed by a ruling few.[6] Like a province which has been conquered by force of arms, the community of prisoners has come to accept the validity of the regime constructed by their rulers but the subjugation is not complete. Whether he sees himself as caught by his own stupidity, the workings of chance, his inability to "fix" the case, or the superior skill of the police, the criminal in prison seldom denies the legitimacy of confinement.[7] At the same time, the recognition of the legitimacy of society's surrogates and their body of rules is not accompanied by an internalized obligation to obey and the prisoner thus accepts the fact of his captivity at one level and rejects it at another. If for no other reason, then, the custodial institution is valuable for a theory of human behavior because it makes us realize that men need not be motivated to conform to a regime which they define as rightful. It is in this apparent contradiction that we can see the first flaw in the custodial bureaucracy's assumed supremacy.

III

Since the Officials of prison possess a monopoly on the means of coercion, as we have pointed out earlier, it might be thought that the inmate population could simply be forced into conformity and that the lack of an inner moral compulsion to obey on the part of the inmates could be ignored. Yet the combination of a bureaucratic staff—that most modern, rational form of mobilizing effort to exercise control—and the use of physical violence—that most ancient device to channel man's conduct—must strike us as an anomaly and with good reason. The use of force is actually grossly inefficient as a means for securing obedience, particularly when those who are to be controlled are called on to perform a task of any complexity. A blow with a club may check an immediate revolt, it is true, but it cannot assure effective performance on a punch-press. A "come-along," a straitjacket or a pair of handcuffs may serve to curb one rebellious prisoner in a crisis, but they will be of little aid in moving more than 1200 inmates through the messhall in a routine and orderly fashion. Furthermore, the custodians are well aware that violence once unleashed is not easily brought to heel and it is this awareness that lies behind the standing order that no guard should ever strike an inmate with his hand—he should always use a night stick. This rule is not an open invitation to brutality but an attempt to set a high threshold on the use of force in

order to eliminate the casual cuffing which might explode into extensive and violent retaliation. Similarly, guards are under orders to throw their night sticks over the wall if they are on duty in the recreation yard when a riot develops. A guard without weapons, it is argued, is safer than a guard who tries to hold on to his symbol of office, for a mass of rebellious inmates may find a single night stick a goad rather than a restraint and the guard may find himself beaten to death with his own means of compelling order.

In short, the ability of the officials to physically coerce their captives into the paths of compliance is something of an illusion as far as the day-to-day activities of the prison are concerned and may be of doubtful value in moments of crisis. Intrinsically inefficient as a method of making men carry out a complex task, diminished in effectiveness by the realities of the guard-inmate ratio,[8] and always accompanied by the danger of touching off further violence, the use of physical force by the custodians has many limitations as a basis on which to found the routine operation of the prison. Coercive tactics may have some utility in checking blatant disobedience—if only a few men disobey. But if the great mass of criminals in prison are to be brought into the habit of conformity, it must be on other grounds. Unable to count on a sense of duty to motivate their captives to obey and unable to depend on the direct and immediate use of violence to insure a step-by-step submission to the rules, the custodians must fall back on a system of rewards and punishments.

Now if men are to be controlled by the use of rewards and punishments—by promises and threats— at least one point is patent: The rewards and punishments dangled in front of the individual must indeed be rewards and punishments from the point of view of the individual who is to be controlled. It is precisely on this point, however, that the custodians' system of rewards and punishments founders. In our discussion of the problems encountered in securing conscientious performance at work, we suggested that both the penalties and the incentives available to the officials were inadequate. This is also largely true, at a more general level, with regard to rewards and punishments for securing compliance with the wishes of the custodians in all areas of prison life.

In the first place, the punishments which the officials can inflict—for theft, assaults, escape attempts, gambling, insolence, homosexuality, and all the other deviations from the pattern of behavior called for by the regime of the custodians—do not represent a profound difference from the prisoner's usual status. It may be that when men are chronically deprived of liberty, material goods and services, recreational opportunities and so on, the few pleasures that are granted take on a new importance and the threat of their withdrawal is a more powerful motive for conformity than those of us in the free community can realize. To be locked up in the solitary confinement wing, that prison within a prison; to move from the monotonous, often badly prepared meals in the mess-hall to a diet of bread and water;[9] to be dropped from a dull, unsatisfying job and forced to remain in idleness—all, perhaps, may mean the difference between an existence which can be borne, painful though it may be, and one which cannot. But the officials of the New Jersey State Prison are dangerously close to the point where the stock of legitimate punishments has been exhausted and it would appear that for many prisoners the few punishments which are left have lost their potency. To this we must couple the important fact that such punishments as the custodians can inflict may lead to an increased prestige for the punished inmate in the eyes of his fellow prisoners. He may become a hero, a martyr, a man who has confronted his captors and dared them to do their worst. In the dialectics of the inmate population, punishments and rewards have, then, been reversed and the control measures of the officials may support disobedience rather than decrease it.

In the second place, the system of rewards and punishments in the prison is defective because the reward side of the picture has been largely stripped away. Mail and visiting privileges, recreational privileges, the supply of personal possessions—all are given to the inmate at the time of his arrival in one fixed sum. Even the so-called Good Time—the portion of the prisoner's sentence deducted for good behavior—is automatically subtracted from the prisoner's sentence when he begins his period of imprisonment.[10] Thus the officials have placed themselves in the peculiar position of granting the prisoner all available benefits or rewards at the time of his entrance into the system. The prisoner, then, finds himself unable to win any significant gains by means of compliance, for there are no gains left to be won.

From the viewpoint of the officials, of course, the privileges of the prison social system are regarded as rewards, as something to be achieved. That is to say, the custodians hold that recreation, access to the inmate store, Good Time, or visits from individuals in the free community are conditional upon conformity or good behavior. But the evidence suggests that from the viewpoint of the inmates the variety of benefits granted by the custodians is not defined as something to be earned but as an inalienable right—as the just due of the inmate which should not turn on the question of obedience or disobedience within the walls. After all, the inmate population claims, these benefits have belonged to the prisoner from the time when he first came to the institution.

In short, the New Jersey State Prison makes an initial grant of all its rewards and then threatens to withdraw them if the prisoner does not conform. It does not start the prisoner from scratch and promise to grant its available rewards one by one as the prisoner proves himself through continued submission to the institutional regulations. As a result a subtle alchemy is set in motion whereby the inmates cease to see the rewards of the system as rewards, that is, as benefits contingent upon performance; instead, rewards are apt to be defined as obligations. Whatever justification might be offered for such a policy, it would appear to have a number of drawbacks as a method of motivating prisoners to fall into the posture of obedience. In effect, rewards and punishments of the officials have been collapsed into one and the prisoner moves in a world where there is no hope of progress but only the possibility of further punishments. Since the prisoner is already suffering from most of the punishments permitted by society, the threat of imposing those few remaining is all too likely to be a gesture of futility.

IV

Unable to depend on that inner moral compulsion or sense of duty which eases the problem of control in most social organizations, acutely aware that brute force is inadequate, and lacking an effective system of legitimate rewards and punishments which might induce prisoners to conform to institutional regulations on the grounds of self interest, the custodians of the New Jersey State Prison are considerably weakened in their attempts to impose their regime on their captive population. The result, in fact, is, as we have already indicated, a good deal of deviant behavior or noncompliance in a social system where the rulers at first glance seem to possess almost infinite power.

Yet systems of power may be defective for reasons other than the fact that those who are ruled do not feel the need to obey the orders and regulations descending on them from above. Systems of power may also fail because those who are supposed to rule are unwilling to do so. The unissued order, the deliberately ignored disobedience, the duty left unperformed—these are cracks in the monolith just as surely as are acts of defiance in the subject population. The "corruption" of the rulers may be far less dramatic than the insurrection of the ruled, for power unexercised is seldom as visible as power which is challenged, but the system of power still falters.[11]

Now the official in the lowest ranks of the custodial bureaucracy—the guard in the cellblock, the industrial shop, or the recreation yard—is the pivotal figure on which the custodial bureaucracy turns. It is he who must supervise and control the inmate population in concrete and detailed terms. It is he who must see to the translation of the custodial regime from blueprint to reality and engage in the specific battles for conformity. Counting prisoners, periodically reporting to the center of communications, signing passes, checking groups of inmates as they come and go, searching for contraband or signs of attempts to escape—these make up the minutiae of his eight-hour shift. In addition, he is supposed to be alert for violations of the prison rules which fall outside his routine sphere of surveillance. Not only must he detect and report deviant behavior after it occurs; he must curb deviant behavior before it arises as well as when he is called on to prevent a minor quarrel among prisoners from flaring into a more dangerous situation. And he must make sure that the inmates in his charge perform their assigned tasks with a reasonable degree of efficiency.

The expected role of the guard, then, is a complicated compound of policeman and foreman, of cadi, counsellor, and boss all rolled into one. But as the guard goes about his duties, piling one day on top of another (and the guard too, in a certain sense, is serving time in confinement), we find that the system of power in the prison is defective not only because the means of motivating the inmates to conform are largely lacking but also because the guard is frequently reluctant to enforce the full range of the institution's regulations. The guard frequently fails to report infractions of the rules which have occurred before his eyes. The guard often transmits forbidden information to inmates, such as plans for searching particular cells in a surprise raid for contraband. The guard often neglects elementary security requirements and on numerous occasions he will be found joining his prisoners in outspoken criticisms of the Warden and his assistants. In short, the guard frequently shows evidence of having been "corrupted" by the captive criminals over whom he stands in theoretical dominance. This failure within the ranks of the rulers is seldom to be attributed to outright bribery—bribery is usually unnecessary, for far more effective influences are at work to bridge the gap supposedly separating captors and captives.

In the first place, the guard is in close and intimate association with his prisoners throughout the course of the working day. He can remain aloof only with great difficulty, for he possesses few of those devices which normally serve to maintain social distance between the rulers and the ruled. He cannot withdraw physically in symbolic affirmation of his superior position; he has no intermediaries to bear the brunt of resentment springing from orders which are disliked; and he cannot fall back on a dignity adhering to his office—he is a *hack* or a *screw* in the eyes of those he controls and an unwelcome display of officiousness evokes that great destroyer of unquestioned power, the ribald humor of the dispossessed.

There are many pressures in American culture to "be nice," to be a "good Joe," and the guard in the maximum security prison is not immune. The guard is constantly exposed to a sort of moral blackmail in which the first signs of condemnation, estrangement, or rigid adherence to the rules is countered by the inmates with the threat of ridicule or hostility. And in this complex interplay, the guard does not always start from a position of determined opposition to "being friendly." He holds an intermediate post in a bureaucratic structure between top prison officials—his captains, lieutenants, and sergeants—and the prisoners in his charge. Like many such figures, the guard is caught in a conflict of loyalties. He often has reason to resent the actions of his superior officers—the reprimands, the lack of ready appreciation, the incomprehensible order—and in the inmates he finds willing sympathizers: They too claim to suffer from the unreasonable irritants of power. Furthermore, the guard in many cases is marked by a basic ambivalence toward the criminals under his supervision and control. It is true that the inmates of the prison have been condemned by society through the agency of the courts, but some of these prisoners must be viewed as a success in terms of a worldly system of the values which accords high prestige to wealth and influence even though they may have been won by devious means; and the poorly paid guard may be gratified to associate with a famous racketeer. Moreover, this ambivalence in the guard's attitudes toward the criminals nominally under his thumb may be based on something more than a *sub rosa* respect for the notorious. There may also be a discrepancy between the judgments of society and the guard's own opinions as far as the "criminality" of the prisoner is concerned. It is difficult to define the man convicted of deserting his wife, gambling, or embezzlement as a desperate criminal to be suppressed at all costs and the crimes of even the most serious offenders lose their significance with the passage of time. In the eyes of the custodian, the inmate tends to become a man in prison rather than a criminal in prison and the relationship between captor and captive is subtly transformed in the process.

In the second place, the guard's position as a strict enforcer of the rules is undermined by the fact that he finds it almost impossible to avoid the claims of reciprocity. To a large extent the guard is dependent on inmates for the satisfactory performance of his duties; and like many individuals in positions of power, the guard is evaluated in terms of the conduct of the men he controls. A troublesome, noisy, dirty cellblock reflects on the guard's ability to "handle" prisoners and

this ability forms an important component of the merit rating which is used as the basis for pay raises and promotions. As we have pointed out above, a guard cannot rely on the direct application of force to achieve compliance nor can he easily depend on threats of punishment. And if the guard does insist on constantly using the last few negative sanctions available to the institution—if the guard turns in Charge Slip after Charge Slip for every violation of the rules which he encounters—he becomes burdensome to the top officials of the prison bureaucratic staff who realize only too well that their apparent dominance rests on some degree of co-operation. A system of power which can enforce its rules only by bringing its formal machinery of accusation, trial, and punishment into play at every turn will soon be lost in a haze of pettifogging detail.

The guard, then, is under pressure to achieve a smoothly running tour of duty not with the stick but with the carrot, but here again his legitimate stock is limited. Facing demands from above that he achieve compliance and stalemated from below, he finds that one of the most meaningful rewards he can offer is to ignore certain offenses or make sure that he never places himself in a position where he will discover them. Thus the guard—backed by all the power of the State, close to armed men who will run to his aid, and aware that any prisoner who disobeys him can be punished if he presses charges against him—often discovers that his best path of action is to make "deals" or "trades" with the captives in his power. In effect, the guard buys compliance or obedience in certain areas at the cost of tolerating disobedience elsewhere.

Aside from winning compliance "where it counts" in the course of the normal day, the guard has another favor to be secured from the inmates which makes him willing to forego strict enforcement of all prison regulations. Many custodial institutions have experienced a riot in which the tables are turned momentarily and the captives hold sway over their quondam captors; and the rebellions of 1952 loom large in the memories of the officials of the New Jersey State Prison. The guard knows that he may some day be a hostage and that his life may turn on a settling of old accounts. A fund of good will becomes a valuable form of insurance and this fund is almost sure to be lacking if he has continually played the part of a martinet. In the folklore of the prison there are enough tales about strict guards who have had the misfortune of being captured and savagely beaten during a riot to raise doubts about the wisdom of demanding complete conformity.

In the third place, the theoretical dominance of the guard is undermined in actuality by the innocuous encroachment of the prisoner on the guard's duties. Making out reports, checking cells at the periodic count, locking and unlocking doors—in short, all the minor chores which the guard is called on to perform—may gradually be transferred into the hands of inmates whom the guard has come to trust. The cell-block runner, formally assigned the tasks of delivering mail, housekeeping duties, and so on, is of particular importance in this respect. Inmates in this position function in a manner analogous to that of the company clerk in the Armed Forces and like such figures they may wield power and influence far beyond the nominal definition of their role. For reasons of indifference, laziness, or naïveté, the guard may find that much of the power which he is supposed to exercise has slipped from his grasp.

Now power . . . once lost is hard to regain. The measures to rectify an established pattern of abdication need to be much more severe than those required to stop the first steps in the transfer of control from the guard to his prisoner. A guard assigned to a cell-block in which a large portion of power has been shifted in the past from the officials to the inmates is faced with the weight of precedent; it requires a good deal of moral courage on his part to withstand the aggressive tactics of prisoners who fiercely defend the patterns of corruption established by custom. And if the guard himself has allowed his control to be subverted, he may find that any attempts to undo his error are checked by a threat from the inmate to send a *snitch-kite*—an anonymous note—to the guard's superior officers explaining his past derelictions in detail. This simple form of blackmail may be quite sufficient to maintain the relationships established by friendship, reciprocity, or encroachment.

It is apparent, then, that the power of the custodians is defective, not simply in the sense that the ruled are rebellious, but also in the sense that the rulers are reluctant. We must attach a new meaning to Lord Acton's aphorism that power tends to corrupt and absolute power corrupts absolutely. The custodians of the New Jersey State Prison, far from being converted into brutal tyrants, are under strong pressure to compromise with their captives, for it is a paradox that they can insure their dominance only by allowing it to be corrupted. Only by tolerating violations of "minor" rules and regulations can the guard secure compliance in the "major" areas of the custodian regime. Ill-equipped to maintain the social distance which in theory separates the world of the officials and the world of the inmates, their suspicions eroded by long familiarity, the custodians are led into a modus vivendi with their captives which bears little resemblance to the stereotypical picture of guards and their prisoners.

. . . The lack of a sense of duty among those who are held captive, the obvious fallacies of coercion, the pathetic collection of rewards and punishments to induce compliance, the strong pressures toward the corruption of the guard in the form of friendship, reciprocity, and the transfer of duties into the hands of trusted inmates—all are structural defects in the prison's system of power rather than individual inadequacies.[12]

ENDNOTES

1. Max Weber, *The Theory of Social and Economic Organization,* edited by Talcott Parsons, New York: Oxford University Press, 1947, p. 337.

2. Just as the Deep South served an a dumping-ground for particularly troublesome slaves before the Civil War, so too can the county jail or mental hospital serve as a dumping-ground for the maximum security prison. Other institutions, however, are apt to regard the Trenton Prison in somewhat the same way, as the report of the Governor's committee to investigate the prison has indicated. *Supra* page 22.

3. *Ibid.,* p. 324.

4. *Ibid.,* Introduction.

5. Failures in this process within the custodial staff itself will be discussed in the latter portion of this chapter.

6. *Ibid.,* p. 149.

7. This statement requires two qualifications. First, a number of inmates steadfastly maintain that they are innocent of the crime with which they are charged. It is the illegitimacy of their particular case, however, rather than the illegitimacy of confinement in general, which moves them to protest. Second, some of the more sophisticated prisoners argue that the conditions of imprisonment are wrong, although perhaps not illegitimate or illegal, on the grounds that reformation should be the major aim of imprisonment and the officials are not working hard enough in this direction.

8. Since each shift is reduced in size by vacations, regular days off, sickness, etc., even the day shift—the largest of the three—can usually muster no more than 90 guards to confront the population of more than 1200 prisoners. The fact that they are so heavily out-numbered in not lost on the officials.

9. The usual inmate fare is both balanced and sufficient in quantity, but it has been pointed out that the meals are not apt to be particularly appetizing since prisoners must eat them with nothing but a spoon. Cf. Report of the Governor's Committee to Examine the Prison and Parole System of New Jersey, November 21, 1952, pp. 74–79.

10. The law of New Jersey stipulates that each prisoner may reduce the sentence he receives from the court by (a) earning one day per week for performing work assignments conscientiously (Work Time); and (b) earning commutation of his sentence, up to 60 days during the first year of imprisonment and in increasing amounts for subsequent years, for orderly deportment and manifest efforts at self-control and improvement (Good Time). Cf. New Jersey Department of Institutions and Agencies, Research Bulletin No. 18 "Two Thousand State Prisoners in New Jersey," Trenton, New Jersey, May 1954.

11. Portions of the following discussion concerning the corruption of the guards' authority are to be found in Gresham M. Sykes, *Crime and Society,* New York: Random House, 1956.

12. Those who are familiar with prison systems such as those of the Federal government or the State of California might argue that I have underestimated the possibilities of improvement which can be won with well-trained, well-paid, well-led guards. They might be right, but I think it is important to stress the serious, "built-in" weaknesses of the prison as a social system.

STUDY QUESTIONS FOR READING 22

1. What makes the guards have almost limitless power? What is the "essential mark of infinite power"? Do guards have it?

2. What is power, according to Max Weber? How great is the power of guards? How might the guards' power, or lack thereof, contribute to what Zimbardo and others called the guards' sadism or "quiet rage"?

3. What is the power of authority (legitimate power) based on? Why don't prison guards have it? Is physical coercion a good substitute on a day-to-day basis or in times of crises?

4. In the end, inmates are controlled through the privilege system: a system of rewards and punishments. What are the problems with this system?

5. The guard's power is corrupted for three key reasons. Identify and explain each.

HOW TO INCREASE THE RATE OF VIOLENCE—AND WHY

JAMES GILLIGAN, M.D.

Within the penal system—in addition to legally executed and morally defended punishments—there is a dark underside to punishment in the prisons. It occurs regularly, knowingly, and more or less universally. It is a predictable consequence of our policies and punishments. The most egregious example of what I am referring to here is the violence that prisoners routinely inflict on one another.

Now I realize that to hold the prison system itself responsible for "inhouse" violence—from the threats, extortion, and robberies to which prisoners are regularly subjected by other prisoners, to the actual mutilations, rapes, and murders that occur in prison—might sound at first like claiming that the "cops" are completely responsible for the violence that the "robbers" commit. This is not my intention. Of course, many prisoners were sent to prison in the first place because they had already made a habit of violence. Still, prison conditions often tolerate and even exacerbate the inmates' pre-existing potential for violence. In fact, the very conditions that occur regularly in most prisons may force prisoners to engage in acts of serious violence in order to avoid being mutilated, raped, or murdered themselves.

All the evidence of which I am aware, both from my own observations, from what I have learned from judges, correctional administrators, prison mental health professionals, and prisoners themselves, and from what has been written, indicates that the responsibility for violence in prisons emanates neither unilaterally from prisoners nor from the prison system alone. It is the predictable and even inevitable outcome of patterns of interaction between prisoners and the penal system. Any characterization of legal punishment as a form of violence, with a symbolism of its own (one it shares more or less interchangeably with "criminal" violence) if it is to be complete must include the violence of prisoners toward each other in the inventory of prison punishment. While that conclusion may seem radical to some, it is supported by a great deal of empirical evidence, some of which I will now review.

Heterosexual deprivation itself leads directly to increased levels of violence, both within the prison and, later, in the community, after the prisoners are released from prison (as ninety percent are). Heterosexual deprivation in itself constitutes a symbolic castration or emasculation of those men who are heterosexual[1]—a shaming of them as men. When coupled with whatever pre-existing homophobia or homosexual panic these men may be vulnerable to, this readily leads to paranoid thoughts and fears, and ultimately, to violent behavior.[2]

But the business of shaming prisoners by symbolically castrating or emasculating them does not end there. Homosexual rape is another even more horrendous and destructive form of punishment endemic to the prisons. For example, in one prison holding close to 700 inmates, one of the prison administrators, who was in a position to know, informed me that out of that total number, probably no more than half a dozen men failed to engage in some form or other of regular sexual encounter with other men. How did he know that? Because in that prison an "observation gallery" overlooks every cell in the three tiers of its maximum-security wing so that the correction officers can observe what goes on within each and every cell.

Since this prison, like almost every other prison in this country, does not permit "conjugal visits," you might assume that such a figure reflects the sexual frustration that must naturally and inevitably accompany a state of enforced heterosexual deprivation. When I first began visiting such institutions, I naively questioned why inmates should not be allowed to participate in sexual relations with each other, as long as they did so voluntarily, since no other sexual relationships were permitted for them. A more experienced colleague answered my question with another: "How could any relationship be 'voluntary' in this kind of environment?" He did not mean that there are no men in prison who voluntarily seek out sexual relationships with other men; a minority of criminals are gay or bisexual, just as a minority of all people are. But all choices and relationships are so constrained and limited in the unfree world of the prison that what is normally meant by such terms as "free" or "voluntary" does not apply. The vast majority of sexual relationships in prison occur in a context of coercion, whether by means of overwhelming physical force and violence, or by means of credible threat of violence. In other words, most such relationships are, in effect, rape. The fact that many of those relationships are relatively stable "marriages" between dominant and submissive partners merely means that they constitute a form of chronic, ongoing, and repeated rape.

But rape is universally acknowledged to be a crime, and it is seldom if ever openly acknowledged as among the forms of legal punishment legitimately prescribed by governmental authorities. So what would lead me to speak of it as "punishment"—as an intrinsic and universal part of the punishments that our government metes out to those whom it labels as "criminal"? I do this for several reasons. First, the relevant legal authorities, from the judges and prosecutors who send people to prison, to the prison officials who administer them, are all aware of the existence, the reality, and the near-universality of rape in the prisons. Indeed, this is one reason why so many conscientious judges are extremely reluctant to send anyone to prison except when they feel compelled to, either by the violence of the crime or, as is increasingly true, by laws mandating prison sentences even for nonviolent crimes, such as drug offenses. Second, the conditions that stimulate such rapes (the enforced deprivation of other sources of self-esteem, respect, power, and sex-

ual gratification) are consciously and deliberately imposed upon the prison population by the legal authorities. Third, all these authorities tacitly and knowingly tolerate this form of sexual violence, passively delegating to the dominant and most violent inmates the power and authority to deliver this form of punishment to the more submissive and nonviolent ones, so that the rapists in this situation are acting as the vicarious enforcers of a form of punishment that the legal system does not itself enforce formally or directly.

THE CASE OF JEFFREY L.

I first gained some acquaintance with the reality of rape in prison, and of the means through which some inmates are forced into the role of sex slave, when I was asked to see one young man, Jeffrey L., because his behavior had become so bizarre that the prison authorities thought he needed to be evaluated for psychiatric illness. The incident that led to this referral had occurred in the prison Visiting Room, a setting in which inmates sit on one side of a long table and their visitors on the other. Jeffrey L.'s mother had just concluded a visit with him, when instead of merely saying good-bye he leaped over the table in an attempt to follow her out of the Visiting Room and out of the prison, crying hysterically, clinging to her, begging her to take him home with her. Since he would not tell either his mother or the correction officers why he had behaved this way, they asked me to see him.

When I interviewed Jeffrey, I noted that he was a slightly built nineteen-year old white man (or boy) who appeared even younger than his stated age, who was visibly trembling and appeared nearly frightened to death. What he described to me was a pattern of repeated gang rapes to which he had been subjected since first arriving in prison. He was sent to prison for a relatively minor, nonviolent offense. After he was convicted in court, he had first been sent to the medium-security prison to which all of the younger prisoners convicted of nonviolent crimes are initially sent for a brief "diagnostic" evaluation, on the basis of which they are assigned or "classified" to whatever long-term prison setting the authorities deem suitable for that particular individual; soon after arriving there, he was raped by a gang of other inmates. Because he felt overwhelmingly ashamed of what had happened to him, and also because he knew enough about the mores of the prison subculture to know that seeking help from the correctional authorities would be seen as informing or "ratting" on his fellow prisoners, and that the penalty for that in the world of the prison is capital punishment (imposed by the inmates themselves, of course, not by the guards), he refused to reveal to anyone what had happened. As ordinarily happens with nonviolent first offenders, he was soon transferred to a minimum-security prison, where he was again gang-raped. In terror of a repetition of that experience, and in order to provoke the prison officials to transfer him elsewhere, he refused a direct order to return to the cell block to which he had been assigned (and in which he had been raped), and thus was transferred to a third (medium-security) prison, where he was promptly subjected to a gang rape for the third time. It was following that experience that he behaved as I described above in the Visiting Room.

After I referred Jeffrey for surgical repair of the anal tears that the rapes had caused, I informed the Commissioner of Correction of what had happened. He was appropriately, and quite sincerely, horrified, and immediately took steps to make sure that this young man was better protected in the future. It was clear, of course, that the administrators had not engaged in any kind of conspiracy to permit inmates to be subjected to this kind of "punishment." But we need to understand the full meaning of Jeffrey L.'s experience in the larger context. First, it is an integral part of the functioning of the prison system, and hence of the punishment to which prison inmates are regularly subjected; it is no anomalous chance event. Consider these additional facts. Jeffrey L. had only been treated this harshly by the other inmates because he refused to submit passively and peacefully. He resisted becoming a sex object. So, many if not most of the inmates who do submit peacefully to being the passive sex objects of stronger, more dominant and violent prisoners are not doing so "voluntarily," but simply in order to avoid being subjected to physically injurious violence of the sort that Jeffrey had suffered.

A second consideration is the degree to which the sexual abuse and exploitation, or rape (though it is not always recognized and identified as rape) of inmates is "permitted," by the line-officers on each cellblock. The practice of tolerating and permitting such relationships is one means by which the officers maintain control of the prison population as a whole. The strategy here can be analyzed into two components: "You scratch my back and I'll scratch yours," and "Divide and conquer." With respect to the first, the officers are entering into an implicit, tacit agreement with the rapists, in which the officers will permit the rapists whatever gratifications they get from raping the weaker prisoners, and the rapists agree in turn to cooperate with these officers by submitting to the prison system as a whole (that is, by renouncing the option of assaulting officers individually, or of collaborating with each other collectively to organize a riot). With respect to the second, that system of mutually agreed upon trade-offs simultaneously prevents the inmates as a whole from uniting with each other, for it divides the inmates into two groups—the rapists and the raped—thus minimizing the chance of their being able to organize an effective protest, rebellion, or not. It becomes a strategy that officers may use to "divide and conquer" the inmates.

Conditions in most prisons are such that the officers as a group have an objective interest in pursuing these two strategies (though the degree to which they actually do pursue them may vary, from one officer or prison to another). First of all, there are never as many officers as there are prisoners, and the officers are perpetually in danger of being overwhelmed by superior numbers, if the inmates unite. And, then the prison officers "buy" themselves an hour or two of peace each day—there is in effect a rest period each afternoon (rest for the officers, that is)—when the inmates are allowed to go into their cells; the whole prison quiets down. The officers know perfectly well what is happening, that roughly half the inmate population submits to being raped.

To what extent are prison officers consciously aware that this is happening, and to what extent do some of them deliberately tolerate these patterns of behavior? All prison officers must be aware of the patterns of prison rape because prisons are small, enclosed communities, and officers form a tightly cohesive clique (of necessity and for their own protection, since those who are not part of that clique do not long survive) so that anything that one officer knows, all know. On the other hand, they are not all equally supportive of the maintenance of this social system; indeed, many are appalled by it. Unfortunately, however, those who disapprove of it cannot stop it, since it is just as dangerous ("suicidal" is perhaps not too strong a word) for an officer to violate the unwritten code of the officers' subculture as it is for an inmate to violate the corresponding (and virtually identical) code of the inmates' subculture—the first principle of which for both is, "Thou shalt not snitch."

I am far from alone in reaching these conclusions. In 1937, Haywood Patterson, chief defendant in the famous Scottsboro rape case, wrote about these behaviors as he observed them at Alabama's Atmore State Prison. In his autobiography, *Scottsboro Boy,*[3] he said that homosexual rape was not only tolerated but actually encouraged by prison authorities, primarily because "it helped them control the men. Especially the tough ones they called devils. They believed that if a devil had a galboy [a sex slave] he would be quiet. He would be a good worker and he wouldn't kill guards and prisoners and try to escape. He would be like a settled married man." He stated that the most valued galboy was a young teenager. "A fifteen-year-old stood no chance at Atmore," he wrote. "I've seen young boys stand up and fight for hours for their rights. Some wouldn't give up"—though eventually they would be overpowered, or lose consciousness. He reported that both prisoners and security guards would watch the assaults with impassive interest. "They knew a young woman was being born. Some just looked forward to using her a little later themselves." Once they were symbolically—socially and psychologically—emasculated in this way, the newly created "galboys" were combination prostitutes and slaves, who could and would be bought and sold by their various pimps, masters, or owners. With reference to the extent of this form of sexual enslavement, Patterson remarked that "I once heard Deputy Warden Lige Lambert tell some state patrolmen that fifty percent of the Negro prisoners in Atmore were galboys—and seventy percent of the white."

Wilbert Rideau, who is himself an inmate at the Angola State Penitentiary in Louisiana, reports that

officers there were equally aware of what was going on. These staff members "used to perform prison marriages in which the convict and his galboy-wife would leap over the broomstick together in a mock ceremony."[4]

In his report on sexual violence among the youngsters in Connecticut's juvenile institutions, Anthony Scacco[5] charged that the "administration knows who the victims and aggressors are, and in many instances, the guards are directly responsible for fostering sexual aggression within the institution." Davis's[6] study of the Philadelphia jail system revealed that many security guards discouraged complaints of sexual assault, indicating that they didn't want to be bothered; and Dinitz, Miller, and Bartollas,[7] in another study of prison rape, charged that "some guards will barter their weaker and younger charges to favored inmates in return for inmate cooperation in keeping the prison under control."

Of course, the active and passive collusion of prison officers and other officials in the vicarious utilization of rape and rapists as a collateral, unofficial supplement to the publicly acknowledged repertoire of punishments that the prison system metes out to inmates does not have to be as overt as these examples suggest, or as overt as the Nazis' delegation of authority to the kapos in the concentration camps, in order to be just as effective in accomplishing the same result. As C. Paul Phelps, the Louisiana Secretary of Correction (and former warden of Angola), shrewdly observed, "Anytime . . . a high level of homosexual rapes and enslavement is taking place, there has to be a tacit trade-off between the inmate power structure and the administration."[8] Most of the trade-off, he says, generally takes place on the lower level of the administration:

> When it gets down to the lower level, it's usually an agreement between the inmates and security officers, and the agreement doesn't have to be verbal. Much of the communication between inmates and between staff and inmates is on the nonverbal level. They have their own peculiar method of communicating what they want to say without really saying it, and each understands exactly what the other is saying. It's probably the most sophisticated nonverbal system of communication ever invented in the world.[9]

Thus, prison officers may "play dumb" when one inmate requests to be put in a cell with another whom he can sexually dominate and exploit; they would purchase peace in the cellblock rather than protect the more submissive inmate from rape. But this purchases a relative degree of peace only for the officers, not for the inmates. There is almost universal agreement that one of the major causes of the violence of inmates toward each other—some would say the major cause—is sexual relationships among inmates.[10] Men will fight—often to the death—both in order to commit rape and to avoid being raped; in order to win one "galboy" from another inmate; because of sexual jealousy; in order to prove that they are "real" men and not homosexuals (as those terms are defined in that macho, homophobic subculture); and because the whole system is so degrading, shameful, and humiliating, so damaging to their self-esteem and so destructive of their sense of masculine sexual adequacy and identity; and finally, because some literally go insane, developing paranoid delusions and hallucinations in response to the continual onslaught to their sense of who they are (i.e., whether they are men), and what, if anything, they are worth. That these patterns of violence follow them onto the street, when they are eventually released from prison, goes without saying.

Nevertheless, prison officers have a vested interest in maintaining the system of prison rape because it deflects the violence of the inmates away from the officers and onto each other. As Wilbert Rideau observed at Angola:

> The . . . natural inclination of the institutional security force is to be tolerant of any type of situation that divides the prisoners into predators and prey, with one group of prisoners oppressing another because such a situation prevents the development of any unity among prisoners that could tear down the institution. A "homosexual" jungle-like state of affairs is perfect for that purpose. It's another, perhaps the most effective, means of control.[11]

Of course, it is also true that rape is not the only means by which this goal can be accomplished; it can also be accomplished by dividing the prisoners along racial lines. Dr. Frank L. Rundle, who has served as the chief psychiatrist of the 2,200-man California Training Facility at Soledad, and also as director of

psychiatry of the Prison Services for all of the correctional institutions, both adult and juvenile, of New York City, observed that the readiness of prison officials to utilize any means to divide inmates from each other went so far as to lead the California prison system to encourage the division of inmates into gangs whose members were selected by race. "The whole system is set up in such a way as to, if not overtly, at least covertly, encourage racial war."[12]

Now, however, I want to return to the symbolism of punishment, as revealed by the phenomenon of rape in prison. The term "rape" is customarily applied to the sexual coercion of a female. The Federal Bureau of Investigation defines the crime of rape as: "the carnal knowledge of a female forcibly and against her will"[13]—a formulation that, in effect, defines the phenomenon of male rape out of existence. Those attitudes toward men and women, from which the definition of rape derives, may teach us something about the symbolism of rape. For this definition implies that to be raped is to be treated as a female. Thus, it is no wonder that rape victims in prison are called "galboys," "whores," and "wives," and that men who have been raped almost universally report that they feel emasculated, castrated, and deprived of their masculinity.

The phenomenon of male rape may be far more common than is revealed by any of the conventional statistics on rape. For reasons I have already indicated, rapes in prison are almost never reported, either to the prison authorities or to the district attorneys in the outside world, and are prosecuted only in the rarest and most extreme cases. For example, in an exhaustive investigation of "Sexual Assault in the Philadelphia Prison System and Sheriff's Vans" by the police department and the district attorney's office, in which more than 3,000 prisoners and 500 staff members were interviewed, the Chief Assistant District Attorney, Allan Davis, after hearing repeated accounts of "brutal gang rapes and victimization of young, inexperienced inmates," concluded that sexual violence was "epidemic." Still, he found that only about three percent of the estimated 1,000 sexual assaults, per year, that he uncovered in the Philadelphia jails alone, were ever reported to his office.[14]

And yet, as I have indicated, the rape of males is one of the most widespread—indeed, virtually universal—features of the penal system as I have observed it, and as many others have confirmed. The findings are legion. I will cite some examples: when the Texas Department of Correction became the subject of an investigation, hearings, and a trial, the federal judge in the case, William W. Justice, determined as a "finding of fact" that the brutalization of inmates by other inmates, including forced coercive sexual assault (rape, by any other name), was a "routine" feature of that penal system.[15]

Another court-ordered investigation of conditions of one Florida prison in 1980 found that

assaults, rapes, robberies, shootings, and stabbings were commonplace even in high-confinement, lockdown areas. So prevalent was the issue of sexual assault that one correction officer quoted in a report to a state legislator said that a young inmate's chances of avoiding rape were "almost zero. . . . He'll get raped within the first twenty-four to forty-eight hours. That's almost standard."[16]

Similarly, in a Pulitzer Prize-winning investigation, Loretta Tofani[17] noted that despite an official figure of less than ten rapes per year among male inmates, on-the-record interviews with ten guards, sixty inmates, and one jail worker indicated that there were "approximately a dozen incidents a week" (or more than 600 per year) in the Prince George County Detention Center alone.

In 1968, mass rapes were admitted to be "routine occurrences at Cook County Jail," in Chicago, by officials of the jail themselves. Dr. Anthony M. Scacco, Jr., a criminologist formerly with the Connecticut Department of Correction, reported that rape and other sexual violence was rampant in juvenile and young-adult institutions in that state. Dr. Frank L. Rundle, of the California Training Facility at Soledad, concluded that rape and other sexual violence is universal in the nation's prisons: "I think that that same picture is true of any prison. It's not just Angola or San Quentin or Soledad. It is a feature of prison life everywhere." The director of security at the Angola State Penitentiary, in Louisiana, estimated that "about seven out of ten inmates here [are] now participating or have participated in homosexual activities at one time or another during their confinement." And, as already stated, most of that behavior cannot be considered "volun-

tary" in any meaningful or legitimate sense, given the atmosphere of threat, danger, and coercion in which it occurs. As C. Paul Phelps, the Louisiana Secretary of Correction, observed, "While the initial rape-emasculation might have been effected by physical force, the ensuing sexual acts are generally done with the galboy's 'consent' and 'cooperation.' "[18]

There are close to two million men in the various penal facilities of this country on any given day, roughly half of whom have already been tried, convicted, and sentenced, while the other half are awaiting trial. And since the turnover of those awaiting trial and those sentenced to short-term incarceration is especially high, the total number of men in custody for at least part of the year, in any one year, comes to more than ten million, with a near equal number released back into our communities.[19]

If any substantial portion of these men are forced to submit to rape, then the number of men who are raped on any given day in America's jails and prisons is astronomical. One investigator estimated some ten years ago, when the total population of the incarcerated was less than half of today's level, that the number was as high as "eighteen adult males raped every minute" of every day.[20] A moment's calculation reveals that that may not be a farfetched figure, particularly with today's even higher rates of incarceration: 18 per minute means roughly 1,000 per hour, 24,000 per day, 168,000 per week, or just under 9,000,000 rapes per year. Even assuming for a moment that the true percentage of those who are raped is below 50 percent; even if some more conservative figure, such as 25 percent, or even 10 percent, is more accurate, the fact remains that most of those who are raped are raped not just once every six weeks, but rather, several times a week (both by their "old man," the rapist to whom they are forced to submit as if they were his "wife," and by those other inmates to whom their "old man" forces them to submit, in exchange for the money or other rewards from those to whom he makes his "whore" available). There is the additional fact that many of those who are raped at the beginning of their sentences, or while they are in short-term incarceration, are gang-raped, so that each incident of rape may incorporate ten or twelve or fourteen individual acts of rape,[21] which would suggest that the figure of 9,000,000 male rapes a year may be, if not conservative, at least not wildly exaggerated. But let us suppose, for the sake of being as conservative as possible, that even that estimate is exaggerated by a factor of ten. That would still leave a total figure of 900,000 (or nearly one million) male rapes a year—as an integral part of the punishment to which prisoners are subjected in the prisons and jails of this country each year.

Is even a figure of ten percent too high? Donald Cotton and Nicholas Groth[22] observed that any "available statistics must be regarded as very conservative at best, since discovery and documentation of this behavior are compromised by the nature of prison conditions, inmate codes and subculture, and staff attitudes." Given that important caveat, with its implication that every estimate is likely to be a significant underestimate, we might note that Daniel Lockwood[23] concluded that 28 percent of the prisoners in one New York state prison had been targets of sexual aggression at least once, and that 20 percent had been targeted more than once. Peter L. Nacci and Thomas Kane[24] estimated that nine percent of state prison inmates nationwide had been "targets" of sexual assault, and Clemens Bartollas and Christopher Sieverdes[25] came up with that same percentage among the children who were inmates of juvenile correctional facilities in the southeastern United States. Even Wilbert Rideau has pointed out that "most of the sexual violence occurring not only in Louisiana but across the nation takes place in the . . . county jails, which act as a sieve filtering the strong from the weak and producing the sexual slaves long before they reach the penitentiaries."[26] Thus, the number of incidents of acts of coercive sex, or forcible rape, may be only a fraction of the actual number of sex acts that are participated in because of a realistic awareness that the only alternative is to be seriously injured, mutilated, gang-raped, or killed. One can only comment that rape by any other name is still as coerced and degrading.

Beyond the question of the frequency or quantity of male rape in prisons, the full extent of which is impossible to measure accurately for all the reasons mentioned, we need to consider its nature—the degree of violence and injury it inflicts, and the symbolic message that it communicates. The mere knowledge that one could become a victim of such atrocities can be enough to have a powerful and destructive impact on the entire population living in an environment in which such acts occur, and in which all are potentially vulnerable. And, lest the reader wonder if my examples of sexual exploitation in prison are drawn only from an atypical prison system, let me quote from another observer's account, that of Dr. Anthony Scacco, Jr.:

> *Many cases could be cited of actual rape of an individual in jail, but one in particular is chosen to let the reader hear the events from an ordinary citizen. He is married with a family, no previous criminal record, and a former Georgia legislator and businessman who found himself the victim of a jail situation. William Laite was indicted and convicted in Texas of perjury relating to a contract he had with the Federal Administration Housing Authority. He was sentenced to the Terrant County Jail in Fort Worth, Texas. The moment he entered the tank, or day room, he was approached by five men. The first comment from one of them was, "I wonder if he has any guts, we'll find out tonight, won't we? Reckon what her name is; she looks ready for about six or eight inches. You figure she will make us fight for it, or is she going to give up to us nice and sweet like a good little girl? Naw, we'll have to work her over first, but hell, that's half the fun, isn't it?" "I couldn't move," said Laite. "I was terrified. This couldn't be real. This couldn't be happening to me." Laite was saved from sexual assault when a seventeen-year-old youth was admitted to the day room as he was about to become the victim of the five men in the tank. The men saw the boy and turned on him, knocked him out, and then, "they were on him at once like jackals, ripping the coveralls off his limp body. Then as I watched in frozen fascination and horror, they sexually assaulted him, savagely and brutally like starving animals after a raw piece of meat. Then I knew what they meant about giving me six or eight inches."*

Laite was shocked by the unconcern shown by the guards. He stated that the "guards were protected from the violent prisoners, but I, an inmate myself, was not. The guards never made an attempt to discipline the prisoners. In fact, I suspected that they might pass the time of day watching the fights and sexual activities from some secluded location."[27]

James Dunn,[28] an inmate at Angola, in Louisiana, has described how he first became a sex slave there. At the age of nineteen, he received a three-year sentence for burglary (a nonviolent crime, it should be emphasized, since it involved only the stealing of property, not physical injury to human bodies).

> *During my first week here, I saw fourteen guys rape one youngster 'cause he refused to submit. They snatched him up, took him into the TV room, and, man, they did everything to him—I mean, everything, and they wouldn't even use no grease. When they finished with him, he had to be taken to the hospital where they had to sew him back up; then they had to take him to the nuthouse at Jackson 'cause he cracked up.*

Three weeks later, Dunn himself

> *received a call to go to the library, where an inmate shoved me into a dark room where his partner was waiting. They beat me up and raped me. That was to claim me. . . . When they finished, they told me that I was for them, then went out and told everyone else that they had claimed me.*

Dunn recalls his reaction as being "one of fear, of wanting to survive. Once it happened, that was it—unless you killed one of them, and I was short [i.e., had a short sentence] and wanted to go home. So I decided I'd try to make the best of it." Because of his memory of the scene of gang rape that he had witnessed, he did not fight back against his own double rape: "Man, I didn't want none of that kind of action, and my only protection was in sticking with my old man, the guy who raped me." As a result, Dunn had to act as his rapist's "wife" or "slave" doing "whatever the hell he wanted me to do"—wash his old man's clothing, make the beds, prepare meals, and generally do all of the menial things that needed doing.

Wilbert Rideau has commented that "few female rape victims in society must repay their rapist for the violence he inflicted upon them by devoting their existence to servicing his every need for years after—but rape victims in the world of prison must."[29] While that may be true for some female victims of rape, one can readily think of at least two situations in which that is not the case—and here I am thinking of battered wives trapped in a vicious cycle of domestic assault, and of girls who are the victims of incest, both

of which are instances of sexually assaulted females who may have to live with their rapists or assaulters, and serve their needs for an ongoing, indefinitely prolonged duration. Those who have worked with victims of incest and with women who have had battering spouses and boyfriends have commented that one of the most stressful aspects of these women's trauma is that they were forced to live with their assaulter and to be at his mercy on a daily basis. That work is highly instructive to those of us who are working with men and boys in penal facilities who are forced to live with their assaulters and to be at their mercy; this is the sort of traumatization which is an intrinsic part of the legal "punishment" meted out by our criminal "justice" system.

What motivates a man to commit rape in the prisons? What does a man hope to accomplish by it? Obviously, rape is intended to be a humiliating, shameful, dishonoring, traumatizing, and violent act. In the prisons, it is quite clear that the act of inflicting humiliation on the rape victim has to do with the transferring of the rapist's fears of personal and sexual inadequacy and impotence onto that of the rape victim, the one who is to be emasculated, reduced, undone, and "turned out"—recast into a "woman." Here again, the work of Wilbert Rideau is highly instructive. Rideau has written probably the closest thing we have to a definitive study of rape in prison. He says that

> *The act of rape in the ultramasculine world of prison constitutes the ultimate humiliation visited upon a male, the forcing of him to assume the role of a woman. It is not sexual and not really regarded as "rape" in the same sense that society regards the term. In fact, it isn't even referred to as "rape." In the Louisiana penal system, both prisoners and personnel generally refer to the act as "turning out," a nonsexual description that reveals the nonsexual ritualistic nature of what is really an act of conquest and emasculation, stripping the male victim of his status as a "man." The act redefines him as a "female" in this perverse subculture, and he must assume that role as the "property" of his conqueror . . . [who] arranged his emasculation. He becomes a slave in the fullest sense of the term.[30]*

One could spend a great deal of time working with this passage of Rideau's, especially if we bear in mind that the prisons are not only a laboratory for the study of violence, but a subterranean index of much of what is both expressed in our wider culture, and, at the same time, buried deep within the collective unconscious of patriarchal culture. Any reader of Rideau cannot fail to see both the deep misogyny and the misanthropy, which is the subtext of prison life, a text which invariably, inevitably accompanies the rampant fear on the part of these men (perhaps most men?) of being shamed by being seen as less than a "man." If for these men, to be "turned out," or turned "into" a "woman" is the ultimate denigration, consummated through an act of rape, then this may tell us something about the patriarchal legacy and making of "manhood" which is at the heart of "civilization" as we have known it, with all its violence between men; its class structure and racial prejudice; and its asymmetrical treatment of women and men.

Another account, this one by Colonel Walter Pence, chief of security at a State Penitentiary at Angola, picks up on the point I am making:

> Rape in prison is rarely a sexual act, but one of violence, politics, and an acting out of power roles. Most of your homosexual rape is a macho thing. It's basically one guy saying to another: "I'm a better man than you and I'm gonna turn you out to prove it." I've investigated about a hundred cases personally, and I've not seen one that's just an act of passion. It's definitely a macho/power thing among the inmates. And it's the basically insecure prisoners who do it.[31]

But "insecure" in what way, about what? Wilbert Rideau answers:

> Man's greatest pain, whether in life or in prison, is the sense of personal insignificance, of being helpless and of no real value as a person, an individual—a man. Imprisoned and left without any voice in or control over the things that affect him, his personal desires and feelings regarded with gracious indifference, and treated at best like a child and at worst like an animal by those having control of his life, a prisoner leads a life of acute deprivation and insignificance. The psychological pain involved in such an existence creates an urgent and terrible need for reinforcement of his sense of manhood and personal worth. Unfortunately, prison deprives those locked within of the normal avenues of pursuing gratification of their needs and

> leaves them no instruments but sex, violence, and conquest to validate their sense of manhood and individual worth.[32]

Or as C. Paul Phelps put it when he was secretary of the Louisiana Department of Corrections, "Sex and power go hand in hand in prison. Deprived of the normal avenues, there are very few ways in prison for a man to show how powerful he is—and the best way to do so is for one to have a slave, another who is in total submission to him."[33]

To understand the psychology and symbolism of punishment, and how it mirrors that of "crime," we need to ask: "What emotional gratification are people seeking when they advocate punishing other people harshly, as opposed to quarantining them in order to restrain them?" I am suggesting that the motives behind crime and punishment are identical: that the greatest fear in each instance is that of being shamed or laughed at; that the subsequent wish or need to dominate and humiliate others is in the service of gaining a swelled sense of pride and power by having dominion over others, including the power to inflict pain on them, punish them, and "give them what they deserve."

This is why the psychology and symbolism of punishment is a mirror of the psychology and symbolism of crime. How could it be otherwise, given that punishment has always been consciously intended to mirror crime ("an eye for an eye," etc.)? Namely, a defense against the fear of being shamed or laughed at, and the positive attainment of feelings of pride, even honor. For example, I vividly recall the comments of a prosecutor who expressed his outrage and chagrin at the fact that one defendant he had prosecuted had been found "not guilty by reason of insanity." The defendant had broken into a priest's house, tied him up, brutally tortured and mutilated him, and blinded him. The prosecutor was in no way appeased or relieved that the defendant was likely to spend the rest of his life in a prison mental hospital. Instead, what mattered to him was that this defendant might be "laughing up his sleeve" at all the legal authorities whom he had "fooled" (and thus "made a fool of") by "deceiving" the court into thinking that he was mad rather than bad.

Not long ago, an "op-ed" piece in the *New York Times*[34] revealed similar feelings—the use of punishment by prison as a defense against the fear of being laughed at and treated with contempt (that is to say, shamed). In this article, the author, Andrew Vachss, who also happened to be an attorney, asserted that "predatory sexual psychopaths" are "monsters" who "lack empathy for other people" and are "narcissistic; *they laugh behind their masks at our attempts* to understand and rehabilitate them. *We have earned their contempt* by our belief that they can change. . . .'"—all of which was part of his argument as to why we should not waste time trying to understand them, or to facilitate their (nonexistent) capacity to change, but should instead lock them up and throw away the key.

I would agree with many of Vachss' points. These men are indeed "narcissistic," but I would stress that that is precisely why they feel the need to commit the very crimes that so appall us—they themselves are afraid of being laughed at and being treated with contempt. Those fears are precisely what motivate sadism—both the sexual psychopaths' sadism toward their victims, and the sadism of many of us toward sexual psychopaths, for whom "no punishment can possibly be too severe."

Two further comments: The ambiguity and imprecision of the word "narcissistic" often leads to confusion and misunderstanding, just as it did in this article, in which the author was unable to see that the criminal's tendency to "laugh" at other people and hold them in contempt was not based on feelings of superiority but rather on its opposite, on feelings of inferiority, of fearing that others would find him ridiculous and contemptible. Attitudes such as arrogance, superiority, and self-importance, to which the term "narcissism" is often attached, and which are so often misunderstood to be the genuine attitudes of the people who hold them, are actually defenses against, or attempts to ward off or undo, the opposite set of feelings: namely, underlying feelings of personal insignificance and worthlessness.

I would agree with the author that sadistic sexual psychopaths are "lacking in empathy" for other people, but I would also want to observe that that is no reason for us to lack empathy for them. A lack of empathy sets anyone on the path to violence. Finally, I would agree with the author of this article that some men (a few, but they do exist) are so badly damaged that it is

unclear whether they can ever change, and are so dangerous to others that I too see no alternative but to "quarantine" them for the foreseeable future. But what is the emotion—the motive—that leads us to see other people as "monsters" rather than as damaged human beings, and to see the attempt to understand them rather than punish them as a waste of time? Interestingly, the motive behind such punitive attitudes turns out to be identical to the motive behind the very crimes that many of us are eager to punish—namely, the fear that one will be laughed at, held in contempt, or made a fool of (i.e., shamed), unless one is sufficiently sadistic. For the most direct way to prevent someone from laughing at you is to make them cry instead, and the most direct way to make them cry is to inflict pain upon them—and "pain," as I said, is what "punishment" means (for both derive from *poena,* the Latin word for pain).

What are the broader implications of this analysis of the symbolism of the violence that is inflicted in the name of justice, rationality, and the law? Punishment is a *form* of violence in its own right—albeit a legally sanctioned form—but it is also a cause of violence, as it stimulates the very same illegal violence that it is ostensibly intended to inhibit or prevent.

The importance of that fact would be hard to exaggerate. Punishment is almost universally rationalized as a means of preventing violence; elections to political office in America are increasingly becoming contests as to which of the candidates is "tougher" on crime. But the conclusion that my analysis leads to is that punishment does not inhibit or prevent crime and violence, it does not lower the rate or frequency of acts of violence. Punishment stimulates violence; punishment causes it. The more punitive our society has become, the higher our rate of violence (both criminal and noncriminal) has become. But if punishment increases the rate of crime and violence, rather than decreasing it, then why do people who say they want to "fight" crime, advocate increasing the amount of punishment that we impose on criminals? The causes of violence are the same, whether the violence is legal punishment or illegal crime, and the symbolism of both forms of violence is identical. Throughout history, the legal system has been as intent on cutting out or otherwise destroying, damaging, despoiling, or dishonoring people's eyes, tongues, genitals, and other body parts—as have criminals. The purpose of both forms of violence—crime and punishment—is the same: to restore justice to the world by replacing shame with pride. And the means by which that is accomplished is the same. The very same acts of violence and mutilation (by which one prevents one's victim from shaming oneself further) serve to shame one's victim, which accomplishes the purpose of transferring one's own shame onto one's victim; for it is shameful to suffer violence (regardless of whether it is called crime or punishment), just as it is a source of pride and honor to be the one who dispenses violence to others.

Finally, I want to ask: What is it about our social class system that holds in place a self-defeating policy of increasingly violent punishment, when we have clearly demonstrated that such policies stimulate violence? A society's prisons serve as a key for understanding the larger society as a whole. One can use the prison system as a magnifying glass through which one might see what is otherwise less easily discernible in the culture—underlying patterns of motivation, symbolization, and social structure that determine the life of the community as a whole. From this perspective, it is worth noting that the rulers of any society, just like the prison guards, have an interest in pursuing the strategies I described earlier: "You scratch my back and I'll scratch yours" and "Divide and conquer." This is accomplished in the macrocosm of society just as it is in the microcosm of the prison, by lulling the middle class into accepting its subordination to, and exploitation by, the upper class, by giving the middle class a class subordinate to itself (the lower class) which it can exploit, and to whom it can feel superior, thus distracting the middle class from the resentment it might otherwise feel and express toward the upper class. The subordinate classes (middle and lower) are divided into predator and prey, respectively, and are more likely to fight against each other than against the ruling class, which makes them easier for the ruling class to control. (E.g., middle class voters are angrier at "welfare queens" than they are at members of the Forbes 400—whom they rather tend to admire, and would like to emulate.)

But how are the members of the lower class set against each other, rather than against the two classes above them who reserve most of the wealth and privileges of society for themselves? In the same way the prison system is ruled, namely, by dividing the citizenry into predators and prey—by dividing the lower class into criminals and victims. It is not in the vested interests of the ruling class to pursue those social policies that would cut down on crime; on the contrary, it is in their interest to keep the crime rate as high as possible. The ruling class (all of whom are white, in America) is responsible, in large part, for the way in which we, as a community, have chosen to distribute our collective wealth (since they, or those who represent their interests, write the laws that constitute those choices), which is in turn responsible for the social inequities that lead to crime and violence. At the same time, it is the ruling class that wages the so-called "war on crime," which is really a war on the poor. . . . Both the perpetrators and the victims of criminal violence are disproportionately the very poor. The kinds of assaults that the very poor suffer from the "criminals" among them (rape, murder, and assault and robbery) are so direct, palpable, and visible, so physically painful, so impossible to ignore, so life-threatening and lethal, that they inevitably distract the very poor from noticing or fighting the more hidden, disguised assaults they suffer from the class system itself. As Representative Charles Schumer recently pointed out, it is in the political interest of the party that represents the interests of the very rich to foster as high a rate of crime as possible; and even to exaggerate what the crime rate is, to foment fear and panic about violent crime far beyond what is realistically appropriate, and so on. For the more that people are worried about crime and violence, the more the middle class will focus its anger and fear on the poor and members of certain minority groups (for most of the violence that is labeled as "crime" is committed by people from those groups); the nonviolent and noncriminal poor will be angry at those other poor people who are violent criminals; and both those classes will be too distracted by their anger at the lower-class criminals to notice that they have much better reasons to be angry at the very rich, and the party that represents the interests of the rich, than at all the violent criminals put together. Ironically, when crime is at its maximum, the party of the rich can even represent itself as the savior of everybody, by promising to "get tough on crime" and by declaring its war on crime (which, as I said, is really a war on the poor—that social class which is seen, in this mystification, as being the ultimate source of most crime and violence), thus distracting attention from the fact that the ultimate source of most crime and violence is actually the upper class—or rather, the class system.

Thus, it is not surprising at all—indeed, it is only to be expected—that those who identify with the interests of the ruling class would be likely to pursue those policies that lead to an increase in the rate of what is legally defined as crime and violence. Such policies include the following:

1. Punishing more and more people (criminals) more and more harshly, by means of more and harsher prisons, capital punishment, and so on. Nothing stimulates crime as powerfully and as effectively as punishment does (since punishment stimulates shame and diminishes guilt, and shame stimulates violence, especially when it is not inhibited by guilt).

2. Outlawing those drugs that inhibit violence (such as marijuana and heroin), while legalizing and advertising those that stimulate violence and cause physical injury and death (such as alcohol and tobacco); and criminalizing those drugs that have no demonstrable direct (pharmacological) effect on violent behavior (such as cocaine), thus spending billions of taxpayers' dollars to stimulate crime and violence by providing an enormous publicly funded subsidy for those organized crime groups who profit from the fact that the smaller the supply of these drugs, the higher their price; and then misinforming the public about the relationship between drugs, crime, and violence, as though crime and violence were caused by illicit drugs (which they are not) rather than by enormously profitable legal drugs such as alcohol (the one drug which has been shown to stimulate violence), all of which distracts the public from noticing that the real cause of violence is not drugs: The real cause of violence is the "war on drugs" (and the social and economic inequities which the "war on drugs" is designed to distract attention from).

3. Manipulating the tax laws and other economic policies so as to increase the disparity in income and wealth between the rich and the poor, for that also stimulates crime and violence, by maximizing the degree to which the poor are subjected to experiences and feelings of being shamed, humiliated, and made to feel inferior.

4. Depriving the poor of access to education (especially if they are in prison), for nothing decreases the rate of crime and violence as powerfully and effectively as does education. We know that the single most effective factor which reduces the rate of recidivism in the prison population is education, and yet education in the prisons is the first item to be cut when an administration "gets tough on crime." Educational achievement provides prisoners in need of rehabilitation with a nonviolent source of self-esteem or pride; it protects them against the vulnerability to shame, and the injuries of structural violence (poverty) that motivate criminal violence.

5. Perpetuating the caste divisions of society that usually fall along racial lines. The poor and members of minority racial and ethnic groups are regularly subjected to maximal degrees of shame, humiliation, and feelings of inferiority by being told that they are innately and inherently stupid and intellectually inferior; that is then turned into a self-fulfilling prophecy by depriving them of the education they would need in order to develop their actual intellectual potential.

6. Exposing the public to entertainment that glorifies violence and holds it out as a source of pride, honor, and masculine self-esteem.

7. Making lethal weapons easily available to the general public.

8. Maximizing the polarization and asymmetry of the social roles of men and women. Nothing stimulates crime and violence more than the division of males and females into the roles of violence object and sex object, respectively.

9. Encouraging the prejudice against homosexuality, by striving to keep homosexuals out of the military, and from positions of leadership within religious institutions. Nothing stimulates violence more powerfully and effectively than homophobia, just as nothing would prevent it more effectively than a more relaxed, tolerant, and respectful attitude toward homosexuality (but what would the raison d'être of the military be without violence?).

10. Perpetuating and legitimizing the exposure of children and youth to violence such as corporal discipline in school and at home, injuries that would be considered assault and battery if inflicted on those who are more mature, and yet are regularly declared legitimate by our highest courts.

11. Regulating the economy so as to ensure that unemployment will never be abolished or even fall below a high enough minimum.

If these are the policies of the white ruling class—then what will we have achieved? We will have attained what we see all around us in America today—a society characterized by three complementary and mutually reinforcing characteristics: 1) the richest and most powerful, secure, and invulnerable upper class in the world; 2) a middle class in collusion with the upper class, yet itself exploited by the latter; and 3) an underclass that commits a higher degree of violence than exists in any other developed nation on earth, with violence committed primarily by the poor against the poor.

Isn't it remarkable how much the social structure of our society as a whole resembles the social structure of the prison, as this analysis of rape in prison reveals it?

These are among the things that the study of the prison system may have to teach us about society as a whole. By applying the patterns of manipulation and control that are easily visible in prisons to the corresponding but more skillfully disguised patterns that exist in the community at large, we can see things about our society that might not otherwise be as obvious.

ENDNOTES

1. I am not alone in reaching this conclusion. Gresham Sykes, in his classic monograph, *The Society of Captives: A Study of a Maximum Security Prison* (Princeton: Princeton University Press, 1958, pp. 70–72), has commented that "the inmate . . . is figuratively castrated by his involuntary celibacy. . . . the psychological problems created by the lack of heterosexual relationships can be even more serious" than the physiological ones associated with castration. For "a society composed exclusively of men tends to generate anxieties in its members concerning their masculinity regardless of whether or not they are coerced, bribed, or seduced into an overt homosexual liaison. . . . an essential component of a man's self conception—his status of male—is called into question." And if the foundation upon which a prisoner's self-concept and self-esteem is built includes as a central component his sense of heterosexuality (as the great majority of men's does, from about the age of three onwards), and they do go on to experience homosexual acts, whether voluntarily or involuntarily, "the psychological onslaughts on his ego image will be particularly acute." But even when sex with men is not part of the prisoner's experience, "the deprivation of heterosexual relationships carries with it another threat to the prisoner's image of himself. . . . The inmate is shut off from the world of women. . . . Like most men, the inmate must search for his identity not simply within himself but also in the picture of himself which he finds reflected in the eyes of others; and since a significant half of his audience is denied him [i.e., the female half], the inmate's self image is in danger of becoming half complete, fractured. . . ." That is, his sense of himself as a man, and a sexually adequate one at that, cannot be reinforced, under conditions of heterosexual deprivation, by its reflection in the eyes of a woman with whom he is sexually involved; so it is no wonder that men in that condition are vulnerable to feelings of having been functionally and symbolically castrated, or emasculated, or transformed into homosexuals.

Since men who are predisposed to committing violence are those who doubt their sexual adequacy in the first place (violence being the ultimate last-resort defense against feelings of masculine sexual inadequacy, when all else fails—the ultimate way to "prove," both to others and to oneself, that one is a man, and not "a wimp, a punk, or a pussy"), the effect of this symbolic castration on the population of violent men is to intensify their violence even further—with effects that are catastrophic, both in prison and after these men return to the community. Thus, to the list of the many ways in which prisons and punishment only endanger the public rather than making it safer, and only stimulate violent crime rather than inhibiting or preventing it, must be added the almost universal American policy of refusing to allow prisoners to have conjugal visits from their wives or lovers.

2. I do not mean to suggest, of course, that all men in prison share a heterosexual orientation. But even gay men are not immune to prison violence; in fact, if they are perceived to be homosexual, they are likely to be even more at risk.

3. Haywood Patterson and Earl Conrad, *Scottsboro Boy* (Garden City, N.Y.: Doubleday, 1950). In Wilbert Rideau

and Ron Wikberg, *Life Sentences: Rage and Survival Behind Bars* (New York, N.Y.: Times Books, 1992), pp. 89–90.
4. Rideau, *ibid.,* p. 90.
5. Anthony M. Scacco, Jr., *Rape in Prison* (Springfield, IL: Charles C. Thomas), 1975.
6. Allan J. Davis, "Sexual assaults in the Philadelphia prison system and sheriff's vans," *TransAction,* Dec. 1968, pp. 8–16.
7. C. Bartollas, S. J. Miller, and S. Dinitz, *Juvenile Victimization: The Institutional Paradox* (Beverly Hills: Sage Publications), 1976.
8. C. Paul Phelps. In Rideau, op. cit., p. 86.
9. Rideau, op. cit., p. 86.
10. Much of this evidence is summarized in Robert W. Dumond, "The sexual assault of male inmates in incarcerated settings," *International Journal of the Sociology of Law,* 20:135–157, 1992, pp. 146–47. S. F. Sylvester, J. H. Reed, and D. Nelson, in their study of *Prison Homicides* (N.Y.: Spectrum Publications, 1977), concluded that sexual assault was the leading motive of inmate murders in American prisons. When E. Herrick analyzed prison violence for *Corrections Compendium* ("The Surprising Direction of Violence in Prison," *14*(6):1–17, 1989), he found that the state of Arkansas reported the highest number of assaults on staff by inmates of any correctional system in the United States (1,113 in 1988); and they identified conflicts over sexual relations as the single biggest cause of violence. Hans Toch, in *Police, Prisons and the Problems of Violence* (Washington, D.C.: National Institute of Mental Health, U.S. Government Printing Office, 1977), also concluded that conflicts over sex and sexual assault in prison are a major cause of inmate violence.
11. Rideau, op. cit., p. 88.
12. Rideau, op. cit., p. 88.
13. *Uniform Crime Reports 1988: Crime in the United States* (Washington, D.C.: Federal Bureau of Investigation, U.S. Department of Justice, U.S. Government Printing Office, 1989), p. 15.
14. Davis, op. cit.
15. *Ruiz* v. *Estelle,* 503 F. Supp. 1265, U.S. District Court.
16. Lerner, Steven, "Rule of the cruel," *Corrections,* Vol. 3, Article No. 38, 1987, Boca Raton, FL: Social Issues Resources Series. In Robert W. Dumond, op. cit., p. 136.
17. Loretta Tofani, "Rape in the county jail," *The Washington Post* (Sept. 26–28, 1982). In Dumond, op. cit.
18. All the quotations in this paragraph are from Rideau, op. cit., p. 85.
19. Testimony of Dr. Carl C. Bell, Chairman of the National Commission on Correctional Health Care, before the Appropriations Committee of the U.S. House of Representatives, Subcommittee on Labor, Health and Human Sciences, Education, and Related Agencies, Washington, D.C., April 28, 1992. In *CorrectCare,* 6(2):1, 1992.
20. Steven Donaldson, "Rape of males: A preliminary look at the scope of the problem," unpublished dissertation, 1984. In Dumond, op. cit.
21. Peter L. Nacci and Thomas Kane, for example, found that *36 percent* of the sexual assaults in prison that their informants described were *gang rapes* (multiple perpetrators against a single victim); see "Sex and sexual aggression in federal prisons," *Progress Reports* (Washington, D.C., U.S. Department of Justice, Federal Bureau of Prisons, June 1982), p. 10.
22. Donald Cotton and Nicholas Groth, "Inmate rape: prevention and intervention," *Journal of Prison and Jail Health,* 2(1):47–57, 1984.
23. Daniel Lockwood, *Sexual Aggression Among Male Prisoners* (Ann Arbor, MI: University Microfilms), 1978.
24. Peter L. Nacci and Thomas Kane, "The Incidence of sex and sexual aggression in federal prisons," *Federal Probation,* 47(4):31–36, 1983.
25. Clemens Bartollas and Christopher Sieverdes, "The sexual victim in a coeducational juvenile correctional institution," *The Prison Journal, 58*(1):80–90, 1983.
26. Rideau, op. cit., p. 90.
27. Dr. Anthony Scacco, Jr., op. cit. In Rideau, op. cit., pp. 91–2.
28. Rideau, ibid., p. 77.
29. Ibid., p. 75.
30. Ibid., p. 75.
31. Ibid., p. 75.
32. Ibid., p. 74.
33. Ibid., p. 75.
34. Andrew Vachss, "Sex predators can't be saved," *New York Times,* Jan. 5, 1993. (Emphases added.)

STUDY QUESTIONS FOR READING 23

1. It has been said that holding prisons responsible for inmate violence is like holding cops responsible for the crimes of the robbers. How does Gilligan respond to this charge?

2. According to Gilligan, does heterosexual deprivation itself lead directly to increased levels of violence—in the prison and upon release? Why or why not?

3. What did a prison administrator tell Gilligan about the number of inmates who avoided regular sexual encounters with other men? How did the prison administrator know?

4. Gilligan once believed that "consensual" sex between inmates was fine, since no conjugal visits are allowed. Why does he now disagree?

5. How does Gilligan feel about stable prison "marriages"? As he discusses much later in the reading, how are these relationships like marriages that involve battering and incest within families?

6. Rape is not a legal form of punishment. Why then does Gilligan refer to it as an intrinsic and universal part of the punishment that our government metes out to those whom it labels as "criminals"?

7. How does Jeffrey L.'s story demonstrate Gilligan's point about the "consensual" nature of prison sexual relationships?

8. Line officers tolerate and permit these sexual relationships for two reasons. Explain each carefully.

9. In Gilligan's view, prison sex doesn't make prisons less violent. How does it change the violence in prison? Explain.

10. What does the very definition of rape show us about how men feel when raped?

11. Why does Warden Phelps say inmates rape each other?

12. Why does Gilligan argue that a lack of empathy in criminals is no reason for us to lack empathy toward them? What is the most direct way of keeping someone from laughing at us? What is the emotion, or motive, that leads us to see other people as "monsters" or incorrigibles, who we should not only incapacitate but punish?

13. Why does Gilligan say that punishment—a form of violence—is rationalized as preventing violence, but actually stimulates it?

14. According to Gilligan, guards control the prison by using the "you scratch my back" and "divide and conquer" methods of management. Describe how Gilligan argues that this works for the upper, middle, and lower classes of society, and for the officers and inmates Levinson referred to as the "heavies" and the "lights."

15. According to Gilligan, what policies will stimulate crime?

16. What are the three key results of policies such as these?

17. Gilligan's thinking closely mirrors the thinking of the author of which earlier reading in the book? How?

18. Dostoevsky said, "You can judge the civilization of a society by the conditions of the prisons." He was writing at the time of the Gulag in the Soviet Union. Why does Gilligan think these words make a sad commentary on our civilization?

"CHEMICAL SHACKLES" AS A CONTROL MECHANISM

VICTOR HASSINE, INMATE AM4737

I met Chaser in 1984, my fourth year at Graterford, when he first arrived to serve time on a robbery conviction. I can still remember the frightened look on his face that first day. As I was adapting to the rapidly changing rules and conditions of a prison in total meltdown, Chaser became the beneficiary of my hard-learned lessons on inmate survival. We managed to forge a mutual friendship.

Many outsiders who have met Chaser would comment, "He doesn't look like he belongs in here." I've heard this often when people encounter an inmate who doesn't have some grotesque feature that neatly fits their preconceived notion of the "criminal look." Experience has taught me that the less an inmate appears like a criminal, the more likely he is to be particularly vicious and unrepentant. Criminals who look like criminals keep people on guard; the honest-looking ones put them at ease, which allows them the greater advantage of misjudgment. But in Chaser's case they were right. He didn't belong in prison, let alone deserve to become a victim of the system.

I did my best to look after my friend until, about nine months later, he was transferred to the Rockview facility. This was a relief for me, since protecting a naive and scared young man from the predators at Graterford was no easy task.

Once he was transferred, I quickly forgot about Chaser. Frankly, it is nearly impossible for me to remember all the people that have come in and out of my life, especially nowadays with the influx of so many frightened young kids. Almost all my relations with fellow inmates today are superficial, as prison life becomes more and more a case of every man for himself.

What Chaser and I didn't know at the time was that prison administrators were feverishly trying to figure out how to stop the imminent collapse of Graterford and other overcrowded prisons. With thousands of new, young Chasers coming in, it was becoming more impossible to feed, house, and clothe them all, let alone rehabilitate them. More importantly to officials, an increasing number of guards and staff were becoming victims of inmate attacks. As employee safety was their first priority, the administrators realized that something had to be done to shore up the cracks in Graterford's foundation—and it had to be quick, cheap, and effective. But Chaser and I never concerned ourselves with the administration's problems. After all, we had swag men to deal with and predators to avoid.

In 1990, as I made my way to chow at Rockview, I ran into Chaser again. He was walking out of the dining hall's special section reserved for the "nuts" whom the administration referred to euphemistically as "special-needs inmates." Chaser walked sluggishly with a disheveled, glassy-eyed appearance. In short, he *looked* like one of the nuts.

"Chaser, is that you?" I asked.

"Hey, Vic," he replied, "I've got to talk to you. It's real important. Meet me in the yard."

That evening in the yard, my old friend explained to me how he had returned to the streets two years earlier, only to lose his wife and son, develop a voracious drug habit, and end up committing burglaries to support his habit.

I was unmoved by Chaser's story, since almost every returning con I've ever met recounts a similar tale of woe. All I wanted to know was why he was on the nut block and why he was taking "brake fluid" [prescribed psychotropic medication]. It was obvious because of his very slow, disjointed movement and his shakes. Another alarming clue was the noticeable scars on his wrists from razor cuts.

Chaser described how his return to prison had exposed him to the "medicate-and-forget-them" system of modern prison maintenance. This new system of mind-altering and mood-altering psychotropic drugs was rapidly becoming the prison administration's "quick, cheap, and effective" solution to warehousing masses of inmates into smaller spaces, while using fewer and fewer support services.

The reasoning seemed to be that every dose of medication taken by an inmate equaled one less fraction of a guard needed to watch that inmate, and one less inmate who may pose a threat to anyone other than himself. Hence, overcrowding had brought about a merging of the psychiatric and corrections communities. The effect on inmates can be best described by Chaser during this 1994 interview.

INTERVIEW WITH CHASER: A MEDICATION ADDICT

"The first time [I came to prison] I was terrified because I didn't know what to expect and I knew no one. I was awkward and didn't know my way around. I had not acquired a prison or inmate mentality. The second time I was much more at ease because I knew a lot of people still in prison and I knew what to expect. I had also learned quite fast how to become as comfortable as possible. I had to take a lot of psychotropic drugs to achieve this comfortable state of mind. . . .

"In November of 1989, after telling the shrink in the county prison that I wished I was dead, I was unknowingly given Sinequan which knocked me out for three days. But since I was in a special quiet section of the jail, I continued the medication, because to me it was better than being in population. . . .

"I think the biggest difference between street drugs and psychotropic drugs is that street drugs give me some kind of feeling of well-being, high, confidence, euphoria, and contentment. But psychotropic

drugs cause all feeling to cease. It stops self-awareness and sucks the soul out of a man. It slows or stops a man from striving to better himself and he stops caring about everything. It also creates total laziness. That laziness becomes his entire attitude and also is 100-percent habit-forming. . . .

"After almost three months at the county prison in Philly, I was sent to Graterford to start my four-to-ten-year sentence. I had abruptly stopped taking the Sinequan and felt totally disoriented. I lasted three weeks in population. Looking for drugs, I ended up taking another inmate's Thorazine at times. I was out of control and all I could think of or look forward to was getting stoned.

"One day I got very drunk and went into a blackout and refused to lock up. Four guards carried me to a room and I was put into restraints. I was given nine months in the Hole. I did five at Graterford and was sent to Rockview to complete it. . . .

"[Getting medication in Rockview] was quite easy. I said I wished I was dead, which was the same thing I said in the county. Every week the shrink would ask, 'How do you feel now?' All I had to do was say, 'Bad,' and ask for more or different meds. I always got what I asked for, as long as I told them I thought of killing myself. . . . I took Sinequan, Melloril, Elavil, Klonopin, first separately, while always asking for Valium. Then in desperation, I mixed the medications and the dosages. The ultimate effect was total numbness. My body was numb. My feelings were numb, and then my mind was numb. I did not care what happened to me and just stopped thinking about anything. . . .

"While taking the meds, I was put on a special block and given a single cell. I got only a reprimand at misconduct hearings and did not have to go to work. I felt I was being placated and given special attention and I liked that. But when I stopped taking the meds, I was shook down [cell-searched] a lot and went to the Hole if I was ever given a misconduct. Once in the Hole, I would say I wish I was dead, and again they'd give me medication. . . .

"I admitted to staff many times that I had a severe drug addiction and that I had an abusive personality. I tried numerous times to get in the drug-therapy groups and on the D and A [Drug and Alcohol] Blocks. I was refused and ignored every time. . . .

"I lost all sense of dignity and self-worth. I had no pride. I lost all interest in the outside world and eventually did not care if I ever returned to it. All I knew or cared about was what times I went to get my fix and hurried to be first in line. I constantly had the shakes and inner tremors. My speech was slurred and slowed, and so was my thinking. I could not think ahead. I was like a small child only looking for instant gratification. My entire metabolism changed, and I gained a lot of weight fast. It damaged my memory, even to this day . . .

"Since I was under constant supervision and being evaluated once or twice a month, pre-release and parole became much harder to obtain. So for the luxury of being comfortable and in a fantasy world, I had to abandon the idea of early release or furloughs. Since my number-one priority was no longer a goal, it became easy for me to forget or stop striving for what was once important to me. The side effects of the medication, such as tremors and shakes, made it impossible for me to get and keep a job. Education, reading, learning, and working to strengthen my mind became things of the past. Giving up became repetitious and habit-forming (not unlike street drugs) and eventually I lost and gave up my self-respect, dignity, and morals until my only interest in life was getting in line three times a day to receive my medication.

"I had given up on all these things, and I woke up one day and realized I was a very sad man. But I was willing to give up on life, because the medications I was taking made me think I was comfortable. . . . I had given up on Chaser. . . .

"I was seeing a shrink two times a week because I was depressed. I was not diagnosed as having any kind of mental illness or chemical imbalance, but despite that I was taking large dosages of Thorazine, Sinequan, Lithium, Elavil, and Melloril. I took them at 7 a.m., 11 a.m., 4 p.m., 8 p.m. . . .

"One night just before lockup, I got another misconduct. I didn't care if I went to the Hole or got cell restriction. What concerned me was that the administration might possibly take away my medication. So after weighing my options, it seemed only logical to kill myself, or at the least, give that appearance. I opened my window, pressed my wrists against the frozen bars, then took an old razor and opened my wrists. I figured that, if I died, that would be fine. But, if I lived, I would definitely get more medication, and that thought satisfied me. I lived this madness and insanity for well over a year, until I ran into you. You offered me your time and energy to explain to me what I was doing to myself and what I was becoming. Within six months, I was totally off the special-needs block and off 99 percent of the medication and my will to live and succeed returned . . . with a vengeance. I never needed the medications for my depressed condition. I just needed someone to say they cared. I needed a friend. I got both from you. I owe you my life, not the prison, and not the medication. . . .

"I have been medication-free for two years now and, although I'm usually uncomfortable with prison conditions, I can look in the mirror and see Chaser looking back with a smile. So to me, giving up the medication was a small price to pay to be myself again.

"[Psychotropic medication] is one of the easiest things to get in prison. It is easier to go to the shrink and ask for 500 mg of Thorazine than it is to get on the phone or get a pass to the Chapel. If a guy goes to the doc saying he feels depressed, violent, or suicidal, the doc will give him one of numerous medications. He is usually given a choice. All the medications are geared to slow a man down or fog his thinking so bad he can't think of why he's depressed, violent, or suicidal. This will continue for years, as long as he says he needs the medications to a staff person once a month. . . .

"I'd say 40 percent of the population here is taking some form of psychotropic medication. They are treated less harshly than those unmedicated. They are seen and talked to by staff much more often than those not on medications. They are given special consideration at misconduct hearings. They are permitted to come in from night yard earlier than the other inmates and, in a lot of cases, are given a single cell. When it comes to working, someone on psychotropic medication can usually pick whatever job he says he can handle. On the other hand, most of us were not required to work at all. . . .

"I believe that, when a guard or any staff member puts on a uniform, they know it stands for authority. So they demand respect and control. When someone rebels or stands up to them, they feel their authority and control is threatened and they take steps to eliminate the rebellion. They put on the appearance of power, so they act cold, mean, negative, and harsh to display this power.

"Now when a guy is on medication, the threat is almost nonexistent. They [the staff] feel safe and secure with the men that are medicated. So the use of force and display of power is not necessary, and they act more leniently to the medicated inmate. They treat these men like children. To staff, a medicated inmate is a controlled inmate and not a threat to them. . . .

"[If all inmates were required to take psychotropic drugs], I would be shocked and scared. It would be like they were turning the prison into a brainwashing institution. I would think they had lost all control and were attempting to gain it back by stopping our wills and brains from functioning properly. I believe they are headed in that direction because of how easy the medications are to get and how many people are taking them. . . .

"I think that, as the prison populations continue to grow and grow, and a younger and more violent crowd comes in, it will become harder and harder for the administration to control all the blocks. I think they are now learning that the best way to control inmates or pacify them is to totally medicate them. It may even become a reward system."

PSYCHOTROPIC DRUGS

Psychotropic drugs are nothing new to the psychiatric community, which has been using them on the mentally ill for years. However, its use in corrections as a population-management tool and behavior modifier is relatively new. The effects of prolonged use of such medication on an ever growing number of inmates are unknown.

Just from the increasing size of medication lines and the growing number of inmates doing the brake-fluid shuffle, I have observed that psychotropic medications (also known as "chemical shackles") are defining the behavior of an increasing percentage of inmates in the general population.

As politicians and bureaucrats continue to debate the loftier issues facing the criminal justice system, the mother of invention has required front-line prison administrators to quickly implement any practice that might help them to keep their prisons intact and functioning. The practice of medicating inmates is rising fast up the ranks of prison-administration hierarchies, since it has proven to be a relatively inexpensive and efficient prison-control tool. The two governing estates of custody and treatment are being pushed aside by the rising third estate of psychiatric medication.

A bureaucratic system that subdues whole populations with drugs must certainly give us pause. The wisdom of turning means into ultimate ends in this way needs to be questioned. Today in prison, I find myself longing for any glimpse of an attempt to rehabilitate, not because I believe in rehabilitation but because I worry about a society that no longer bothers to consider its possibility.

In my opinion, today's prison managers are only interested in their ability to contain an ever-increasing number of people for an ever-longer period of time. Since there is only so much that can be done in terms of cell and prison design, the search for solutions has focused not on changing the nature of prisons but on changing the nature of prisoners. With medication, breaking down a man's mind is much easier and more economical than breaking ground on a new institution. Besides, if a prison system only has to develop a more cost-efficient way to create a better inmate rather than a better citizen, who would really know the difference? Who would really care?

As of this interview, Chaser has been off medication for about two years. He has successfully gone through drug-rehabilitation therapy and is soon due for release. Once released, he will join a growing number of mind-altered men who are leaving prison and entering the mainstream of society. Only time will tell whether chemically treated inmates do in fact make acceptable citizens. But, if you ask me, we should go back to trying to build a better mousetrap and, for God's sake, leave the mice alone.

STUDY QUESTIONS FOR READING 24_____

Editor's Note: It is not known how often inmates take psychotropic drugs. In one study of more than 3,000 female and 14,000 male inmates, women were on psychotropic drugs almost twice as often as men (16 percent *v.* 9 percent), and this difference held even when various explanatory factors were accounted for (see Morash, Haarr, and Rucker, "A Comparison of Programming for Women and Men in U.S. Prisons in the 1980s," *Crime and Delinquency, 40*(2), April 1994, 197–221).

1. What are some examples of psychotropic drugs?

2. According to the research cited above, how common is the use of psychotropic drugs? Is the use of these drugs expected to rise or fall?

3. What was Chaser's "tale of woe," and why didn't Victor Hassine care about it?

4. How could Hassine tell Chaser was on psychotropic medication?

5. What is the "medicate-and-forget-them" system of prison management? Why is it increasingly popular?

6. How did Chaser get his medications?

7. What does Chaser say happened when he repeatedly admitted to staff that he had a severe drug addiction and an abusive personality and wanted to get into drug-therapy groups?

8. Chaser tried to kill himself when he was taken to the Hole. Why?

9. Chaser was addicted to psychotropic drugs for over a year. What does he say he really needed?

10. According to Chaser, how easy is it to get psychotropic drugs in prison?

11. According to Chaser, how does taking psychotropic drugs change the way the staff treats an inmate?

12. To staff, a medicated inmate is what kind of inmate? As a result, inmates call psychotropic drugs what?

CHANGES IN PRISON CULTURE: PRISON GANGS AND THE CASE OF THE "PEPSI GENERATION"

GEOFFREY HUNT, STEPHANIE RIEGAL, TOMAS MORALES, AND DAN WALDORF

. . .

Prison authorities see gangs as highly undesirable and have argued that an increase in extortion, intimidation, violence, and drug trafficking can be directly attributed to their rise. In responding to prison gangs, the California Department of Corrections (CDC) introduced a number of strategies and policies, for example, using "confidential informants," segregating gang members in different buildings and prisons, intercepting gang communications, setting up task forces to monitor and track gang members, locking up gang leaders in high security prisons, and "locking down" entire institutions. These changes were perceived by our respondents who saw the CDC as increasingly tightening its control over the prison system and the gangs.

PRISON GUARDS

In spite of the "official" view that gangs should be eradicated, many prison authorities hold a more pragmatic view and feel that the gangs have "had little negative impact on the regular running of prison operations" (Camp and Camp 1985:xii). Moreover, as Cummins (1991) has noted, there is often a considerable discrepancy between the official stance and what takes place within particular prisons. This point was emphasized by our respondents who portrayed guards' attitudes toward the gangs as complex and devious, and saw the guards as often accepting prison gangs and in some cases even en-

couraging them. In supporting this view, they gave three reasons why guards would allow gangs to develop or continue.

First, some noted guards' financial incentive to encourage gang behavior. They suggested that guards are keen to create "threats to security" which necessitate increased surveillance and, consequently, lead to overtime work.

> *They have a financial interest in getting overtime. . . . Anything that was "security" meant that there were no restrictions in the budget. So if there are gangs, and there are associations, if there is some threat in that focus of security, they make more money (Case 17).*

Others went even further and told us that some guards benefited from gangs' illegal activities.

> *Well, you know the guards, aren't . . . you'd be surprised who the guards affiliated with. Guards have friends that's in there. They have their friends outside, you know. Guards'll bring drugs in. Sell 'em. Guards will bring knives in, weapons, food. The guards play a major role (Case 7).*

Not only were guards involved in illegal activities, but the practice was often overlooked by other guards. For example, as one respondent philosophically replied in answer to our question: "Were individual guards involved in illegal gang activities?"

> *Well, I think you have guards that are human beings that . . . don't really want to do more than they have to. So if they see a guard doing something a little*

shady, it's easy to turn a blind eye because of the hassle it would take to pursue it (Case 16).

Finally, in addition to these financial incentives, some believed that guards encouraged gang activities and conflict in order to control the prison inmates more effectively and "keep the peace out of prisons" (Case 32).

> *They perpetuated the friction because, for instance, what they would do is . . . give false information to different groups. . . . Something to put the fear so that then the Latino would prepare himself for a conflict. . . . And so everybody's on point and the next thing you know a fight would break out and the shit would come down. So it was to their interest to perpetuate division amongst the inmates so that they would be able to better control the institution. Because if you are spending your time fighting each other you have no time . . . to fight the establishment (Case 34).*

This divide and rule policy was emphasized by many of our respondents and was seen as a major contributory factor in prisoner conflicts.

JACKETING AND THE USE OF CONFIDENTIAL INFORMANTS

According to our respondents, another prison administration tactic was "jacketing"—officially noting in a prisoner's file that he was a suspected gang member. Once identified as a gang member, a prisoner could be transferred to a high security prison or placed in a special housing unit. "Jacketing," which is similar to the "dirty jacket" procedure outlined by Davidson (1974), was seen by our respondents as a particularly arbitrary process and one in which the prisoner had little or no recourse.

> *Like I said, if you're a sympathizer you could be easily jacketed as a gang member. You hang around with 'em. You might not do nothing. But hang out with 'em. Drive iron with 'em. Go to lunch with 'em (Case 1).*

Many respondents felt the process was particularly unfair because it meant that a prisoner could be identified as gang member and "jacketed" purely on the basis of information from a confidential informant.

Confidential informants or "snitches" supplied intelligence information to prison authorities about inmate activities, especially gang-related activities.

> *Now let's say you and I are both inmates at San Quentin. And your cellie gets in a fight and gets stabbed. So all of a sudden, the Chicano who is a friend of your cellie says that he'll get the boys and deal with this. They talk about it but nothing happens. All of a sudden one of the snitches or rats, says I think something is cooking, and people are going to make a move to the administration. What will happen is that they [the administration] will gaffel up you and me and whoever else you associate with and put us all on a bus straight to Pelican Bay. They will say we have confidential reliable information that you guys are planning an assault on Billy Bob or his gang. . . . And you're wondering, you've never received a disciplinary infraction. But by God now, information is in your central file that you are gang affiliated, that you're involved in gang violence (Case 16).*

Our respondents distinguished between two types of snitching—dry and hard.

> *Dry snitching is a guy who will have a conversation with a guard and the guard is just smart enough. He'll say you talk to Joe, don't ya? You say, oh, yeah, Joe's a pretty good ol' boy, I heard he's doing drugs but don't believe it. He might smoke a few joints on the yard, but nothing hard. He just dry snitched. He indirectly dropped a lug on Joe. And then you got the guy who gets himself in a jam and goes out and points out other inmates (Case 16).*

Dry snitching could also refer to a prisoner supplying general information to guards without implicating anyone by name. This allowed the prisoner to develop a "juice card" or a form of credit with the guard.

> *A "juice card" is that you have juice [credit] with a particular guard, a lieutenant, a sergeant or somebody that is part of staff. . . . Let's say that somebody is dry snitching. By dry snitching I mean that they might come up to their juice man that has a "juice card," let's just say it is a sergeant of the yard, and they might go up there and say, "Hey I hear that there is a rumble coming down. I can't tell you more than that but some shit is going to come down tonight." So they alert the sergeant right. The sergeant tells him, "I owe you*

one." *Now the guy might come up to the sergeant and say, "Hey remember you owe me one, hey I got this 115 [infraction] squash it. "Okay I will squash it." That is the "juice card" (Case 34).*

Many of our respondents felt there was a growing number of snitches (also see Stojkovic 1986). A key factor promoting this growth was the pressure exerted by the guards—a point denied by the prison authorities in Stojkovic's research.

Pressure could be applied in a number of ways. First, if for example a prisoner was in a high security unit, he often found himself unable to get out unless he "debriefed"; i.e., provided information on other gang members. Many respondents felt that this was an impossible situation because if they didn't snitch their chances of getting out were minimal. As one respondent remarked:

They [the guards] wanted some information on other people. . . . So I was put between a rock and a hard place. So I decided I would rather do extra time, than ending up saying something I would later regret (Case 10).

Second, if the guards knew that a prisoner was an ex-gang member, they might threaten to send him to a particular prison, where he would be attacked by his own ex-gang.

See there is a lot of guys in there that are drop outs from whatever gang they were in, and they are afraid to be sent to a joint where some other tip might be. They even get threatened by staff that if they don't co-operate with them they will be sent to either Tracy, or Soledad and they are liable to get hit by their own ex-gang, so they cooperate (Case 40).

However, it would be inaccurate to suggest respondents accused only the prison authorities, since many also pointed out other developments within the prison system, and especially within the prison population, to explain what they described as a deteriorating situation.

. . .

REFERENCES

California Department of Corrections. 1991. Historical Trends: Institution and Parole Population, 1970–1990. Offender Information Services Branch. Data Analysis Unit. Sacramento.

Camp, George, M., and Camille G. Camp. 1985. Prison Gangs: Their Extent, Nature and Impact on Prisons. U.S. Department of Justice, Office of Legal Policy, Federal Justice Research program. Washington, D.C.

Cummins, Eric. 1991. "History of gang development in California prisons." Unpublished paper.

Davidson, R. Theodore. 1974. Chicano Prisoners: The Key to San Quentin. Prospect Heights, Ill.: Waveland Press, Inc.

Stojkovic, Stan. 1986. "Social bases of power and control mechanisms among correctional administrators in a prison organization." Journal of Criminal Justice 14:157–166.

STUDY QUESTIONS FOR READING 25

1. In the earlier reading by Gilligan, a psychiatrist at Soledad prison said that the California system encouraged the division of inmates into racially divided gangs: "The whole system is set up in such a way as to, if not overtly, at least covertly encourage racial war." In contrast, what is the "official view" about prison gangs as discussed here? Do all prison authorities hold this view? How do you know?

2. The authors of this reading interviewed a snowball sample of ex-inmates from the California system. These inmates say that some officers may accept and even encourage prison gangs for three reasons. What are these reasons?

3. What is "jacketing"? How can it cause an inmate to be sent to a control unit, such as Pelican Bay in California?

4. In fairness, the released inmates interviewed in this reading gave several other reasons for the growth of prison gangs. What were they?

CONTROL UNITS AS A CONTROL MECHANISM

FAY DOWKER
GLENN GOOD

INTRODUCTION

The term "control unit" was first coined at United States Penitentiary (USP) at Marion, Illinois in 1972 and it has come to designate a prison, or part of a prison, that operates under a "super-maximum security" regime. Control unit prisons may differ from each other in some details but all share certain defining features:

1. *Prisoners in a control unit are kept in solitary confinement in tiny cells (6' by 8' is common) for between 22 and 23 hours a day. There are few, if any, work opportunities, no congregate exercise, and no congregate religious services.*

2. *These conditions exist permanently (temporary lockdowns occur at almost every prison) and as official policy.*

3. *The conditions are officially justified not as punishment for prisoners but as an administrative measure. Prisoners are placed in control units in administrative moves and since there are no rules governing such moves (in contrast to punitive moves), prisoners are denied any due process and prison officials can incarcerate any prisoner in a control unit for as long as they choose, without having to give any reason.[1]*

The authors are members of the Committee to End the Marion Lockdown. They would like to thank all the prisoners who have provided information on control units. They welcome comments on this article as well as more information or inquiries concerning control units. Please write c/o CEML, P.O. Box 578172, Chicago, Illinois 60657-8172.

This article is structured as follows. The first section will begin with a discussion on the imminent replacement of Marion by a new, purpose-built control unit prison in Florence, Colorado. The second section will document the proliferation of control units, modeled on Marion, in state prison systems across the country. In the third section, we will analyze the function of control units, contrasting the official claims with the facts. In the fourth section, we broaden the analysis to look at imprisonment in the United States as a whole, and we draw conclusions as to the true purpose of prisons. The fifth section describes the state of public opinion on issues regarding prisons, and the role of the media in shaping and maintaining that opinion. The last section is a brief summary.

MARION TO BE REPLACED BY FLORENCE

USP-Marion was not originally built as a control unit prison. It has thus been inadequate for the task of implementing the even tighter control of prisoners which Bureau of Prisons (BOP) Director, J. Michael Quinlan, in testimony before a Congressional subcommittee in the fall of 1989, said would constitute an improvement upon Marion's existing regimen (Lehman 1990:36–7).

The BOP has decided to replace Marion with a control unit prison in Florence, Colorado, specifically designed to achieve this goal. Scheduled to open in 1993, the prison's state-of-the-art technology will help to eliminate even the minimal levels of human contact

223

prisoners have at Marion. It has proved very difficult to find out exact details of the new control unit prison to be built at Florence. When a Freedom of Information Act request for information on plans for Florence was submitted to the BOP, the BOP denied the request on the basis that the plans did not yet exist.[2] If that is the case, then the local newspapers appear to know more about the new prison than its designers. The following information comes from such newspapers (Miniclier 1991:A1; O'Keefe 1991; Chronis 1990:B1; Harmon 1991:B2; Associated Press 1990; Ritter 1991:13).

The Marion replacement is one of a complex of four federal prisons being built just south of Florence. The control unit will house 550 prisoners and it is designed so that one guard will be able to control the movements of numerous prisoners in several cell-blocks by way of electronic doors, cameras, and audio equipment. "We'll be able to electronically open a cell door, shut it behind the inmate and move him through a series of sliding doors," according to Russ Martin, project manager for the Florence prison. Prisoners will be even more restricted than at Marion, according to the Pueblo, Colorado *Chieftain:* "Inmates won't have to travel nearly as far in the new Florence prison." At Marion, the prisoners can at least shout to each other through their bars. At Florence, solid cell doors will make that difficult or impossible, and there will be no windows in the cells.[3]

Just five miles from the prison site, in Lincoln Park, is the Cotter Corporation, a uranium milling company owned by Commonwealth Edison of Chicago, Illinois. The area surrounding the mill and nearby railroad has been extensively contaminated with radioactivity. Uranium tailings dumped in unlined ponds have poisoned the underground aquifer and the nearby Arkansas River. Dried radioactive dust is carried for miles by the high winds.The contamination of the water alone has caused the Lincoln Park area to be on the Environmental Protection Agency National Priorities List since 1984, and it has been designated a Superfund site for contamination clean-up (O'Keefe 1991:10).

The political landscape around Florence is equally bleak. Florence is in Fremont County where more than one in ten of the work force is employed by the Colorado Department of Corrections in the nine prisons clustered around Canon City (ibid.: 10). Prisoners constitute more than ten percent of the population of the county (Miniclier 1991:A1).

Florence itself is an economically devastated community of 3,000 where unemployment stands at seventeen percent and the prospect of about 1,000 temporary and 750–900 new permanent jobs has proved irresistible. Ninety-seven percent of respondents to one local mail-in poll were in favor of the building of the Florence complex. The citizens raised $160,000 to purchase the 600 acres for the site; 400 locals gathered for the ground-breaking; t-shirts bearing a map of the site were "sold out" at $7.99; a housewarming barbecue, hosted by the BOP, was attended by 1,000 local residents. Now, Pueblo Community College is offering criminal justice courses customized to suit the needs of the federal prison.

PROLIFERATION OF CONTROL UNITS

The model for the new control unit at Florence is the Security Housing Unit (SHU) at Pelican Bay State Prison in California (Wilson 1991:2). The SHU, which opened in December 1989, was designed as the ultimate facility for the implementation of Marion-style repression. Built to hold 1,056 prisoners in near-total isolation, it is already 20% over capacity (Smith 1991:1). Prisoners are confined to their 8' by 10' cells with solid steel doors for 22.5 hours a day. They are allowed out only for a ninety minute "exercise" period alone in an empty concrete yard the size of 3 cells with 20' high walls and metal screens overhead. Guards open the sliding doors by remote control, and they use loudspeakers to direct the prisoners in and out. Prisoners, moved off the cell-block for any reason, are shackled and flanked by two guards wielding truncheons. Except for the sound of a door slamming or a voice on a speaker, the SHU is silent. Prison officials, not the courts, "sentence" prisoners to SHU terms (Corwin 1990:A1). Often, confidential tips from other prisoners serve as the basis for a disciplinary hearing to determine whether to send the prisoner to the SHU, and these hearings have few safeguards of due process. Many prisoners are sent there for filing grievances, lawsuits, or for otherwise opposing prison injustices (Weinstein 1990). SHU prisoners report the use of "hog-tying" (the intertwining of handcuffs and ankle-cuffs on a prisoner), "cock-fights" in which guards double-cell enemies or otherwise allow them to attack each other, and forced cell moves using Taser stun-guns, 38 mm guns, and batons.[4]

Conditions, such as those at the SHU and Marion, are replicated in state control units throughout the country. Many of these prisons feature their own innovations in controlling and dehumanizing prisoners. At a second California control unit prison at Corcoran, armed guards patrol the Plexiglas ceilings over the cells, and peer in at prisoners through Plexiglas cell walls (Wilson 1991:2). At Colorado's Centennial Prison in Canon City, the administrative segregation unit has been expanded to include the whole prison (Foster 1990; Ruark 1991). A priest hired by the prison delivers communion through a small, knee-high food slot in a solid steel cell door. "If you ain't wrapped too tight, 23-hour lockdown can be enough to make you explode," says the priest. Guards are armed with "nut-guns," wide-bore guns that fire wildly caroming, acorn-sized "nuts" at prisoners from close range. "It's a miniature cannon," the priest explains. "The recommended technique is to fire at the floor so that the acorn ricochets." Prisoners hit by the nuts can be maimed. "One guy lost his eye, and since I arrived here three years ago, an acorn took off a guy's nose and plastered it to his cheek" (Johnson 1990:12). A specially constructed, $44 million control unit prison, scheduled to be opened near Canon City in early 1993, will hold 500 prisoners, with an additional 250 capacity expansion part of the prison's design (Lemons 1991).

At Lebanon, Ohio, prisoners under administrative control are held in 8′ by 6′ isolation cells. Each cell has a second door so that prisoners can be locked in the extreme back, darkened portion of the cell. A prisoner describes being leg-shackled, having his arms cuffed to a belt about his waist, and being escorted by three guards whenever he is moved from his cell. Other prisoners are forbidden to speak to him (Perotti 1991).

In Missouri, the state prison at Potosi is run by Warden Paul K. Delo, a Vietnam War veteran who, by Missouri law, doubles as the state's executioner since Death Row is at Potosi. Says Delo of his secondary duties, "One of our officers had an analogy. He said it's just like at your own house. Nobody likes to take out the garbage, but somebody has to" (Uhlenbrock 1991:1). Perhaps inspired by Delo's army experience, prison officials apply the "double-litter restraint" to recalcitrant prisoners. The prisoner's hands are cuffed behind his back; his ankles are cuffed; and he is forced to lie face-down on an Army-type cot, his head turned to the side. A second cot is then tightly strapped upside-down over the prisoner and the ends are strapped shut, totally enclosing and immobilizing him. Carl Swope, a 21-year-old sentenced to 7 years for credit card fraud, filed suit after being held in the restraint for three hours (Bryant 1991:A3).

Other state control unit prisons are at Ionia, Michigan; Southport, New York; McAlester, Oklahoma; Baltimore, Maryland; Florence, Arizona (Jacobson 1991:A3); Starke, Florida; Walla Walla, Washington; Westville, Indiana (*Associated Press* 1991a); and Trenton, New Jersey (Page 1991). A survey by BOP found that 36 states now operate some form of super-maximum security prison or unit within a prison (Lassiter 1990:80). The list continues to grow. Colorado (Lemons 1991) and Connecticut (Cardaropoli 1991) have control unit prisons under construction, and Indiana is building a second control unit prison at Sullivan.

Control unit technology is even trickling down to the local level. The Jefferson County Detention Center in Colorado holds each prisoner in an 80-square-foot cell equipped with a concrete bed with a mattress on top, sink, toilet, and concrete table. Everything, from the lights to the locks on the doors, is operated electronically by guards in control booths. The jail was designed to allow for a range of control measures, including nearly round-the-clock cell confinement (McGraw 1986). New York City's Central Punitive Segregation Unit on Riker's Island holds 300 people under 21- to 23-hour-a-day lockdown with no television or radio. Most of those in the "Bing," as the unit is informally known, are detainees awaiting trial. The city plans to expand the unit to hold 900 (Raab 1991a:12).

Control unit prisoners have resisted the brutality they are subjected to with the means at their disposal.

Prisoners at the Pelican Bay SHU flooded the federal court with over 300 civil rights petitions, forcing an unusual meeting between federal judges and the prison's warden to discuss prison conditions. Lawyers for the prisoners have since filed a class action lawsuit charging, among other things, that the extreme isolation violates constitutional safeguards against cruel and unusual punishment (Mintz 1991). At Southport, New York, prisoners capped months of resistance by taking guards hostage and holding three of them for 26 hours until the prisoners' grievances were aired over local television (Raab 1991b).

Probably the most sustained resistance has occurred at the Maximum Control Complex (MCC) at Westville, Indiana, which opened in April, 1991. Sixteen of the 35 prisoners in the MCC launched a hunger strike in September to expose conditions in the prison: 23.5-hour daily cell time, extremely cold temperatures, denial of mail, constant bright lighting of the cells, and severely restricted visitation. The announced minimum stay in the unit is 3 years. Four of the prisoners continued the strike for 37 days, eating only after prison officials obtained a court order allowing them to force-feed the prisoners (Associated Press 1991b). The hunger strikes continued intermittently. One prisoner severed off his fingertip with a razor, and a second tried unsuccessfully to do the same. The protests garnered coverage in papers across the nation (Associated Press 1991c; 1991d). Prison officials responded by having guards brutally beat prisoners, sometimes while they were in shackles, assigning some of the prisoners to isolation where they are clothed only in their underwear and socks, and obstructing attempts by lawyers to gain entry (Carmody 1992).

THE FUNCTION OF CONTROL UNITS

To understand the reasons for the spread of control units, we must determine what function they serve, what it is that they achieve. We will examine what is claimed about control units by prison officials and compare those statements with what is known. We will analyze 3 specific claims repeatedly made by prison officials, all over the country, and reported in any media coverage of control unit issues:

1. Control units contain the most violent prisoners, the "worst of the worst," who have proved too violent to be held at other prisons.
2. Control units reduce violence at other prisons by isolating the most violent prisoners.
3. The reduction of violence allows security at these other prisons to be relaxed.

The first claim is the major one, on which the other two rest; so we will concentrate on it. The facts of Marion show that the claim is false. Federal prisons used to be given a security rating from 1 through 6, 1 being the least secure and 6 being the most secure. In 1984, Marion was the only level 6 prison in the federal system, and prisoners there were supposed to have a corresponding level 6 rating. However, a 1984 report by consultants hired by a congressional oversight committee stated that 80% of prisoners at Marion did not deserve that level of security according to BOP security and custody classification procedures (Breed and Ward 1985). In fact, prisoners are sent to Marion for a variety of reasons, and sometimes for no reason at all. For example, the US District Court ordered a cap on prisoner population and as a result, so many prisoners convicted of felonies in the District of Columbia have been moved to Marion to relieve overcrowding that they constituted 17% of Marion's population in 1990 (Lassiter 1990:80). Virtually all of these prisoners are Blacks.

There is, however, a trend to be seen. While many prisoners have been sent to Marion on accusations, and even conviction, of violent or escape related actions, many others have been transferred for initiating "too many" lawsuits, for protesting the brutality of the prison system, or for angering prison officials in some other way. In addition, among the many political prisoners who have been in Marion, American Indian Movement leader, Leonard Peltier; Sekou Odinga, member of the Black Liberation Army; Alan Berkman, Tim Blunk, and Ray Levasseur were sent directly to Marion from court (*Can't Jail The Spirit* 1989; O'Keefe 1991) thereby disproving the claim that prisoners at Marion have been violent at other prisons.

The Prison Discipline Study initiated in 1989 by the Prisoner Rights Union of Sacramento, California, investigated the question of which prisoners were most often disciplined and how (Prisoner's Rights Union 1991). The report showed that solitary confinement was the most common disciplinary action. Included in this report were testimonies by prisoners that prisoners exhibiting personal integrity are singled out for brutal treatment. Respondents to the survey described this group as: "those with principles or intelligence;" "those with dignity and self-respect;" "authors of truthful articles;" "motivated self-improvers;" those "verbally expressing . . . [their] opinion," "wanting to be treated as a human being," and/or "reporting conditions to people on the outside." The study shows, therefore, that a practice such as sending prisoners to control units, that is based on arbitrary and subjective judgments by guards and other officials, will target prisoners who are most likely to be challenging the prison system.

In fact, BOP rules for determining who gets sent to Marion are far broader than the "violent at other prisons" line given to the media. In the aforementioned "1 through 6" security-rating system, prisoners were assigned their security rating on a number of factors: Type of Detainers, Severity of Current Offense, Projected Length of Incarceration, Types of Prior Commitments, History of Escapes or Attempts, and History of Violence (Breed and Ward 1985:35). Although this rating system is obviously broader than the "violent" formula and open to a certain amount of interpretation, the finding that 4 out of 5 prisoners at Marion did not have the required level-6 rating meant the BOP had to find another, more vague system.Therefore, they have revised their rules, and now classify institutions as minimum, low, medium, and high security. Prisoners must be "high" security to be sent to Marion, which is determined by pre-commitment factors such as severity of offense. In addition, prisoners at Marion should have a "maximum" custody rating, that is determined by post-commitment criteria such as "disciplinary record" (Dove 1991). Having revised these rules, the BOP changed the classification of everyone at Marion to "high-max" (Dunne 1991).

It is admitted at the highest level that a prisoner's political beliefs are basis for assigning that prisoner to a control unit. In a letter to Congressperson Kasten-

meier, the then Chair of the Congressional subcommittee that oversees the BOP, Michael Quinlan, the Director of the BOP, stated: "A prisoner's past or present affiliation, association or membership in an organization which has been documented as being involved in acts of violence [or] attempts to disrupt . . . the government of the United States . . . is a factor considered in assessing the security needs of an inmate" (Quinlan 1987). We may ask what constitutes "association" with an organization, or what is meant by trying to "disrupt" the government.[5] In a case brought in Sacramento by a prisoner in the Security Housing Unit (SHU) at the California state prison, Chief Justice Karlton made it clear that prisoners are sent to the SHU for reasons that have nothing to do with discipline. He noted that the plaintiff, who was challenging the prison's forbidding him to practice his Native American religion, was in the SHU for being "an associate" of a prison gang, the Mexican Mafia, and that "given that [he] is in the SHU by virtue of his status rather than as punishment for a particular act, there is no apparent way for him to work his way out" (*Sample* v. *Borg*, 675 F.2d 574 [E. D. Cal. 1987]).

As a last point in our argument against the claim the Marion contains the "worst of the worst," we note that, for this to be true, all or most prisoners who satisfy their criteria must be at Marion. For example, Oscar Lopez Rivera, a Puerto Rican Nationalist, is in Marion for "conspiring to escape." Since he is there, then other prisoners who "conspire to escape" should be there as well as all the prisoners who actually try to escape, as well as all the prisoners who actually *do* escape and are apprehended. Are they? There are prisoners at Marion who have assaulted guards (not in itself an indication of anything negative, if the guard had been harassing and abusing the prisoner). Are all prisoners who have assaulted guards, or even killed guards, at Marion? Obviously the answer is no.

Finally, let us address the two other claims made by officials about control units. Prison officials claim that Marion, Pelican Bay, and the other control units reduce violence in the rest of the prison system. Since we have shown that the control units do not hold the most violent prisoners, this cannot be true, and there is no evidence that is has happened. Moreover, all the evidence points to the contrary. Most of the prisoners will, however, be released at some stage, either back into the general prison population or into society. It is known that control-unit conditions produce feelings of resentment, rage, and mental deterioration (Korn 1988). Prisoners will have been so deprived of human contact that it will be hard for them to cope with social situations again. The inhumanity of control units cannot reduce violence; it can only increase it. Evidence includes the high level of violence at Marion during the period before the lockdown, when controls were being tightened but not yet to the extent of complete physical incapacitation of the prisoners. The tighter controls certainly did not have a calming effect on the prison. In addition, the guard deaths of 1983 occurred in the Control Unit itself.

The claim that control units allow security to be loosened at other prisons is also invalidated because of the truth about which prisoners go there. And again, there is no evidence that the situation in other prisons has improved. Furthermore, Marion has been the model for the numerous state control units.[6] A delegation of the US House Subcommittee on Courts, Intellectual Property, and the Administration of Justice that visited Marion in May 1990, cited the need to "develop a more humane approach to the incarceration of the maximum-security prison population. This is particularly true because the Federal Bureau of Prisons serves as a model for state prisons and for other countries in the world" (Lassiter 1990:90). Incredibly, similarity to Marion is now a defense against suits brought to contest inhuman conditions at other prisons.[7] The existence of Marion has not improved conditions at other prisons; its example has dragged them downwards toward greater brutality.

. . .

[Incarceration] figures are even more striking when analyzed in terms of race. The incarceration rate for Black men is 3,370 per 100,000—more than seven times that for White men (Whitman 1991). We do not have current data on the rates of incarceration for other non-white peoples; however, through 1976–78, Indians were arrested at a rate more than 10 times that of White people (US Census of Population, 1976–1978). The United States incarcerates Black men at a rate 5 times higher than South Africa does (Mauer

1992:1). Just as control units suppress the prison population, so prisons act in our poor, Black, Latin, and Native communities. It is no exaggeration to say that hardly anyone in these communities escapes the shadow of the "criminal justice system."

The devastation can be expressed in many ways. Black people are 12% of the US population, 43% of the prison population (Wicker 1991). Using data based on a single day in mid-1989, a study by Marc Mauer for the Sentencing Project in Washington, DC, found that about 1 in 4 Black men in their twenties were under some kind of control by the criminal justice system, and about 1 in 12 were actually behind bars (Mauer 1990). In 1985, the US Bureau of Justice Statistics published the results of a 1979 survey that sought to determine the probability that a person in the United States would go to prison in his/her lifetime (Langan and Greenfeld 1985). Using the data in this report, it can be calculated that in 1979 the probability that a Black man would go to prison, sometime during his life, was 22%. In 1992 we can surmise that this is higher, so that, probably, 1 in 4 Black men will go to prison during his lifetime.

What must this mean for the Black community? Families suffer financially and emotionally. Whatever few jobs might have been available to Black men will be further out of reach for an "ex-con." Prisoners rejoin their communities from prisons which do not even pretend to rehabilitate and where conditions encourage violence and criminality. Moreover, those pressed to escape poverty and oppression through crime, in the absence of other options, are frequently those with intelligence and initiative and who are less demoralized. Thus, their descent into criminality and imprisonment robs the community of a particularly valuable resource. Having to pay lawyers, spend time in courts and visitation, and preparing for the inevitable confrontations with the various elements of the apparatus of oppression also amounts to a tax on these communities that sucks up time, energy, and scarce resources that might otherwise go into self-development.

Faced with the questions "Why do Black people go to prison at a rate 7 times higher than White people?" we can answer in three different ways. One is that Black people commit 7 times as much crime and are genetically disposed to do so. The second is that Black people commit 7 times as much crime and something about their disadvantaged social situation is responsible for this. The third is that Black people do not commit that much crime but the criminal justice system is racist enough to make sure they end up in prison that often.

Rejecting the first alternative, the truth must lie somewhere in between the last two answers, and, although it is impossible to determine how much weight to give to each, one cannot escape the conclusion that US society is extremely racist. If the imprisonment rate accurately reflects the crime rate, one is led to conclude that to effectively combat crime, poverty and racism must be eliminated (even if one is not interested in eliminating them for any other reason).

The other alternative, that in fact Black people do not commit such a disproportionate amount of crime, is indicated by much evidence, although it is impossible to calculate the degree of the disparity. For example, the number of crimes committed is so overwhelming that actual imprisonments only account for a small fraction of the people who perpetrate them. The crime rate is difficult to determine and the two major national sources of crime data disagree significantly on both quantity and trends. However, they both show that the magnitude of crime frequency is very high: in 1986, between 13[8] and 34[9] million crimes were committed. Thus from a huge pool of potential prisoners, i.e., people who have committed crimes, the criminal justice system singles out those who will go to prison. This is done mainly through policing policy. One major example, that shows how racist this is, is the "War on Drugs," in which police target poor, Black neighborhoods even though the great majority of drug users are White people. It is estimated by the government that, by 1995, 69% of people in prison will be drug offenders (Mauer 1992:7). A front page story in the *Los Angeles Times* said that while about 80% of the nation's drug users are White people, the majority of those arrested for "drug crimes" are Black people (Harris 1990). Racism also explains why the 1986 Federal Anti-Drug Abuse Act equates selling 5 grams of crack co-

caine worth about $100 with 500 grams of powdered cocaine worth about $50,000, both crimes drawing mandatory prison terms of 5 years. Black drug users often choose cheaper crack cocaine, while White drug users more often use the relatively expensive powder which is the real profit-maker for the drug trade (McPherson 1992).

Crime is a problem that must be tackled. However, there is no evidence that high imprisonment rates are the answer to the problem of crime. Indeed, study after study shows that prisons do not deter crime (Blumstein, et al. 1978; Visher 1987: 513–14) and, remarkably, we know of no research that indicates that they do. (The only slight reduction in the crime rate due to incarceration is by the incapacitation of those imprisoned, but the conclusion of the studies referenced above is that massive increases in the imprisonment rate have only a tiny effect on the crime rate). Imprisoning large numbers of people in order to stop crime has been a spectacular and massively expensive failure. Academic research shows this, and even prison officials sometimes admit to the reality of the situation. According to the Director of Corrections of Alabama, "We're on a train that has to be turned around. It doesn't make any sense to pump millions and millions into corrections and have no effect on the crime rate" (Ticer 1989: 80).

Prisons do not reduce crime, so what do they do? They cause direct suffering to prisoners and their families. More subtly, though more significantly to our discussion, they are a major cause of the deterioration of communities of poor people, especially people of color. If one decides that the purpose of prisons cannot be to stop crime, because they do not and this has been known for many years, then one can conclude that this devastation is the real intention. The consequent suppression of active protest amongst people of color against the injustices of a society based on the maximization of profit is obviously a gain for those with a vested interest in such a society.

CONTROL OF PUBLIC OPINION

Control units seriously violate prisoners' rights. The facts about Marion show that they serve to suppress dissent among the prison population. Imprisonment does not reduce crime but brutalizes entire communities. The "War on Drugs" has no effect on the problem of drug abuse, but is a war on poor people and especially people of color. These truths never appear on our televisions or in our newspapers, even though crime and prisons are practically a media obsession.

The present system of mass incarceration with the accompanying specter of more and more control units can only be maintained with at least the tacit approval of society as a whole. So it is not surprising that those of the population least likely to experience the brutality of prison are also subjected to appropriate control procedures. We have already described how the media repeat the falsehoods concerning control units. Newspaper articles often do not even bother to attribute claims to prison spokespeople but make statements such as "Florence will become the inheritor of the worst of the worst in the federal prison system" ("Editorial" 1990:4A) as if they were facts.

We face a constant barrage of racist anti-crime and anti-drug hysteria from the establishment. Prisoners are portrayed as incorrigible, dangerous, and undeserving of even the most basic human rights. Politicians and the mainstream media never even mention, let alone intelligently discuss, underlying problems of poverty, inequality, and racism. Debate is thus limited to how to manage the ever-increasing flood of prisoners, the necessity of creating such a flood being taken as given.

The reality of the role of control units is carefully hidden from public view. Most control units and other newly constructed prisons are located in isolated, economically depressed, rural areas. This serves several purposes. The ardent support of local people, who rely on the prison for desperately needed jobs, is secured, and prisoners are isolated from their families and friends.

Political figures support increased imprisonment, since most of them thrive on "tough-on-crime" platforms. Nor can the courts be relied upon. In *Bruscino* vs. *Carlson,* Marion prisoners sought compensation for the attacks which occurred during the October 1983 shakedown and relief from the ongoing conditions of the lockdown. A 1985 Magistrate's Report for this case was approved by the full US District Court for Southern Illinois in 1987. The decision found that 50 prisoners, who testified to beatings and other brutalities, were not credible witnesses, and that only the single prisoner who testified that there were no beatings was believable. When the prisoners appealed the decision, the ruling of the Seventh Circuit Court of Appeals described conditions at Marion as "ghastly," "sordid and horrible," and "depressing in the extreme," but maintained that they were necessary for security reasons and that they did not violate prisoners' constitutional rights.

Finally, there is no discussion of what should be considered a crime and who is to be considered a criminal. The Black drug addict who sells drugs to keep up his habit, the poor man who robs a drug store at gun point, the woman who kills her abusive husband—they are all sent to prison and considered dangerous. However, the violation of safety codes by slum landlords and mine owners; embezzlement and fraud by savings and loan executives; pollution of land, seas, and atmosphere by oil and chemical company directors; the bombing of schools, hospitals, and water purification plants by US presidents; the aggressive marketing of cigarettes (the most deadly narcotic in the world, causing almost 200 times as many deaths as cocaine in the US in 1988 according to C. Everett Koop, Reagan's surgeon general [Shalom 1992: 15]) across the world by US tobacco companies cause excessively more death, injury, and impoverishment. Yet these crimes are rarely punished by imprisonment. Crimes against humanity and the environment are not illegal if committed by the powerful.

SUMMARY

We have described the development of control unit prisons in the United States and we have shown how this is an attempt by prison authorities to suppress protest and dissent within the prison system. The entire prison system is an attack on oppressed people, the poor, and especially people of color, rendering them less able to organize and struggle for their rights and their liberation.

ENDNOTES

1. An example of how this works in practice is the case of an Ohio prisoner who was charged with "inciting to riot" for getting other prisoners at his medium-security prison to sign a statement of grievances against the prison for bad conditions. The prison disciplinary committee found him guilty and recommended a punitive transfer to a control unit at another prison in Ohio. However, all transfers must be approved at Central Office in Columbus. In this case, the approval was denied, since under the law, the prisoner could not be punished for what he had done by such a transfer. So, the warden at his prison responded by requesting that Central Office approve an administrative transfer instead. The transfer was approved without question (Reed 1992).

2. Letter from Wallace H. Cheney, General Counsel for the Federal Bureau of Prisons, to Jan Susler, Attorney for the People's Law Office, Chicago, IL, December 31, 1990. The entire text of the letter read: "This is in response to your request for information related to the Florence, Colorado project. The issues you enquired about have not yet been decided. Therefore, no records exist at this time pertaining to your request. I trust you [sic] will find this information useful."

3. This assumes that this aspect of the model for Florence, the Pelican Bay State Prison Security Housing Unit, is copied. See e.g. Wilson (1991:2) and Corwin (1990:A1).

4. Letter from Pelican Bay SHU prisoner Thomas Fetters, to the authors, June 30, 1991. Fetters writes that he was transferred to the SHU for filing a lawsuit after being injured by a guard who assaulted him while he was in physical restraints. Letter from SHU prisoner Robert Lee Davenport, to the authors, September 28, 1990. Davenport reports being hog-tied and left on his cell-floor for ten hours and witnessing other prisoners left like that for twenty hours.

5. Federal District Judge, Barrington Parker, stated in a decision not long ago: "It is one thing to place persons under greater security because they have escape histories and pose special greater risks to our correctional institutions. But consigning anyone to a high-security unit for past political associations they will never shed unless forced to renounce them is a dangerous mission for this country's prison system to continue." On September 8, 1989, the US Court of Appeals in Washington, DC expressly rejected Judge Parker's opinion and reversed his decision.

6. See Smith (1991), a full-page plea, masquerading as a news report, for the Illinois prison system to build its own version of Marion.

7. For example, in an affidavit filed in the case of *Perotti* v. *Seiter, et al.* (civil no. C-1-84-1285, US District Court for the southern District of Ohio, Western Division), in which prisoners alleged that the control unit complex at the Southern Ohio Correctional Facility in Lucasville violates the United Nations' *Standard Minimum Rules for the Treatment of Prisoners,* Stephen T. Dillon, the control unit supervisor and administrator, in defense of the prison officials, stated that the Ohio control unit does not violate prisoners' rights because it "is based on modern and common corrections procedure and is similar to the . . . maximum security facility of the US Bureau of Prisons at Marion, Illinois."

8. "Uniform Crime Reports" in *Sourcebook of Criminal Justice Statistics—1987,* Washington, DC: USGPO, 1989.

9. Bureau of Justice Statistics, "National Crime Survey" in *Households Touched by Crime—1988,* Washington, DC: USGPO, 1989.

REFERENCES

Associated Press 1990. "Scientist Recommends Health Risk Study of Lincoln Park Area." *Pueblo Chieftain,* December 8.

—. 1991a. "Civil Libertarians Might Sue Over Maximum Security Prison." *Fort Wayne News Sentinel,* October 25.

—. 1991b. "Court Order Ends 37-Day Hunger Strike at Prison." *Indiana Post Tribune,* October 31, Gary, IN.

—. 1991c. "Inmates Refuse Food for 26th Day." *San Francisco Chronicle,* October 19.

—. 1991d. "Indiana Inmates' Hunger Strike Nears a Month." *New York Times,* October 20.

Blumstein, A., J. Cohen, and D. Nagin, eds. 1978. *Deterrence and Incapacitation: Estimating the Effects of Criminal Sanctions on Crime Rates.* Washington, DC: National Academy of Sciences.

Breed, A. F., and D. Ward. 1985. *The United States Penitentiary Marion, Illinois, Consultants' Report Submitted to the Committee of the Judiciary, U.S. House of Representatives, December 1984 in Marion Penitentiary.*

Bryant, T. 1991. "Encased: Prison's Use of 'Cocoon' is Challenged in Suit Here." *St. Louis Post-Dispatch,* January 26.

Can't Jail the Spirit. 1989. 1st Edition, Chicago: Editions El Coqui.

Cardaropoli, A. M. 1991. " $26 Million Bid Appears Lowest to Construct 'Supermax' Prison." *Hartford Journal Inquirer,* September 18.

Carmody, C. 1992. "Chicago Lawyers Barred from Visiting Ind. Inmates." *Chicago Daily Law Bulletin,* March 17.

Chronis, P. G. 1990. " 'Baddest of the Bad' Coming to New Federal Prison." *Denver Post,* May 11.

Corwin, M. 1990. "High-Tech Facility Ushers in New Era of State Prisons." *Los Angeles Times,* May 1.

Dove, D. 1991. Letter from Chief, BOP Office of Public Affairs Dove to CEML, August 15.

Dunne, B. 1991. Letter from Marion prisoner Dunne to the Committee to End the Marion Lockdown.

"Editorial." 1990. *Pueblo Chieftain,* December 26.

Foster, D. 1990. "Maximum Security to Live Up to Its Name." *Rocky Mountain News,* May 5.

Harmon, T. 1991. "Prison Construction Work Swells Florence Area Population." *Pueblo Chieftain,* March 24.

Harris, R. 1990. *Los Angeles Times,* April 22.

Jacobson, D. 1991. Letters from Arizona State prisoner Jacobson to the authors 27 July and 27 September.

Johnson, R. 1990. "Parish Behind Bars." *Denver Post,* November 11.

Korn, R. 1988. "The Effects of Confinement in the High Security Unit at Lexington." *Social Justice, 15*(1).

Langan, P., and L. Greenfeld. 1985. *Prevalence of Imprisonment.* Washington, DC: US Department of Justice.

Lassiter, C. 1990. "Roboprison." *Mother Jones,* September/October.

Lehman, S. 1990. "Lockdown." *Wigwag,* September.

Lemons, J. 1991. "DOC Official: New Prison to Be 'Much Better.' " *Colorado Daily Record,* August 2, Canon City.

Marion Penitentiary. 1985. *Oversight Hearing before the Subcommittee on Courts, Civil Liberties and the Administration of Justice.* Washington, DC: USGPO.

Mauer, M. 1990. *Young Black Men and the Criminal Justice System: A Growing National Problem, Sentencing Project.* Washington, DC.

—. 1992. *Americans Behind Bars: One Year Later, Sentencing Project.* Washington, DC.

McGraw, P. 1986. "Safety for Both Guards, Prisoners Designed into Jeffco's High-Tech Jail." *Denver Post,* September 7.

McPherson, L. 1992. "News Media, Racism and the 'Drug War.' " *Extra!,* April/May.

Miniclier, K. 1991. "Florence Pins Hopes on Prisons." *Denver Post,* April 4.

Mintz, H. 1991. "Pelican Bay Litigation Attacks Prison's Mission." *The Recorder,* October 29.

O'Keefe, M. 1991. "Big House on the Prairie." *Westword (Denver),* April 24–30.

Page, P. 1991. " 'Modules' or 'Cages'? TSP [Trenton State Prison] Enclosures Stir Protest." *The Times (Trenton, New Jersey),* August 17.

"Pennsylvania Senate Committee Calls for a 'Super-Maximum' Prison." 1990. *Criminal Justice Newsletter,* December 17.

Perotti, J. 1991. *Prison News Service (Toronto),* March/April.

Prisoners' Right Union. 1991. *Prison Discipline Study.* Sacramento, CA.

Quinlan, M. 1987. Letter from BOP director Quinlan to Congressperson Robert W. Kastenmeier about the Lexington control unit.

Raab, S. 1991a. "New York City's Maxi-Maxi Dungeon: Too Brutal?" *New York Times,* August 4.

—. 1991b. "The Inmate's View of a Riot: A Reaction to Jail Brutality." *New York Times,* June 26.

Reed, Little Rock. 1992. Letter from Reed to the authors, February 12.

Ritter, J. 1991. "Colorado Suit Accuses Edison of Radiation Pollution." *Chicago Sun-Times,* February 18.

Ruark, T. 1991. Letter from Colorado State prisoner Ruark to the authors, August 5.

Sample v. *Borg* 675 F.Supp. 574 (E.D. Cal. 1987).

Shalom, S. R. 1992. "Made in the U.S.A.: Deadly Exports." *Z Magazine,* April 1.

Smith, W. 1991. "State Puts Low Priority on High-Security Prison." *Chicago Tribune,* April 1.

Ticer, S. 1989. "The Search for Ways to Break Out of the Prison Crisis." *Business Week,* May 8.

US Census of Population: 1976–1978.

Uhlenbrock, T. 1991. "Soft-Spoken Executioner to Run New Prison." *St. Louis Post-Dispatch,* January 26.

Visher, C. A. 1987. "Incapacitation and Crime Control: Does a 'Lock 'Em Up' Strategy Reduce Crime?" *Justice Quarterly,* 4.

Weinstein, C. 1990. "Supermax Blues at Pelican Bay SHU." *California Prisoner,* August.

Whitman, S. 1991. "The Crime of Black Imprisonment." *Prison News Service,* July, Toronto.

Wicker, T. 1991. "The Iron Medal." *New York Times,* January 9.

Wilson, N. K. 1991. "Hard-Core Prisoners Controlled in Nation's High-Tech Prisons." *Chicago Daily Law Bulletin,* April 25.

STUDY QUESTIONS FOR READING 26_____

1. When and where did control units first come into being?

2. What are the three defining characteristics of control units?

3. How did inmates communicate at Marion? Will the cell design allow this at Florence?

4. How does the priest administer communion? What does he tell us about "nut-guns" and their effects during his three years in Colorado?

5. At the time of this article, in 1993, how many states had this kind of control unit or maxi-max prison?

6. What are the three claims for control units that their supporters make?

7. According to these authors, control units do not house the worst of the worst, as shown by Marion in 1984. In 1984, when Marion was the only maxi-max prison in the federal system, what were the security ratings given to prisoners by the BOP? What percentage of prisoners at Marion were rated as requiring the highest security by the BOP (according to the findings of the congressional oversight committee)? What did the BOP do as a result?

8. In the view of these authors, control units do not reduce violence in other prisons or on the outside. Why not? Instead, how have control units changed the situation in state prison systems?

PART THREE: ESSAY QUESTIONS

In your answers, be sure to use one sentence at the end of your first paragraph to offer a clear thesis statement—that is, a statement of your point of view and your arguments for it. Then, in each paragraph of your answer, give evidence to support one of your arguments. Cite specific authors and give specific, concrete support for your point of view by offering statistics, case studies, examples, quotations, expert opinions and so on.

1. Compare and contrast the assumptions and practices of the inmate participation and control models. What do experts on both sides of the debate say? In your view, which model is better and why?
   - Setting rules for inmates versus giving inmates a chance to help make the rules
   - Doing your own time versus building community
   - The paramilitary aspects of prison life versus normalizing prison life
   - Inmates as convicted criminals versus inmates as incarcerated citizens
   - Teaching inmates to live in a tightly controlled prison society versus teaching inmates to live in a representative democracy

2. Discuss whether prisons should be more participatory or more controlling. In your discussion, include the ideas of several authors on each side of the debate.

WEBSITES

www.corrections.com/aca
The American Correctional Association

www.corrections.com/aja
The American Jail Association

www.spr.org
Stop Prison Rape is an organization committed to combating the rape of male and female prisoners and to helping survivors of jailhouse rape; here, they provide much useful information on the topic of prison rape.

DO PRISONS WORK? DOES REHABILITATION WORK?

Part Four presents a debate on whether prisons work in terms of meeting their goals of incapacitation, deterrence, retribution, and, especially, rehabilitation. Orville Pung argues that prisons meet these goals, with the possible exception of rehabilitation. Donald Newman disagrees, arguing instead that prison construction should be halted because prisons do not meet their goals: they incapacitate only temporarily; they do not effectively deter; and, instead of rehabilitating, they make inmates more dangerous. Next, James Q. Wilson argues that rehabilitation does not work; it is unreasonable to expect it to work; and it is probably more practical to put our efforts into controlling inmates rather than attempting to reform them. Elliott Currie vehemently disagrees with Wilson and argues that rehabilitation has never been tried seriously on a large scale, but it can work.

In the first reading, Orville Pung defends prisons by arguing that although no social institution meets all of its goals perfectly, prisons do provide incapacitation, deterrence, and retribution. He points out that schools do not educate all their students, hospitals do not cure all their patients, and churches do not make all their members devout—but none of these failures results in pressure to close schools, hospitals, or churches. He goes on to argue that although it is difficult to estimate how many people are deterred by prison, prison does deter some people, it extracts retribution from prisoners, and, at least for the period of incarceration, it reduces the ability of offenders to commit crimes against the public.

Donald Newman disagrees completely, arguing that prison construction should be halted because prisons do not effectively deter, rehabilitate, or incapacitate offenders, and because we have effective alternatives that are cheaper. Newman points out that inmates serve only two years before their release, and 98 percent will return to the free world some day. Therefore, incapacitation is only temporary. Worse, time spent in confinement makes many inmates a higher risk and even more dangerous when they return to the community. In fact, prison is probably the last place any sensible treatment expert would choose for rehabilitation. Newman notes that the idea of rehabilitation in prison has been called the "noble lie." Although it is logical that prisons *should* deter, the evidence shows that an increased number of prisoners has not been accompanied by a decrease in crime. Fortunately, cost-effective alternatives to prison do exist in the community. Even hard-line prison authorities agree that twenty percent of inmates could be effectively and safely placed in these alternative environments, and less jaundiced observers say 50 percent or more could be so housed. Therefore, Newman says, we should explore alternatives to prison that are just as effective and far cheaper.

The next reading features a selection from James Q. Wilson's book *Thinking About Crime*. Wilson argues that rehabilitation doesn't work, it is unreasonable to expect it to work, and our efforts should be directed at controlling offenders, rather than reforming them. He believes the popular characterization of Robert Martinson's work, that "nothing works" when it comes to rehabilitation is reasonably accurate; after reviewing hundreds of rehabilitation studies, Martinson found only "hints here and there" of success. Further, Wilson states that it is "naive to think that criminal rehabilitation can turn unwilling people away from crime under conditions of duress and indifference." Therefore, he believes we probably should focus our attention on controlling offenders, rather than reforming them.

In the last reading in Part Four, Elliott Currie responds from his book *Confronting Crime*. Currie points out that Robert Martinson himself withdrew his claim that rehabilitation doesn't work. And the National Academy of Sciences questioned Martinson's findings when they wrote, "When it is asserted that 'nothing works,' the Panel is uncertain as to just what has even been given a fair trial." In Currie's view, rehabilitation has never been tried seriously on a large scale—but it can work. Even in the 1960s, in the heyday of rehabilitation, rehabilitation programs both inside and outside of prisons were "attempted only sporadically, and never on a scale that could remotely be said to have tested the potential of rehabilitation itself." For example, among prisons throughout the country, the youth prisons of Washington, D.C., were widely thought to be among the most committed to rehabilitation. However, the resources these prisons actually devoted to the task were minuscule. For example, over 2,000 youths were served by a psychiatric staff consisting of only two workers, one full time and one part time. But rehabilitation can work. For example, in studies by Charles Murray and Louis Cox, delinquent boys spent six to sixteen weeks in nice "camps" that were nothing like traditional institutions. These camps helped turn troubled youth around and were superior to traditional imprisonment, even for serious delinquents.

A DEFENSE OF PRISONS

ORVILLE B. PUNG

Since the first incarcerative institutions were constructed, there have been voices raised calling for their abolition or modification, yet we continue to use prisons. This paper presents some of the reasons prisons have proved to be such an enduring social institution.

Every society has established institutions which reflect its fundamental values, aspirations or commitment to ideals. In modern industrial society we have built elaborate, expensive school buildings to which we point proudly as evidence of our commitment to education, while realistically we know that learning is a lifelong process which may have little to do with the presence or absence of school buildings. We also know that a significant number of people who attend school have never become "educated."

To fulfill our need for religion we build churches which stand as symbols of our belief in a supreme being. Few would attempt to correlate the presence or number of church buildings in a community with the religious commitment of its citizens. Religion tends to be an individual value system which may include church attendance as an outward manifestation of commitment. The failure of churchgoers to live up to the ideals of their God does not result in pressure to close churches.

Another basic institution present in our society in large and expensive numbers is the hospital. Hospitals do not always cure people as most people who die do so in hospitals. Despite this, we do not clamor to close hospitals, because we feel that they exist for the general good of our community.

Finally, we have prisons. As in each of the other institutions, the expectations we have are not often met. In the case of prisons, however, there continues to be a clamoring in some quarters to close or at least not build any more prisons because "prisons don't work."

Perhaps this criticism is a result of the prison's failure to adapt and change with the times. Medicine, for example, has progressed from leeches to laser surgery. Religion has gone from the circuit-riding preacher to closed circuit television, and education from the one-room schoolhouse to the omnipurpose learning centers of today. Auburn Penitentiary has, for the most part, remained Auburn Penitentiary, despite a few name changes.

Perhaps criticism is based on a failure to change but, more likely, criticism that prisons don't work is the result of disagreements about what they are supposed to work towards (Morris, 1978, p. 2). Indeed, the very stability of the prison in the face of sweeping social and temporal change suggests that it does in fact work very well at something.

Any assessment of the utility of prisons is dependent upon an identification of the purposes to be served by imprisoning criminal offenders. Traditionally, four purposes of the prison have been identified: *rehabilitation, deterrence, retribution,* and *incapacitation* (O'Leary, et al. 1975). These are not the only purposes served by prisons (Reasons and Kaplan, 1975), but they are the most commonly accepted. Most of the recent criticism of prisons has centered around the one goal of rehabilitation (Martinson, 1974).

Rehabilitation is a medical term that has little or no practical application within the institution of the prison. "To restore to a previous state," the classic definition of rehabilitation, may imply that the inmate can and should return to a life of crime from whence he or she came. However, prison can and should provide access to programs during incarceration which can assist the offender after release. The prison should have available some of the same opportunities that exist in the general community—for example, formal education, vocational training, or employment. This is not rehabilitation but basic opportunities that can *habilitate*. For some inmates no training is necessary as the skills they possess are more than adequate to function in society in a successful or legal way. For these inmates, work opportunities to earn money are the most appropriate.

Prison for countless offenders has been a positive turning point in their lives. From educated and influential persons like Charles Colson of Watergate fame to long-time drifters like Merle Haggard, the prison experience has provided an opportunity to take stock of one's life, to reassess what the future could be. This is not to advocate that people should go to prison to find themselves, but rather to point out that the prison experience is not always the damaging and ruining experience conventional wisdom would have one believe.

Certainly if the goal of a prison is only to rehabilitate (as schools are to completely educate and hospitals are to always cure), then prisons do not work very well. If, on the other hand, prisons represent the symbolic social expectation that when one breaks the law punishment will follow, then it can be said that prisons work fairly well.

Deterrence relates to a threatened sanction for criminal offenses which causes would-be offenders to refrain from crime as a result of fear of the penalty. The symbolic presence of the prison has intrinsic value as a social statement affirming society's belief in, and willingness to uphold, its rules or laws (Gibbs, 1978, p. 42). The prison can serve deterrent purposes both in the general symbolic message to every member of society and the specific deterrent to the potential offender.

In the absence of a massive research effort to determine how many people did not break the law because of potential prison consequences, we will never know how effective deterrence has been (Zimring and Hawkins, 1973). Nonetheless, it seems reasonable to suggest that the prison represents a harsh enough penalty to deter potential offenders.

Retribution (punishment) is a basic tenet of any justice model (Fogel, 1975; Von Hirsch, 1976). While one can certainly argue that the conditions found in many prisons result in more retribution than justice would demand, that issue addresses the conditions of a specific prison rather than the concepts of the institution itself. Indeed, it has been argued that a major fault with our system of justice lies in its uneven application of the prison sanction rather than its general reliance upon imprisonment (Twentieth Century Fund, 1976). That is, more people should be imprisoned but for lesser periods of time rather than fewer people imprisoned for substantial periods.

Incapacitation is the final generally accepted goal of imprisonment. To the extent that prisons reduce the opportunities for offenders to commit crimes, they are successful in achieving the goal of incapacitation. At least for the period of their incarceration, criminal offenders are prevented from victimizing people in the free community.

Since the dawn of history, society has had its problems dealing with members who for some reason become dangerous or predatory. While the churchman can claim the cause is original sin, scientists can identify bad genes, educators can suggest learning disabilities, psychiatrists can point to faulty parents, and sociologists can blame television programs, the fact remains that these dangerous and predatory people must be controlled or incapacitated. This kind of person represents only a small percentage of the general population but accounts for a disproportionate number of violent acts and miscellaneous crime (Johnson, 1978). Some individuals account for so many acts of violence that simple incapacitation becomes the mission of the prison.

Unfortunately, within a majority of our prisons incapacitation is not fully achieved as all too frequently some offenders continue to commit acts of violence, but now against fellow inmates and prison staff. A victim is a victim, whether the person is an innocent citizen or an innocent inmate or staff person. Prisons must be designed and operated to provide for the safe incapacitation of the dangerous and predatory individual. Nonetheless, in terms of the general public, imprisonment incapacitates offenders and does this very well considering that only two percent of prison inmates manage to escape (U.S. Department of Justice, 1981).

This review of how well the prison serves the four traditional goals of imprisonment indicates that it is neither a total success nor a total failure at any of them. On balance, it appears the prison is relatively successful as a punishment. Given the inappropriateness of rehabilitation, the prison is useful for deterrence and relatively successful at retribution and incapacitation. There are still more purposes of the prison which recommend its continued use as a response to crime.

Among a number of social, economic and political benefits which can be derived from the continued use of prisons, two major functions of imprisonment stand out. First, the prison can and does provide an alternative to more severe or more troublesome responses to crime. Second, the prison serves as an incentive to offenders subjected to less drastic sanctions.

PRISON AS AN ALTERNATIVE

Too often those who condemn the prison and call for the abolition of imprisonment forget that the prison was created as an alternative to more gruesome criminal penalties (Rothman, 1971, p. 62). Prior to the invention of the penitentiary, penalties for criminal behavior included whipping, branding, maiming and death. The prison was developed initially as an alternative to these barbaric sanctions. As Professor Graeme Newman noted (1978):

> Those who press for abolition of prison do not understand the powder keg upon which prisons are built. To eradicate prisons would be to eradicate an important and valuable part of our culture—as seamy as it is, it is far less seamy than it might have been. We are capable of much worse, as the history of our exploits with criminals . . . clearly demonstrates (p. 286).

The presence of a sanction as severe and unpleasant as incarceration provides an alternative to even more severe sanctions such as torture and death. Indeed, the possibility of imprisonment may reduce reliance on capital punishment, vigilante justice, and other perhaps equally frightening sanctions. Dean Donald J. Newman has observed, " . . . incarceration has been a major alternative to the death sentence in serious crime cases . . . " (1974).

Two of those more terrifying solutions to the problem of crime are psychological conditioning and electronic control. It is difficult to suggest that either of these two would represent an advance over incarceration. We may have the technology in contemporary society to control human behavior, but these controls are more potentially damaging to fundamental freedom than incarceration could ever be.

Anyone who has seen the movie, *A Clockwork Orange*, has a general idea of the potential of psychological conditioning for the control of behavior. Whether one opts for reward psychology or aversive therapy may be a philosophical question, but the threat of "mind control" is real. Psychotropic drugs coupled with a system of rewards and penalties can be used to effectively shape behavior.

This option may be more effective in controlling criminal activity than the prison, but the cost in self-determination is exorbitant. How many among us would sacrifice the ability to choose among courses of action, the right to make decisions about our lives, in order to avoid a sentence to imprisonment? Even if we elected to replace the prison with mind control, who should we entrust with this awesome power?

Similarly . . . our surveillance capabilities are enormous. It is possible to clearly photograph individual people at their daily activities through cameras placed in satellites orbiting Earth. Closed circuit television, magnetic scanners, and two-way mirrors are commonplace today. Anyone who has gone to a bank, flown in an airplane, or even shopped in a department store recently has been subjected to these types of surveillance.

Beyond these monitoring devices which are innocuous by comparison, we have the capability to "follow" and control individuals electronically and by computer. It is possible to implant telemetric devices in criminal offenders and monitor their every activity as well as to use radio transmitted electronic shocks to sanction them for misbehavior (Ingraham and Smith, 1972).

There are, of course, other alternatives to incarceration which can also be envisioned. Banishment to penal colonies was one historical alternative which may arise in the future, especially given a resurgence in the space program. Before this idea is dismissed outright, one should remember that the federal government still deports alien criminal offenders. We can also always rely on civil commitment of criminal offenders to mental hospitals. Neither of these, however, would appear to be effective alternatives to incarceration.

In short, prisons were designed as a humanitarian response to what were perceived as overly harsh criminal penalties in the early 19th century. This original purpose may be even more necessary in modern society than it was nearly 200 years ago.

PRISON AS AN INCENTIVE

Proponents of prison abolition often suggest that prisons can be abandoned because they are not needed (Rector, 1975). They argue that most, if not all, criminal offenders can be effectively controlled and sanctioned through the use of a variety of non-incarcerative penalties such as probation, fines, restitution, and the like. Surely this is true.

Many offenders do not require a prison term for either punishment or incapacitation. Both the offender and the victim in these cases may well be better served by a restitutive penalty than by incarceration in prison. The difficulty arises, however, in securing the offender's compliance with the court order (Connolly, 1975).

The most frequently used alternative to the prison is a sentence to probation. Probation sentences require the offender to adhere to a set of standards for conduct while residing in the free community under the supervision of a probation officer. If probation is going to work, it requires a credible threat of incarceration.

Imagine a penal system in which there is no prison. In this system, a sentencing judge may sanction criminal offenses by ordering the offender to either serve a term of probation, pay restitution or a fine, seek counseling services, obtain employment, or a variety of other such actions. What is this judge to do if he or she orders an offender to pay a fine and the offender refuses? It is possible the judge could then order probation, a more restrictive sentence. Of

course, the offender could always refuse to abide by the conditions of probation.

Implicit in every sentence less severe than prison is the phrase, " . . . or else you will be sentenced to prison." If this "or else" is removed, these less severe sanctions will prove to be ineffectual. It may be said that all sentences less harsh than imprisonment depend upon the possibility of a prison term. This is an important component of any system of justice.

The concept of justice demands that an extensive array of retributive penalties be available in response to various levels of offense and offender culpability. Thus, probation, fines, community service programs, restitution, halfway houses or a combination of all are needed. This continuum must have as an option the most severe sanction, i.e., the prison. Without the presence of the prison, the death penalty becomes the last option. This option is clearly inappropriate to enforce a minor penalty for a minor crime. Prison represents a negative alternative to motivate the offender to take part in community programs or respond to probation (Wilson, 1977, p. 59).

THE PRISON RESPONSE

The Quaker development of the penitentiary to replace the cruel practices of beating, dunking, maiming and torturing offenders was idealistic and noble, but flawed. The penitentiary concept was modeled after the cloistered monastery with cells, meditation and the Bible as the basic ingredients to effect change. The ability to determine when this change actually occurred was impossible and relied on subjective evaluation or verbal assertion by the offender.

Release when it seemed that the penitent was sufficiently sorry was later replaced by the "release when cured" treatment model. This vague and ambiguous approach resulted in the convict learning to "con." Treatment programs replaced the Bible and both were subject to abuse as the assurance of conversion to the warden later became claims of being rehabilitated or cured to the parole board (American Friend's Service Committee, 1971).

After years of agonizing not only over how prisons should be run but, more importantly, how inmates should be released, the reemergence of some basic and almost simple principles has occurred (Fogel, 1975). The most obvious is the concept of punishment fitting the crime, i.e., the justice model of determinate sentencing. The recognition that the medical model was flawed is another.

Recent trends which view the basic functions of a prison as incapacitation, retribution, and public safety will go far in placing the role of the prison in perspective. Much of the recent criticism of prison has been based on the failure of the prison to meet the goal of rehabilitation. Coupling these renewed goals with social deterrence and the provision of self-improvement programs for those who wish to avail themselves may well round out the appropriate role of the prison.

Another set of arguments against the prison has centered not so much on the institution of the prison itself as it has on the use of the institution. This argument asserts that too many people go to prison for too long a time. This is an unfortunate outgrowth of two centuries of cloudy goals, excessive expectations, and inertia. Many people now in prison do not themselves "need" to be in prison either for their own benefit or for the protection of society. The difficulty arises here in that we have a tradition of prison. Many offenders are in prison because we "need" to put them there. To much of the American public, the punishment for crime is prison. Anything less is leniency.

An essential requirement for our society is the development of an extensive continuum of sanctions to deal with the various offenders so that those who do in fact go to prison are those who actually require retribution or incapacitation at that level. By limiting prison populations to only those who require imprisonment, we will help assure that these specialized and essential institutions of last resort will fulfill their function.

Prisons are a basic and needed institution in our society. The only questions are: How many are needed and for whom? These are fundamentally moral and social issues which will be decided in the political arena. The law-abiding majority will continue to determine what are appropriate uses of the prison. They will do this with reference to the American tradition of incarceration.

The institution of the prison must be seen in its proper perspective. It is part of the criminal justice system, not the mental health industry. It has a long tradition as an appropriate, indeed humanitarian, response to crime. It has little to do with crime rates or issues of broad social control except in a general or symbolic sense. Until the viruses of crime, poverty, discrimination and exploitation are eliminated and the utopian condition is achieved, prisons will exist and be necessary. Thus, the prison exists as did the iron lung—a response, not a solution.

REFERENCES

American Friend's Service Committee (1971). *Struggle for Justice.* (New York: Hill and Wang).

Connolly, Paul K. (1975). "The Possibility of a Prison Sentence is a Necessity." *Crime and Delinquency,* 21(4), pp. 356–359.

Fogel, David (1975). *" . . . We are the living proof. . . ."* (Cincinnati: Anderson Publishing Co.).

Gibbs, Jack P. (1978). "Preventive Effects of Capital Punishment Other than Deterrence." *Criminal Law Bulletin,* 14(1), pp. 34–50.

Ingraham, Barton L. and Gerald W. Smith (1972). "Electronic Surveillance and Control of Behavior and Its Possible Use in Rehabilitation and Parole." *Issues in Criminology,* 7, pp. 35–52.

Johnson, Perry M. (1978). "The Role of Penal Quarantine in Reducing Violent Crime." *Crime and Delinquency,* 24(4), pp. 465–485.

Martinson, Robert (1974). "What Works?—Questions and Answers About Prison Reform." *The Public Interest,* (Spring), pp. 22–54.

Morris, Norval (1978). "Conceptual Overview and Commentary on the Movement Toward Determinacy." In *Determinate Sentencing.* (Washington, D.C.: Government Printing Office), pp. 1–10.

National Council on Crime and Delinquency (1982). *Criminal Justice Newsletter* 13(14), pp. 6–7.

Newman, Donald J. (1974). "In Defense of Prisons," *Psychiatric Annals,* 4(3), pp. 6–17.

Newman, Graeme (1978). *The Punishment Response.* (Philadelphia: J. B. Lippincott).

O'Leary, Vincent, Michael Gottfredson and Art Gelman (1975). "Contemporary Sentencing Proposals." *Criminal Law Bulletin,* 11, p. 555.

Reasons, Charles E. and Russell L. Kaplan (1975). "Tear Down the Walls?: Some Functions of Prisons." *Crime and Delinquency,* 21(4), pp. 360–72.

Rector, Milton G. "The Extravagance of Imprisonment." *Crime and Delinquency,* 21(4), pp. 323–330.

Rothman, David J. (1971). *The Discovery of the Asylum.* (Boston: Little, Brown).

Twentieth Century Fund Task Force on Criminal Sentencing (1976). *Fair and Certain Punishment.* (New York: McGraw-Hill).

U.S. Department of Justice (1981). *Prisoners in State and Federal Institutions on December 31, 1979.* (Washington, D.C.: Government Printing Office).

Von Hirsch, Andrew (1976). *Doing Justice.* (New York: Hill and Wang).

Wilson, Rob (1977). "Supervision (the Other Parole)." *Corrections Magazine,* 3(3), pp. 56–59.

Zimring, Franklin and Gordon Hawkins (1973). *Deterrence.* (Chicago: University of Chicago Press).

STUDY QUESTIONS FOR READING 27

1. According to Pung, why is it unfair to say that prisons should be closed because they don't work?

2. In what ways have prisons failed? In what ways do they work fairly well?

3. How does prison actually help prison alternatives work?

4. Who should be sent to prison? How long will we need prisons?

PRISONS DON'T WORK

DONALD J. NEWMAN

. . .

This author opposes the construction of additional prisons, particularly maximum security prisons, for the following reasons: (1) prisons do not deter, rehabilitate, or effectively incapacitate offenders; (2) an expanded prison system will be unnecessary in a few years; (3) prisons are permanent and create an inflexible correctional system; (4) prison expansion is excessively costly and there are cost effective alternatives; and (5) prisons perpetuate brutality and racism.

PRISONS DO NOT DETER, REHABILITATE, OR EFFECTIVELY INCAPACITATE OFFENDERS

All advocates of the use of incarceration have a mixture of rationales.[1] For some, imprisonment is a last resort, necessary to incapacitate dangerous offenders to protect the community from further depravations. Indeed, to have and to hold is one of the most traditional purposes of imprisonment. And perhaps the best case can be made for incapacitation as a useful purpose of imprisonment. Prisons, particularly maximum security prisons, are cleverly designed so that few inmates escape and to this extent local communities are protected during the time these offenders are held in confinement. Apart from frequent crimes committed within the prison itself, a more troublesome issue is the long-range capacity of prisons to protect potential victims by holding offenders.[2] Most prisoners serve less than two years before first release and well over ninety-eight per cent of all inmates eventually return to the free world. Incapacitation, except for a handful of lifers, is only a temporary thing. In spite of some sporadic attempts to make prison sentences completely indeterminate,[3] ranging from one day to life for all offenses, most prison sentences in our society are for periods less than life imprisonment. The allowed length of a prison term depends upon the seriousness of the crime as determined by legislative provisions and by judicial sentencing practices. In the best traditions of Blackstone and Bentham,[4] our criminal codes provide different sentence lengths for different types of crimes and for different degrees of culpability within each crime category.

Not only is incapacitation usually temporary, but time spent in confinement makes many inmates higher risks and more dangerous when they do return to the community. Prison is always a brutalizing experience and necessarily involves removing an offender from community ties, including family and employment. At the benefit of temporary incapacitation, prisons return to communities offenders who are disenfranchised, disengaged from employment and family, damaged, brutalized, and likely to be more brutal after the prison experience.[5]

For some advocates of incarceration, including some sentencing judges, the primary use of prisons is simply to punish. "Just deserts" is a common theme in crime control processing today.[6] If proportionate punishment is a legitimate objective of sentencing, there are many ways this can be accomplished without building more costly, ineffective and cruel prisons. Building new prisons to punish individuals is overkill. Imprisonment is indeed punishment but at an excessive economical and social cost.

It is evident that imprisonment does not deter others from committing crimes, at least not more than other non-incarceration sanctions currently available.[7] In violent crimes, such as homicides, rapes, and the like—the very crimes most prison advocates desire to prevent—it is clear that incarceration does not deter potential violators.[8] If it did, then why do we continue to have a steady stream of persons committing such crimes and going to prison? The same is true for lesser crimes, including most property violations. While it seems logical to law-abiding persons, including most legislators and judges, that imprisonment should deter people from stealing, using narcotics, and assaulting one another, it is apparent that it does not work this way. Deterrence, if it works at all, is a much more complex process than a direct-line relationship between sanctions and conformity.[9] Crimes continue unabated no matter how fast we arrest, convict and incarcerate, no matter how broad we throw our net and how severely we react in imposing sanctions. From the law-abiding citizen's perspective, prisons *should* deter; in the everyday world of crime control processing it is only too clear that they do not.

Another alleged objective of incarceration is rehabilitation of offenders. On its face, this is ludicrous. A prison for rehabilitation is probably the last setting that would be chosen by any sensible treatment expert. Prisons collect the offenders of our ordered society, hold them in a single-sex, repressive environment which is walled off from the outside world. With all the social degradation that goes on in prisons, it would be a near miracle if someone were rehabilitated in such an environment. In fact, it is remarkable that more prisoners do not come out more sullen, dangerous and brutal than they were when they entered. Nonetheless, for many years rehabilitation was advocated as one of the major goals of correctional systems. In part, this hope grew out of a sincere belief that the application of social science would cause people to change, whether in authoritarian settings or not.[10] Over time, however, rehabilitation became simply a catch-word of correctional administrators who sought to soften the cruel conditions of imprisonment. They used rehabilitative claims in order to win funding concessions from legislatures that, it appears, are never swayed solely by appeals for civility. Rehabilitation has been called the "noble lie" of corrections, used, not cynically, to win better prison conditions by administrators who knew its actual achievement was ephemeral.[11]

In spite of years of dedicated attempts to develop rehabilitative programs inside the walls, and in spite of some small pockets of success, the rehabilitative ideal has been discredited.[12] Few professionals today would advocate rehabilitation as even a secondary purpose of imprisonment. This does not mean that there should not be training and treatment programs within prisons. Given the fact that many offenders will be incarcerated for years, it is in societal self-interest that attempts be made to treat serious personality disorders, to educate, and to equip offenders to better take their place in the economic order when they are released. But treatment and training as a *purpose* of imprisonment is advocated nowhere today. The prison in our modern society is anachronistic. It has never accomplished *any* of the purposes for which it was intended. To expand a prison system is simply to finance foreordained failure.

An Expanded Prison System Will Be Unnecessary in a Few Years

The burgeoning of prison populations today is partly an artifact of shifts in the age demography of our general population. Prison inmates fall mostly into the age range of eighteen to twenty-four and thus are roughly age cohorts with college students (who otherwise differ, of course, coming from a higher socioeconomic stratum). But whether middle or lower class, black or white, all population projections past the year 2000 indicate a *decline* in this age segment of our population.[13] Colleges are predicting a steady decline in the population base from which students are recruited. The prisoner age base will also decline. No one would think of building a new college today. We made a mistake in overbuilding grade schools, high schools and colleges in the post-World War II era. At present, we are closing grade schools and merging high schools. We should not make the same mistake with prisons. Prison overcrowding is a temporary phenomenon, resulting from peculiarities in the age distribution in our general population and will gradually reduce if left alone. This is not much consolation in terms of current conditions. On the other hand, new construction is years from completion. If new cells are needed today, they should have been planned and executed some years ago to accommodate the prisoner population at peak. To begin planning or construction now is foolish. By the time new prisons are finished they will not be needed, yet there will be pressures to keep all prisons full once they are constructed.[14] Parkinson's Law affects prisons as well as other institutions in our society.

PRISONS ARE PERMANENT AND CREATE AN INFLEXIBLE CORRECTIONAL SYSTEM

It is comparatively easy to open a prison, but nearly impossible to close one. When a new prison is suggested for a particular community, a common response is outrage, anger, and opposition. Once the prison has been built, however, the anger and outrage of those opposed to its construction are insignificant compared with citizen responses if the prison is threatened with closure. In many small communities in which prisons are typically built, the prison tends to become a major industry, not only as the largest employer, but as an important purchaser of goods and services from the community. Under such conditions, closing a prison would wreak an economic hardship on these small communities.

Whether for economic self interest or otherwise, the fact remains that very few American prisons have ever been closed. There are a few exceptions.[15] Alcatraz was closed and replaced by the Federal Correctional Institution at Marion, Illinois, and the Ohio State Penitentiary was closed as archaic and replaced by a new correctional facility not too far away. Nevertheless, most prisons, even those opened a century and a half ago, remain active today. The prototype maximum security prison which was built in Auburn, New York, between 1819 and 1823 is still operating in the same location today.[16] In fact, in New York State, which is one of the largest and most maximum security of all correctional systems, *no* prison has ever been closed since the opening of Auburn. Although prisons may be failures from many perspectives, from simple longevity and continuous operation they are remarkably successful.

Correctional systems, like all other responses to social problems, should be able to respond to variations in the crime problem and in sentencing patterns by expanding or contracting as the need for secure restraint varies over time. A correctional system that is heavily reliant on the prison as a centerpiece does not have this flexibility. Once the capital commitment to prisons is made, and prisons become entrenched in the economic and social life of communities, the correctional system loses flexibility. The life expectancy of prisons is usually as long as the structural integrity of the building allows. They not only are virtually impossible to close but, by the nature of prison construction, nearly as impossible to modify or remodel. In those locations where prisons have become big business, there will be many pressures to continue to perpetuate a high incarceration rate. Legislatures have committed capital and few judges will risk electorate unpopularity by sentencing offenders to prison. In short, if we build more prisons, we will have them forever, and the tendency will be to utilize them even after the current crisis has passed.

Prison Expansion Is Excessively Costly and There Are Cost-Effective Alternatives

Prison construction is among the most expensive type of architectural endeavors in modern society. Prisons must not only efficiently house inmates but must be secure from escapes and from internal disturbances. Security considerations alone, both on the prison perimeter and internally, cause construction costs to skyrocket. Even using all modern electronic security devices, including heat sensors, wired perimeter fences, electric eyes, laser beams, closed circuit television and automatic locking devices, the per-bed cost of a prison approaches the price of a middle-class home. With some variation from place to place, modern prisons cost in excess of $100,000 per cell.[17]

Prisons are "total institutions" requiring that inmates be clothed, fed, have access to medical care, fire protection, and ironically, police protection, as well as other services to meet all living needs of highly diverse populations. Building a prison is roughly comparable to building an apartment complex for reluctant, hostile, and dangerous persons who must be fed and totally cared for while continuously observed, searched and otherwise monitored during the time they live in the apartment. It requires a complex

Chinese box architecture that is intrinsically grotesque and excessively expensive. Furthermore, it is an expense that has no social utility. For all of the reasons discussed above, new prison construction is not only foolish but socially and economically dysfunctional.

Most authorities, even hard-line prison administrators, admit that a relatively high proportion of persons presently incarcerated could be as effectively and safely held in the community if there were sufficient alternatives. The extent of this proportion is thought to be rarely below twenty per cent. Less jaundiced observers believe, with some reason, that current prison populations could be reduced by half or more if other alternatives were available.

One rather obvious solution to prison overcrowding would be to release more prisoners on parole earlier in their sentences. This, of course, is exactly the opposite of the current trend toward longer sentences with fixed terms and no possibility of parole. Even though it may be politically difficult, it is a feasible and safe alternative. We certainly need to use prisons in our crime control efforts, but there is no reason to incarcerate as many offenders for as long as we do. The United States has the longest sentences of any civilized country in the world.[18] There is absolutely no evidence that six years incarceration is better than four, or two years better than six months; "better" measured on any scale.[19] Length of sentence is unrelated to recidivism, to deterrence, to long-range community safety and even to punishment. The first few days, even hours, of incarceration are the most punitive, after that adjustment begins and prisoners settle down to do time. In fact, long sentences necessarily lead to "institutionalization," the process where offenders gradually accept the prison world as a way of life.[20] There is no other way prisoners can serve long terms and survive, emotionally or physically.

Some states, having abolished parole, and now faced with overcrowding are in the process of reinstating it.[21] A "Board of Prison Terms" is the favored new euphemism for parole board. And, as sentence lengths increase, there is a tendency to liberalize "good time" credits, allowing more time off for good behavior, thus moving the prison population through incarceration more quickly. In a few places, the prison population has been "capped" at or near capacity. In such situations every time a new prisoner is received, one is released, thus achieving homeostasis based on cell capacity rather than reasoned, meritorious release policies.[22]

Whether parole, good time, or in-put/out-put capping are utilized, the result is the same: shorter sentences for many offenders and system-wide relief from excessive overcrowding. And this can occur without increasing the risk to the community. Why then, build expensive new prisons to expand the incarceration capacity?

In addition to these techniques, all of which use imprisonment as the sentence of first choice, there are other alternatives which bypass imprisonment altogether. Though they are nonincarcerative, at least in maximum security settings, all *are* sentences and to this extent satisfy the punitive "just deserts" mandate of the criminal law. None of the techniques is lenient, rather they are simply varieties of security less than maximum. These alternatives include intensive probation supervision, halfway houses located in the community, residential treatment centers, work release dormitories, intermittent incarceration such as weekend lock-up in local jails, drug rehabilitation centers, and the like. The primary and central core of community-based corrections is intensive probation supervision. This has the obvious advantage of being flexible, having no capital investment. Probation can expand or contract at a fraction of the cost of even other community alternatives such as halfway houses.

For a number of years California had a probation subsidy program as an alternative to incarceration.[23] Under this subsidy program an incarceration norm would be determined for each county. This would be calculated as the average number of persons from a particular county sent to state prisons annually over a five-year period. If a county sent a number less than this norm to prison in future years, the county would receive state funds of approximately one third the cost of housing an offender in prison. For instance, if County A sent 100 offenders to prison annually (on average over the past five years), the norm for this county would be set at 100. In future years, for every offender under 100 sent to prison from this county, local officials would receive approximately $4,000 from state funds to be spent to assist the people in the community. For instance, if ten less persons were sent to prison from this county in a given year, the county would receive $40,000 for community crime control efforts. In turn, the state would save about $80,000, for if these ten had gone to prison, the annual cost would come to roughly $120,000 at $12,000 per inmate. This type of subsidy program builds economic incentives for judges and other county officials to retain offenders in the community. However, the California subsidy program had a flaw. While the money returned to the counties was to go solely to development of probation services, the retaining of inmates in the community put strains on other resources, including the police and local jails. It would have been better and much more effective if the monies returned to the county had been apportioned among all agencies in the local criminal justice system to better enable them to absorb these offenders.

There are, of course, political obstacles to the development of state (or national) subsidy programs. In an era of "get tough" crime control, it is always difficult to convince state lawmakers that prisons are financial disasters in the long run and that resources returned to communities for local criminal justice systems are not only cheaper but more effective. It would require a sophisticated state legislature to opt for a long-range savings by supporting local options. In the present public opinion climate it is probably too much to ask. It seems increasingly clear that crime control, including imprisonment and other alternatives, is beyond state as well as local coping capacity and what is needed is a national effort to meet the crime problem and to alleviate prison overcrowding.

Prisons Perpetuate Brutality and Racism

Prisons are inherently the cruelest institutions we have devised in our society. Everything from the basic architecture of walled, turreted, maximum-security facilities to internal rules and regulations derived from constant concern for security combine to create an environment that is degrading, repressive and punitive. Even in the heyday of the rehabilitative ideal, prisons were not designed or operated to convey a beneficial purpose. Prisons are more than simply a collection of the worst among us; they are the symbolic embodi-

ment of the awesome power of the state to compel conformity. Prisons represent the public statement that crime does not pay, and are designed to deter those outside as well as to repress and incapacitate those held within. Everyone familiar with American prisons—whether inmates or not—agree that euphemistically titled "correctional facilities," particularly maximum security prisons, are brutal by their nature.[24] The major effect of imprisonment on those serving time is shattered self esteem and acceptance of brutality as a way of life. Few people who serve sentences can avoid being hurt—more often by fellow inmates than guards—for homosexual rapes, extortion, intimidation, assaults and beatings are normal fare in the prison world. Few persons who serve time can escape becoming brutal. Hardness is an esteemed virtue and muscle is the way to the top of the prison social order.

Recidivism is commonly used to measure the effectiveness of prisons but most observers agree that it is an improper test, indicating little about the nature and pains of imprisonment. Apart from deciding how recidivism is to be measured (whether released inmates commit new crimes and, if so, whether these crimes are of the same kind or more serious than the ones for which they were incarcerated; how long after release the crime must be committed; and the like) there are basic questions of the relationship of imprisonment to recidivism.[25] Even if released prisoners commit other offenses, it is hard to demonstrate that imprisonment failed in some way. Conversely, if parolees do not recidivate, it is equally difficult to demonstrate that some aspect of imprisonment caused them to go straight. Recidivism can only be measured when the "normal" crime rate in populations with demographic characteristics similar to inmates is taken into account. That is, to more accurately assess recidivism (without answering the causal question) it is necessary to establish the normative crime rate of persons with similar traits and backgrounds and measure any increment or decline in crimes among releasees with the same traits. . . .

Few measures of the effects of imprisonment other than the statistical artifact of new offenses are used to measure the effects of incarceration. Yet it is clear to all who deal with ex-inmates that the experience of imprisonment affects the majority in a negative fashion. Their lives remain shattered, their sensibilities dulled and the code of the prison jungle becomes a common value-set which is carried on to the outside.

The bulk of prison inmates are made up of the lowest socioeconomic status persons in our society. Prison populations have always been overrepresentative of the ignorant, poor and discriminated in our society.[26] Prison populations of the past represented successive waves of immigrants and their first generation offspring. Today it is blacks and Spanish-speaking persons who fill our prisons and jails. Because of this,

in public opinion, being black, Puerto Rican or Chicano has become synonymous for being criminal. Immigration has all but ceased, so that blacks and the Spanish-speaking are the end of the line of successive waves of newcomers. They are unlikely to be pushed out of low status positions by any new immigrant groups. As long as we have prisons, and certainly if we expand them, we will continue to perpetuate the racism fostered by prison labelling.[27]

To expand, at great cost, a demonstrably ineffective crime control institution is sheer madness. To build more prisons in a desperate attempt to meet our crime problem, itself borders on the criminal.

ENDNOTES

1. *See generally* J. Wilson, Thinking About Crime (1975); *and* E. Van Den Haag, Punishing Criminals (1975) [hereinafter cited as Punishing Criminals]. *See also* G. Hawkins, *The Prison: Policy and Practice* 30–38 (1976).

2. *Mandatory Sentences, supra* note 9, at 604–15.

3. For an example of the impact which transition to determinate sentencing has on a highly indeterminate sentencing structure, *see* Cassos & Taugher, *Determinate Sentencing in California: The New Number's Game*, 9 Pacific L.J. 5 (1978).

4. W. Blackstone, Blackstone's Commentaries on the Law 749-754 (B. Gavit, ed. 1941); J. Bentham, *An Introduction to the Principles of Morals and Legislation* in The Utilitarians 169–77 (1973; orig. pub. 1789).

5. For a statement on the destructive impact of prison on the incarcerated, *see* Corrections, *supra* note 18, at 1–2, 223–24, 343. Several subsequent studies have indicated that the brutalizing aspects of incarceration, especially with regard to racial tension, have intensified. *See, e.g.,* J. Irwin, Prisons in Turmoil (1980); *and* J. Jacobs, Stateville (1977).

6. *See generally* A. Von Hirsch, Doing Justice (1976); Twentieth Century Fund, Fair and Certain Punishment (1976); D. Fogel, We are the Living Proof (2d ed. 1979); *and* Punishing Criminals, *supra* note 22.

7. For a compendium of deterrence research, *see* D. Beyleveld, A Bibliography on General Deterrence Research (1980). *See also* F. Zimring & G. Hawkins, Deterrence (1973) [hereinafter cited as Deterrence]; Andenaes, *Does Punishment Deter Crime?* 2 Crim. L.Q. 76 (1968); *and* Gibbs, *Assessing the Deterrence Doctrine,* 22 Am. Behavioral Scientist 672 (1979).

8. *See generally* J. Gibbs, Crime, Punishment and Deterrence (1975); *and* A. Blumstein, J. Cohen & D. Nagin, Deterrence and Incapacitation: Estimating the Effects of Criminal Sanctions on Crime Rates (1977).

9. *See* Deterrence, *supra* note 28, at 75–89; *and* Erickson, Gibbs & Jensen, *The Deterrence Doctrine and the Perceived Certainty of Legal Punishments,* 42 Am. Soc. Rev. 316 (1977).

10. *See generally* D. Rothman, The Discovery of the Asylum (1971).

11. N. Morris, *The Abandonment of the "Noble Lie"* in The Future of Imprisonment 20–27 (1974).

12. *See generally* D. Lipton, R. Martinson & J. Wilks, The Effectiveness of Correctional Treatment: A Survey of Treatment Evaluation Studies (1975); *and* Martinson, *What Works? Questions and Answers About Prison Reform,* 35 The Public Interest 25 (1974).

13. *See* Bureau of Census, U.S. Dept of Commerce, 1980 Census of Population Supplementary Reports (1981); *Projections of Prison Populations, supra* note 6, at 23; *and* 1 American Prisons, *supra* note 10, at ch. 4.

14. 1 American Prisons, *supra* note 10, at 92–95. *See also* Am. Friends Service Committee, Struggle for Justice 172–73 (1971).

15. Policy Choices, *supra* note 8, at 10.

16. For a discussion of the development of Auburn Prison, *see* H. Barnes & N. Teeters, New Horizons in Criminology 505–47 (rev. ed. 1945). For information regarding the current operating condition of Auburn Prison, *see* Am. Correctional A., Directory: 1981 Juvenile and Adult Correctional Departments, Institutions, Agencies and Paroling Authorities 179 (1981).

17. *See generally* D. McDonald, The Price of Punishment: Public Spending for Corrections in New York (1980).
18. R. Carter, D. Glaser & L. Wilkins, Correctional Institutions 41–60 (2d ed. 1977).
19. M. Gottfredson & D. Gottfredson, Decisonmaking in Criminal Justice: Toward the Rational Exercise of Discretion 250–57 (1980).
20. *See, e.g.,* E. Goffman, Asylums (1961); Schrag, *Leadership Among Prison Inmates,* Am Soc. Rev. 11 (1960); G. Sykes, The Society of Captives: The Study of a Maximum Security Prison (1958); *and* D. Clemmer, The Prison Community (1958).
21. B. Ney & W. Nagel, Release Procedures 5 (1980). *See also* American Prisons, *supra* note 10, at 123.
22. *See* A. Von Hirsch & K. Hanrahan, Abolish Parole? 15 (1981).

23. For a description and study of the California Subsidy Program, *see* E. Lemert & F. Dill, Offenders in the Community (1978).
24. *See generally* J. Irwin, Prisons in Turmoil (1980); *and* J. Jacobs, Stateville (1977).
25. *See* Deterrence, *supra* note 28, at 234–36; *and* G. Kassebaum, D. Ward & D. Wilner, Prison Treatment and Parole Survival 14 (1971).
26. U.S. Dep't of Justice, Prisoners in State and Federal Institutions on December 31, 1979 at 4–5 and Profiles of State Prison Inmates: Sociodemographic Findings from the 1974 Survey of Inmates of State Correctional Facilities 4–8 (1979).
27. *See* Christianson, *Our Black Prisons,* 27 Crime and Delinquency 364 (1981).

STUDY QUESTIONS FOR READING 28

1. Which prison goal does prison best attain? Why? What are its limitations?

2. Do we need more prisons to punish (or give "just deserts" or retribution)? Why or why not?

3. In Newman's view, do prisons deter? How does he know?

4. Newman says it is ludicrous to claim that rehabilitation is a *goal* of prisons. Why?

5. According to Newman, should training and treatment programs be available in prisons? In your view, *will* training and treatment programs be offered if rehabilitation is *not* a goal of corrections? Why or why not?

6. Do longer prison sentences generate more punishment, more deterrence, or less recidivism than shorter sentences? Do prisons work better than lower-cost alternatives in the community?

REHABILITATION

JAMES Q. WILSON

The first edition of this book [*Thinking About Crime*] appeared in 1975 on the heel of an article by the late Robert Martinson in which he reviewed the result of well over two hundred separate efforts to measure the effects of programs designed to rehabilitate the convicted offender. Martinson's article[1] was a summary of what he, with Douglas Lipton and Judith Wilks, had published in a massive volume that had initially been commissioned by the New York State Governor's Committee on Criminal Offenders.[2] That volume systematically examined virtually all of the studies available in print between 1945 and 1967 that met various modest tests of methodological adequacy. The major conclusion of that review as stated in Martinson's article soon became familiar to almost everyone even casually interested in crime-control programs: "With few and isolated exceptions, the rehabilitation efforts that have been reported so far have had no appreciable effect on recidivism."[3]

It did not seem to matter what form of treatment in the correctional system was attempted—whether vocational training or academic education; whether counseling inmates individually, in groups, or not at all; whether therapy was administered by social workers or psychiatrists, whether the institutional context of the treatment was custodial or benign; whether the sentences were short or long; whether the person was placed on probation or released on parole; or whether the treatment took place in the community or in institutions. Indeed, some forms of treatment (notably a few experiments with psychotherapy) actually produce an *increase* in the rate of recidivism.

The Martinson review was unique in its comprehensiveness but not in its findings. R. G. Hood came to much the same conclusion in a review published in 1967;[4] Walter C. Bailey, after examining one hundred studies of the efficacy of treatment and especially the fifty or so that claimed positive results, concluded in 1966 that the "evidence supporting the efficacy of correctional treatment is slight, inconsistent, and of questionable reliability";[5] Leslie T. Wilkins observed in 1969 that "the major achievement of research in the field of social psychology and treatment has been negative and has resulted in the undermining of nearly all the current mythology regarding the effectiveness of treatment in any form."[6]

In retrospect, little of this should have been surprising. It requires not merely optimistic but heroic assumptions about the nature of man to lead one to suppose that a person, finally sentenced after (in most cases) many brushes with the law, and having devoted a good part of his youth and young adulthood to misbehavior of every sort, should, by either the solemnity of prison or the skillfulness of a counselor, come to see the error of his ways and to experience a transformation of his character. Today we smile in amusement at the naïveté of those early prison reformers who imagined that religious instruction while in solitary confinement would head to moral regeneration. How they would now smile at us at our presumption that conversations with a psychiatrist or a return to the community could achieve the same end. We have learned how difficult it is by governmental means to improve the educational attainments of children or to restore stability and affection to the family, and in these cases we are often working with willing subjects in moments of admitted need. Criminal rehabilitation requires producing equivalent changes in unwilling subjects under conditions of duress or indifference.

By the end of the 1970s, politicians and scholars alike had by and large learned the same message—"nothing works." In fact, that is not quite an accurate summary of what Martinson and the others found or said. His article and their book contained many hints that *some* reductions in criminality for *some* kinds of offenders under *some* circumstances were possible. But the exaggeration contained in the popular conclusion was pardonable, for even giving the most generous possible interpretation to the hints of success here and there did not allow one to find any clear and consistent rehabilitative effect on which a public policy might be based.

And it would take strong evidence of such an effect to ease the growing philosophical doubts that many persons were beginning to entertain about criminal court sentences that depended on the presumption of rehabilitation for their justification. If rehabilitation is the goal, and persons differ in their capacity to be rehabilitated, then two persons who have committed precisely the same crime under precisely the same circumstances might receive very different sentences, thereby violating the offenders' and our sense of justice. The indeterminate sentence, widely used in many states, is expressive of the rehabilitation ideal: a convict will be released from an institution, not at the end of a fixed period, but when someone (a parole board, a sentencing board) decides he is "ready" to be released. Rigorously applied on the basis of existing evidence about what factors are associated with recidivism, this theory would mean that if two persons together rob a liquor store, the one who is a young black male from broken family, with little education and a record of drug abuse, will be kept in prison indefinitely, while an older white male from an intact family, with a high school diploma, and no drug experience, will be released almost immediately. Not only the young black male, but most fair-minded observers, would regard that outcome as profoundly unjust.

In practice, the system does not work as its theory implies. But neither does it work well. The decision when to release a prison inmate is, in many states, given over to a parole board from which few if any appeals are possible. In New York State, for example, the twelve members of the board of parole, who in the early 1970s had jurisdiction over all prisoners serving more than ninety days (a total well in excess of twenty thousand) could, among other things, decide when to release a prisoner who was serving an indeterminate sentence. Supposedly the board examined all aspects of the prisoner's life and behavior to decide if he is "ready" for release. If it were capable of and had the time for such profound judgments, it might well behave in the way described in the aforementioned liquor store example. But of course no board can make profound judgments about the thousands of cases it hears every year, with the result that it adopts instead a rule of thumb: if a prisoner is thought to be "rehabilitated," he will be released when he has served one-third of his sentence or three years, whichever is less. The board decided who was rehabilitated and who was not by reviewing a file of reports and questioning the inmate for ten or fifteen minutes at an interview. If parole was denied, the inmate was not told the reason; if he objected, there was no appeal.

The Citizen's Inquiry on Parole and Criminal Justice in New York City prepared in 1974 a study of the results of this parole system. For a four-year period, the percentage of prisoners returned to prison within one-year was calculated for those who were granted parole and those who, by being denied parole, were required to serve their full sentence. Overall there was no statistically significant difference between the return to prison rates of those paroled and those not—about 10 or 11 percent of each group went back to prison within the year.[7] Clearly, the parole board was unable to guess who had been rehabilitated and who had not.

As the scientific basis for the possibility of rehabilitation was shown wanting, the philosophical rationale for making it the chief goal of sentencing began collapsing. By the latter part of the 1970s, there appeared a revival of interest in the deterrent, incapacitative, and retributive functions of the criminal justice system.

But not everyone was convinced that rehabilitation had failed. During the 1960s, there had developed in California a remarkable concentration of talent and energy devoted to finding and testing rehabilitation programs, especially ones designed to treat delinquents in the community. Marguerite Q. Warren, Ted Palmer, and others not only used advanced psychological testing to classify delinquents by personality type and employed skilled counselors to provide intensive community supervision, they randomly assigned delinquents to the treatment and control groups in order to insure the best possible scientific evaluation of the results.

At first, these results were encouraging, so much so that the President's Commission on Law Enforcement and Administration of Justice, in its 1967 report to Lyndon Johnson, endorsed the Community Treatment Program (CTP) of the California Youth Authority, describing it as having reduced delinquency (as measured by parole revocation) from 52 percent among youth who were incarcerated before release to 28 percent among those given intensive counseling in the community.[8]

The Martinson article was particularly critical of these claims. In their reanalysis of the California data, Lipton, Martinson, and Wilks concluded that Warren and her colleagues had substantially undercounted the number of offenses committed by the youth in the experimental community program. Apparently, probation officers assigned to these delinquents developed such close relations with their charges, and were so eager to see their program succeed, that they failed to report to the authorities a number of offenses committed by the experimentals, whereas youth assigned to the control groups had their offenses reported in the normal way by probation and parole authorities.

Given the resources devoted to the California project and the publicity it had received, it is hardly surprising that its leaders counterattacked. Ted Palmer published in 1975 a rebuttal to the Martinson article, claiming that it overlooked or downplayed a number of success stories in the rehabilitation literature and that in particular it misrepresented the CTP. Palmer conceded that the youth in the experimental program had a number of offenses overlooked by counselors, but argued that these were largely minor or technical violations, many of which were detected simply because the youth were under closer observation and some of which involved merely the failure to partici-

pate regularly in the intensive supervision program. Moreover, the Martinson review ended in 1967; if it had continued through 1973, Palmer said, the differences between experimentals and controls, at least for serious offenses, would have been clear.[9]

Martinson responded vigorously to this challenge, and the battle was joined.[10] In the midst of the verbal pyrotechnics of Palmer and Martinson—they were nothing if not spirited adversaries—a new and, as it turned out, more weighty voice was heard. Paul Lerman, a Rutgers sociologist, published a book-length evaluation of the CTP (as well as of the California probation subsidy program) in which he concluded, after a painstaking analysis of the published data, that "the CTP did not have an impact on youth behavior that differed significantly from the impact of the control program."[11] Moreover, the "community" focus of the experimental program turned out to be somewhat exaggerated—in fact, the great majority of experimental youth were placed in detention at least once and many were detained repeatedly in order to maintain control over them. Indeed the youth in the experimental "community" program were more likely to be sent to detention centers than the control group supervised by regular parole officers. Finally, Lerman found strong evidence that, though the CTP had tried to match experimental and control groups by randomly assigning youth to each, over the many years the program operated the two groups began to differ markedly in their characteristics as persons dropped out of the program for one reason or another. In particular, the experimental group came to be composed disproportionately of persons who were older, had higher IQ's, and were diagnosed as "neurotic" (rather than as "power-oriented"). This intriguing finding, largely buried in an appendix to the Lerman book, raises issues to which we shall return presently.

Lerman had made many of these points earlier in a 1968 article; he made them more elaborately in the 1975 book. Curiously, Palmer, who continued to protest against the Martinson article, appears to have taken little notice, at least publicly, of the Lerman criticisms. Palmer's book length attack on Martinson and his reassertion of the claims of the CTP appeared in 1978; there is no mention of Lerman in it.[12]

While the debate in correctional journals raged, the public view, insofar as one can assess it from editorials, political speeches, and legislative initiatives, was that Martinson was right. Because of this widespread belief that "nothing works," the National Research Council, the applied research arm of the prestigious National Academy of Sciences, created in 1977 a Panel on Research on Rehabilitative Techniques, chaired by Professor Lee Sechrest, then of the Department of Psychology of Florida State University. The panel was charged with reviewing existing evaluations of rehabilitative efforts to see if they provided a basis for drawing any conclusions about the effectiveness of these efforts. Its first report—on efforts to rehabilitate in correctional institutions—was issued in 1979; a second report, on how to design better efforts, appeared two year later.[13]

Owing to the importance in the public debate of the review by Lipton, Martinson, and Wilks (LMW), that book was made the focus of the panel's attention. In addition, the report examined reviews that analyzed studies appearing after 1968, the cutoff date for the LMW review. Among the papers commissioned by the panel was a detailed reanalysis of a sample of the studies analyzed by LMW, carried out by two scholars not identified with the ongoing debate, Stephen Fienberg and Patricia Grambsch.

The conclusion of the panel is easily stated: by and large, Martinson and his colleagues were right. More exactly, "The Panel concludes that Lipton, Martinson, and Wilks were reasonably accurate and fair in their appraisal of the rehabilitation literature."[14] If they erred at all, it was in being overly generous. They were sometimes guilty of an excessively lenient assessment of the methodology of a given study. Moreover, the evaluations published since 1968 provide little evidence to reverse this verdict. For example, David F. Greenberg's 1977 review of the more recent studies comes to essentially the same conclusion as Martinson.[15] S. R. Brody's survey in England on the institutional treatment of juvenile offenders agrees.[16]

The panel looked in particular at Palmer's argument that nearly half the studies cited by Martinson showed a rehabilitative effect. The panel was not persuaded: "Palmer's optimistic view cannot be sup-

ported, in large part because his assessment accepts at face value the claim of the original authors about effects they detected, and in many instances those claims were wrong or were overinterpretations of data. . . ." In any event, "we find little support for the charge that positive findings were overlooked."[17]

The conclusion that Martinson was right does not mean that he or anyone else has proved that "nothing works," only that nobody has proved that "something works." There is always the chance, as the panel noted, that rehabilitative methods now in use but not tested would, if tested, show a beneficial effect and that new methods yet to be tried will prove efficacious.

RECIDIVISM, RATES, AND RESTRICTIVENESS

The most dramatic new argument in the continuing debate over rehabilitation, however, comes from two authors who do not, at first glance, appear to be writing about rehabilitation at all. Charles A. Murray and Louis A. Cox, Jr., members of a private research organization, were retained to find out what happens to chronic delinquents in Chicago who are confronted by sanctions of varying degrees of restrictiveness.[18]

The Chicago authorities wanted to know if any of the programs offered in that city (ranging from commitment to a conventional juvenile reformatory, to newer programs that left the delinquent in the community or sent him to a program) changed the rate at which delinquents committed offenses. Such studies have been done many times, usually with the negative results reported by Martinson. But Murray and Cox redefined the outcome measure in a way that seems to make a striking difference. Until now, almost all students of recidivism "rates" or rehabilitation outcomes have measured the success or failure of a person by whether or not he was arrested for a new offense (or was convicted of a new offense, or had his parole revoked) after leaving the institution or completing the therapeutic program. "Success" was an either-or proposition: if you did not (within a stated time period) get into trouble again, you were a success; if you did get into trouble—*even once*—you were a "failure." Though the evaluators of rehabilitation programs typically speak of "recidivism rates," in fact they do not mean "rate" at all; they mean "percent who fail." More accurately, they use "rate" in the sense of "proportion," as in the "birth rate" or the "tax rate." But there is a different meaning of rate: the *frequency* of behavior per unit of time. Even a cursory glance through the studies reviewed by Lipton, Martinson, and Wilks reveals that almost all of them use "recidivism rate" to mean "the proportion who fail."

It was Murray's and Cox's happy thought to use rate in the sense of frequency and to calculate how many arrests per month were charged against a given group of delinquents before and after being exposed to Chicago juvenile treatment programs, and to do so separately for each kind of program involved. They examined three groups of youth.

The first was composed of 317 serious delinquents. They had been arrested an average of 13 times prior to being sent to the Department of Corrections, which was when Murray and Cox first started to track them. They were young (the average age was sixteen) but active: they had been charged with 14 homicides, 23 rapes, over 300 assaults and 300 auto thefts, nearly 200 armed robberies, and over 700 burglaries. The boys entered the study by having been sentenced by the court to a state correctional institution where they served an average of about ten months. Murray and Cox followed them for (on the average) seventeen months after their release.

By the conventional measure of recidivism, the results were typically discouraging—82 percent were rearrested. But the *frequency* with which they were arrested during the follow-up period fell dramatically— the monthly arrest rate (that is, arrests per month per 100 boys) declined by about *two-thirds*. To be exact, the members of this group of hard-core delinquents were arrested 6.3 times each during the year before being sent away but only 2.9 times each during the seventeen months on the street after release.

The second group consisted of 266 delinquents who were eligible to go to a state reformatory but who instead were diverted to one of several less custodial programs run by the Unified Delinquency Intervention Services (UDIS), a Cook County (Chicago) agency created to make available in a coordinated fashion noninstitutional, community-based programs

for serious delinquents. Though chosen for these presumably more therapeutic programs, the UDIS delinquents had criminal records almost as severe as those sent to the regular reformatories—an average of over 13 arrests per boy, of which 8 were for "index" (that is, serious) offenses, including 9 homicides, over 500 burglaries, and over 100 armed robberies. Nonetheless, since these youths were specially selected for the community-based programs, one would expect that in the opinion of probation officers, and probably in fact, they represented somewhat less dangerous, perhaps more amenable delinquents.

Despite the fact the UDIS group may have been thought more amenable to treatment, the reduction in their monthly arrest rates was *less* than it had been for the group sent to the reformatories (about 17 percent less). In general, UDIS did not do as well as the regular Department of Corrections. Even more interesting, Murray and Cox found that the more restrictive the degree of supervision practiced by UDIS, the greater the reduction in arrest rates. Youths left in their homes or sent to wilderness camps showed the least reduction (though some reduction nonetheless); those placed in group homes in the community showed a greater reduction; and those put in out-of-town group homes, intensive-care residential programs, or sent to regular reformatories showed the greatest reduction. If this is true it implies that how strictly the youth were supervised rather than what therapeutic programs were available, had the greatest effect on the recidivism rate.

Ordinarily, we do not refer to the crime-reduction effects of confinement as "rehabilitation." Technically, they are called the results of "special deterrence" ("special" in the sense that the person deterred is the specific individual who is the object of the intervention, and not the general delinquent population). "Rehabilitation" usually refers to interventions that are "nice," benevolent, or well intended, or that involve the provision of special services. A psychologist might say that rehabilitation involves "positive reinforcements" (such as counseling) rather than "negative reinforcements" (such as incarceration). Indeed, the National Research Council Panel defines rehabilitation as the result of "any planned intervention" that reduces further criminal activity, "whether that reduction is mediated by personality, behavior, abilities, attitudes, values, or other factors," provided only that one excludes the effects of fear or intimidation, the latter being regarded as sources of special deterrence.

Although the distinction has a certain emotional appeal, it makes little sense either scientifically or behaviorally. Scientifically, there is no difference between a positive and negative inducement; behavioral psychologists long ago established that the two kinds of reinforcements have comparable effects. (It is not generally true that rewards will change behavior more than punishments, or vice versa.) Behaviorally, it is not clear that a criminal can tell the difference between rehabilitation and special deterrence if each involves a comparable degree of restriction. Rehabilitation can (and usually does) involve a substantial degree of coercion, even of intimidation ("be nice or you won't get out," "talk to the counselor or stay in your cell," "join the group discussion or run the risk of being locked up"). Behavior-modification therapy can involve the simultaneous use of positive reinforcers ("follow the rules and earn a token") and negative ones ("break the rules and lose a token"). It might help the discussion of offender-oriented programs if the distinction between rehabilitation and special deterrence were collapsed.

The real issue raised by the Murray-Cox study is not, however, what to call the effect they observe, but whether they have actually observed any effect at all. A number of criticisms have been made of it, but two are of special importance. First, does the decline in arrests indicate a decline in actual criminality or merely an increase in skill at avoiding apprehension? Second, if there is an actual decline in criminality, might this not be explained by the maturation of youth, that is, growing out of crime as they become older? Michael D. Maltz, Andrew C. Gordon, and their colleagues made these and other criticisms in response to a preliminary report of the Murray-Cox findings.[19] In their later, book-length treatment of the Chicago project, Murray and Cox responded.

The second criticism seems the easiest to answer. Murray and Cox were able to show that the decline in rearrest rates existed for all incarcerated serious delinquents regardless of age. As an additional check, the authors examined a third group—nearly 1,500 youth born in Chicago in 1960 and arrested at least once by the Chicago Police Department before their seventeenth birthdays. Since this group was chosen at random from all arrested youth of the same age, it naturally is made up primarily of less serious offenders. Indeed, only 3 percent of this group was ever referred to UDIS or the Department of Corrections. When the monthly arrest rates for this group were examined, the data showed a more or less steady increase throughout the teenage years. Being arrested or being placed on probation had no apparent effect on subsequent delinquency. By all the tests they used, therefore, the decline in arrest rates for those delinquents given strict supervision cannot be explained by the fact that they were simply getting older.

The other criticism is harder to answer. Strictly speaking, it is impossible to know whether arrest data are a reasonable approximation of the true crime rate. No one argues, of course, that every crime results in an arrest. All that is at issue is whether a more or less constant fraction of all crimes result in arrests. There are two possibilities: either having been arrested before draws police attention to the boy (he is "stigmatized" or "labeled"), thus making him *more* likely to be arrested for subsequent crimes; or the arrest and subsequent punishment increases his skills at avoiding detection (the system has served as a "school for criminals"), thus making him *less* likely to be arrested for a given offense.

Now it is obvious that the first of these two possibilities—the "labeling" effect of being arrested—cannot be true, for as we have seen, delinquents who are placed under supervision have their subsequent arrest rates *decline*. If the police "pick on" previously arrested youth, either they do so without making an arrest (by keeping an eye on "troublemakers," for example) or they try harder to arrest them but find the youth are not committing as many crimes as before.

The other possibility—that boys become skilled at avoiding arrest—is impossible to disprove, but Murray and Cox raise some serious questions as to whether this gain in skills, if it occurs at all, could explain the decline in arrest rates. Perhaps their most telling argument is this: one must not only believe that correctional institutions are "schools of crime," one must believe they are such excellent schools that they produce a two-thirds gain in arrest-avoiding skills. This would make reformatories and group homes the most competent educational institutions in the country, since no one has yet shown that conventional schools, with the best available educational technology, can produce comparable gains in learning non-criminal skills. And all this must be accomplished within the ten-month period that is the average length of detention. It is still possible, of course, that the "schools of crime" hypothesis is true, but it requires one to make some heroic assumptions in order to sustain it: that large numbers of boys learn more during ten months reformatory than they learn in ten years on the street; that the great majority, despite their statements to the contrary made to interviewers, increase their commitment to crime as a way of life (rather than as an occasionally profitable activity) as a result of incarceration; and that the object of their efforts when back on the street is to employ their sharpened skills at avoiding apprehension while committing relatively unprofitable crimes rather than attacking more profitable (and riskier) targets.

Though Murray and Cox make a persuasive case for the validity of their findings, it cannot be taken as a conclusive study. For one thing, we would like to know what happens to these delinquents over a much longer period. Most studies of rehabilitation suggest that any favorable effects tend to be extinguished by the passage of time (though such extinction usually appears within the first year). We would also like to know more about the kinds of offenses for which these persons were arrested, before and after court intervention (perhaps they change the form of their criminal behavior in important ways). And above all, we would like to see such a study repeated in other settings by other scholars. It may even be possible to do this retrospectively, with data already in existence but never before analyzed using frequency of offending (rather than proportion of failures) as the measure of outcome.

In fact, long before the Murray-Cox study, LaMar T. Empey and Maynard L. Erickson had reported on the Provo Experiment in Utah, an effort to reduce delinquency that was evaluated by arrest rates before and after treatment—the same outcome measure used by Murray and Cox (indeed, the latters' book contains a foreword by Empey). The Provo Experiment was, in principle at least, an even better test of changing recidivism rates than the Chicago project because the former, unlike the latter, randomly assigned delinquent boys to either treatment or control groups and kept detailed records (in addition to before-and-after measures) of what actually happened to the boys in the treatment programs. The experimental program was community-based, but, unlike conventional probation or even group homes, involved an intensive level of participation in a supervised group discussion program, absence from which was promptly penalized by being locked up. The program was in time killed by community opposition (many persons thought it excessively punitive, others quarreled over who should pay for it). The four years worth of data which could be gathered, however, indicate that there have been substantial reductions in arrest rates that cannot be explained by maturation or social class differences for all boys. This was true of both those incarcerated and those left in the community, with the greatest reductions occurring among boys in the experimental programs.[20] Though open to criticism, the Provo data provide some support for the view that, if one measures offense *frequency,* some kinds of programs involving fairly high degrees of restrictiveness and supervision may make some difference.

The Murray-Cox and the Empey-Erickson studies are important, not only because they employ rates rather than proportions as the outcome measure or even because they suggest that something might work, but also because they suggest that the study of deterrence and the study of rehabilitation must be merged—that, at least for a given individual, they are the same thing. Until now, the two issues have been kept separate. It is not hard to understand why: welfare and probation agencies administer "rehabilitation," the police and wardens administer "deterrence"; advocates of rehabilitation think of themselves as "tender-minded," advocates of deterrence see themselves as "tough-minded"; rehabilitation supposedly cures the "causes" of crime, while deterrence deals only with the temptations to crime; psychologists study rehabilitation, economists study deterrence. If Murray-Cox and Empey-Erickson are correct, these distinctions are artificial, if not entirely empty.

The common core of both perspectives is, or ideally ought to be, an interest in explaining individual differences in the propensity to commit crime, or changes in a single individual's propensity over time. The stimuli confronting an individual can rarely be partitioned neatly into things tending to produce pain and those likely to produce pleasure; most situations in which we place persons, including criminals, contain elements of both. If explaining individual differences is our object, then studying individuals should be our method. Studies that try to measure the effect on whole societies of marginal changes in aggregate factors (such as the probability of being imprisoned, or the unemployment rate) are probably nearing the end of the line—even the formidable statistical methodologies now available are unlikely to overcome the gross deficiencies in data that we shall always face.

Policy makers need not embrace the substantive conclusions of Murray and Cox (though it is hard to see how they could reasonably be ignored) to appreciate the need to encourage local jurisdictions to look at the effect of a given program on the rate of behavior of a given set of offenders. If they do, they may well discover, as Murray and Cox feel they discovered in Chicago, that for the serious, chronic delinquent, the strategy of minimal intervention (probation, or loosely supervised life in the community) fails to produce any desirable changes (whether one calls those changes deterrence or rehabilitation), whereas tighter, more restrictive forms of supervision (whether in the community or in an institution) may produce some of these desired changes, or at the very least not produce worse delinquency through "labeling" or "stigmatization." It is hard to imagine a reason for not pursuing this line of inquiry.

ENDNOTES

1. Robert Martinson, "What Works?—Questions and Answers About Prison Reform," *The Public Interest* (Spring 1974): 22–54.

2. Douglas Lipton, Robert Martinson, and Judith Wilks, *The Effectiveness of Correctional Treatment: A Survey of Treatment Evaluation Studies* (New York: Praeger, 1975).

3. Martinson, "What Works," p. 25.

4. R. G. Hood, "Research on the Effectiveness of Punishments and Treatments," in *Crime and Justice,* vol. 3, ed. Leon Radzinowicz and Marvin E. Wolfgang (New York: Basic Books, 1971), pp. 159–182.

5. Walter C. Bailey, "Correctional Outcome: An Evaluation of 100 Reports," in Radzinowicz and Wolfgang, *Crime and Justice,* p. 190.

6. Leslie T. Wilkins, *Evaluation of Penal Measures* (New York: Random House, 1969), p. 78.

7. Citizens' Inquiry on Parole and Criminal Justice, *Report on New York Parole* (March 1974). See also Robert W. Kastenmeier and Howard C. Eglit, "Parole Release Decision-Making," *American University Law Review* 22 (Spring 1973): 477–525.

8. *The Challenge of Crime in a Free Society,* A Report by the President's Commission on Law Enforcement and Administration of Justice (Washington, D.C.: U.S. Government Printing Office, 1967), p. 170.

9. Ted Palmer, "Martinson Revisited," *Journal of Research in Crime and Delinquency* 12 (July 1975): 133–152.

10. Robert Martinson, "California Research at the Crossroads," *Journal of Research in Crime and Delinquency* 13 (April 1976): 180–191.

11. Paul Lerman, *Community Treatment and Social Control* (Chicago: University of Chicago Press, 1975), p. 67.

12. Ted Palmer, *Correctional Intervention and Research* (Lexington, Mass.: Lexington Books/D.C. Health, 1978). Some hesitant support for Palmer's position is provided in a review of the Lerman book by Eugene Bardach in *Policy Analysis* 3 (1977): 129–136.

13. Lee Sechrest et al., eds., *The Rehabilitation of Criminal Offenders* (Washington, D.C.: National Academy of Sciences, 1979); Lee Sechrest et al., *New Directions in the Rehabilitation of Criminal Offenders* (Washington, D.C.: National Academy of Sciences, 1981).

14. Sechrest, *The Rehabilitation of Criminal Offenders,* p. 5.

15. David F. Greenberg, "The Correctional Effects of Corrections: A Survey of Evaluations," in *Corrections and Punishment,* ed. David F. Greenberg (Beverly Hills, Calif.: Sage Publications, 1977), pp. 111–148.

16. S. R. Brody, *The Effectiveness of Sentencing—A Review of the Literature,* Home Office Research Report No. 35 (London: HMSO, 1976).

17. Sechrest et al., *The Rehabilitation of Criminal Offenders,* p. 31.

18. Charles A. Murray and Louis A. Cox, Jr., *Beyond Probation* (Beverly Hills, Calif.: Sage Publications, 1979).
19. Michael D. Maltz, Andrew C. Gordon, David McDowall, and Richard McCleary, "An Artifact in Pretest-Posttest Designs: How It Can Mistakenly Make Delin-quency Programs Look Effective," *Evaluation Review* 4 (1980): 225–240.
20. LaMar T. Empey and Maynard L. Erickson, *The Provo Experiment* (Lexington, Mass.: Lexington Books/D.C. Heath, 1972).

STUDY QUESTIONS FOR READING 29

Editor's Note: According to Wilson, there is no evidence that prison makes inmates worse, and some that it deters certain kinds of offenders, especially certain young ones. Interviews with prisoners reveal no relationship between the number of crimes committed and whether the offenders had served a prior prison term. At least, there is no evidence that the net effect of prison is to increase the crime rates of ex-cons enough to cancel out the gains from incapacitation. (These ideas come from elsewhere in Wilson's book, *Thinking About Crime,* p. 147.)

1. After Martinson reviewed hundreds of rehabilitation studies, he never quite said "nothing works," but most scholars and politicians heard him say that. How does Wilson describe what Martinson *did* say? Does he think this popular characterization of Martinson was fair? Why or why not?

2. According to Wilson, is it easy to change criminals? Why or why not?

3. According to Wilson, what did the Murray and Cox study show about various kinds of punishment?

READING 30

REHABILITATION CAN WORK

ELLIOTT CURRIE

Some of the same considerations that prompt greater attention to middle-range sanctions also suggest a related point: that an effective anticrime program must reconsider the recently fashionable rejection of rehabilitating offenders. Again, one of the most unfortunate aspects of the conservative approach to crime is that it provides no middle ground—nothing that we can do with offenders short of either warehousing them in prisons or simply letting them go, to cope with their problems on their own. There are times when either of those options is doubtless the right one. Some criminals surely cannot be much helped by anything we know how to do; others pose no real danger to the rest of society and would be better off with a minimum of interference. But those are extremes. In the middle are vast numbers of people who appear before the courts suffering from a wide variety of personal and social problems. Our current practice is generally to let them go until they do something bad enough or often enough to justify imprisoning them. Once they are behind bars, little or nothing is done with them before they get out, at which point they are either resolutely neglected by the larger society or, if they cause enough further damage, are thrown back behind bars with much self-righteous headshaking. This is one tragic consequence of a world-view that cannot envision a significant role for public authorities other than the reactive power to coerce and punish.

But liberal criminology, too, has had a hand in creating this situation. The liberal wariness about the claims and motives of many programs ostensibly designed to rehabilitate offenders was often well founded. But it is one thing to criticize the oppressive or trivial character of so much of what has passed for treatment of criminals and delinquents, another to throw out the idea of rehabilitation altogether. For doing the latter requires us to believe either that criminal offenders (unlike most of the rest of us) do not have problems deep enough to require help in overcoming them, or that the larger society has no responsibility for seeing to it that they get such help if they need it. This is a clear instance of what I've called the liberal failure to acknowledge pathology—the unwillingness to confront the fact that people who do violent things to others often have a great deal wrong with them.

There is scattered evidence that doing nothing at all may even be the worst course of all for some violent offenders. This was one conclusion of a Harvard University evaluation of the well-known experiment in closing the youth training schools in Massachusetts in the seventies. The study did show that even very dangerous youths could be safely treated in smaller, community-based facilities, and that the need for conventional youth prisons had been much exaggerated. But it also found that to leave these youths without *any* services was likely to increase their rates of delinquency.

The ideological attack on the concept of rehabilitation has usually been accompanied by the argument that nothing more constructive can be done anyway—that we have "tried" rehabilitation and discovered that it "doesn't work." But the reality is considerably less discouraging. To begin with, while it was true that rehabilitation carried far more rhetorical weight in the sixties than it did in the next decade, in practice serious rehabilitation programs, either inside or outside the prisons, were even then attempted only sporadically, and never on a scale that could remotely be said to have tested the potential of rehabilitation itself. In the sixties, for example, the youth prisons of the District of Columbia were widely thought to be among the most advanced in the country in terms of their commitment to rehabilitating rather than simply warehousing the youth under their care. But as the President's Commission on Crime in the District of Columbia pointed out at the time, the resources they actually devoted to that task were minuscule; the youth facilities "lacked even the rudiments of essential diagnostic and clinical services"; there was "little time for individual counseling and no group therapy" in the juvenile institutions. The District of Columbia Children's Center had one full-time psychiatric staff member and one part-time to serve over two thousand youths.

The conclusion that rehabilitation had failed was based in part on a series of studies reviewing the scattered evaluations of rehabilitation programs up through the mid-sixties, of which the best known was done by Robert Martinson and his colleagues at the City University of New York. Summarizing that research in 1974, Martinson concluded that "with few and isolated exceptions, the rehabilitative efforts that have been reported so far have had no appreciable impact on recidivism." Martinson's conclusion, already gloomy enough, was amplified considerably in the less careful accounts of his work by the media, which quickly began to proclaim that, when it came to rehabilitating criminals, "nothing works."

Similar conclusions had been offered by earlier reviews of the evidence, such as it was, on rehabilitation programs before the sixties. But these conclusions were much stronger than the data warranted, and their enthusiastic reception had at least as much to do with ideology as with evidence. For the critique of rehabilitation, in this sweeping and categorical form, was attractive to both ends of the political spectrum. To the criminological Right, it offered further testimony that the only feasible response to criminal offenders was increased efforts at deterrence and incapacitation, and it served in a deeper sense to confirm the view that crime reflected fundamental flaws in human nature or in the constitution of offenders. In spite of all our best efforts, the research seemed to say, you can't do anything with these people after all, so you shouldn't try.

For the Left, on the other hand, the apparent failure of rehabilitation frequently supported a very different argument: that given the deep social and economic sources of crime in the United States little could be gained (and much abuse would be encouraged) by tinkering with offenders in the name of "individual treatment."

But both of these extreme views strained credibility. As Donald West remarks, "Fashionable as it has become, there is a certain implausibility" about the conclusion that "nothing works." "It seems to imply that nothing one does to delinquents, however kind or however nasty, makes the slightest difference." By the late seventies, there was already some fragmentary but significant evidence for a more encouraging view, and it has grown since. In 1979 the criminologists Paul Gendreau and Bob Ross published a survey of more recent evaluations of rehabilitative programs, arguing that some of them had indeed worked, at least for some offenders. In the same year, the National Academy of Sciences came to similar conclusions, only a bit more restrained. A Rand Corporation report in 1976 had already suggested that the "nothing works" verdict had been too hasty, and cited several programs whose positive results seemed to have survived hard scrutiny. Moreover, Charles Murray and Louis Cox's evaluation of the UDIS program in Illinois. . . . seemed to suggest—although this was not necessarily their intention—that indeed everything worked: that programs ranging from community based counseling services to residential camps and intensive psychiatric care all reduced delinquency among hardened young offenders. And by the end of the seventies, Martinson himself had changed his mind dramatically; on the basis of new evidence, he "withdrew" his earlier conclusion that "rehabilitative efforts have no appreciable effect on recidivism."

These more positive assessments center on two points. They find considerably more evidence of success in some kinds of programs, under some conditions, than the earlier studies—in part, because they examine more recent programs that are more intensive and more carefully evaluated. But even more importantly, they also suggest that we know something about *why* rehabilitation "fails," when it does; and that the reasons don't lie solely with the unregenerate human material with which the programs must contend, but also with intrinsic limitations in the programs themselves and in the larger community to which offenders must return.

To begin with, many rehabilitation programs simply didn't do what they were designed on paper to do. Most lacked what Gendreau and Ross call *therapeutic integrity;* that is, they failed to follow through on their theoretical assumptions about what rehabilitation would actually require (if they had theoretical assumptions at all). The programs cited by Martinson and other critics as evidence that rehabilitation did not work were often not only underfunded and understaffed, but typically staffed by poorly trained and often unmotivated people. The early critics of rehabilitation made little effort to separate reasonably serious and intensive programs from those—vastly more common—that at best offered minimal counseling or tutoring to people who were otherwise allowed to languish in the enforced bleakness of institutions or in the shattered, dead-end communities from which they had come. This led a National Academy of Sciences (NAS) panel, in their 1979 review, to conclude that "when it is asserted that 'nothing works,' the Panel is uncertain as to just what has even been given a fair trial."

By the same token, however, the rather unsurprising failures of most conventional rehabilitation programs suggest some of the requirements for success. From the scattered evidence collected by Gendreau and Ross, by the NAS panel, by the supported work experiments, and by others, it's possible to piece together some of the characteristics of those programs that are likely to be successful, and which, therefore, seem worthy of serious further exploration.

Interestingly, most of the positive assessments of rehabilitation suggest that what distinguishes promising from unpromising approaches is not so much any specific program or therapeutic technique. Robert Martinson argued in 1979 that "the most interesting general conclusion is that no treatment program now used in criminal justice is inherently either substantially helpful or harmful." The "critical fact seems to be the *conditions* under which the program is delivered." More concretely, the evidence suggests that the "strength and integrity of treatments," as the NAS

panel put it, is crucial; whatever the specific technique used in treatment programs, the most important issue is whether it is implemented intensively, seriously, and for a reasonable length of time. When these conditions are met, the results can be impressive. We've seen this already in the case of supported work for addicted offenders. And the principle is affirmed in Murray and Cox's evaluation of the UDIS program. For what's striking about the various alternatives to imprisonment UDIS offered is how mild and short-range most of them—even those defined as "most restrictive" or "intensive"—really were in practice. One of the most effective programs, according to Murray and Cox, was the out-of-town residential camps. These camps were hardly regimented, intrusive, "total institutions." In one of them, youths were put to work at construction and painting; they attended classes in an alternative school and went on overnight camping trips, hikes, and riding excursions, along with swimming and other sports. Another camp was designed around the theme of exploring rural life: hiking, camping, talking with farmers, and observing farm life. It also had an urban component along the same lines, which included exploring city neighborhoods and going to museums. In the first camp, the average youth stayed two to four months; in the second, about six weeks. Yet these relatively limited experiences were superior, measured by their effects on later delinquency, to traditional imprisonment—even for very serious delinquents.

The "strength and integrity" of the programs, then, is clearly one factor in whether rehabilitation "works" or not. Another is whether the program is closely linked with other community resources—schools, employers, social-service agencies, networks of relatives, and neighborhood organizations. This finding makes considerable sense in light of the clear importance of "informal" communal institutions in crime prevention, a finding we've encountered at several points. Linking delinquents with the range of available services in the community was a central principle of the UDIS program and a major ingredient in its success. Similarly, in evaluating the sources of success or failure in programs developed in Massachusetts, Robert Coates argues that the more successful programs were those that closely involved the surrounding community and the delinquents' families on a day-to-day basis, rather than being "community" programs only in the sense of being located in a neighborhood rather than an institution. As Coates puts it, what is important is "working with youth in the context of their networks":

The youngster is a participant in numerous networks (family, peer groups, school, work) that influence his or her behavior and at times compete for his or her allegiance. To expect that directing short-term treatment only at the individual will dramatically alter those network relationships that have been shaped over many years is unrealistic at best and foolhardy at worst.

Thus it is important to think of rehabilitation not so much as something that takes place only within the minds of individual offenders, but also as a process of strengthening their relationships with the communal and familial institutions that most influence their lives.

Communities, however, cannot function well in this capacity unless they can offer a modicum of stability and the means for a decent and dignified life as the fruit of respectable and cooperative behavior. And it is this problem . . . that bedevils even truly serious rehabilitative programs and that most tellingly reminds us that what appears to be "failure" on the surface is often less a failure of the programs themselves than of the institutions of the larger community. This obvious but often overlooked reality is illustrated most dramatically in a recent study by William McCord and Jose Sanchez of the careers of 1950s graduates of New York's Wiltwyck School for delinquents. This research is worth examining in some detail, because it offers a compelling look at both the genuine potential of serious efforts at rehabilitation and the roots of their frequent failure.

McCord and Sanchez compared two groups of men who had been institutionalized as adolescents either at Massachusetts's Lyman School—a conventional, punitive, regimented youth prison—or at Wiltwyck, a school for severely disturbed boys that offered an intensive and supportive therapeutic environment. The two institutions were about as far apart in philosophy and practice as they could be.

Wiltwyck offered its residents what its founders called "disciplined love." It emphasized the avoidance of punitive discipline, the encouragement of self-government, and the development of a "community of understanding." The school's basic aim was "to increase the child's understanding of the consequences of his behavior, to enhance his self-esteem, and to offer him a degree of emotional security." As McCord and Sanchez note, "Since the children usually came from brutal urban environments, the unwalled school provided a totally new milieu." Wiltwyck's departure from conventional prison practice won it considerable liberal support in the state, including that of Eleanor Roosevelt; its graduates included Claude Brown and Floyd Patterson.

On the other hand, at Lyman—the first American reform school and one of the most typical—"the slightest deviation from the rules—such as talking when not allowed, 'stubbornness,' or disobedience—resulted in physical punishment and a sentence to the 'disciplinary cottage,' " in which "the master maintained absolute silence." "Those children who avoided harsher discipline," McCord and Sanchez write, "typically spent their time in a silent classroom or in a field where they shovelled manure." In this respect, Lyman was "neither better nor worse" than the average youth prison in America. As in most of them, the aim was "to mold children through punitive discipline and rudimentary education," emphasizing the principles of "punishment, incapacitation, and severity" over the "therapeutic milieu" attempted at Wiltwyck.

McCord and Sanchez traced the histories of all 175 boys who had been at Wiltwyck for eighteen months or longer between 1952 and 1955, as well as a random sample of 165 boys who had graduated from Lyman in the same years. By the beginning of the 1980s, they were in their late thirties or early forties. How had they fared in the meantime? The results, as measured by commitments for serious criminal offenses, were at first quite confusing. For the first five years after release, the Wiltwyck graduates had very low rates of recidivism, particularly as compared with the Lyman youths. At earlier and more crime-prone ages, McCord and Sanchez point out, the Wiltwyck approach seemed "significantly effective in preventing felonies." Wiltwyck's policies appeared to work— at first—even for the most troubled youths, those who had been defined as "psychopathic" and were often "violent, impulsive, and aggressive." At ages fifteen to nineteen, for example, the Wiltwyck graduates diagnosed as "psychopathic" were rearrested for felonies after graduation at a rate of just 11 percent; the Lyman graduates, 79 percent. But though the Wiltwyck boys never reached as high a level of recidivism as the Lyman youths had at the beginning, their troubles with the law, *after* the first five years beyond graduation, increased steadily with age. Those of the Lyman graduates, on the other hand, generally *decreased* with age and, by the late twenties, were lower than those of the Wiltwyck group.

What accounted for the curious pattern of early success and later declines among the Wiltwyck graduates? Only one difference in the characteristics of the two groups seemed to matter: "the person's ethnic background." The increases in recidivism in the Wiltwyck boys took place entirely among black and Hispanic graduates; with increasing age, the rates for *white* graduates declined. And this ethnic difference explained much of the variance in the patterns of recidivism over time between Wiltwyck and Lyman, because the Wiltwyck boys were more often black and Hispanic, the Lyman boys more often of European descent—Irish, Italian, or French-Canadian. It was this ethnic mix, McCord and Sanchez argue on the basis of official records as well as interviews with some of the graduates, that largely accounted for the fact that "in contrast to the Wiltwyck group, many of the men from Lyman found it relatively easy to deal with life on the outside." They quote one Lyman graduate of Irish descent, a retired policeman, to the effect that "I fooled around a lot when I was a kid. . . . But then I got an uncle on the force. When I was twenty, he got me my first job as a traffic man. And look at me now—sitting on this porch and enjoying life. It helps to have the Irish connection." By contrast, the positive effects of the Wiltwyck experience for the school's heavily minority graduates deteriorated because of the deprivation and discrimination they encountered in their communities of origin. They had nothing comparable to the "Irish connection." Interviews with these men in later life

suggested that all of the men remembered Wiltwyck fondly—perhaps, in a sense, too fondly. The sojourn at Wiltwyck offered a welcome relief from "real" society. As the years passed, experiences at Wiltwyck became largely irrelevant. The blacks and Hispanics encountered discrimination in education, jobs, and housing—a feeling of frustration which dashed the hopes Wiltwyck had engendered.

"In fact," the authors conclude, "Wiltwyck rehabilitated most of its boys." But by ten years after graduation, they "faced the all-too-tangible barriers of prejudice and lost the advantages given them by the treatment at Wiltwyck." And the lesson that McCord and Sanchez draw is surely the correct one: not that rehabilitation is doomed to fail, even for severely troubled youths, but that "effective treatment in childhood must be accompanied by a fundamental change in opportunities and intergroup relations."

STUDY QUESTIONS FOR READING 30

Editor's Note: Currie places much faith in the argument that prisons are "schools for crime." He cites Dinitz and Conrad who found that the more formal the intervention, the quicker the delinquent returned to arrest, even when controlling for offense, age, sex, race, and socioeconomic status. He also cites West who found that for those delinquents who were convicted, delinquency rose by 16 percent, but for those who were not convicted, but had reported the same rates of delinquency earlier, delinquency fell by 14 percent. (These ideas come from earlier in Currie's book, *Confronting Crime*, pp. 78–80.)

1. According to Currie, has rehabilitation been "tried" and found "not to work"? Why or why not? In your answer, discuss the caseload of the "model" youth prisons in D.C.

2. To Currie, the work of Murray and Cox suggested, although this was not necessarily their intention, that instead of saying "nothing works" it would be safer to
   say what?

3. What were the camp programs like in the Murray and Cox Study? According to
   Currie, how effective were these programs compared to "total institutions"? How
   does this differ from Wilson's view?

4. Currie points out that Martinson himself withdrew what previous conclusion he
   made about rehabilitation?

5. Wilson said the National Academy of Sciences ruled that Martinson was right,
   when they said Martinson was "reasonably accurate and fair in their appraisal of
   the rehabilitation literature." In stark contrast, what does Currie quote the National
   Academy of Sciences as saying?

6. Compare Wiltwyck to Lyman school for boys. Which one "rehabilitated" its boys?
   Which one had lower long-term recidivism? How do the authors explain this?

ESSAY QUESTIONS FOR PART FOUR

In your answers, be sure to use one sentence at the end of your first paragraph to offer a clear thesis statement—that is, a statement of your point of view and your arguments for it. Then, in each paragraph of your answer, give evidence to support one of your arguments. Cite specific authors and give specific, concrete support for your point of view by offering statistics, case studies, examples, quotations, expert opinions, and so on.

1. In your opinion, should we build more prisons based on the extent that prisons meet each of the following goals:
    *   rehabilitation
    *   incapacitation
    *   deterrence
    *   retribution

    In your answer, be sure to include and evaluate information from this part of the book, as well as earlier parts. Be sure to respond to the arguments and evidence of those with whom you disagree.

2. Does rehabilitation work? Can it work? In your answer, be sure to include the insights of both Wilson and Currie.

PART FIVE

DO ALTERNATIVES TO PRISON WORK?

Alternatives to prison are designed to reduce prison overcrowding and save money; at the same time, they are intended to provide rehabilitation and sufficient incapacitation, deterrence, and retribution. The critics of alternatives charge that some of these programs may not meet these goals. Furthermore, instead of providing an alternative to prisons, they may instead replace *probation,* or "widen the net." In Part Five, we explore the extent to which the stated goals of prison are met by several prison alternatives: boot camps, mediation, shaming, community service, restitution, probation, and probation with various enhancements.

The authors of the first reading argue that boot camps do not reduce prison crowding or recidivism, although they do provide other benefits to offenders. Current boot camps seem to be designed for men, not women, and they pose special problems for juveniles. Although boot camps do not ordinarily reduce prison crowding, they can if they serve as early-release mechanisms for offenders who would otherwise have been sent to prison. Boot camp inmates do not recidivate less than prisoners or probationers do. However, some programs do reduce recidivism—those that schedule more than three hours per day for counseling, drug treatment, and education, and that provide some community follow-up after release. Boot camps do offer other benefits: Offenders leave boot camps drug free and physically healthy, and they are optimistic about the future. However, the authors oppose boot camps for juveniles because nonviolent juveniles would not be incarcerated, so net-widening is a real problem. And nonviolent and status offenders do not belong in the "destructive environment" of juvenile institutions. Further, women do not fare well in men's camps; if women can't go to boot camp, however, they will have fewer opportunities for therapeutic programming and early release. Therefore, these authors favor separate boot camps for women that offer programs designed to address women's needs: employment and vocational training, treatment for substance abuse, domestic violence and sexual assault counseling, parenting education, life skills education, and community reintegration. Men also have these needs, so the authors suggest that all boot camps should be redesigned to meet these needs.

The next reading examines work in a boot camp in Maryland. Officers choose boot camps for some of the same reasons inmates do: They think the atmosphere will be better than a regular prison, and they think the discipline will do them good. Most officers who attend training are excited about the program but unprepared for its challenges. Training to work (and working) in boot camps for offenders is rigorous, but successful officers learn to lead by example. Officer training consists of a month of grueling sixteen-hour days, in which officers run hundreds of miles and do thousands of pushups and sit-ups. As one officer puts it, "Army boot camp was nothing compared to this." Out of thirty-nine officers who started the program in Maryland, only fourteen graduated. "A few failed out. Most quit." The training is designed to help officers teach by example; once employed, officers cannot ask inmates to do anything they cannot do. One officer says, inmates "see a 44-year-old man out here doing it, and they know they can do it." Recidivism has been low, and there are other measures of success, including the cleanliness of the camp's grounds, the respect between staff and inmates, and the absence of disturbances and vandalism.

In the following reading, several federal probation officers explain a day in their lives. They tell moving stories of their clients who range from the tragic to the despicable, and they discuss whether probation significantly reduces crime. One officer talks with emotion about his clients, including a mentally ill client named Sheila. Sheila's mother hates her and has done things to her that have been

> *so destructive [and] so malicious . . . as to be almost beyond comprehension. . . . Sheila's mother hates her, but she has never been able to leave her. . . . Entering this house is like walking into a den of hate. . . . In all the years . . . I have never witnessed a kind word, seen a gentle touch, or heard genial laughter.*

Another officer writes about a fraudulent client who is a danger to the public:

> *[He] has made a career out of defrauding the public . . . [and has] sold fraudulent oil leases, rare coins, precious stones, and vacation time shares. [He] will no doubt return to some sort of criminal activity the day after he gets off supervision. In his case, a term of probation is truly protecting the public.*

One officer, however, expresses concern that protecting the public is the exception, not the rule:

> *I sometimes wonder, as all probation officers do, if anything I do really ever makes a difference. Do I ever do anything that prevents a man from being murdered, a child from being abused, a woman from being raped? I don't know. I can probably* never *know. I can only hope.*

Another officer emphasizes the importance of supervision and verification, which she argues can hold the offender accountable and can reduce crime.

The next reading is about intensive probation supervision (IPS) in Georgia. This program requires offenders to meet with their probation officers face-to-face five times a week, undergo random drug and alcohol testing, become and remain employed, and perform 132 hours of community service. IPS was found to cost less than prison, to divert offenders from prison, and to cause offenders to commit fewer and less serious crimes than regular probationers or parolees. IPS in Georgia was found to be a true alternative to prison, rather than an alternative to regular probation. Researchers also found that IPS saves almost $7,000 for each offender diverted from prison, even when the costs of prison construction are not included. Further, the authors point out that any estimation of program costs should include the value of the community service performed by IPS offenders. The authors assert that "IPS offenders commit fewer and less serious crimes." These offenders also absconded at a lower rate than regular probationers. However, IPS offenders had a higher rate of rearrest and reconviction than regular probationers because they were arrested more often for minor repeat offenses such as marijuana possession, and probation officers were likely to detect these offenses, given the higher level of surveillance.

Shaming is another way to enhance probation and avoid prison. Shaming seems to have certain advantages; it is cost-effective and retributive, and it may be rehabilitative and a deterrent. Douglas Litowitz argues, however, that shaming is neither rehabilitative nor a deterrent because it is negative and conveys the message that the offender is "thoroughly contemptible." Although Litowitz acknowledges that prisons are also unsuccessful as a deterrent, he asserts that if drug dealers are not deterred by ten- or twenty-year prison sentences, they will probably not be deterred by being forced to "walk around city hall in a T-shirt proclaiming that they are drug dealers." As for public confessions, he suspects that only voluntary apologies are rehabilitative; when the confession is forced, the offender simply goes through the motions. If shaming is to show any promise at all, the focus must be on reintegration after the shaming, by helping the offender rejoin society successfully, which is conspicuously absent from American shaming. Litowitz concludes that we should look to more promising sanctions instead of "dusting off methods of punishment from the dark ages."

Probation can also be enhanced by requiring community service. In the next reading, Julie Martin argues that community service can save money, but only when it *replaces* prison as a punishment. For community service to be cost-effective for other offenders, it must yet be proven to sufficiently rehabilitate, punish, and deter. Most community service clients are "extremely unlikely candidates for imprisonment." And it is only when the clients are prison-bound offenders that the programs save money. One such program in New Mexico spent only $85,000 and saved $1.4 million in prison costs. In contrast, one study found that another community service program for juveniles cost $3 for every $1 worth of labor donated. However, many people believe in community service for reasons other than cost savings. One probation officer wrote, "[Community service] is satisfying to the public because they see the offenders out there doing something, and it's good for the offenders because they feel justice is being done." One offender stated, "I don't like working without pay, but when you compare ten days of this with ninety days of Rikers [jail]—whew, there's no choice." But does community service rehabilitate? Some experts think so, but others disagree. Nonetheless, one judge takes a strong stand that community service raises self-esteem and keeps offenders connected with the community. In one study, 71 percent of offenders felt they had benefitted from community service.

Restitution programs require the offender to perform community service or to pay money to the victim and/or the justice system or both; Richard Lawrence concludes that the Texas restitution program saves money compared to prison, and it helps rehabilitate offenders. He assumes, however, that all 3,000 offenders in Texas who were placed in the restitution program would have gone to prison, and he points out that the restitution program is cheaper than prison for a variety of reasons. Prison costs $37 a day, but the program Lawrence discusses costs only $30. Offenders live in restitution centers and repay victims and the community while they work and pay for room and board, transportation, taxes, and court and probation costs. Offenders pay about half a million dollars per year toward these costs. At night and on weekends, offenders perform community service. If this service is valued at minimum wage, these offenders contribute $1.6 million per year. The Texas program also seems to be successful in terms of rehabilitation. Seventy-five percent of offenders were unemployed at the time they entered the program, but only 25 percent were unemployed at the time of their release. In the first five years of the program, 60 percent of offenders were discharged successfully, 12 percent were discharged for rule or technical violations, and only 2 percent were discharged for new offenses, most of which were misdemeanors.

Some restitution programs are set up by the justice system, and may require offenders to pay restitution to the system or to the victim, but restorative justice requires mediation between the victim and offender, with those two parties agreeing on the type and amount of restitution. Restorative justice differs from retributive justice, and works through mediation programs that are popular with victims, offenders, and the public. In the retributive system, crimes are seen primarily as a violation of "the King's Peace," rather than the victim. In restorative justice, the offender is not asked to pay an abstract debt to society by being punished, but to make things right by paying a debt directly to the victim. Restorative justice emphasizes restoring the victim to his or her former state, rather than using punishment to hurt the offender as badly as the victim was hurt. Restorative justice works through mediation: The mediator meets with the victim and offender separately, listens to both stories, explains the program and encourages participation. The actual mediation session lasts about one hour. During the mediation session, victims and offenders talk about what happened and how each party feels about the offense. Victims ask questions such as, "Why me?" and "How did you get into our house?," and "Were you stalking us and planning on coming back?" Finally, losses and restitution are discussed. Afterwards, victims often report that they are relieved: The offender often bears little resemblance to the frightening "criminal" they had imagined. Offenders report that mediation is difficult, but allows them to express remorse in a direct and personal way. Ninety-five percent of mediation sessions result in a written agreement for restitution. In addition, surveys show that more than 80 percent of the public would participate in mediation if they were a victim of a nonviolent property crime committed by a juvenile or young adult, which describes the vast majority of crimes.

EVALUATING CORRECTIONAL BOOT CAMP PROGRAMS
ISSUES AND CONCERNS

ANGELA R. GOVER
GAYLENE J. F. STYVE
DORIS LAYTON MacKENZIE

Boot camp prisons require offenders to serve a short term in a prison or jail in a quasi-military program similar to boot camp or basic training in the military. Today, many local and state governments as well as the Federal Bureau of Prisons are using this correctional option for adult as well as juvenile offenders. The programs are characterized by a structured environment that promotes order and discipline. Inmates rise early in the morning and follow an intensive schedule of daily activities. Boot camp advocates expect the regimented environment to instill discipline in youthful offenders.

Components of boot camp programming vary depending on the philosophy of the institution. Some programs may devote nearly five hours per day to military activities such as drill and ceremony, marching, and physical labor. Other programs with more of a rehabilitative focus may devote more time to activities such as counseling, academic education, or drug treatment. In addition to programming differences, other differences among boot camp models include program capacities, program location, participant eligibility criteria and selection practices, program duration, populations served, and community aftercare components. These differences, especially the emphasis placed on programming components and goals, will have an effect on participants' successful completion of the program. From a research perspective, such diversity among programs makes it difficult to generalize findings from an individual site evaluation to other programs.

This [reading] reviews the research on correctional boot camps for adults and juveniles. The research to date has been disappointing to boot camp advocates because there is no evidence that these programs have had long-term impacts on participants. In examining the research, it becomes obvious that we do not have a good grasp of what components of the boot camps are expected to change offenders. Literature reviews and meta-analyses provide some consensus about the components of effective rehabilitation programs. However, there is little available information on whether boot camps incorporate these components into their environments.

A DAY IN THE LIFE OF A BOOT CAMP INMATE

Upon arrival at the boot camp prison, male inmates have their heads shaved (females may be permitted short haircuts) and they are informed of the strict program rules. At all times they are required to address staff as "Sir" or "Ma'am," to request permission to speak, and to refer to themselves as "this inmate." Punishments for minor rule violations are summary and certain, frequently involving physical exercise such as push-ups or running; major rule violations may result in dismissal from the program.

In a typical boot camp prison, the ten- to sixteen-hour day begins with a predawn reveille. Inmates dress quickly and march to an exercise yard where they participate in an hour or two of physical training followed by drill and ceremony. Then they march to breakfast where they are ordered to stand at parade rest while waiting in line and to exercise military movements when the line moves. Inmates are required to stand in front of the table until commanded to sit and are not permitted to make conversation while eating. After breakfast they march to work sites where they participate in hard physical labor that frequently involves community service, such as cleaning state parks or highways. When the six- to eight-hour work day is over, offenders return to the compound where they participate in more exercise and drill. A quick dinner is followed by evening programs consisting of counseling, life skills training, academic education, or drug education and treatment.

Boot camp inmates gradually earn more privileges and responsibilities as their performance and time in the program warrants. A different color hat or uniform may be the outward display of their new prestige. Depending upon the facility, somewhere between 8 and 50 percent will fail to complete the program. For those who successfully complete the program, an elaborate graduation ceremony occurs with visitors and family invited to attend. Frequently awards are given for achievements made during the program. In addition, the inmates often perform the drill and ceremony they have practiced throughout their time in the boot camp.

DIFFERENT PERSPECTIVES ON CORRECTIONAL BOOT CAMPS

Boot camps are controversial for a variety of reasons (MacKenzie and Souryal, 1995a; MacKenzie and Parent, 1992; Meachum, 1990; Morash and Rucker, 1990). Much of the controversy has to do with an instinctive reaction toward the military atmosphere. It is important, however, to separate this instinctive reaction from the debates that occur among people who are more knowledgeable about the programs and corrections in general. Here, there is a much more interesting debate. One perspective exhibited by many knowledgeable correctional experts is a "Machiavellian" point of view (MacKenzie and Souryal, 1995b). These individuals expect little direct benefit from the military atmosphere of the boot camp programs, but

are willing to support the concept to achieve two ends: early release for nonviolent offenders and additional funding for treatment programs (both inside and outside prison). In their opinion, the popularity of the boot camps with policy makers and the public allows early release and treatment that would not otherwise be available to these offenders.

Opponents of the boot camp model fear dangers associated with this correctional option. Many psychologists who are experienced in both corrections and behavioral change take this position when examining boot camp programs. They believe that the potential dangers of the military model are too great to compromise for early release or funds for treatment. Furthermore, they argue that boot camps cannot provide a mechanism for treatment because many of the characteristics of the programs (confrontation, punishment instead of reward, etc.) are antithetical to treatment. The confrontational interactions may be particularly damaging for some individuals such as those who have been abused in the past or others who have problems with dependency in relationships. Morash and Rucker (1990) contend that aspects of the boot camps may actually inflict damage on participants. Additionally, boot camp opponents fear that even though some programs may be used as early release mechanisms, most have a serious potential for widening the net (i.e., adding to the overall numbers of offenders in confinement—perhaps drawing more from those who would be subject to probation than from those who would serve prison sentences). The net-widening issue is particularly critical for the newly developing juvenile programs.

There are some additional concerns about using these programs for juveniles. Juveniles may be in a different stage of development. It may be difficult for the juveniles to obey authority figures if they do not believe that such obedience is in their own best interest. They may rail against the injustice of group punishment. Some juveniles, such as those who have been victimized in the past, may have additional problems that make the boot camps a harmful experience for them. An additional fear is that the program will greatly increase the number of juveniles incarcerated due to the fact that they appear to many to be the perfect solution for an unruly and undisciplined juvenile.

Another perspective argues that the military atmosphere is an effective model for changing offenders. Persons who have worked in drug treatment programs—where strict rules, discipline, and confrontational interactions are common—seem to be more comfortable with the military model. Military personnel assert that the leadership model of basic training provides new and appropriate techniques for correctional programming. Of course, many of those responsible for the development and implementation of individual boot camp programs are committed to and believe in the viability of this approach. They argue that the stress created in boot camp may shock the inmates and make them amenable to change and thus take advantage of the treatment and aftercare programs offered. Further, the military atmosphere of boot camp may actually enhance the effectiveness of this treatment by keeping the offenders physically and mentally healthy while enabling them to focus on their education, treatment, and therapy.

So the debate continues. What is clear is that these boot camps are proliferating across the nation, yet we have limited knowledge about their effects on the individuals involved and the impact on correctional systems. The main point may be that we need to identify the beneficial aspects of the camps as well as the potential drawbacks. Certainly, we can assume that the effect of the camps will differ depending upon the needs of the individuals involved. Further, we need detailed information on the specific components of the programs and how these components affect those involved. Lastly, we need to learn what type of boot camp is (or is not) effective for specific types of offenders.

EMPIRICAL RESEARCH EXAMINING THE EFFECTIVENESS OF BOOT CAMP PROGRAMS

Research examining correctional boot camps focuses on the impact of the programs on: (1) prison crowding and costs; (2) changes made by participants during the time they are in the boot camps; (3) women participants; (4) recidivism and adjustment of the participants when they return to the community; and, (5) juvenile offenders.

Impact on Prison Crowding

Many correctional programs are designed to be intermediate sanctions which are less restrictive than prison but more restrictive than probation (Morris and Tonry, 1990). Because boot camp prisons are commonly considered not to be more restrictive than prison, they are often categorized this way. The problem is that intermediate sanctions may, on the one hand, have a net-widening effect and, on the other, require a greater degree of structured control over the offender's daily activities. The former adds to the cost of corrections due to the increased overall number of offenders, the latter due to the necessary increase in staff time. While boot camps may not involve a significantly smaller degree of control, they may reduce the amount of time that the offender is incarcerated and thus reduce correctional costs.

On the other hand, if offenders who would normally be given probation are being sent to the boot camps then we might expect both the costs and prison crowding to increase. MacKenzie and Piquero (1994) examined the impact of adult boot camps on prison crowding using a statistical model that weighted the impact of factors such as program size, number of dismissals, and recidivism rates. In the models, they varied the percent of the offenders who would have been given sentences of probation or prison. The results indicated that boot camps can reduce prison crowding if they are designed as early release mechanisms for offenders who would have been sent to prison. However, while the programs may have the potential to reduce prison crowding, in actuality they seldom do. For example, in the multi-site evaluation completed by MacKenzie and her colleagues, only two of the five boot camp programs examined appeared to save prison beds (MacKenzie and Piquero, 1994; MacKenzie and Souryal, 1994). In the remaining three states, the boot camp programs appeared to increase the need for prison beds. Thus, the evidence that boot camp prisons reduce crowding and the associated costs is not extremely persuasive.

The Impact of the Programs on the Participants

To date, research examining boot camps has shown very little negative impact from the programs.

Offenders have reported being drug free and physically healthy when they leave the boot camps (MacKenzie and Souryal, 1994). Participants have also reported that the program helped them and they were optimistic about the future. This was true of the "enhanced" boot camp programs that emphasized treatment as well as programs that predominantly focused on military training, hard labor, and discipline. Also, when MacKenzie and Souryal (1995a) examined changes in antisocial attitudes they found that participants in the boot camps, as well as the comparison samples of prisoners, became less antisocial. Again, results on the effectiveness of the boot camps are mixed and we are left with questions about the specific components of the camps that lead to positive change. In an exploratory analysis, these authors found some evidence that participants became less antisocial in boot camps that devoted more time to rehabilitation, had higher dismissal rates, and were voluntary (Ibid.).

Women in Boot Camps

The majority of the boot camp participants are male. For this reason, most of the research examining boot camps has focused on male offenders. In a 1992 survey of state prisons, MacKenzie et al. (1996) found thirty-nine boot camps for adults operating in twenty-five states. Only thirteen of these states had female participants who comprised a mere 6.1 percent of the total number of incarcerated boot camp offenders. Most of the female inmates were integrated into programs along with the male participants. Only four states operated separate programs for women.

MacKenzie and Donaldson (1996) studied six boot camps that had female participants. In direct interviews, the women reported difficulties keeping up with the physical demands of the program. They further reported experiencing extensive emotional stress because the majority of the boot camp staff and inmates were male. It is for this reason that some researchers and practitioners argue that it is not appropriate to integrate female boot camp inmates with male inmates and drill instructors as a high proportion of incarcerated women have past histories of abuse by men (MacKenzie et al., 1996). This abuse factor com-

bined with the highly confrontational environment of boot camps is likely to trigger emotions associated with past feelings of mental and physical abuse for many women. Furthermore, when comparing programs that integrated men and women to programs with women only, women in separate programs reported less emotional and physical stress. Therefore, it is important to consider the potential effects of gender integration on program participants during the early stages of program development.

Some of the boot camp programs do offer increased opportunities for therapeutic programming such as drug treatment and parent training. Others offer participants a way to obtain early release. These opportunities may not be available to inmates in regular prison. Therefore, if women are excluded from participation in boot camps they may not have the same chance for similar therapeutic programming or early release.

Previous descriptive studies of women offenders have identified some of their major needs as the following: employment or vocational training to prepare them to support themselves and their children; treatment for substance abuse; domestic violence and sexual assault counseling; and education/training on issues related to family obligations such as parenting, life skills, and community reintegration (American Correctional Association, 1993). MacKenzie and Donaldson (1996) found the characteristics of the female boot camp inmates to be similar to the characteristics of the typical female inmates identified in these earlier studies. Therefore, in their opinion, these characteristics should be programming considerations for boot camps with female populations.

Nearly all of the female inmates interviewed in the MacKenzie and Donaldson study had children for whom they would be financially responsible when returning to the community. Programs with lenient visitation policies would help establish, reunite, and maintain relationships between mothers and their children while they are incarcerated. Also, since a large proportion of female boot camp inmates reported having some type of serious problem associated with drug use, the provision of drug treatment and services is a key component of an effective treatment model. Yet, many of the boot camps did not incorporate components that would address the needs of women offenders. After examining the boot camps, MacKenzie and Donaldson conclude that most boot camps are designed with the male inmates in mind, and women are placed in the camps as an afterthought. Therefore, they suggest all programs be designed for females. Such programs would emphasize parenting skills and responsibilities, or education about spousal abuse. Those developing boot camps should ask themselves why such programs are not appropriate for men.

Recidivism and Community Adjustment of Adult Boot Camp Releasees

At this point in time there have been no experimental studies examining the impact of boot camps on the community adjustment and recidivism of adult offenders. In a recent report looking at the effectiveness of crime prevention programs, Sherman and colleagues examined both the scientific rigor and the results of the research on the recidivism of boot camp participants (1997). They found few studies reached moderate levels of scientific quality, although some of the research made use of statistical controls to adjust for the original differences between the boot camp releasees and comparison groups. In general, the results demonstrated no significant difference in recidivism between offenders who were sent to the boot camps and those who were given probation or prison sentences. The recidivism rates of offenders who served time in the boot camps were approximately the same as the rates of offenders who had served other sentences such as prison or probation.

After reviewing the results of the adult and juvenile boot camp research, Sherman and colleagues concluded there was no evidence that the military atmosphere, structure, and discipline of correctional boot camps significantly reduced the recidivism of releasees in comparison to other correctional sanctions (1997). However, in some programs where a substantial number of offenders were dismissed from the boot camp prior to completion, the recidivism rates for those who completed the program were significantly lower than the rates for those who were dismissed. Thus, although there is no evidence that the boot camps actually change offenders, there is some indi-cation that the programs can be used to "signal" which offenders will have difficulty completing probation or parole. From this perspective, offenders who remain in the program and complete it are less at risk for recidivism than those who are dismissed (by either voluntarily dropping out or being expelled for misbehavior).

In one exploratory analysis examining program differences and recidivism rates, MacKenzie et al. (1995) found some commonalities among programs where the boot camp releasees had lower recidivism rates than comparison groups on some but not all measures of recidivism. These programs scheduled more than three hours per day for therapeutic activities such as counseling, drug treatment, and education. The programs also required inmates to volunteer for participation and provided some type of community follow-up after release. Since these are components of treatment programs that have been found to be effective, the researchers ended with the question: "Does the military atmosphere add anything above and beyond a short-term, quality prison treatment program?" They were careful to warn the reader that these results are tentative until more research is completed.

In another study, MacKenzie and Brame (1995) found that boot camp releasees adjusted more positively than comparison samples during community supervision in only one of five sites. Thus, both the recidivism studies and the positive adjustment studies suggest that there may be some programs that have positive impacts on participants. However, the specific components that lead to positive change remain unclear.

Correctional Boot Camps for Juveniles

As boot camp programs have moved from adult prisons to local jails and juvenile populations, new issues have arisen (Cronin, 1994; Austin, Jones and Bolyard, 1993). For example, while adult programs could target nonviolent offenders in prison, nonviolent juveniles are much less likely to be incarcerated. Thus, net-widening and the associated costs have become critical issues in the development of juvenile programs. This is particularly relevant given the history of concern with the destructive environment of detention centers for nonviolent juveniles or status offenders. The deceptively seductive idea of providing discipline and structure for disruptive juveniles means there is a real threat that increasingly large numbers of juveniles will be placed in boot camps, regardless of whether it is a suitable alternative sanction. Furthermore, in contrast to adult boot camps, academic and therapeutic programming as well as aftercare are viewed as necessary components in juvenile programs. In fact, besides the military atmosphere, there are questions about how much the boot camp programs actually differ from other residential facilities for juveniles.

The emergence of juvenile boot camps has been a recent and explosive trend. In June of 1995, MacKenzie and Rosay (1996) surveyed state and local juvenile correctional administrators and identified a total of thirty-seven programs operating at that time. Only one of these programs opened prior to 1990 with nearly all of them opening during or after 1993. The passage of the 1994 Crime Act permitted the Department of Justice to allocate a substantial amount of funding for juvenile boot camps; twelve jurisdictions were awarded grants to develop boot camp programs for juveniles and another twelve jurisdictions received funds for the renovation of existing facilities or the construction of new ones. Thus, the number of juveniles in boot camps will most likely continue to increase in the next few years.

The type of juveniles participating in boot camp programs tend to be fairly similar. Unlike adult boot camps, juvenile programs are rarely limited to individuals convicted of their first serious offense and who volunteer. The typical juvenile boot camp inmate was a nonviolent male between the ages of fourteen to eighteen who was placed in the program by a juvenile court judge. However, only about half of the boot camps were solely limited to nonviolent offenders while the other half accepted offenders convicted of violent crimes. Differences among programs can be found in population capacities and program length. The capacities of juvenile boot camps ranged from 12 to 396 and program length ranged from one day to one year.

Almost all boot camps for juveniles emphasized a military atmosphere with drill and ceremony, platoon grouping, and discipline. About half used military ti-

tles and uniforms for both staff and juveniles. In addition to the military atmosphere, the majority included physical labor in the daily activities. Youth also engaged in physical fitness, sports activities, and some type of challenge or adventure programming. Overall, juveniles spent between one and ten hours per day in physical training, military drill, and work. In comparison they spent, on average, about six and a half hours in educational classes or counseling. Because of this heavy emphasis on education and counseling, it comes as no surprise that juvenile boot camp administrators rated rehabilitation as a very important goal of their programs. Reducing recidivism was also rated as very important.

In the crime prevention report authored by Sherman et al. (1997), MacKenzie further reviewed the research examining the impact of juvenile boot camps on delinquent recidivism. The quality of these studies was rated as high since juveniles were randomly assigned to the boot camps or comparison groups. Four random assignment studies examining boot camps in California, Alabama, Colorado, and Ohio were located. In three of the sites there were no significant differences between the boot camp youth and the control groups. In one site the youths released from the boot camp recidivated more than those in the control group. The juvenile recidivism research parallels adult boot camp research; there is no evidence demonstrating the effectiveness of these programs in reducing recidivism.

Summary of the Research

This short review of the literature on boot camp programs for juveniles and adults demonstrates that most research has focused on individual programs and the impact of these programs on subsequent criminal activities. The fact that programs differ dramatically in their goals and components is problematic. Thus, knowledge about the effectiveness of one program may be dependent upon very atypical aspects of the program or even a charismatic leader, and not necessarily be related to boot-camp-type characteristics of the program. The research results may show us that one program works but not *why* that program works. To understand why the program works we need to know more about the relationship between the specific components of the program and the impacts on the individuals involved. Questions revolve around the specific conditions of confinement or the environment of the boot camps. How do conditions of a boot camp differ from traditional prisons and detention centers? What are the impacts of these conditions on those involved? If they do indeed differ for juveniles, there are questions about the effectiveness of the camps for certain types of offenders (e.g., higher risk, older, those with a high number of prior commitments). Furthermore, some are fearful that aspects of the camps may be particularly damaging for some individuals such as those with certain past histories (e.g., juveniles who have been physically or sexually abused).

REFERENCES

American Correctional Association. 1993. *Female Offenders: Meeting Needs of a Neglected Population*. Laurel, MD: American Correctional Association.

Andrews, D. A., I. Zinger, R. D. Hoge, J. Bonta, P. Gendreau, and F. T. Cullen. 1990. Does correctional treatment work? A clinically-relevant and psychologically-informed meta-analysis. *Criminology,* 28:369–404.

Austin, J., M. Jones, and M. Bolyard. 1993. A survey of jail-operated boot camps and guidelines for their interpretation. In *Correctional Boot Camps: A Tough Intermediate Sanction.* D. L. MacKenzie and E. E. Herbert, eds. Washington, DC: National Institute of Justice.

Cronin, R. C. 1994. Boot Camps for Adult and Juvenile Offenders: Overview and Update. National Institute of Justice Research Report, Washington, DC: National Institute of Justice.

Gendreau, P. and R. R. Ross. 1987. Revivification of rehabilitation: Evidence from the 1980's. *Justice Quarterly.* 4:349–407.

Lipsey, M. W. 1992. Juvenile delinquency treatment: A meta-analytic inquiry into the variability of effects. In *Meta-Analysis for Explanation: A Casebook.* T. Cook, H. Cooper, D. S. Cordray, H. Hartman, L. V. Hedges, R. Light, T. A. Louis, and F. Mosteller, eds. New York: Russell Sage Foundation.

MacKenzie, D. L. and R. Brame. 1995. Shock incarceration and positive adjustment during community supervision. *Journal of Quantitative Criminology,* 11:111–142.

MacKenzie, D. L., R. Brame, D. McDowall, and C. Souryal. 1995. Boot camps and recidivism in eight states. *Criminology,* 33:327–357.

MacKenzie, D. L. and H. Donaldson. 1996. Boot camp for women offenders. *Criminal Justice Review,* 21:21–43.

MacKenzie, D. L., L. Elis, S. S. Simpson, and S. B. Skroban. 1996. Boot camps as an alternative for women. In *Correctional Boot Camps: A Tough Intermediate Sanction.* D. L. MacKenzie and E. E. Herbert, eds. Washington, DC: National Institute of Justice.

MacKenzie, D. L. and D. Parent. 1992. Boot camp prisons for young offenders. In *Smart Sentencing: The Emergence of Intermediate Sanctions.* J. N. Byrne, A. J. Lurigio, and J. Petersilia, eds. London: Sage.

MacKenzie, D. L. and A. Piquero. 1994. The impact of shock incarceration programs on prison crowding. *Crime and Delinquency,* 40:222–249.

MacKenzie, D. L. and A. Rosay. 1996. Correctional boot camps for juveniles. In *Juvenile and Adult Boot Camps.* Laurel, MD: American Correctional Association.

MacKenzie, D. L. and C. Souryal. 1994. Multi-Site Evaluation of Shock Incarceration: Executive Summary. Report to the National Institute of Justice. Washington, DC: National Institute of Justice.

MacKenzie, D. L. and C. Souryal. 1995a. Inmates' attitude change during incarceration: A comparison of boot camp with traditional prison. *Justice Quarterly,* 12:325–354.

MacKenzie, D. L. and C. Souryal. 1995b. A "Machiavellian" perspective on the development of boot camp prisons: A debate. *University of Chicago Roundtable.* Chicago: University of Chicago Press.

Meachum, L. M. 1990. Boot camp prisons: Pros and cons. Paper presented at Annual Meeting of American Society of Criminology, Baltimore, MD.

Morash, M. and L. Rucker. 1990. A critical look at the ideal of boot camp as a correctional reform. *Crime and Delinquency,* 36:204–222.

Morris, N. and M. Tonry. 1990. *Between Prison and Probation: Intermediate Punishments in a Rational Sentencing System.* New York: Oxford University Press.

Sherman, L. W., D. Gottfredson, D. L. MacKenzie, J. Eck, P. Reuter, and S. Bushway. 1997. *Preventing Crime: What Works, What Doesn't, What's Promising.* A report to the U.S. Congress prepared for the National Institute of Justice (NCJ-165366).

1. How do boot camps for offenders resemble military boot camps?

2. What does a typical day involve in boot camp?

3. What percentage of inmates fail to complete the program? For those who finish, what type of ceremony is involved?

4. How can boot camps reduce prison crowding? Do they? How do you know?

5. How does boot camp impact participants? Be specific in your answer.

6. Are co-ed boot camps appropriate for women? Single-sex boot camps? Why or why not?

7. What are the needs of women offenders? Do men have these needs too? Do the authors think changing boot camps to address women's needs would help men too?

8. Do boot camp inmates recidivate less than prisoners or probationers? How is recidivism affected by program differences between boot camps?

9. How do juveniles differ from adults who are sent to boot camps? How does programming differ for juveniles as compared to adults? Do juvenile boot camps reduce recidivism?

10. Why do the authors seem to oppose boot camps for juveniles?

WORKING IN A BOOT CAMP

LINDA R. ACORN

Corrections Officer Kevin McKenney chose to work at the Herman L. Toulson Boot Camp in Jessup, Md., for some of the same reasons inmates volunteer to go there: He thought the atmosphere there would be better than in a regular prison, and he knew the discipline involved would do him some good.

McKenney had worked for 11 months at Patuxent Institution, a nearby maximum security facility, and had served in the U.S. Army. He was confident he would have little trouble adjusting to working at a boot camp for youth demeanants.

Six weeks later, after running hundreds of miles, forming thousands of push-ups and sit-ups, and spending weeks learning military drills in the camp's grueling training program, McKenney assesses his choice: boot camp was nothing compared to this.

According to his commander, Maj. Robert Clay, McKenney's reactions to the camp are typical of the officers who ask to work there. Most are excited about the program, but at first are unprepared for the strict behavior code and the rigors of training, he says.

"In the beginning, they can't wait," Clay says. "They think all they've got to do is show up and that they're automatically going to pass."

But the officers quickly learn that working in a boot camp is as demanding as serving time in one. Because the Maryland program requires officers to be able to carry out all of the commands they give the inmates, their training is merciless.

Aside from the intense physical regimen—which includes running at least six miles daily, regardless of the weather—the officers go through intensive skills preparation to ensure they are capable of handling the inmates. They observe the more experienced staff. They learn military lingo. They memorize word-for-word a set of "teach backs"—explanations of how to perform various drill commands and the purpose of each command. And all the while they are treated like military recruits.

"There's a lot of discipline involved," Clay says. "We holler at them and put them through the same regimentation we put the inmates through."

One result of this get-tough training has been that out of the 39 officers who started this year's training program, only 14 graduated. A few failed out. Most quit.

"I think that may be a trait of young people now," says Clay, who is 44. "They just think they can do everything and that it's just going to happen because they showed up. When the realization hits them that it takes hard work and perseverance to make things happen, they quit."

STARTING UP THE CAMP

Clay, a former Marine sergeant who served in Vietnam and a 21-year veteran of the Maryland Division of Correction, helped start up the Jessup boot camp in the summer of 1990. He began by contacting the Marine Corps officer candidate school in Quantico, Va., to set up a training program for himself and six other corrections workers. Their month-long training, which consisted of 16-hour days of constant physical and mental exercise, was at least as tough as the current on-site training, Clay says. By Aug. 5, 1990, he and his staff were ready for the arrival of Maryland's first boot camp inmates.

The six-month camp is open to first-time, nonviolent male offenders ages 17 to 32. It is administered much like boot camp programs in other states, combining military-style discipline and hard work with education and counseling.

The current staff consists of 87 correctional officers, 10 of whom are women. All but one—an officer who came straight from Maryland's corrections academy—worked in other prisons before volunteering to transfer to the camp. Officers at the camp receive the same pay and benefits as staff in regular prisons, but, they say, their roles are very different.

Sgt. Jose Fernandez, who formerly worked at the Baltimore City Correctional Center and the Jessup Pre-release Unit, says officers at the camp are much more actively involved in offenders' lives. "I've worked for seven years for the Division of Correction," he says. "Officers in other prisons—they lose control. There are so many repeat offenders. You get tired of seeing them come back, you get tired of reading about them in papers, but there's nothing you can do. Here we can show them there is another way of life."

LEADING BY EXAMPLE

Officers at the boot camp talk a lot about leading by example. It is this philosophy that makes their training and their daily work with the inmates so demanding.

According to Capt. Stanley Christian, a 20-year corrections veteran, staff must display both physical and mental fortitude to gain the inmates' respect.

"You can lecture people all day, but if you don't practice what you preach, they really won't listen," he says. "The only thing they recognize is strength. We've got to show them we're just as strong as they are . . . if not stronger."

Displaying strength is particularly important during exercise drills. Requiring the inmates to do hundreds of push-ups and sit-ups, even on hot, humid summer days, may seem harsh, Clay says, but he never asks them to perform any exercise he won't perform right along with them, and he regularly joins them in their daily physical regime.

"They see a 44-year-old man out here doing it, and they know they can do it," he says.

All staff follow military codes of discipline throughout the camp, standing at attention to salute the major and addressing him as "sir." They use military jargon—referring to floors as decks and windows as portholes, for example—and they require the inmates to use those terms throughout their stay.

"The reason we have the inmates use Marine Corps terminology is that it teaches them to think before they talk," Clay says. "If we let them use the same street jargon they used when they came here, they wouldn't think. They'd just run their mouths, which gets them into trouble."

Staff also teach inmates how to pack their footlockers in military fashion, and they give them drill formation commands during marching exercises.

About 70 percent of the staff have previous military experience; most are former members of the Marine Corps or served in special Army units, according to Clay. For those who never served, the work is that much more difficult.

Officer Brenda Canceran, a former Patuxent Institution employee who came to the camp with no military background, said learning the teach backs was one of the hardest parts of training. "There's so much to know," she says. "But the discipline is good for you as a person. And so is the exercise—you're always in shape."

Staff not only have to be physically fit and well-disciplined; they also need to demonstrate strong character. At times they must show the inmates their authority, while at others they must offer them compassion.

The inmates expect to be disciplined, Clay says, citing evaluations the inmates complete halfway through their stay. The inmates point out which officers are too easy on them and which ones give them too many chances, Clay says. And at graduation, the inmates most often thank the toughest members of his staff, he says.

The officers must be careful not to take their discipline too far, however. The program allows no hitting or pushing. Clay once dismissed an officer from the program because he was too aggressive. "I'm not like that," he says. "They have to take care of these kids. When everything is just hard, hard, hard, there's no balance. I can't use a person that doesn't have balance."

The ideal balance resembles a good instructor/student relationship, Clay believes. This allows the staff to give inmates guidance, discipline and care without sacrificing authority, he says.

ASSESSING THE BENEFITS

In spite of the many demands on the officers, most like their jobs. The tough training they undergo builds comradery. Officer Canceran says she might never have graduated had it not been for support from her class and her drill instructors.

The officers also believe they can make a difference at the camp in a way they couldn't in other prisons. As Christian says, "We don't get any more money for this. We don't have to go out there. I have over 20 years. I could have retired or I could be sitting in an office somewhere delegating authority. But that shows the kids even more how much you care—that some people really want to help."

No studies have been completed on the still-young Jessup camp, but Clay said the recidivism rate has been low, with only five new arrests among the 300 offenders who graduated in the program's first year. He doesn't consider recidivism a complete measure of success, though, citing the cleanliness of the camp's grounds, the respect between staff and inmates, and the absence of disturbances or vandalism as valuable achievements. He also points to the individual success cases he knows of—former inmates who have called or written with stories of employment and crime-free activities.

Most important, he says, is that he and his staff deliver what the Division of Correction promises.

"If you're just warehousing an inmate and he gets out and commits a crime, maybe it's partly your fault," he says. "Here I know I've shown them the way, and if they don't do it, it's their fault. I've done my part."

STUDY QUESTIONS FOR READING 32

1. How does one correctional officers compare Army boot camp to training to work in boot camps for offenders?

2. Of the 39 officers who started the training, how many finished? Did the others fail or quit?

3. These officers believe they can make a difference in the lives of others. What has recidivism been in the first year? What other measures of success do they offer?

WORKING AS A FEDERAL PROBATION OFFICER

E. JANE PIERSON, THOMAS L. DENSMORE, JOHN M. SHEVLIN,
OMAR MADRUGA, AND TERRY D. CHILDERS

ENHANCED SUPERVISION—NOT NECESSARILY "TAIL 'EM, NAIL 'EM, AND JAIL 'EM"

E. Jane Pierson

Not so long ago, probation officers made home contacts based on a predetermined schedule, whether or not there were any issues to address in that particular case. The "classification" of the case, not the issues, determined the officer's contacts. So when the time came for a "visit" the officer got in his or her car and drove to the residence. Then, the officer would proceed to talk with the "client" about that person's children, spouse, job, school, the weather, or whatever, while leaning against his or her car, "kicking the tire." In those cases, there were no real issues to be addressed.

The above scenario is not likely to be repeated with the implentation of "enhanced supervision." Meaningless "tire kicking" or "quota system" contacts as well as the "monthly reporting ritual" or "assembly line," as this officer referred to it, have been abandoned for a more commonsense approach to supervision. Enhanced supervision is grounded in statutory authority which mandates that the probation officer accomplish certain objectives. Enhanced supervision provides for the officer's evaluation and re-evaluation of issues in each individual case. Issues to be addressed rather than a quota to meet now occupy the officer's day. And occupied it is!

Verification appears to be a key word in enhanced supervision, but then it always has been or, at least, should have been. Verification of the offender's resi-dence; employment and specific job duties; finances; roommates; new charges, disposition of old charges; fine, restitution, and penalty assessment payments; travel requests; attendance at counseling sessions; performance of community service hours; and so on, all have their place in a day's work. Verification by the officer equates to accountability of the offender. Officer verification and offender accountability do not necessarily equate to "tail 'em, nail 'em, and jail 'em," as it may superficially appear. Verification is consistent with this officer's statutory duty to "keep informed . . . as to the conduct and condition of a probationer or a person on supervised release" (title 18, section 3603(2)).

Verification and more verification proved essential in one particular case in which a female, convicted of bank embezzlement, obtained employment as a receptionist. The sentencing judge had imposed a special condition that she must disclose her conviction to her employer if she handled cash or negotiables. The offender did not notify her employer because her job duties, she claimed, did not include the handling of cash or negotiables. Employment was verified in the usual ways—pay stubs, phone calls, and contact at the job site. Her employment seemed in order until this officer requested a copy of the offender's most recent employee evaluation, wherein it was noted that she was progressing well in payroll training! Following this officer's near coronary at learning this bit of information, direct contact with the employer revealed that the offender's payroll training consisted of her learning how to input employee work hours into a computer only. The offender did not lose her job, and she has since confided that she feels more comfortable and secure in her employment now that her employer is aware of her conviction.

By demanding accountability from the offender via verification, officers enforce the conditions and thus protect the community, but an officer is also charged with aiding the offender. How, you say, since we, as enhanced supervision officers, obviously have no trust in the offender? Yet, we do trust the offender—it is simply his or her creditability we must verify. We aid the offender in much the same way we always have—by referral and by providing services ourselves. Referrals are for employment services; vocational rehabilitation; education; parenting classes; marital/family counseling; credit counseling; food and/or clothing from social service agencies and/or churches; Alcoholics Anonymous; Narcotics Anonymous; contract drug aftercare providers; residential treatment programs. And we follow up to ensure that services were provided or additional referrals were made to assist the offender and to enforce the conditions—although it was somewhat perplexing, yet humorous, when I received a letter from a destitute and homeless offender I had modified [sent] into a community corrections center, to see that it was addressed to the attention of "Mrs. Prison."

When noncompliance is detected, a violator's warrant is not automatically requested; in the majority of cases, interim sanctions are applied. If this strategy is not successful, then the offender meets with the supervising officer and supervising U.S. probation officer for a nonjudicial compliance hearing. Usually additional sanctions are imposed on the offender. Every effort is made by the officer to bring the offender into compliance prior to court or Parole Commission action. One nonjudicial compliance hearing ended with the offender indicating that he understood his responsibilities much clearer, and he made the comment, "You people are really serious about this." To date, he remains in compliance.

When all else fails, the violator's warrant is requested and issued. The offender is then taken into custody, which seems to provide the most pathetic and the most humorous of situations. For example, a parolee, who was arrested early one morning while still in his underwear, very irately stated, "You are treating me like a common criminal." Another parolee who came into the office asked "How much trouble am I in?" And upon seeing the deputy U.S. marshals answered his own question, "Big trouble."

And the last but certainly not the least aspect of our job is keeping the court and the United States Parole Commission informed of the offender's behavior or, in most cases, his misbehavior and what has been done in attempts to correct noncompliance. Paperwork can easily be deemed the probation officer's nemesis.

My day consists of any combination of, and occasionally it seems all of, the above and more (i.e., surveillance, search, home confinement/electronic monitoring, modifications, community corrections center referrals, court appearances, and the demon telephone—I have a *lot* of co-dependent offenders). The list is by no means complete. Overall, the day of an enhanced supervision officer is stressful, frustrating, and too long with too many things to do, but it is also challenging, exhilarating, and humorous. There is little that is more professionally rewarding than knowing that you have been instrumental in helping to prevent another victim statistic or in helping an individual overcome his or her self-defeating behavior simply by doing your job.

We, as enhanced supervision officers, are Jacks and Janes (no pun intended) of all trades and specialists in each separate aspect that comprises supervision. Enhanced supervision has provided us supervision proponents with the validity and legitimacy that had for too long taken second place in the order of importance of the duties of the probation officer. I, for one, say it was about time for supervision to quit being the stepchild of the system.

ONE HOT DAY AT A TIME: DAILY MEDITATIONS OF A DRUG SPECIALIST

Thomas L. Densmore

Is it hot—104 in the shade! But then, it's always hot here. Heat never stops the duties of a drug specialist in the United States Probation Office. Being about the Government's business in the cause of therapy does not succumb to the weather. "Neither rain, nor snow, nor sleet . . . nor heat."

The only concession you make to the heat is to work early in the day or late at night. In the middle of the day, find shade. I start early enough today to see "Tony" before he goes to work. He is 35, recently released from 6 months in treatment, on his own for the first time, working his first real job at a grocery store. He is having a hard time figuring out how to be a clean and sober 35-year-old. He last saw life sober at age 10. He's missed a lot since then, such as basic survival skills. We do a budget. He spends $17 a week on cigarettes; $18 on food; $7 on incidentals. I persuade him to let the rest go into the credit union so that he can pay his rent, phone, and lights at the end of the month. He agrees. Relapse can be brought on by something as simple as the thought: "It's not fair that I don't make enough money to even pay my rent." He'll entertain himself by going to an AA group and playing dominoes after group. Tony gives me a urine specimen to prove his sobriety.

A quick call to the office. "Ken" is avoiding treatment. He missed a urine call last night. He is already at work. I leave a message with his wife ("Tell Ken to be ready to give me a u/a when he gets home tonight." I sweat through a couple more stops. No one is home. Everyone is already at work. I need to find some coolness in a productive way.

I guess I'll take a few hours to check on the five clients at our residential program. The counselor fills me in on each client's progress. "Fawn" doesn't want to be here. "Lee" has just written a letter to the judge saying "I'm trapped in treatment. Please send help." Interesting, since the judge sent him here. "Terri" is moving into a new phase of treatment which requires that she give her life story, an eye-opening event for her. "Ernest" is looking for treatment support in the community. "Amado" is ready to graduate. I talk with each client. Fawn decides to try for one more week. Lee changes his mind that treatment is worse than prison. Terri explains how frightening it is to see your life without being high. She is overwhelmed by how much she has lost, especially time. Ernest is encouraged that he can find people who care for him outside of treatment. Amado is excited/scared about his graduation next week.

We have just finished hiring our contract counselors for next year. We did real good. We got great counselors. So now I can pretend that I'm a counselor/line officer again. This is fun. I love working in the field, even in the heat. I might not even check into the office.

It's still hot outside. Guess I'll go to the office, do paperwork, hope it's cool. At the office, my secretary has been working hard. She has all of the therapy bills for June ready for me to check and sign. After paying the bills, I begin the age-old game of phone tag. I return eight messages. I talk to three recording machines and five people. I will have to testify next Thursday that high blood pressure and hemorrhoid medications can't combine to result in a u/a positive for cocaine. The defense will have a doctor to testify that in this defendant's body, these medications create cocaine metabolite. Where do they find these doctors anyway? I also agree to do: a training session for new counseling staff; a speech at a networking meeting for counselors; and an audit trip to West Texas. One counselor wants to complain that I deducted too much from his last bill. I should have stayed in the field and sweltered.

Despite the heat, I head on out. All strapped up and ready to go, the boss gives me the latest from Washington. Somebody messed up. Washington needs $24 million to pay for defense attorneys. Every district has to contribute what they can from their current drug therapy budget. In the middle of this heat, everything is frozen. No new treatment. Everything is cut back until further notice. Get the word out. Hold the drug budget for fiscal 1993. So much for the rest of this day.

Another 10 calls. Dallas will do a "freeze group" and Saturday workshops. Arlington will do only the Saturday workshops. Fort Worth will do a group and get free therapy for new clients. Lubbock will get free therapy until the freeze is over. The West Texas people will use AA until the "Freeze of 92" thaws. The heat and the field are forgotten. Let's figure this out. How much money do we have left for counseling? How much can I risk sending back? Will the clients relapse? I hope not. I am whipped. I'm going home. This day started out with such promise. Just a nice day of seeing people, driving around, acting important, and sweating. This "freeze in July" is going to make things "hot" for us until Christmas.

One more step to get that u/a from Ken and then I'm done. He'd better be ready.

Finally, home. Oh, no! I forgot the u/a's in my car. They must be boiling by now. I either have to mail them tonight after this terrible hot day or keep them cold in our refrigerator. ("Honey, I have some u/a's I forgot to mail. I have to keep them cold until I can mail them tomorrow. I vote for our refrigerator. How do you vote?")

Just one more stop at the post office and THEN I'm done.

A SPECIAL OFFENDER SPECIALIST HITS THE ROAD

John M. Shevlin and Omar Madruga

It is 7 A.M. on Monday, and I am where we park the Government cars. I will be spending the day in the field with my supervisor. He periodically rides in the field with me as he does with the other officers assigned to the Special Offender Unit in the United States Probation Office in Miami, Florida. Our unit supervises offenders involved in violent crimes, major drug conspiracies, racketeering, money laundering, and major frauds. We also supervise offenders associated with criminal organizations, public corruption, and other sensitive cases.

Our first stop of the day is with an individual relocated to our district, an offender who formerly cooperated with the Government. We have gotten an early start so that we can see this offender at home before he leaves for work. He is a difficult case to supervise for many reasons. Based upon his cooperation with the Government, he feels that he need not follow the conditions of supervision like any other offender. Also, he frequently suggests that it would be in his best interest to return to the district in which he was sentenced. After questioning him in reference to residence, employment, and other personal circumstances, I once again persuade him to discard any thought of returning to the district of his sentencing.

Our next stop is a car dealership where Mr. Udall is a salesman. He is a criminal who has made a career out of defrauding the public. He has sold fraudulent oil leases, rare coins, precious stones, and vacation time-shares. In those few instances where delivery was actually made to a customer, the product was incredibly overpriced. Once again, Mr. Udall makes his usual request to enter into a self-employment situation. Once again, I deny him permission to do so. He appeals to the supervisor who also indicates that he may not enter into a self-employment situation. As we depart the car dealership, I comment to my supervisor that Mr. Udall will no doubt return to some sort of criminal activity the day after he gets off supervision. In his case, a term of probation is truly protecting the public from additional criminal activity.

Before our next stop, I do a "drive by" of the area. I do this because Mr. Rodriguez is an active confidential informant for the Government. He has been approached by some narcotic traffickers to utilize his place of business, a building supply corporation, to launder narcotic proceeds. Unbeknown to the narcotic traffickers, the offender is involved with the Government in a "sting" operation. After driving by the business, I see an automobile which I do not recognize. Using the cellular phone, I conduct a check of the license plate. The vehicle is registered to Mr. Rodriguez' wife. As the car appears to be brand new, I assume that Mr. Rodriguez has driven the car to work himself. Once again using the cellular phone, I call Mr. Rodriguez at his place of business. He confirms my finding that the vehicle is his, and then my supervisor and I go into the business. As there are no customers in the business at the moment, Mr. Rodriguez is able to discuss freely his confidential informant activities. Because he speaks only Spanish, I translate for my supervisor who speaks only English. We review his confidential informant activities, and all appears to be in order. Due to the sensitive nature of the case, Mr. Rodriguez is only seen at his place of residence or employment. I do not have him report to the office.

Mr. Francois is our next stop. I go to his residence, and he is once again at home. Based upon his cooperation with the Government, he received a term of probation as opposed to the mandatory 5-year term of incarceration that he was facing. The issue as to his unemployment is once again addressed. I have been repeatedly instructing him to secure employment, and he has been repeatedly doing everything in his power to avoid securing employment. Mr. Francois then requests permission to travel to the Turks and Caicos Islands. These islands, located in the Caribbean, are known as a haven for drug trafficking and money laundering. His request to travel to this area is denied. I explained to Mr. Francois that his denial is based upon the fact that he has been convicted of importation of cocaine, he has a history of criminal activity associated with importing cocaine, and he is in technical violation of his supervision by not being employed. He becomes extremely irate and states that he intends to have his attorney file a motion with the court. I explain to Mr. Francois that he can file anything with the court that he wants. However, I give him an employment search log and instruct him to fill out the log. Also, based upon the fact that he is unemployed, he is to report on a weekly basis. Mr. Francois will make good on his threat to file a motion with the court. After leaving, my supervisor and I discuss what our response to the judge will be.

Mr. Perez is our next stop. He has an extremely lengthy prior record. If he is once again convicted of drug trafficking, he will be classified as a career offender. He is now working at a construction site as a painter. After briefly reviewing his situation, I take a urine sample from him. He has had a history of drug use. Nevertheless, this has not been a problem as of late.

We then stop at "calle ocho" in an area of Miami known as Little Havana. Once again, I translate for my supervisor as we order our Cuban lunch. At the conclusion of lunch, we use the cellular telephone to check with the office to see if there are any messages. I am advised that Mr. Francois' attorney has left two messages: one for me and one for my supervisor. After finishing our lunch with some cafe Cubano, we resume our field day.

Yesterday, I had organized an itinerary to make the best use of the day. Our next stop is at the Federal Bureau of Investigation office where I locate Agent Kennedy. I explain to him that I have received a copy of a travel permit from the Southern District of New York in reference to a well-known organized crime figure. My special offender colleague in the Southern District of New York always advises me when this individual travels to Miami. The organized crime figure owns an expensive condominium in a prestigious apartment building located on Biscayne Bay. Agent Kennedy thanks me for the information and indicates that he will advise other law enforcement officials who may want to know about the presence of this individual in our district.

Mrs. Marcus is our next contact. She is the wife of a former attorney who is under my supervision. He was one of several attorneys involved in a scheme to bribe state court judges. He is now on a term of supervised release after having received a sentence of incarceration and a large fine. Payment of the fine has been a major issue for Mr. Marcus. He has repeatedly indicated that he does not have enough assets to pay the fine. Mr. and Mrs. Marcus are presently involved in a hotly contested divorce trial. She called yesterday to advise me that she has some financial information that may prove of interest to the probation office. I thank Mrs. Marcus for the documentation and indicate to my supervisor that this documentation will prove interesting to compare to the Personal Financial Statement that Mr. Marcus gave me last month.

Our next three stops do not result in personal contacts with offenders. A former police officer convicted of providing protection to narcotic traffickers has called in sick to the hotel where he is now employed as a chef. Mr. Gonzalez, convicted of unlawfully exporting military armaments, is not at his place of business, a company that sells cellular phones and beepers. His employment has been a problem since his release from prison. In his next office interview, I will suggest to him that he secure another job.

The last stop of the day is with Mr. Adler. Like many of the offenders in the Special Offender Unit, he takes issue with employment. He is a career offender who throughout his life has held virtually no legitimate employment. He is not at the residence, and Mrs. Adler indicated to me that he is out looking for work. Sure, Mrs. Adler! In any event, I ask Mrs. Adler to have her husband call me tomorrow morning at 9 A.M. My supervisor and I then return to the area where the Government cars are parked. While doing the paperwork for the field day, I staff some of the cases with my supervisor. He and I agree on courses of action in reference to several of the stops made today. It has been a typical day in working with the offenders I supervise. It is challenging work, work I enjoy.…

A MENTAL HEALTH SPECIALIST'S DAY IN THE FIELD

Terry D. Childers

"WHO IS IT?"

The voice boomed from behind the closed door in response to my insistent knocking.

"Federal Probation Officer."

Silence.

Then, "WHADDYA WANT?"

"I'd like to speak to Donald Jones, please."

"WHO?"

"Donald Jones."

"NOBODY NAMED THAT LIVE HERE!"

I couldn't believe that I had the wrong address. Not that I couldn't be mistaken. It's rather difficult to find an address in some sections of Chicago's West Side because few of the buildings are numbered. I don't know whether it's the result of intent or neglect, but most of the addresses have obviously been ripped from the structures. The numbering section in Chicago is such that all even numbered addresses are on the north or south side of the streets, and all the odd numbered addresses are on the south or east side of the streets. So, you could usually find a particular address just using that system. Unfortunately, there are so many empty lots on the West Side (resulting from burned out buildings) that it is still quite difficult to know if you have found the correct address. There was always some guesswork involved, but I was confident I was in the right building.

"Is this 3524 W. Crenshaw?" I asked the disembodied voice.

"YEAH!"

"Is this the third floor?"

"YEAH!"

"And is this the only apartment on this floor?"

"YEAH!"

"But Donald Jones doesn't live here?"

"RIGHT!"

"Well, do you *know* anybody named Donald Jones?"

"UH UH!"

I seemed to be at a dead end. I stepped away from the door and glanced at my field book. The card for Donald Jones revealed that I was at the correct building and on the right floor. I was about to turn around and leave when I noticed that there was an alias for Donald on the field card: "Snatch." This was probably a name that Donald had used during his days of running afoul of the law. I figured that I should at least give it a chance.

"Is Snatch there?"

"WELL YEAH, SNATCH'S HERE," the voice answered in a tone suggesting I had asked is grass green, water wet, or the Pope Catholic. "WHY DON'T YOU JUST ASK FOR SNATCH, MAN?" he yelled. "YOU CONFUSE ME!"

"Sorry," I apologized, "my mistake. Could you just tell Donald that his PO is here to see him please?"

The voice mumbled something and then bellowed, "HEY, SNATCH, YOUR PO'S HERE, MAN!" I wondered if this guy ever said anything in a moderate voice.

A few moments passed, and then I heard the beginning of the sound that almost always welcomes a person to any closed door on the West Side. It was the litany of locks unlocking, latches unlatching, and chains unchaining. Clink, clink. Clank, clank. Clack, clack. Then the door opened and Donald's smiling gaze peered out at me. "Hey, Mr. Childers! How you doin'?"

"I'm fine, Donald. How are you?" I answered. We were still separated by a steel security gate covering the entire door, and as Donald struggled with the huge padlock, I studied his composure. He looked calm, alert. His hands trembled slightly, but I had seen him when he couldn't even hold a coffee cup without spilling the contents all over himself. From a cursory glance, he looked pretty good.

I gazed behind Donald into the apartment. It appeared disheveled and messy, and there seemed to be people sleeping in chairs, on sofas, and on the floor. I had never been to this apartment before. Donald had only moved there last week. Like many others on my caseload, Donald never really *lived* any place; he just *stayed* places. He tells me that the people he lives with are his cousins, but if this is true, Donald's aunts and uncles were incredibly procreant people. From the way he talks, one out of every three people on the West Side is Donald's cousin.

He finally removed the padlock from the security gate and pulled it aside to let me in. As I had never been to this apartment before, I asked Donald to give me a brief tour. It didn't take long, as the apartment was quite small. I walked through the various rooms, gingerly stepping over the sleeping forms, and finished the tour in the tiny kitchen where Donald and I both sat down at the green formica table. I noticed only one other person moving around in the apartment, a young man who I presumed to be "the voice." He was scurrying around the apartment, emptying the contents of all the ashtrays into a shipping bag, intent upon his task. I doubted that he was embarrassed about cigarette butts. Subtle fellow.

I asked Donald to bring me all of the medication he was taking. He left and shortly returned with several bottles of medicine. I noted the dates of the prescriptions, as well as the dosages, physician's name, address, and telephone number, and number of pills. I asked Donald if he was taking his medication, and he said he was. Until recently, he was taking Thorazine, an antipsychotic medication. Donald responded well to Thorazine, but developed severe side effects, including tardive dyskinesia, uncontrolled spasms of the facial muscles. He was given Cogentin and other medication to ease the side effects, but they were not effective. I had discussed this with his psychiatrist some weeks before, and the doctor suggested substituting the Thorazine with Haldol, another antipsychotic major tranquilizer that did not seem to cause the same kind of irritating side effects. I was extremely concerned about this, as Donald had a tendency to stop taking his medication if he felt the least bit uncomfortable.

"How's the new medication, Donald?" I asked.

"Oh, oh, it's good Mr. Childers. Yeah, yeah, real good. That other stuff, that was just too strong, you know? It made me all tense and all tired at the same time. And it gave me the twitches. I hate the twitches, man. Yeah. I walk down the street and people look at me twitchin' and they think I'm crazy, you know? So yeah, yeah, this is much better. Yeah. Absolutely."

"And how are the voices, Donald?" I asked. Donald often suffered auditory hallucinations when he stopped taking his medication.

"Oh, better, better, much better," he answered. "Like they're not telling me to do things no more, you know? Yeah, really. It's like they're hardly voices anymore. Just a kind of buzzing. No words. Just buzzzzzzzzzzz. And I can watch TV again. Don't think that Dan Rather's talkin' special to me anymore, you know? Can listen to the news and not be in it. Yeah, yeah, like that news."

As I listened to him, I emptied his bottle of Haldol and carefully counted all the tablets. It was immediately apparent that there were twice as many tablets as there should be. I could only surmise that Donald was not taking the medication as he was supposed to. I confronted him with my conclusion and he replied it was true. He was not taking the medication as it was prescribed. He was supposed to take one 2 mg tablet in the morning and another 2 mg tablet at bedtime. He was only taking the one before bed. I explained to him my concern about this, recalling how this pattern had previously led to severe decompensation, and told Donald that I expected him to take the medication as prescribed. He responded that taking the tablet in the morning made him groggy and sluggish for the rest of the day, and I replied that he should discuss this with his psychiatrist at their next meeting. But, in the meantime, I expected him to take the medication as ordered. I also told Donald that I was going to go to the clinic where he receives treatment and talk to his social worker about his progress. Donald had a pervasive pattern in which he would stop taking his medication, become depressed and anxious, use cocaine (to self-medicate), become paranoid, decompensate further, and then be hospitalized. It is a pattern shared by many of the offenders on my caseload.

I was always concerned about drug use. Donald assured me that he was clean, and all of the results of his urinalysis tests supported this. However, I was now troubled by his new living situation and the possibility that somebody who lived there might be using drugs. The ashtray emptier had left an impression on me. Donald responded that, to his knowledge, his cousin did not use drugs, and if any other people were to use drugs in the apartment, they would be reminded of

Donald's parole status and told to leave. I asked him who all of the other people sleeping in the apartment were, and he said that they were all friends of his cousin. I obtained all the ID information on the cousin and would run a name check with NCIC and the Chicago Police Department within the next week.

I left Donald's numberless building and drove directly to the mental health clinic about a mile away. I spoke to his social worker for some time, sharing my concerns that Donald might relapse to his old pattern of not taking his medication and begin using drugs. She suggested that within the next week we all meet together and explain to Donald our expectations and possible consequences for not following them. We agreed that it was essential that all of us—me, Donald, the social worker, the psychiatrist, and the nurse—attend this meeting. A date was established, and the social worker assured me that she would monitor the situation closely.

I left the clinic and headed to my next appointment which was on the South Side of Chicago. It's a curious thing, but it seems that the South Side has a much worse reputation than it deserves. I often hear vistors to Chicago express fear and trepidation about venturing into the South Side, and some of that is justified if you don't know the city very well. But in reality, the West Side is far worse. The closest thing that I have ever seen to Chicago's West Side is the South Bronx in New York. All of the West Side is dangerous, but there are pockets on the South Side that are really very nice. Unfortunately, the person who I was now about to visit did not live in one of those pockets.

I parked in front of Sheila Bonds' house, surveyed the block to see if there was any suspicious activity around, and walked up to her porch. I have known Sheila for over 6 years and have violated her parole three times, always for drug use. She had most recently been reparoled 10 months ago and so far had exhibited no signs of abuse.

I knocked on the door and Sheila opened it. She had on a nightgown. Nothing else. No robe, no housedress, just a nightgown. This is not unusual, Sheila *always* has on a nightgown. For the 6 years that I have been making visits to her home, Sheila has never answered the door dressed in anything else but a night-gown. Regardless of the time of day, regardless of the season or weather, Sheila has had on a nightgown. It might be 7 A.M. or 7 P.M., it might be a sweltering 96 degrees or a frigid 10 below zero, and Sheila has on a nightgown. We always go through the same ritual. She answers the door in her nightgown. She murmurs "just a minute," disappears for a few seconds, and reappears in different apparel. Sometimes a robe, sometimes a housedress, sometimes slacks and a shirt, but it is always evident that the nightgown is still on underneath.

There is nothing seductive about any of this. Sheila is hardly a seductive woman. Weighing over 260 pounds, she cares little about her appearance and less about her aroma. Her personal hygiene is dismal.

Sheila rarely frowns. She rarely smiles. Her face is, if you can imagine, without expression. It is what clinicians would describe as "flat" or "shallow" affect. She is a psychiatric phenomenon and has been in and out of mental institutions since the age of 13. She has been labeled with almost every psychiatric disorder found in DSM-III-R, the psychiatric bible: schizophrenia, schizophreniform, schizo-affective, delusional disorder, manic-depressive, major depression, dysthemia, borderline personality disorder, schizoid personality disorder, and even suggestion of some obsessive-compulsive disorders. She has been in every kind of psychiatric program imaginable and has been maintained on a variety of psychotropic medications. She's a real mess.

Her mother hates her. I do not say this lightly. I am fully aware of the impact of words, and I realize that "hate" is subjective and laden with philosophical and even theological overtones. It should probably not even be in my vocabulary, either as a clinician or as a law enforcement official. But it is the only word that conveys the intensity of the relationship of this mother and daughter. Sheila's mother has done things to her that have been so destructive, so malicious, and so purposefully intentful, as to be almost beyond comprehension. This woman makes Sybil's mother look like Saint Anne. Countless efforts have been made over the years by psychiatrists, social workers, and others to involve this woman in treatment, but she has always resisted it. Worse, she sabotages any gains that Sheila makes in treatment. Sheila's mother hates her, but she has never been able to leave her.

As I'm musing about this hateful situation, Sheila returns in more appropriate attire, shorts and a blouse, the nightgown stuffed haphazardly into the shorts. I follow her into the house, a single family home that Sheila shares with her mother and, occasionally, other relatives. Entering this house is like walking into a den of hate. The air is heavy with it, a presence that makes you feel tired and old, that makes you want to flee to the air and light outside. In all the years that I have known Sheila, in all the times I have been in this house, I have never witnessed a kind word, seen a gentle touch, or heard genial laughter.

I went through the same routine with Sheila as I had with Donald. I counted the number of tablets of all of her medications, determined that she was probably taking them as she was supposed to, and told her that I was in weekly contact with her counselor and was aware that so far she had been making all of her therapy appointments. Sheila responded to any of my statements with a series of murmurs or grunts, which was the norm for her. I told her to be in my office for an appointment 2 weeks from today, and she walked me to the door. Just before I entered my car I glanced back at her house and Sheila was standing motionless on her porch, staring at a spot somewhere just above my head, still neither smiling nor frowning, one of the saddest creatures I have ever known.

I left Sheila's neighborhood behind and drove north on Lake Shore Drive to a far more fashionable neighborhood on the North Side. I was there to meet with a sex offender who was procrastinating about submitting to a psychological evaluation. In addition to supervising offenders who have very serious psychiatric problems, I am also responsible for the supervision of most of the sex offenders in my district. They almost always live in better areas than my psychiatric cases; they almost always have more going for them in terms of finances and employment; and they almost always cause more human pain than any other kind of offender with whom I have ever dealt. Jim Anderson, at whose apartment I had just arrived, has caused more pain than most.

I buzzed his apartment and his voice responded over the intercom system "Yes, who is it?" The voice was controlled, modulated, almost a whisper.

"Terry Childers."

"You're 10 minutes late, Mr. Childers. I just called your office to see if you had forgotten about me. You *know* this is my lunch hour, and you *promised* me you'd be on time. Now it's almost time for me to go back. Are you trying to get me in trouble?"

"Look, Jim," I answered, "I really don't want to stand here in the hallway having a discussion with the intercom, so just buzz me in, OK?" The door buzzed, and I let myself into the mirror-covered corridor leading to the elevators. Jim lived on the fifth floor in a 20-story building, and I entered the bank of elevators that serviced the first 10 floors. I exited the elevator, walked to his apartment #505, and knocked on the door.

"Who is it?"

"Give me a break, Jim. It's Childers. Would you just open the door, please?"

The door cracked open and Jim's face, a dark, hard, but rather handsome face, peered out. The chain was still on the door.

"Are you by yourself?"

"Yes, Jim, I'm by myself. Were you expecting me not to be?"

"You can just never be too careful, that's all," he uttered, releasing the chain and opening the door.

I entered an apartment that was so neat, it was eerie. It wasn't that everything was clean and fresh and sparkling, though it all was. It was more like everything had its own exact place. I moved a magazine that was on the kitchen table to set down my briefcase. Jim lifted up my briefcase, placed it on one of the kitchen chairs, and put the magazine back to its original location—*exactly*.

It was time to get down to business. "Jim, the last time we talked, I gave you the name of the psychologist to call for the evaluation. Have you talked to him yet?"

"Yes, I talked to him, and I think there's a problem."

"And what might that be?" I queried.

"Well, he has an office at The University of Chicago, and he wants me to meet him there."

"And what's the problem with that?"

"It's just too far!" he cried.

"Jim, it's 15 minutes away from your front door! You live practically next to Lake Shore Drive, and that takes you straight there."

"But that's not the only problem," he whined. "It's also in a dangerous neighborhood. If I go down there I might get hurt. I just can't do it."

"Hyde Park (where The University of Chicago is located) is one of the safest areas on the South Side. I simply don't buy your argument about it not being safe. The bottom line is you must get this evaluation in order to comply with the conditions of your parole, and I expect you to do it."

"There's also another problem," he said.

Why was I not surprised? "OK, what other problem?"

"This psychologist expects me to talk to him about all the stuff that happened years ago, when I got in trouble. And he wants to talk to me about my sex life and stuff, and I see no need to do that."

Feeling that we had finally arrived at the real issue, I answered as carefully as I could. "Jim, you were convicted of a sexual offense against a child. The purpose of this evaluation is to see if there has been a change in your basic sexual orientation and patterns of arousal. It is what we expect anybody convicted of a similar offense to have."

"I was not convicted of a sexual offense," he answered.

"What?" I asked, incredulous.

"I was convicted of kidnapping."

"Well, that might be true, but the kidnapping involved you taking a 6-year-old child against his will, holding him captive for over 12 hours, and repeatedly sexually attacking him. I'd say that was a sexual offense."

"I don't want to talk about that! It makes me painful! It makes me painful! You have no right to try and make me talk about things that make me painful!"

"Are you telling me that you refuse to cooperate with this evaluation?" I demanded.

"No," he responded. "I am willing and even welcome the chance to talk to somebody who is sympathetic to me and will help me with some of my problems, but I see no need for this kind of testing."

"Well, this is the kind of testing that we are going to suggest that you have, Jim."

"I've already talked to my attorney, and he told me not to do anything without talking to him first."

"You may certainly talk to your attorney if you wish, but neither you nor your attorney are going to be the ones who determine what kind of testing or counseling you receive. I know that the psychologist is in his office today. I expect you to call him and make an appointment today and to call me tomorrow and let me know when that appointment is. Understand?"

"This is harassment," he spat.

"I don't think so," I replied. "I'll be in my office tomorrow by 8:30. I expect to hear from you by 9:00."

"I have to talk to my attorney first."

"9:00," I repeated, and let myself out of the apartment.

I felt a certain sense of relief when I walked out of the apartment building onto the street. Things were definitely getting a little tense in Jim's apartment. I again reminded myself to discuss with my supervisor the idea of joining up with another U.S. probation officer when visiting the more dangerous and volatile offenders on my caseload like Jim Anderson.

I proceeded to the Special Investigations Unit of the Chicago Police Department located in Cook County Juvenile Court. This is the specialized unit that investigates child sexual abuse cases. I had established an excellent relationship with the unit, as I had with other Federal and local law enforcement agencies that focus on this issue. I spoke to the sergeant for some time, who acknowledged that all of the offenders that we shared in common were not suspects in any cases at this time. After I left there, I made several other stops, some to offenders' homes, some to mental health clinics, and then prepared for my last visit of the day. It would be very different from most of the visits I make in the field. It would be with a victim.

I have on my caseload an offender named John Smith. John had been convicted of a child pornography offense and had recently been released to parole supervision following a 2-year period of incarceration. There was a special condition for mental health aftercare, and I had referred him to a clinic specializing in the evaluation and treatment of sex offenders.

John was convicted for receiving child pornography through the mail. However, when the agents searched his apartment, they found a number of home-made videotapes depicting John having sex with what appeared to be a young teenage girl. As it turned out, the girl was his stepdaughter, Brigid. He was never charged, federally or locally, for this behavior. He acknowledged that the girl on the tapes was his stepdaughter, but at the time the tapes were discovered by the agents, the girl was no longer a minor.

Of course, one of the first things I asked John when he was released from prison was if he had any contact with Brigid anymore. Although he continues to live with the girl's mother, he assured me that he never has any contact of any kind with Brigid and that he does not plan to. He was unsure of where she might live, but thought that it might be in Blue Island, a southern suburb of Chicago.

The problem now was that John was telling the psychologist doing his evaluation that Brigid had been an active and willing participant in their sexual encounters. He states that she was in no way coerced or manipulated and, as a matter of fact, initiated the sexual relationship herself. According to the psychologist, it was crucial to know the degree to which the girl's participation was voluntary or coerced. John had given us both written permission to speak to Brigid. The trouble was finding her. There was no longer any communication between the girl and her mother.

A check through the phone book for Blue Island had been unsuccessful, as had been directory information. There was no one by the name of Brigid Johnson listed. So I decided to check with the Blue Island Police department to see if they might have any information on this girl. As it turned out there was no criminal history for a Brigid Johnson, but there had been some traffic violations issued to a person by that name. The identification information revealed Brigid to be a 21-year-old white female, which fit the description of the Brigid I was looking for. I proceeded to the address on the ID card and walked up to the modest apartment building. There were no names on the mailboxes or doorbells. I rang the bell for the first-floor apartment. A young blonde woman, dressed in a Grateful Dead T-shirt and blue sweatpants, opened the door.

"Brigid?" I asked.

"Yes?"

I showed her my badge and ID. "Federal probation officer. May I speak to you a moment, please?"

"What's this about?" she asked. I could see the worry on her face.

"John Smith," I answered.

The worried expression on her face changed to something else. Anger? Fear? I couldn't be sure. She looked at me hard for several seconds and then, without a word, opened the door and let me in. She gestured for me to sit down on the sofa in the tiny living room, and she took a chair opposite me.

"I knew he was out," she said.

I nodded.

"I haven't seen him in years. Or my mother either. But I still hear stuff about them, you know?" She was silent for a while, staring intently at the carpet. "He doesn't know where I live, does he? I don't want him to know where I live. Or her either."

"He told me that he heard you lived here in Blue Island. He said he didn't know the exact address. I won't tell him where you live, I can promise you that." I explained to her how I obtained her address and also explained to her the purpose of my visit. I took my time doing so, making sure that she understood that she was in no way bound to do any of this if she didn't want to.

"So the bottom line," I concluded, "is that the psychologist would like to talk to you about what happened between you and John—about the stuff that is on the videotape. It could be done by telephone. You wouldn't even have to leave the house. Or if you don't want to talk to the psychologist about it, you could talk to me, and I would relay the information to her. But it's entirely up to you."

She stood up and went to the window. She crossed her arms across her chest and hugged her shoulders. She was completely silent. Finally, she turned around to face me.

"No," she said. "I can't do it. I won't do it. It happened a long time ago and it's taken me a long time to get my life back together. Things are finally going OK for me. I'm engaged now. I'm supposed to get married next year. My fiancé doesn't know anything about this. Can you imagine what might happen if he found out? If anybody found out? Nobody in my life now knows anything about this, and that's the way I want it to stay. It's my own dirty little secret, one that I have to live with every day of my life, one that I still cry about, but only when I'm alone. The memories are not dead yet, but they're buried in a place and nobody but me knows about them. No. I won't do it. I won't talk about it. Not to the psychologist. Not to you. Not to anybody. Not ever."

She had begun to cry, her body quaking with silent sobs. She bent down toward me, her hands making a pleading gesture.

"I was just a little girl!" she moaned. "Just a little girl."

I was beginning to feel like an ogre. I was afraid that I had opened up old wounds that had never really begun to heal. "Look," I said, "I'm sorry that I've upset you, which I obviously have, but I can't help but think from your reaction that you might still have a lot of unresolved issues about all of this. There are counselors that specialize in this kind of thing, you know, victims of child sexual abuse. I would be more than happy to give you some of their names and—"

"NO!" she shouted. "It's over. It's dead. It's buried. I just want to make it go away and never come back. No counselors. No help. Nothing. I just want it to go away."

She was silent for a while, again staring out the window, and then addressed me in what sounded like a defeated, listless voice. "I'm sorry. I can't help you. I hope you understand."

"It's OK. I do understand." I took one of my business cards out of my badge case and handed it to her.

"Here, this is one of my cards. If you should change your mind, or if there's anything I can help you with, just call me. And if John ever contacts you or begins to bother or harass you in any way, call me and we'll take care of it."

"Thank you," she said, taking the card without looking at it.

I let myself out the door and was almost to my car, when I heard her call out behind me.

"Hey, Mister?"

I turned around. She was leaning out of the open door.

"Don't let him hurt anyone else, OK? Don't let him hurt anyone else."

Before I could answer, she closed the door.

My field day was over. As I drove home, I pondered Brigid's request. "Don't let him hurt anyone else." How many similar requests I have heard in the past 16 years. Don't let him rob another bank, don't let him sell another drug, don't let him steal another check, and on and on. I sometimes wonder, as all probation officers do, if anything I do really ever makes a difference. Do I ever do anything that prevents a man from being murdered, a child from being abused, a woman from being raped? I don't know. I can probably *never* know. I can only hope.

STUDY QUESTIONS FOR READING 33_____

1. Jane Pierson believes that verification is the most important part of enhanced supervision. Why?

2. Thomas Densmore reports that "Tony" has just been released from 6 months in treatment and is on his own and working a real job for the first time. However, Tony is finding it hard to be a clean-and-sober 35-year-old. When was he last sober? What is his weekly budget in order to have money for rent, phone, and lights at the end of the month?

3. John Shevlin tells us about Mr. Udall and his past crimes and what he predicts for Udall's future.

4. Terry Childers tells the story of trying to locate "Snatch." What is remarkable about Snatch's living conditions? What is his pattern, so common among Childers' clients, which results in regular trips to the mental hospital?

5. Discuss Childers' encounter with Jim Anderson's denial of both his sex crimes and his need for help.

6. Discuss the plea made by Brigid, the victim of child sexual abuse, and how Terry Childers ponders the request.

INTENSIVE PROBATION SUPERVISION

BILLIE S. ERWIN
LAWRENCE A. BENNETT

Georgia's Intensive Probation Supervision (IPS) program, implemented in 1982, has stirred nationwide interest among criminal justice professionals because it seems to satisfy two goals that have long appeared mutually contradictory: (1) restraining the growth of prison populations and associated costs by controlling selected offenders in the community and (2) at the same time, satisfying to some extent the demand that criminals be punished for their crimes. The pivotal question is whether or not prison-bound offenders can be shifted into Intensive Probation Supervision without threatening the public safety.

A new research study, partially funded by the National Institute of Justice, suggests that intensive supervision provides greater controls than regular probation and costs far less than incarceration. The study was conducted by the Georgia Department of Corrections, Office of Evaluation and Statistics, and was assisted by an Advisory Board funded by the National Institute of Justice. This reading summarizes the findings.

THE GEORGIA PROGRAM

The IPS program began in 1982 as a pilot in 13 of Georgia's 45 judicial sentencing circuits. By the end of 1985, it had expanded to 33 circuits and had supervised 2,322 probationers.

While probation programs with varying degrees of supervision have been implemented throughout the country, Georgia's IPS is widely regarded as one of the most stringent in the Nation. Standards include:

- Five face-to-face contacts per week;
- 132 hours of mandatory community service;
- Mandatory curfew;
- Mandatory employment;
- Weekly check of local arrest records;
- Automatic notification of arrest elsewhere via the State Crime Information Network listing;
- Routine and unannounced alcohol and drug testing.

The supervision standards are enforced by a team consisting of a Probation Officer and a Surveillance Officer. The team supervises 25 probationers. In some jurisdictions, a team of one Probation Officer and two Surveillance Officers supervises 40 probationers.

The standards are designed to provide sufficient surveillance to control risk to the community and give a framework to treatment-oriented counseling. The counseling is designed to help the offender direct his energies toward productive activities, to assume responsibilities, and to become a law-abiding citizen.

Most offenders chosen for the IPS pilot program were already sent to prison, presented an acceptable risk to the community, and had not committed a violent offense. A risk assessment instrument was used to screen offenders. While the majority of those selected fell into the category of nonviolent property offenders, a large number of individuals convicted of drug- and alcohol-related offenses also were included as the program developed. Some of these offenses also involved personal violence.

Of the 2,322 people in the program between 1982 and 1985, 370 (or 16 percent) absconded or had their probation revoked. The remaining 1,952 were successfully diverted from prison; many are still under some form of probationary supervision. Some have successfully completed their sentence.

THE EVALUATION FINDINGS

The evaluation evidence strongly suggests that the IPS program has played a significant role in reducing the flow of offenders to prison. The percentage of offenders sentenced to prison decreased and the number of probationers increased. The kinds of offenders diverted were more similar to prison inmates than to regular probationers, suggesting that the program selected the most suitable offenders. IPS probationers committed less serious crimes during their probation than comparable groups of regular probationers or probationers released from prison. The extensive supervision required seems to exert significant control and thus gives better results.

The cost of IPS, while much greater than regular probation, is considerably less than the cost of a prison stay, even when construction costs are not considered. In addition, society receives thousands of hours of community service from IPS offenders. Criminal justice practitioners seem to accept the program as suitable intermediate punishment. Judges particularly like it because it increases local control.

The evaluation addressed seven major issues:

1. Did the program divert offenders from prison to an alternative operation? The evidence indicates that intensive probation supervision diverted a substantial number of offenders from prison.

Georgia sentencing statistics from 1982 through 1985 show a 10-percent reduction in the percentage of felons sentenced to incarceration. At the same time, the percentage of offenders placed on probation increased 10 percent (from 63 percent in 1982 to 73 percent in 1985). Jurisdictions with intensive supervision teams showed an increase of 15 to 27 percent in the percentage of offenders on probation, markedly higher than the statewide average increase of 10 percent.

A 10-percent reduction in the percent of felons who were incarcerated represents major progress in easing prison crowding. The precise extent of the impact of intensive probation supervision cannot be determined, however, because many factors influenced judges' decisions to consider alternative sentences. Nevertheless, in view of the shift toward increased use of probation, the influence of intensive supervision must be considered substantial.

2. Would the felons who were placed in the IPS program have gone to prison if the program had not existed? Because Georgia does not have determinate or presumptive sentencing guidelines, the judicial circuits historically have exhibited a great deal of sentencing disparity. In general, sentences in the rural circuit are more severe than in urban circuits. For this reason, selecting offenders for the program according to crime type or risk measure may not have achieved equal impact among the various circuits in diverting offenders from prison.

Hence, IPS administrators targeted a particular type of offender—specifically serious but nonviolent offenders who, without the intensive supervision option, would have gone to prison in the jurisdiction where they were sentenced. This carefully reasoned decision reflected the administrators' desire to achieve maximum support from the judiciary.

The evaluation results indicate that 59.4 percent of the IPS cases were more similar to those incarcerated than to those placed on probation. The results also suggest that 24.6 percent of those actually incarcerated were very similar to those probated. The evidence seems clear: the offenders actually sentenced to IPS resembled these incarcerated more than those who received probation.

3. Was risk to the community reduced? The experience suggests that IPS sufficiently controls offenders so that risk to the community is markedly limited. The recidivism rates are considerably better for IPS offenders than for groups under regular probation and for those released from prison. IPS offenders commit fewer and less serious crimes.

Of the 2,322 offenders sentenced to the IPS program:

Box 34.1

The Intensive Probation Supervision Evaluation Methodology

Developers of innovative programs generally view the results of their work enthusiastically; others tend to be skeptical. To ensure an objective evaluation, the National Institute of Justice provided an independent advisory board of experienced correctional practitioners and researchers. The board worked with the Office of Evaluation and Statistics of the Georgia Department of Corrections to assess the Intensive Probation Supervision program. The evaluation employed solid measurement techniques and standard statistical approaches. The evaluators consulted probation officials in other States who assisted in formulating evaluation questions about the ease with which the program could be transferred.

The evaluation analyzed data on all probationers processed through the program between 1982 and 1985. The evaluators used several different samples depending on the issue being assessed:

- To evaluate some issues (community safety for example), the evaluators analyzed characteristics of the entire sample under supervision no matter how long the individual had been in the program.
- To evaluate other issues, selected samples were drawn of offenders with comparable sentencing dispositions.
- To assess the general effectiveness of the program, the evaluators sampled groups of offenders with matching characteristics.

Using constructed samples makes conclusions fairly tentative, but applying truly experimental conditions is often not possible in operational situations.

Comparison groups were tracked for 18 months, and the evaluators measured the number of arrests, convictions, and incarcerations.

Such measures cannot quantify the precise extent of criminal activity, but because the measures are applied to each of the various samples, they probably represent a fair comparative assessment. Also, because of the close contact between the Surveillance Officers and the probationers in the IPS program, the actual amount of criminal activity might be presumed to be somewhat less than for those under regular probation supervision or for those released from prison.

To determine the extent to which offenders were diverted from prison, the researchers analyzed a set of factors that would best predict the prison-versus-probation decision. To ensure that offenders accepted into the IPS program were true diversions from prison, the staff screened offenders who had already been sentenced to prison. Staff then recommended sentence modification for those selected. Some success was achieved: about half the cases assigned to IPS had their sentences modified—a technique that provided obvious evidence that the offender was diverted from prison.

Many judges—even those who were committed to the program and its criteria—declined to amend sentences as a regular procedure. For those cases, special procedures were developed to screen cases and make recommendations prior to sentencing. These cases appeared to represent cases diverted from prison, but it is difficult to determine this with certainty.

Characteristics were analyzed of all offenders sentenced in the 26 districts that had IPS programs during calendar year 1984. The characteristics included age, race, sex, risk score, need score, crime type, and location of the district (rural or urban).

For offenders sentenced during 1983, the first year the program was fully operational, evaluators compared the profiles of three groups: IPS probationers, regular probationers, and prison releasees. A computer selected the sample of 200 regular probationers and 200 IPS probationers matched by age, sex, race, crime type, risk score, and need score. These two groups were tracked from the date they were assigned to community supervision. To select the group of incarcerated offenders, newly admitted inmates were screened at the institutional intake centers; 176 were selected. Of this group, 97 were eventually released and tracked for 18 months from the date they were released.

Since the risk assessment instrument, based on a Wisconsin instrument, had been validated on Georgia offenders as a predictor of recidivism, each of the groups was divided into four risk categories. Risk scores are (0–7) Low Risk, (8–14) Medium Risk, (15–24) High Risk, and (25 and over) Maximum Risk.

The decision to include cases with low risk scores has caused some reviewers to ask if Georgia's intensive program has taken less serious cases. It is important to note that an offender without a serious previous criminal history may score low on the risk scale; but the nature of the instant offense may be so serious the offender would be considered for incarceration by existing standards in the sentencing jurisdiction. The low risk scores for 5.2 percent of the incarcerated cohort confirm this reality. However, the criterion for selecting offenders and evaluating the effects of the program was this question: "Would this offender go to prison without the program?"

- 68 percent are still on probation under IPS or regular probation caseloads;
- 15 percent have successfully completed their sentences;
- 1 percent were transferred to other jurisdictions;
- 16 percent have been terminated from the program and returned to prison for technical violations or new crimes.

Only 0.8 percent of the IPS probationers have been convicted of any violent personal crimes (including simple battery, terroristic threat, etc.). Most new crimes have been drug- and alcohol-related offenses. To date, no IPS probationer has committed a subsequent crime that resulted in serious bodily injury to a victim. Of the 2,322 cases admitted to the program, the following serious crime convictions have resulted: 1 armed robbery, 6 simple assaults, 4 simple battery offenses, 1 terrorist threat, 18 burglaries, 19 thefts, and 3 motor vehicle thefts.

Table 34.1 shows the number and percent of rearrests, reconvictions, and reincarcerations for selected samples of offenders sentenced during 1983. Prison releasees had the highest rate of rearrest in all risk categories. IPS probationers had a higher rate of rearrest than regular probationers, which is not surprising considering the higher level of surveillance.

TABLE 34.1   Outcomes for Offender Groups after 18-Month Tracking by Risk Classification[a]

OFFENDER CLASSIFICATION	NO. OF CASES	REARRESTED		RECONVICTED		SENTENCED TO JAIL OR PRISON		INCARCERATED IN STATE PRISON	
		No.	%	No.	%	No.	%	No.	%
Low risk									
IPS probationers	12	5	41.6%	3	25.0%	3	25.0%	2	16.7%
Regular probationers	11	3	27.0%	0	0.0%	1	9.1%	1	9.1%
Prison releasees	13	6	46.2%	5	38.5%	4	30.8%	3	23.1%
Medium risk									
IPS probationers	62	21	33.9%	10	16.1%	10	16.1%	9	14.5%
Regular probationers	58	20	34.5%	14	24.1%	9	15.5%	6	10.3%
Prison releasees	12	7	58.3%	6	50.0%	4	33.3%	2	16.7%
High risk									
IPS probationers	69	24	34.5%	19	27.5%	14	20.3%	11	15.9%
Regular probationers	73	22	30.1%	18	24.7%	13	17.8%	10	13.7%
Prison releasees	47	27	57.4%	21	44.7%	10	21.3%	6	12.8%
Maximum risk									
IPS probationers	57	25	43.6%	15	26.3%	12	21.1%	11	19.3%
Regular probationers	58	26	44.8%	16	27.6%	11	19.0%	8	13.8%
Prison releasees	25	16	64.0%	9	36.0%	7	28.0%	6	24.0%
Total for all risk groups									
IPS probationers	200	80	40.0%	37	18.5%	39	19.5%	33	16.5%
Regular probationers	200	71	35.5%	48	24.0%	34	17.0%	25	12.5%
Prison releasees	97	56	57.8%	41	42.3%	25	25.8%	17	17.5%

[a]Numbers and percentages do not add across the columns because the categories are separate but not mutually exclusive. A percentage of those offenders arrested are convicted. Some of those convicted are placed in jail while others are returned to prison.

Risk scores are based on a Wisconsin instrument; scores are (0–7) Low Risk, (8–14) Medium Risk, (15–24) High Risk, and (25 and over) Maximum Risk.

The recidivism pattern that begins to emerge from Table 34.1 involves greater intervention (e.g., more incarceration, tighter supervision) paired with more negative outcomes. This pattern tends to hold for most risk groups except offenders with high risk classifications. Offenders with high risk classifications who had been incarcerated showed the lowest percentage of reincarcerations in State prison; however, this same subgroup had the highest rate of rearrest, reconviction, and reincarceration in jail.

The apparent variation in the go-to-prison rate may be attributed to some unknown factor rather than differences in offenders' behavior. For example, it is not unusual for a Georgia judge to decide that an offender may have been released from prison too soon. When that individual appears before the judge on a subsequent offense, the judge will often use jail, county work camps, or some other method of detention and supervision to ensure more direct control over the offender and the period of incarceration.

Recidivism patterns also may be affected by the selection process for the incarcerated sample. This group included only those who had been released for 18 months at the time of the study. Because screening for this group was done in December 1983, only those offenders who were released before July 1984 could be tracked. Thus, those tracked had experienced a short period of incarceration—2 to 6 months. The

early release means they were apparently deemed less serious offenders. This suggests that comparisons with more serious offenders released from prison would reflect an even more favorable view of the IPS group.

Table 34.2 shows the number of convictions for various crimes for the three groups of offenders. The IPS group was convicted of fewer serious new crimes against persons than either of the other two groups. Although not shown in Table 34.2, minor repeat offenses, primarily marijuana possession, were numerous. Judges reacted strongly in such cases since they felt the offender had already been given his last chance. Serious offenses were, however, remarkably infrequent.

While many IPS probationers were convicted for possession of marijuana and habitual alcohol-related offenses, the most serious new offenses were 4 burglaries and 1 armed robbery in which no one was injured. The regular probationers had more serious offenses; they committed 8 burglaries, 1 rape, and 2 aggravated assaults in addition to other less serious new crimes. The prison releasees were convicted of the most new crimes: 13 burglaries, 3 aggravated assaults, 2 rapes, and 2 armed robberies. This comparison suggests that IPS surveillance provided early detection of uncooperative behavior or substance abuse and effectively reduced danger before citizens were harmed.

TABLE 34.2   New Serious Crimes Committed during 18-Month Followup Period

TYPE OF CRIME	IPS PROBATIONERS (NO. = 200)		REGULAR PROBATIONERS (NO. = 200)		PRISON RELEASEES (NO. = 97)	
	No.	%	No.	%	No.	%
Sale of Marijuana	0	0.0%	1	0.5%	0	0.0%
Sale of Cocaine	0	0.0%	1	0.5%	0	0.0%
Theft by Taking	4	2.0%	4	2.0%	3	3.2%
Auto Theft	0	0.0%	1	0.5%	0	0.0%
Burglary	4	2.0%	8	4.0%	13	14.0%
Aggravated Assault	0	0.0%	2	1.0%	3	3.2%
Robbery	0	0.0%	2	1.0%	0	0.0%
Armed Robbery	1	0.5%	0	0.0%	2	2.2%
Rape	0	0.0%	1	0.5%	2	2.2%

TABLE 34.3   Comparison of Costs per Offender (Average Days Incarcerated or under Supervision)

Incarcerated Offenders	Cost
255 days @ $30.43 = $7,759.65	$7,759.65
(Excludes capital outlay)	
IPS Probationers	$984.66
196 days @ $4.37 under IPS = $856.22	
169 days @ $.76 under regular probation = $128.44	
Cost avoidance per IPS probationer = $6,774.69	

Although more IPS probationers violated the conditions of probation than regular probationers (7 percent compared to 4.5 percent), this might be anticipated because IPS probationers were so closely supervised. What might not be expected is the very low number who absconded. Only one of the sample of 200 IPS probationers absconded compared to four of the 200 regular probationers.

4. How much did the program cost? Preliminary estimates suggest a savings of $6,775 for each case diverted from prison (see Table 34.3). If all 2,322 offenders placed in IPS through the end of 1985 were diverted, considerable savings were realized—more than $13 million.

It should be noted that these estimates are based on incarceration costs ($30.43 per day) and supervision costs only. The estimates do not include any capital outlay, which could quite legitimately be included because the prisons in Georgia are full. If the 1,000 offenders under the IPS program at any given time had been incarcerated, they would have filled two moderate-sized prisons which, if constructed, would have cost many millions of dollars.

Another benefit of IPS is the thousands of hours of public service IPS offenders provide. If these hours are valued at even minimum wage, the contribution to society would be considerable.

Probation supervision fees were critical to financing IPS. In 1982, the Georgia Department of Corrections instituted a policy that allowed judges to order probationers to pay supervision fees. The fees cur-

rently range from $10 to $50 per month. The policy followed an Attorney General's ruling that existing statutes permitted court-ordered fee collection if the fees were used to improve probation supervision. IPS was implemented at the same time the probation fee collection system was initiated. No funds were requested from the legislature.

Judges, who had been vocal in requesting stricter supervision standards, were advised that intensive supervision would be phased in using resources made available through fee collection. The amount of money collected from fees exceeded expectations. Over the 4 years of operation, the money collected for probation fees exceeded IPS costs and was used for numerous additional special probation needs. This does not mean that IPS probation fees alone have supported the program—regular probation fees also were included. Georgia judges impose probation fees on a case-by-case basis. (The issue of probation supervision fees is of considerable interest—what level of fees should be levied on which offenders; what is the most effective collection process; and what kinds of penalties are imposed for nonpayment—but represents an entire study outside the scope of this reading.)

5. What kinds of cases have been assigned to the IPS program? Looking at the 2,322 offenders sentenced to the program through 1985, the following profile emerges: 68 percent were white, 89 percent were male, 46 percent were 25 years old or younger, and another 24 percent were between 26 and 30 years old. Forty-three percent were convicted of property offenses, 41 percent of drug- and alcohol-related offenses, and 9 percent were convicted of violent personal crimes.

6. What kinds of cases were most successful in the IPS program? Drug offenders responded better to the IPS program than they did to regular probation (90 percent success rate during the 18-month followup study). Frequent contact during the evening and on weekends and the urinalysis monitoring may be particularly effective in supervising drug offenders.

The finding that offenders convicted of drug- and alcohol-related offenses had the highest success rates raises interesting questions because the program initially considered discouraging substance abuse offenders from being accepted in the program. But judges were obviously looking for constructive alternatives for substance abuse cases; hence staff training and urinalysis capabilities were increased.

Females succeeded at a slightly higher rate than males, as they did under regular supervision. There was no significant difference in outcome by race.

The evaluators used discriminant analysis techniques to predict which offenders might be most effectively supervised under an intensive program. These techniques enabled the evaluators to predict 64 to 68 percent of the variation in outcome. The analysis identified risk score as the most important variable in predicting that a probationer is likely to fail in the IPS program. Being a property offender was the next most important predictor. Sex of the offender, need score (a scale depicting the social needs of the probationer), race, and drug possession each made small additional contributions to the predictions.

7. How well has the program been accepted? Judges are now among the strongest supporters of the program in part because the program has a high degree of accountability. A judge can contact an IPS officer about a case knowing that the officer has had direct, recent contact with the offender. The officer knows what the offender is doing and how he is adjusting.

IPS staff have maintained high morale throughout the life of the program despite long, irregular work hours and heavy paperwork. Few have abandoned the program; most who leave the program have been pro-

moted to other jobs. Probation Officers who are interested in joining the program must add their names to a waiting list.

THE STAFF

Conflicts between the treatment and enforcement functions of a Probation Officer are well documented. One of the most interesting findings of the IPS evaluation is the near impossibility of separating treatment from enforcement. The Georgia design places the Probation Officer in charge of case management, treatment and counseling services, and court-related activities. Surveillance Officers, who usually have law enforcement or correctional backgrounds, have primary responsibility for frequently visiting the home unannounced, checking curfews, performing drug and alcohol screening tests using portable equipment, and checking arrest records weekly. The Surveillance Officer becomes well acquainted with the family and the home situation and is often present in critical situations. Both the Probation and Surveillance Officers report a great deal of overlap of functions and even a reversal of their roles.

Because the Surveillance Officer is in frequent contact with the probationer, a close supportive relationship often develops. The Probation Officer spends a great deal of time with court matters and screening potential cases and is thus sometimes viewed as the representative of the repressive aspects of probation. Such divergent roles could lead to conflict and general dysfunction. However, the small caseloads contribute to close, often daily communication among the staff. Thus the probationer's needs—whether for control or support—are clearly identified and the team develops a coordinated plan and follows it closely.

The evaluators report that one major benefit of the team approach may be the support that officers give one another. This enables them to maintain high morale in very demanding jobs. During the evaluation period, each officer became absorbed in attaining the goals of the cases rather than simply performing according to the job description. Roles overlapped and officers exhibited an impressive, cooperative team spirit. Some officers interchanged roles whenever circumstances required scheduling adjustments. Staff seemed to function with mutual respect and concern for each other and for the continuity of supervision.

Smooth staff functioning, however, was not achieved by accident. The program's Probation Officers were selected from among the most experienced and best available. The Surveillance Officers were hired by the Probation Division specifically for the new program. In addition, true teams might not have emerged without careful attention to training. A National Institute of Corrections grant supported concentrated staff training coordinated through the Criminal Justice Department of Georgia State University. The freshly trained and invigorated staff were seen as emissaries of the new intensive supervision, and their energetic and dedicated response to the program may well have contributed significantly to the program's success.

IPS IS A SUCCESSFUL OPTION IN GEORGIA

IPS has proven itself to Georgia officials and has become an integral part of the corrections system. Intensive Probation Supervision is a highly visible probation option that satisfies public demand for a tough response to crime while avoiding the costs of prison construction.

The cost of IPS, while much greater than regular probation, is considerably less than the cost of a prison stay, even when construction costs are not considered. In addition, society receives thousands of hours of community service from those in the IPS program. Criminal justice practitioners seem to accept the program as a suitable intermediate punishment. Judges particularly like it because it increases local control.

In Georgia, IPS is seen as one option on a continuum of increasing levels of control. Probation administrators, mindful of the public's increasing demand that probation clearly demonstrate appropriate punishment, have responded with a creative range of options. The options have varying degrees of severity and intrusiveness.

One rapidly growing alternative is the Community Service Program in which probationers perform court-ordered community service under the conditions of regular probation. The Community Service Program is far less intensive and less costly than most and is therefore able to manage a large volume of cases. Other alternative sanctions include placement in a community diversion center and Special Alternative Incarceration, which is a 90-day "shock" incarceration program.

By providing a series of graduated options, Georgia's Department of Corrections has responded seriously to repeat violators but also has shown a commitment to alternatives to prison whenever possible. Instead of a stark prison-versus-probation decision, judges have a wider choice of sanctions. A highly innovative state has taken the initiative to use the full range of options.

The attention focused on approaches developed in Georgia for identifying and diverting offenders from prison is well deserved. Georgia has exhibited ingenuity and commitment to try new ways to address a nationwide problem. The lessons gained through Georgia's experience are applicable in other locations that are experiencing similar problems with prison costs and crowding, although the population of offenders who could be diverted may vary a great deal. Jurisdictions that are considering implementing programs such as IPS should not only study Georgia's program; they should also define the target group in terms of their own needs. There is no magic formula, but Georgia's experience demonstrates that enough people can be diverted to achieve significant cost savings without serious threat to the community.

STUDY QUESTIONS FOR READING 34

1. What does Intensive Probation Supervision (IPS) in Georgia require from offenders in terms of face-to-face meetings with their probation officers, drug and alcohol testing, employment, and community service?

2. What evidence do the authors give that IPS reduced the number of offenders sent to prison, rather than the number placed on regular probation?

3. How much less did IPS cost per offender than prison? How did this estimate - account for prison construction costs and community service performed by probationers?

4. Compare the serverity and frequency of recidivism of the IPS probationers to regular probationers and parolees.

5. The IPS probationers had a higher rate of re-arrest and re-conviction. How did the authors explain this difference?

SHAMING OFFENDERS

DOUGLAS LITOWITZ

One of the latest trends in criminal sentencing is the imposition of "scarlet letter" punishments,[1] where the defendant must submit to some type of public humiliation. The infamous scarlet letter depicted by 19th-century novelist Nathaniel Hawthorne was a large red "A" emblazoned on the dress of an adulteress. In recent times, the following noteworthy cases have received national attention:

- In Illinois, a man convicted of criminal battery was ordered to post a sign on his driveway stating, "A violent felon lives here. Travel at your own risk."[2]
- In Boston, men caught soliciting prostitutes are sentenced to clean the streets under the district attorney's "Operation John Sweep" program."[3]
- A judge in South Carolina ordered a 15-year-old girl shackled to her mother for a month as punishment for various petty crimes.[4]
- A thief in Texas was sentenced to shovel horse manure,[5] while another was sentenced to carry a sign in front of a bookstore stating, "I stole from this store."[6]
- In Milwaukee, a convicted drunk driver was offered a reduced jail sentence for agreeing to walk through the business district wearing a sandwich board proclaiming his crime.[7]
- In Houston, a man convicted of domestic violence was forced to publicly apologize at the entrance to City Hall.[8]

Shaming punishments typically arise when a defendant qualifies for a prison term but is sentenced to probation instead. Judges are generally allowed to fashion conditions of probation on a case-by-case basis if the conditions satisfy certain statutorily enumerated goals, such as rehabilitation, protection of the public, restitution, and deterrence.[9] Public humiliation is supposed to satisfy these conditions: it is rehabilitative because it forces an offender to admit his guilt, it protects the public because it announces that the offender is dangerous, it is restitutive because the offender must apologize or perform a public service, and it acts as a deterrent because the ritual of humiliation is so distasteful.

Scarlet letter sentences have attracted support from prosecutors, judges, and conservative groups across the country. For example, columnist George Will has argued that "the sting of shame" is a cost-effective alternative to imprisonment.[10] In response, the American Civil Liberties Union and other liberal groups have argued that public humiliation is mean-spirited and will only make criminals more hardened.[11]

The resurgence of shaming penalties raises two key questions: Will these sentences be upheld by the appellate courts, and will they be more effective than our existing methods of punishments?

On the first question, it appears that shaming sentences will survive legal challenge and will probably gain in popularity over the next several years. On the second, there is very little hard data, so at this point we are left with mere conjecture. But from what is known about criminal psychology, it seems unlikely that shaming penalties will have the intended effect of lessening crime and rehabilitating offenders.

THE LEGAL CHALLENGE

Shaming punishments have been challenged in the appellate courts on three fronts: (1) that they violate the

Eighth Amendment ban on cruel and unusual punishment, (2) that they violate the First Amendment by compelling defendants to convey a judicially scripted message (in the form of forced apologies, warning signs, newspaper ads, and sandwich boards), and (3) that shaming punishments are not specifically authorized by state sentencing guidelines and therefore constitute an abuse of judicial discretion. The first two challenges might appear stronger since they have a basis in the Constitution, yet they have proven less successful in the appellate courts.

The Eighth Amendment challenge was rejected by a Florida appellate court in a case where a drunk driver was sentenced to affix a bumper sticker to his car reading "CONVICTED D.U.I.—RESTRICTED LICENSE." The court reasoned that "[t]he mere requirement that a defendant display a 'scarlet letter' as part of his punishment is not necessarily offensive to the Constitution."[12] Since the Supreme Court has ruled that the death penalty is not cruel and unusual punishment, it is doubtful that shaming penalties will be found to violate the Eighth Amendment.

Shaming punishments will also probably withstand the challenge that they are a form of state-compelled speech. The freedom of speech argument might seem convincing in light of the Supreme Court's 1977 ruling that the State of New Hampshire could not compel a Jehovah's Witness to display the state motto ("Live Free or Die") on his license plate.[13] Although one would think that requiring criminals to publish confessions scripted by judges would violate the criminal's right to free speech, state and federal courts have rejected this argument.[14]

The final challenge, that shaming penalties exceed the scope of available sentencing options, has met with mixed success. In April 1997, the Illinois Supreme Court used this rationale to strike a probation condition requiring an offender to place a warning sign in his front yard.[15] The Illinois decision looked favorably upon a 1996 decision of the Tennessee Supreme Court that struck a similar warning sign at the home of a child molester, on the grounds that the sentencing guidelines did not authorize such "breathtaking departures from conventional principles of probation."[16] Similarly, the New York Court of Appeals

struck a sentence requiring a drunk driver to carry a special tag on his license plate.[17] On the other hand, the Oregon Supreme Court let stand a sentence requiring an offender to post a warning sign at his home,[18] and the Georgia Court of Appeals upheld a probation condition requiring a drunk driver to wear a fluorescent pink bracelet.[19]

When a court vacates a shaming sentence because it is not authorized under the probation guidelines, the court's decision can be trumped if the legislature amends the probation statute to specifically authorize shaming penalties as a condition of probation. Once this occurs, there will be few remaining grounds for challenging such sentences, leaving us with the all-important question: Assuming that shaming punishments will survive legal challenge in the appellate courts, will they constitute an advancement over existing methods of punishment, such as imprisonment, fines, community service, and home monitoring?

There is no hard data on this question because shaming penalties are a very recent development. However, from what we know about criminal psychology, it seems that shaming punishments will prove almost completely ineffective as a method of punishment in the great majority of cases. To see this point, we must first understand why shaming punishments were abandoned in the 19th century, and why they are inappropriate for contemporary society.

SHAMING'S DEATH AND REBIRTH

In Colonial days, the courts favored primitive methods of punishment such as the whipping post, the pillory, stocks, branding, banishment, the dunking stool, and a device known as the "brank," a metal mask that wrapped around the face of a woman who talked too much.[20] More serious offenses were dealt with by public hanging. While many of these sentences had a physical component, they also had a strong symbolic and psychological element, which explains why they were meted out in a public forum. For example, the stocks physically restricted offenders, but it also immobilized them in a public place where they could be pelted with rotten vegetables and stones. The criminal law of the time possessed a strong religious component and punished activities that are now considered private affairs, such as blasphemy, adultery, failing to observe the Sabbath, and general laziness. Since there was no clear line between church and state, punishments were designed to instill religious precepts and make the offender a good Christian. Little attention was paid to the commitments that motivate punishment today, such as deterrence, rehabilitation, and protection of the public. Although the Colonial shaming rituals seemed primitive and harsh, they were often followed by the reabsorption of the offender back into the community.

In Colonial times, courts did not impose shaming penalties in lieu of prison sentences, since the Colonists had no conception that prolonged imprisonment could itself operate as a criminal punishment. Prison as we know it (as a "house of correction" where people "serve time") was virtually nonexistent until the late 18th century. The Colonial prison was often a co-educational facility for debtors and defendants awaiting trial.[21]

Imprisonment replaced public shaming during the 19th century, probably for two reasons. First, under the increasing influence of the Quakers, there was a growing sense that criminality was not caused by sin, but rather by evil influences in the criminal's environment. Instead of shocking criminals into redemption, the logical approach was to remove criminals from their environment and teach them good habits so that they could return to society. The second notion, derived from the work of Italian criminologist Cesare Beccaria and popularized by various founding fathers, was that flamboyant punishments were not as effective as swift and certain punishments of lesser strength.[22] Gradually, public spectacle was replaced by deprivation of liberty (imprisonment), isolation, rigid work schedules, and education.

Shaming punishments also declined because they seemed inappropriate for an increasingly atomistic, impersonal, secular, and industrial society. Shaming punishments may have been appropriate for close-knit communities united by a common religious faith, where individuals were subordinated to the group and where the government freely intruded into private affairs. However, shaming punishments proved less appropriate for an increasingly diverse American society that placed a premium on individual autonomy and privacy. For example, in the days of *The Scarlet Letter*, the birth of an illegitimate child was deemed a public matter affecting the whole town, hence the punishment was public and involved a strong religious component. Nowadays, we feel that when someone commits a crime, it is a private matter between the perpetrator, the victim, and the criminal justice system. To make a spectacle of punishment in front of perfect strangers seems an invasion of privacy, an affront to individual dignity.

If shaming punishments were long ago relegated to the dust bin of history, why are they being revived in courtrooms across the country? Without doubt, the rebirth of shaming penalties is related to the growing realization among judges that the dominant method of punishment—imprisonment—is expensive and ineffective. Statistics from the Department of Justice indicate that as of July 1994, 1 in 128 Americans was incarcerated on any given day, with 1 in 38 under some form of correctional supervision.[23] The total number of Americans in prison is now twice the number of 1985, and the entire prison population is growing at 8.4 percent annually (doubling every 11 or 12 years).[24] The Sentencing Project has reported that one in three young African-American males is tied up in the criminal justice system, either in prison or jail, or on probation or parole; in Baltimore and Washington, D.C., the figures are closer to 50 percent, a condition akin to a police state.[25] While it is true that every society has its lawbreakers, America now has the highest incarceration rate of any industrial Western nation, with no end in sight. Yet even as we are building more prisons and dealing out harsher sentences, we do not feel any safer.

Accordingly, judges have begun to explore alternatives to imprisonment. Apart from shaming, the two most likely alternatives are fines and community service, but each has serious flaws. Fines can send a powerful message, but a fine resembles a license fee, where an offender pays a fee for the privilege of causing harm. Fines also send the message that a criminal action is not serious enough to warrant jail time, thereby weakening respect for the legal system and eroding the deterrent effect of criminal sentenc-ing. Finally, fines seem to discriminate in favor of wealthy offenders who can better afford a monetary setback.

Community service is a possible sentencing op-tion, but it too has serious drawbacks. Most notably, it carries unwanted positive connotations of charity and philanthropy, especially when the offender is working side-by-side with non-criminal volunteers. Many judges feel that community service does not satisfy the public's sense of retribution—it fails to convey the message that the offender has broken a serious rule and must pay for his actions.

Because of the problems with fines and commu-nity service, shaming is being touted as one of the few remaining alternatives to imprisonment. In a promi-nent article dealing with alternative sentencing, Pro-fessor Dan Kahan of the University of Chicago Law School identifies four broad types of shaming sen-tences.[26]

- *Stigmatizing publicity.* The defendant's crime is communicated to neighbors, for example by pub-lishing a list of "johns" in a local newspaper, or by forcing the defendant to publish his picture with a description of his wrongdoing;
- *Literal stigmatization.* The offender must wear a public badge of humiliation, for example, a sand-wich board or T-shirt proclaiming the nature of his crime;
- *Self-debasement.* This requires a publicly de-grading physical action, for example by requiring slumlords to spend a night in their own slums, re-quiring "johns" to clean the streets in bright uni-forms, or requiring offenders to shovel horse manure;
- *Contrition.* This requires some form of apology, and self-effacement, for example by forcing the offender to publicly apologize and beg forgive-ness or to hold a press conference and admit his wrongdoing.

Professor Kahan thinks that shaming penalties are sometimes appropriate because they are cheaper than imprisonment while conveying the same message of moral outrage. (This element is missing from fines and community service, which convey a somewhat benign message of disapproval.) Shaming, then, would seem an ideal alternative. If it worked as planned, it would be cheaper than prison while hav-ing the same deterrent and retributive value, and it also expresses community outrage in a public forum. The problem, however, is that shaming will not work in this way.

WHY SHAMING WON'T WORK

The premise behind public shaming is that crime is caused by the offender's lack of shame, so the sham-ing ritual operates to create this missing sense of shame. Public humiliation is supposed to force the of-fender to recognize the error of his ways and deter him from future crimes.

But this cuts against everything we know about how shame operates as a human emotion. A sense of shame is not something that the state can create out of thin air—one either has a sense of shame or one does not, and a shaming punishment will not likely create a conscience simply by exposing the criminal to public ridicule. Psychologists have pointed out that a sense of shame arises very gradually, only after one has built up a set of values and aspirations and then subse-quently fails to meet these aspirations. A person can-not be shocked into feeling a complex emotion like shame. It is much more likely that a person will re-spond with reactive emotions like anger, frustration, and rage.

Judges who impose shaming penalties make the false assumption that criminals share the average per-son's view of the legal system. Since the average per-son would feel shame at being publicly humiliated for breaking the law and would adjust their behavior ac-cordingly, judges presume that criminals will react in the same way. Yet this is wrong—many criminals (es-pecially in urban areas) believe that the legal system is illegitimately biased against them and that they were forced to break the law because of their circum-stances. Such people are impervious to public humil-iation because they see it as another piece of confirming evidence that the entire system is corrupt and cruel.[27] If these people are to be reached, it cannot be done with new and bizarre punishments, but only by measures taken before the crime is committed, by instilling enough values in the criminal that he or she has a sense of shame in the first place.

Many urban criminals see *themselves* as victims, a point brought out in Eldridge Cleaver's comments about black prisoners:

> One thing that the judges, policemen, and administrators of prisons seem never to have understood, and for which they certainly do not make any allowances, is that Negro convicts, basically, rather than see themselves as criminals and perpetrators of misdeeds, look upon themselves as prisoners of war, the victims of a vicious dog-eat-dog social system that is so heinous as to cancel out their own malefactions.[28]

If one takes Cleaver seriously, prisoners in urban areas are not likely to feel shame at violating the laws of a system that, they feel, has delivered them over to poverty and hopelessness.

Another factor to consider is that lawbreakers tend to carve out exceptions and excuses for their behavior, so even if sentenced to public humiliation, they are not likely to become convinced that they are the problem. Charles Starkweather, one of the most notorious mass killers in American history, told a court psychiatrist that he shot a police officer in "self-defense" because, after all, the police were chasing him![29] This type of attitude can be changed only by education and rehabilitation; public shaming will make such people hold fast to their excuses.

It might be argued that shaming sentences are appropriate for people who are not alienated from the system and are basically law-abiding, for those who made a wrong turn and ran afoul of the law, such as the teenager who steals a book at the shopping mall, the insurance salesman who is caught driving after too many drinks, and for the quick-tempered construction worker who gets into a bar brawl.

But if these people are generally law-abiding, it is hard to see what we gain from making them submit to *public* humiliation—certainly, some sort of private ritual seems more appropriate. Consider the case of the teenager who steals a book: rather than humiliate him publicly, we might require him to pay a fine or work at

the bookstore, in which case he might develop sympathy with the store owners, thereby instilling the values that will prevent him from committing a future crime.

It would seem, then, that shaming penalties will not work on hardened "career criminals" who are totally outside the legal system, and they are superfluous when dealing with first and second-time offenders. This means that shaming would be appropriate only in a narrow band of cases, and even in those cases such punishments might cause more harm than good.

CREATING MORE CRIMINALS

For one thing, it is entirely possible that shaming punishments would become a badge of distinction among criminals, functioning as a right of passage into the outlaw world. Since the shaming ritual is purely negative, it conveys the message that the offender is thoroughly contemptible to the core of his being, that he is not a valuable and worthy person. This could result in a type of "labeling disorder," where the offender is branded as an outcast and then forms an identity around this label.

Judging from newspaper accounts of shaming rituals, there is reason to doubt whether shaming penalties will have any positive effect on repeat offenders. For example, *The New York Times* reported that a man who was required to keep a warning sign in his driveway felt that the sign was illegal.[30] Similarly, a child molester who was required to publish a confession in a local newspaper felt that the sentence was a "useless gesture" that did not accomplish anything.[31] And a nationwide television audience watched as the rapist-killer of Polly Klaas stood before a packed California courtroom and instead of admitting his shameful action, accused Polly's father of molesting her. In these cases, public exposure failed to bring about an attitude of shame and contribution—it only made the offenders more hardened and more alienated from the legal system.

It is also questionable whether shaming punishments are appropriate for crimes that are not so much "shameful" as "unseemly" and "embarrassing," like soliciting a prostitute, buying stolen furniture, cheating on taxes, or selling marijuana. These cases are probably better handled with fines, community service, home monitoring, or forcing the offender to attend educational seminars. Since the activities in question are not viewed as deeply shameful by many Americans, it seems excessive to make a public spectacle of the defendant's guilt.

Consider the decision to publish the names of men who are convicted of soliciting prostitutes. Many of these men probably feel that prostitution should be legal, as it is in Nevada and many European countries. The "john" will be ashamed when his name is plastered in the newspaper, and the release of this information may ruin his marriage (if it is not already ruined), but it is hard to see what society gains by making a public announcement of private affairs, especially when the criminal activity is simply driven further underground or rerouted to a new part of town. The only way to really cut down on this activity is through education, for example by teaching "johns" that prostitution is abusive, exploitative, and dangerous.

The same analysis applies in drug cases, which constitute a major percentage of recent convictions. When a drug dealer is arrested, several others step in to take his or her place because the trade is so lucrative. If these people are not deterred by 10- or 20-year sentences, they will probably not be deterred by being forced to walk around City Hall in a T-shirt proclaiming that they are drug dealers.

The point here is that shaming penalties would not seem appropriate for many cases that clog court dockets. Although shaming seems at first blush like a dramatic and powerful alternative to prison sentences, in reality there are very few opportunities where shaming would be appropriate, let alone effective.

THE REHABILITATIVE COMPONENT

Although probation is supposedly aimed at rehabilitating the offender, it is hard to see how shaming penalties are rehabilitative. Forcing the criminal to publicly confess may give the impression of rehabilitation, but if the offender is simply going through the motions mechanically, there is no genuine rehabilita-

tion. Subjecting the offender to public scorn reminds him of society's disapproval, but it has no component of teaching or instruction to help him become a better person. Not only does the shaming ritual fail to prepare offenders for re-entry into society, it actually marks them as persons of lesser worth in the eyes of their neighbors (it also stigmatizes their families). As a result, shaming sentences seem mean-spirited because they are motivated by the public's hunger to see offenders suffer, not by any attempt to rehabilitate. If there was a genuine concern to help criminals and to lessen criminality, then the shaming ritual would have to be complemented with a positive ritual that brings the offender back into the community.

Sociologist John Braithwaite has suggested one avenue in this direction by making an important distinction between "reintegrative shaming" and "stigmatizing shaming." Writing in *The British Journal of Criminology,* Braithwaite argues that the first type of shaming might work, whereas the second type will fail:

> For shaming to obtain its maximum effectiveness, it must be of a reintegrative sort, avoiding stigmatization. Stigmatization is shaming which creates outcasts where "criminal" becomes a master status trait that drives out all other identities, shaming where bonds of respect with the offender are not sustained. Reintegrative shaming in contrast is disapproval dispensed with an ongoing relationship with the offender based on respect[,] where degradation ceremonies are followed by ceremonies to decertify deviance, where forgiveness, apology and repentance are culturally important.[32]

Braithwaite's distinction between reintegrative shaming and stigmatizing shaming helps to explain why, if our goal is to lessen crime and to deter criminality, the shaming ritual must be followed by a reintegrating ritual, perhaps by having defendants meet with their victims and with people whom they respect, who can convey their disappointment at past conduct and their hope for future behavior. This element of reintegrative shaming is notably absent from the shaming sentences that have recently captured national attention, which tells us that public shaming is not really about stopping crime so much as venting public anger.

The resurgence of flamboyant shaming sentences has diverted attention from other nonincarcerative options that are perhaps less glamorous but more effective. The National Criminal Justice Commission has recommended several promising alternatives that appear more effective than prison, including intensive probation, drug treatment, halfway houses, day reporting centers, and work release programs.[33] These alternatives might combine the least intrusiveness and the lowest cost with the greatest potential for rehabilitation, yet we have heard very little about these options precisely because they lack the element of vengeance and retribution that accompanies public humiliation. To be sure, retribution and vengeance are important components of punishment, but it would be foolish to choose a method of punishment that satisfies only these goals at the expense of rehabilitation.

*****

There is a mean and gratuitous quality to the scarlet letter sentences that are gaining favor in courtrooms across the country. Although shaming is rationalized as a return to traditional values, its real motivation is simply to vent frustration. Shaming rituals are as close to a good old-fashioned whipping as contemporary society will allow.

It is true that a strong sense of shame prevents a person from committing a crime, but shame is a fall from grace, and a person who lacks self-esteem in the first place cannot fall very far. A better tactic in fighting crime is to elevate the criminal class to the point where they have something to lose by committing an illegal act. Focusing attention on the root causes of crime would be more fruitful than dusting off methods of punishment from the Dark Ages.

ENDNOTES

1. Reske, *Scarlet Letter Sentences,* ABA Journal, January 1996, at 16. *See also* McMurry, *For Shame: Paying for Crime Without Serving Time, but with a Dose of Humility,* Trial, May 1997, at 12.
2. Hoffman, *Crime and Punishment: Shame Gains Popularity,* New York Times, January 16, 1997, at Al.
3. El Nasser, *Paying for Crime with Shame: Judges Say "Scarlet Letter" Angle Works,* USA Today, June 25, 1996, at 1A.
4. Smith, *Judge Orders South Carolina Girl, 15, Shackled to Mother,* Chicago Sun-Times, December 15, 1995, at 30.
5. Reske, *supra* n. 1, at 16.
6. Spaid, *Humiliation Comes Back As Criminal Justice Tool,* The Christian Science Monitor, December 17, 1996, at Al.
7. *Id.*
8. *Id.* at 18.
9. *See, e.g.,* West's Ann. Cal. Penal code, secs. 1202.7, 1203.1(j).
10. Will, *The Sting of Shame,* Washington Post, February 1, 1996, at A21.
11. *Public Humiliations for Crimes: Ain't That a Shame,* ACLU News and Events, June 25, 1995, available on the World Wide Web.
12. Goldschmitt v. State, 490 So.2d 123, 125 (Fla. Dist. CL. App. 1986).
13. Wooley v. Maynard, 430 U.S. 705, 97 S.Ct. 1428, 1435 (1977).
14. *Supra* n.12 at 125–6; Lindsay v. State, 606 So.2d 652, 657 (Fla. Dist. Ct. App. 1992); U.S. v. Clark, 918 F.2d 843, 847 (9th Cir. 1990), *overruled on other grounds,* U.S. v. Keys, 95 F.3d 874, 878 (9th Cir. 1996).
15. State v. Meyer, 680 N.E.2d 315 (Ill. 1997).
16. State v. Burdin, 924 S.W.2d 82, 86 (Tenn. 1996).
17. People v. Letterlough. 86 N.Y.2d 259, 655 N.E.2d 146, mot. den. 655 N.E.2d 698 (1995).
18. State v. Bateman, 95 Or. App. 456, 771 P.2d 314, cert. den. 777 P.2d 410 (1989).
19. Ballenger v. State, 210 Ga. App. 627, 436 S.E.2d 793 (1993).
20. Andrews, *Punishments in Olden Times* (Littleton, Colorado: Fred B. Rothman & Co., 1993, orig. 1881).
21. Rothman, "Perfecting the Prison," in Morris and Rothman, eds., *The Oxford History of the Prison* (New York: Oxford University Press, 1995).
22. Beccaria, *On Crimes and Punishments* 46–47. Trans. David Young (Indianapolis: Hackett 1986).
23. These statistics are reprinted in Dozinger, ed., *The Real War on Crime* 35 (New York: HarperCollins, 1996).
24. *Inmate Count Doubles: Hit 1.6 Million in '95,* The Arizona Republic, August 19, 1996.
25. *Supra* n.23, at 102.

26. Kahan, *What Do Alternative Sanctions Mean?*, 63 U. Chi. L. Rev. 591, 631 (1996).

27. *See* Massaro, *Shame, Culture, and American Criminal Law,* 89 Mich. L. Rev. 1880, 1944 (1991), arguing that shaming punishments are cruel and will not be effective.

28. Cleaver, *Soul on Ice* 58 (New York: McGraw-Hill, 1968).

29. Allen, *Starkweather: The Story of a Mass Murderer* (Boston: Houghton Mifflin, 1976).

30. *See supra* n.2. at A11.

31. *See* Reske, *supra* n.1, at 17.

32. Braithwaite, *Shame and Modernity,* 33 Brit. J. Criminology 1 (1993).

33. *Supra* n.23, at 200.

STUDY QUESTIONS FOR READING 35

1. Litowitz describes a variety of shaming punishments, including one for a man convicted of criminal battery and another for a 15-year-old girl convicted of various petty crimes. Describe these two punishments.

2. Under what circumstances are shaming punishments typically imposed?

3. How is public humiliation supposed to meet each of the statutorily required goals of punishment?

4. Why were shaming punishments more appropriate in Colonial times than they are today? What has changed?

5. Why are shaming punishments being used again today?

6. What are the problems with fines for criminal offenses?

7. What are the problems with community service for criminal offenses?

8. What kind of shaming would help rehabilitate offenders—reintegrative shaming or stigmatizing shaming? What does the absence of shaming tell us?

9. Litowitz says "Shame is a fall from grace, and a person who lacks self-esteem in the first place cannot fall very far." What does he mean by this? What would be a better tactic for reducing crime than shaming punishments? Why?

COMMUNITY SERVICE
FOR OFFENDERS

JULIE C. MARTIN

Neither slavery nor involuntary servitude, except as a punishment for crime whereof the party shall have been duly convicted, shall exist within the United States, or any place subject to their jurisdiction. U.S. Const., amend. XIII, §I.

Community service has been a part of the United States criminal justice system since drunkards were sentenced to chop wood in colonial Boston Common, chain gangs were sent out to build interstate highways,[1] and youths were given the choice between going to jail or going to fight in World War II.[2] The first modern community service program began in Alameda County, California, in 1966 when the court started a program for indigent female traffic offenders.[3] The municipal court judges had been reluctant to put the women in jail because of the hardship it would cause them and their families.[4]

Many programs began in the United States in the late 1970s and early 1980s with grants from the federal Law Enforcement Assistant Administration (LEAA); however, federal resources have since dwindled.[5] As of 1982 there were at least 100 community service programs for adults and an estimated 100 to 200 for juveniles across the United States.[6] By 1987 one-third of all states had passed legislation encouraging community service as an alternative to imprisonment.[7] The United States Congress has been slower to define appropriate uses of community service, but in the *Comprehensive Crime Control Act and Criminal Fine Enforcement Act of 1984*, Congress mandated that felons who received a sentence (not for a class A or B felony) must be ordered to pay a fine, make restitution, and/or work in community service.[8]

Community service has become an attractive component of the "community corrections alternative" in the United States. It has been seen as a solution to the overcrowding of prisons and the rising costs of imprisonment. In one state a sheriff was elected because he opposed the building of a new jail facility and promised to substitute jail time with community service work.[9] The community is said to benefit not only from the lesser implementation costs but also from the value of the community services provided. A judge from Tennessee wrote, "Certainly there is plenty of public and charitable work to be done that is not being done in every city and town in America."[10]

Supporters of community service have also hailed its effectiveness at punishing, deterring, and rehabilitating offenders. A newspaper in Rockland, New York, wrote that community service is better than prison because "some sweat is extracted" and with the work comes a "realization that crime does not pay. . . . That message does not always get through to the person sitting in a jail cell, twiddling his thumbs."[11] The argument for rehabilitation has been that criminals can be "corrected" if placed into a life that resembles normal life "rather than the bleak deprivation and rigid authoritarianism of the prison."[12] The East Boston District Court also described these goals in a proposal to begin a community service project:

> *[I]t is anticipated that the offender will become fully aware of the seriousness of his actions, especially as it pertains to the plight of his victim(s). . . . [H]e will be realistically aware of his transgressions and will be prepared to adequately and effectively complete a socialization process for his re-entry into the mainstream of a law abiding society."[13]*

But have the community service programs been meeting these expectations? In this paper, I will look specifically at whether community service programs save the community money, punish and deter the offender, and rehabilitate the offender. I will then consider the implications of these findings.

SAVING THE COMMUNITY MONEY

Incarcerating offenders has become an expensive enterprise. In 1986 the Second Annual Conference on Probation and Correctional Alternatives for the state of New York reported that it spends $26,500 per year for each inmate.[14] New prison facilities cost $160,000–$165,000 per new prison bed. New York now spends an estimated $1.3 billion each year in operating costs.[15] With such large costs, it is not surprising that a sheriff could win an election by opposing the building of a new prison and by supporting a community service program. However, community service has been given mixed reviews as to whether it solves the problem of rising costs and overcrowding of prisons.

Community service programs have been criticized for not keeping offenders out of prison but merely functioning as a control device used in conjunction with probation. One study found, "community service programs, like their pretrial counterparts, have been used to increase state control over offenders who would not have been imprisoned in any case and would not have committed new crimes."[16] In another study, criminologist Alan Harland concluded:

The offender sentenced to community service does not typically avoid incarceration thereby. Instead, the service is imposed in addition to his normal penalty, or at best, in lieu of monetary sanctions. . . . Community service programs . . . almost exclusively deal . . . with offenders who . . . are extremely unlikely candidates for imprisonment.[17]

Instead of lightening the load, community service has increased the caseloads of probation officers and not lessened the number of sentences to prison.[18] Such criticism leads to the conclusion that community service is not saving the community money but may in fact be costing the community more money

due to the increased supervision by probation officers. However, there are additional factors that need to be considered.

First, some narrowly tailored programs exist that do in fact keep offenders out of prison and thus save the community money. The sheriff, described above, began a community service program after he was elected. He reported that in the program offenders did 15,000 hours of work, which saved the county from paying for 2,500 jail days, or $75,000.[19] Another example of a program that is narrowly tailored is the Prisoner and Community Together (PACT) program in Elkhart County, Indiana. It has been specifically designed so that the program is only available to convicted offenders who have been sentenced to prison time.[20] In 1983 the program diverted 2,363 days from jail/prison time and thus reduced prison overcrowding.[21] Another program, in New Mexico, is tailored similarly so that only those offenders convicted of a "prison-bound felony" are referred to the program.[22] The program used less than $85,000 in state and federal grants and developed nonprison and prison-reduced sentences for more than 100 offenders, which saved the state close to $1.4 million in prison costs.[23]

There is also some anecdotal evidence that narrowly tailored community service programs save the community money by keeping offenders' families together and off public assistance. Many offenders who were employed are able to continue working part-time while completing their community sentences.[24] Judge Ferrino, the presiding justice of the East Boston District Court, has stated that this helps many offenders and their families maintain financial stability and avoid going onto welfare, which would be a drain on the community's resources.[25]

An additional factor to be considered is that while the community service programs may not be keeping offenders out of prison, they are providing labor to the community. The worth of this labor, it is argued, outweighs the cost of implementing the program. Surely if the program is narrowly tailored like the PACT program in Elkhart, Indiana, the community is not only saving money but "making money." The 1983 study in Elkhart estimated that 14,069 hours of free work were being done at a $101,480 economic benefit to the county.[26] Thus the Elkhart community received

$101,480 as well as saving money from the 2,363 hours diverted from prison time.[27]

On the other hand, the Restitution to Victims of Crime (REVOC) program in the East Boston District Court is not a narrowly tailored program because it does not divert a significant number of people from prison.[28] Community service is often given to people: 1) unable to pay fines, 2) as a condition to probation or continuance without a finding, or 3) as a restitution.[29] In 1989 offenders worked a total of 14,183 hours. From January to October 1990, they worked 13,807.5 hours,[30] a pace which will net 16,569 hours by the end of the year. The average value of the offenders' work has been estimated at five dollars per hour. However, this estimate may be low as it does not consider the benefits from offenders skilled in a trade.[31] For 1989, the five-dollars-per-hour estimate would mean the community received an estimated $70,915 in community service, while the program has been estimated to cost the court approximately $50,000 per year.[32] Such calculations would mean the community service saves the community money regardless of whether the program is used in lieu of incarceration or in addition to probation.

Despite the East Boston Court's ability to make money for the community through offenders' labor, "[f]ew community service programs assert that the value of the work that offenders do outweighs the expense of assigning and supervising them."[33] A study by the Institute for Policy Analysis found that a juvenile restitution and community service program spent three dollars for every one dollar in restitution paid or community service worked (figures are not available for community service alone).[34]

Community service, regardless of whether it is in lieu of incarceration or in conjunction with probation, may save the community money in the long run if it is successful in its goals of deterrence and rehabilitation (as discussed below, it is not clear whether community service successfully meets these goals). If community service is found to be a deterrent both to the individual offender and to the community at large, it will keep people from committing crimes and out of the judicial system—both of which would save the community money. Further if community service is found to rehabilitate offenders, these of-fenders will not only stay out of the judicial system but will become productive members of the community. For example, in East Boston an offender who is a single mother used to be on welfare. Now, however, her community placement has offered to hire her (as long as their budget does not get cut), and she will not have to continue receiving welfare.[35]

PUNISHING AND DETERRING THE OFFENDER

"The idea of work as a punishment for crime goes back a long way in the United States."[36] Seeing offenders working has been a part of the "public's consciousness of crime."[37] Much of the public is satisfied with this as a form of punishment. As described above, community service has been seen by many as a better punishment than sending an offender to prison.[38] United States district judge Joseph L. Tauro wrote, "[A] meaningful, closely supervised public service sentence can provide a daily reminder to the offender that he has in fact committed serious anti-social behavior."[39]

As noted above, community service has not been used exclusively for offenders who would have otherwise gone to prison. Community service has become a punishment that can be added on to probation. As Andrew Klein, the chief probation officer of the Quincy court stated, "Community service is the ideal middle ground between probation and prison. . . . It's satisfying to the public because they see the offenders out there doing something, and it's good for the offenders because they feel justice is being done."[40]

Community service programs have also been found to be a form of punishment when the court had no other alternative. The Supreme Court encouraged community service programs when it held, in 1971, that indigent defendants could not be imprisoned for nonwillful failure to pay fines.[41] In 1983 the Supreme Court found that the courts are not powerless because of their inability to force payments and specifically noted that they could order community service.[42] In response to the Supreme Court rulings, many jurisdictions began developing community service programs. One state enacted a statute that allows fines and restitution to be converted into "day fines," which are worked off in community service hours.[43] The East

Boston District Court has developed a uniform practice of converting fines five dollars to one hour of community service when the offender is unemployed.[44]

Of course, the community service program is not a successful form of punishment unless the offender completes his or her hours. Whether doing community service in lieu of incarceration or in addition to probation, approximately two-thirds of the offenders sentenced to community service will complete their hours without any prodding.[45] The rest usually need "encouragement" from the judge or a probation officer who threatens to send the offender to jail if he or she does not complete the hours. Usually this threat works, and only 5 to 10 percent are sent to prison for failing to complete the hours.[46] In East Boston, no formal studies have been done on percentage completion, but it has been estimated that over 90 percent of the offenders complete their hours.[47] In a program in Arizona, 97.7 percent of the offenders completed the program successfully.[48]

For those offenders that need prodding, it has been found that the "encouragement" must be a real threat. A probation officer must be willing to enforce the community service; the judge must be willing to order the offender to prison; and there must be space to accommodate the offender in the prison. In one juvenile community service program area, the county's juvenile detention center had been demolished, and it took several months before the new one was built. During that period, the percentage of completion of hours went from 90 percent to only 50 percent.[49] As David Steenson, the director of the program said, "Word gets out on the grapevine. . . . Unfortunately, in America, the most benign sentence has to have something worse lurking behind it."[50]

Though community service may be seen as an effective form of punishment to many, there are those who find it to be too much like a reward. For example, the Manhattan district attorney's office is not satisfied with the several community service programs that exist in Manhattan.[51] Robert Holmes, an assistant district attorney in charge of a program that tries to put chronic property offenders in prison for up to a year, said "You are not punishing them by letting them loose and giving them a job . . . If we can postpone another victim of crime for nine months instead of the

ridiculous 70 hours of community service, then we're doing our jobs."[52] Mary De Bourbon, a spokeswoman for Manhattan's district attorney Robert Morgenthau, said, "There are far too few jail sentences given out in criminal court anyway. . . . For things like cleaning up your own graffiti, community service is fine, but putting somebody into community service who steals for a living is inappropriate."[53]

In addition to the goal of punishment, community service programs have had the goal of serving as a deterrent to the offender as an individual and to society in general. A Maryland politician discussed community service as a deterrent in his political campaign:

> We want to develop the idea that you can't just get away with breaking the law. The first time you do something here, something is going to happen to you, and it's not just going to be a slap-on-the-wrist probation. . . . You have got to have the courage to do something unpleasant to people if they don't conform.[54]

Few, if any, studies have looked at the rate of crime in a community before and after the implementation of community service to see if it serves as a general deterrent. The first problem with community service acting as a general deterrent is that many would-be offenders are not aware of the programs. With regard to a program in Manhattan, many of the offenders were surprised that such a program existed.[55]

For those would-be offenders who would serve in community service in lieu of incarceration, knowledge of community service may serve as less of a deterrent than incarceration. Many offenders have expressed that they prefer community service programs over incarceration. This preference also fuels the debate over whether community service is more of a punishment than incarceration. One offender stated, "I don't like working without pay, but when you compare ten days of this with 90 days at Rikers [New York City's prison]—whew, there's no choice."[56] An offender in Georgia who was sentenced to community service was able to reserve Sundays for leisure and family. "The offender highly valued these Sundays, reporting them to be the major benefit of community service in lieu of imprisonment."[57] However, for those would-be offenders aware that they may be sentenced to community service in addition to probation, there may be more deterrence. As the Maryland politician pointed out, the would-be offenders become aware that they will get more than the "slap-on-the-wrist probation."

Studies regarding recidivism can give some indication of individual deterrence though the results cannot be divorced from any effects rehabilitation may have on the offender (as will be discussed below). One study looked at a group of British offenders. In Great Britain, convicted offenders can be sentenced to do 40 to 240 hours of community service in lieu of a prison term.[58] 44.2 percent of those who did community service were reconvicted within one year versus 33.3 percent of those who were detained in prison.[59] Such a study would suggest that community service neither rehabilitates nor deters offenders. A study of juvenile offenders had different results. The study found that community service did seem to have a better short-term effect as 33 percent of those offenders who did community service were reconvicted within six months while 54 percent of noncommunity service offenders were reconvicted.[60] However, the community service recidivists were convicted of more serious offenses than the noncommunity service recidivists."[61]

REHABILITATING THE OFFENDER

Lauren Pete, the director of a community service project in the Bronx, stated that while the primary purpose of the program is punishment, it is what she calls:

> [H]opeful punishment. I'm not saying we can rehabilitate somebody in 70 hours, but I think the work experience can help set somebody on the right track. . . . It shows them that they can get up in the morning, and they can go to work. . . . Some of our people get a tremendous sense of pride when they find they're working hard and doing something for somebody else.[62]

Judge Dennis A. Challeen, of Winona, Minnesota, finds that community service programs should not be considered a form of punishment at all but strictly as programs for rehabilitating the offender.[63] Judge Challeen describes the typical offender not as a shrewd, clever criminal but as a "loser," and a misfit—a chemically dependent, unemployable person who commits crimes out of impulse.[64] He describes the effects of incarceration on such people:

> When we punish or incarcerate these people, we only reinforce the losing traits that make up their negative characters. They become more angry and more frustrated. We further destroy their self-worth. We give them reasons to be more anti-authoritarian, and we take away all their responsibilities. We allow them to blame others, including the courts and the justice system. . . . We give them no priority system, and we totally alienate them from our communities.[65]

To Judge Challeen, community service programs are part of a workable alternative to incarceration. Community service is a turn back to the "work ethic" and the idea that the work will produce accountability and self-worth. The program creates self-esteem through the "work ethic" and "positive, humanitarian efforts" instead of destroying it like incarceration does.[66]

A study done in New England on the effects of community service on offenders supports Judge Challeen's propositions.[67] In this study, 71 percent of the offenders felt that they had benefitted from completing the community service.[68] Eighteen percent mentioned that they had a positive experience from meeting new people: the people in the agencies they worked for and the people who the agencies served.[69] Three percent specifically stated that they felt that people did not treat them like criminals but gave them a chance.[70] Thirteen percent mentioned personal gains: "self-respect, a sense of responsibility and trustworthiness, 'an open mind,' re-establishing communication with other people, and 'feeling better' about themselves."[71] Eleven percent of the offenders felt that the community service had given them work experience and got them into a work discipline.[72]

There were also several anecdotal stories of those offenders who have been "rehabilitated" after doing community service. In the New Zealand study, one offender stated that society had benefited from the community service program because he was no longer an "active crime."[73] In the East Boston District Court, one offender was sentenced to do work at a church homeless shelter.[74] He had a serious alcohol problem but began to attend Alcoholics Anonymous meetings at the church. He also had been homeless and started to stay at the church rectory. After his community service was completed, he continued to work at the church, attend AA meetings, and live in the rectory.[75] The overall rehabilitative benefits of community service can be questioned, however, when looking at the recidivism rates discussed above with regard to deterrence.

The rehabilitation benefits of community service also raise the question of whether community service can be seen as a punishment and deterrent at the same time. If the offender perceives the program as helpful will it serve as a deterrent for future crimes and will it be a punishment? The New Zealand study seems to indicate that offenders could appreciate that community service programs have a variety of aims, such as benefiting the community, benefiting the offender, integrating the community and the offender, punishing the offender, and providing an alternative sentence.[76] Benefit to the offender was the largest perceived aim, and as mentioned above, a majority of the offenders felt this aim was met.[77] Punishing the offender was one of the smaller perceived aims, but 100 percent of the offenders who found it to be an aim thought it was accomplished.[78]

RESPONDING TO THE EVALUATIONS OF GOALS

Thomas Tubbs, director of the corrections division at LEAA, stated, "Corrections will always be a reflection of what the public wants."[79] For courts such as the East Boston District Court, the community service programs have been able to reach their initial goals. When the East Boston program was developed, the court realized it would not be used for diverting people from prison terms. However, it has still managed to save the community money. Moreover, there are those anecdotal stories that it has served the purpose of deterring and rehabilitating. However, not every community service program may be an accurate reflection of the public's desires or the desires of those involved in corrections reform. From the discussion above, it can be concluded that while community service programs may be beneficial, they may not be addressing all the goals they were intended to address.

Many community service programs do not seem to be solving the overcrowding problem in prisons to the extent originally expected or saving the public the amount of money originally intended. Only those programs that are narrowly tailored to offenders who would otherwise be sent to prison seem to be saving the community significant money. Other community service programs may be saving the community money, such as the program in the East Boston District Court, but not to the same extent as those narrowly tailored for offenders sentenced to prison terms.

After these initial findings about the overall costs, those involved in corrections reform are faced with decisions. First, they must determine whether these goals are as important to them now as they were when programs were first being implemented. If so, they may consider modeling their programs after those found in Elkhart, Indiana, or in New Mexico. Others may conclude that they will not do this either because their courts do not have jurisdiction over many prison-bound offenders or because they do not wish to use their programs for prison-bound offenders. These reformers may decide to implement or continue the programs in addition to probation because of the ability to save some money or because of the success they have seen in reaching other goals.

It is critical that those involved in corrections reform review the above studies when formulating or reformulating their goals for and structure of community service programs. For example, the legislatures that are operating in some communities have not taken into consideration the evaluations regarding money. Many legislatures "are requiring more community service sentences but not providing funds for new programs"[80] Without understanding the programs and the evaluations of them, legislatures may be taking community service programs away from their intended goals. Lucy MacKenzie, legislative action director of the New Jersey Association on Correction, said:

> The legislators have got it into their heads that community service is the shining light, the one alternative sentence that's going to help uncrowd the jails. . . . If they think it's such a great idea, they're going to have to spend some money on it. . . . We're very happy to see this being used, but they don't understand the fragility of it. The programs are going to go downhill, and the sanction is going to lose its credibility before it really gets established if they don't give us more than a few crumbs off the table.[81]

In addition to understanding the evaluations regarding money, reformers must look at the evaluations of punishment, deterrence, and rehabilitation. It is questionable whether these goals are being met for the programs used in lieu of incarceration. The programs have been criticized as a result of the relatively short sentences given and the recidivism rates. Reformers need to evaluate whether these goals are as important when compared to the success of saving the community money, which the programs in lieu of incarceration have proven they can do. Reformers may find that longer sentences and/or additional requirements such as counseling and job training could help the programs meet these goals.

For those programs that are used in addition to probation or in lieu of fines, reformers must look at the evaluations differently as much of the criticism regards those programs used in lieu of incarceration. These reformers may find that while it appears that community service programs are successful at punishment, deterrence, and rehabilitation, additional studies should be performed. For example, the East Boston District Court should consider doing a study regarding recidivism rates. They may also find that the longer sentences and additional requirements may be helpful. Once again, these reformers must also balance the success of these goals with the costs of implementing the program. Some may find that the costs are outweighed by the benefits received from the punishment, deterrence, and rehabilitation. They may also find that the costs are minimal based on the financial success of such courts as the East Boston District Court.

Since the first modern community service program was developed in Alameda, California, in 1966, the public and corrections reformers have had expectations about the effects of community service programs. As many studies and evaluations have shown, community service programs have met certain goals with varying degrees of success depending upon the particular characteristics and needs of those courts involved. The next set of evaluations and studies need to clarify some of the questionable results but more importantly need to look at how the public's and corrections reformers' goals can be tailored in light of the current evaluations.

ENDNOTES

1. A. Klein, Alternative Sentencing 175 (1998).
2. Maher and Dufour, *Experimenting with Community Service: A Punitive Alternative to Imprisonment,* 51 Federal Probation 22 (1987).
3. A. Klein, *supra* note 1.
4. *Id.*
5. Krajick, *Community Service: The Work Ethic Approach to Punishment,* 8, Corrections Magazine 6, 7 (1982). LEAA invested more than $1 billion in community corrections in its 12 years of existence. Blackmore, *Does Community Corrections Work?,* 7 Corrections Magazine 15 (1981).
6. K. Krajick, *supra* note 5, at 8.
7. Maher and Dufour, *supra* note 2, at 23.
8. *Id.*
9. A. Klein, *supra* note 1, at 178
10. Id. at 179, quoting Brown, *Community Service as a Condition of Probation,* 41 Federal Probation, 7 (1977).
11. Id. at 286 quoting *Seek Alternatives to Jail Sentences,* Rockland Journal-News, June 16, 1984.
12. Blackmore, *Community Corrections,* 6 Corrections Magazine 4 (1980).

13. East Boston District Court Probation Department's Proposal for Restitution to Victims of Crime (Project REVOC) (1978).
14. E. Wutzer and S. Layton, Community Corrections: Making it Work in New York State 43 (1986).
15. *Id.*
16. Blackmore, *supra* note 12, at 11.
17. Krajick, *supra* note 5, at 10.
18. *Id.* at 8.
19. Klein, *supra* note 1, at 178.
20. M. Umbriet, Crime & Reconciliation 108 (1985).
21. *Id.* at 110.
22. *Alternative Sentencing Found Cost-Effective in New Mexico,* 18, Criminal Justice Newsletter 5 (1987).
23. *Id.*
24. See Maher and Dufour, *supra* note 2, at 25.
25. Interview with Judge J. Ferrino, Presiding Justice in East Boston District Court, in East Boston, Massachusetts, October 11, 1990.
26. M. Umbreit, *supra* note 20, at 110.
27. *Id.*

28. Interview with Ann Marie Lewis, project director of REVOC in East Boston District Court, East Boston, Massachusetts, November 29, 1990.

29. *Id.* The court requires restitution in situations such as crimes against property, failure to pay child support, and welfare fraud. *Id.*

30. Interview with Bunny Dean-Murray, administrative assistant to presiding justice in East Boston District Court, East Boston, Massachusetts, November 29, 1990.

31. For example, an offender who had carpentry skills constructed several bathrooms in a women's and children's shelter. *Id.*

32. *Id.*

33. Krajick, *supra* note 5, at 9.

34. *Id.*

35. Interview with A. Lewis, *supra* note 28.

36. Krajick, *supra* note 5, at 8.

37. *Id.*

38. See text accompanying n. 11.

39. Maher and Dufour, *supra* note 2, at 24.

40. Krajick, *supra* note 5, at 7.

41. *Tate v. Short,* 401 U.S. 395, 398 (1971).

42. *Bearden v. Georgia,* 461, U.S. 660, 672 (1983).

43. A. Klein, *supra* note 1, at 176.

44. Interview with Judge Ferrino, *supra* note 25.

45. Krajick, *supra* note 5, at 16.

46. *Id.*

47. Interview with B. Murray, *supra* note 30.

48. Blackmore, *supra* note 12, at 10, 11.

49. Krajick, *supra* note 5, at 16.

50. *Id.*

51. *Id.* at 18.

52. *Id.*

53. *Id.*

54. *Id.* at 10.

55. *Id.* at 19.

56. *Id.*

57. Maher and Dufour, *supra* note 2, at 22.

58. Blackmore, *supra* note 5, at 19.

59. *Id.*

60. R. Wiebush, Recidivism in the Juvenile Diversion Project of the Young Volunteers in Action Program (1985).

61. *Id.*

62. Krajick, *supra* note 5, at 18.

63. *An Interview with Dennis A. Challeen: Turning Society's Losers Into Winners,* 19, The Judges' Journal 4 (1980).

64. *Id.* at 6.

65. *Id.*

66. *Id.* at 8.

67. J. Leibrich, B. Galaway and Y. Underhill, Community Service Orders in New Zealand 116 (1984).

68. *Id.*

69. *Id.*

70. *Id.*

71. *Id.*

72. *Id.*

73. *Id.*

74. Interview with B. Murray, *supra* note 30.

75. *Id.*

76. J. Leibrich, B. Galaway and Y. Underhill, *supra* note 67, at 112.

77. *Id.*

78. *Id.*

79. Blackmore, *supra* note 12, at 14.

80. Krajick, *supra* note 5, at 12.

81. *Id.* at 13.

STUDY QUESTIONS FOR READING 36

1. Most community service clients are "extremely unlikely candidates for imprisonment." Do programs for clients who are not prison bound save money? Do programs for prison-bound offenders save money? If so, how much money is saved?

2. What percentage of offenders complete their hours of service on their own? What percentage complete their hours after threats of incarceration from a probation officer or a judge?

3. One probation officer says that community service satisfied the public for reasons other than cost savings. What are these reasons?

4. Offenders seem to prefer community service to prison or jail. Why?

5. What percentage of offenders say they benefitted from community service? How does one judge describe these benefits?

RESTITUTION PROGRAMS

RICHARD LAWRENCE

Crowded prisons have led to countless lawsuits against departments of corrections, forcing states to build more prisons and find other ways to punish offenders.

Expense is another factor that has forced states to seek alternatives, in addition to expanding their prisons. The cost for new prison construction ranges from $50,000 to $150,000 per bed. The annual cost to keep an inmate in prison averages about $15,000.

Probation has been the traditional alternative, but caseloads have become so enormous that probation officers cannot maintain reasonably close control and supervision. New alternatives must reduce prison populations, preserve public safety, and punish and deter offenders. Many forms of community corrections have not met these goals.

PAYING BACK THE VICTIM

Restitution as a criminal sanction in the American judicial system is a fairly new development. Restitution sentences may require the offender to pay money to the victim and/or the justice system or perform some public or community service (Galaway, 1977; McDonald, 1988).

Minnesota developed a restitution program in 1972, allowing convicted property offenders a chance to avoid prison if they worked and paid restitution to their victims (McDonald, 1988). Courts throughout the United States began adopting the idea. A recent survey estimates there are from 500 to 800 restitution programs for juvenile offenders in this country (Schneider, 1985), and an estimated 250 to 500 restitution programs serving the criminal courts (Hudson and Galaway, 1977).

Restitution seems to be gaining popularity and acceptance among the public, legislators, judiciary and corrections personnel because it seems to fulfill sentencing goals as well as or better than other punishments.

- Retribution—Restitution requires that offenders pay for crime, the damages and loss incurred. Court-ordered monetary and community-service restitution help satisfy victims' and the public's need for "just deserts."
- Deterrence—Restitution programs require greater demands and offender accountability than probation alone. Many believe that paying more for crime will be a greater deterrent.
- Rehabilitation—Restitution aims to confront offenders with the consequences of their crime. It often changes criminal thinking and behavior patterns. Victim-offender restitution programs (VORP) bring the victim and offender together to resolve losses and damage. Such programs often result in greater offender responsibility.
- Reintegration—Offenders who pay restitution often get more positive responses and acceptance from the victim and community. Restitution programs benefit the offender by maintaining community ties. Eliminating the problems of post-prison adjustment and overcoming the "ex-con" label may reduce subsequent criminal behavior, making it one of restitution's greatest benefits.

MAKING IT WORK

Is restitution really an effective alternative to prison? Can it achieve the goals of sentencing, reduce prison crowding, and still avoid risk to public safety? An examination of one state's program may help answer these questions.

The Texas Restitution Center Program began in 1983. In six years, it has grown to 17 centers with a combined bed capacity of more than 700 residents. The primary purpose of the program is to serve as a cost-effective form of punishment. The Texas program is applicable to other states with large, crowded prison populations, which tend to have high incarceration rates.

Texas was faced with a crowded prison system, decreased state revenues, and a federal court order to reduce crowding (Ruiz v. Estelle, 1982). The courts divert non-violent felony offenders to the centers, where they repay victims and the community while continuing to work and pay taxes.

The bill emphasized community protection and community input in developing the centers. Residents' activities are carefully monitored by the center's staff and by the probation department. During the day, the residents go to work in the community and return to the centers afterwards. The residents use their wages to pay for room and board, transportation, court and probation costs, victim restitution and child support. They perform community service restitution during evening and weekend hours.

From 1983 to 1988 more than 3,000 offenders who would have been sentenced to Texas prisons were diverted to the restitution centers. For the five-year period from 1984–1988, an average of 60.5 percent of the residents were successfully discharged or successfully participating in the centers. The average percentage of residents discharged for technical or rule violations from 1984–1988 was 11.7 percent. Only 1.9 percent of the residents were discharged for a new offense, and 65 percent of those arrests were for misdemeanors. The vast majority of the diverted offenders did not increase the risk to public safety.

Most of the offenders got jobs during their stay at the restitution centers. While 75 percent were un-

employed when they arrived at the centers, only 25 percent were unemployed at the time of discharge. Thousands of hours of community service restitution are performed by the residents each year. From 1984–88, nearly half a million hours of community service were performed by the residents—an average of 96,900 hours per year. Translated into savings to the community at the minimum wage rate, those hours would equal over $1.6 million.

The residents also pay a considerable amount of monetary restitution. From 1984–88, a total of $480,866 was paid to crime victims; $376,548 went for court costs, fines and fees; and $368,440 was paid for probation fees. The residents paid a total of $931,454 to support their dependents and personal savings; and $340,924 to other financial obligations in the community.

The operating cost to the state was reduced significantly by the total of $4,530,081 paid by the residents (1984–88) for room, board and transportation.

Considering the incarceration costs in the Texas Department of Corrections, the restitution center program is a success. The operating cost for Texas prisons is reported to be $37.50 per day per inmate. This figure includes only operating expenses, not the more than $50,000 per cell for new prison construction. Cost to the Texas Adult Probation Commission for operating the Restitution Center Program averages $30 per day per bed space. In addition to lower operating costs, the monetary restitution paid by the residents helps make a strong case for the program.

Restitution programs have grown rapidly in the past decade. The program in Texas has shown that states known for their massive prison populations can use restitution to reduce prison crowding and the costs of incarceration, without compromising public safety. Many citizens, judicial and probation personnel seem to have readily accepted the idea of restitution as a unique method of meting out punishment with a visible benefit to the community.

REFERENCES

Galaway, Burt. 1977. "The Use of Restitution," *Crime and Delinquency,* 23 (1):56–57.

Hudson, Joe, and Burt Galaway. 1977. *Restitution in Criminal Justice.* Lexington Books.

McDonald, Douglas C. 1988. *Restitution and Community Service.* Washington. D.C.: National Institute of Justice.

Schneider, Anne L. 1985. *Guide to Juvenile Restitution.* Washington, D.C.: U.S. Government Printing Office.

STUDY QUESTIONS FOR READING 37

1. What does Lawrence assume about all 3,000 offenders in the Texas program? If his assumption is correct, how much does this restitution program save compared to prison?

2. Where do offenders live while in the program? What do they spend their wages on? How do they spend their time on the weekends?

3. Lawrence asserts that "The program also seems to be successful in terms of rehabilitation." What statistics does he give to support this?

4. What percentage of offenders were unemployed when they started the program compared to when they were discharged?

RESTORATIVE JUSTICE AND MEDIATION

MARK S. UMBREIT

Linda and Bob Jackson had their house broken into while they were away visiting friends in another city. The frustration, anger, and growing sense of vulnerability they felt far exceeded the loss of their television set and stereo. The young person, Allan, who committed this crime was caught and entered a plea of guilty. When the Jacksons were invited to participate in a program that allowed them to meet their offender, they were eager to get answers to questions such as "why us?" and "were you watching our movements?" The mediation session allowed them to get answers to these and other questions, let Allan know how personally violated they felt and negotiate a plan for him to pay them back. While nervous at first, Allan felt better after the mediation. Everyone treated him with respect even though he had committed a crime, and he was able to make amends to the Jacksons. Linda and Bob felt less vulnerable, were able to sleep better and received payment for their losses. All parties were able to put this event behind them.

The Jacksons are among many thousands of people who have been victimized and have been given the opportunity to experience a radically different way of "doing justice." Through their participation in a victim-offender mediation program, they were able to experience firsthand what the emerging theory of restorative justice is about.

Our contemporary understanding of social theory related to crime and victimization can be traced back to a major paradigm shift that occurred during the Norman invasion of Britain in the twelfth century. This marked a turning away from viewing crime as a victim-offender conflict within the context of community. Crime became a violation of the king's peace,

and upholding the authority of the state replaced the practice of making the victim whole.

One of the most significant current developments in our thinking about crime is the growing interest in restorative justice theory (Mackey, 1990; Umbreit, 1993a, 1991b; Umbreit and Coates, 1993; Van Ness, 1986; Van Ness et al., 1989; Wright, 1991; Wright and Galaway, 1989; Zehr, 1990, 1985; Marshall and Merry, 1990; Galaway and Hudson, 1990; Messmer and Otto, 1992), which is based upon principles that were widely practiced prior to the Norman invasion of Britain. At a time in modern society when the current paradigm of justice has demonstrated very little positive impact on offenders, crime victims or the larger community, it is understandable that a promising theory of criminal justice is increasingly being embraced in a growing number of communities throughout the world.

Restorative justice theory provides an entirely different theoretical framework for responding to crime. Rather than defining "the state" as the victim, restorative justice theory postulates that criminal behavior is first a conflict between individuals. The person who was violated is the primary victim, and the state is a secondary victim. The current retributive paradigm of justice focuses on the actions of the offender, denies victim participation and requires only passive participation by the offender. The very definition of "holding offenders accountable" changes when viewed through the lens of restorative justice. As Zehr (1990) notes: "Instead of 'paying a debt to society' by experiencing punishment, accountability would mean understanding and taking responsibility for what has been done and taking action to make things right. Instead of owing an abstract debt to society, paid in an abstract way by experiencing punishment, the offender would owe a debt to the victim, to be repaid in a concrete way."

Restorative justice places both victim and offender in active problem-solving roles that focus upon the restoration of material and psychological losses to individuals and the community following the damage that results from criminal behavior. Whenever possible, dialogue and negotiation serve as central elements of restorative justice. This is true primarily of property crimes, although also of a growing number of more violent offenses. Problem solving for the future is seen as more important than establishing blame for past behavior. Public safety is a primary concern, yet severe punishment of the offender is less important than providing opportunities to: empower victims in their search for closure and healing; impress upon the offender the human impact of their behavior; and promote restitution to the victim.

By far the clearest distinction between the old paradigm of retributive justice and the new paradigm of restorative justice has been developed by Zehr (1990), as outlined in Table 38.1.

While clearly more difficult to apply in violent crimes, the principles of restorative justice theory are having an increasing impact on social policy. Many of these principles can also be seen in the pioneering work of an Australian scholar who addresses the issues of crime, shame and reintegration. Braithwaite (1989) argues for "reintegrative shaming," a type of social control based upon informal community condemnation of wrongdoing, but with opportunities for the reintegration of the wrongdoer back into the community. He states that the most effective crime control requires active community participation "in shaming offenders, and, having shamed them, through concerted participation in . . . integrating the offender back into the community" (Braithwaite, 1989). Braithwaite notes that societies with low crime rates consist of people who do not mind their own business, where there exist clear limits to tolerance of deviance and where communities have a preference for handling their own problems.

While Braithwaite does not specifically address restorative justice or victim-offender mediation, he argues for principles of justice which emphasize personal accountability of offenders, active community involvement, and a process of reconciliation and reaffirmation of the offender that directly relates to the restorative justice paradigm.

VICTIM-OFFENDER MEDIATION

The clearest expression of restorative justice theory is seen in the emerging field of victim-offender mediation (Fagan and Gehm, 1993; Galaway, 1989, 1988; Galaway and Hudson, 1990; Umbreit, 1993a, 1986; Zehr, 1990, 1980). Developed extensively in recent years, it represents one of the most creative efforts to: hold offenders personally accountable for their behavior; emphasize the human impact of crime; provide opportunities for offenders to take responsibility for their actions by facing their victim and making amends; promote active victim and community involvement in the justice process; and enhance the quality of justice experienced by both victims and offenders. There are more than 120 victim-offender mediation programs in the U.S., 26 in Canada and an even larger number in Europe (Umbreit, 1991b), as noted in Figure 38.1.

A widespread network of victim-offender mediation programs is now developing throughout the U.S., Canada, England, Germany, France, Austria, Norway and Finland. While interest in restorative justice theory has grown extensively throughout North America and Europe, there exists a significant lack of empirical research to assess the impact of the theory.

The ultimate strength of any social theory is to be found in how accurately it captures the reality of people who are subject to it. Restorative justice theory makes bold claims about the needs of people affected by crime within community structures. Its validity as a new social theory must be grounded in empirical evidence offered by those most affected by crime—victims and offenders. Should restorative justice fail to become a "grounded theory" (Glazer and Strauss, 1967) from the bottom up, it risks the likelihood of becoming an abstraction—a philosophical exercise in

TABLE 38.1   Paradigms of Justice—Old and New

OLD PARADIGM	NEW PARADIGM
1. Crime defined as violation of state.	1. Crime defined as violation of one person by another.
2. Focus on establishing blame based on guilt, on past (did he/she do it?).	2. Focus on problem solving, on liabilities/obligations, on future (what should be done?).
3. Adversarial relationship and process are normative.	3. Dialogue and negotiation are normative.
4. Imposition of pain to punish and deter/prevent future crime.	4. Restitution as means of restoring both parties; goal of reconciliation/restoration.
5. Justice defined by intent and process: right rules.	5. Justice defined as right relationships; judged by outcome.
6. Interpersonal, conflictual nature of crime obscured, repressed; conflict seen as individual versus the state.	6. Crime recognized as interpersonal conflict; value of conflict is recognized.
7. One social injury replaced by another.	7. Focus on repair of social injury.
8. Community on sidelines, represented abstractly by state.	8. Community as facilitator in restorative process.
9. Encouragement of competitive, individualistic values.	9. Encouragement of mutuality.
10. Action directed from state to offender. • victim ignored, • offender passive.	10. Victim and offender's roles recognized in problem/solution: • victim rights/needs recognized, • offender encouraged to take responsibility.
11. Offender accountability defined as taking punishment.	11. Offender accountability defined as understanding impact of action, and helping to decide how to make things right.
12. Offense defined in purely legal terms, devoid of moral, social, economic, political dimensions.	12. Offense understood in whole context—moral, social, economic, political.
13. "Debt" owed to state and society in the abstract.	13. Debt/liability to victim recognized.
14. Response focused on offender's past behavior.	14. Response focused on harmful consequences of offender's behavior.
15. Stigma of crime unremovable.	15. Stigma of crime removable through restorative action.
16. No encouragement for repentance and forgiveness.	16. Possibilities for repentance and forgiveness.
17. Dependence upon proxy by professionals.	17. Direct involvement by participants.

Reprinted with permission from Howard Zehr.

criminal justice policy reform with little relevance to the reality of how justice is actually done in a free and democratic society. On the other hand, a grounded theory of restorative justice contains the powerful and prophetic potential for a fundamental change in how society understands and responds to crime in the community.

This book [*Victim Meets Offender*] will offer such empirical grounding for the theory of restorative justice. It will report on the largest and most extensive multi-site analysis of victim-offender mediation to occur in North America (Umbreit, 1991a, 1993b; Umbreit and Coates, 1992, 1993). Over a two-and-one-half-year period, victim-offender mediation programs

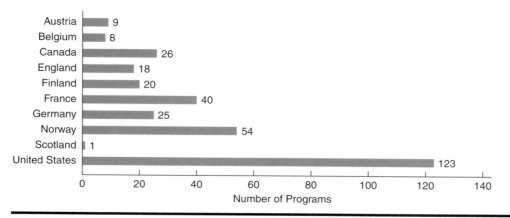

FIGURE 38.1   International Development of Victim-Offender Mediation
Austria has a federal policy making victim-offender mediation available for youths in any of its 143 cities, within its 9 provinces.

working with the juvenile courts in Albuquerque (NM), Austin (TX), Minneapolis (MN) and Oakland (CA) were examined. A total of 1,153 pre- and post-mediation interviews with victims and offenders were conducted. Two different comparison groups were used to examine the impact of mediation, along with numerous interviews with court officials and program staff, a review of court and program records, and 28 observations of actual mediation sessions.

The conclusions that emerged from this multi-site study, as will be noted in the final chapter [of *Victim Meets Offender*], are consistent with a growing body of literature, particularly two recent studies conducted in England (Dignan, 1990; Marshall and Merry, 1990). Together, these studies provide important empirical evidence to support the basic propositions put forth by the restorative justice paradigm.

THE MEDIATION PROCESS

Victim-offender mediation and reconciliation programs differ in a variety of ways related to referral source, diversion versus post-adjudication referral, case management procedures, use of volunteer mediators, etc. A basic case management process, however, tends to be present in most of the programs in the U.S. and Canada, particularly those that have been influ-

enced by the VORP (Victim Offender Reconciliation Program) model (Umbreit, 1988).

Nearly all victim-offender mediation and reconciliation programs focus upon providing a conflict resolution process that is perceived as fair to both parties. It is the mediator's responsibility to facilitate this process. First, the parties are given time to address informational and emotional needs. Once questions have been answered and feelings expressed, the mediation session then turns to a discussion of losses and the possibility of developing a mutually agreeable restitution plan (i.e., money, work for victim, work for victim's choice of a charity, etc.).

The process typically begins when judges, probation staff, prosecutors or victim assistance staff refer juvenile or adult offenders (most often those convicted of such crimes as theft and burglary) to the victim-offender mediation program. Many programs accept referrals after a formal admission of guilt has been entered with the court. Some programs accept cases that are referred prior to formal admission of guilt, as part of a deferred prosecution or diversion effort. Each case is then assigned to either a staff or volunteer mediator. Prior to scheduling the mediation session, the mediator meets with both the offender and victim separately. These individual meetings with each party play a very important role in the mediation process.

The mediator listens to the story of each party, explains the program and encourages their participation.

Usually mediators meet first with the offender. If he or she is willing to proceed with mediation, they meet later with the victim. In addition to collecting information about the criminal event and explaining the program, these individual meetings provide an opportunity for the mediator to build rapport and trust with the individuals involved. Particularly since both parties are likely to have already been dealt with in an impersonal fashion by a variety of criminal justice officials, having the mediator meet with both individually before even scheduling the mediation is extremely important. It tends to humanize the justice process and result in a higher "getting-to-the-table" rate of actual mediation participation. These preliminary meetings, held separately with victims and offenders, require effective listening and communication skills. They are critical to building rapport and trust with both parties.

While crime victims are encouraged to consider the possible benefits of mediation, they must not be coerced into participating. To do so, even with the best of intentions, would be to revictimize them. Voluntary participation by crime victims and offenders—although for offenders it is a choice within a highly coercive context—is a strong ethical principle of the victim-offender mediation process. Presenting the mediation process as an option helps victims and offenders to feel empowered.

Program literature in the field implies that offender participation in the mediation process is also totally voluntary. Actual practice suggests something quite different. A rather significant amount of state coercion is exercised when offenders are ordered to participate in mediation by the court, via probation, or are diverted from prosecution if they complete the program. One early study (Coates and Gehm, 1985) found that offenders certainly did not perceive the process as voluntary. A more recent and much larger study (Umbreit and Coates, 1992, 1993), as will be reported in this book, found the vast majority of offenders believed they had a choice as to whether to participate in mediation.

A more honest approach is used by programs that attempt to secure offender participation in the least co-

ercive manner possible. Offenders who are strongly opposed to participating are allowed to bow out of the program, while those who are determined by the program staff to be inappropriate for mediation are referred back to the referral source.

Once the victim and offender have indicated their willingness to participate, the mediator then schedules a face-to-face meeting. The mediation session begins with the mediator explaining his or her role, stating any communication ground rules that may be necessary, and stating the agenda for the meeting (first to talk about what happened and how they felt about it, and then to discuss losses and negotiate restitution).

During the first part of the mediation session, the focus is on the facts and feelings related to the crime. Crime victims are given the unusual opportunity to express their feelings directly to the person who violated them. They can get answers to questions such as "why me?", "how did you get into our house?", and "were you stalking us and planning on coming back?" Upon seeing their offender, victims are often relieved. This "criminal" usually bears little resemblance to the frightening character they may have conjured up in their minds.

Facing the person they violated is not easy for most offenders. While it is often an uncomfortable position for offenders, they are given the equally unusual opportunity to display a more human dimension to their character. For many, the opportunity to express remorse in a very direct and personal fashion is important. The mediation process allows victims and offenders to deal with each other as people, oftentimes from the same neighborhood, rather than as stereotypes and objects.

When both parties have concluded discussing the crime and how they felt about it, the second part of the meeting is then initiated. The losses incurred by the victim are reviewed, and a plan for making things right is discussed. The principles of fairness and realism are emphasized during the final negotiation of the restitution agreement. When courts refer cases to mediation, they do not usually order a specific restitution amount. Cases in which the parties are unable to agree upon the amount or form of restitution are referred back to the referral source, with a good likelihood that the offender will be placed in a different program. Mediators do not impose a restitution settlement.

Most programs report that in more than 95% of all mediation sessions a written restitution agreement has been successfully negotiated and signed by the victim, offender and mediator. Joint victim-offender meetings usually last about one hour, with some meetings in the two-hour range.

It is important to note that there exist a number of significant exceptions to the "typical" process described, particularly among many community dispute resolution centers that have mediated quite a few disputes among crime victims and offenders, but that did not frame the mediation as a "victim-offender mediation." For example, many of these community dispute resolution centers would have staff be responsible for all of the case development work, including any separate meetings or conversations with the parties prior to mediation. The mediator would first meet the victim and offender at the time of the mediation session.

IS THE PUBLIC INTERESTED?

Even in view of the empirical evidence in support of restorative justice theory and mediation, the question remains "Is the larger public really interested?" Certainly the data that have emerged from examination of a number of individual programs are rather persuasive. Yet is there evidence of public support for the principles of restorative justice? The strong "law-and-order" and "get-tough" rhetoric that dominates most political campaigns would suggest not. After all, how often have we heard ambitious politicians or criminal justice officials state that "the public demands that we get tougher with criminals?" This perception—or some would argue, misperception—fuels the engine that drives our nation toward ever-increasing and costly criminal punishments, as seen in lengthy sentences and the highest per capita incarceration in the world (Mauer, 1991).

There is, however, a growing body of evidence to suggest that the general public is far less vindictive than often portrayed and far more supportive of the basic principles of restorative justice than many might think. A recent statewide public opinion survey, conducted by the University of Minnesota (Pranis and Umbreit, 1992) using a large probability sample, challenges conventional wisdom about public feelings related to crime and punishment.

A sample of 825 Minnesota adults, demographically and geographically balanced to reflect the state's total population, were asked three questions with implications for restorative justice as part of a larger omnibus survey. A sampling of this size has a sampling error of plus or minus 3.5 percentage points. The first question was: Suppose that while you are away, your home is burglarized and $1,200 worth of property is stolen.

"The burglar has one previous conviction for a similar offense. In addition to 4 years on probation, would you prefer the sentence include repayment of $1,200 to you or 4 months in jail?" Nearly three of four Minnesotans indicated that having the offender pay restitution was more important than a jail sentence, as indicated in Figure 38.2.

To examine public support for policies that address some of the underlying social problems that often cause crime, a concern that is closely related to restorative justice, the following question was asked: "For the greatest impact on reducing crime, should additional money be spent on more prisons, or spent on education, job training and community programs?" Spending on education, job training and community programs rather than on prisons to reduce crime was favored by four of five Minnesotans, as seen in Figure 38.3.

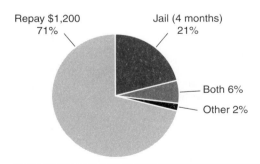

FIGURE 38.2 Public Support for Sentencing Burglar
Minnesota State sample, 1991

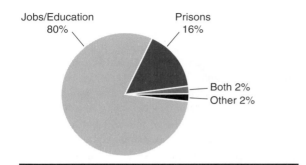

FIGURE 38.3   Public Support for Crime Prevention
Minnesota State sample, 1991

The third and final question related to restorative justice addressed the issue of interest in victim-offender mediation. This question was presented in the following manner: "Minnesota has several programs which allow crime victims to meet with the person who committed the crime, in the presence of a trained mediator, to let this person know how the crime affected them, and to work out a plan for repayment of losses. Suppose you were the victim of a non-violent property crime committed by a juvenile or young adult. How likely would you be to participate in a program like this?"

More than four of five Minnesotans expressed an interest in participating in a face-to-face mediation session with the offender. This finding is particularly significant in that criminal justice officials and program staff who are unfamiliar with mediation often make such comments as "there is no way in the world that victims in my community would ever want to confront the offender," or "only a small portion of victims would ever be interested." The finding is particularly important since the vast majority of crime is committed by either juveniles or young adults. Some would suggest that the victim-offender mediation process is likely to be supported only for crimes involving juvenile offenders. This is certainly not the case in Minnesota. As noted in Figure 38.4, 82% of respondents indicated they would be likely to participate in a program that would allow them to meet the juvenile or young adult who victimized them.

A picture of a far less vindictive public than often portrayed emerges from this statewide survey. Respondents indicated greater concern for restitution and prevention strategies that address underlying issues of social injustice than for costly retribution. Holding offenders personally accountable to their victim is more important than incarceration in a jail. Public safety is understood to be more directly related to investing in job training, education and other community programs than incarceration.

While it might be tempting to suggest that this public opinion survey simply reflects the rather unique liberal social policy tradition of Minnesota, its findings are consistent with a growing body of public opinion research across the U.S. (Bae, 1991; Gottfredson, Warner and Taylor, 1988; Clarke, 1985; Public Agenda Foundation, 1987, 1989, 1991; Public Opinion Research, 1986). These previous studies have found broad public support for payment of restitution by the offender to their victim instead of incarceration for property crimes, and support for crime prevention strategies instead of prison strategies to control crime. The studies did not explicitly ask respondents if they supported "restorative justice." The questions asked, however, addressed important underlying principles that are fundamental to the theory of restorative justice, which places far more value on crime prevention and restoration of physical and emotional losses than on retribution and blame for past behavior.

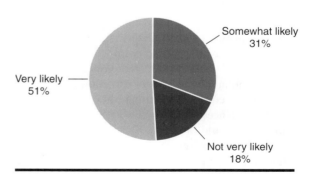

FIGURE 38.4   Support for Victim-Offender Mediation
Minnesota State sample, 1991

REFERENCES

Bae, I. (1991). "A Survey on Public Acceptance of Restitution as an Alternative to Incarceration for Property Offenders in Hennepin County, Minnesota." In: Heinz Messmer and Hans-Uwe Otto (eds.), *Restorative Justice on Trial*. Dordrecht, NETH: Kluwer Academic Publishers.

Braithwaite, J. (1989). *Crime, Shame and Reintegration.* Cambridge, MA: Cambridge University Press.

Clarke, P. (1985). *Perception of Criminal Justice Surveys: Executive Summary.* The Michigan Prison and Jail Overcrowding Project.

Coates, R. B. and J. Gehm (1985). *Victim Meets Offender: An Evaluation of Victim Offender Reconciliation Programs.* Valparaiso, IN: PACT Institute of Justice.

Dignan, J. (1990). *Repairing the Damage.* Sheffield, UK: Centre for Criminological and Legal Research, University of Sheffield.

Fagan, H. and Gehm, J. (1993). *Victim-Offender Reconciliation and Mediation Program Directory.* Valparaiso, IN: PACT Institute of Justice.

Galaway, B. (1988). "Crime Victim and Offender Mediation as a Social Work Strategy." *Social Service Review* 62:668–683.

———— (1989). "Informal Justice: Mediation Between Offenders and Victims." In: P. A. Albrecht and O. Backes (eds.), *Crime Prevention and Intervention: Legal and Ethical Problems.* Berlin: Walter de Gruyter.

———— and J. Hudson. (1990). *Criminal Justice, Restitution, and Reconciliation.* Monsey, NY: Criminal Justice Press.

Gottfredson, S. D., B. D. Warner and R. B. Taylor (1988). "Conflict and Consensus about Criminal Justice in Maryland." In: N. Walker and M. Hough (eds.), *Public Attitudes to Sentencing: Surveys from Five Countries.* Aldershot, UK: Gower.

Glazer, B. G. and A. Strauss (1967). *The Discovery of Grounded Theory.* Chicago: Aldine.

Mackey, V. (1990). *Restorative Justice, Toward Nonviolence.* Louisville, KY: Presbyterian Criminal Justice Program.

Mauer, M. (1991). *Americans Behind Bars: A Comparison of International Rates of Incarceration.* Washington, DC: The Sentencing Project.

Marshall, T. F. and S. Merry (1990). *Crime and Accountability.* London: Home Office.

Messmer, H. and Hans-Uwe Otto (1992). *Restorative Justice on Trial: Pitfalls and Potentials of Victim-Offender Mediation—International Research Perspectives.* Dordrecht, NETH: Kluwer.

Pranis, K. and M. S. Umbreit (1992). *Public Opinion Research Challenges Perception of Widespread Public Demand for Harsher Punishment.* Minneapolis, MN: Citizens Council.

Public Agenda Foundation (1987). *Crime and Punishment: The Public's View.* New York: Edna McConnell Clark Foundation.

———— (1989). *Punishing Criminals: The Public's View, An Alabama Survey.* New York: Edna McConnell Clark Foundation.

———— (1991). *Punishing Criminals: The People of Delaware Consider the Options.* New York: Edna McConnell Clark Foundation.

Public Opinion Research (1986). *Report Prepared for the North Carolina Center on Crime and Punishment.* Washington, DC.

Umbreit, M. S. (1986). "Victim Offender Mediation: A National Survey." *Federal Probation* 50(4):53–56.

———— (1988). "Mediation of Victim Offender Conflict." *Journal of Dispute Resolution* 85–105.

———— (1991a). "Mediating Victim Offender Conflict: From Single-Site to Multi-Site Analysis in the U.S." In: H. Messmer and H.-U. Otto (eds.), *Restorative Justice on Trial.* Dordrecht, NETH: Kluwer Academic Publishers.

———— (1991b). "Having Offenders Meet With Their Victim Offers Benefits for Both Parties." *Corrections Today* (July):164–166.

———— and R. B. Coates (1992). "The Impact of Mediating Victim Offender Conflict: An Analysis of Programs in Three States." *Juvenile & Family Court Journal* 43:21–28.

———— (1993a). "Crime Victims and Offenders in Mediation: An Emerging Area of Social Work Practice." *Social Work* 38(1):69–73.

———— (1993b). "Juvenile Offenders Meet Their Victims: The Impact of Mediation in Albuquerque, New Mexico." *Family and Conciliation Courts Review* 31(1):90–100.

———— and R. B. Coates (1993). "Cross-Site Analysis of Victim Offender Mediation in Four States." *Crime & Delinquency* 39(4):565–585.

Van Ness, D. W. (1986). *Crime and Its Victims.* Downers Grove, IL: Intervarsity Press.

———— D. Carlson, T. Crawford and K. Strong (1989). *Restorative Justice Theory.* Washington, DC: Justice Fellowship.

Wright, M. and B. Galaway (1989). *Mediation and Criminal Justice*. London: Sage.

Wright, M. (1991). *Justice for Victims and Offenders*. Philadelphia, PA: Open University Press.

Zehr, H. (1980). *Mediation the Victim-Offender Conflict*. Akron, PA: Mennonite Central Committee.

——— (1990). *Changing Lenses, A New Focus for Crime and Justice*. Scottsdale, PA: Herald Press.

STUDY QUESTIONS FOR READING 38

1. Compare the adversarial (retributive) system to the restorative system by crossing out the word or words that are not appropriate for restorative justice. Replace them with the appropriate words.
   a. Crime is defined as violation of the state
   b. Focus on establishing blame and guilt in the past
   c. The norm is an adversarial relationship between parties
   d. Punishment used to deter future crime
   e. Justice defined by intent and process: right rules
   f. Conflict seen as between the individual and the state
   g. One social injury (crime) is replaced by another (punishment)

2. What crimes are most often referred to victim-offender mediation? What are some of the common questions victims have? Why do victims feel relieved to see the offenders?

3. How long do the meetings last? What percentage of meetings result in a formal, written agreement for restitution?

4. What fraction of the public surveyed said that having burglars pay restitution was more important than a jail sentence? What fraction of the public surveyed said that they would be willing to participate in a face-to-face encounter with the offender?

ESSAY QUESTIONS FOR PART FIVE_____

In your answers, be sure to use one sentence at the end of your first paragraph to offer a clear thesis statement—that is, a statement of your point of view and your arguments for it. Then, in each paragraph of your answer, give evidence to support one of your arguments. Cite specific authors and give specific, concrete support for your point of view by offering statistics, case studies, examples, quotations, expert opinions, and so on.

1. How effective are the various alternatives to incarceration in terms of the goals listed below? Why?
- retribution
- deterrence
- incapacitation
- rehabilitation

2. Which of the alternatives to incarceration listed below do you see as the most promising for the future? Which do you see as the least promising? Why?
- boot camps
- traditional probation
- intensive probation supervision
- public shaming
- community service
- restitution
- mediation as a form of restorative justice

CREDITS

Reading 1: Gray, Tara. *"America's Imprisonment Binge: An Overview of the Book by John Irwin and James Austin." Justice Quarterly, 11* (4), 729–733, 1994. Reprinted with permission of the Academy of Criminal Justice Sciences.

Reading 2: Chesney-Lind, Meda. "The Forgotten Offender—Women in Prison: From Partial Justice to Vengeful Equity." *Corrections Today,* December 1998. Reprinted with permission of the American Correctional Association, Lanham, MD.

Reading 3: Walker, S., C. Spohn, and M. DeLone. "Corrections: A Picture in Black and White." From *The Color of Justice: Race, Ethnicity, and Crime in America,* 2nd edition. © 2000. Reprinted with permission of Wadsworth, an imprint of the Wadsworth Group, a division of Thomson Learning. Fax 800-730-2215.

Reading 5: Zupan, Linda L. "The Persistant Problems Plaguing Modern Jails." From *Jails: Reform and the New Generation Philosophy.* Copyright © 1991 by Anderson Publishing Co./Cincinnati, OH. Reprinted with permission of Anderson Publishing Company.

Reading 6: Metz, Andrew. "Life on the Inside: The Jailers." *Newsday,* March 21, 1999: A5, A50, A52. Newsday, Inc. © 1999. Reprinted with permission.

Reading 7: Webb, Gary L., and David G. Morris. "Working as a Prison Guard." From *Prison Guards: The Culture and Perspective of an Occupational Group.* © 1978. Reprinted with permission of Gary L. Webb.

Reading 9: Bartollas, Clemens. "Living in a Juvenile Prison." Originally titled "Survival Problems of Adolescent Prisoners." From *The Pains of Imprisonment,* Robert Johnson and Hans Toch, eds. © 1982. Reprinted with permission of Clemens Bartollas.

Reading 10: Johnson, R. "Life In the Belly of the Beast." From *Hard Time: Understanding and Reforming the Prison,* 2nd edition. © 1997 by Wadsworth, a division of Thomson Learning. Reprinted with permission of Random House, Inc.

Reading 11: Abbott, Jack Henry. "The Hole: Solitary Confinement." From *In the Belly of the Beast.*

© 1981 by Jack Henry Abbott. Used by permission of Random House, Inc.

Reading 12: Johnson, Robert. "Living and Working on Death Row." From *Death Work: A Study of the Modern Execution Process,* 1st edition. © 1990. Reprinted with permission of Wadsworth, an imprint of Wadsworth Group, a division of Thomson Learning. Fax 800-730-2215.

Reading 13: Siegal, Nina. "Lethal Lottery." *POZ,* November 1998. © 1998 POZ Publishing, L. L. C. Reprinted with permission.

Reading 14: Baunach, Phyllis Jo. "Critical Problems of Women in Prison." From *The Changing Roles of Women in the Criminal Justice System: Offenders, Victims, and Professionals,* 2nd edition, by Imogene Moyer. Prospect Heights, IL: Waveland Press, Inc., 1992. Reprinted by permission of Waveland Press, Inc. All rights reserved.

Reading 15: Siegal, Nina. "Stopping Abuse in Prison." *The Progressive,* April 1999, 31–33. © 1999 by The Progressive, Inc. Reprinted with permission.

Reading 16: Gray, Tara and Jon'a Meyer. "Why Inmate Participation is Better When Managing Prisons." Originally titled "Prison Administration: Inmate Participation versus the Control Model." From *Correctional Contexts: Contemporary and Classical Readings,* James W. Marquart and Jonathan R. Sorensen, eds. © 1997 by Roxbury Publishing Company. Reprinted with permission.

Reading 17: DiIulio, John J., Jr. "Why More Control Is Better When Governing Prisons." Originally titled "Governing Prisons in Three States." From *Governing Prisons: A Comparative Study of Correctional Management.* © 1987 by The Free Press. Reprinted with permission of The Free Press, a division of Simon & Schuster, Inc.

Reading 19: Peters, Tom. "The Missing 'X-Factor': Trust." From *Liberation Management.* © 1992 by Excel, a California Limited Partnership. Reprinted by permission of Alfred A. Knopf, a division of Random House, Inc.

Reading 20: Shireman, Charles. "Group Norms in a Reform School *Without Locks and Bars:* An

Overview of the Book by Grant R. Grissom and William L. Dubnov." Originally titled *"Without Locks and Bars: Reforming Our Reform Schools.* By Grant R. Grissom and William L. Dubnov." *Social Service Review 64,* December 1990, 660–664. Reprinted with permission of Charles Shireman.

Reading 21: Meyer, Jon'a. "Readaptation: Work and Family in a Mexican Prison Village." Originally titled "Mexico's La Mesa Penitentiary: An Experiment in Humanity." *American Jails,* July/August 1995, 101–104. Reprinted with permission.

Reading 22: Sykes, Gresham. "The Need for More Control in the Society of Captives." Originally titled "The Defects of Total Power." From *The Society of Captives: A Study of a Maximum Security Prison.* © 1958 by Princeton University Press. Reprinted by permission of Princeton University Press.

Reading 23: Gilligan, James. "How to Increase the Rate of Violence—and Why." From *Violence: Reflections on a National Epidemic.* © 1996 by James Gilligan. Used by permission of Grosset & Dunlap, Inc., a division of Penguin Putnam, Inc.

Reading 24: Hassine, Victor. " 'Chemical Shackles' as a Control Mechanism." Originally titled "Interview with Chaser: A Medication Addict." From *Life Without Parole: Living in Prison Today.* © 1996 by Roxbury Publishing Company. Reprinted with permission.

Reading 25: Hunt, Geoffrey, Stephanie Riegel, Tomas Morales, and Dan Waldorf. "Changes in Prison Culture: Prison Gangs and the Case of the 'Pepsi Generation.' " *Social Problems, 40* (3), August 1993, 398–409. Reprinted with permission.

Reading 26: Dowker, Fay and Glenn Good. "Control Units as a Control Mechanism." Originally titled "The Proliferation of Control Unit Prisons in the United States." From the Committee to End the Marion Lockdown homepage, http://www-unix.oit.umass.edu/~kastor/ceml_articles/cu_in_us.html. Reprinted with permission of the Committee to End the Marion Lockdown, P.O. Box 578721, Chicago, IL 60657-8172.

Reading 27: Pung, Orville B. "A Defense of Prisons." From *Corrections: An Issues Approach,* 2nd edition, Lawrence Travis, Martin Schwartz, and Todd Clear, eds. Copyright © 1980 by Anderson Publishing Co. Reprinted with permission of Anderson Publishing Company.

Reading 28: Newman, Donald J. "Prisons Don't Work." Originally titled "A Critique of Prison Building." *New England Journal on Prison Law, 8* (1), 121–139, 1982. Reprint permission courtesy of the *New England Journal on Criminal and Civil Confinement.*

Reading 29: Wilson, James Q. "Rehabilitation." From *Thinking About Crime,* revised edition. © 1975, 1983 by Basic Books, Inc. Reprinted by permission of Basic Books, a member of Perseus Books, L. L. C.

Reading 30: Currie, Elliott. "Rehabilitation Can Work." From *Confronting Crime: An American Challenge,* pp. 235–244. © 1985 by Elliott Currie. Reprinted by permission of Pantheon Books, a division of Random House, Inc.

Reading 31: Gover, Angela R., Gaylene J. F. Styve, and Doris Layton MacKenzie. "Evaluating Correctional Boot Camp Programs: Issues and Concerns." From *The Dilemmas of Corrections: Contemporary Readings,* 4th edition, by Kenneth C. Haas and Geoffrey P. Alpert. Prospect Heights, IL: Waveland Press, Inc., 1999. Reprinted by permission of Waveland Press, Inc. All rights reserved.

Reading 32: Acorn, Linda R. "Working in a Boot Camp." *Corrections Today,* October 1991. Reprinted with permission of the American Correctional Association, Lanham, MD.

Reading 33: Pierson, E. Jane, Thomas L. Densmore, John M. Shevlin, Omar Madruga, and Terry D. Childers. "Working as a Federal Probation Officer." Originally titled "A Day in the Life of a Federal Probation Officer—Revisited." *Federal Probation,* December 1992, 18–28. Reprinted with permission from *Federal Probation.*

Reading 34: Erwin, Billie S. and Lawrence A. Bennett. "Intensive Probation Supervision." Originally titled "New Dimensions in Probation: Georgia's Experience with Intensive Probation Supervision (IPS)." *National Institute of Justice Research in Brief,* January 1987. This article was funded by the National Institute of Justice and the United States Department of Justice. Points of view or opinions expressed in this publication are those of the authors and do not necessarily represent the official position or policies of the U.S. Department of Justice. Reprinted with permission.

Reading 35: Litowitz, Douglas. "Shaming Offenders." Originally titled "The Trouble with 'Scarlet Letter' Punishments." *Judicature, 81* (2), 1997. Reprinted with permission of *Judicature,* the journal of the American Judicature Society.

Reading 36: Martin, Julie C. "Community Service for Offenders." Originally titled "Community Service: Are the Goals of this Alternative Sentencing Tool Being Met?" *Court Review,* Winter 1991, 5–11. Reprinted with permission from *Court Review,* the journal of the American Judges Association.

Reading 37: Lawrence, Richard. "Restitution Programs." Originally titled "Restitution Programs Pay Back the Victim and Society." *Corrections Today,* February 1990. Reprinted with permission of the American Correctional Association, Lanham, MD.

Reading 38: Umbreit, Mark S. "Restorative Justice and Mediation." From *Victim Meets Offender: The Impact of Restorative Justice and Mediation.* Monsey, NY: Criminal Justice Press, Willow Tree Press, 1994. Reprinted with permission.

INDEX